Latinos in the American Political System

Latinos in the American Political System

An Encyclopedia of Latinos as Voters, Candidates, and Office Holders

VOLUME I: A–M

Jessica L. Lavariega Monforti, Editor

ABC-CLIO™

An Imprint of ABC-CLIO, LLC
Santa Barbara, California • Denver, Colorado

Library of Congress Cataloging-in-Publication Data

Names: Lavariega Monforti, Jessica, editor.
Title: Latinos in the American political system : an encyclopedia of Latinos as voters, candidates, and office holders / Jessica L. Lavariega Monforti, editor.
Description: Santa Barbara, California : ABC-CLIO, 2019. |
    Includes bibliographical references and index.
Identifiers: LCCN 2018030432 (print) | LCCN 2018033924 (ebook) |
    ISBN 9781440853470 (ebook) | ISBN 9781440853463 (set : alk. paper) |
    ISBN 9781440853487 (vol. 1 : alk. paper) | ISBN 9781440853494 (vol. 2 : alk. paper)
Subjects: LCSH: Hispanic Americans—Politics and government—Encyclopedias. |
    Hispanic American politicians—Biography—Encyclopedias. | United States—
    Politics and government—Encyclopedias.
Classification: LCC E184.S75 (ebook) | LCC E184.S75 L3677 2019 (print) |
    DDC 973/.0468—dc23
LC record available at https://lccn.loc.gov/2018030432

ISBN: 978-1-4408-5346-3 (set)
        978-1-4408-5348-7 (vol. 1)
        978-1-4408-5349-4 (vol. 2)
        978-1-4408-5347-0 (ebook)

23 22 21 20 19   1 2 3 4 5

This book is also available as an eBook.

ABC-CLIO
An Imprint of ABC-CLIO, LLC

ABC-CLIO, LLC
147 Castilian Drive
Santa Barbara, California 93117
www.abc-clio.com

This book is printed on acid-free paper ∞

Manufactured in the United States of America

This work is dedicated to my students, past and present, some of whom have contributed to these volumes. Many of my students shattered the largely negative statistics used to describe them and predict their futures; their progress is our progress. Unfortunately, they have rarely been exposed to the historical or contemporary political engagement and political successes of Latina/o communities in the United States. Nevertheless, like many of the elected officials, activists, and organizations covered in this research, my students have demonstrated resilience in the face of struggle, persistence through adversity, and muchas ganas de sobresalir *(strong desire to excel or overachieve). Both groups, my students and the people and groups written about here, have shown themselves to be* enprendedores y inovadores *(entrepreneurs and innovators).*

José Martí once wrote, "Es pecado no hacer lo que uno es capaz de hacer" *(It is a sin not to do what one is capable of doing). I am sure that not too far in the distant future, academics and scholars will write about the political work, successes, and legacies these students leave behind as they blaze new trails of their own. I have been humbled and honored to learn with and from amazing student scholars at the University of Texas-Pan American, Pace University, and California Lutheran University. They often pushed and inspired me, and my hope is that they and students like them can use this work to enrich their knowledge about Latinas and Latinos in U.S. politics.*

Contents

Essays

A–Z Entries

VOLUME 1

VOLUME 2

Contents

Contents

Primary Documents

Guide to Related Topics

ACTIVISTS AND ORGANIZERS

Alvarado, Pablo (see National Day Laborer Organizing Network)

Arellano, Elvira

Avila, Joaquín

Baez, Joan

Cantú, Norma Elia

Cantú, Norma V.

Cartagena, Juan (see Latino Justice PRLDEF)

Chávez, César

Chavez-Thompson, Linda

Corona, Humberto "Bert"

Dawson, Rosario

Dickerson Montemayor, Alicia

Fererra, America

Fierro de Bright, Josefina

Gonzales Parsons, Lucy

Gonzales, Rodolfo "Corky"

Gutiérrez, José Ángel

Huerta, Dolores

Kumar, María Teresa

Longoria, Eva

Méndez, Sylvia

Moreno, Luisa

Murguía, Janet

Peña, Albert, Jr.

Pérez García, Héctor

Pimentel, Norma

Romero, Anthony D.

Rosales, Rosa

Schomburg, Arturo Alfonso

Tenayuca, Emma

Tijerina López, Reies

COURT DECISIONS

Alexander v. Sandoval (2001)

Balzac v. Porto [sic] *Rico* (1922)

Botiller v. Dominguez (1889)

Del Rio Independent School District v. Salvatierra (1930)

Delgado v. Bastrop I.S.D., et al. (1948)

Espinoza v. Farah (1973)

Evenwel v. Abbott (2016)

Hernandez v. New York (1991)

Hernández v. Texas (1954)

Immigration and Naturalization Service (INS) v. Cardoza-Fonseca (1987)

Johnson v. De Grandy (1994)

Lau v. Nichols (1974)

Mendez v. Westminster (1947)

Miranda v. Arizona (1966)

Plyler v. Doe (1982)

San Antonio Independent School District v. Rodriguez (1973)

United States v. Brignoni-Ponce (1975)

United States v. Verdugo-Urquidez (1990)

ELECTED AND APPOINTED OFFICIALS

Acosta Bañuelos, Romana (Treasurer of the United States)

Badillo, Herman

Becerra, Xavier

Berriozábal, María Antoinetta

Bush, George Prescott

Cardozo, Benjamin Nathan (Associate Justice of the U.S. Supreme Court)

Castro, Julián (U.S. Secretary of Housing and Urban Development)

Castro, Raúl Héctor. (U.S. Ambassador to Argentina)

Cavazos, Jr., Dr. Lauro "Fred" (U.S. Secretary of Education)

Cisneros, Henry G. (U.S. Secretary of Housing and Urban Development)

Cruz, Rafael Edward ("Ted")

de la Garza, Eligion "Kika"

de León, Kevin

Díaz, Jr., Rubén, Jr.

Díaz-Balart, Lincoln

Diaz-Balart, Mario

Echaveste, Maria (U.S. Presidential Advisor and White House Deputy Chief of Staff to Bill Clinton and White House Deputy Chief of Staff)

Espaillat, Adriano

Fariña, Carmen (New York City Schools Chancellor)

Ferreras-Copeland, Julissa

Gallego, Ruben

Giménez, Carlos

Gómez, Cruz

Gonzales, Alberto R. (U.S. Attorney General)

González, Charles Augustine "Charlie"

González, Henry B.

Grijalva, Raúl M.

Gutiérrez, Luis

Herrera Beutler, Jaime

Hinojosa, Rubén

Larrazolo, Octaviano A.

Luján, Ben Ray

Lujan Grisham, Michelle

Marín, Rosario (Treasurer of the United States)

Mark-Viverito, Melissa

Martinez, Susana

Menendez, Robert "Bob"

Napolitano, Grace Flores

Negrete McLeod, Gloria

Otero-Warren Adelina "Nina"

Peña, Federico (U.S. Secretary of Energy)

Perez, Thomas "Tom" Edward (U.S. Secretary of Labor)

Pierluisi Urrutia, Pedro

Rendón, Anthony

Richardson, William "Bill"

Ros-Lehtinen, Ileana

Roybal, Edward R.

Roybal-Allard, Lucille

Rubio, Marco

Ruiz, Raúl

Salazar, Kenneth Lee "Ken" (U.S. Secretary of the Interior)

Salinas Ender, Elma Teresa

Sánchez, Linda

Sanchez, Loretta

Serrano, José E.

Solis, Hilda

Sotomayor, Sonia Maria (Associate Justice of the U.S. Supreme Court)

Taveras, Angel

Torres, Norma

Van de Putte, Leticia

Velázquez, Nydia

Villaraigosa, Antonio, Jr.

CAMPAIGN AND POLITICAL PARTY STAFF AND CONSULTANTS

Aguilar, Jorge (Pelosi staff)

Aristimuño, José (O'Malley campaign)

Mallea, Jose (2016 Bush campaign)

Praeli, Lorella (2016 Clinton campaign)

Ramos, Paola (2016 Clinton campaign)

Renteria, Amanda (2016 Clinton campaign)

Silva, Jorge (2016 Clinton campaign)

Solis Doyle, Patti (2008 Obama campaign)

Sosa, Lionel (Republican strategist/ consultant)

Villarreal, Jose H. (2016 Clinton campaign)

LEGISLATION, PUBLIC POLICY, AND LANDMARK EVENTS

Affordable Care Act of 2010 and Latinos

Asylum Seekers

Balseros/Rafters (1994)

Bilingual Education, National Day Laborer Organizing Network (NDLOS)

Border Wall

Brown Power Movement/Chicano Civil Rights Movement

Catholicism and Latino/a Politics

Central American Migration

Chicano Moratorium (1970)

Cuban Adjustment Act of 1966

Deferred Action for Childhood Arrivals (DACA)/Deferred Action for Parents of Americans and Lawful Permanent Residents (DAPA)

Delano Grape Strike (1965–1970)

Depression-Era Repatriation of Mexicans

Discrimination against Latinas/os

DREAM Act

DREAM Act at the State Level

Education and Latinos

El Teatro Campesino

Election of 2016 and Latinos

Environmental Justice and Latinos

Family Leave and Reproductive Policy

Immigration and Customs Enforcement (ICE), Expanded Powers of (2000s)

Immigration as a Policy Issue

Immigration Reform and Control Act (IRCA)

Jones Act (1917)

Latina/o Gender Gap

Latina/o Identity Politics

Latina Political Leadership in the South

Latinas in U.S. Politics

Latino Political Power

MEDIA AND JOURNALISTS

ORGANIZATIONS

Central American Resource Center (CARECEN)

Coalition for Humane Immigrant Rights of Los Angeles (CHIRLA)

Community Service Organization (CSO)

Congressional Hispanic Caucus Institute (CHCI)

Crusade for Justice

DACA Sin Miedo

Equal Voice Network (EVN)

Hispanic Association of Colleges and Universities (HACU)

Immigrant Youth Justice League (IYJL)

La Raza Unida Party (LRU)

Latin Builders Association (LBA)

LatinoJustice PRLDEF

League of United Latin American Citizens (LULAC)

LIBRE Initiative

Mexican American Legal Defense and Educational Fund (MALDEF)

Mexican American Political Association (MAPA)

Mexican American Youth Organization (MAYO)

Mi Familia Vota

Movimiento Estudiantil Chicanx de Aztlán (M.E.Ch.A.)

National Association of Latino Elected and Appointed Officials (NALEO) Educational Fund

National Hispanic Caucus of State Legislators (NHCSL)

National Hispanic Leadership Agenda (NHLA)

National Immigration Law Center (NILC)

National Institute for Latino Policy (NiLP)

National Latina Institute for Reproductive Health (NLIRH)

#NotOneMore

Organized Communities against Deportations (OCAD)

Political Association of Spanish-Speaking Organizations (PASSO)

Salvadoran Humanitarian Aid, Relief, and Education Foundation (S.H.A.R.E.)

Southwest Voter Registration Education Project (SVREP)

UnidosUS

United Farmer Workers (UFW)

United We Dream

University of Missouri–Kansas City (UMKC) Hispanic Advisory Board

Viva Kennedy! Clubs

Voto Latino

Young Lords

Preface

Latinos in the American Political System: An Encyclopedia of Latinos as Voters, Candidates, and Office Holders is a two-volume collection of primary documents, essays, and short entries that takes an extensive view of Latinas/os and their involvement and impact on the U.S. political system. Accurate and readily available information about Latinas/os in U.S. politics has been wanting. The need to fill the void of information on the subject was the impetus to create this encyclopedia. Composed of a variety of materials, *Latinos in the American Political System* provides readers with information that is accessible and that imparts insights into many dimensions of the Latina/o political experience in the United States.

This work brings together current research on areas of major concern and debate in the fields of political science, sociology, anthropology, ethnic studies, American studies, and other social sciences in relation to the most prominent groups of people of Latin American descent in the United States. Although the encyclopedia attempts to cover as broad a range of Latina/o contributions to and experiences with politics as is possible, it does not purport to cover every conceivable issue in the field. The idea is to focus on the experiences of the largest ethnic group in the country, including major milestones, accomplishments, and policy, for which data are available. Mexican American communities comprise the largest proportion of the Latino population and have had the largest presence in the United States. Hence, a significant portion of the encyclopedia concentrates on this subgroup. However, substantial effort was made to include the experiences and contributions of relatively smaller, but growing, groups like Dominicans and Central Americans.

Latinos in the American Political System is a resource to disseminate information on an important and much-neglected topic. The experts, scholars, practitioners, and others who contributed to this encyclopedia amassed materials that add to the literature in a variety of social science disciplines. Although the editor is conscious of the need for ongoing research in these areas, this encyclopedia is designed to serve as a reference and resource on Latina and Latino experiences with the U.S. political system. It is intended to expose a broader audience of readers, including high school students and college and university undergraduates, to a variety of critical analyses and information in a relatively concise manner, and also to serve as a quick reference for those readers seeking to identify areas for further research.

HOW THIS ENCYCLOPEDIA IS ORGANIZED

Latinos in the American Political System contains four long topical essays that provide depth of analysis, synthesis, and content context for such broad topics as Latino/a elected officials and office holders at the state and federal levels, Latino/a mayors, and Latino political mobilization and voter turnout. The encyclopedia also contains almost 240 alphabetically arranged short entries on specific topics and individuals. Over 20 primary document selections are included to expose readers to important historical concepts and provide unfiltered access to the record of social and political thought and policy. All essays, entries, and document selections are cross-referenced to related items throughout the encyclopedia. A Guide to Related Topics will help users trace broad themes and topics across the entries. While each entry and long essay conclude with a bibliography of print and electronic information resources specific to the topic, a bibliography of important general works is also included in the back matter for quick reference. The encyclopedia also offers an annotated guide to Latino organizations across the U.S. political landscape and a chronology of important events in Latino political history in the United States. The various components of the encyclopedia—long essays, short entries, primary documents, the annotated list of organizations, and the general bibliography and chronology—all help provide the reader with a range of information about the subject matter. These components also provide an overview of and information about topics that are not readily available elsewhere in one publication.

TERMINOLOGY

The question of which term is more appropriate to use when referring to Latinas/os has been a subject of much debate. Formally adopted by the U.S. government in the late 1960s, "Hispanic" has been the category used by government agencies. This is a term that identifies a person by tracing their ancestry to Spain and from those countries that were part of the former Spanish colonial empire. Because this term identifies people based on their colonial experience, or that of their ancestors, some people prefer to use different terminology, such as Latino, Latina, or Latinx.

Latina/o refers to persons of Latin American origin (i.e., Mexico, Central and South America, and the Iberian Peninsula) as well as those who identify as being of these experiences that includes language and cultural beliefs and practices. It is a collection of persons from different parts of the world and different histories, having experiences and contact with each other to form common bonds, encounters, and cultural practices, including the experience of societal mistreatment, to form a community in the United States. Latinx (plural Latinxs) is a gender-neutral term often used in lieu of Latino or Latina (referencing Latin American cultural or racial identity). The x replaces the standard o/a ending in Spanish and Portuguese forming nouns of the masculine and feminine genders, respectively. Both Hispanic and Latina/o/x are pan-ethnic terms that are used to group various ethnic subgroups together based on their related cultural origins and/or geographic, linguistic, religious, or racial similarities.

Research indicates that when given the option, Latinas/os prefer to identify themselves by their country of origin—Mexican, Dominican, Cuban, Puerto Rican, and so on—but many share a sense of belonging to a community of Latinas/os and/or Hispanics. "Hyphenated identity" such as Mexican American, Cuban American, and Salvadoran American are also sometimes utilized. And terms like *Chicana/o/x* or *Mexicana/o* are chosen to identify some Mexican Americans in the United States.

The terms most often used by contributors to this encyclopedia are "Latina" or "Latino" or the gender-neutral version of this word. The term Hispanic is also used interchangeably with Latina/o/x. As an ethnoracial minority group, Latinas/os are sometimes referred to as a "minority group." This is typically employed to identify the group as a disadvantaged ethnoracial group in the United States, and therefore "people of color" or "communit(ies) of color" are most often used instead.

PEER REVIEWERS

This encyclopedia was supported by the efforts of peer reviewers who provided invaluable insights and comments on longer essays included in these volumes. I extend my appreciation to them for their assistance and inspiring work. Responsibility for the contents of this book resides solely with the editor and not the reviewers.

Jessica L. Lavariega Monforti

Acknowledgments

In an undertaking like this two-volume encyclopedia, there are many moving parts and myriad people to thank. First, I would like to thank ABC-CLIO for inviting to lead this project, which would simply not be possible without the contributing authors and ABC-CLIO staff. A full list of contributing authors is available at the end of the encyclopedia. *Mil gracias* (many thanks) to all of you. Your dedication to this project through drafts and edits to the final project is greatly appreciated. I would also like to thank colleagues for useful comments, recommendations, and suggestions throughout the development of this work.

I would also like to thank the many Latina and Latino candidates, activists, leaders, and elected officials without whom this encyclopedia would simply not exist. Thank you for breaking down barriers and choosing to actively participate and shape our democracy. Your experiences inspire this work, as well as demonstrate what remains to be done.

The work would simply not be possible without the encouragement and patience of my family. Thank you to *mi querido esposo* (my dear husband), Belsay, and my daughters for your love and the support you've shown me throughout this project. In many ways, publishing this work is a result of our combined efforts.

Introduction

For at least the last decade, scholars and pundits alike have been pointing to the swell of Latina/o population growth in the United States and the potential for this population to influence the country's political landscape. Since 1960, the nation's Latino population has increased nearly ninefold, from 6.3 million then to 56.5 million by 2015, and, by 2065, the population is projected to expand to 107 million. The Latino immigrant population has increased to nearly 20 times its size over the past half-century, from less than 1 million in 1960 to 19.4 million in 2015. After increasing for at least four decades, the share of the Hispanic population that is foreign born began declining after 2000. Among all Hispanics, the share that was born in another country was 34.4 percent in 2015, down from a peak of about 40 percent earlier in the 2000s. The share of adult Hispanics who are foreign born began declining a bit later—47.9 percent of Hispanic adults were born in another country in 2015, down from a peak of 55.0 percent in 2007. The U.S.-born Latino population increased sixfold over this same period; there are about 32 million more U.S.-born Latinos in the country today (37.1 million) than there were in 1960 (5.5 million). This growth has pushed seismic demographic change in U.S. society and its politics. The Hispanic population is more and more visible across the country, and its growth is increasingly controversial in some places. Some claim that Latinos are the future of U.S. politics, while others claim that these communities will contribute to the downfall of American culture. Regardless of the position people take on this question, all sides seem to agree that Latino influence on U.S. society and in politics is significant.

As the Hispanic population increases in size, so does the number of potential Latino voters. This is a very young population that is growing fast, and the two elements feeding that population growth—births and immigration—do not immediately translate into growth in the number of eligible voters. Nearly two-thirds (63%) of the people added to the Hispanic population lacked one of the two requirements for voting: age and citizenship. Hispanics are a fast-growing population and a fast-growing political presence at a time when other major segments of the rest of the U.S. population are growing slowly, if at all. Of the 5.7 million Hispanics added to the U.S. population between the last two presidential elections, 1.7 million persons, or 30 percent, were under 18 years old. Most are native-born U.S. citizens and hence will eventually become eligible voters. And when they do, they will join the electorate at a rapid rate. While the number of Latino voters jumps up in each successive election, the ballot-box clout of Latinos grows very little despite hitting record-breaking turnout. Since 2012, the number of Hispanic eligible voters has increased by 4 million, accounting for 37 percent of the growth in all eligible voters during that span. In other words, as the number of Latino eligible voters has reached new highs with each election, so has the number of Latino voters. But the number of Latinos who do not vote reached new highs as well. In 2008, a then-record 9.8 million Latino eligible voters did not vote. That number rose to 12.1 million in 2012, despite record turnout of Latino voters. At the state and local levels, the same is true. For example, in the 2018 Texas primary election, where Latinos comprise 40 percent of the state's population, Latino voter turnout surged but still lags behind that of the wider electorate. While Latinos have favored the Democratic Party over the Republican Party in every presidential election since at least the 1980s, their electoral impact has long been limited by low voter turnout and a population concentrated in non-battleground states.

Latinos also affect U.S. politics as elected and appointed officials. As of 2016, there were over 6,000 Latinos among the more than half a million elected officials in the United States. The majority serve as school board members and local officials, such as mayors, commissioners, and judges. The number of Latinos in government positions increased 61 percent over the past 20 years, but the level of representation has not kept pace with population growth more broadly. Despite being the nation's largest minority group, Hispanics are still largely underrepresented in politics: they are almost a fifth of the population but make up only 1 percent of all elected and appointed officials in the United States. Nevertheless, Latinos have achieved political power in elected and appointed positions across different branches of government over the past two decades.

These data indicate that Latino communities are engaged in political behavior, with the potential for increased mobilization and engagement over the short and long terms. What people, events, and policies got us to this point? What are the major trends in Latino politics? What have been the major contributions of Latino communities and individuals to the development of U.S. politics? These are some of the questions answered in *Latinos in the American Political System: An Encyclopedia of Latinos as Voters, Candidates, and Office Holders*.

Jessica L. Lavariega Monforti

Chronology

1848
The Treaty of Guadalupe Hidalgo is signed, ending the Mexican-American War (1846–1848) and forcing Mexico to cede the present-day Southwest, including California, Nevada, Utah and parts of Arizona, New Mexico, Colorado, and Wyoming.

1889
The U.S. Supreme Court decision in *Botiller v. Dominguez* addresses the validity of Spanish and Mexican land in territories annexed from Mexico under the terms of the Treaty of Guadalupe Hidalgo.

1914
The Colorado National Guard and guards of the Rockefeller family–owned Colorado Fuel & Iron Company attack 1,200 striking coal miners in what would come to be known as the Ludlow Massacre. Several dozens were killed, including wives and children of Latino origin.

1917
Congress passes the Jones Act, granting U.S. citizenship to the residents of Puerto Rico. It also created a separation of powers between the executive, judiciary, and legislature branches and established a bicameral legislature.

1922
The U.S. Supreme Court renders a decision in *Balzac v. Porto* [sic] *Rico*—one of the so-called "Insular Cases," which pertain to the relationship between U.S. territories and the U.S. mainland.

1926
The Spanish-language daily newspaper *La Opinión* is founded by Ignacio Eugenio Lozano, Sr. *La Opinión* becomes the major print news outlet for Spanish-speaking Latinos living in Southern California.

1928–1929
Octaviano Larrazolo, the former governor of New Mexico (1919–1921), becomes the first Mexican American to serve in the U.S. Senate.

1929
The League of United Latin American Citizens (LULAC), a civil rights organization, is established in Corpus Christi, Texas.

1930

Texas courts consider the segregation of students of Mexican descent in Texas schools in *Del Rio Independent School District v. Salvatierra*.

1932

President Herbert Hoover names Benjamin Cardozo to the Supreme Court of the United States.

1942

The Bracero Program is initiated, bringing millions of Mexican guest workers into the United States before its termination in 1964.

1943

The Zoot Suit Riots erupt in Los Angeles. These were a series of conflicts that occurred between U.S. servicemen, Mexican American youths, and other minorities.

1946

Mendez, et al. v. Westminster [sic] School District of Orange County, et al. is a U.S. Court of Appeals case that challenges the remediation and segregation of schools attended by Mexican American students.

1947

The Community Service Organization (CSO), a California Latino civil rights organization, is formed to mobilize disenfranchised Mexican American residents in East Los Angeles. It is famous for training César Chávez and Dolores Huerta.

1948

Hector Pérez García and other Mexican American leaders create the American GI Forum, a civil rights organization, in Corpus Christi, Texas. The Forum is dedicated to addressing discrimination and inequities for Latino veterans.

1948

In *Delgado v. Bastrop*, Texas courts once again consider the remediation and segregation of Mexican American students in Texas schools.

1954

Hernández v. Texas is a case involving racial and ethnic discrimination against Mexican Americans in jury selection. It is the first and only Mexican civil rights case to be tried by Mexican American lawyers before the U.S. Supreme Court.

1954

The U.S. Immigration and Naturalization Service (INS) launches Operation Wetback, an immigration law enforcement initiative created in cooperation with the Mexican government that resulted in the mass deportation of Mexican nationals.

1960s

Chicano youth in the barrios of Los Angeles establish the Brown Berets, a community-based social justice organization modeled after the Black Panther Party.

1960

The Mexican American Political Association (MAPA) is a civic rights organization formed in Fresno, California, whose mission was to place more Mexican Americans in elected and appointed offices.

1960

The Viva Kennedy! Movement is initiated to support John F. Kennedy's campaign for president. It is composed of a series of clubs operating in Latino communities throughout the Southwestern United States, the upper Midwest, and New York.

1961

Henry González (D) is elected to the U.S. House of Representative from the 20th congressional district in Texas.

1962

César Chávez and Dolores Huerta form the National Farm Workers Association (NFWA), known today as the United Farm Workers (UFW).

1962

Edward R. Roybal (D) is elected to the U.S. House of Representatives from the 25th congressional district in East Los Angeles, California.

1964

Kika de la Garza (D) is elected to the U.S. House of Representatives from the 15th congressional district in Texas. He serves in the House for 32 years (1965–1997).

1965–1970

The Delano grape strike, a five-year confrontation between farm workers and California grape growers, is led by César Chávez and the United Farm Workers (UFW). The strike involves walkouts, marches, and consumer boycotts.

1965

El Teatro Campesino, or Farmworkers Theatre, is launched by Luis Valdez as part of the Delano grape strike.

1966

Rodolfo "Corky" Gonzales founds the Crusade for Justice, a Mexican American social and political organization, in Denver, Colorado.

1966

In the landmark case *Miranda v. Arizona,* the U.S. Supreme Court extends and clarifies the protections of those accused of a crime.

1966

Congress passes the Cuban Adjustment Act (CAA), which allows any native or citizen of Cuba who entered the United States after January 1, 1959, to adjust their status to legal permanent residents after being present in the United States for at least two years.

1966
Farm workers strike against La Casita Farms and other large melon growers in Rio Grande City and other towns in Starr County, Texas

1967
The Mexican American Youth Organization (MAYO), a civil rights organization, is founded in San Antonio, Texas, by five graduate and undergraduate students at Saint Mary's University.

1968
Congress passes the Bilingual Education Act (BEA) to address the needs of limited-English-speaking-ability (LESA) students.

1968
The East Los Angeles School Walk Outs are organized by Chicano students to protest the poor and inadequate educational conditions in their high schools.

1968
The Mexican American Legal Defense and Educational Fund (MALDEF), a civil rights organization, is founded by Pete Tejerina and Mario Obledo in San Antonio, Texas.

1968
UnidosUS, the largest national Hispanic civil rights and nonpartisan advocacy organization in the United States, is founded as the Southwest Council of La Raza.

1969
The Movimiento Estudiantil Chicanx de Aztlan (M.E.Ch.A.), a student-led organization, is established to promote unity and empowerment via political action.

1970
The La Raza Unida (LRU), a political party centered on Chicano (Mexican American) nationalism, is founded in Texas.

1971–1974
Romana Acosta Bañuelos becomes the first Latina to serve as treasurer of the United States during the Nixon administration.

1970
The Chicano Moratorium protests the deaths of Chicano soldiers in Vietnam.

1970
Herman Badillo (D) is elected to the U.S. House of Representatives, becoming the first Puerto Rican–born voting member to serve in the House (1971–1977).

1971
The Latin Builders Association (LBA), the largest Hispanic construction association in the United States, is founded in Miami, Florida.

1972
The Puerto Rican Legal Defense and Education Fund (PRLDEF), a national Latinx civil rights litigation and advocacy organization, is founded by three Puerto Rican

attorneys from New York. Today, the organization is known as Latino Justice PRLDEF.

1973

In *Espinoza v. Farah,* the U.S. Supreme Court considers whether Title VII of the Civil Rights Act of 1964 affords protections to both citizens and noncitizens.

1973

Decided by the U.S. Supreme Court, *San Antonio Independent School District v. Rodriguez* is the first case involving Mexican Americans that challenges how the state of Texas uses local property taxes to fund public education.

1974

Congress passes the Equal Educational Opportunities Act.

1974

The U.S. Supreme Court declares in *Lau v. Nichols* that the lack of supplemental instruction for students with limited English-speaking ability in public schools violated the Civil Rights Act of 1964.

1974

Raúl Castro (D) becomes the first Mexican-born U.S. citizen elected governor of Arizona.

1974

The Southwest Voter Registration Education Project (SVREP), the largest and oldest nonpartisan Latino voter participation organization in the United States, is founded in San Antonio, Texas.

1975

In *United States v. Brignoni-Ponce,* the U.S. Supreme Court declared that it was unconstitutional for Border Patrol to stop vehicles based on drivers appearing to be of Mexican descent. This is the first racial profiling case of its kind involving Latinos.

1976

Five Latino members of Congress establish the Congressional Hispanic Caucus.

1976

Congressman Edward R. Roybal (D) of California founds the National Association of Latino Democratic Officials, which is later renamed the National Association of Latino Elected and Appointed Officials (NALEO) Educational Fund. NALEO is a nonpartisan membership association of the nation's elected and appointed Latino public officials.

1977

El Nuevo Herald, one of the largest Spanish-language newspapers in the United States, begins as a weekly Spanish insert in the *Miami Herald.*

1978

U.S. Representatives and Congressional Hispanic Caucus members Edward Roybal, E. "Kika" de la Garza, and Baltasar Corrada del Rio create the Congressional

Hispanic Caucus Institute, Inc., to provide educational opportunities for the Hispanic community.

1979

La Voz de Houston, a Spanish-language newspaper, is founded in Houston.

1979

The National Immigration Law Center (NILC), a U.S.-based nonprofit, nonpartisan organization, is established to defend and advance the rights of low-income immigrants and their families.

1980

Fidel Castro allows over 100,000 Cuban exiles, known as "Marielitos," to leave the island from the port of Mariel, en route to the United States.

1981

The Salvadoran Humanitarian Aid, Relief and Education Foundation (S.H.A.R.E.) is founded in Washington, D.C.

1982

The Institute for Puerto Rican Policy (IPR) is founded in New York. The nonpartisan, nonprofit organization is later renamed the National Institute for Latino Policy, Inc. (NiLP).

1982

The landmark decision by the U.S. Supreme Court in *Plyler v. Doe* made it unconstitutional for any state to deny students a free public education on account of their immigration status.

1985

The newspaper *El Especialito* is founded in Union City, New Jersey, by Cuban immigrant Antonio Ibarria.

1986

President Ronald Reagan signs the Immigration Reform and Control Act (IRCA).

1986

The Coalition for Humane Immigrant Rights of Los Angles (CHIRLA) is founded to protect immigrant rights following passage of the Immigration Reform and Control Act (IRCA).

1986

The Hispanic Association of Colleges and Universities (HACU), an association of colleges and universities, is founded to improve educational opportunities for Hispanic students.

1987

In *Immigration and Naturalization Service (INS) v. Cardoza-Fonseca,* the U.S. Supreme Court considers questions of asylum and deportation for immigrants.

1988–1990

Lauro Fred Cavazos, Jr., becomes the first Hispanic to serve in a U.S. cabinet as secretary of education under Presidents Ronald Reagan and George H. W. Bush.

1989

Former Colorado state senator Larry Trujillo founds the National Hispanic Caucus of State Legislators (NHCSL), a nonpartisan member organization of the National Hispanic Leadership Agenda (NHLA) that represents Hispanic elected state officials.

1989

Ileana Ros-Lehtinen (R) is elected to the U.S. House of Representatives from the 27th congressional district in Florida.

1991

The National Hispanic Leadership Agenda (NHLA), a nonprofit and nonpartisan coalition of 40 major Hispanic national organizations and Hispanic leaders, is founded.

1991

In *Hernandez v. New York*, the U.S. Supreme Court renders a decision regarding the right to an impartial jury as called for by the Sixth Amendment.

1992

Maria Hinojosa and Maria Martin launch *Latino USA,* a weekly NPR show focused on Latinos.

1992

Lincoln Díaz-Balart (R) is the first Cuban American elected to the U.S. House of Representatives from the 21st congressional district in Florida. He serves in Congress until 2011.

1992

Lucille Roybal-Allard (D) is elected to the U.S. House of Representatives from the 40th congressional district in California.

1992

Luis Gutiérrez (D) becomes the first Latino elected to the U.S. House of Representatives from the 4th congressional district in Illinois.

1993

The Border Patrol conducts Operation Hold the Line, originally named Operation Blockade, to prevent undocumented border crossings in the El Paso sector of the U.S.-Mexican border.

1993–1997

Henry G. Cisneros, a former mayor of San Antonio, Texas (1981–1989), serves as secretary of Housing and Urban Development (HUD) under President Bill Clinton.

1993–1997

Federico Peña serves as secretary of transportation in the Clinton administration. He will go on to serve in the same administration as secretary of energy (1997–1998).

1994

Over 32,000 Cubans leave the island for the United States without documents on rafts or small boats. They become known as the *balseros.*

1994

The National Latina Institute for Reproductive Health (NLIRH), a nonprofit advocacy organization that provides reproductive health services for underserved Latina populations, is founded.

1994

The Immigration and Naturalization Service launches Operation Gatekeeper to halt illegal immigration at the U.S.–Mexico border near San Diego.

1994

California voters overwhelmingly approve Proposition 187, a ballot initiative aimed at prohibiting undocumented immigrants from using health care, public education, and other social services.

1995

Linda Chavez-Thompson is elected executive vice-president of the American Federation of Labor–Congress of Industrial Organizations (AFL-CIO).

1996

Rubén Hinojosa (D) is elected to the U.S. House of Representatives from the 15th congressional district in Texas. He serves until 2017.

1997

President Bill Clinton signs the Nicaraguan Adjustment and Central American Relief Act (NACARA).

1998–2001

Maria Echaveste serves as deputy chief of staff in the Clinton White House.

2000

Mi Familia Vota, a nonprofit civic engagement organization, is founded in Los Angeles.

2001

In the *Alexander v. Sandoval* decision, the U.S. Supreme Court rules that Title VI of the Civil Rights Act of 1964 does allow private lawsuits based on evidence of disparate impact; in this case, the plaintiff sought to sue the Alabama Department of Public Safety (DPS) for its failure to adopt a driver's license exam for non-English speakers.

2001

The Development, Relief, and Education for Alien Minors (DREAM) Act is introduced into Congress but not passed; the bill was designed to grant legal status to undocumented immigrants, especially those who arrived in the United States as children and pursued higher education or military service.

2001

Anthony D. Romero becomes executive director of the American Civil Liberties Union (ACLU), the country's leading civil rights litigation and advocacy organization.

2001
The National Day Laborer Organizing Network (NDLON) is founded in Northridge, California.

2001–2003
Rosario Marín serves as treasurer of the United States under President George W. Bush.

2002
Norma V. Cantú founds the Mexican American Legislative Leadership Foundation, an organization that helps Mexican American students develop leadership skills in the Texas legislature.

2002
Mario Díaz-Balart (R) is elected to the U.S. House of Representatives from Florida's 25th congressional district.

2002
Bill Richardson (D) is elected governor of New Mexico. He serves until 2011.

2002
Raúl Grijalva (D) is elected to the U.S. House of Representatives from Arizona's 3rd congressional district.

2004
Rosario Dawson and MSNBC political pundit Maria Teresa Kumar cofound Voto Latino, a political outreach organization seeking to raise awareness of issues of importance to Latinos.

2005
Antonio Villaraigosa is elected the 41st mayor of Los Angeles. He became the first Latino mayor of Los Angeles since 1872.

2005
Jointly conducted by the Department of Homeland Security and the Department of Justice, Operation Streamline employs a "zero-tolerance" approach to unauthorized border crossing by conducting criminal prosecutions of those engaging in such crossings.

2005–2007
Alberto Gonzales serves as attorney general of the United States under President George W. Bush.

2006
President George W. Bush signs the Border Fence Act, which begins construction of a border wall along portions of the U.S.–Mexican border.

2006
Los Angeles school walk-outs are organized to protest passage by the U.S. House of Representatives of the Border Protection, Anti-terrorism, and Illegal Immigration Control Act. The act later failed to pass in the Senate.

2006

U.S. immigration protest marches, known as Mega Marchas, are launched in various cities across the nation.

2006

Robert Menendez is elected to the U.S. Senate from New Jersey.

2007

United We Dream, the largest youth-led immigrant advocacy network in the United States, is founded.

2008

Ben Ray Luján (D) is elected to the U.S. House of Representatives from New Mexico's 3rd congressional district.

2009

Julissa Ferreras-Copeland is elected to the New York City Council from the 21st district, becoming the first Latina ever elected to represent Queens.

2009

Rubén Díaz, Jr. (D) is elected president of the Borough of the Bronx in New York City.

2009

The Immigrant Youth Justice League (IYJL), a Chicago-based nonprofit, is founded by undocumented youth.

2009

President Barack Obama nominates Sonia Sotomayor as an associate justice of the U.S. Supreme Court. She becomes the first Latina and first justice of Puerto Rican descent to serve on the Court.

2009–2013

Ken Salazar, former U.S. senator from Colorado, serves in the Obama administration as secretary of the interior.

2009–2013

Hilda Solis serves as labor secretary under President Barack Obama, becoming the first Latina to serve in a cabinet-level position.

2009–2016

Pedro Pierluisi Urrutia serves as the resident commissioner for Puerto Rico.

2010

Arizona governor Jan Brewer signs Senate Bill 1070 (SB 1070), known as the Support Our Law Enforcement and Safe Neighborhoods Act of 2010. This measure is one of the strictest and most controversial immigration laws of its time.

2010

Jaime Herrera Beutler (R) becomes the first Latina elected to the U.S. House of Representatives from Washington State's 3rd congressional district.

2010
Susana Martinez becomes the first Latina to be elected governor of New Mexico and in the United States.

2010
Marco Rubio is elected to the U.S. Senate from Florida.

2010
Angel Taveras is elected mayor of Providence, Rhode Island, becoming the city's first Latino mayor.

2011
Juan Cartagena becomes president and general counsel of Latino Justice PRLDEF.

2011
Carlos Giménez is elected mayor of Miami-Dade County in Florida.

2012
Rafael Edward "Ted" Cruz (R) is elected to the U.S. Senate in the state of Texas.

2012
Michelle Lujan Grisham (D) is elected to the U.S. House of Representatives from New Mexico's 1st congressional district.

2012
By executive action, President Barack Obama grants DREAMers—children brought to the United States at a young age—a two-year work permit and protection from deportation through the Deferred Action for Childhood Arrivals (DACA) program.

2012
Organized Communities against Deportations (OCAD) is founded in Chicago.

2013
The National Day Laborer Network (NDLON) launches the #NotOneMore project.

2013–2017
Tom Perez serves as secretary of labor in the Obama administration. He becomes chair of the Democratic National Committee in 2017.

2014
Carmen Fariña becomes chancellor of the New York City Department of Education, the largest public school district in the United States.

2014
George P. Bush, the grandson of former president George H. W. Bush and who is of Mexican descent on his mother's side, is elected commissioner of the Texas General Land Office.

2014
Kevin de León (D) is elected president pro tempore of the California State Senate.

2014

Various nonprofit groups, including the Catholic Legal Immigration Network (CLINIC), found the CARA Family Detention Pro Bono Project. The Project offers training and information on immigration matters affecting low-income immigrants.

2014

Ruben Gallego (D) is elected to the U.S. House of Representative from Arizona's 7th congressional district.

2014–2017

Julián Castro serves as U.S. secretary of Housing and Urban Development (HUD) under President Barack Obama.

2016

Adriano Espaillat (D) is elected to the U.S. House of Representatives from New York, becoming the first Dominican American and first formerly undocumented immigrant to be elected to Congress.

2016

In the presidential election, 79 percent of Latinos vote for Hillary Clinton (D), while 18 percent vote for Donald Trump (R).

2016

Xavier Becerra (D), a former member of the U.S. House of Representatives (1993–2017), is elected attorney general of California.

2016

President Barack Obama signs the Puerto Rico Oversight, Management, and Economic Stability Act (PROMESA), which attempts to mitigate Puerto Rico's debt.

2017

President Trump signs Executive Order 13767, calling for Immigration and Customs Enforcement (ICE) to hire 10,000 immigration officers to help ICE carry out its functions.

2017

President Trump ends the Deferred Action for Childhood Arrivals (DACA) program for DREAMers established under President Barack Obama in 2012.

2018

The Trump administration announces that it will use $1.6 billion in congressional appropriations to create and replace about 100 miles of wall along the U.S.–Mexico border.

Jaime Dominguez

Latino Elected Officials on the Federal Level

INTRODUCTION

The number of Latinos serving nationwide in the year 2017 is at a record high. According to the National Association of Latino Elected Officials (NALEO), a total of 6,600 Latinos have been elected to serve in the U.S. Congress, in the executive and the legislative powers of many states, and in multiple local governments. Approximately 36 percent of them (2,401) are women. More concretely, 321 Latinx elected officials serve in the state legislatures of 38 states—many of which did not have important concentrations of Latino populations in the recent past. Texas, California, New Mexico, and Arizona are the states with the highest number of Latino officials.

From all perspectives, this is a dramatic change and a clearly significant improvement from the situation that prevailed at the beginning of the 1960s, when Latinx were still a segregated, largely disfranchised, and economically disadvantaged community. They lived and worked then far from the centers of national power in the United States. With the notable exception of the state of New Mexico, Latinos and Latinas were almost politically invisible during the first five decades of the 20th century.

It is evident that the growing political influence that Latinos have at all levels of the American government today allows, on one hand, very optimistic views: some scholars see the political activity and relevance of the group in terms of a process of progressive mainstreaming. Clearly, Latinos and Latinas have been constantly breaking one glass ceiling after another with almost every election year. For example, in the 2016 election, a granddaughter of Mexican immigrants and former attorney general from Nevada, Catherine Cortez Masto (D), became the first Latina ever elected to serve in the U.S. Senate—a legislative body particularly notorious for the scarce presence of minorities throughout its history. The new Latina senator won the seat that former Senate Democratic minority leader, Harry Reid, had left vacant in the upper chamber of the national legislature. Meanwhile, that same year, Adriano Espaillat (D-NY) became the first Dominican American ever to be elected to the U.S. House of Representatives. Ruben Kihuen (D), is the first Latino ever to represent the state of Nevada, and Darren Soto (D) is the first Puerto Rican to represent Florida.

Yet despite gains, there are some relevant setbacks that clearly suggest that the full inclusion of Latinos into the American political system is still a work in progress. For instance, former congresswoman Loretta Sanchez lost a senatorial race in the state of California in 2016—and she also left the seat that she had had in the House of Representatives since 1996, having decided not to run for reelection. Loretta Sanchez and her sister Linda were the first Latina sisters ever to serve together in the history of the U.S. Congress. At the state level, two Latinos lost their seats in Kansas and four more lost their seats in the lower chambers of New Mexico, New York, Illinois, and Alaska. It is also remarkable that the Trump administration is the first one since the 1980s that does not have a Latinx person appointed to a cabinet position—not to mention the notorious anti-Latino and anti-immigrant messages that defined the president's political campaign.

Three points are critical to understand the ascent of Latinos to federal positions. The first is that the change in the access of Latinx politicians to the federal government is historically related to the Voting Rights Act changes approved in 1975. This post–Civil Rights legislation extended to Latinos and other language minorities provisions that eliminated old barriers to vote and created spaces where minority candidates would be able to run successfully.

Second, while Latinos continue to open political spaces and claim success in areas that were unthinkable only five decades ago, their access into the political institutions of mainstream America cannot be seen in terms of a progressive and unequivocal line of success. This is instead a process where a combination of success and failure occurs. Many Latinx candidates continue to face significant political obstacles and keep making decisions about their family names and the extent to which they should advertise or not their Latino background; some have difficulties getting the support of local leaders or face financial constraints to be electorally competitive. Some others have little chances to win in overcrowded primaries; many simply lose their electoral races.

The full understanding of the election of Latino officials today requires an accurate assessment of the contexts and strategies that determine the success of ethnic candidates. It is essential to account for failures and the reasons why such failures occur. That altogether may reveal a clearer picture of the limits that the Latino political power faces in today's American politics.

The third important point is related to concepts and ideas. Scholars have often used the theory of representation created by Hannah Pitkin in 1967 to understand the election of Latinos to federal positions. Pitkin identified several forms of representation. One of them, *descriptive representation* referred to the extent a body of elected officials reflects the sociodemographic characteristics of the population. It is from this perspective that analysts say that Latinx people are underrepresented: 17 percent of the population of the United States is Latinx, and yet, only 1 percent of all elected positions in the country are held by politicians of this group. Pitkin also considered that *substantive representation* refers to the extent to which elected officials take actions that advance the interests of minorities. Representation occurs in this way when elected officials advocate, express, and symbolize other people's preferred policies. Responsiveness is the key point here, or whether the work of those who are elected effectively reflects the interests of those who elected them.

Yet our theories are in need of updates. Despite their extended use and wide acceptance, these concepts are not necessarily useful to advance empirical research. They are isolated precisely from the framework where decisions occur, that is, elections. Additionally, they cannot account for the diversity of Latinos or for the fact that representatives and voters are not a monolithic group. It is worth mentioning, for instance, that three book-length works have been written on Latinos and Latinas in the U.S. Congress in the last decades, and all three have had to modify the concept of representation in one way or another. Moreover, the concept of representation is currently being seriously revisited and challenged by political theorists and by feminist theory scholars.

While analysts from the field of Latino studies have not fully revised the idea of representation, many are utilizing alternative concepts such as political incorporation or political inclusion to guide their studies. Both refer broadly to the process through which outsiders are integrated into the political structures of mainstream institutions. Given the complexities of Latinx participation in the American system, I use the latter concepts in that same broad way.

The sections that follow are predominantly concentrated on the election of Latinos to Congress, but also make reference to other significant victories at the state and local levels, in order to provide a deeper understanding of the political incorporation of the Latinx community, and the challenges that lie ahead.

POLITICAL PIONEERS

The access of outsiders to elected positions generally starts with individual cases of political inventiveness or bold ambition. In the case of Latinx, some important, isolated victories took place in the decade of the 1960s.

Between 1880 and 1960, New Mexico was the only state that sent Hispanics to serve in the U.S. Congress. In New Mexico, the preexistent Hispanic elites were able to maintain their political power throughout the first decades of the 20th century, which was exceptional in the political landscape of the Southwest. In addition to elite influence and the presence of large segments of Hispanic and Indian populations, there was unmistakable political intention: leaders like Octaviano Larrazolo (1859–1930) fought staunchly to defend the voice of the group and for its fair share of political influence and representation. Consequently, New Mexico sent more candidates of Hispanic origin to the national legislature than any other state during the first half of the 20th century. (Hispanics in the state, however, have usually emphasized more their Spanish heritage than the Latino one.)

Octaviano Larrazolo was the first politician of Mexican origin to serve in the U.S. Senate in 1929. A former governor of the state and a devoted fighter of Latino rights all his life, he served during a very brief period due to poor health. In 1934, after having served two terms in the House of Representatives, Dennis Chavez was appointed to the U.S. Senate to fill a vacancy. Chavez became a very important political figure; he ranked fourth in seniority in the upper chamber when he died in 1962. Another four Hispanic-origin politicians served in the lower chamber between 1911 and 1963 representing the state: Benigno C. Hernandez, Néstor Montoya, Antonio M. Fernández, and Joseph Montoya.

Outside New Mexico, the relations between Latinos and the mainstream society were largely unequal during the postwar period. Latinos suffered residential and school segregation, disenfranchisement, and high levels of racial prejudice. Nevertheless, the group also experienced—just like many other Americans—a gradual process of urbanization and some social mobility, which eventually translated into some modest political success.

Some Latinos made their mark in the states of California and Texas in the turbulent decade of the 1960s. In 1962 Philip Soto and John Moreno were elected to the California Assembly, which had not had a Latino member since 1907. Edward Roybal was an important influence in those elections. Roybal, a former health worker, community organizer, public health educator, and councilman from Los Angeles (between 1949 and 1962), won the race to represent the area of East Los Angeles in the House of Representatives. He was the first Latino to represent the state of California in the Congress since 1879. Roybal was decisively active in Latino affairs and inspired a whole generation of Mexican Americans in the state. In 1976, he was one of the key founding members of the Congressional Hispanic Caucus (CHC). The CHC is an organization of congresspersons of Latino descent ruled by the House of Representatives.

Other isolated victories were remarkable in Texas. Henry B. Gonzalez and Eligio "Kika" de la Garza were elected to serve in the U.S. House of Representatives in 1961 and 1964, respectively. Gonzalez was born in the city of San Antonio in 1916; he received a law degree and later won an election to the city council of San Antonio. He became a Texas state senator in 1956—the first Mexican to do so since 1846. As a state senator, he received considerable attention for his filibuster to stop passing discriminatory bills that were meant to circumvent the decision related to the *Brown v. Board of Education* case. His election to the U.S. Congress was supported by the "Viva Kennedy" clubs that had been formed then and by Lyndon B. Johnson, then vice-president of the United States, personally. Gonzalez had a colorful personality and was a staunch liberal, but he had particular perspectives that were often contrary to those of several Latino leaders of his generation. He was particularly critical of some strategies of the Chicano Movement and favored paths of assimilation rather than contestation. He served in Congress until 1988.

Eligio de la Garza was born in Mercedes, Texas. He also had a law degree and served in the Korean War. Upon his return to Texas, he was elected to the Texas House of Representatives. He was much closer to the prevalent political elites in Texas than Gonzalez. Beyond the mainland, there was also a representative of Cuban origin elected from Hawaii in 1962: Thomas Ponce Gil (D). He served for just one term.

Toward the end of the decade, in 1968, Manuel Luján, a politician from New Mexico, was the first Republican Latino to join the group of Hispanic congresspersons in Washington. He belonged to an important family in New Mexico that had a prominent insurance business. Republican Latinos at that time were fully incorporated into the elites of their states, and it is not surprising that Congressman Luján was more conservative than his Latino peers in Congress. He served for 10 terms in this position and was appointed secretary of the interior during the administration of George H. W. Bush in 1993.

Most Latino elected officials were affiliated with the Democratic Party during those years, and the Republican Party did not have Latino candidates elected in states other than New Mexico. In this context, Representative Luján received considerable attention from his national party leaders, representing the symbolic presence of Latinx Republicans in general. A few years later, Henry Bonilla, from Texas, was in a similar case. A former TV anchor and producer, he was recruited by the Republican Party leaders of Texas to unseat Albert Bustamante, a Democratic incumbent who was under federal grand jury investigation. Bonilla was elected to the House of Representatives in 1993 and remained in his seat until 2007. He was a fiscal conservative who favored anti-immigrant agendas.

If access to electoral positions was scarce for Latinos, it was even more so for Latinas. Yet Latinas were active at different levels as well. Dolores Huerta was a prominent activist who worked for the rights of agricultural workers; many other Latinas were also participating in a variety of community organizations during the 1960s, and some of them took relatively visible leadership roles. Virginia Musquiz was the first woman to run for the city council in Crystal City, Texas, in 1963, and also the first Latina to run for a seat in the Texas House of Representatives in 1965. Both bids were unsuccessful, but in 1974, she won an election as clerk in a Texan county. Before then, she was the national chair for the Raza Unida Party (1972–1974). In subsequent years, however, the parties that grew out of the Chicano Movement disappeared, and Latinos and Latinas increasingly worked within the framework of the two major parties.

In California, Linda Benitez worked actively in the Los Angeles Central Committee of the Democratic Party, becoming a member of its executive board in the middle of the 1960s. Another Latina, Julia Luna Mont, and was one of the founders of the Peace and Freedom Party; she ran unsuccessfully for the Los Angeles School Board in 1967. Puerto Rican women worked with the Young Lords, and several Cuban Americans participated in multiple organizations predominantly related to policies regarding Cuba during the 1960s.

As the decade was reaching its end, some important changes had taken place for Latinos in the United States. First of all, the Chicano Movement had attracted, in one way or another, a degree of national attention that Latinx people never had before; for the first time, the presence of Latinos was recognized by the political elites of Washington. Furthermore, other important demographic changes were also taking place: the Latino population started to grow because of higher birth rates than the mainstream population, added to increasing migration from Latin America. The patterns of geographic distribution of Latinos were changing too, given that newcomers settled in areas beyond the Southwest after 1965. All these factors were even more relevant in the context of the new rules of decennial redistricting that were taking place, which made the Latino presence more politically relevant overall.

Latino officials who served during those years had experienced considerable social mobility, but they have also suffered or witnessed different forms of discrimination. Their socialization instilled in that generation an acute sense of commitment to advance the goals of their co-ethnics.

THE TURNING POINT: THE VOTING RIGHTS ACT AND BEYOND

Some isolated victories took place in the 1970s, but the following decade would mark a clear point of change for Latinx political inclusion in the United States. In 1975, the provisions of the Voting Rights Act (VRA)—a critical piece of legislation approved in the aftermath of the Civil Rights Movement—were also extended to Latinos and Asians. This legislation sought to eliminate the barriers that prevented blacks in the United States from enfranchisement and from fully participating in the electoral process.

The 1975 Voting Rights Act extensions also created the electoral spaces where minorities could win congressional elections: the majority-minority districts; they are the reason why the presence of Latino officials increased in truly unprecedented numbers in subsequent years. Change, however, did not happen immediately: in Congress, for instance, the real representation of Latinos in a sustained pattern of access started only in the following decade, that is, during the 1980s. Then, the decennial redistribution of the number of seats that each state receives was completed (reapportionment), and the state legislatures had finished creating the boundaries of their new districts (redistricting).

At the start of the 1970s, Herman Badillo, from New York, became the first Puerto Rican–born congressperson to be elected to the U.S. House of Representatives. (Puerto Ricans have a resident commissioner who represents the voice of the island in Congress but lacks the voting power that state representatives have.) Badillo served there until 1977, when he resigned to take a position of deputy mayor of New York City. He was succeeded by another young and energetic Latino of Puerto Rican background, Robert Garcia, who just like Badillo, became a very active member of the Congressional Hispanic Caucus.

As scholar Rodolfo de la Garza accurately stated, the Latino presence in Congress at that time was merely a sign of the incipient presence of the ethnic group at the national level. These Latinos were actually part of the first group of Latinx national legislators ever in the United States. More broadly, their presence suggested the existence of an incipient Latino middle class as well.

Until the 1990s, New Mexico was the only state that elected Hispanic governors. Yet that does not mean that the presence of Latinos in such office was always frequent. Jerry Apodaca, elected in 1975, was the first Latino to serve in such a position since 1918. Apodaca had previously served as a state legislator for eight years. Later, in 1983, Toney Anaya also became a governor of the state in 1983.

Raul H. Castro (D-AR) was the first Latino governor elected outside New Mexico; he served from 1975 to 1977. Born in Mexico, he was raised in a large family of modest means; his father died when he was a young adolescent. Castro nonetheless won a fellowship that allowed him to attend college while performing different jobs; later he earned a law degree as well. He practiced law in Tucson, Arizona, before starting his political career. In 1954, Castro won an election as a county attorney and later became a county superior court judge. When his reputation grew, he met the aide of an Arizona senator, who was able to connect him with the highest power circles in Washington. President Lyndon B. Johnson appointed him ambassador to El Salvador, and he also served in Bolivia afterward. Upon his return to Arizona, Castro had an unsuccessful bid as governor in 1970, but he ran again and succeeded in 1974.

The presence of Latinos in statewide executive offices was infrequent as the end of the century approached (and it remains so to this date). In 1990, for instance, there was only one Spanish-speaking governor serving in the entire country, Robert Martinez (Florida), but his background was actually Spanish, not Latino.

The direct influence of the Voting Rights Act in the election of minority candidates to Congress is clear and indisputable: virtually all Latinx candidates who were elected during the last two decades of the century ran in newly created districts. The number of majority-Latino districts was directly related to the number of Latino members of Congress. Among them, Matthew Martinez and Esteban Torres won their races in Los Angeles, California. Salomon Ortiz was elected in the area of Brownsville/Corpus Christi, Texas, and Albert Bustamante was elected in San Antonio, Texas, and several others followed. Bill Richardson (D-NM) was elected in 1984 to represent a newly created, largely white district of New Mexico. Richardson claims Latino background through his mother. His father was an American bank executive who lived with his family in Mexico City for several years for business reasons. Richardson served in Congress for seven terms, being an innovative force in the Congressional Hispanic Caucus, and reaching the position of deputy Democratic whip in the House of Representatives.

Other Latino candidates continued to open new spaces of inclusion at the state and local levels. In Miami, Florida, Maurice Ferré was elected mayor in 1973. Ferré was the first candidate of Puerto Rican descent elected to that position—in a city where the Cuban population dominates. He had a long tenure in office, serving until 1985. He was succeeded by Xavier L. Suarez, who was the first Cuban-born mayor of the city.

As more Latinx people were enfranchised and more Latino candidates channeled their ambitions through the political arena, there were more celebrated victories during those years. Henry Cisneros was elected mayor of the city of San Antonio in 1981—the first Latino to hold that position since 1842. Cisneros later gained higher national visibility when he was appointed as secretary of Housing and Urban Development during the Clinton administration; he served in that position from 1993 to 1997.

In Denver, Colorado, Federico Peña won the mayoral election in 1983. He was the first Latino to hold such a position in the city's history. In subsequent years, he was appointed secretary of transportation (1993–1997) and secretary of energy, where he served between 1997 and 1998.

In California, Gloria Molina became the first Latina elected to the Los Angeles City Council in 1987. Later, Miguel Cruz Bustamante became the first Latino Speaker of the assembly in California (in 1996). Two years later, in 1998, Bustamante was elected lieutenant governor, being the first Mexican American in such a position in more than 100 years. He was the highest-ranking Latino state official until 2003, when Bill Richardson was elected governor of New Mexico.

In other positions, Joseph Carrillo became the first Latino to serve in the Arizona senate in 1974. In Texas, Dan Morales was the first Latino to serve as state treasurer in 1990. Nonetheless, success was still elusive for many Latinx who lived in the Northeast and the Midwest. Latinos have been present in Michigan from the early decades of the century, but no Latino was present in the state legislature until Belda Garza, born in Mexico City and a longtime resident in Detroit, was elected in 1998. In New Jersey, Latinos also found considerable barriers to access elected offices. A Republican, Jorge Rod—born Jorge Rodriguez—was the first Latino ever to win a seat in this state assembly in 1981. Robert Menendez was the first Latino to be elected to the New Jersey state senate in 1992. Menendez is a Republican of Cuban background who has served in the U.S. Senate since 2006.

The first Latina ever elected to the House of Representatives was Ileana Ros-Lehtinen (R-FL), elected in 1989; she was also the first Cuban American to serve in the national legislature. Representative Ros-Lehtinen was born in Havana, Cuba, but her family immigrated to the United States when she was seven years old. Currently serving in the Congress, she has recently announced that she will not seek reelection in 2018. After Ros-Lehtinen was elected, other women followed: Nydia Velázquez (D-NY) and Lucille Roybal-Allard (daughter of Edward Roybal, D-CA) were elected in 1992; Loretta Sanchez, Grace Napolitano, and Hilda Solis, all Democrats from California, followed them in 1996, 1998, and 2000, respectively.

Focusing on the election of first-timers offers a good point of view to study the progressive inclusion of Latinos and Latinas in the political structures of the U.S. government. This perspective, however, allows a very limited analysis of the political careers of these officials or their responsiveness or commitment to Latino interests in the long term; it also neglects the fact that some of these first-timers were, unfortunately, not exempt from political controversies or personal scandals of a diverse nature in subsequent years.

Nonetheless, the presence and the visibility of Latinos were unprecedented at the dawn of the new century. Between 1984 and 2001, the number of Latinos elected to the government nationwide went from 3,128 to 5,138. The Latino electorate was also seen in a different way: analysts considered it a "sleeping giant," a force with significant potential to influence the results of presidential elections, particularly in swing states.

THE NEW MILLENNIUM

The term Latinx includes persons with different nationalities, experiences of immigration, and party affiliations; their views are shaped by the sociopolitical and cultural environments of the states where they live. Consequently, the Latino electorate is not a unified giant, but a complex group with many political preferences and diverse forms of political behavior. Latinx politicians reflect such complexity.

While Latinx officials continue to access positions of power, they do so with political views and styles that no longer reflect the common experiences of socialization that scholars observed in the 1970s. One case that illustrates this diversity is that of presidential primaries. In the course of one decade, three Latino politicians have participated in presidential primaries, but their political profiles, preferences, and bases of political support cannot be more dissimilar. Bill Richardson was a candidate in the Democratic primary from which Barack Obama was eventually nominated in 2008. Richardson had a stellar resume: U.S. representative, governor of New Mexico, ambassador to the United Nations, and secretary of energy; he also was a high-level negotiator with Iraq and North Korea. Although he sees himself as a person of multicultural influences, he has worked for the Latino agenda in many instances, including his tenure in Congress and his active role as chairman of the Congressional Hispanic Caucus.

Conversely, the two Latinos who ran in the 2016 Republican primary, Ted Cruz (R-TX) and Marco Rubio (R-FL), are children of Cuban immigrants, conservative Republicans, and both were in their first term in the U.S. Senate when they entered their party primaries. Both politicians had support from the Tea Party Movement in their senatorial races, and both have anti-immigrant views. During the primary season, Cruz was a successful fundraiser who relied on social conservatives and libertarian conservative groups. He is the first Latino to win a caucus or presidential primary, with victories in Iowa and 10 more states.

Several scholars have demonstrated in previous studies that despite the different pressures that elected Latinos face from their districts and party leaders, many still show some visible levels of group consciousness. The question is, however, how the increasing mainstreaming of candidates and their political differences will affect the Latino interests and agendas in the years to come.

As of 2017, according to the National Association of Latino Elected Officials, there are 4 Latinx senators—including 1 woman, Catherine Cortez Masto—and 34 representatives (including 9 women). Two senators and 27 representatives are Democrats, whereas 2 other senators and 7 more representatives are affiliated with the Republican Party. Thirteen Latinx are currently serving as state officials, 80 as state senators, and 246 as state representatives. Latinas have also taken significant steps. They went from holding 907 offices to 2,202 in 2017. Currently, they are filling one-third of all positions held by Latinx elected officials.

At the level of urban politics, Antonio Villaraigosa (D) attracted national attention in 2005, when he succeeded in his election as mayor of Los Angeles. This was clearly an important victory: he was the first Latino mayor of the city since 1872.

Susana Martinez (R-NM) is the first Latina governor in the history of the United States. As of 2017, Governors Martinez and Brian Sandoval (R-NV) are the only two Latinx serving in such positions. Another minority governor, David Ige (D-HI), has an Asian background. There are no African American governors serving currently; the other 47 governors are white.

There have been other siblings serving simultaneously in Congress in recent years. In addition to Loretta Sanchez and Linda Sánchez, mentioned before, Mario and Lincoln Diaz-Balart—both Republicans from Florida—served together for four terms before Lincoln's retirement in 2011. John Salazar (D-CO) and his brother Ken Salazar (D-CO) served as representative and senator, respectively, from 2005 to 2009.

In Congress, some Latino representatives have gained prominence within the institution. Former representative Xavier Becerra (D-CA) was appointed assistant to the Speaker of the House of Representatives in 2007, and chairman of the House Democratic Caucus between 2013 and 2017. He resigned his congressional seat to become the first Latino attorney general in California in 2017. Other congresspersons are known for their purposeful work on particular issues. Luis Gutierrez (D-IL) is a prominent figure in the debates on immigration in the U.S. Congress. (He has announced, however, that he will not seek reelection in 2018.)

Furthermore, scholars have also shown that beyond policy action or roll call votes, Latinx congresspersons participate in different tasks of oversight, debate, and agenda setting, that is, issues behind the scenes or the public eye. They also help in the process of socialization of incoming peers, and even though they are a minority in the larger context of Congress, they keep alive the agenda of Latino topics in the national legislature.

From a broad normative perspective, it is evident that the advancement of democracy requires that groups that have been denied political membership are fully included in the political process. Moreover, there are important effects on the Latino electorate, as some scholars have demonstrated. The presence of Latinx in positions of power increases the sense of efficacy of Latinx constituents and makes voters more confident in contacting their representatives. The election of Latino and Latina officials has positive effects even in terms of voter turnout.

From this perspective, the election of Latinx officials is clearly not a matter of representation, but one that relates to a process of full inclusion into the life of the American political system.

Miriam Jiménez

FURTHER READING

Casellas, Jason P. 2011. *Latino Representation in State Houses and Congress*. Cambridge: Cambridge University Press.

Cruz, José E. 2004. "Latinos in Office." In Navarro, Sharon A., and Armando Xavier Mejia, eds. *Latino Americans and Political Participation. A Reference Handbook*. Santa Barbara, CA: ABC-CLIO, pp. 173–226.

de la Garza, Rodolfo O. 1984. "'And Then There Were Some . . .'" Chicanos as National Political Actors, 1967–1980." *Aztlán: A Journal of Chicano Studies* 15, no. 1 (Spring): 1–24.

de la Garza, Rodolfo O., & David Vaughan. 1984. "The Political Socialization of the Chicano Elites: A Generational Approach." *Social Science Quarterly* 65, no. 2: 290–307.

Dovi, Suzanne. 2002. "Preferable Descriptive Representatives: Will Just Any Woman, Black, or Latino Do?" *American Political Science Review* 96, no. 4 (December): 729–43.

Espino, Rodolfo, David L. Leal, & Kenneth J. Meier, eds. 2007. *Latino Politics: Identity, Mobilization, and Representation*. Charlottesville: University of Virginia Press.

Espino, Rodolfo, III. 2005. "Political Representation." In Suzanne Oboler and Deena J. González, eds. *The Oxford History of Latinos and Latinas in the United States*, vol. 3. New York: Oxford University Press, pp. 424–31.

Garcia, F. Chris, & Gabriel Sanchez. 2008. *Hispanics and the U.S. Political System: Moving into the Mainstream*. Upper Saddle River, NJ: Prentice Hall.

Geron, Kim. 2005. "Today's Latino Elected Officials." In *Latino Political Power*. Boulder, CO: Lynne Rienner Publishers, pp. 189–204.

House of Representatives, Office of the Historian and Office of the Clerk. 2013. *Hispanic Americans in Congress, 1822–2012*. Washington, D.C.: U.S. Government Printing

Office, pp. 482–86. https://www.gpo.gov/fdsys/pkg/GPO-CDOC-108hdoc225/pdf /GPO-CDOC-108hdoc225.pdf.

Jiménez, Miriam. 2015. *Inventive Politicians and Ethnic Ascent in American Politics: The Uphill Elections of Italians and Mexicans to the U.S. Congress.* London: Routledge.

Minta, Michael D. 2011. *Oversight: Representing the Interests of Blacks and Latinos in Congress.* Princeton, NJ: Princeton University Press.

NALEO. 2017. *National Directory of Latino Elected Officials* Los Angeles: NALEO Educational Fund.

Pitkin, Hanna Fenickel. 1967. *The Concept of Representation.* Berkeley: University of California.

Wilson, Walter Clark. 2017. *From Inclusion to Influence: Latino Representation in Congress and Latino Political Incorporation in America.* Ann Arbor, MI: University of Michigan Press, 2017.

Latino Mobilization and Voter Turnout: An Overview of Experimental Studies

Latino voters have attracted considerable attention from researchers as well as political candidates and operatives in recent election cycles in the United States. The literature commonly uses the term Latino to describe voters of Latino/Hispanic origin and is being used here as a gender-neutral term. The growth in the Latino population in recent decades, along with corresponding increases in the number of eligible Latino voters, especially in key states, have been accompanied by a rise in mobilization efforts targeting this segment of the electorate. Despite the intensification of Latino outreach in political campaigns, particularly through the use of Spanish-language advertisements, Latinos persistently vote at lower levels compared to other racial and ethnic groups, including African Americans. The wide gap between the number of eligible Latino voters and the number that actually goes to the polls on Election Day continues to disappoint expectations regarding democratic ideals for participation.

A good deal of research has been conducted on Latino voter turnout and mobilization through the analysis of observational data. This body of literature has focused on resource models of participation (Verba, Schlozman, & Brady, 1995), examinations of the impact of living in a majority-minority geography (Barreto, Segura, & Woods, 2004; Brace, Handley, Niemi, & Stanley, 1995; Henderson, Sekhon, & Titiunik, 2016; Rocha, Tolbert, Bowen, & Clark, 2010), examinations of the impact of Latino group consciousness (Stokes, 2003), and the impact of co-ethnic candidates (Barreto et al., 2005; Barreto et al., 2007; Barreto, 2010) on turnout, among other approaches. A handful of these observational studies of Latino electoral participation assess the impact of mobilization efforts, including the effectiveness of contact by Latino organizations (Shaw, De la Garza, & Lee, 2000), partisan contact (Nuño, 2007), and the differential effects of direct and indirect contact (Barreto, Merolla, & Soto, 2011).

Recent scholarship has also deployed experimental approaches to study Latino political engagement and participation. These studies, focusing on Latino mobilization in elections, are the focus of this chapter. Next we present an overview of

Latino turnout in recent election cycles as well as a summary of key findings produced from randomized experiments on Latino mobilization.

LATINO TURNOUT: A STORY OF UNREACHED POTENTIAL

Electoral participation among Latinos in the United States continues to trail voter participation among white and black Americans despite becoming the largest minority group in the country at the turn of the century. According to the U.S. Census Bureau, the share of Latino voters nationally grew to 9.2 percent in the 2016 election cycle, up from 8.4 percent in 2012 (File, 2017). Overall, turnout among Latino voters in the 2016 general election was slightly lower than in 2012 (when 23.3 million Latinos were eligible to vote): 47.6 percent compared to 48 percent, respectively. By contrast, 59.6 percent of blacks voted in November 2016 (down from 66.6% in 2012), and 65.6 percent of non-Hispanic whites voted in 2016, slightly higher than in 2012, when 64.1 percent of white voters voted (File, 2017). Excitement surrounding the Obama candidacy helped to drive nearly one in two eligible Latino voters (49.9%) to the polls on Election Day in the 2008 general election (File, 2017). Since 1980, the highest rate of Latino turnout in general elections was registered in the 1992 election, when 51.6 percent of eligible Latinos voted, but even in that election cycle Latino turnout was still lower than for other racial groups (70.2% of whites and 59.3% of blacks voted in November 1992) (File 2017). Relatively lower rates of turnout among Latino voters is also observed in midterm election cycles; in the November 2014 elections, for example, the Pew Research Center found that turnout among eligible Latino voters fell to a record low of 27 percent (Krogstad, et al., 2016).

Still, Latinos continue to be touted as a key electorate in U.S. politics with the potential to be decisive in current and future elections. Three competitive states in the 2016 presidential race, Arizona, Florida, and Nevada, were among the top 10 states with the highest Latino populations in the Unites States (31%, 24%, and 28%, respectively (Stepler & Hugo López, 2016). Democratic candidate Hillary Clinton lost two (Florida and Arizona) of those three states; had she won all three states, she would have won the presidency. According to exit polls conducted by Edison, 66 percent of Latino voters nationally voted for Clinton over Trump in the 2016 presidential election; in Florida, 62 percent of Latino voters supported Clinton. It is conceivable that if Latinos across the country had voted at rates comparable to, or perhaps even higher than, whites or even other racial minorities, it could have been consequential, altering the outcome of the presidential election.

Historically, major party mobilization efforts have largely overlooked Latinos (Hero et al., 2000; Stevens & Bishin, 2011; Verba, Schlozman, & Brady, 1995). In recent election cycles, the growing number of untapped Latino voters has prompted greater interest from major parties and candidates seeking to mobilize supporters (Abrajano, 2010; Barreto, 2010; De la Garza, 2004). Few studies, however, until recently systematically examined the effectiveness of various mobilization strategies designed to target Latino voters. In recent years, scholars have turned their attention to this enterprise, and some of the more promising findings have been yielded by studies that deploy randomized experimentation to test a wide range of strategies, tactics, and approaches.

EXPERIMENTS ON MOBILIZATION IN POLITICAL SCIENCE

Experimental methods are widely considered to be the gold standard to demonstrate causal relationships in political phenomena and have become an influential research approach in the discipline of political science. Druckman and colleagues (2006) noted that use of experimental designs has been on the rise since the 1970s as researchers place a premium on approaches that enable them to make reliable claims about causal relationships. Observational studies, such as survey research, can reveal important associations, but they cannot reliably disentangle cause and effect because they cannot rule out the possibility that unobservable factors are driving the results. Experimental approaches that randomly assign units to treatment and control conditions enable researchers to do so because they can be assured that each of these groups is similar, on average, with respect to both observable and unobservable characteristics. In this way, any differences studies reveal between treatment and control groups can only be attributed to an intervention, such as a campaign ad, a visit by a canvasser, or a postcard mailing. Overall, more than 20 studies of which we are aware deploy experimental methods to study aspects of Latino politics.

Experimental methods offer researchers tremendous control over aspects of their studies, including recruitment, random assignment to experimental groups, treatment (administration of stimuli), and measurement of the treatment effect. Some experiments are conducted in laboratory settings, which allow for high levels of control and offer strong internal validity. Other experiments are conducted in the context of surveys. In these, some, randomly selected respondents are exposed to one version of a question while others see a different version, and researchers compare the responses of each group to a common question of interest to determine the effects of this random variation. By contrast, field experiments are conducted in real-world settings where researchers have less control over the conditions in which their experiments occur, but external validity is maximized. Field experiments trade off internal for external validity since the experimenter conducts their research in a natural setting or political context, controlling only for the most central aspects of random assignment and treatment (McDermott, 2002). Field experiments have become increasingly popular to study a wide range of political phenomena, but perhaps especially in the area of voter mobilization in which researchers seek to examine the real-world impact of specific approaches.

Gosnell (1927) conducted the first field experiment testing the effect of mailers on turnout in Chicago. Results from this study showed a positive effect on households that were treated with a nonpartisan message that encouraged them to vote. Nevertheless, few field experiments in the voting domain were conducted in the seven decades that followed. Interest in field experimentation became renewed after the publication of Gerber and Green's (2000) seminal article that compared effects of different types of voter contact strategies (direct mail, phone calls, and door-to-door canvassing) on turnout in elections. By documenting the effectiveness of various tactics, this study reinforced conventional wisdom about campaigning, but it also dispelled common misconceptions by showing, for example, that phone calls and even direct mail had only minimal, if any, effects on voting. Researchers quickly followed suit to apply field experimental approaches to study many aspects of voter mobilization and political participation (e.g., Gerber & Green, 2008; Gerber, Green, & Larimer, 2008; McNulty, 2005; Nickerson et al., 2006; Ramírez, 2005; Wong, 2005). Many of these studies focused on Latino engagement, mobilization, and electoral participation.

EXPERIMENTS IN LATINO MOBILIZATION

Scholarship about Latino politics includes field, laboratory, and survey experiments that study a wide range of topics. Laboratory experiments in Latino politics touch on political empowerment (Gutierrez, 1995), co-ethnic voting (McConnaughy, White, Leal, & Casellas, 2010), and attitudes toward government (Trujillo & Levy Paluck, 2012), while survey experiments in Latino politics have investigated group consciousness (Junn & Masuoka, 2008), Latino vote choice (Jackson, 2011; Lavariega Monforti, Michelson, & Franco, 2013), and candidate evaluation (Adida, Davenport, & McClendon, 2016). When it comes to the study of Latino electoral mobilization, field experiments have dominated inquiries regarding the efficacy of mobilization campaign strategies designed to get members of this pan-ethnic group to the polls. Researchers have leveraged field experiments to examine the effects of varying the type of tactic, the message, the delivery, the source, the language, or other elements or cues that can potentially influence voter responsiveness.

Michelson's (2003, 2005) work represents the first incursions in the use of field experimental designs to study Latino voter mobilization, focusing exclusively on the use of in-person canvassing as a mobilization tactic. During a 2001 school board election, Michelson (2003) conducted a field experiment in Dos Palos, California, employing a nonpartisan door-to-door canvassing strategy on Latino and non-Latino registered voters. (Canvassing is a campaign tactic that typically refers to individuals visiting voters at their homes to deliver a persuasive message or mobilization appeal). Individuals assigned to the treatment condition received either a civic duty message or an ethnic solidarity message from Latino bilingual canvassers. The civic duty message resulted in a 7.1 percentage point boost in turnout among Latino Democrats, and the ethnic solidarity message resulted in a 10.6 percentage point boost in turnout among Latino Democrats. Canvassing of Latino non-Democrats did not boost turnout. This study was re-published in 2005 along with three additional Latino mobilization field experiments that sought to improve upon the original Dos Palos study. The additional experiments included two canvassing field experiments conducted in Fresno, California, and one in Maricopa County, California. The first Fresno study, conducted in 2002 during a statewide election, tested whether employing canvassers from multiple races and ethnicities had differential effects on Latino turnout, finding that non-Latino canvassers were more effective in mobilizing Latino registered voters than Latino canvassers. The second Fresno study, conducted in 2003 during a gubernatorial recall election, yielded null results and was designed to test how the content of mobilization messages—partisan versus nonpartisan—might have contrasting results on Latino turnout. Similarly, the third study conducted in Maricopa County during a recall election in 2003 also tested partisan versus nonpartisan messages in door-to-door canvassing. This time, the use of a partisan message in canvassing increased turnout in Latino households by 6.9 to 8.5 percentage points, while the use of a nonpartisan message increased turnout in Latino households by 8.5 to 14.1 percentage points.

As we noted earlier, field experiments on Latino mobilization have employed many different types of strategies, including door-to-door canvassing (García Bedolla, & Michelson, 2012; Matland & Murray, 2012; Michelson, 2003, 2005, 2006; Michelson et al., 2011), direct mail (Abrajano & Panagopoulos, 2011; Binder et al., 2014; Matland & Murray, 2012; Ramírez, 2005), radio advertisements (Panagopoulos & Green, 2011), and phone banking (García Bedolla & Michelson, 2012; Ramírez, 2005). Only two of these studies used experimental designs to compare the effectiveness of different contact strategies. First, Ramírez (2005) conducted a multisited field experiment across the United States during the 2002 general election. Over 400,000 Latino registered voters in six high-density Latino population areas in California (two sites), Colorado, New Mexico, New York, and Texas were randomly assigned to treatment groups that would receive appeals encouraging voter turnout through one of three modes of communication: direct mail, robotic phone calls, and live calls (bilingual). Ramírez found that prerecorded phone calls (called robocalls) were not an effective mobilization technique, while direct mail and live phone calls by volunteers seemed to be more effective. Phone banking was particularly effective, increasing turnout by 4.6 percentage points on average. Second, Matland and Murray (2012) conducted a field experiment in Brownsville, Texas, where the population was 90 percent Latino during the 2004 general election. The researchers randomly assigned registered voters to canvassing (bilingual), mail, and control groups. Canvassing resulted in a statistically significant increase in turnout of 1.63 percentage points on average, while mailers raised turnout by 2.9 percentage points on average. Latino voters assigned to be canvassed voted at a rate that was 7.3 percentage points higher on average compared to subjects in the control condition. Individuals in both treatment conditions received either a Latino empowerment message or a civic duty message to encourage voter mobilization. The civic duty message was more effective in the direct mail treatment, while the Latino empowerment appeal was more effective when voters were canvassed, but these differences were not statistically significant. These studies suggest that direct mail campaigns, phone banking, and door-to-door canvassing can effectively mobilize Latino voters, particularly when these voters are contacted in person.

Though not exclusively focused on Latinos, García Bedolla and Michelson (2012) explored multiple strategies for the effective mobilization of Latinos, Asian Americans, and African Americans, including the use of direct mail, leaflets and door hangers, phone banks, and door-to-door canvassing. In their book *Mobilizing Inclusion*, the authors conducted over 260 randomized field experiments to study the mobilization of underrepresented racial and ethnic groups in collaboration with community-based organizations in California. Thirty of those experiments focused primarily on Latino mobilization using phone banking (24 experiments) and door-to-door canvassing (6 experiments) in both low- and high-salience elections between 2006 and 2008. The authors found that follow-up phone calls to intended voters resulted in a significant increase in voter turnout among Latinos. However, García Bedolla and Michelson found null results in the field experiments that implemented door-to-door canvassing targeting low-income Latinos residing in urban areas. In additional experiments that contacted eligible voters in mixed Latino and African American communities, the authors found that "door-to-door campaigns are effective in getting low-propensity voters from communities of color out to vote" (p. 125).

The use of appeals to co-ethnicity is commonplace in Latino mobilization experiments. In the same vein as scholars of African American politics (Dawson, 2003; Tate, 2003) some scholars use ethnic group identity to explain Latino electoral behavior and partisanship (Barreto, 2007, 2010; Barreto & Nuño, 2011; Nuño, 2007; Shaw et al., 2000). These scholars cite Bobo and Gilliam's (1990) "empowerment hypothesis," which predicts increased political involvement of minority voters when viable minority candidates are running for office, and Tate's (2003) research on how African American mayoral candidates increase voter turnout among African Americans to predict similar results for Latino voters. Following this logic, Binder and colleagues (2014) examined the mobilizing effect of co-ethnic leadership while varying the language of mailers sent to voters during California's 2010 statewide primaries. The treatment takes advantage of the candidacy of then lieutenant governor Abel Maldonado and his authorship of an initiative that would be on the ballot during the same primary. A total 6,000 postcards were sent to Latino registered voters in San Bernardino County, California, varying the message and the language in which the message was delivered. Findings show that Latinos whose dominant language was English and were assigned to receive English-language postcards experienced a significant boost in turnout, though Maldonado's co-ethnic candidacy did not result in a significant increase of turnout among Latinos overall.

A variation of the co-ethnic hypothesis of mobilization was implemented in Michelson's (2006) study of Latino youth mobilization. In this in-person canvassing field experiment, the author targeted a population with very low propensity to turn out to vote. She explains that while Americans between the ages of 18 and 25 already have low levels of participation, Latinos of the same age group turn out at even lower levels, often below 30 percent. The experiment was conducted in Fresno, California, during the 2002 gubernatorial election. Registered Latino voters between the ages of 18 and 25 were randomly assigned to a control group and a treatment group. In the treatment condition, individuals were either contacted by Latino or non-Latino canvassers and they also randomly received either a civic duty message or an ethnic group solidarity message. Latino canvassers were able to contact 13 percent more young Latino registered voters than non-Latino canvassers. This suggests that co-ethnicity between Latino voters and canvassers can facilitate contact, a necessary requirement for communication of get-out-the-vote messages. Canvassing resulted in a statistically significant rise in turnout of 2.4 percentage points on average, even though turnout overall was very low (7% in the control group and 9.4% in the treatment group). Perhaps surprisingly, the experiment also revealed that non-Latino canvassers were more effective than Latino canvassers in mobilizing young Latinos, despite the fact that Latino canvassers contacted subjects at a higher rate than non-Latino canvassers. Accordingly, the results do not appear to support the co-ethnic mobilization hypothesis.

Though some experiments provide for Spanish-speaking phone banking volunteers and canvassers as a matter of convenience (Matland & Murray, 2012; Michelson, 2003; Ramírez, 2005), some studies randomly vary the use of Spanish language in their appeals as part of their experimental design (Abrajano & Panagopoulos, 2011; Binder et al., 2014; Panagopoulos & Green, 2011). Panagopoulos and Green conducted a field experiment in which Spanish-language get-out-the-vote radio advertisements were randomly assigned to be broadcasted in 36 congressional districts in 28 states during the 2006 general elections in the United States. The authors argued that Spanish-language radio had the potential to provide a unique opportunity to reach potential Latino voters. These districts were exposed to a 60-second nonpartisan Spanish-language get-out-the-vote advertisement; media buys were varied for exposure (50, 75, and 100 gross ratings points of advertising). The authors found that the purchase of 100 gross ratings points raised turnout among Latinos within the treated districts by 4 to 5 percentage points on average. This study demonstrates that the use of Spanish-language media can be effective in getting Latinos to participate at higher rates in American elections overall, compared to no exposure to such advertisements, but the researchers were unable to compare the effectiveness of similar ads in English.

An experiment designed, in part, to test whether appeals in Spanish or English are more effective in mobilizing Latino voters was conducted by Abrajano and Panagopoulos (2011) in the context of a special election to fill a vacancy on the New York City council in 2009. Either Spanish- or English-language nonpartisan get-out-the-vote appeals were delivered to registered Latino voters living in single-voter households via direct mail. Postcards in both languages raised turnout on average, but the English-language version appeared to be more effective, raising turnout by about 1.6 percentage points on average compared to 0.65 percentage points for the Spanish version. These results confirm the results of other field experiments that found direct mail can be an effective way to mobilize Latino voters (Matland & Murray, 2012; Ramírez, 2005), but the findings also suggest that Spanish-language appeals may not necessarily be superior to English-language appeals in seeking to mobilize Latino voters.

IMPLICATIONS

From a scholarly perspective, the experimental studies summarized here shed a great deal of light on Latino voter behavior. In many ways, Latino voters resemble non-Latino voters in terms of their responsiveness to various mobilization tactics and approaches. But in other ways, Latinos may be unique. There is much still to learn, for example, about if, how, and why they respond differently to messages delivered in Spanish versus English. Insights gleaned from studies that examine these differences systematically may reveal much about the sociopsychology of voting by Latino voters. Moreover, and as many of the details related to the studies described show, Latinos are not a monolithic group of voters. Documenting and understanding the heterogeneity that exists across subgroups of Latino voters in terms of their responsiveness to political messages and mobilization tactics remains an important, but unfinished, enterprise.

From a practical perspective, the experimental study of Latino mobilization has real-world implications for electoral politics in the United States. The evidence described here can inform decision making in partisan as well as nonpartisan organizations that seek to expand democratic participation among underrepresented groups. Partisan electoral campaigns that seek to target Latinos will surely be interested in implementing the most effective strategies, especially in competitive settings in which Latino votes can be decisive. Experimental findings also enable campaigns to pursue efficient resource allocation by calculating the cost-effectiveness of various approaches. For example, Ramírez (2005) and Panagopoulos and Green (2011) used the results of their experiments to estimate the cost-effectiveness of the campaign strategies tested in their respective studies. Ramírez (2005) calculated the monetary costs per vote that a campaign would incur when using direct mail, robocall, and live phone call campaigns. Live phone calls were the most cost-effective mobilization technique, with a cost of $22 per vote, while robocalls cost $275 per vote and mailers cost more than $600 per vote. Though live phone banking may be an expensive service overall, the evidence shows it is a worthwhile investment, at least compared to robocalls and mailers. In their study, Panagopoulos and Green (2011) calculated that the purchase of 100 gross ratings points, at an average of $88 cost per point in an average-sized district, increased turnout by 978 votes on average, implying a cost of only $9 per vote.

As the number of Latino voters in the United States climbs, we expect scholars will remain interested in the underpinnings of Latino political behavior and continue to deploy experimental approaches, and especially field experiments, to study aspects of Latino participation in elections. Nevertheless, no single experiment, no matter how well designed and implemented, can definitely isolate the impact of any specific approach. Experimentation depends on ongoing replication and extension; in other words, experiments, even identical experiments, need to be conducted over and over again, in similar and different settings and conditions, to get a clear sense of how the results differ in different contexts or when they are conducted among different populations. As a result, researchers have only scratched the surface when it comes to exploring Latino voter mobilization using experimental methods, but the findings to date are promising and intriguing enough to raise many new and fascinating questions that beg for further exploration in their own right.

Ivelisse Cuevas-Molina and Costas Panagopoulos

FURTHER READING

Abrajano, Marisa. 2010. *Campaigning to the New American Electorate: Advertising to Latino Voters.* Stanford, CA: Stanford University Press.
Abrajano, Marisa, & Costas Panagopoulos. 2011. "Does Language Matter? The Impact of Spanish Versus English-Language GOTV Efforts on Latino Turnout." *American Politics Research* 39, no. 4: 643–63.

Adida, Claire L., Lauren D. Davenport, & Gwyneth McClendon. 2016. "Ethnic Cueing across Minorities: A Survey Experiment on Candidate Evaluation in the United States." *Public Opinion Quarterly* 80, no. 4: 815–36.

Barreto, Matt A. 2007. "¡Sí Se Puede! Latino Candidates and the Mobilization of Latino Voters." *American Political Science Review* 101, no. 3: 425–41.

Barreto, Matt A. 2010. *Ethnic Cues: The Role of Shared Ethnicity in Latino Political Participation.* Ann Arbor: University of Michigan Press.

Barreto, Matt A., Jennifer Merolla, & Victoria Defrancesco Soto. 2011. "Multiple Dimensions of Mobilization: The Effect of Direct Contact and Political Ads on Latino Turnout in the 2000 Presidential Election." *Journal of Political Marketing* 10, no. 4: 303–27.

Barreto, Matt A., & Stephen A. Nuño. 2011. "The Effectiveness of Coethnic Contact on Latino Political Recruitment." *Political Research Quarterly* 64, no. 2: 448–59.

Barreto, Matt A., Gary M. Segura, & Nathan D. Woods. 2004. "The Mobilizing Effect of Majority–Minority Districts on Latino Turnout." *American Political Science Review* 98, no. 1: 65–75.

Barreto, Matt A., Mario Villarreal, & Nathan D. Woods. 2005. "Metropolitan Latino Political Behavior: Voter Turnout and Candidate Preference in Los Angeles." *Journal of Urban Affairs* 27, no. 1 (2005): 71–91.

Binder, Michael, Vladimir Kogan, Thad Kousser, & Costas Panagopoulos. 2014. "Mobilizing Latino Voters: The Impact of Language and Co-Ethnic Policy Leadership." *American Politics Research* 42, no. 4: 677–99.

Bobo, L., & F. D. Gilliam. 1990. "Race, Sociopolitical Participation, and Black Empowerment." *American Political Science Review* 84, no. 2: 377–93.

Brace, Kimball, Lisa Handley, Richard G. Niemi, & Harold W. Stanley. 1995. "Minority Turnout and the Creation of Majority-Minority Districts." *American Politics Quarterly* 23, no. 2: 190–203.

Cassel, Carol A. 2002. "Hispanic Turnout: Estimates from Validated Voting Data." *Political Research Quarterly* 55, no. 2: 391–408.

Dawson, Michael C. 2003. *Black Visions: The Roots of Contemporary African-American Political Ideologies.* Chicago: University of Chicago Press.

De la Garza, Rodolfo O. 2004. "Latino Politics." *Annual Review of Political Science* 7: 91–123.

DeSipio, Louis. 1998. *Counting on the Latino Vote: Latinos as a New Electorate.* Charlottesville: University of Virginia Press.

Druckman, James N., Donald P. Green, James H. Kuklinski, & Arthur Lupia. 2006. "The Growth and Development of Experimental Research in Political Science." *American Political Science Review* 100, no. 4: 627–35.

File, Thom. 2017. "Voting in America: A Look at the 2016 Presidential Election." U.S. Census Bureau, May 10. https://www.census.gov/newsroom/blogs/random-samplings/2017/05/voting_in_america.html.

Garcia Bedolla, Lisa, & Melissa R. Michelson. 2012. *Mobilizing Inclusion: Transforming the Electorate through Get-Out-the-Vote Campaigns.* New Haven, CT: Yale University Press.

Gerber, Alan S., & Donald P. Green. 2000. "The Effects on Canvassing, Telephone Calls, and Direct Mail on Voter Turnout: A Field Experiment." *American Political Science Review* 94, no. 3: 653–63.

Gerber, Alan S., & Donald P. Green. 2008. "Field Experiments and Natural Experiments." In Janet M. Box-Steffensmeier, Henry E. Brady, and David Collier, eds. *The Oxford Handbook of Political Methodology.* New York: Oxford University Press, pp. 357–403.

Gerber, Alan S., Donald P. Green, & Christopher W. Larimer. 2008. "Social Pressure and Voter Turnout: Evidence from a Large-Scale Field Experiment." *American Political Science Review* 102, no. 1: 33–48.

Gosnell, Harold F. 1927. *Getting Out the Vote: An Experiment in the Stimulation of Voting*. Chicago: University of Chicago Press.

Green, Donald P., & Alan S. Gerber. 2015. *Get Out the Vote: How to Increase Voter Turnout*. Washington, D.C.: Brookings Institution Press.

Green, Donald P., Alan S. Gerber, & David W. Nickerson. 2003. "Getting Out the Vote in Local Elections: Results from Six Door-to-Door Canvassing Experiments." *Journal of Politics* 65, no. 4: 1083–96.

Gutierrez, Lorraine M. 1995. "Understanding the Empowerment Process: Does Consciousness Make a Difference?" *Social Work Research* 19, no. 4: 229–37.

Henderson, John A., Jasjeet S. Sekhon, & Rocío Titiunik. 2016. "Cause or Effect? Turnout in Hispanic Majority-Minority Districts." *Political Analysis* 24, no. 3: 404–12.

Hero, Rodney, F. Chris Garcia, John Garcia, & Harry Pachon. 2000. "Latino Participation, Partisanship, and Office Holding." *PS: Political Science & Politics* 33, no. 3: 529–34.

Jackson, Melinda S. 2011. "Priming the Sleeping Giant: The Dynamics of Latino Political Identity and Vote Choice." *Political Psychology* 32, no. 4: 691–716.

Junn, Jane, & Natalie Masuoka. 2008. "Identities in Context: Politicized Racial Group Consciousness among Asian American and Latino Youth." *Applied Development Science* 12, no. 2: 93–101.

Krogstad, Jens Manuel. 2016. "Key Facts about the Latino Vote in 2016." Pew Research Center, October 14. http://www.pewresearch.org/fact-tank/2016/10/14/key-facts-about-the-latino-vote-in-2016.

Lavariega Monforti, Jessica, Melissa Michelson, & Annie Franco. 2013. "¿Por Quién Votará? Experimental Evidence about Language, Ethnicity and Vote Choice (among Republicans)." *Politics, Groups, and Identities* 1, no. 4: 475–87.

Malhotra, Neil, Melissa R. Michelson, Todd Rogers, & Ali Adam Valenzuela. 2011. "Text Messages as Mobilization Tools: The Conditional Effect of Habitual Voting and Election Salience." *American Politics Research* 39, no. 4: 664–81.

Manuel, Jens, Mark Hugo Lopez, Gustavo López, Jeffrey S. Passel, & Eileen Patten. 2016. "Looking Back to 2014: Latino Voter Turnout Rate Falls to Record Low." Pew Research Center. http://www.pewhispanic.org/2016/01/19/looking-back-to-2014-latino-voter-turnout-rate-falls-to-record-low/

Matland, Richard E., & Gregg R. Murray. 2012. "An Experimental Test of Mobilization Effects in a Latino Community." *Political Research Quarterly* 65, no. 1: 192–205.

McConnaughy, Corrine M., Ismail K. White, David L. Leal, & Jason P. Casellas. 2010. "A Latino on the Ballot: Explaining Coethnic Voting among Latinos and the Response of White Americans." *The Journal of Politics* 72, no. 4: 1199–1211.

McDermott, Rose. 2002. "Experimental Methods in Political Science." *Annual Review of Political Science* 5, no. 1: 31–61.

McNulty, John E. 2005. "Phone-Based GOTV—What's on the Line? Field Experiments with Varied Partisan Components, 2002–2003." *The Annals of the American Academy of Political and Social Science* 601, no. 1: 41–65.

Michelson, Melissa R. 2003. "Getting Out the Latino Vote: How Door-to-Door Canvassing Influences Voter Turnout in Rural Central California." *Political Behavior* 25, no. 3: 247–63.

Michelson, Melissa R. 2005. "Meeting the Challenge of Latino Voter Mobilization." *The Annals of the American Academy of Political and Social Science* 601, no. 1: 85–101.

Michelson, Melissa R. 2006. "Mobilizing the Latino Youth Vote: Some Experimental Results." *Social Science Quarterly* 87, no. 5: 1188–1206.

Nickerson, David W. 2006. "Volunteer Phone Calls Can Increase Turnout: Evidence from Eight Field Experiments." *American Politics Research* 34, no. 3: 271–92.

Nuño, Stephen A. 2007. "Latino Mobilization & Vote Choice in the 2000 Presidential Election." *American Politics Research* 35, no. 2: 273–93.

Oberholzer-Gee, Felix, & Joel Waldfogel. 2009. "Media Markets and Localism: Does Local News En Espanol Boost Hispanic Voter Turnout?" *The American Economic Review* 99, no. 5: 2120–28.

Panagopoulos, Costas, & Donald P. Green. 2011. "Spanish-Language Radio Advertisements and Latino Voter Turnout in the 2006 Congressional Elections: Field Experimental Evidence." *Political Research Quarterly* 64, no. 3: 588–99.

Ramírez, Ricardo. 2005. "Giving Voice to Latino Voters: A Field Experiment on the Effectiveness of a National Nonpartisan Mobilization Effort." *The Annals of the American Academy of Political and Social Science* 601, no. 1: 66–84.

Ramírez, Ricardo. 2007. "Segmented Mobilization Latino Nonpartisan Get-Out-the-Vote Efforts in the 2000 General Election." *American Politics Research* 35, no. 2: 155–75.

Rocha, Rene R., Caroline J. Tolbert, Daniel C. Bowen, & Christopher J. Clark. 2010. "Race and Turnout: Does Descriptive Representation in State Legislatures Increase Minority Voting?" *Political Research Quarterly* 63, no. 4: 890–907.

Shaw, Daron, Rodolfo O. De La Garza, & Jongho Lee. 2000. "Examining Latino Turnout in 1996: A Three-State, Validated Survey Approach." *American Journal of Political Science* 44, no. 2 (April): 338–46.

Stepler, Renee, & Mark Hugo López. 2016. "U.S. Latino Population Growth and Dispersion Has Slowed Since Onset of the Great Recession: Ranking the Latino Population in the States." Pew Research Center: Hispanic Trends, September 8. http://www.pewhispanic.org/2016/09/08/4-ranking-the-latino-population-in-the-states.

Stevens, Daniel, & Benjamin G. Bishin. 2011. "Getting Out the Vote: Minority Mobilization in a Presidential Election." *Political Behavior* 33, no. 1: 113–38.

Stokes, Atiya Kai. 2003. "Latino Group Consciousness and Political Participation." *American Politics Research* 31, no. 4: 361–78.

Tate, Katherine. 2003. ""Black Opinion on the Legitimacy of Racial Redistricting and Minority-Majority Districts." *American Political Science Review* 97, no. 1: 45–56.

Trujillo, Matthew D., & Elizabeth Levy Paluck. 2012. "The Devil Knows Best: Experimental Effects of a Televised Soap Opera on Latino Attitudes toward Government and Support for the 2010 US Census." *Analyses of Social Issues and Public Policy* 12, no. 1: 113–32.

Verba, Sidney, Kay Lehman Schlozman, & Henry E. Brady. 1995. *Voice and Equality: Civic Voluntarism in American Politics.* Cambridge, MA: Harvard University Press.

Wong, Janelle S. 2005. "Mobilizing Asian American Voters: A Field Experiment." *The Annals of the American Academy of Political and Social Science* 601, no. 1: 102–14.

Latina/o Mayors

The face of the United States is changing and so is its city politics. As late as the early 1960s, Latinas/os were almost totally excluded from city politics. By the early 1980s, as Browning, Marshall, and Tabb (1984, 4) documented, "Latinos rose from exclusion to positions of authority as mayors, council members, and top managers and administrators" in local governments. Today, the vast majority (67%) of Latina/o elected officials in the United States serve at the municipal level. The number of Latina/o mayors, in particular, has increased steadily over the past 30 years—from 139 in 1984 to 252 in 2016, an increase of 81 percent (NALEO, 2016). Although Latina/o mayors are concentrated in the West and Southwest, cities around the country, in the Northeast, Midwest, and the South, have also elected Latina/o mayors. Latinas/os have been elected mayor in large cities, including Albuquerque, New Mexico; Miami, Florida; El Paso, Texas; Denver and Colorado Springs, Colorado; and Los Angeles and San Jose, California; among others. Most Latina/o mayors in the United States have been elected in the postindustrial era—a period that has different political and economic realities compared to mayors in the previous industrial and redevelopment eras.

Latina/o mayors face a dramatically different situation than the mayors who governed during previous eras. From roughly the 1830s through about the 1930s, the city was the epicenter of American industry. This was the period of the industrial city. A key function of the industrial city was to provide the infrastructure necessary for industrial growth. Roads and bridges for transportations, massive sewers to carry off industrial waste, and large supplies of water to furnish the huge factories were among some of the public work projects required for large-scale industrial production. In other words, mayors of the industrial city were heavily involved in city building (Kantor, 1995).

Industrialization brought an urban explosion as factories sprang up in waterfront cities and diverse populations flocked to work in them. As the nation's urban population continued to grow, the industrial city became an increasingly complex economic, political, and social organization. By the 1860s and 1870s, a new style of city politics emerged in most large U.S. cities. Before the huge waves of European immigrants, political power in many American cities was controlled by a very small group of economic elites composed of white Anglo-Saxon Protestants or Yankees (Kantor, 1995). As the industrial city emerged, new kinds of political leaders emerged. These new leaders were less affluent career politicians whose base of support was lodged in the segregated ethnic wards. In order to organize voters within and across the ethnic-based wards and to ensure their support, the new career politicians depended on the city budget (i.e., patronage jobs and contracts) to provide for the needs of their constituents. Patronage became the mechanism that held the political organizations, or "machines," together (Erie, 1990; Trounstine, 2008). The industrial city was a place of opportunity and social mobility for millions of European immigrants and their offspring, and mayors of industrial cities were fortunate to occupy city hall during the era when cities had strong urban manufacturing economies capable of creating a "powerful stream of wages and investment capital to energize the city" (Rae, 2003: 18).

URBAN CHANGES

By the 1940s, the industrial city began to experience a transition into a redevelopment city. Deindustrialization, suburbanization, and the emergence of automobiles transformed cities (Bluestone & Harrison, 1984; Teaford, 1990). The automobile caused businesses and people to push out farther from downtown, away from what was the central core of the industrial city. Census figures for 1940 confirmed that many U.S. cities, including Boston, Philadelphia, and Cleveland, suffered a decline in population.

Mayors of the postwar redevelopment era worked to revitalize their cities within the context of deindustrialization. During the industrial city era, goods were almost entirely produced in large factories in a single city and then shipped to consumers and producer markets. However, after World War II, and especially after the mid-1960s, the increased mobility of capital allowed corporations to locate and relocate with much more flexibility, leading to the economic decline of many central cities. Technological developments would fundamentally alter the manufacturing process so that ever larger portions of the labor force would find work in the service sector of the economy. Soon the service sector of the city economy grew at a rate that quickly surpassed manufacturing employment, the key labor market during the era of the industrial city. Numerous communities that were dependent on manufacturing suffered a long-term decline.

Unlike the industrial period, mayors of the redevelopment city had to do more than focus on routine service provisions. The context had changed. The Housing Act of 1949, and later the urban renewal programs of the 1960s, heightened the federal government's involvement in urban economic development. Cemented on the one side by the city's access to federal funding and on the other by the commitment of local businesses to invest in downtown, mayors formed strong coalitions with downtown corporate interests. Mayors now were in the center of the effort to demolish and change the urban landscape with the hope of redeveloping the city's economically troubled downtown (Salisbury, 1964). Blocks and blocks of slum housing were razed. Roads were rerouted, and miles and miles of interstate highways were laid. Large, transformational endeavors with heavy involvement from city hall became routine in the redevelopment city (Fainstein, Fainstein, Hill, Judd, & Smith, 1986; Stone & Sanders, 1987).

Black mayors emerged in the redevelopment era and came to power in a different context of urban constraints and opportunities than when the European immigrants began to pursue political incorporation in the early 20th century. During the late 1890s and into the early 20th century, millions of African Americans from the rural South migrated to the cities of the urban North and West. Historians began to call this the Great Black Migration (Lemann, 1991; Wilkerson, 2010). During the Great Depression, black in-migration to northern urban centers slowed but picked up again during the 1940s and did not begin to taper off until the 1970s. By the 1970s, it is estimated that 5 million African Americans had left the rural small towns of the South and made residence in Washington, D.C., New York, Newark, Philadelphia, Chicago, Detroit, and in newer cities out west such as Oakland and Los Angeles. Blacks also made their way out of rural southern towns and into southern cities like Atlanta, Birmingham, and Memphis.

As whites fled the cities, the percentage of the black population increased— giving African American voters electoral clout. A strong sense of racial-group consciousness and a desire for equality were central factors for the political mobilization of blacks during the first half of the 20th century (Dawson, 1994; Shingles, 1981). The passage of the 1964 Civil Rights Act opened public accommodations to blacks, and the 1965 Voting Rights Act outlawed the legal tactics used to restrict black voter participation. From the mid-1960s to the late 1970s, specially targeted voter education and registration drives in southern and northern cities resulted in adding millions of blacks to the eligible voter rolls. Black voters formed the bases for a new black politics (Preston, Henderson, & Puryear, 1987; Walton, 1971). The symbol of the new black urban politics became the African American mayor. The election of big-city African American mayors began first in Cleveland (Carl Stokes) and Gary, Indiana (Richard Hatcher), in 1967. In 1970, Newark elected Kenneth Gibson as its first black mayor. Black mayors were elected for the first time in Detroit, Atlanta, and Los Angeles in 1973 and in Washington, D.C., in 1974. Black mayors signaled the gradual institutionalization of black political power in urban America.

THE POSTINDUSTRIAL CITY

By the 1980s, the redevelopment city began a transition into a postindustrial city. One of the distinguishing features of the postindustrial city is the rise and dominance of large multilocational corporations in local economies (Kantor, 1995: 77–111; Sassen, 2001; Savitch, 1988). These corporations are much larger than the businesses that dominated the economy during the industrial city era. These huge multilocational corporations "control the movement of most goods, services, and capital throughout the United States" (Kantor, 1995: 90). Because of their large size, many of the postindustrial corporations have multiple administrative and operational units often scattered across several locations.

The restructuring of the urban economy transformed the city's labor market. In the postindustrial city, the polarization of city occupations is more apparent.

Educated and skilled workers benefit from the service-oriented economy. There are a number of high-end and high-skilled positions for managers and professionals at the top and more low-paying service jobs (cleaning, cooking, waiting tables, stocking shelves) at the bottom. The entire economic restructuring process has left unskilled and semiskilled inner-city workers with significantly fewer opportunities for gainful employment. This has posed a particular dilemma for blacks and Latinas/os, two of the last racial/ethnic groups to arrive in the cities in large numbers (Wilson, 1996). Blacks and Latinas/os are also underrepresented among those with higher education. Cities, which had once served as processing centers for lesser-skilled immigrants preparing themselves for economic advancement, now have become large repositories for workers with lessened economic prospects.

Latina/o mayors are emerging as significant players in the postindustrial city, and the politics of the postindustrial city differs from earlier eras. The tight coalition of downtown commercial interests of banks, railroads, department stores, and local newspapers that Salisbury (1964) found held great sway during the postwar redevelopment era pulled back their involvement in civic and political affairs. In the postindustrial city, universities, medical centers, nonprofit foundations, metropolitan business associations, environmental groups, and cultural institutions are taking a leadership role in local affairs (Katz & Bradley, 2013; Maurrasse, 2001; Rodin, 2007; Stoker, Stone, & Horak, 2015). Nonprofit foundations are also playing critical roles in the postindustrial city. In Baltimore, Pittsburgh, Chicago, and other cities, program officers and staffers of large foundations like the Annie E. Casey Foundation and the Ford Foundation are seeding programs devoted to improving housing and addressing other needs in poor neighborhoods, providing research and data analysis on important policy matters, and helping empower low-income communities struggling to survive the changes and challenges of the postindustrial city.

The postindustrial city is occurring within the context of a "back-to-the-city" movement, where young professionals are carving out urban space within the central city (Ehrenhalt, 2013; Hyra, 2008). In recent years, developers and real estate agents are selling young hipsters the idea that it's not necessary to move downtown to achieve a sense of urbanity. The young professionals pulled to the city by the huge multilocational corporations want to stay in happening places in neighborhoods that offer activities. During the postwar redevelopment period, the class divide played out at the neighborhood level in many U.S. cities and featured battles over downtown renewal and slum clearance. The class cleavage was between a corporate elite determined to make the downtown attractive to the middle class and to business and poor, working class people resisting neighborhood displacement (Stone 1976; Ferman 1996). Back then the class struggle over neighborhoods was symbolized by the bulldozer. Today, in the postindustrial city, displacement remains an issue, but now the issue is gentrification. More middle-class families (often whites), particularly single people and young married couples priced out of more expensive areas, have moved to formerly poor areas of the city, especially into neighborhoods that are close to the work and entertainment opportunities of downtown (Freeman, 2006; Hyra, 2013).

DEMOGRAPHIC CHANGE

Without question, demographic change prepares the ground for political change. One of the most significant changes in U.S. politics over the past 30 years has been the demographic transformation of Latina/o populations. The most significant transformation has been the size and proportion of Latinas/os living in the United States. Latina/o communities in the United States grew nearly 60 percent between 1990 and 2000 and increased 43 percent between 2000 and 2010. The 2010 Census showed that Latinas/os are now the fastest-growing and largest (at 16.3 percent of the population versus 12.6 percent for African Americans) minority group in the country, and this increase is largely fueling the trend toward whites being less than 50 percent of the U.S. population around 2050.

The demographic change is being felt across the country. Over half of the U.S. Latina/o population is concentrated in the Southwestern states. Latinas/os, mostly of Mexican origin, have always had a significant presence in the Southwest, but over the past 40 years, the number of Latina/o immigrants from Mexico and Central and South American countries has increased in states like Texas, New Mexico, Arizona, and California. Between 1980 and 2015, the immigrant population from Central America grew from 354,000 to 3,385,000 (U.S. Census Bureau, 2015). Latinas/os of Puerto Rican descent have been a significant presence in parts of New York, Florida, and Illinois since the middle of the 20th century. Florida has been home to a large population of Cuban immigrants who came to the United States after Fidel Castro's rise to power in 1959.

The most important observation for these population changes is that Latinas/os are more dispersed than ever before. In addition to the major Latina/o destination cities like Los Angeles, New York City, and San Antonio, Latinas/os have also moved in large numbers to places like Lawrence, Massachusetts; Durham, North Carolina; Cicero, Illinois; Manchester, New Hampshire; and Providence, Rhode Island.

Every year, all of the nation's largest cities become more Latina/o than the year before. Indeed, the current growth in the Latina/o population is driven not by immigration but by native population birth. Between 2000 and 2008, the increase in native births was almost double that of foreign-born. Of the nearly 47 million persons of Hispanic origin living in the United States, about 29 million were born in the United States. The native born now represent approximately 62 percent of all Latinas/os (Fraga, et al., 2012: 4–11). As Fraga and his colleagues (2012: 8) observe, "Latinos are substantially younger than the overall population, and Latinos born in the United States are younger than those immigrating from abroad; as a result, Hispanics will disproportionately contribute future population growth in the United States for the foreseeable future."

Demographic change is very important in shaping urban politics. However, as discussed in Erie's (1990) book in the case for the Irish of the industrial city and African Americans in the era of the redevelopment city, capturing the mayor's office requires more than population numbers. The increasing political presence of Latina/o communities in cities throughout the United States and the election of Latina/o mayors have been aided by the role of community organizations. When

Browning, Marshall, and Tabb (1984) studied black and Latina/o politics in 10 California cities during the turbulent decades of 1960–1980, they found that community organizing played an important role in the process of Hispanics achieving political incorporation. A typical pattern saw the development of community organizations that would first mobilize Latina/o residents around community issues (policing, schools, housing, etc.) then work toward Latina/o political incorporation (Burns, 2006; Jones-Correa, 1998). In addition, community organizations taught Latina/o citizens how to become active in local elections. Studies show that in most cases, Latinas/os were able to reach the mayor's office largely as a result of the mobilization of Hispanic voters by Latina/o community–based organizations prior to their election (Orr & Morel, 2018). In short, demography is very important but must be understood alongside such factors as organization and leadership.

Latina/o group consciousness is another variable that intervened with the changing demography to bring forth Latina/o political incorporation. In the postindustrial city, the massive influx of Latina/o immigrants into cities created a critical mass of people who share language, traditions, and social circumstances. Despite the increased diversity among them, Latinas/os now see themselves as a group. In 2006, the Latina/o National Survey found a large majority of Latina/o respondents felt a sense of shared commonality between and among Latinas/os and Latina/o subgroups (Fraga, et al., 2012). In other words, Latinas/os are increasingly exhibiting what Michael Dawson (1994) has called "linked fate." The majority of individual Latinas/os in the United States now believe that their own self-interest is associated with the interest of Latinas/os as a group. The growing sense of group consciousness and group identity among Latinas/os has important political implications for city politics (Sanchez, 2006). Latina/os' youthfulness, the matter of nativity, low levels of trust in government, alienation from political institutions, and lack of political knowledge all combine to reduce the potential political influence of Latina/o communities (Abrajano & Alvarez, 2010; DeSipio, 1996; Fraga, et al., 2012; Garcia, 2011; Garcia & Sanchez, 2008; Hero, 1992; Hero, Garcia, Garcia, & Pachon, 2000). However, research has shown that group consciousness, or "linked fate," can influence political behavior and facilitate group political mobilization. The expectation is that as Latinas/os gain a sense of groupness, it would translate into united activism to advance Latina/o group interests.

As the electorate shifted to reflect the changing demography of cities, the increasing size of the Latina/o population gave Latina/o politicians an additional opportunity to exercise political influence and clout within cities. In 1981, Henry Cisneros, from San Antonio, became the first Latina/o mayor of a large U.S. city. In 1983, Federico Peña was elected mayor in Denver (1983). Following Cisneros, Edward Garza (2001) and Julian Castro (2009) were also elected mayor in San Antonio. In 2005, Antonio Villaraigosa was elected mayor in Los Angeles. Mayors in other central cities, including Nelda Martinez in Corpus Christi (2012) and Angel Taveras (2011) and Jorge Elorza (2015) in Providence, Rhode Island, have been elected as well. In 2016, 252 localities had Latina/o mayors (see Figure 1).

In recent election cycles, Latina/o mayoral candidates have mounted credible candidacies in a number of major cities. For example, Latina/o candidates have sought the mayor's office in Houston, New York City, and San Diego. In Chicago,

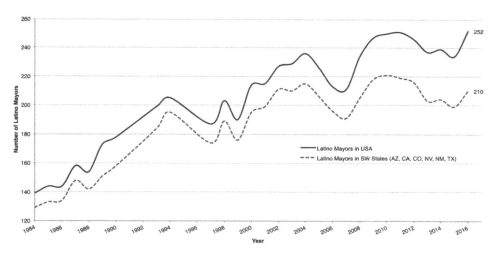

Figure I Total Latino Mayors, 1984–2016. (National Association of Latino Elected Officials, 2016). Adapted from Cuéllar, Carlos. 2018. "Patterns of Representation: A Descriptive Analysis of Latino Mayor Cities in the U.S." In Marion Orr and Domingo Morel, eds. *Latino Mayors: Political Change in the Postindustrial City.* Philadelphia, PA: Temple University Press, pp. 33–70.

Jesus "Chuy" Garcia, a Mexican American, finished second in Chicago's 2015 mayoral election, forcing a head-to-head runoff vote between himself and incumbent mayor Rahm Emanuel. Garcia lost but received a respectable 44 percent of the vote against Mayor Emanuel. As the demographics continue to shift, it is likely that more cities will elect Latina/o mayors. Additionally, the leadership experience and visibility that come with being mayor is likely to create an important pipeline for Latinas/os seeking higher office at the state and federal level. For instance, former San Antonio mayors Henry Cisneros and Julian Castro were appointed to cabinet positions in the Clinton and Obama administrations. In Rhode Island, former mayor Angel Taveras ran for governor.

Although Latina/o mayors have been elected in several major U.S. cities, in 2016, 63.8 percent of all Latina/o mayors served in cities with populations under 17,000 residents (Cuellar, 2018). In 2016, roughly three-quarters (76.2%) of all Latina/o mayors served in municipalities located in three states: Texas (37.7%), California (24.6%), and New Mexico (13.9%) (Cuellar, 2018). Indeed, the majority of all Latina/o mayors (83%) are from Southwestern states (Arizona, California, Nevada, New Mexico, and Texas) (Cuellar, 2018). However, the number of Latina/o mayors is growing in other regions of the United States. Between 2000 and 2010, the largest increase in Latina/o mayors came from states in the South and Northeast regions (Cuellar, 2018).

Like the Irish, Italian, and African American communities before them, Latinas/os expect that Latina/o mayors will address issues and needs of their community. Millions of immigrants from Mexico, Central America, and the Caribbean migrated to Los Angeles, Providence, Miami, Denver, Hartford, San Antonio, and many other cities, expecting unrestricted economic opportunities. Despite their expectations, the postindustrial city with its less labor-intensive political economy, presents a different challenge for some newcomers. Unlike the industrial city era, the postindustrial city has a serious jobs development problem. This was also true for the urban redevelopment era of the 1970s and 1980s. Today's Latina/o mayors are in the vortex of this economic transformation.

Domingo Morel

See also: Taveras, Angel (1970–)

FURTHER READING

Abrajano, Marisa A., & R. Michael Alvarez. 2010. *New Faces, New Voices: The Hispanic Electorate in America*. Princeton, NJ: Princeton University Press.

Bluestone, Barry, & Bennett Harrison. 1984. *The Deindustrialization of America*. New York: Basic Books.

Browning, Rufus, Dale Rogers Marshall, & David Tabb. 1984. *Protest Is Not Enough: The Struggle of Blacks and Hispanics for Equality in Urban Politics*. Berkeley: University of California Press.

Burns, Peter F. 2006. *Electoral Politics Is Not Enough: Racial and Ethnic Minorities and Urban Politics*. Albany: State University of New York Press.

Clarke, Susan E., Rodney E. Hero, Mara S. Sidney, Luis R. Fraga, & Bari A. Erlichson. 2006. *Multiethnic Moments: The Politics of Urban Education Reform*. Philadelphia: Temple University Press.

Cuéllar, Carlos. 2018. "Patterns of Representation: A Descriptive Analysis of Latino-Mayor Cities in the United States." In Marion Orr and Domingo Morel, eds. *Latino Mayors: Political Change in the Postindustrial City*, Philadelphia, PA: Temple University Press.

Dawson, Michael. 1994. *Behind the Mule: Race and Class in African-American Politics*. Princeton, NJ: Princeton University Press.

DeSipio, Louis. 1996. "Making Citizens or Good Citizens? Naturalization as a Predictor of Organizational and Electoral Behavior among Latino Immigrants." *Hispanic Journal of Behavioral Sciences* 18, no. 2: 194–213.

Ehrenhalt, Alan. 2013. *The Great Inversion and the Future of the American City*. New York: Vintage Press.

Erie, Steven P. 1990. *Rainbow's End: Irish Americans and the Dilemmas of Urban Machine Politics, 1840–1985*. Berkeley: University of California Press.

Fainstein, Susan S., Norman I. Fainstein, Richard C. Hill, Dennis Judd, & Michael Smith. 1986. *Restructuring the City: The Political Economy of Urban Redevelopment*. New York: Longman Publishers.

Ferman, Barbara. 1996. *Challenging the Growth Machine: Neighborhood Politics in Chicago and Pittsburgh*. Lawrence, KS: University Press of Kansas.

Fraga, Luis Ricardo, & Ann Frost. 2011. "Democratic Institutions, Public Engagement, and Latinos in American Public Schools." In Marion Orr and John Rogers, eds. *Public Engagement for Public Education*. Stanford, CA: Stanford University Press, pp. 117–38.

Fraga, Luis Ricardo, John A. Garcia, Rodney E. Hero, Michael Jones-Correa, Valerie Martinez-Ebers, & Gary M. Segura. 2010. *Latino Lives in America: Making It Home*. Philadelphia: Temple University Press.

Fraga, Luis Ricardo, John A. Garcia, Rodney E. Hero, Michael Jones-Correa, Valerie Martinez-Ebers, & Gary M. Segura. 2012. *Latinos in the New Millennium*. New York: Cambridge University Press.

Freeman, Lance. 2006. *There Goes the 'Hood: Views on Gentrification from the Ground Up*. Philadelphia: Temple University Press.

Frug, Gerald F., & David J. Barron. 2008. *City Bound: How States Stifle Urban Innovation*. Ithaca, NY: Cornell University Press.

Garcia, F. Chris, & Gabriel R. Sanchez. 2008. *Hispanics and the U.S. Political System: Moving into the Mainstream*. Upper Saddle River, NJ: Prentice Hall.

Garcia, John A. 2011. *Latino Politics in America: Community, Culture, and Interests*. Lanham, MD: Rowman and Littlefield.

Henig, Jeffrey, & Wilbur C. Rich, eds. 2004. *Mayors in the Middle: Politics, Race, and Mayoral Control of Urban Schools*. Princeton, NJ: Princeton University Press.

Hero, Rodney E. 1992. *Latinos and the Political System: A Two Tiered Pluralism*. Philadelphia: Temple University Press.

Hero, Rodney E., F. Chris Garcia, John Garcia, & Harry Pachon. 2000. "Latino Political Participation and Office Holding." *PS: Political Science and Politics* 33, no. 3 (September): 529–34.

Hyra, Derek S. 2008. *The New Urban Renewal: The Economic Transformation of Harlem and Bronzeville*. Chicago: University of Chicago Press.

Jones-Correa, Michael. 1998. *Between Two Nations: The Political Predicament of Latinos in New York City*. Ithaca, NY: Cornell University Press.

Kantor, Paul. 1995. *The Dependent City Revisited: The Political Economy of Urban Development and Social Policy*. Boulder, CO: Westview Press.

Katz, Bruce, & Jennifer Bradley. 2013. *Metropolitan Revolution*. Washington, D.C.: Brookings Institution.

Lemann, Nicholas. 1991. *The Promised Land: The Great Migration and How It Changed America*. New York: Alfred A. Knopf.

Maurrasse, David J. 2001. *Beyond the Campus: How Colleges and Universities Form Partnerships with Their Communities*. New York: Routledge.

National Association of Latino Elected and Appointed Officials (NALEO). 2016. *National Directory of Latino Elected Officials*. Los Angeles, CA: NALEO Educational Fund.

Orr, Marion, & Domingo Morel. 2018. "Managing Fiscal Stress in Providence: The Election and Governance of Mayor." In Marion Orr and Domingo Morel, eds. *Latino Mayors: Political Change in the Postindustrial City*. Philadelphia: Temple University Press.

Orr, Marion, & John Rogers, 2011. "Unequal Schools, Unequal Voice: The Need for Public Engagement for Public Education." In Marion Orr and John Rogers, eds. *Public Engagement for Public Education: Joining Forces to Revitalize Democracy and Equalize Schools*. Palo Alto, CA: Stanford University Press, pp. 1–26.

Preston, Michael B., Lenneal J. Henderson, Jr., & Paul L. Puryear. 1987. *The New Black Politics: The Search for Political Power*. New York: Longman Publishers.

Rae, Douglas W. 2003. *City: Urbanism and Its End*. New Haven, CT: Yale University Press.

Rich, Wilbur C. 1996. *Black Mayors and School Politics: The Failure of Reform in Detroit, Gary, and Newark*. New York: Garland Press.

Rodin, Judith. 2007. *The University and Urban Revival*. Philadelphia: University of Pennsylvania Press.

Salisbury, Robert. 1964. "Urban Politics: The New Convergence of Power." *Journal of Politics* 26, no. 4 (November): 775–97.

Sanchez, Gabriel R. 2006. "The Role of Group Consciousness in Political Participation among Latinos in the United States." *American Politics Research* 34, no. 4: 427–51.

Sassen, Saskia. 2001. *The Global City: New York, London, Tokyo*. Princeton, NJ: Princeton University Press.

Savitch, H. V. 1988. *Post-Industrial Cities: Politics and Planning in New York, Paris, and London*. Princeton, NJ: Princeton University Press.

Shingles, Richard. 1981. "Black Consciousness and Political Participation: The Missing Link." *American Political Science Review* 75: 76–91.

Stoker, Robert P., Clarence N. Stone, & Martin Horak. 2015. "Contending with Structural Inequality in a New Era." In Clarence N. Stone and Robert P. Stoker, eds. *Urban Neighborhoods in a New Era: Revitalization Politics in the Postindustrial City.* Chicago: University of Chicago Press, pp. 209–49.

Stone, Clarence Nathan. 1976. *Economic Growth and Neighborhood Discontent: System Bias in the Urban Renewal Program of Atlanta.* Chapel Hill: University of North Carolina Press.

Stone, Clarence N., & Heywood T. Sanders, eds. 1987. *The Politics of Urban Development.* Lawrence: University Press of Kansas.

Stone, Clarence N., & Robert P. Stoker. 2015. *Urban Neighborhoods in a New Era: Revitalization Politics in the Postindustrial City.* Chicago: University of Chicago Press.

Teaford, Jon C. 1990. *The Rough Road to Renaissance: Urban Revitalization in America, 1940–1985.* Baltimore: Johns Hopkins University Press.

Trounstine, Jessica. 2008. *Political Monopolies in American Cities: The Rise and Fall of Bosses and Reformers.* Chicago: University of Chicago Press.

U.S. Census Bureau. 2015. 2015 American Community Survey. American FactFinder. https://factfinder.census.gov/faces/nav/jsf/pages/index.xhtml.

Viteritti, Joseph P., ed. 2009. *When Mayors Take Charge: School Governance in the City.* Washington, D.C.: Brookings Institution.

Walton, Hanes, Jr. 1971. *Black Politics: A Theoretical and Structural Analysis.* Philadelphia: J. B. Lippincott Company.

Wilkerson, Isabel. 2010. *The Warmth of Other Suns: The Epic Story of America's Great Migration.* New York: Vintage.

Wilson, William J. 1996. *When Work Disappears: The World of the New Urban Poor.* New York: Vintage Press.

Wong, Kenneth K., Francis X. Shen, Dorothea Anagnostopoulos, & Stacey Rutledge. 2007. *The Education Mayor: Improving America's Schools.* Washington, D.C.: Georgetown University Press.

Hispanic Office Holders at the State and Local Levels

INTRODUCTION

Latina/o candidates for elective office continue to reshape the political landscape in the United States, emerging victorious in contests at all levels of government and in both political parties. Existing research showed that prior to the 2014 midterm election, nearly 6,100 Latinas/os were serving in elected office nationwide. "This is up from the 4,853 Latino elected officials who held office in 2004, an increase of 25 percent" (NALEO, 2016). At the time, the four states with the largest number of Latino elected officials were Texas, California, New Mexico, and Arizona. At the national level, the current session of Congress saw the election and/or reelection of 38 Latinos, including 34 members of the U.S. House of Representatives and 4 members of the U.S. Senate (1 is Latina). Despite this continuous increase of Latino representation at the national level, the largest contingent of Hispanic elective officials is found at the municipal and county levels. Specifically many of these officials have been elected to positions on city governments as well as school boards.

This essay will provide an overview of previous research related to Latina/o office holders at the local levels, as well as discuss the benefits of having Latinas/os in elective office such as descriptive and substantive representation. Specifically, it briefly discusses the factors that deter potential Latina/o candidates from running for office as well as factors that help them overcome these potential challenges.

THE ROLE OF THE VOTING RIGHTS ACT

Prior to the passage of the Voting Rights Act (VRA) of 1965, racial and ethnic minorities encountered many forms of institutionalized racism. This form of racism was permitted under state laws. Many states (primarily in the South) created restrictive and demeaning laws that promoted segregation and discrimination at the expense of the racial and ethnic minorities living in those states. These laws were commonly referred to as "Jim Crow Laws." In order to combat the existence of Jim Crow segregation, President Lyndon B. Johnson's administration signed the Civil Rights Act of 1964 and the Voting Rights Act of 1965. Although the Civil Rights Act was primarily focused on helping the federal government force non-compliant states to allow racial and ethnic minorities to vote (a right given to them under the Fifteenth Amendment in the U.S. Constitution), the federal government was not given enough authority to enforce the law. However, with the creation of the VRA, the federal government was given the authority it needed to fully enforce the law. It has been extended six times since it was originally created. In 1975, Section 4 was amended to require that all election-related materials, including ballots, be bilingual in communities where minority populations, including Hispanic, Asian, or Native American groups, are at least 5 percent of the population. This provision allowed these groups more opportunities to participate within American politics. One of the prominent sections of the law, Section 5, required approval from the U.S. Department of Justice for states that wanted to change laws that affected voting in areas with a large population of minority voters. This section was especially significant for Southern states, where racism and discrimination were prevalent. Unfortunately, *Shelby County v. Holder* (2013) resulted in the U.S. Supreme Court ruling that Section 4 of the VRA, which identified the states that had to comply with Section 5, was no longer constitutional. Therefore, the Southern states that were forced to comply with Section 5 were now able to create and enforce restrictive electoral laws that have hurt racial and ethnic minority members' abilities to vote.

The VRA has been amended five times: 1970, 1975, 1982, 1992, and 2006. The purpose of these amendments was to preserve parts of the original act that were going to expire. Among these amendments is the provision requiring states and cities to provide bilingual ballots in areas where a single-language population that is larger than 5 percent of the area's population and is of voting age resides. This provided more opportunities for Hispanic and Asian groups to engage in political participation. The provision, included in the original law and then expanded in 1975, required these areas to provide bilingual ballots. Another component under this provision was for local and state officials to make every effort to prevent voting discrimination from occurring.

Descriptive versus Substantive Representation. The 1982 amendment to the VRA proposed a solution for discriminatory laws: the creation of majority-minority or single-member districts. The purpose of the majority-minority districts was the expectation that majority African American and Latino populations living in these districts would be able to elect minority representatives to the U.S. Congress, with the added benefit of gaining substantive representation. The first scholar to distinguish between descriptive (or physical) and substantive representation was Pitkin (1967). Descriptive representation consists of being represented by someone who shares a physical quality with his or her constituent. The expectation is that sharing the same physical characteristics increases his or her ability to represent the constituents' interests. Substantive representation focuses on being represented by someone who will pursue constituents' interests, regardless of his or her physical characteristics or gender.

Some scholars argue that although majority-minority districts increase descriptive representation in Congress, minority groups, including Latinos, do not gain substantive representation as a result of member election. Lublin (1997) uses Poole-Rosenthal scores to analyze representatives' ideologies and interest group ratings of roll-call votes. He finds that majority-minority districts lower substantive representation in the South because white Democratic and Republican representatives from surrounding districts become more conservative due to the wishes of their white constituents. In addition, majority-minority districts cause a loss of Democratic seats in Congress, which hurts substantive representation for African Americans and Latinos. Thus, minority representatives' voices are not heard once they get to Congress (see also Guinier, 1991). In the North, white representatives tend to vote for policies that are favorable to minorities. He also argues that when African American and Latino populations are less than 40 percent in a district, white representatives become more aware of his or her minority constituents' concerns. They will also adopt more liberal positions on issues that are important to minorities. This finding is supported by Hutchings (1998), who argues that representatives pursue minority interests if their districts consist of some minorities.[1] The common solution promoted by Lublin is for minorities to gain substantive representation from white Democratic representatives (see also Guinier, 1991; Swain, 1995).

Over time, researchers have identified several benefits that underrepresented groups (including minorities) gain from descriptive representation (Dovi, 2002; Mansbridge, 1999). Mansbridge argues that racial- and gender-defined groups gain several benefits from descriptive representation. First, representatives are able to articulate concerns that were not clearly defined. Second, descriptive representatives can dispel previous stereotypes about the groups, including assumptions that the group was "unfit to rule." Second, as the number of minority representatives increases, their constituents feel as if they are active participants. In her analysis, Dovi argues that not only can descriptive representation provide adequate representation for underrepresented groups, but subgroups can (and should) receive adequate representation as well. She encourages the representatives to actively pursue relationships with members of the subgroups in order to demonstrate that their interests will also be pursued. The next section presents a literature review that begins with a discussion of benefits and costs of descriptive representation at the national and state levels. It concludes with a discussion of factors that reduced Latino representation on city councils and school boards.

---

1. Griffin and Newman (2006) provide a counter-argument to Lublin. Their analysis of roll-call votes demonstrates that white representatives' roll-call votes are more complimentary to white ideological views and that minority groups' ideological concerns are ignored (see Griffin, Newman, & Wolbrecht, 2012).

DESCRIPTIVE REPRESENTATION ACROSS ALL LEVELS OF GOVERNMENT

National Government. At the national level, scholars have engaged in a debate about the merits of descriptive representation gained through majority-minority districts. Mansbridge (1999) suggests that descriptive representation should occur through the "most fluid" of methods, including proportional representation and affirmative action policies. In contrast, she identifies majority-minority districts and quotas as the "least fluid" strategies. Casellas (2009a) finds that at the national level, Latino representatives are more likely to be elected from majority-minority districts. However, a challenge encountered by minority members of Congress is related to how they are viewed by the institution and those who control the institution. Hawkesworth (2003) finds that minority congresswomen in the 103rd and 104th Congresses encounter "racing-gendering" in response to their efforts to introduce and gain support for welfare reform legislation. Hawkesworth argues that white members of Congress challenge their efforts to introduce successful legislation through disrespect and efforts to spin their legislation as bills that promote the interests of a specific group.

In their examination of Latino representation, scholars have identified several benefits associated with majority-minority districts (Hero, Garcia, Garcia, & Pachon, 2000). Hero, et al. (2000) confirm previous findings that Latino politicians increase the amount of employment opportunities, teachers, and political empowerment. Another benefit is that descriptive representation reduces the barriers of participation for Latinos and reduces political alienation among Latinos (Affigne, 2000; Arviszu & Garcia, 1996; Baretto, 2007; Baretto, Segura, & Woods, 2004; Pantoja & Segura, 2003). Affigne (2000) notes that political participation rates are declining steadily among Latinos. Barreto, et al. (2004) analyze voter registration records for counties in California and find that majority-minority districts increase Latino turnout while decreasing white turnout. Barreto (2007) examines voters in 6,776 precincts and finds that Latino voters have higher turnout rates and more support for Latino candidates in co-ethnic elections. Pantoja and Segura (2003) find evidence that descriptive representation decreases the level of political alienation felt by Latinos in the United States. However, they also find evidence that other factors, including socioeconomic and political factors, reduce political alienation.

One of the first examinations of how Latino members of Congress provide substantive representation for their constituents was completed by Welch and Hibbing (1984). They analyze roll-call votes for white and Latino members of Congress whose districts have large Latino constituencies. They find that Latino representatives provided strong substantive representation for their Latino constituents. Latino representatives demonstrate more liberal positions than their white peers. Overall, Latinos receive substantive representation from Latino representatives and white Democratic representatives. Their conclusions were re-examined by Hero and Tolbert (1995) who reached different conclusions. They mailed a survey to members of the 100th Congress, asking them how they would vote on issues that were important to Latinos. They conclude that Latino constituents gained more substantive representation from having a Democratic representative outside of the Southwest than from having a Latino representative. Casellas (2002) builds upon Hero and Tolbert. Although he finds support for their conclusions about Latino representatives from the 100th Congress, his analysis of the 87th to 104th Congresses demonstrates that Latinos receive some substantive representation from their Puerto Rican and Mexican American representatives as well as from Democratic representatives. In an analysis of scorecards from the National Hispanic Leadership Agenda for Latino members of Congress from the 108th Congress, Knoll (2009) finds support for the conclusion that Latinos gain substantive support from Democratic representatives. Wallace (2014), however, finds that in the 111th Congress, Latino constituents were more likely to gain more substantive representation from Democratic representatives as well as African American representatives. She argues that descriptive representatives (Latinos) only provided substantive representation on issues of high importance, including immigration, but not on issues of low importance.

State Government. At the state legislature level, scholars have found conflicting results regarding the benefits gained from descriptive representation. The presence of Latino legislators increases the introduction of policies that are important to Latinos, including health care services and education (Bratton, 2006). In states where the Latino population is higher than 10 percent, the presence of Latino legislatures reduces "backlash" toward Latino-interest policies (measured as welfare policies) (Preuhs, 2007). Although minority constituents can receive substantive representation from their minority legislators, there is evidence that minority legislators face many challenges once they are elected.

At the state level, a factor that affects minorities' chances of winning elections is their population within a state (Casellas, 2007; 2009b). Casellas finds that when the Latino population in a state is interacted to legislative turnover rates and legislative professionalization, states with high turnover rates and citizen legislations increase Latinos' chances of winning office (Casellas, 2009b). In his examination of the California state legislature, Casellas finds that partisanship does not increase the likelihood of a Latino candidate being elected. Although the percentage of Latinos in a district or state has been shown to affect Latino candidates' chances of winning elections, it does not demonstrate having an impact upon how Latino representatives vote on policies once they are in office (Casellas, 2007; Hero & Tolbert, 1995; Knoll, 2009).

The Local Level. Although descriptive representation has been shown to provide *some* substantive representation at the national and state levels, scholars have found that minorities receive many benefits at the local level. First, the presence of minorities in government bureaucracies increases the likelihood that minorities will gain access to resources and that minority-friendly policies will be pursued, without hurting the interests of whites (Hindera, 1993a; Meier, Wrinkle, & Polinard, 1999; Selden, Brudney, & Kellough, 1998).

Second, the presence of minorities and females on city councils increases the number of minorities and female municipal employees (Dye & Renick, 1981). For African Americans and Latinos, their likelihood of getting administrative, professional, and protective jobs depends upon their proportion of the population in cities and the number of African Americans and Latinos on city councils. For female job candidates, their likelihood of being employed in administration and professional jobs decreases in cities with highly educated residents and in larger cities. Mladenka (1989) finds that African American and Latino membership on the city council increases municipal employment opportunities for these groups; however, having a minority mayor in office does not. Hispanic municipal employment is affected more by Hispanic membership on the city councils. Dye and Renick (1981) provide some evidence that having African Americans and Latinos on city councils increases the likelihood that they will gain administrative or professional jobs.

Third, scholars have found that minority membership on school boards provides benefits for African Americans and Latinos. In general, minority board members have been shown to increase the numbers of minority administrators, which has increased the number of minority teachers in classrooms (Meier, Gonzalez-Juenke, Wrinkle, & Polinard, 2005). Latino school board members increase the numbers of Latino teachers, which reduces the levels of second-generation discrimination experienced by Latino students (Leal, Martinez-Ebers, & Meir, 2004; Meier, 1993; Polinard, Wrinkle, & Longoria, 1990). Similar results are also seen for African Americans (Meier & England, 1984). Having African American and Latino school board members increases the number of minority administrators, which increases the number of minority teachers, which helps minority students' test scores, reduces second-generation discrimination rates, and provides other benefits (Leal, et al., 2004; Meier, 1993; Meier, Doerfler, Hawes, Hicklin, & Rocha, 2006; Meier & England, 1984; Polinard, et al., 1990; Rocha & Hawes, 2009). Meier, et al. (1999) analyze whether minority students could gain benefits from minority teachers at the expense of white students. Analyzing standardized test scores from 350 school boards in Texas, they conclude that white students had higher test scores if they had minority teachers. However, minority students' test scores were only improved if the teaching staff consisted of 22 percent of minority faculty. Meier and England (1984) argue that for Latinos, school board membership affects the number of Latino administrators who are hired in schools (also see Meier, et al., 2005). Meier, et al. (2006) confirm previous findings that minority and low-income students benefit from having minority teachers. Rocha and Hawes (2009) find that African American and Latino teachers reduce the amount of second-generation discrimination experienced by African American and Latino students. However, the following factor—turnout in local elections—has an impact upon the level of representation that Latinos and other minorities can gain.

The Impact of Turnout upon Minority Representation. Scholars have shown that turnout levels in school boards and political elections affect the descriptive representation that minorities receive. It is important to study how turnout affects minority representation at the local level. Hajnal and Trounstine (2005) argue that turnout at the national level is higher and that it is beneficial to study how turnout rates among minority groups vary at different levels of government. Low turnout levels for school board elections lead to underrepresentation of minorities on school boards. Allan and Plank (2005) examine the turnout levels among four school districts in Michigan. Of the four, two hold "consolidated" school elections, or elections occur at the same time as municipal elections in November. The other two districts hold "special" elections or separate elections (Allan & Plank, 2005: 512). They find that consolidated elections increase turnout levels across all elections, as well as turnout levels of minorities for school board elections. This is significant because higher turnout rates among minorities increase their descriptive representation. Hajnal and Trounstine (2005, 2010) find that turnout among Latinos and Asian Americans increases as their population size increases. They also find that increasing turnout among these groups significantly increases their representation on city councils. The next section will discuss several factors that have decreased the likelihood of competing for office by Latino candidates.

FACTORS THAT AFFECT LATINO DECISIONS TO BECOME CANDIDATES

Scholars have examined the presence of Latino candidates who attempt to pursue interests that appeal to voters of all races. Gonzalez-Juenke and Sampaio (2010) test the concept of deracialization in the context of contests for seats in the U.S. House and Senate. The authors acknowledge that deracialization has been used to examine local-level elections and that their analysis is the first to apply it to a different context. This strategy is used in areas where the minority group of the candidate has not reached majority size. In their analysis, Gonzalez-Juenke and Sampaio examine the campaigns of Ken and John Salazaar who ran for seats in the U.S. Senate and House, respectively, in 2004. Their analysis demonstrates the brothers deracialized their respective campaigns because many of the voters in Colorado were rural Republicans. Some strategies that they used included not associating themselves with vote drives aimed toward Latino voters, visiting voters in rural areas, and other methods.

Scholars have assessed how factors including electoral structure, the size of minority groups in districts, and others have affected Latino candidates' decisions to run in elections at all levels of government. In an examination of U.S. House primary elections between 1994 and 2004, Branton (2009) argues that the growth of the Latino population in a district increases the number of Latino candidates who compete in Democrat and Republican primary elections. It also increases the number of quality challengers who are members of these groups and makes Democratic primary races more competitive. Casellas (2007) examines factors that affect Latino candidates' chances of being elected to the California state legislature. He confirms previous findings that candidates (including Latinos) are more likely to compete for a legislative seat where there are open seats, when incumbents retire at the end of their terms, and if they are able to raise campaign funds. The availability of public funds did not increase the likelihood that female, minority, or working-class candidates would run for office (La Raja, 2007). Among potential Latino candidates in non-Latino majority wards, Krebs (1999) finds that Latino candidates were less likely to run for office in districts where they would have to build a coalition of support in order to win a city council seat. Although the factors discussed earlier have caused potential Latino candidates to defer from competing for office, many have overcome these factors and not only run for office but have also been elected for office. The final section will focus exclusively on factors that have allowed these candidates to successfully win elections at the local level.

FACTORS AFFECTING LATINO CANDIDATE SUCCESS AT THE LOCAL LEVEL

Progressive reformers tried to argue that at-large elections would provide adequate representation for the residents of the city as a whole (Banfield & Wilson, 1963). However, research has shown that white candidates received more representation, since white candidates were more likely to win city council seats. Returning to ward-based elections was a solution used in vote dilution cases (Davidson & Korbel, 1981). The purpose was to allow citizens in districts to vote for representatives from those districts, as opposed to the entire city (Karnig & Welch, 1982). Supporters of the use of district elections argued that district representatives would address the interests of the residents of their district instead of the interests of the residents of the entire city. This portion of the literature review will provide a discussion of how electoral structures affect descriptive representation for African Americans and Latinos on city councils and school boards.

City Councils. Scholars have found evidence that several other factors affect minority office holding. Latinos and other minority groups are underrepresented in the South and Southwest, smaller cities, and areas where the residents are less educated (Robinson & Dye, 1978; Taebel, 1978). For Latino representation, the size of the council has a stronger effect than the type of election that is used (Taebel, 1978). Taebel (1978) argues that at-large elections and small council sizes decrease descriptive representation for African Americans and Latinos.

School Boards. School board members are elected through at-large elections or district elections, or they are appointed (Leal, et al., 2004). The type of election that is used to elect school members is important for Latino descriptive and substantive representation. Having at-large or ward-based elections can determine the number of minorities on school boards and the number of Latino administrations (Meier, et al., 2005). They also find that the size of the Latino population in an area not only affects school board membership but also the number of Latino administrators and teachers in schools. Leal, et al. (2004) and Meier, et al. (2005) find that at-large elections reduce the amount of Latino members on school boards and consequently reduce descriptive representation. Meier, et al. (2005) find that at-large elections lower Latino candidates' chances of being elected to school boards. However, they conclude that at-large elections hurt school board membership and lower the number of minority administrators and teachers for both African Americans and Latinos. Rocha (2007) finds that Latinos can gain more representation on school boards in areas where the residents of Latino communities have higher levels of education and in areas where they are the majority of the population. He does not find evidence that Latinos gain more descriptive representation through ward-based elections.

As was seen for minority candidates in city council elections, minority school board candidates' chances of winning elections is limited by the use of at-large elections versus ward-based elections. Latino population and school board membership vary in a nonlinear fashion; school board membership is affected when the Latino population reaches a 5.2 percent threshold (Leal, et al., 2004; Meier, et al., 2005). Latinos can win at-large elections when they are the majority population (Leal, et al., 2004). Overall, Latinos gain descriptive and substantive representation from district elections (Leal, et al., 2004; Meier, 1993; Meier, et al., 2005; Polinard, et al., 1990).

CONCLUSION

In this essay, the benefits of having Latinos in office across all levels of government were discussed. The main categorization of these benefits was descriptive representation, which describes the idea that having a candidate that looked like his or her constituents provided many benefits, including substantive representation. The essay then transitioned to a discussion of factors that affected potential Latino candidates' decisions to run for office as well as factors that helped and/or limited their success at the local level.

Natasha Altema McNeely

See also: Latina/o Mayors; Latino Elected Officials on the Federal Level

FURTHER READING

Affigne, Tony. 2000. "Latino Politics in the United States." *PS: Political Science & Politics.* 33: 520–27.

Allen, Ann, & David N. Plank. 2005. "School Board Election Structure and Democratic Representation." *Educational Policy* 19, no. 3: 510–27.

Arviszu, John R., & F. Chris Garcia. 1996. "Latino Voting Participation: Explaining and Differentiating Latino Voting Turnout." *Hispanic Journal of Behavioral Sciences* 18: 104–28.

Banfield, Edward C., & James Q. Wilson. 1963. *City Politics.* Cambridge. MA: Harvard University Press and the M.I.T. Press.

Barreto, Matt. A. 2007. "Si Se Puede! Latino Candidates and the Mobilization of Latino Votes." *American Political Science Review* 101: 425–41.

Barreto, Matt A., Gary M. Segura, & Nathan D. Woods. 2004. "The Mobilizing Effect of Majority-Minority Districts on Latino Turnout." *The American Political Science Review* 98: 65–75.

Branton, Regina P. 2009. "The Importance of Race and Ethnicity in Congressional Primary Elections." *Political Research Quarterly* 62, no. 3: 459–73.

Bratton, Kathleen A. 2006. "The Behavior and Success of Latino Legislators: Evidence from the States." *Social Science Quarterly* 87, no. 5: 1136–57.

Burnham, Robert A. 1997. "Reform, Politics, and Race in Cincinnati: Proportional Representation and the City Charter Committee, 1924–1959." *Journal of Urban History* 23: 131–63.

Casellas, Jason P. 2002. "Latino Representation in the U.S. Congress: To What Extent Are Latinos Substantively Represented?" Presented at the 2002 Meeting of the Southern Political Science Association, Savannah, Georgia, November 6–9.

Casellas, Jason P. 2007. "The Election of Latinos to the California Legislature Pre- and Post-2000 Redistricting." *California Politics & Policy* 11: 21–38.

Casellas, Jason P. 2009a. "The Institutional and Demographic Determinants of Latino Representation." *Legislative Studies Quarterly* 34: 309–26.

Casellas, Jason P. 2009b. "Coalitions in the House? The Election of Minorities to State Legislatures and Congress." *Political Research Quarterly* 62: 120–31.

Davidson, Chandler, & George Korbel. 1981. "At-Large Elections and Minority Group Representation: A Re-examination of Historical and Contemporary Evidence." *Journal of Politics* 43: 982–1005.

Dovi, Suzanne. 2002. "Preferable Descriptive Representatives: Will Just Any Woman, Black or Latino Do?" *American Political Science Review* 96: 729–43.

Dye, Tomas R., & James Renick. 1981. "Political Power and City Jobs: Determinants of Minority Employment." *Social Science Quarterly* 62: 475–86.

Gonzalez Juenke, Eric, & Anna Christina Sampaio. 2010. "Deracialization and Latino Politics: The Case of the Salazar Brothers in Colorado." *Political Research Quarterly* 63, no. 1: 43–54.

Griffin, John D., Brian Newman, & Christina Wolbrecht. 2012. "A Gender Gap in Policy Representation in the US Congress?" *Legislative Studies Quarterly* 37, no. 1: 35–66.

Guinier, Lani. 1991. "The Triumph of Tokenism: The Voting Rights Act and the Theory of Black Electoral Success." *Michigan Law Review* 89, no. 5: 1077–154.

Hajnal, Zoltan, & Jessica Trounstine. 2005. "Where Turnout Matters: The Consequences of Uneven Turnout in City Politics." *The Journal of Politics* 67, no. 2: 515–35.

Hajnal, Zoltan L., & Jessica Trounstine. 2010. "Who or What Governs? The Effects of Economics, Politics, Institutions, and Needs on Local Spending." *American Politics Research* 38, no. 6: 1130–63.

Hawkesworth, Mary. 2003. "Congressional Enactments of Race–Gender: Toward a Theory of Raced–Gendered Institutions." *American Political Science Review* 97, no. 4: 529–50.

Hero, Rodney. 1987. "The Election of Latinos in City Government: An Examination of the Election of Federico Pena as Mayor of Denver." *Political Research Quarterly* 40: 93–105.

Hero, Rodney E., F. Chris Garcia, John Garcia, & Harry Pachon. 2000. "Latino Participation, Partisanship, and Office Holding." *PS: Political Science and Politics* 33: 529–34.

Hero, Rodney E., & Caroline J. Tolbert. 1995. "Latinos and Substantive Representation in the U.S. House of Representatives: Direct, Indirect, or Nonexistent." *American Journal of Political Science* 39: 640–52.

Hindera, John J. 1993a. "Representative Bureaucracy: Imprimis Evidence of Active Representation in the EEOC District Offices." *Social Science Quarterly* 74: 95–108.

Hindera, John J. 1993b. "Representative Bureaucracy: Further Evidence of Active Representation in the EEOC District Offices." *Journal of Public Administration Research and Theory* 3: 415–29.

Hutchings, Vincent L. 1998. "Issue Salience and Support for Civil Rights Legislation among Southern Democrats." *Legislative Studies Quarterly* 23, no. 4 (November): 521–44.

Karnig, Albert K., & Susan Welch. 1982. "Electoral Structure and Black Representation on City Councils." *Social Science Quarterly* 63, no. 1: 99.

Knoll, Benjamin R. 2009. "¿Amigo de la Raza? Reexamining Determinants of Latino Support in the U.S. Congress." *Social Science Quarterly* 90: 179–95.

Krebs, Timothy B. 1999. "The Political and Demographic Predictors of Candidate Emergence in City Council Elections." *Urban Affairs Review* 35, no. 2: 279–300.

La Raja, Raymond J. 2007. "Sunshine Laws and the Press: The Effect of Campaign Disclosure on News Reporting in the American States." *Election Law Journal* 6, no. 3: 236–50.

Leal, David L., Valerie Martinez-Ebers, & Kenneth J. Meier. 2004. "The Politics of Latino Education: The Biases of At-Large Elections." *Journal of Politics* 66: 1224–44.

Lublin, David. 1997. "The Election of African Americans and Latinos to the US House of Representatives, 1972–1994." *American Politics Quarterly* 25, no. 3: 269–86.

Mansbridge, Jane. 1999. "Should Blacks Represent Blacks and Women Represent Women? A Contingent 'Yes.' " *The Journal of Politics* 61, no. 3: 628–57.

Meier, Kenneth J. 1993. "Latinos and Representative Bureaucracy: Testing the Thomson and Henderson Hypothesis." *Journal of Public Administration Research and Theory, PART* 3: 393–414.

Meier, Kenneth J., Carl Doerfler, Daniel Hawes, Alisa K. Hicklin, & Rene R. Rocha. 2006. "The Role of Management and Representation in Improving Performance of Disadvantaged Students: An Application of Bum Phillips's 'Don Shula Rule' 1." *Review of Policy Research* 23, no. 5: 1095–110.

Meier, Kenneth J., & Robert E. England. 1984. "Black Representation and Educational Policy: Are They Related?" *American Political Science Review* 78, no. 2: 392–403.

Meier, Kenneth J., Eric Gonzalez Juenke, Robert D. Wrinkle, & Jerry T. Polinard. 2005. "Structural Choices and Representation Biases: The Post-Election Color of Representation." *American Journal of Political Science* 45: 758–68.

Meier, Kenneth J., Paula D. McClain, Jerry L. Polinard, & Robert D. Wrinkle. 2004. "Divided or Together? Conflict and Cooperation between African Americans and Latinos." *Political Research Quarterly* 57: 399–409.

Meier, Kenneth J., Robert D. Wrinkle, & Jerry L. Polinard. 1999. "Representative Bureaucracy and Distributional Equity: Addressing the Hard Question." *The Journal of Politics* 61: 1025–39.

Mladenka, Kenneth D. 1989. "Blacks and Latinos in Urban Politics." *American Political Science Review* 83: 165–92.

National Association of Latino Elected & Appointed Officials (NALEO). 2016. *National Directory of Latino Elected Officials*. Los Angeles: NALEO Educational Fund.

Pantoja, Adrian D., & Gary M. Segura. 2003. "Does Ethnicity Matter? Descriptive Representation in Legislatures and Political Alienation among Latinos." *Social Science Quarterly* 84: 441–60.

Pitkin, Hanna Penichel. 1967. *The Concept of Representation*. Berkeley: University of California Press.

Polinard, Jerry L., Robert D. Wrinkle, & Thomas Longoria. 1990. "Education and Governance: Representational Links to Second Generation Discrimination." *Western Political Science Quarterly* 43: 631–46.

Polinard, Jerry L., Robert D. Wrinkle, Thomas Longoria, & Norman Binder. 1994. *Electoral Structure and Urban Policy: The Impact on Mexican American Communities*. Armonk, NY: M. E. Sharpe.

Preuhs, Robert R. 2007. "Descriptive Representation as a Mechanism to Mitigate Policy Backlash: Latino Incorporation and Welfare Policy in the American States." *Political Research Quarterly* 60, no. 2: 277–92.

Robinson, Theodore P., & Thomas R. Dye. 1978. "Reformism and Black Representation on City Councils." *Social Science Quarterly* 59, no. 1: 133–41.

Rocha, Rene R. 2007. "Black-Brown Coalitions in Local School Board Elections." *Political Research Quarterly* 60: 315–27.

Rocha, Rene R., & Daniel P. Hawes. 2009. "Racial Diversity, Representative Bureaucracy, and Equity in Multiracial School Districts." *Social Science Quarterly* 90: 326–44.

Selden, Sally Coleman, Jeffrey L. Brudney, & J. Edward Kellough. 1998. "Bureaucracy as a Representative Institution: Toward a Reconciliation of Bureaucratic Government and Democratic Theory." *American Journal of Political Science* 42: 717–44.

Swain, Carol Miller. 1995. *Black Faces, Black Interests: The Representation of African Americans in Congress.* New Haven, CT: Harvard University Press.

Taebel, Delbert. 1978. "Descriptive Representation on City Councils: The Impact of Structure on Blacks and Hispanics." *Social Science Quarterly* 59: 142–52.

Wallace, Sophia J. 2014. "Examining Latino Support for Descriptive Representation: The Role of Identity and Discrimination." *Social Science Quarterly* 95, no. 2: 311–27.

Welch, Susan. 1990. "The Impact of At-Large Elections on the Representation of Blacks and Hispanics." *Journal of Politics* 52: 1050–76.

Welch, Susan, & John R. Hibbing. 1984. "Hispanic Representation in the U.S. Congress." *Social Science Quarterly* 65: 328–35.

A

Acosta Bañuelos, Romana

(1925–2018)

A Republican businesswoman born in Arizona, Romana Acosta Bañuelos served as the first Latina treasurer of the United States from 1971 to 1974 during the Nixon administration. She was also the owner of Ramona's Mexican Food Products, Inc., a multimillion-dollar business, and co-founder of the Pan American Bank, the first bank for Mexican Americans in California (Reyes-Velarde, 2018). She passed away on January 15, 2018, at the age of 92 of pneumonia in Redondo Beach, California.

Romana Acosta Bañuelos was born in Miami, Arizona, on March 20, 1925, to Mexican immigrant parents, Juan Francisco Acosta and Teresa Lugo, natives of Sonora, Mexico. In 1932, during the Depression, she and her family were deported to Mexico as part of an anti-immigrant backlash and relocated to the Mexican states of Sonora and Chihuahua. In Mexico at the age of 15 she married her first husband, Nepomuceno Torres, with whom she had two sons, Martin and Carlos, and whom she divorced by the age of 18. A decade after her deportation she returned to the United States and relocated to Los Angeles, California, where she met her second husband, Alejandro Bañuelos Tapia, with whom she, and two Mexican brothers, began a tortilla business. By 1947, she had bought out her tortilla business partners and began expanding Ramona's line of products to include packaged and frozen foods.

In 1963, she was approached by a group of businessmen seeking to establish a bank for the Latino community in the East Los Angeles and Boyle Heights areas. The following year, in 1964, she and the businessmen established the Pan American National Bank in East Los Angeles (Hassan, 2018). The bank was constructed in 1965 and is now recognized as the oldest Latinx-owned bank in California that serves East Los Angeles and "Boyle" Heights community. Moreover, the bank helped foster a closer relationship between the Latino community and the financial institutions by providing the community with financial education.

By 1969, Bañuelos was appointed the chairperson of the Pan American National Bank's board of directors and was awarded the Outstanding Business Woman of the Year Award by the city of Los Angeles. In that same year, Los Angeles mayor Samuel William Yorty presented her with a commendation from the Los Angeles County Board of Supervisors.

The following year, in 1970, Bañuelos was contacted by White House officials and asked if she would consider placing her name as a nominee for the position of the 34th treasurer of the United States (EWB). On September 20, 1971, President Richard Nixon personally nominated her to be treasurer of the United States and to succeed the late 33rd treasurer of the United States, Dorothy Andrew Kabis, who passed away on July 3, 1971.

Subsequently, on October 6, 1971, her nomination came under scrutiny as her food plant in suburban Gardena was raided by federal immigration agents and 36 undocumented immigrants were arrested. Bañuelos stated that "the raid might have been part of an attempt by Democrats to block my nomination as Treasurer of the United States," and her nomination went before the Senate (Hassan, 2018). The Senate committee ruled that she "had no knowledge of the workers and that she had been unfairly targeted in order to embarrass the Nixon administration."

On December 17, 1971, she took office and became the 34th treasurer of the United States, the first Latina in the position, and the highest-ranking Mexican American in the government. She served one term as treasurer and left office in 1974 to dedicate more of her time to her business, family, and philanthropic pursuits.

In 1979, Bañuelos became a founding member of Executive Women in Government, and by that year she helped further expand Ramona's Mexican Food Products, Inc., which became instrumental in popularizing Mexican cuisine throughout the United States. Throughout the 1980s and 1990s she remained president of Ramona's Food Products, Inc., and Pan American National until the late 1990s, when her three children took over daily operations of both organizations.

José E. Mendoza Vazquez

See also: Marín, Rosario (1958–)

Further Reading

The American Presidency Project. 1981. "Richard Nixon: Statement Announcing Nomination of Romana A. Bañuelos as Treasurer of the United States." September 20. John T. Woolley and Gerhard Peters, University of California Santa Barbara. http://www.presidency.ucsb.edu/ws/index.php?pid=3148.

Hassan, Adeel. 2018. "Romana Acosta Bañuelos, U.S. Treasurer Under Nixon, Dies at 92." *The New York Times*, February 5. https://www.nytimes.com/2018/02/05/obituaries/romana-acosta-banuelos-us-treasurer-under-nixon-dies-at-92.html.

Henderson, Andrea. 2005. "Bañuelos, Romana Acosta." *Encyclopedia of World Biography*. 2nd ed. Vol. 24. Detroit: Gale, pp. 40–42. http://go.galegroup.com/ps.

Los Angeles Conservancy. 2016. "Pan American Bank." https://www.laconservancy.org/locations/pan-american-bank.

Reyes-Velarde, Alejandra. 2018. "Romana Acosta Bañuelos, First Latina U.S. Treasurer and Mexican American Pioneer, Dies at 92." *Los Angeles Times*, January 22. http://www.latimes.com/local/obituaries/la-me-romana-acosta-banuelos-20180119-story.html.

Affordable Care Act of 2010 and Latinos

The Patient Protection and Affordable Care Act (ACA) was signed into law by President Barack Obama on March 23, 2010. A sweeping overhaul of the U.S. health insurance system, its primary goal was to expand access to subsidized health insurance coverage to the estimated 47 million uninsured individuals. The ACA provided a critical opportunity to improve health for Latino populations in the

Tania Ruiz, with La Clinica del Pueblo, helps José Morales as he considers signing up for health care. Morales has insurance but it doesn't meet the standard to qualify for coverage under the ACA. The National Council of La Raza (NCLR) hosted an Affordable Care Act outreach event for Latinos in February 2014. Latinos represent the nation's largest uninsured population. (David Paul Morris/Bloomberg via Getty Images)

United States, who face a number of specific disparities, high rates of uninsurance, and lack of adequate access to care. Politically contentious since its inception, the ACA faced targeted attacks to repeal or replace the law by Republicans in Congress since its passage, and especially under the Trump administration beginning in 2017.

The law included several key provisions to expand health insurance access, including the expansion of Medicaid to those earning up to 133 percent of the federal poverty level (FPL), new state-based health insurance exchanges, insurance market reforms, premium subsidies for individuals with incomes below 400 percent of the FPL, cost-sharing subsidies for individuals with incomes below 250 percent of the FPL, and a requirement for individuals to obtain health insurance coverage or face a penalty when filing their income taxes. The coverage expansions were at the center of the law and were accompanied by a number of other reforms, including a standardized minimum benefit package, meaning that all insurance products must include a comprehensive set of basic services; the elimination of exclusions or higher prices for people with preexisting health conditions; the prohibition of gender rating, which meant that women could no longer be charged more for insurance than men; the elimination of "excision" practices so that insurance companies could no longer cancel policies after they are issued; and a provision allowing dependents to remain on their parents' insurance plan until their 26th birthday. The ACA also reauthorized the Office of Minority Health, which works to improve the health of racial and ethnic minority populations through improved data reporting and collection, identification of health disparities, and the development of health policies and programs to improve health care outcomes for Latinos and other minority communities in the United States.

The ACA created online health insurance "marketplaces," which opened in 2013 at the website HealthCare.gov. While 32 states expanded Medicaid coverage to those at 138 percent or below of the federal poverty level, some states rejected this provision following a 2012 Supreme Court ruling, which held that states would not lose Medicaid funding if they didn't expand Medicaid under the ACA. Several states with large Latino populations, such as Texas, opted out of the Medicaid expansion. This deprived millions of working adults access to medical insurance and left large numbers of people to fall into the "coverage gap" that was created. This battle set the tone for many years of political attempts to repeal and replace the law.

Because of the diversity of Latino populations, rates of uninsurance prior to the ACA varied widely based on state of residence, country of origin, legal status, gender, age, and socioeconomic status. Nonetheless, as a whole, Latinos had the highest rate of uninsured persons in the nation prior to the reform, comprising nearly a third of the entire uninsured population at 16 million people and at a rate nearly three times that of non-Hispanic whites. In most states, Latinos represented the majority of the eligible uninsured populations, ranging between 25 percent and 50 percent of persons who stood to benefit from the ACA. While half of all uninsured Latinos resided in California, Florida, and Texas, some of the highest levels of uninsured are in southeastern states, which are experiencing relatively recent but rapid growth in the Latino population. Because of this pattern of uninsurance, the ACA provided an unprecedented opportunity to improve coverage and health care access for Latino populations. The law has enjoyed favorable opinions among Latinos, with approval ratings in this group among the highest in the nation, ranging from 47 percent to 61 percent across the years since implementation.

A number of ACA enrollment challenges emerged for Latino populations in particular. These included a high prevalence of immigrant households, barriers associated with low incomes, and language barriers. While many are eligible for assistance with insurance affordability, such as subsidies, an estimated one in five Latinos are "unbanked," meaning they lack checking accounts. This required creative solutions, such as the ability to pay insurance premiums through alternative methods (such as money order, cashier check, or prepaid card). Language was initially a major obstacle in the enrollment process, since nearly 40 percent of Latinos eligible for the health insurance marketplace are Spanish-speaking. However, this resulted in an unprecedented collaboration with Spanish-language media outlets and Latino-owned businesses urging communities to enroll and the creation of a Spanish-language website, CuidadoDeSalud.gov. In addition, the ACA employed bilingual enrollment specialists, Spanish-language print materials, and a hotline to assist Spanish speakers.

Noncitizens are among the most likely to lack coverage in the United States. Prior to the ACA, three in five Latino noncitizens and nearly half of all noncitizen Latino children were uninsured. Under the ACA, legal categories of immigration status had as much impact on eligibility as means-tested categories such as income, thus disproportionately affecting Latino populations. The law relied on and reproduced eligible categories of legal status to determine eligibility for programs, specifically distinguishing between "qualified" and "nonqualified" immigrants for the purpose of federal benefits. These are based on categories constructed by Congress in 1996 as part of the Personal Responsibility and Work Opportunity Reconciliation Act (PRWORA). Under the ACA, eligibility for marketplace coverage first distinguished between "lawfully present immigrants" (which includes both "qualified" and some "nonqualified" categories from the PRWORA framework) and "not lawfully present immigrants."

The ACA expressly excluded undocumented immigrants from participating in the federally subsidized state health exchanges and in obtaining Medicaid; at the same time, they were exempt from the individual mandate requiring insurance coverage. Lawfully present noncitizen immigrants include permanent residents, refugees, asylees, Cuban and Haitian entrants, victims of domestic violence and trafficking survivors and their derivatives (that is, the spouse, child, sibling, or parent), persons granted withholding of deportation or removal, people with temporary protected status, lawful temporary residents, individuals with nonimmigrant status (including people with worker and student visas), those with deferred enforced departure or deferred action status (with the exception of Deferred Action for Childhood Arrivals [DACA]), and applicants for any of these statuses. These individuals were made eligible for exchange subsidies, premium tax credits, and cost-sharing tax credits. However, not all lawfully present persons were considered "qualified" persons under the ACA. Nonimmigrants, including students, visitors, and temporary guest workers, are considered legally present but not legal permanent residents and are thus ineligible for ACA benefits and the ability to purchase coverage on the exchanges. In addition, for lawfully present noncitizen immigrants, eligibility for Medicaid remained restricted under the ACA, with "qualified" immigrants barred for the first five years. Lawfully residing adults who have been in the country less than five years were not eligible for Medicaid (in states that expanded adult Medicaid), while in some states lawfully residing immigrant children who have been in the country less than five years could be eligible at the discretion of the state. In other words, opportunities for Medicaid coverage for both children and adults varied depending on the state in which they live. In addition, DACA recipients were explicitly excluded from all key components of ACA program eligibility and remained in the same category as undocumented immigrants, even though they are considered lawfully present. Because eligibility for insurance coverage is affected by legal status, the ACA increased immigrants' exclusion within the U.S. health care system and codified differential opportunities between immigrants and citizens in the United States.

Unique to the Latino population in the United States is the high number of mixed-status families, which contain varied constellations of citizens, permanent legal residents, undocumented immigrants, and individuals in legal limbo such as temporary protected status or DACA. There were direct and indirect impacts of the ACA on the estimated 2.3 million mixed-status families in the United States. Prior policy shifts that considered immigration status as part of eligibility requirements resulted in a number of problematic issues: children with undocumented parents accessed benefits at a lower rate than those with citizen parents, despite their eligibility for benefits such as Medicaid and the State Children's Health Insurance Program, and families expressed fear of interacting with authorities or of jeopardizing future chances at legalization, which led some mixed-status families to limit or delay services for children or even withdraw from programs altogether. In addition, changes accompanying the ACA had the long-term effect of exacerbating existing health disparities since access to services for the uninsured was expected to be reduced, as those not eligible for coverage through the purchase of subsidized insurance from health insurance exchanges became more isolated from the general population as public support for programs that treat the uninsured diminished. Furthermore, variable eligibility within mixed-status families created ripple effects on others, resulting in reduced overall household resources.

In the years since its passage, the ACA made significant progress toward increasing health care access, affordability, and quality. Between 2010 and 2015, the uninsured rate in the United States declined by 43 percent, accompanied by significant improvements in affordability, financial security related to health care debt, and a reduction in the amount of nonelderly adults reporting fair or poor health. However, the successes of the ACA health care reform were uneven. Latino populations remained disproportionately uninsured across the country. In addition, the ratio of those enrolled compared to those eligible to enroll varied widely by locality, and uninsurance and underinsurance has remained especially high in heavily Latino communities.

Heide Castañeda

See also: Obama, Barack (1961–) and Latinos

Further Reading

Garfield, Rachel, & Anthony Damico. 2016. *The Coverage Gap: Uninsured Poor Adults in States That Do Not Expand Medicaid.* Kaiser Family Foundation Issue Brief. http://files.kff.org/attachment/issue-brief-the-coverage-gap-uninsured-poor -adults-in-states-that-do-not-expand-medicaid-an-update-2.

Garrett, Bowen, & Anuj Gangopadhyaya. 2016. *Who Gained Health Insurance Coverage under the ACA, and Where Do They Live?* Urban Institute. www.urban.org.

McMorrow, Stacey, Sharon K. Long, Genevieve M. Kenney, & Nathaniel Anderson. 2015. "Uninsurance Disparities Have Narrowed for Black and Hispanic Adults under the Affordable Care Act." *Health Affairs* 34, no. 10: 1774–78.

Mulligan, Jessica, & Heide Castañeda, eds. 2017. *Unequal Coverage: The Experience of Health Care Reform in the United States.* New York: New York University Press.

Obama, Barack. 2016. "United States Health Care Reform: Progress to Date and Next Steps." *Journal of American Medical Association* 316, no. 5: 525–32.

Robert Wood Johnson Foundation (RWJ). 2011. *Issue Brief: How Does the Affordable Care Act Address Racial and Ethnic Disparities in Health Care?* www.rwjf.org.

Aguilar, Jorge

(1988–)

Since May 2017, Jorge Aguilar has been executive director of Nancy Pelosi for Congress at the Democratic Congressional Campaign Committee (DCCC). Aguilar, a

Mexican American, began his career in public service in his hometown of Laredo, Texas. After graduating college, he went on to work for the then-majority leader Harry Reid as his Congressional Hispanic Caucus Institute (CHCI) fellow in 2011, and in 2012 he worked on President Obama's re-election campaign in Las Vegas, Nevada. Jorge later returned to Washington, D.C., to work for Speaker of the House of Representatives, Nancy Pelosi.

Prior to his current position at the DCCC, Aguilar held several positions in Nancy Pelosi's Washington, D.C., press office. Most recently, he served as her press secretary and director of Hispanic media. During his tenure as press secretary, Aguilar served as her spokesperson and traveled with the Democratic leader all around the country, as well as multiple international congressional delegations to Cuba, Haiti, Dominican Republic, Tibet, Hong Kong, Beijing, Japan, Mexico, Chile, and Peru. Notably, the House of Representatives delegation to Cuba was the first of its kind in the aftermath of President Obama's plans to normalize relations with the Caribbean country. During these domestic and international trips, Jorge organized press events and utilized his bilingual skills to manage Pelosi's media presence in both English and Spanish media outlets.

Before making his way to the national political stage, Jorge Aguilar was the first in his family to graduate from college in 2011 with a bachelor's of arts degree in political science from Texas A&M International University (TAMIU). After graduating, he began his professional experience in public service at the city council and mayor's office in Laredo, Texas. As mentioned, Jorge was then chosen to be a Public Policy Fellow for the prestigious CHCI, where he worked for the former Senate majority leader, Harry Reid. After his stint in the Senate—and before returning to work for the first woman ever elected to be Speaker of the House of Representatives—Aguilar went on to work in President Obama's 2012 re-election campaign as a field organizer in Las Vegas, Nevada.

Jorge Aguilar is one of six siblings, and was born and raised at the U.S.–Mexico border in Laredo and Rio Bravo, where he attended South Texas public schools and where his parents still reside. While he now lives in Washington, D.C., Aguilar is proud of his upbringing and heritage, which is why he remains committed to the Latina/o community and to the plight of working-class families. He has received numerous recognitions. In 2015, Huffington Post named him one of 40 Latinas/os under 40 to watch out for in American politics. Moreover, his hometown school district honored Jorge's contributions to the community by presenting him with the 2015 League of Legends Award for distinguished alumni.

Aileen Cardona-Arroyo

See also: Congressional Hispanic Caucus Institute (CHCI)

Further Reading

Belloc, Mauricio. 2014. "Laredense Es El Hombre De Confianza De Nancy Pelosi." *El Mañana*, March 17. http://elmanana.com.mx/noticia/26617/Laredense-es-el-hombre -de-confianza-de-Nancy-Pelosi.

Lopez Calderon, Josue. 2015. "40 under 40: Latinos in American Politics." Huffington Post, September 21. https://www.huffingtonpost.com/josue-lopez-calderon/40-under-40 -latinos-in-am_1_b_8168364.html.

Alexander v. Sandoval

(2001)

Alexander v. Sandoval is a 2001 U.S. Supreme Court decision that held that a regulation enacted under Title VI of the Civil Rights Act of 1964 did not include a private right of action to allow private lawsuits based on evidence of disparate impact.

This case began when Martha Sandoval failed an English-only driver's license exam and was prevented from obtaining an Alabama driver's license. Martha filed a lawsuit in the U.S. District Court for the Middle District of Alabama and alleged that the Alabama Department of Public Safety (Alabama DPS) English-only exam violated the Civil Rights Act, Title VI, Sections 601 and 602 (the Act). The Act prohibits federal financial assistance programs from enforcing policies that are discriminatory toward assistance recipients based on race, color, or national origin. Specifically, Martha pled that (1) Alabama DPS accepted federal funding and (2) the Alabama DPS English-only driver's license exam subjected non-English speakers to discrimination based on their national origin.

In *Sandoval v. Hogan*, the Middle District Court agreed with Martha and enjoined (or stayed) the policy, thereby ordering that the Alabama DPS accommodate non-English speakers. An appeal of the Middle District Court's decision was affirmed by the U.S. Court of Appeals for the Eleventh Circuit. Both courts rejected the Alabama DPS defense that Title VI did not provide Martha a cause to prevent disparate-impact discrimination.

Unsatisfied with the results, Alabama DPS made its final plea and petitioned for review before the U.S. Supreme Court. After oral arguments were presented, Supreme Court justice Scalia issued the Court's majority opinion finding in favor of Alabama DPS. The majority opinion held that individuals did not have a private right of action to prevent disparate-impact discrimination. This opinion reversed the decisions held by the Middle District and the Court of Appeals for the Eleventh Circuit.

Specifically, the Supreme Court analyzed (1) whether private individuals may sue to enforce Section 601 of Title VI and obtain both injunctive relief and damages; (2) whether Section 601 prohibits only intentional discrimination; and (3) whether regulations promulgated under Section 602 of Title VI may proscribe activities that have a discriminatory disparate impact on racial groups, even if such activities are permissible under Section 601.

The Supreme Court's majority opinion held that (1) private individuals may sue to enforce Section 601 (preventing intentional discrimination) and (2) Section 601 only prevents intentional discrimination.

However, most of the Court's opinion focused on whether Section 602 conferred a private right of action for Martha, and similarly situated individuals, to enforce regulations against disparate-impact discrimination. In other words, in addition to having their funding revoked by the governing federal agency, can private individuals require that Alabama DPS implement policies that do not have a discriminatory disparate impact on protected classes?

Here, although the Supreme Court held that Section 601 established that "no person . . . shall . . . be subjected to discrimination," it also held that Section 602 establishes that "each federal department and agency . . . is authorized and directed to effectuate the provisions of [Section 601]."

In summary, the Supreme Court held that Section 602 was phrased as a directive to federal agencies engaged in the distribution of public funds to not discriminate, intentionally or unintentionally, against any protected class. Therefore, agencies adopting any discriminatory practices may have their funding revoked. Still, the Supreme Court did not extend the additional remedy to individuals to prevent these agencies from adopting those policies that would create disparate-impact discrimination against a protected class. In this case, Martha, as an individual, was not allowed to force Alabama DPS to adopt a driver's license exam for non-English speakers.

Victor A. Flores

See also: Environmental Justice and Latinos

Further Reading

Alexander v. Sandoval 532 U.S. 275 (2001).

Galalis, David J. 2004. "Environmental Justice and Title VI in the Wake of *Alexander v. Sandoval*: Disparate-Impact Regulations Still Valid under Chevron." *Boston College Environmental Affairs Law Review* 31: 61.

La Londe, Kyle W. 2004. "Who Wants to Be an Environmental Justice Advocate: Options for Bringing an Environmental Justice Complaint in the Wake of *Alexander v. Sandoval*." *Boston College Environmental Affairs Law Review* 31: 27.

Rosenbaum, Sara, & Joel Teitelbaum. 2002. "Civil Rights Enforcement in the Modern Healthcare System: Reinvigorating the Role of the Federal Government in the Aftermath of *Alexander v. Sandoval*." *Yale Journal Health Policy Law & Ethics* 3: 215.

Sandoval v. Hogan, 7 F.Supp.2d 1234 (M.D.Ala. 1998).

Alvarado, Pablo. *See* National Day Laborer Organizing Network (NDLON)

American GI Forum

The American GI Forum is a civil rights organization created in 1948 by Dr. Hector Pérez García and other Mexican American leaders in Corpus Christi, Texas. The main purpose of the organization was to defend the rights of Mexican American military veterans and ensure their access to educational, medical, employment, and housing benefits provided under the GI Bill of 1944. The organization quickly expanded to become a civil rights organization, as Forum members not only advocated for Mexican American veterans' rights, it also carried out a broad-based civil rights campaign to fight systemic discrimination against Mexican Americans in the areas of education, political representation, employment, health care, and criminal justice. Led by Mexican American leaders dubbed the Mexican American Generation by historian Mario T. García, the American GI Forum was among the foremost civil rights organizations of the postwar era.

New officers of the Mile-Hi Chapter of the American GI Forum in January 1966. Front row (left to right) are Ruben Valdez, Ernest Martinez, James Maestas; back row are Frank Hernandez, Albert Herrera, Frank Manzanares. Other new officers are John Padilla, treasurer, and Richard Padilla, secretary. (Denver Post via Getty Images)

After World War II ended, millions of soldiers returned to their communities in the United States, including hundreds of thousands of Mexican Americans and other Latinos/as who served in the war. Many racial and ethnic minorities who served in the armed forces retuned to a nation that still practiced legal racial segregation in schools, housing, swimming pools, theaters, hotels, restaurants, and other public accommodations. These veterans returned with a keen awareness of the contradictions of fighting for democracy abroad while many Americans at home were relegated to second-class citizenship. Their heightened sense of social justice and leadership motivated veterans such as Hector P. García to engage in civil rights and political activism in the postwar era. García, an immigrant who was born in Tamaulipas, Mexico in 1914, became a physician prior to entering the armed services during World War II. After serving as a military doctor and returning from the war, García joined the League of United Latin American Citizens (LULAC) and began working to improve the health and living conditions for Mexican Americans in his hometown of Corpus Christi.

After learning that Mexican American veterans were not receiving medical and health care benefits under the GI Bill, García organized a group of veterans to form the American GI Forum as a veterans' rights group to promote civic engagement and equality for Mexican Americans. The Forum's principal tenets included patriotism, family, religious faith, nonviolence, democracy, and education. The Forum touted itself as a family-oriented organization and took pride in this. It especially welcomed the membership, participation, and leadership of youth and women in the Ladies Auxiliary and Junior GI Forum. Women played key roles in voter registration drives, Forum newspapers, board meetings, Forum-sponsored events and programs, local and state Forum conferences, and establishing new chapters.

In December 1948, when the owner of a funeral home in Three Rivers, Texas, denied Beatriz Longoria the use of his chapel to wake her deceased husband, Felix Z. Longoria, a soldier who was killed in the war, García and the American GI Forum rallied the Mexican American community in support of Mrs. Longoria's request. The case, known as *the Longoria Affair*, catapulted the Forum to the national political arena and highlighted discrimination against Mexican Americans, especially after Senator Lyndon B. Johnson arranged for Longoria's burial at Arlington National Cemetery with full military honors. The Forum quickly expanded its civil rights agenda to not only challenge discrimination against Mexican Americans but also to fundamentally change U.S. society by making it more democratic.

Promoting educational reform was among the Forum's primary objectives in the 1950s. In fact, the Forum's motto was "Education Is Our Freedom and Freedom Should Be Everybody's Business." The organization worked with LULAC to establish the Little Schools of the 400 to teach Mexican American children English and increase reading levels among Mexican American children before they started first grade. This program inspired both the Texas legislature and the federal government to establish similar programs, which became a model for Head Start. Forum members also challenged unequal school financing, facilities, and instruction; culturally and linguistically biased testing; and the widespread practice of segregating Mexican Americans in "Mexican" schools. In 1947, Forum members Gus García, James DeAnda, and Carlos Cadena sued the Bastrop, Elgin, Martindale, and Travis Independent School Districts in the case of *Delgado v. Bastrop Independent School District (1948)*, resulting in the abolition of arbitrary segregation of Mexican children based on their ethnicity. Other lawsuits were filed against the Carrizo Springs, Kingsville, and Mathis Independent School Districts and Driscoll Consolidated Independent School District between 1954 and 1957.

With the support of the American GI Forum, LULAC, and other Mexican American community leaders, Gus García filed and won one of the most important legal cases to challenge jury discrimination in 1954, *Hernández v. Texas*. Garcia, the first Mexican American to argue before the U.S. Supreme Court, successfully argued that Mexican Americans were treated as a "separate class," despite their status as rightful citizens as provided in the Treaty of Guadalupe Hidalgo of 1848. By the late 1950s, the American GI Forum became more actively involved in electoral politics, leading voter registration drives and Viva Kennedy Club campaigns to rally support for the election of John F. Kennedy. After Kennedy was assassinated, Forum members supported Lyndon B. Johnson in his 1964 bid for reelection, as well as his civil rights agenda and War on Poverty programs. Several Forum members, including Hector García and Vicente Ximenes, played key roles in advising Johnson on issues of concern for Mexican Americans, including the appointment of Mexican Americans to important federal agencies.

During the civil rights years, Forum members continued their activism and supported the farm workers' struggle in California and Texas and the call to end the Bracero Program because of its abusive nature and exploitation of Mexican and Mexican American workers. Members also supported the grape and lettuce strikes in northern California and the melon strike in South Texas and joined the marches from Delano to Sacramento (1965) and Rio Grande City to Austin (1966). In Colorado, Forum member Rodolfo "Corky" Gonzales created the Crusade for Justice to address racial discrimination against Mexican Americans in Colorado and supported the boycott against Coors Brewery in the 1970s for employment discrimination. The American GI Forum continued its activism through the 1970s and 1980s. However, by the mid-1980s, national organizations such as the National Council for La Raza, Mexican American Legal Defense and Education Fund, and National Association of Latino Elected Officials dominated the national scene in the struggle for Mexican American/Latina/o civil rights. Despite its decline in the political arena, the American GI Forum still exists to promote the rights of all veterans. At the height of its activism, the organization was a formidable vehicle that played a significant role in abolishing segregated schools; fighting discrimination against Mexican Americans; and promoting social, economic, political, and educational justice.

Maritza De La Trinidad

See also: Brown Power Movement/Chicano Civil Rights Movement; Crusade for Justice; *Delgado v. Bastrop I.S.D. et al.*; Gonzales, Rodolfo "Corky" (1928–2005); *Hernández v. Texas* (1954); League of United Latin American Citizens (LULAC); Mexican American Legal Defense and Educational Fund (MALDEF); National Association of Latino Elected and Appointed Officials (NALEO) Educational Fund; Pérez García, Héctor (1914–1996); Treaty of Guadalupe Hidalgo of 1848; UnidosUS; Viva Kennedy! Clubs

Further Reading

Allsup, Carl. 1982. *American G.I. Forum: Origins and Evolution*. Austin: University of Texas Press.

American GI Forum of Texas, Inc. 2015. *American GI Forum of Texas*. http://agiftx.com /index.php?page=home.

Carroll, Patrick J. 2003. *Felix Longoria's Wake: Bereavement, Racism, and the Rise of Mexican American Activism*. Austin: University of Texas Press.

Felts, Jeff, producer. 2007. *Justice for My People: The Dr. Hector P. García Story*. KEDT South Texas Public Broadcasting System, Inc.

Garcia, Ignacio M. 2003. *Hector P. Garcia: In Relentless Pursuit of Justice*. Hispanic Civil Rights. Houston: Arte Público Press.

Kells, Michelle Hall. 2006. Héctor P. García: Everyday Rhetoric and Mexican American Civil Rights. Carbondale: Southern Illinois University Press.

Ramos, Henry A. J. 1998. *The American GI Forum: In Pursuit of the Dream, 1948–1983*. Houston: Arte Público Press.

Valadez, John J., dir. 2010. *The Longoria Affair*. Color DVD. Narrated by Tony Plana. Independent Lens.

Arellano, Elvira

(1975–)

Elvira Arellano is an immigrant activist from Mexico who is known for fighting her deportation from a Chicago church. Prior to her deportation in 2007, Arellano was one of millions of undocumented Latinas living and working in the United States in low-wage jobs. When she received a deportation order in 2006, Arellano took refuge for 12 months in the United Methodist Church of Adalberto in Chicago and became an immigrant rights activist calling for the right of families to remain together. In 2007, she traveled to Los Angeles and spoke publicly about the injustice of her deportation as a mother of a U.S. citizen and was promptly arrested by Immigration and Customs Enforcement (ICE) agents and deported to Mexico. In 2014, Arellano applied for asylum in the United States and was permitted to return and reunite with her son while awaiting her hearing. Elvira Arellano has become a symbol of resistance for undocumented people in the United States, especially undocumented parents whose families are torn apart through deportation.

Arellano's migration took a route common to many migrants. In the 1990s, she left her home state of Michoacán due to unemployment in the wake of neoliberal structural reforms and migrated to Tijuana to work in the maquiladoras (factories). In 1997, when the availability of work in Tijuana had become unreliable, Arellano crossed into the United States without authorization and initially worked in the state of Washington, where she gave birth to her first son in 1998, Saúl, before moving to Chicago and joining a cleaning crew at O'Hare Airport (Toro-Morn, 2013). For years, Arellano supported herself, her son, and her extended family in Mexico while making mortgage payments on her home in Chicago by working two low-wage jobs. Following the 9/11 attacks, Arellano was targeted for deportation through Project Tarmac, an operation of the federal government to identify undocumented airport employees nationwide. ICE agents showed up at the home of Arellano in the early morning hours to arrest her for working with a false Social Security number. Arellano was asked to report for deportation in 2006 but instead took refuge in the Adalberto Memorial Church in the Puerto Rican Humboldt Park neighborhood of Chicago. In the 1980s this church was central to the Sanctuary Movement for Central Americans fleeing the violence of war. Elvira Arellano and her then seven-year-old son Saul quickly became the faces of the renewed Sanctuary Movement in opposition to family separation through deportation.

While in sanctuary, Arellano's story was covered regularly in the *Chicago Tribune,* and she was interviewed and photographed by numerous other media outlets. Her story drew support from many, but it also attracted hate mail, threats, and picketing from antimigrant rights forces. In August 2007 Arellano left the church and traveled to a migrant rights rally in Los Angeles, where she was one of many migrant rights speakers. After she spoke and left the rally, ICE agents arrested her and she was deported to Tijuana, Mexico. Reflecting back on her decision to leave sanctuary and speak in public, Arellano said, "I could not sit here, arms crossed, observing while other working mothers like myself and millions of children like Saúl faced the destruction of their families" (Toro-Morn, 2013: 51).

In Mexico, Arellano continued advocating for migrant rights, criticizing the violation of rights of Central American migrants as they pass through Mexico to declare asylum in the United States. Her activism and critical voice in Mexico once again drew opposition and threats. Arellano participated in the "Migrant Movement of MesoAmerica," and in 2014 she led a group of asylum seekers in a protest on the U.S.–Mexico border. During the protest Arellano again entered into the United States without inspection, this time in order to petition for asylum on the grounds of the "credible fear test." Arellano now has a work permit and works two jobs in Chicago while awaiting her asylum hearing.

Teresa Carrillo

See also: Immigration as a Policy Issue; National Security State and Latinos

Further Reading

Brachear Pashman, Manya. 2017. "Son of Immigration Activist Who Sought Sanctuary in Chicago Church to Graduate High School." *Chicago Tribune*, March 15. http://www.chicagotribune.com/news/immigration/ct-saul-arellano-graduates-high-school-met-20170614-story.html.

Ortiz Healy, Vikki. 2017. "Immigration Activist Arellano Allowed to Remain in United States for Another Year." *Chicago Tribune*, March 15. http://www.chicagotribune.com/news/immigration/ct-elvira-arellano-ice-update-20170315-story.html.

Toro-Morn, Maura. 2013. "Elvira Arellano and the Struggles of Low-Wage Undocumented Latina Immigrant Women." In Nilda Flores González, Anna Romina Guevarra, Maura Toro-Morn, and Grace Chang, eds. *Immigrant Women in the Neoliberal Age*. Chicago: University of Illinois Press.

Zamudio, María Inés. 2014. "Elvira Arellano: From Undocumented Immigrant to International Activist." *The Chicago Reporter*, January 16. http://www.chicagoreporter.com/elvira-arellano-undocumented-immigrant-international-activist/.

Aristimuño, José

(1988–)

Jose Aristimuño is CEO and principal at NOW Strategies, a public affairs firm that specializes in communications, political consulting, and multicultural outreach. A bilingual Spanish-language commentator and political strategist, he also worked as an immigration columnist for Telemundo and as the director for Hispanic media at DSG Latinovations, a public affairs firm created in 2007 by the Dewey Square Group to help the public and private sectors build relationships with the Latino populations (Calderon, 2015). His primary efforts focused on the effects of climate change on Latino communities, the expansion of Internet access, and Latino voter participation. Aristimuño is also the CEO and founder of Latino Giant, a Latino issues media company committed to empowering Latinos to reach the American Dream.

During the 2016 election cycle, Aristimuño was hired by Maryland governor Martin O'Malley to serve as national director of Hispanic media for his presidential campaign. Prohibited from serving another term as governor because of term limits, O'Malley left office in early 2015 and expressed interest in running for president. Aristimuño, who initially started working with the campaign as a volunteer, was charged in his role of national director with leading the campaign's Latino outreach and engagement efforts. A key part of his strategy was to ensure that the campaign reached out to the Latino community in a culturally-sensitive way, recognizing the differences between Latinos in the United States (Collins, 2015). The campaign also spoke directly to Latinos in their communities and spoke about Latino issues and progressive immigration policy. At the time of Aristimuño's appointment, O'Malley was not well known and was the only Democratic candidate polling with a negative favorability rating from Latinos despite showing a significant interest in and commitment to Latino issues (Collins, 2015). While the candidate's name recognition among Latinos improved somewhat, the campaign was suspended in February 2016 after a third-place finish in the Iowa Caucuses.

Aristimuño has held several government positions, serving as deputy national press secretary for the Democratic Party in 2016. He played a central role in implementing the party's media strategy, which included significant spending on Spanish-language radio and television ads and highlighting the failure of the GOP to boost outreach to Latinos (Gamboa, 2016). Prior to this position, he worked at the Department of Health and Human Services as director of Specialty Communications and Spokesperson.

Aristimuño, who is Venezuelan American, graduated from American University in 2012 with a BA in political science and is pursuing a law degree from American University Washington College of Law. He also attended Broward Community College, and his father is a writer in Caracas, Venezuela.

Atiya Kai Stokes-Brown

See also: Election of 2016 and Latinos

Further Reading

Burton, Michael J., & Daniel M. Shea. 2010. *Campaign Craft: The Strategies, Tactics, and Art of Political Campaign Management*. Santa Barbara, CA: Praeger.

Calderon, Josue Lopez. 2015. "The Huffington Post/40 under 40: Latinos in American Politics." Huffington Post, September 22. http://corporate.univision.com/press/univis ion-in-the-news/2015/09/22/the-huffington-post-40-under-40-latinos-in-american -politics/.

Collins, Eliza. 2015. "O'Malley Hires a Director of Hispanic Media." Politico, September 1. http://www.politico.com/story/2015/09/martin-omalley-director-hispanic -media-2016-213233.

Dulio, David A. 2004. *For Better or Worse: How Political Consultants Are Changing Elections in the United States*. Albany: State University of New York Press.

Gamboa, Suzanne. 2016. "Democrats Spending $500,000 to Air Radio Ad Where 'Latinos Are Listening.'" NBC News, October 7. http://www.nbcnews.com/news/latino /clinton-democrats-spending-500-000-air-radio-ad-where-latinos-n662221.

Johnson, Dennis W. 2007. *No Place for Amateurs: How Political Consultants Are Reshaping American Democracy*. 2nd ed. New York: Routledge.

Thurber, James A., & Candice J. Nelson. 2013. *Campaigns and Elections American Style: Transforming American Politics*. 4th ed. Boulder, CO: Westview Press.

Trent, Judith S., Robert V. Friedenberg, & Robert R. Denton. 2015. *Political Campaign Communication: Principles and Practices*. 8th ed. New York: Rowman & Littlefield Publishers.

A young Salvadoran woman seeking asylum carries her child from a bus at the McAllen, Texas, bus station after being released by the Border Patrol, 2017. The Border Patrol releases Central American asylum seekers with family in the United States pending their Immigration Court hearing dates. (vichinterlang/iStockphoto.com)

Asylum Seekers

Political asylum is an often-overlooked aspect of the immigration debate that has important implications for Latinas/os. The recent "surges" (2014–2016, 2018) of migrants from Central America on the U.S. border have refocused attention on border security and political asylum. Many of these migrants include family units, adding the politically challenging issue of housing minors and even some unaccompanied minors.

The U.S. government distinguishes between refugees who are outside the United States and asylum seekers who already reside in the United States or at a port of entry (POE). According to the Department of Homeland Security (DHS), in 2014 there were 69,975 refugees admitted to the United States, primarily from Iraq, Burma, Somalia, and Bhutan. In 2014, 23,533 individuals were granted asylum. Of the top 10 nations from which U.S. asylums originated, only 3 were Latin American and ranked near the bottom. These included Mexico (2.5%), Haiti (2.3%), and Guatemala (2.1%).

Typically, it is easier to get asylum if an individual fears political persecution in his or her home country than if an individual is under threat from organized crime–related violence. According to U.S. Citizenship and Immigration Services (USCIS), people can seek asylum based on persecution for one of five criteria: "race, religion, nationality, membership in a particular social group, [or] political opinion." For example, Cubans once had automatic asylum claims and a path to citizenship in the United States because of specific laws passed following Castro's communist revolution in Cuba. This policy, known as "wet-foot, dry-foot," was ended by the Obama administration in late 2016 as part of the normalization of relations with Cuba. On the other hand, asylum seekers from Mexico and Central America fearing organized crime violence are far less likely to receive asylum in the United States despite greater potential threat.

To apply, an asylum seeker typically requests asylum and is given a "credible fear" interview in which a customs official interviews the applicant to ascertain whether the individual has a credible fear of returning to their home country and is not seeking asylum protection for purely economic reasons. There have been recent media reports that immigration officials have not been granting credible fear interviews, thus preventing people from applying for asylum.

The U.S. federal government handles the asylum process. Asylum caseworkers and federal immigration judges in administrative hearings then hear immigration cases. There are major backlogs in the system in most jurisdictions, resulting in burnt-out judges and lawyers, and long detentions. Deportation can be stopped if the individual can demonstrate that she or he is under threat of torture or death in their home country. Deporting an individual who would be killed or tortured would be a violation of the UN Convention against Torture, to which the United States is a signatory. Unlike criminal cases, individuals are not guaranteed access to legal representation if they cannot afford it. Thus, the outcome of these cases can hinge upon the individual's ability to pay for legal representation and hire expert witnesses on the country conditions of their home country or get access to free legal assistance. One legal standard known as "internal relocation" that plays a role in these cases is that if an individual can return to another area of their home country and be safe, they can be deported. This forces a potential deportee to show that there is no safe place in the home country the individual can be deported to.

DETENTION CENTERS

While in the asylum process, many applicants are detained. Detention centers are widely described as overcrowded, especially in relation to their ability to handle unaccompanied minors during "surges." Individuals could leave voluntarily but only to return to their home countries.

According to *The New York Times*, some Central American asylum seekers are not aware that they can request asylum in Mexico and are thus deported. United Nations (UN) programs have aimed to increase awareness of the potential to be considered refugees in Mexico (Semple, 2016).

Providing asylum can be in the national security interest of the U.S. government. For example, the ability to promise asylum, reward money, and witness protection can be used to entice informants to provide information against major drug trafficking organizations, thus leading to their dismantlement. Reward money is not much of an incentive if the informant is not physically safe in their home country.

Nathan P. Jones

See also: Immigration as a Policy Issue; National Security State and Latinos; United States–Cuban Relations

Further Reading

Igielnik, Ruth, & Jens Manuel Krogstad. 2017. "Where Refugees to the U.S. Come From." Pew Research Center, February 3. http://www.pewresearch.org/fact-tank/2017/02/03/where-refugees-to-the-u-s-come-from.

Learn about the Asylum Application Process. 2015. U.S. Citizenship and Immigration Services, August 6. https://www.uscis.gov/humanitarian/refugees-asylum/asylum.

Mossaad, Nadwa. 2016. "Refugees and Asylees: 2014." *Annual Flow Report.* Office of Immigration Statistics. April. https://www.dhs.gov/sites/default/files/publications/Refugees_Asylees_2014.pdf.

Obtaining Asylum in the United States. 2015. U.S. Citizenship and Immigration Services, October 19. https://www.uscis.gov/humanitarian/refugees-asylum/asylum/obtaining-asylumunited-states.

Preston, Julia. 2016. "Tension Simmers as Cubans Breeze across U.S. Border." *The New York Times*, February 12. http://www.nytimes.com/2016/02/13/us/as-cubans-and-centralamericans-enter-us-the-welcomes-vary.html.

Semple, K. 2016. "Fleeing Gangs, Central American Families Surge Toward U.S." *The New York Times*, November 12. http://www.nytimes.com/2016/11/13/world/americas/fleeing-gangs-central-americanfamilies-surge-toward-us.html.

United Nations Office on Drugs and Crime (UNODC). 2018. "UNODC Report on Human Trafficking Exposes Modern Form of Slavery." http://www.unodc.org/unodc/en/human-trafficking/global-report-on-trafficking-in-persons.html.

U.S. Citizenship and Immigration Services, Department of Homeland Security. https://www.uscis.gov.

Avila, Joaquín

(1948–2018)

Joaquín Avila was a litigator and advocate from East Los Angeles, California, who specialized in voting rights law. He served as staff attorney (1974–1976), director of political access litigation and associate counsel (1976–1978), and president and general counsel (1982–1985) of the Mexican American Legal Defense and Educational Fund (MALDEF). Avila was successful in arguing several appeals before the U.S. Supreme Court that involved enforcing special provisions of the federal Voting Rights Act of 1965. Avila argued *Lopez v. Monterey County* 519 US 9 (1996) in front of the Supreme Court and received a favorable unanimous verdict.

Avila received a bachelor's degree from Yale University and a juris doctorate from Harvard University Law School. Avila drafted the California Voting Rights Act of 2001. His work centered on giving minority neighborhoods a fair and adequate chance to participate in elections. When constituents vote by electoral districts, only voters who reside in the district are permitted to vote. In at-large elections, a candidate is elected to represent the whole membership of the body (e.g., a city, state, nation) as opposed to a subset of that membership (e.g., a district). Avila was able to change certain elections from at-large to district to provide representation to smaller communities. Through this action, he gave neighborhoods that consisted of mostly minorities the ability to win elections instead of focusing on representing larger and more well-known communities.

Avila taught law school and served as a coach to students who competed in the National Black Law Students Association's Frederick Douglass Moot Court Competition. During his first year as coach of the team, one of his student teams came in second regionally and then moved on to qualify for the top eight teams in the national competition. The following year his team won first place regionally.

Avila was later an assistant law professor at the Seattle University School of Law, where he won the Outstanding Faculty Award from the Black Law Students Association. Avila was also able to start a faculty and student law review that was pivotal in the creation of an election reform symposium entitled, "Where's My Vote?—Lessons Learned from Washington State's Gubernatorial Election." Outside of university relations, Avila worked in private practices that were committed to protecting the voting rights of minorities across the United States. Avila died on March 9, 2018.

Jessica L. Lavariega Monforti

See also: Mexican American Legal Defense and Educational Fund (MALDEF); Voting Rights Act of 1975

Further Reading

Avila, Joaquin G., Eugene Lee, & Terry M. Ao. 2007. "Voting Rights in California: 1982–2006." *Southern California Review of Law & Social Justice* 17: 131.

Avila, Joaquin G., Barbara Phillips, & Molly Matter. 2016. "How a Targeted Triggering Approach Can Repair the Voting Rights Act: Congress Can Eliminate the Blight of Voting Discrimination Once and for All." *Mississippi Law Journal* 85: 1163.

De la Garza, Rodolfo O., & Louis DeSipio. 1992. "Save the Baby, Change the Bathwater, and Scrub the Tub: Latino Electoral Participation after Seventeen Years of Voting Rights Act Coverage." *Texas Law Review* 71: 1479.

"Joaquin Avila." Seattle University School of Law. https://law.seattleu.edu/faculty/profiles/visiting-and-affiliated/joaquin-avila.

"MacArthur Fellows Program." RSS. https://www.macfound.org/fellows/528/.

Rebellious Law. 2015. "Joaquin Avila, Rebellious Lawyer." Rebellious Lawyering Institute and 2016 Rebellious Lawyering Conference—#RebelliousLawyering. https://rebelliouslawyeringinstitute.org/joaquin-avila-rebellious-lawyer-2.

Rubin, Sara Hayley. 2015. "Meet Voting Rights Champ and Genius Joaquin Avila." *Monterey County Weekly.* April 22. http://www.montereycountyweekly.com/blogs/news_blog/meet-voting-rights-champ-and-genius-joaquin-avila/article_b9c30bee-4854-11e5-b03b-77584fe8beb7.html.

B

Badillo, Herman

(1929–2014)

Herman Badillo was the first Hispanic borough president in New York City and the first Puerto Rican–born voting member elected to the U.S. House of Representatives. He served as Bronx Borough president from 1965 to 1969 and U.S. Representative from New York (D) from 1971 to 1977. He was also the first Puerto Rican to run for mayor in the continental United States when he ran for mayor of New York City in 1969—he had subsequent mayoral campaigns in 1973, 1977, 1981, and 1985. In 2001 he sought the Republican mayoral nomination, losing to Michael Bloomberg. Badillo was appointed deputy mayor by Mayor Ed Koch in 1977 and held that position through 1979.

The beginning of Badillo's political career coincided with the growing influence of Puerto Ricans in the city, and he held his first political position in 1958, when he joined the Caribe Democratic Club. In 1960, Badillo chaired John F. Kennedy's campaign committee for East Harlem and then two years later he took over as commissioner of the Department of Housing and Relocation. That position made him the highest-ranking Hispanic official in the city. Badillo stepped down from that position in 1965 to run for Bronx Borough president, where he served for four years.

After his election to Congress in 1970, Badillo served on the Committee on Education and Labor. He made significant contributions to job training for unemployed non–English-speaking citizens via the Comprehensive Manpower Act of 1973. Badillo also served on the Banking, Finance and Urban Affairs Committee and the Small Business Committee, where he had a seat on the Minority Enterprise and General Oversight Sub-committee. During his time in office, he supported legislation intended to counteract various types of discrimination in employment, including discrimination based on age and marital status. In December 1976, he was one of five Latino members of Congress who established the Congressional Hispanic Caucus. More generally, Badillo also advocated for equal rights for residents of Puerto Rico, and consistently supported initiatives to help his many disadvantaged constituents, including legislation regarding increased employment, comprehensive childcare, and community development programs.

In 1986, Badillo unsuccessfully ran for a statewide comptroller position. In 1993, he joined Rudy Giuliani's Republican-Liberal fusion ticket as a candidate for city comptroller. Though Giuliani narrowly won the mayoral election, Badillo lost to New York Assembly member Alan Hevesi. In 1998, Badillo officially switched his party affiliation to Republican. He said, "As a lifelong Democrat, I did not make this decision lightly." Consistent with his long-standing interest in education, he served as a trustee for the City University of New York (CUNY); Badillo served as vice-chairman of the board from 1997 to 1999 and as chairman from 1999 to 2001. In his last campaign, Badillo lost the Republican mayoral primary to Mayor Michael Bloomberg in 2001.

Badillo was born in Caguas, Puerto Rico, and migrated to New York in 1941 with his aunt, having lost both of his parents to tuberculosis in the 1930s. His father, Francisco Badillo, taught in a public school, and his mother, Carmen Rivera, spent her time on charitable activities. His aunt's financial problems after arriving in New York City forced Badillo to move first to Chicago to live with an uncle, and then to California to stay with another family member. Back in New York City by 1944, he attended Haaren High School. He then attended the City College of New York where he majored in business and graduated with a bachelor's degree in business administration in 1951, and received his Bachelor of Laws from Brooklyn Law School. He was also a certified public accountant. In 1949, Badillo married Norma Lit. They had a son, David Alan, before divorcing in 1960. A year later Badillo married Irma Liebling, who had two children from a previous marriage. After Irma's death in 1996, Badillo married Gail Roberts, a New York City schoolteacher.

Jessica L. Lavariega Monforti

See also: Congressional Hispanic Caucus Institute (CHCI); Discrimination against Latinas/os

Further Reading

Badillo, Herman. 2006. *One Nation, One Standard: An Ex-Liberal on How Hispanics Can Succeed Just Like Other Immigrant Groups*. Foreword by Rudolph W. Giuliani. New York: Sentinel, pp. 139–75.

Biological Directory of the United States Congress. Collection of the U.S. House of Representatives: Badillo, Herman. http://bioguide.congress.gov/scripts/biodisplay.pl?index=B000025.

McFadden, Robert D. 2014. "Herman Badillo, Congressman and Fixture of New York Politics, Dies at 85." *New York Times*, December 4. https://www.nytimes.com/2014/12/04/nyregion/herman-badillo-fixture-of-new-york-politics-dies-at-85.html.

Mitchell, Alison. 1993. "Green Wins Nomination for Advocate Post–Dinkins Has 68%." *New York Times*, September 15, A1.

Nagourney, Adam. 1998. "Badillo Is Said to Be Switching to the Republicans." *New York Times*, June 25, B1.

Baez, Joan

(1941–)

Joan Baez is a singer, songwriter, author, and sociopolitical activist. Her songs promote social justice, human and civil rights, and pacifism. Her performances—both in English and Spanish—are part of some of the most iconic moments of the United States' cultural history. As an activist she has been key in the establishment of international organizations, such as the U.S. section of International Amnesty and Humanitas International. During her adult life she has received several honors recognizing both her artistic career and her commitment to social causes.

Joan Chandos Baez was born in Staten Island, New York, on January 9, 1941. She is the daughter of Joan (Bridge) Baez and Albert Vinicio Baez, a renowned

Legendary singer, songwriter, activist, and Rock & Roll Hall of Fame inductee Joan Baez (ca. 1963). (Library of Congress)

Mexican-born American physicist. In one of her books Joan Baez wrote that she and her sisters were raised by a father with a clear conscience and that the legacy they inherited from him was decency: he refused to participate in the lucrative growth of the military industry during his professional life, including the Manhattan Project to develop the first atomic bomb. Instead he collaborated with the United Nations Educational, Scientific and Cultural Organization (UNESCO) and other nongovernmental organizations dedicated to improving the quality of life in Latin American countries through scientific and educational projects. This proved to have a profound impression on Joan Baez's early in life and influenced her adult career as an activist.

From an early age, Baez showed interest in both music and social engagement. When she was 15, she listened for the first time to Dr. Martin Luther King, Jr. In the future, they would become friends, and she would sing during the civil rights rallies he organized. As a teenager she was part of the rebirth of folk music, playing in the Boston musical scene. At 17 she gave her first concert at the Club 47 in Massachusetts. A few years later, during the turbulent 1960s, she established a career as a folk singer and was a continuous presence at demonstrations for social change. In 1963 she sung "We Shall Overcome" in the March on Washington for Jobs and Freedom, and throughout the 1960s she participated in many concerts, rallies, and protests against the Vietnam War, in favor of freedom of speech, and supported equal rights for African Americans. During those years she participated in several acts of civil disobedience, including tax resistance, protesting against U.S. military expenditures and blocking the entrance of the Armed Forces Induction Center in Oakland, California, which led to her arrest twice in 1967. During that decade Baez released several records and her popularity grew, although her message suffered both censorship and sabotage.

In the 1970s she released *Gracias a la Vida,* a studio album almost entirely in Spanish. Baez dedicated this album to those suffering under the dictatorship in Chile. She strongly criticized U.S. involvement in the Southern Cone and worked to bring attention to human rights violations in the region committed by military regimes. During the last few decades, Baez has kept her status as an artist by offering concerts, writing books, recording albums, and participating in movie soundtracks. As an activist, she has been involved in social causes in the United States such as fighting for LGBT rights, the abolition of the death penalty, opposing the Iraq War, and supporting Occupy Wall Street. In 2011 she was the inspiration for the creation of the Joan Baez Award for Outstanding Inspirational Service in the Global Fight for Human Rights by Amnesty International.

Pamela Fuentes Peralta

See also: Military Participation and Latinos; Politics of a Latinx Lesbian, Gay, Bisexual, and Transgender Identity

Further Reading

Baez, Joan. 1987. *And a Voice to Sing With: A Memoir.* New York: Summit Books.

Hadju, David. 2001. *Positively Fourth Street: The Lives and Times of Joan Baez, Bob Dylan, Mimi Baez Farina, and Richard Farina.* New York: Farrar, Straus and Giroux.

Balseros/Rafters

Balseros, or "rafters," from the Spanish word *balsa*, which means "raft," is the name given to Cuban nationals who emigrate without documents from the island to a neighboring state, generally the United States, in self-constructed and flimsy vessels. Rafts are commonly made of inner tubes or large metal cans tied together and surmounted by wooden planks, often driven with oars but sometimes propelled by an engine from a lawnmower or a motorcycle. Only 90 miles separate Cuba from the island of Key West in Florida, but the trip is perilous. The Florida Straits are stormy and shark-infested, and the Gulf Stream can push a raft beyond the Florida peninsula and send it adrift into the Gulf of Mexico. It is estimated that one out of four *balseros* perishes in the journey, for a total of possibly 25,000 people over time. At the very least, those rescued are routinely treated for dehydration, burns, hypothermia, and bites from sea creatures. Still, the rafter phenomenon has characterized modern Cuban history since the 1959 revolution led by Fidel Castro (1926–2016) because of limitations imposed by the regime on legal travel and the United States' policy during the Cold War of rescuing rafters and welcoming them as refugees from a Communist country. During the second Obama administration, in fact, the possibility of an end to the special status enjoyed by Cuban immigrants has led to a resurgence of illegal maritime migration, which had abated after the mid-1990s.

To solidify and maintain his power, Castro often resorted to exporting dissenters to the United States. From 1959 until the missile crisis in 1962, and then from 1965 to 1973, discontented Cubans were permitted to emigrate legally. Even during these periods, however, the Cuban Interior Ministry would not grant an exit permit to anybody with technical skills needed on the island or suspected of crimes against the revolution. Thousands who could not leave legally left clandestinely on rafts. Upon rescue by the U.S. Coast Guard, they would be "paroled," or granted permission to be on U.S. territory; receive aid, including food stamps, cash assistance, and medical care through the Cuban Refugee Program, and be able to change their status to permanent resident after only one year through the Cuban Adjustment Act of 1966. The next massive wave of Cuban immigrants, the 125,000

"Marielitos" that Castro allowed Cuban American exiles to pick up by boat from the port of Mariel in 1980, enjoyed much of the same benefits even though they were given the ambiguous status of "entrants: status pending" rather than refugees and were the recipients of negative media attention because of rumors Castro had used the boatlift to empty the island's prisons and mental institutions.

The perception that Cubans were leaving the island for economic rather than for political reasons, a diminished interest after the collapse of the Soviet Union in rescuing fugitives from Communist countries, and the realization that the U.S. policy of embracing disaffected Cubans may have contributed to the longevity of Castro's rule, all combine to explain the fate of the over 32,000 *balseros* who departed from Cuba in the summer of 1994. The economic situation of Cuba had been deteriorating since 1989, when the Soviet Union became unable to buy Cuban sugar in exchange for oil. Following riots in Havana against the scarcity of essential goods, on August 12, Castro announced the Cuban Coast Guard would not prevent anybody from leaving, thereby prompting the largest maritime exodus from the island to date. People left despite President Bill Clinton's response that migrants intercepted at sea would be refused entry and brought to the U.S. naval base of Guantanamo Bay in Cuba. Initially, the United States tried to persuade the Guantanamo detainees to return to Cuba voluntarily and apply for a U.S. visa there. Only 800 migrants, however, agreed to repatriation. Faced with the high costs of detaining them indefinitely, the Clinton administration eventually agreed to grant humanitarian parole to most of the Cubans at Guantanamo but to henceforth repatriate Cubans intercepted at sea, in what has been called the "wet foot/dry foot policy" (1995). However, Cubans who succeeded in reaching U.S. shores were generally paroled.

This new policy changed the trajectory and the means of maritime migration. Cubans started landing on the Yucatan peninsula and entering the United States from Mexico. Those who had the means hired smugglers with fast speedboats, in Spanish *botas*, and were called *boteros* rather than *balseros*. However, the number of Cubans trying to reach the United States in small unsafe vessels rose dramatically once more after President Barack Obama and Fidel's successor, Raúl Castro, agreed to restore diplomatic relations between the two countries. Under the perception that there was a limited window of opportunity before the United States eliminated favorable immigration policies for Cubans, thousands took to the sea by whatever means they could find. The U.S. Coast Guard interdicted 2,924 Cubans in 2015, compared to only 422 in 2010. In 2017, Obama announced the immediate end of the wet foot/dry foot policy. Undocumented Cuban immigrants are now subject to removal proceedings, regardless of where they are intercepted. To date, the Trump administration has not reversed Obama's order.

Paola Gemme

See also: Cuban Adjustment Act of 1966; Immigration as a Policy Issue; Obama, Barack (1961–) and Latinos

Further Reading

Balseros. 2002. Directed by Charles Bosch and Josef M. Domènech. Documentary. Bausann Films.

Fernández, Alfredo A. 2000. *Adrift: The Cuban Raft People*. Houston: Arte Publico Press.

García, María Cristina. 1996. *Havana USA: Cuban Exiles and Cuban Americans in South Florida, 1959–1994*. Berkeley: University of California Press.

Henken, Ted. 2005. "*Balseros, Boteros* and *El Bombo*: Post-1994 Cuban Immigration to the United States and the Persistence of Special Treatment." *Latino Studies* 3, no. 3: 393–416.

University of Miami Libraries. 2014. "The Cuban Rafters Phenomenon: A Unique Sea Exodus." http://balseros.miami.edu.

Balzac v. Porto [sic] Rico

(1922)

Balzac v. Porto [sic] *Rico* is a U.S. Supreme Court case that forms part of the "Insular Cases"—a group of Supreme Court decisions pertaining to the relationship between U.S. territories and the U.S. mainland. The case unfolded after newspaper editor Jesús M. Balzac was accused of libel—a misdemeanor. The code of Criminal Procedure of Puerto Rico did not guarantee a jury trial for misdemeanor cases. Balzac argued that as a U.S. citizen, his Sixth Amendment right—which guarantees a trial by jury—had been violated. The court ruled against Balzac by reasoning that the rights allotted in the Constitution were bound by locality and thus did not apply to an unincorporated territory such as Puerto Rico.

In the 1901 Supreme Court decision of *Downes v. Bidwell*, Justice White reasoned that Puerto Ricans were not entitled to citizenship at the time because citizenship is tied to territorial incorporation to the United States (Perez, 2008). Almost two decades later, the Jones Act of 1917 resurfaced this debate by granting naturalization to residents of Puerto Rico. Up to that point, the move to grant citizenship to residents of a territory without an envisioned path to territorial incorporation was unprecedented. Thus, judicial questions emerged pertaining to how the Jones Act changed (or not) the relationship of the island to the United States (Venator-Santiago, 2017; Venator-Santiago and Meléndez, 2017).

Out of all of the cases that attempted to make sense of changes to the United States–Puerto Rico relationship, the 1922 Supreme Court case of *Balzac v. People of Porto Rico* represents the most consequential in terms of setting a precedent for the judicial understanding of Puerto Rico's political status (Torruella, 2017). The case reflects the claims of a newspaper editor accused of committing criminal libel after publishing an article with offensive statements about the governor of Puerto Rico at the time. Although the Code of Criminal Procedure of Puerto Rico would have entitled Balzac to a trial had he committed a felony, that right was not guaranteed in his case because he faced a misdemeanor (Levinson, 2017).

Balzac alleged that, as a U.S. citizen, the Sixth Amendment of the Constitution gave him the right to a trial by jury (Torruella, 2017). Specifically, his claims were rooted in the notion that by extending U.S. citizenship to Puerto Rico, the Jones Act of 1917 had de facto incorporated Puerto Rico into the United States (Perez, 2008). Thus, the Supreme Court had to decide whether the protections of the Constitution under the Sixth Amendment applied to citizens who were residents of Puerto Rico (Levinson, 2017).

The Supreme Court ruled against Balzac. The unanimous decision—redacted by Chief Justice Taft—argued that the rights of the Sixth Amendment were rooted in locality, not citizenship status (Torruella, 2017). Overall, then, *Balzac v. Porto Rico* effectively settled that the Jones Act of 1917 had not resulted in the incorporation of Puerto Rico into the United States. Despite naturalization, the island remained an unincorporated territory. What this means is that whereas U.S. citizens in Puerto Rico certainly had the right to move to one of the U.S. states and enjoy the full protections of citizenship, they were not entitled to them as long as they remained residents of the unincorporated territory (Levinson, 2017).

Overall, *Balzac v Porto Rico* legitimized two classes of citizenship with different rights and claims to the protections of the Constitution by making the case that citizenship in Puerto Rico is anchored not on the Fourteenth Amendment, but on a congressional statute (Levinson, 2017). Judicial questions pertaining to the nature of Puerto Rican citizenship persist today (Venator-Santiago and Meléndez, 2017).

Aileen Cardona-Arroyo

See also: Primary Documents: The Preamble and Articles I and II of Constitution of the Commonwealth of Puerto Rico (1952) [in English and Spanish]

Further Reading

Balzac v. People of Porto Rico, 258 U.S. 298 (1922).

Downes v. Bidwell, 182 U.S. 244 (1901).

Levinson, Sanford. 2017. "Citizenship and Equality in an Age of Diversity: Reflections on Balzac and the Indian Civil Rights Act." *Centro Journal* 29, no. 1: 76.

Perez, L. M. 2008. "Citizenship Denied: The Insular Cases and the Fourteenth Amendment." *Virginia Law Review* 94, no. 4: 1029–81.

Torruella, J. R. 2017. "To Be or Not to Be: Puerto Ricans and Their Illusory US Citizenship." *Centro Journal* 29, no. 1: 108.

Venator-Santiago, Charles. 2017. "Mapping the Contours of the History of the Extension of US Citizenship to Puerto Rico, 1898–Present." *Centro Journal* 29, no. 1: 38.

Venator-Santiago, Charles. R., & Edgardo Meléndez. 2017. "US Citizenship in Puerto Rico: One Hundred Years After the Jones Act." *Centro Journal* 29, no. 1: 14.

Becerra, Xavier

(1958–)

Xavier Becerra is a Democratic U.S. politician who served in the California state legislature (1991–1993), in the U.S. House of Representatives (1993–2017), and as California attorney general (2017–). He first entered public service as a member of the California state legislature, but would go on to become the highest-ranking Latino representative in the House of Representatives as the chair of the Democratic Caucus. He would make history as the first Latino to ever hold the position of California attorney general after being appointed by Governor Jerry Brown in December 2016.

Becerra was born to Manuel and Maria Becerra, Mexican migrants who raised him and his three sisters in a working-class home in Sacramento. He is the first in his

Xavier Becerra, attorney general of California
(2017–). Becerra served as a member of the U.S.
House of Representatives for California's
34th congressional district from 1993 to 2003,
and for California's 31st congressional district
from 2003 to 2017. (U.S. House of
Representatives)

family to attend college, graduating from Stanford University with his bachelor's degree in economics in 1980, and again with his juris doctorate in 1984. Becerra's wife is Dr. Carolyn Reyes, a physician, whom he originally met while attending Stanford. They have three daughters together.

In 1986, he began working in government as a staffer for California state senator Art Torres, who represented a legislative district in East Los Angeles (Morain, 2015). He spent the late 1980s working in the state of California's Department of Justice as a deputy attorney general under state attorney general Jack Van de Kamp. Becerra would officially begin his own career as an elected official after winning a seat in the California State Assembly representing the Latino-majority 59th assembly district located in East Los Angeles (Acuna, 1990). He was encouraged to run for this seat by his former boss, state senator Art Torres.

Becerra would run for Congress in 1992 to replace the groundbreaking Latino Congress Member Edward Roybal with the support of prominent Los Angeles Latino politicians, including then state assembly member Gloria Molina (McGreevey, 2017). He would represent his East Los Angeles district through various rounds of redistricting (through which the state of California must redraw congressional boundaries after every census), where his district was designated the 25th, 31st, and finally, the 34th. Becerra's congressional district has always been Latino majority, working class, and heavily Democratic (Acuna, 1990; Morain, 2015).

During Becerra's time in Congress he ascended into leadership positions. His first prominent leadership position was as chair of the Congressional Hispanic Caucus, a congressional member organization composed of Latino Democrats, from 1997 to 1999. He was the first Latino member of Congress to serve on the Ways and Means Committee. Becerra would serve in party leadership, by first being elected by his fellow House Democrats to the position of vice-chair of the House Democratic Caucus in 2009. He would serve in this capacity until 2013 when he was elected chair of the House Democratic Caucus in 2013. Becerra would become the highest-ranking Latino representative in the House ever. The duties of the caucus chair include presiding over meetings of House Democrats and setting the agenda (French and Palmer, 2015). Becerra served on the National Commission on Fiscal Responsibility and Reform, where he represented the House Democrats at the behest of Democratic minority leader Nancy Pelosi.

In 2016, California governor Jerry Brown appointed Becerra to fill the remaining term of former attorney general Kamala Harris, who had just been elected to the U.S. Senate in November 2016. The California State Senate confirmed Becerra in January 2017, upon which he officially resigned from Congress. Before he was appointed to the position, Becerra had originally hoped to become the highest-ranking House Democrat on the Ways and Means Committee. In 2018 he was elected to served as California's attorney general again.

Matthew S. Mendez

See also: Congressional Hispanic Caucus Institute (CHCI); Roybal, Edward R. (1916–2005); *Primary Documents:* Excerpt of an Oral History Interview of Congressman Edward Roybal (1975)

Further Reading`

Acuna, Rudolfo. 1990. "The Candidate Who Upset Latino Politics: Xavier Becerra Owes His Victory to the People, Not the Blessings of a *Papacito.*" *Los Angeles Times,* June 8. http://articles.latimes.com/1990-06-08/local/me-535_1_xavier-becerra.

Acuna, Rudolfo. 1996. *Anything But Mexican: Chicanos in Contemporary Los Angeles.* New York: Verso.

Barreto, Matt A., Mario Villarreal, & Nathan D. Woods. 2005. "Metropolitan Latino Political Behavior: Voter Turnout and Candidate Preference in Los Angeles." *Journal of Urban Affairs* 27, no. 1: 71–91.

French, Lauren, & Anna Palmer. 2015. "Becerra in a Box." *Politico,* December 17. http://www.politico.com/story/2015/12/xavier-becerra-democrats-house-216783.

Garcia Bedolla, Lisa. 2005. *Fluid Borders: Latino Power, Identity, and Politics in Los Angeles.* Berkeley: University of California Press.

McGreevey, Patrick. 2017. "For Attorney General Nominee Xavier Becerra, Immigration Is a Personal Issue." *Los Angeles Times,* January 18. http://www.latimes.com/politics/la-pol-ca-xavier-becerra-immigration-snap-20170118-story.html.

Morain, Daniel. 2015. "Family, Future Mingle as Becerra Eyes Senate Run." *Sacramento Bee,* January 31. http://www.sacbee.com/opinion/opn-columns-blogs/dan-morain/article8838875.html.

Berriozábal, María Antonietta

(1941–)

María Antonietta Berriozábal is a community activist and political leader, and the first Mexican American woman elected to the San Antonio City Council. Born in Laredo, Texas, to immigrant parents from Mexico, she was totally immersed in her church and community as a young person. Because of this foundation in her development, her politics were always guided by culture and history, and the people they represent. Her first venture into politics was at 17 years old when she went to work as a secretary for a Bexar County judge, Blair Reeaves. In her words, she did this "to allow her brothers to continue their schooling."

She eventually met Manuel Berriozábal, a math professor at the University of Texas at San Antonio (UTSA), and married. In her thirties, she began her university education at UTSA where she met Professor Richard Gambitta, who guided María through several studies that were instrumental in sharpening her analysis of politics from a community perspective. More important, this study brought her to focus on women. Why aren't there any Chicanas in political positions? In her words, she called this period her "search," where she connected her political studies with an historical memory of the struggle and the suffering of her people.

In her political gatherings with fellow Chicanas, they collectively decided to run for a seat on the city council to replace Henry Cisneros, who was running for mayor. María was talked into running. She won in a run-off. In her 10 years as a city councilwoman she set a different path where she emphasized a role for community in economic development policy. Immediately most of the economic development "experts" criticized María for her lack of knowledge of economic development. Her approach was to bring spokespeople in to speak for the community there, emphasizing the role of community in speaking to issues as opposed to the "experts." As she put it, "it was a good ole boy network" that represented what was good for the city and it excluded community. In the process, María found that even the Democratic Party was hierarchical and run from the top to bottom and had no room for the voice of the community.

Eventually she organized the Mexican American Business and Professional Women (MABPW) to address the problems of isolation and neglect that Chicanas found in the business and professional world. After 10 years on the city council, María Berriozábal ran for mayor. Her race against Nelson Wolff was very close, but she lost to the big money interests of San Antonio. Interestingly the issue of Applewhite, a water reservoir in the Southside that she opposed because it was intended to allow greater economic development over the Edwards Aquifer, San Antonio's only water source, lost her the election.

Today María is a leader in opposing economic development, as well fighting for housing for neglected communities. She also joined in the union fight in the hotel industry with other women leaders such as Rosa Rosales. Aside from her fierce struggle to bring women into the politics that goes into governing the city, her legacy is one of popular rule from the bottom up, which in her political philosophy emphasized the role of community women.

Rodolfo Rosales

See also: Catholicism and Latino/a Politics; Cisneros, Henry G. (1947–)

Further Reading

Berriozábal, María Antonietta. 2012. *María, Daughter of Immigrants*. San Antonio, TX: Wings Press, 2012.

Castañeda, Antonia. 2003. "Introduction: Gender on the Borderlands." *Frontiers: A Journal of Women Studies* 24, no. 2: xi–xix.

Gutiérrez, José Ángel. 1993. "Oral History Interview with María A. Berriozábal." http://library.uta.edu/tejanovoices/xml/CMAS_033.xml.

Rosales, Rodolfo. 2000. *The Illusion of Inclusion: The Untold Political Story of San Antonio*. Austin: University of Texas Press.

Bilingual Education

Addressing the needs of English Language Learners (ELLs) or Limited English Proficient (LEP) students in grades K–12 is a significant issue for the Latino community. Of the 17.9 million Latinos under the age of 18, 3.7 million are engaged in bilingual education in U.S. public schools (Patten, 2016). Bilingual education has evolved from the 19th century—moving from a mechanism for assimilation, where native language retention was not only neglected but discouraged, to immersion programs where non-native English speakers were separated from the rest of the students for English instruction, to bilingual education, where both English and the ELL students' native languages were used in instruction. The latest development is the creation of dual immersion programs that focus on teaching both Spanish and English to all students in the classroom, ideally resulting in a bilingual student body.

The two major federal acts in regard to bilingual education are the Bilingual Education Act (BEA) of 1968 and the Equal Educational Opportunities Act of 1974. The BEA was a Title VII amendment to the Elementary and Secondary Education Act (a federal act emphasizing equal access and achievement standards for elementary and secondary schools) and was the first federal law that recognized the unique needs of LEP students. The BEA had limited success; school participation was voluntary, funding emphasized teaching English with no regard for native language retention or utilization, and funding was primarily directed at students ages three to eight in spite of the act's original emphasis on deterring high school dropouts among LEP students.

The Equal Educational Opportunities Act of 1974 was significant for, among other things, increasing funding to the Bilingual Education Act and requiring English-language instruction in public schools. This act was the result of *Lau v. Nichols* (1974), a Supreme Court decision that found a lack of language assistance had a discriminatory effect on LEP students, thereby violating the Civil Rights Act of 1964.

Until the 1970s, the most common form of bilingual education was an English-only approach, commonly referred to as "submersion" or the "sink or swim" method. This form of education encouraged students to forget their native language and step away from their native culture, seeing both as necessary for assimilation into American society. Studies have repeatedly found this method of instruction is not effective, although it remains a common form of English instruction in areas that have a small non-native English population or a population of non-native speakers from a variety of language traditions.

The second approach is known as English as a Second Language (ESL) or English for Speakers of Other Languages (ESOL). This involves removing non-English speakers from the classroom for one-on-one or group English-language instruction. ESL/ESOL is neutral on the matter of native language retention—it neither promotes cultural assimilation nor encourages native language retention. Instead, ESL advanced bilingual education by acknowledging that students learn English better when they receive individualized attention, rather than being submerged into an English-only classroom with little to no preparation.

Third came the "bilingual" educational model; students are instructed in both English and their native language, with a gradual phase-out of native-language instruction. A small percentage of these programs value the retention and usage of students' native languages and choose to retain—rather than phase out—bilingual instruction throughout the entirety of the academic program. These are referred to as "maintenance" or "developmental bilingual" programs. Students completing a bilingual program tend to have higher educational outcomes than ESL and immersion students (Kim, Hutchison, and Winsler, 2015).

Lastly, dual immersion or two-way immersion programs combine native English speakers and language-minority students in the same classroom, emphasizing the acquisition of a second language for all students. Dual immersion is designed to span the duration of the educational program in order to facilitate fluency. Spanish is the most common language for dual immersion programs on account of Latinos being the largest ELL population (77.1% of 4.6 million ELL students; Kena, et al., 2016). Dual immersion produces the highest language achievement rates of all the forms of bilingual education, and have been growing in popularity among both public and private schools.

Kiku E. Huckle

See also: Official English Movement

Further Reading

Alanis, Iliana, & Mariela A. Rodriguez. 2008. "Sustaining a Dual Language Immersion Program: Features of Success." *Journal of Latinos and Education* 7, no. 4: 305–19.

Corpora, F. V., & L. R. Fraga. 2016. "¿Es Su Escuela Nuestra Escuela? Latino Access to Catholic Schools." *Journal of Catholic Education* 19, no. 2: 112–139. http://dx .doi.org/10.15365/joce.1902062016.

Dunlop, Velez, ed. 2016. *The Condition of Education 2016 (NCES 2016–144).* Washington, D.C.: National Center for Education Statistics, U.S. Department of Education.

Kena, Grace, William Hussar, Joel McFarland, Cristobal de Brey, Lauren Musu-Gillette, Xiaolei Wang, Jijun Zhang, et al. 2016. "The Condition of Education 2016. NCES 2016-144." *National Center for Education Statistics.* https://nces.ed.gov/pubs2016 /2016144.pdf.

Kim, Yoon Kyong Kim, Lindsey A. Hutchison, & Adam Winsler. 2015. "Bilingual Education in the United States: An Historical Overview and Examination of Two-Way Immersion." *Educational Review* 67, no. 2: 236–52.

Patten, Eileen. 2016. "The Nation's Latino Population Is Defined by Its Youth." http://www .pewhispanic.org/2016/04/20/the-nations-latino-population-is-defined-by-its-youth/.

Bisexual Identity. *See Politics of a Latinx Lesbian, Gay, Bisexual, and Transgender Identity*

Border Wall

Also known as "El Muro," or "the wall," or border fence, the sections of wall along the U.S.–Mexico border were built from 1994, and continued after President George W. Bush signed the Border Fence Act of 2006. The Border Wall was

Construction workers erect a border wall just north of the Rio Grande River in the Rio Grande Valley in deep south Texas to deter undocumented immigrants from entering the United States. The effectiveness of the wall is a matter of dispute, as immigrants continue to enter illegally on a daily basis. (vichinterlang/iStockphoto.com)

intended to provide increased border security and reduce unauthorized crossing by undocumented immigrants and illegal crossing of contraband, but has proved to be a political statement that threatened the lives of unauthorized immigrants attempting to migrate to the United States and hindered the natural habitat of native species. Shortly after passage of the law, the federal government sent notices to property owners to notify them that their lands, or parts of them would have to be sold to the government for the construction of the wall. The most recent additions to the Border Wall started sporadic construction in 2007 alongside the U.S.–Mexico border from Brownsville, Texas, to San Diego, California. The materials used to build the wall vary from fortified metal to concrete fences. Under President Donald Trump, construction of the Border Wall has resumed. According to the Government Accountability Office (GAO), there have been over 9,200 breaches of the wall since 2010.

The construction of the Border Wall brought opposition from local residents whose properties were being taken away by the government to build the wall. Under eminent domain laws, the federal government has the right to seize private properties under fair market value. However, property owners claimed illegal seizing and unfair compensation, which led families to lose their life savings and source of income, prompting lawsuits against the U.S. federal government; to date, hundreds of litigations continue in the courts. In certain areas "El Muro" cuts through farmland, wildlife refuge parks, Native American reservations, and private citizens' backyards. The claim against the Border Wall is not only that of inefficiency but also of the immorality in taking away the livelihood of U.S. citizens and displacing animals from their natural habitats under the claim of national security.

The Border Wall was an attempt by the Department of Homeland Security to update surveillance mechanisms along the U.S.–Mexico border. While constructing the Border Wall, sophisticated equipment was place in certain sectors to record activity. There are no accurate dollar amounts on the total construction cost of the Border Wall, but according to conservative news sources like Reuters, the total cost of the Department of Homeland Security investment in border protection from 2006 to 2009 is estimated to be $2.4 billion for 670 miles of a single-layer border fence, as per a U.S. GAO report.

As mentioned, under President Trump's administration, there is an initiative to resume construction of the Border Wall and in certain areas adding a second layer of border fence. The first phase of the Border Wall did not provide a continuous wall, which aggravates the inefficiency of the project. In efforts to resume construction, the federal government is using the Border Fence Act of 2006 despite lack of new funding support by Congress. Since taking office, the Trump administration has placed an open request for a proposal for the second phase of the Border Wall.

Among many residents in border communities, "El Muro" is no more than a political statement. Unfortunately, it is a political statement that provides a vivid physical reminder of being treated as a second-class citizen because of skin color and ethnicity. Human rights and environmental activist groups have united their efforts in the fight against the construction of the Border Wall, taking to the streets in protest and before Congress to speak against the Border Wall.

Tania Chavez

See also: Immigration as a Policy Issue; National Security State and Latinos; Secure Communities Program; Trump, Donald J. (1946–) and Latinos

Further Reading

Jones, Reece. 2012. *Border Walls: Security and the War on Terror in the United States, India, and Israel.* London: Zed Books.

Botiller v. Dominguez

(1889)

Botiller v. Dominguez is a U.S. Supreme Court opinion addressing the validity of Spanish and Mexican land grants in the aftermath of the U.S. annexation of southwestern territories under the terms of the Treaty of Guadalupe Hidalgo of 1848. This opinion created a double standard limiting the ability of the descendants of Spanish and Mexican landowners to inherit land in the Mexican territories annexed by the United States.

On October 1, 1834, before the U.S. War with Mexico, the Mexican government granted Nemecio Dominguez and Domingo Carrillo, both citizens of Mexico, ownership of the land known as Rancho Las Virgenes. This property was located in Los Angeles County, Mexico (later part of California).

Questions about land grants and the right to property in the territories annexed by the United States in the aftermath of the War of 1898 were settled in the Treaty of Guadalupe Hidalgo. Specifically, Article VIII of the treaty established that property rights of any kind held by Mexicans and their heirs in the newly annexed U.S. territories would be "inviolably respected." The treaty did not stipulate a time frame and presumably protected the rights of all heirs of the original Mexican landowners. Two years later, amidst an ongoing gold rush, Congress admitted California as a state of the Union. In 1851, Congress further enacted legislation for California requiring all persons holding "perfect" or undisputed titles of land to present them to a land commission for certification. The act of 1851 gave all landowners in California two years to comply with the law.

Sometime during the early 1880s, Dominga Dominguez inherited her grandfather's land without a perfect title or without any legal challenges to her right to own the land. When she sought to claim Rancho Las Virgenes, she found that Brigido Botiller and other squatters had taken possession of her land and refused to leave. She sued in the California court system and won every case. The case was appealed to the Supreme Court in 1887.

In the Supreme Court, Botiller argued that no one in the Dominguez family had registered Rancho Las Virgenes with the land commission created by the act of 1851. Dominguez, however, argued that Article VIII of the Treaty of Guadalupe Hidalgo guaranteed her right to inherit her family's land. The Supreme Court sided with Botiller and reversed the California rulings for Dominguez.

Three of the reasons offered by the Court have important implications for Latino/a descendants of residents of conquered territories who held land grants acquired prior to the U.S. annexation. First, *Botiller* established that Congress could enact legislation modifying Article VIII of the Treaty of Guadalupe Hidalgo, and for that matter, any treaty. Second, the Court established that even people who held "perfect titles" to land would not be guaranteed a right to inherit such land. Third, the *Botiller* ruling applied a discriminatory legal standard to Mexican landowners. Whereas the Court had previously allowed white squatters with an "imperfect title" to claim a title over land in California, the Court now established that Mexican descendants with "perfect titles" to land were not necessarily guaranteed a right to inherit the land of their ancestors. Finally, *Botiller* established that a U.S. citizen could not sue to protect her or his property rights under the treaty—only the Mexican government could sue on her or his behalf.

Charles R. Venator-Santiago

See also: Treaty of Guadalupe Hidalgo (1848); *Primary Documents:* Excerpts from the Treaty of Guadalupe Hidalgo (1848)

Further Reading

Botiller v. Dominguez, 130 U.S. 238 (1889).

Soltero, Carlos R. 2006. *Latinos and American Law: Landmark Supreme Court Cases.* Austin: University of Texas Press.

United States General Accounting Office. 2004. *Treaty of Guadalupe Hidalgo: Findings and Possible Options Regarding Longstanding Community Land Grant Claims in New Mexico.* GAO-04-59. Washington, D.C.: Government Printing Office.

Brown Berets

The Brown Berets were a community-based social justice organization that formed as part of the Brown Power or Chicano Movement that flourished in the 1960s. Composed of young adults based in Los Angeles, the Brown Berets followed the model of the Black Panthers in Oakland. The organization planned and acted in support of upward mobility for people of Mexican descent through positive social change in the community. Largely active from 1966 to 1973, its members were very vocal in calling for an end to racism in schools, police harassment and brutality, unemployment, poverty, and the Vietnam War. In recent years some of their members, as well as some organizations modeled after the original group, have called attention to the rights of undocumented immigrants and have stood in solidarity with Black Lives Matter demonstrations.

In the late 1960s, the Chicano Movement developed throughout the states of California, Arizona, New Mexico, Colorado, and Texas. It encompassed a vast array of issues, from political rights to combating negative stereotypes of Mexicans in the U.S. cultural context. During those years, the population of Mexican descent had notably increased in the aforementioned states due to migration waves and the post–World War II population boom. Large numbers of women and men from these new generations lived in impoverished communities and faced struggles in several realms. In school, for instance, they studied in poor facilities, lacking books, encountering administrators and teachers who made racist comments, and counselors who questioned their capacities for success. Also, during the Vietnam era, young Mexican American soldiers from California were killed in disproportionate numbers.

The official beginning of the Brown Berets was in April 1966 when the Los Angeles County Commission sponsored the Mexican American Young Leadership Conference, which congregated high school–aged young leaders to discuss issues regarding their communities, values, beliefs, and the term "Mexican American." The students formed the Young Citizens for Community Action (YCCA) the following month. The organization adopted the term "Chicano" because to use "American" as part of their identity was seen as assimilation with their oppressor. First, they focused on discussing the flaws of the school system, but gradually moved to other topics, such as police brutality and the quality of life in their communities. They counted on the support of an ever-growing network of urban groups and leaders who collaborated with them. Such was the case of Father John B. Luce, who provided financial help to open "La Piranya"—a coffeehouse on East Olympic Boulevard. La Piranya served as an office and meeting place for student leaders from nearby colleges and the Chicano Movement, as well as African American leaders. The gatherings also attracted the attention of the Los Angeles Police Department, who harassed those that visited the coffeehouse. As a result, the YCCA organized protest demonstrations at the sheriff's station. Exactly at that time, the original leadership of the group began to change because some of them had begun college studies. The new president, David Sánchez, insisted on a more militant stance, so the YCCA adopted khaki military attire and berets, with an emblem proclaiming "La Causa" ("The Cause"). Initially, it was police who started calling them Brown Berets, but with time the YCCA members adopted the name as well.

They participated in student protests, such as the Chicano blowouts or walkouts of 1968, and created their own newspaper: *La Causa*. Among their most notable achievements are the creation of a free medical clinic and their participation in the Chicano antiwar effort. The group separated in 1973, after several social achievements, but also after constant police harassment, infiltration of FBI agents, and disagreements among the members in regard to Sanchez's leadership. Some scholars have also highlighted the militaristic, masculine, and hierarchical structure of the group as a possible contribution to the disbanding of this organization.

Pamela Fuentes Peralta

See also: Brown Power Movement/Chicano Civil Rights Movement; Los Angeles School Walkouts (1968, 2006)

Further Reading

Chávez, Ernesto. 2002. *"¡Mi Raza Primero!" (My People First): Nationalism, Identity, and Insurgency in the Chicano Movement in Los Angeles, 1966–1978*. Berkeley and Los Angeles: University of California Press.

Haney Lopez, Ian. 2004. *Racism on Trial: The Chicano Fight for Justice*. Cambridge, MA: Harvard University Press.

Brown Power Movement/Chicano Civil Rights Movement

The Chicano Movement became one of the pivotal periods for social change during the 1960s and remains today an important era for the advancement of civil rights for Chicanas/os. Indeed, a growing unrest was occurring among Mexican Americans. Mexican Americans gained access to the middle class, in part as a result of their military service during World War II. Former Mexican American military war veterans used the GI Bill to buy new homes or go to college. Despite these gains, the children of these former war veterans would take further steps. Coming of age, the next generation of Mexican Americans would find themselves promoting a new sense of racial identity, which would become known as Brown Power. The Brown Power slogan would serve as an expression for promoting a new generation of ethnic political power and effectively establishing access to institutions that had historically denied Chicanas/os full access, such as schools of higher education. In short, Brown Power would instill in Mexican Americans a sense of ethnic nationalism. Brown Power also coincided with direct empowerment for the betterment of the community. The term also carried with it a new militant stance not seen before among Mexican Americans. The new militancy for Mexican Americans could be found among Chicano youths not only in the traditional Southwest, but would extend itself among Chicanos in the Midwest. A "new" urban Chicano reflected a change from the stereotypical poor, rural Chicano of the past, even going as far as changing their identity from Mexican American to Chicano. One of the most infamous events involving Chicanos and their assertion of Brown Power was the East Los Angeles High School Blowouts that occurred in 1968. The walkouts among high school students would promote Brown Power by Chicanas and Chicanos in what they considered the indifferent manner school administrators held toward them. Chicanas and Chicanos had among the highest dropout rates. The school

The Brown Power Movement, or Chicano Movement, extended the Mexican American civil rights movement of the 1960s with the stated goal of achieving empowerment. Many organizations were formed to pursue this goal, such as the Brown Berets, who are seen here saluting as the casket of civil rights activist Ricardo Falcon passes, Fort Lupton, Colorado, 1972. (Dave Buresh/The Denver Post via Getty Images)

walkouts would be monitored by the presence of the Brown Berets, an element of the Brown Power militancy. The term "Brown Power" could be heard shouted among the social protests by Chicana and Chicano activists during the walkouts.

Throughout the 1960s and 1970s larger social issues would be confronted and contested in what scholars would encapsulate as the Chicano Movement or El Movimiento. Critical of their second-class status Chicanos and Chicanas would assert their right to organize against the historical denial of their civil rights. Similar to the Black Civil Rights Movement, the Chicano Movement would engage the Chicano community through historical political social change. Not all events that occurred would be tied the Chicano Movement, but they were so impactful scholars often associated the events under its umbrella. For example, the rise of the United Farm Workers union struggle led by César Chávez and Dolores Huerta was not considered by Chávez or Huerta as part of the largely student-led Chicano Movement. However, the struggle to organize farm workers cannot be dismissed because it was a groundbreaking effort toward offering some of the poorest workers in the United States a decent wage and better working conditions. Other notable events considered part of the Chicano Movement would be the East Los Angeles Blowouts, the New Mexico Land Struggle, the Vietnam War, the War on Poverty, and the culmination of the Chicano Moratorium. The long-term effects of the Chicano Movement helped establish a permanent class struggle among working-class

Chicanos, college students, farm workers, community activists, high school students, and other activists. In short, it established a permanent placement of Chicana/o activists who continued to engage in social change through the institutions they joined after completing college and establishing careers. Now many years later the Chicano Movement no longer has the strong advocacy it once had. Former leaders such as Carlos Muñoz, Jr., or Rodolfo "Corky" Gonzales who led various struggles as part of the Chicano Movement have become part of the establishment they sought to challenge back in the 1960s and 1970s. But that is not to say the Chicano Movement has disappeared completely. Residuals of the Chicano Movement today include the social activism to organize immigration reform for the 6 million undocumented immigrants, which continues to concern the Chicano community as they seek a sound and reasonable solution.

Paul López

See also: Brown Berets; Chávez, César (1927–1993); Chicano Moratorium (1970); Delano Grape Strike (1965–1970); Gonzales, Rodolfo "Corky" (1928–2005); Gutiérrez, José Ángel (1944–); Huerta, Dolores (1930–); La Raza Unida Party (LRU); Los Angeles School Walkouts (1968, 2006); United Farm Workers (UFW)

Further Reading

Acuna, Rodolfo. 2014. *Occupied America: A History of Chicanos*. London: Pearson.

Blackwell, Maylei. 2011. *¡Chicana Power!: Contested Histories of Feminism in the Chicano Movement*. Chicana Matters Series. Austin: University of Texas Press.

Munoz, Carlos, Jr. 2007. *Youth, Identity, Power: The Chicano Movement*. London: Verso.

Bush, George Prescott

(1976–)

George P. Bush was sworn in as the 28th commissioner of the Texas General Land Office on January 2, 2015. Bush won the 2014 Texas General Election with over 60 percent of the vote against Democrat and former mayor of El Paso, John Cook (*New York Times*, 2014). The commissioner is responsible for Texas land, mineral rights, and Permanent School Fund management, as well as preservation of the office's historic archives and the Alamo (George P. Bush, n.d.). The office was established in 1836, making it the oldest state agency in Texas (Texas General Land Office, n.d.). George Prescott Bush is thought to be a rising star in the Republican Party, as he is a member of the Bush family dynasty.

Bush earned his bachelor's degree in history from Rice University in 1998 and became a public high school teacher in Florida. After receiving his juris doctor from the University of Texas School of Law, he worked for a U.S. District judge, Honorable Sidney A. Fitzwater. He served as an intelligence officer in the U.S. Naval Reserves and served on several diplomatic missions to Turkey (2012), Saudi Arabia (2011), Brazil (2007), and Nicaragua (2002) (Courier of Montgomery County, 2013). In the meantime, he entered several business ventures and cofounded Pennybacker Capital LLC and St. Augustine Partners LLC.

The commissioner is the son of former governor of Florida Jeb Bush and Columba Garnica Gallo. His mother is a naturalized citizen from Guanajuato, Mexico, and daughter of migrant worker José María Garnica (Glaister, 2004). He is also the grandson of former president George H. W. Bush and nephew of former president George W. Bush. Bush spoke at the 1992 and 1998 Republican National Conventions and campaigned alongside his uncle in both of his presidential campaigns. Bush cofounded the Hispanic Republicans of Texas in 2009, a political action committee (PAC) whose goal is to successfully elect candidates of Hispanic heritage. In 2012, Bush was promoted within the Republican Party of Texas to the deputy finance chairman position (Republican Party of Texas, n.d.).

As a self-identified Latino, Bush has rejected the Democrats' assertion that their party better represents Latinos and the younger generations, as Bush claims both of those identities (*Huffington Post*, 2014). He is fluent in Spanish and has appeared in Spanish-language television commercials. In fact, Bush believes that the politically incorrect rhetoric of the 2016 Trump presidential campaign did not harm the Republican Party's chances of garnering the Hispanic vote going forward and was one of the few members of the Bush family to vote for Donald Trump (Weissert, 2016).

Bush emphasized that his support of President Donald Trump proves that he is his own man despite his link to the Bush dynasty. Bush's grandmother, Barbara Bush, warned him about entering politics without first making a name for himself in some other field. His grandmother's advice is credited for his strong background in business and in government prior to entering the political realm. The commissioner ran a successful re-election campaign in 2018.

Outside of politics, Bush is heavily involved with educational organizations. He sits as the Tarrant County chairman for Uplift Education, a public nonprofit charter school to reduce the achievement gap in inner-city schools. He is also the co-chairman of the Dallas-Fort Worth Celebration of Reading and co-chaired a $30 million capital campaign for local Big Brothers Big Sisters chapters (Courier of Montgomery County, 2013). Bush married classmate and attorney, Amanda (née Williams) in Maine on April 7, 2004. The Bush family lives in Houston, Texas, with their two children, John and Prescott.

Stephanie L. DeMora and Loren Collingwood

See also: Trump, Donald J. (1946–) and Latinos

Further Reading

Bush, George P. n.d. "Biography." http://www.georgepfortexas.org/about/.

Castro, Tony. 2013. "George P. Bush Future in Politics, Trying to Win the Hispanic Vote." *Huffington Post,* February 9. http://www.huffingtonpost.com/2013/02/09/george-p -bush-future-in-politics_n_2652510.html.

"George P. Bush Elected Texas Land Commissioner." 2014. *Huffington Post*, November 5. http://www.huffingtonpost.com/2014/11/05/george-p-bush-elected_n_6104924.html.

Glaister, Dan. 2004. "He's Young, Good Looking, and Hispanic—Could He Be the Next George Bush in the White House?" *The Guardian,* August 31. https://www .theguardian.com/world/2004/aug/31/uselections2004.usa1.

"NSRW to Host George P. Bush at Bentwater." 2013. *Courier of Montgomery County*, October 12. http://www.yourconroenews.com/news/article/NSRW-to-host-George-P -Bush-at-Bentwater-9271252.php.

Republican Party of Texas. n.d. "George P. Bush Nominated to Be Deputy Finance Chair." https://www.texasgop.org/george-p-bush-nominated-to-be-deputy-finance-chair.

"Texas Election Results." 2014. *New York Times*, December 17. http://www.nytimes.com /elections/2014/texas-elections.

Texas General Land Office. n.d. "The Texas Land Office Is the Oldest State Agency in Texas, Established by the Constitution of the Republic of Texas." http://www.glo .texas.gov/the-glo/about/overview/index.html.

Weissert, Will. 2013. "George P. Bush Starts Small Amid High Expectations." *Associated Press,* July 22. https://www.yahoo.com/news/george-p-bush-starts-small-amid-high -expectations-122933798.html.

Weissert, Will. 2016. "George P. Bush Says Name Isn't Liability after Trump's Win." *Associated Press,* November 10. https://elections.ap.org/content/george-p-bush-says -name-isnt-liability-after-trumps-win.

Cantú, Norma Elia

(1947–)

Norma Elia Cantú is a prominent Chicana and Latina cultural studies scholar, author, folklorist, teacher, and activist. The oldest of 11 children, she was born in Nuevo Laredo, Tamaulipas, Mexico, and moved to the United States as an infant. Of humble upbringing, Cantú has made education a primary tool for both self-empowerment and Latinx community development.

Cantú has achieved wide national recognition for her acclaimed teaching, research, and creative writing career in Latino/a Studies, Chicano/a Literature, Border Studies, Folklore, Women Studies, and Cultural Studies. Her work depicts relentless "*fronteriza* consciousness," making an impact in both literature and social change, inside and outside the academy. She has been recognized as Outstanding Latina of Kansas City (2015), Exceptional Texas Woman (2010), and National Association of Chicana and Chicano Studies Scholar of the Year (2008). She is a board member and fellow of the American Folklore Society, from which she received the Américo Paredes Award. In 2016, Trinity University in Texas appointed her the Norine R. and Frank Murchison Endowed Professor in Humanities. She has generously and effectively mentored generations of Latinx students, scholars, artists, and professionals.

The concern and activism for social justice started very early in Norma Cantú's life. As a laborer in a factory for smelting antimony from its ore, her father was active in labor unions, and she became aware of injustices as a child. She participated in the Chicano Movement in the 1960s, regularly mobilizing for progressive causes after working hours. Cantú soon became involved in international causes, for example, the war in Nicaragua and the opposition to Pinochet in Chile. As she studied both English and political science at Texas A&I (now A&M), Kingsville, her initial intent had been to become a lawyer to fight for human rights and social justice. Yet while discerning about her future career, she attended a pivotal retreat in Sarita, Texas, in 1974, where Cantú decided to become a writer, accepting and embracing her vocation for language and poetry instead of law as an instrument for justice. Community/family storytellers and authors Sor Juana Inés de la Cruz, Miguel de Cervantes, William Shakespeare, Gloria Anzaldúa, and Cherríe Moraga were major influences.

The decision brought her back to Laredo, Texas, to teach and continue her involvement in political activity. She became a member of the Action League of Laredo to institute change at the grassroots level. A TV station in Laredo contacted her to institute a literacy program in the 1980s, a cause she passionately embraced. Cantú founded Literacy Volunteers of Laredo and recruited her students to go out to the colonias of Texas—residential areas along the U.S.–Mexico border that often lack some basic services, such as potable water and sewer systems, electricity, paved roads, and safe housing. There, they worked with people who lacked Spanish and/or English literacy at a time when there were no English as Second Language classes available. This program is still ongoing and has expanded at a community college. Cantú also started a group of Amnesty International, working with abused women and incarcerated immigrants at detention centers. She supported letter-writing campaigns that were instrumental in helping achieve the release of prisoners. One of Cantú's brothers was killed in the Vietnam War, which made her an engaged pacifist involved in antiwar struggles.

Cantú has founded and has been an energetic member of several writers' collectives that support Latinxs and Chicanxs, particularly women. She is a founding member of the Macondo Writing Workshop in 2009 and cofounder of CantoMundo, a national organization that cultivates a community of Latinx poets and provides a space for the creation, documentation, and critical analysis of Latinx poetry. All throughout her career, Cantú has taken her writing seriously as a form of service and activism. She believes art and poetry need to be part of the movement for change.

Cantú earned her doctorate from the University of Nebraska-Lincoln and master's degree in English with minor in Political Science and a bachelor's degree in Education (English/Political Science) from Texas A&M, Kingsville. She was professor of Latina/o Studies and English at the University of Missouri, Kansas City. She is also professor emerita at University of Texas, San Antonio, and has also taught at Georgetown University; Texas A&M International University; Laredo State University, Texas; and University of Nebraska, Lincoln.

Clara E. Irazábal-Zurita

See also: University of Missouri-Kansas City (UMKC) Hispanic Advisory Board

Further Reading

Anzaldúa, Gloria. 1987. *Borderlands, La Frontera: The New Mestiza.* San Francisco: Aunt Lute Books.

Cantú, N. E. 1995. *Canícula: Snapshots of a Girlhood en la Frontera.* Albuquerque: University of New Mexico Press.

Cantú, N. E., ed. 2010. *Moctezuma's Table: Rolando Briseño's Chicano Tablescapes.* San Antonio: Texas A&M University Press.

Cantú, N. E., ed. 2014. *Ofrenda: Liliana Wilson's Art of Dissidence and Dreams.* College Station: Texas A&M University Press.

Cantú, N. E. 2015. *Transcendental Train Yards: A Collaborative Suite of Serigraphs.* Art by M. Sanchez. San Antonio, Texas: Wings Press.

Cantú, N. E., & O. Nájera-Ramirez, eds. 2002. *Chicana Traditions: Continuity and Change.* Urbana: University of Illinois Press.

Gutiérrez, G. y Muhs, ed. 2017. *Word Images: New Perspectives on Canicula and Other Works by Norma Elia Cantú.* Tucson: The University of Arizona Press.

Hernández-Avila, I., & N. E. Cantú, eds. 2016. *Entre Guadalupe y Malinche: Tejanas in Literature and Art.* Austin: University of Texas Press.

The Latina Feminist Group. 2001. *Telling to Live: Latina Feminist Testimonios.* Durham, NC: Duke University Press.

Moraga, C., & G. Anzaldúa. 1983. *This Bridge Called My Back: Radical Writing by Women of Color.* New York: Kitchen Table/Women of Color Press.

Nájera-Ramírez, O., N. E. Cantú, & B. Romero, eds. 2010. *Dancing across Borders.* Urbana: University of Illinois Press.

Cantú, Norma V.

(1954–)

Norma V. Cantú is a Texas civil rights attorney and professor at the University of Texas at Austin, where she has taught courses on disability law and on cases that have promoted school reform. She served as regional counsel for the Mexican American Legal Defense and Educational Fund (MALDEF) and as the assistant secretary of education for the Office for Civil Rights during the Clinton administration, where she implemented governmental policy for civil rights in U.S. education and increased resolved complaints on discrimination by more than 20 percent. In 1983, Cantú worked as a staff attorney on the Chicana Rights Project and became the national director of the Carnegie Endowment–funded Education, Litigation, and Advocacy Project at MALDEF where she treated cases on educational funding, disability rights, educational access for English Language Learners, and racial and sexual harassment in the classroom. She has been named among one of the most influential 100 Hispanics in the United States by *Hispanic Business Magazine*; the American Bar Association's Commission on Racial and Ethnic Diversity in the Profession awarded her with the Spirit of Excellence Award in 2004.

In 2002, Cantú founded the Mexican American Legislative Leadership Foundation, an organization dedicated to supporting Mexican American students in developing leadership skills in the Texas state congress. She has also broadly written on Latino civil rights.

The following are cases that she took part in: the 1980 case *Edgewood v. Kirby*, which prompted the Texas legislature to reform its school funding laws and redistribute funds to poor school districts. In the 1983 case, *Graves v. Barnes*, the court ruled the state of Texas needed to comply with the federal Voting Rights Act. Cantú also worked on several cases regarding the educational services available for Limited English Proficient students: *Diaz v. San José Unified School District, Keyes v. School District No.1, Denver, and Gomez v. State Board of Education of Illinois.* She has also generally worked on cases to address school desegregation, namely in the United States, including *Crucial v. Ector County Independent School District*.

She has published testimonies before the Subcommittees on Postsecondary Education and Labor, a guide for schools on sexual and racial harassment, several articles on Latino empowerment, advocacy, and briefings on civil rights surveys of all school districts. Cantú has been recognized several times by the University of Texas-Pan American (now the University of Texas Rio Grande Valley) with their Distinguished Alumnus Award, was honored by the Women's Institute on Sports and Education Hall of Fame, and the Reynaldo G. Garza Award of Merit in 1993, among many more. Some of her most prestigious speeches include the keynote at the Elie Wiesel Foundation and Commencement at the University of Texas at San Antonio in 2000. In 2017, Cantú received Harvard Law School's Cele-bration of Latino Alumni Award for her mentorship, professorship, and commit-ment to human rights.

The eldest of six children and fluent in Spanish, Cantú was born in Browns-ville, Texas, in 1954. She earned her bachelor's degree summa cum laude from the University of Texas-Pan American and her law degree from Harvard Law School.

Kimberly Cárdenas

See also: Education and Latinos; Mexican American Legal Defense and Educational Fund (MALDEF); Voter ID Laws, Impact of; Voting Rights Act of 1975

Further Reading

Cantu, Norma V. 1996. "Ho Perspectives: Hispanic Outlook in Higher Education: A Question of Clarity." *The Hispanic Outlook in Higher Education* 6: 16.

Galvan, Armando. 1991. "Diaz v. San José Unified School District." *La Raza Law Journal* 4: 98.

Glaze, Melissa. 2003. "In Recognition of Norma Cantu." *Texas Hispanic Journal of Law & Policy* 9: 3.

Tedin, Kent L. 1994. "Self-Interest, Symbolic Values, and the Financial Equalization of the Public Schools." *The Journal of Politics* 56, no. 3: 628–49.

CARA Pro Bono Project

The CARA Family Detention Pro Bono Project was established in 2014 by mem-bers of several nonprofit organizations, including the Catholic Legal Immigration Network (CLINIC), the American Immigration Council, the Refugee and Immi-grant Center for Education and Legal Services (RAICES), and the American Immi-gration Lawyers Association (AILA). Headquartered in Silver Spring, Maryland, CLINIC is affiliated with "the largest network of nonprofit immigration service providers" (CARA Pro Bono, n.d.). Its attorneys provide training and information related to immigration problems encountered by low-income immigrants. The organization has also created a book titled *Representing Clients in Immigration Court*, which explains how to provide the best representation for clients who are immigrants. It is available through AILA. An online course was created in order to help volunteer attorneys learn how to represent unaccompanied children who had been detained at the U.S.–Mexico border. AILA was founded in 1946 and is headquartered in Washington, D.C. It is the member association for all of the lawyers who practice and/or teach immigration law (approximately 14,000 mem-bers). Although one of the organization's main goals is to help end the detention of families, it also provides legal aid to U.S. businesses who seek foreign employees, helps immigrants gain their permanent residence, and helps asylum seekers and foreign students, among many others. RAICES was founded in 1986 to help the residents of San Antonio, Texas, learn more about the plight of Central American immigrants who were fleeing the civil wars. Over time, the organization has been able to provide legal assistance to immigrants in the immigration court and in the U.S. Citizenship and Immigration Services office. Based in Washington, D.C., the American Immigration Council helps change how immigrants are perceived by the native populace. This is achieved by emphasizing the role of immigration within America's history as well as the contributions made by immigrants.

The impetus for this project was the opening of several privately-owned family detention facilities in Texas and New Mexico. The organizations that are part of CARA seek to address the challenges posed by detaining children and their mothers in detention centers. The first detention center was in Dilley, Texas. It was known as the South Texas Family Residential Center (CARA Pro Bono Project, n.d.) and opened in December 2014. The next to open was in Karnes City; an existing all-male detention center was converted to house women and small children. Respectively, these facilities could hold 2,400 individuals and approximately 1,100. The next facility to open was in Artesia, New Mexico. Upon its opening in July 2014, many volunteers, including lawyers, made the journey there in order to provide pro bono (complimentary) legal aid and other services to the detainees. New groups of volunteers arrived weekly, thus allowing existing caseloads to be transferred smoothly between volunteers who were leaving after their period ended and those who arrived to continue their work. All of the lawyers did this, regardless of the monetary costs, including airfare, car rental, lost billable hours, etc. The facility in Artesia was closed after five months.

Although the detention center in Artesia closed, the volunteer model continued to be used as volunteers helped detainees at the facility in Karnes, Texas. Many volunteers, including lawyers, advocates, and members of the religious community, have made every effort to address the needs of the mothers and children who are detained there. Not only has legal aid and advice been provided, but the Karnes chapter of the pro bono project has raised $200,000. These funds have been used to help the women and children pay their bonds and provided basic essentials including clothes, food, and hygiene products. The funds have also been used to help pay for the transportation needs once the women and their children have been released.

Overall, the volunteers provide legal counsel and other services. They also have the shared goal of advocating for these individuals, as well as ending the use of family detention centers and the reliance upon controversial deportation policies.

Natasha Altema McNeely

See also: Minors, Unaccompanied and Undocumented (2010s); National Immigration Law Center (NILC)

Further Reading

Ackerman, Alissa R., & Rich Furman. 2013. "The Criminalization of Immigration and the Privatization of the Immigration Detention: Implications for Justice." *Contemporary Justice Review* 16, no. 2: 251–63.

American Immigration Council. n.d. https://www.americanimmigrationcouncil.org/.

American Immigration Lawyers Association. 2017. http://www.aila.org.

Cara Pro Bono. n.d. http://caraprobono.org/partners/.

Catholic Legal Immigration Network. n.d. 2016. https://cliniclegal.org.

Hernandez, David Manuel. 2008. "Pursuant to Deportation: Latinos and Immigrant Detention." *Latino Studies* 6: 35–63.

Kalhan, Anil. 2010. "Rethinking Immigration Detention." *Columbia Law Review* 110: 24.

Refugee and Immigration Center for Education and Legal Services. 2017. https://www.raicestexas.org.

Cardozo, Benjamin Nathan

(1870–1938)

Benjamin Cardozo was an esteemed jurist, a pivotal figure in the development of American common law, and a distinguished contributor to U.S. jurisprudence (i.e., the philosophy of law). In the legal community, Cardozo is viewed as setting the standard of judicial excellence that we continue to use for judges. Given his social consciousness, elegant judicial opinions, and jurisprudential writings, Cardozo remains one of the most revered and influential 20th-century judges.

Cardozo was born on May 24, 1870, in New York City to Rebecca Nathan and Judge Albert Jacob Cardozo, a prominent affluent Sephardic Jewish family. The extent to which Cardozo self-identified as Hispanic has been debated, with Andrew Kaufman, author of the 1998 biography of Cardozo, indicating that Cardozo regarded himself as a "Sephardic Jew whose ancestors came from the Iberian Peninsula" (Lewis, 2009). Although many consider Justice Sonia Sotomayor to be the first Hispanic U.S. Supreme Court justice, given his known Spanish-Portuguese heritage, some consider Cardozo the first Hispanic U.S. Supreme Court justice.

In 1885, Cardozo enrolled at Columbia University at the age of 15, after receiving private tutelage from Horatio Alger, a prolific 19th-century American writer. In 1889, he graduated with honors in four subjects: Latin, Greek, political economy, and philosophy, and in 1890, Cardozo earned his master's degree in political science. In 1891, after studying for two years at Columbia Law School, he was admitted to the New York bar. Cardozo worked as an attorney in private practice in New York City (1891–1914), where he gained recognition for being an expert in commercial law. In 1914, Cardozo began his judicial career when he was elected to the New York Supreme Court, the state's trial bench. Shortly after his election, he was appointed to the New York State Court of Appeals, the state's highest tribunal.

In 1917, Cardozo ran and won the retention election, which allowed him to keep his seat on the New York State Court of Appeals. He served as both associate judge (1917–1926) and chief judge (1926–1932). According to legal scholars, it is his judicial opinions written during his tenure on this court that are most

Justice Benjamin N. Cardozo served (1932–1938) as an associate justice of the Supreme Court of the United States. Previously, he had served as the chief judge of the New York Court of Appeals. (Harris & Ewing, Collection of the Supreme Court of the United States)

often cited by other judges, discussed by legal scholars, and reprinted in case-books. In *MacPherson v. Buick Motor Co.* (1916), Cardozo abolished the requirement of privity of contract for duty in negligence actions, making it possible for manufacturers of products to be held liable for injuries to consumers. This doctrine left its imprint on the law of torts and was later adopted throughout the United States and Great Britain. Cardozo also authored the opinion in *Palsgraf v. Long Is. R.R. Co.* (1928), the landmark decision in American tort law that redefined the concept of negligence by establishing the concept of proximate cause. Based on his opinions, Nathan Roscoe Pound, a renowned American legal scholar, considered Cardozo one of the 10 best legal minds in U.S. history.

President Herbert Hoover (R) appointed Cardozo in 1932 to the Supreme Court of the United States to succeed Justice Oliver Wendell Holmes. Cardozo served six years on the court until his death at the age of 68. While serving on the Hughes court, Cardozo belonged to the liberal bloc of justices known as the Three Musketeers—the other two members were Justices Louis Brandeis and Harlan Fiske Stone. This group generally supported executive and legislative efforts to improve social and economic conditions. While on the U.S. Supreme Court, Cardozo wrote majority opinions concerning President Franklin Delano Roosevelt's New Deal agenda, including *Helvering v. Davis* (1937), which upheld the federal Social Security program. Additionally, during his tenure on the U.S. Supreme Court Cardozo is credited for shaping the direction of criminal law and voting rights. For instance, in *Palko v. Connecticut* (1937), Cardozo set precedent regarding the due process clause that lasted through the 1960s, and in *Nixon v. Condon* (1932), Cardozo helped abolish the all-white primaries that were prevalent in Southern states.

Cardozo, a legal pragmatist, detailed his philosophies on the law in several books. Cardozo's first and most prominent book, *The Nature of the Judicial Process* (1921), is considered by some to be a "canonical exposition" (Posner, 1990: ix). In the book, Cardozo describes how judges' decisions are informed by both the law and extralegal factors such as societal conditions, which was a radical assertion during that period. He later published several other books, including *The Growth of the Law* (1924), *The Paradoxes of Legal Science* (1928), and *Law Is Justice* (1938). Some legal scholars consider his "rare insight into and eloquent statement of the moral values in the law" the most significant aspects of Judge Cardozo's contributions to legal literature (Hall, 1947: v).

In addition to his work as judge and scholar, Cardozo served on the board of the American Jewish Committee and was cofounder and vice-president of the American Law Institute. Although he never married and never had any children, Cardozo lived with his older sister Nell until her death in 1929. In his honor, numerous law schools have been named after him. Cardozo died on July 9, 1938, and is buried in Beth Olom Cemetery (also known as Congregation Shearith Israel Cemetery) in Brooklyn, New York.

Taneisha N. Means

See also: Sotomayor, Sonia Maria (1954–)

Further Reading

Cardozo, Benjamin Nathan. 1921. *The Nature of the Judicial Process.* New Haven, CT: Yale University Press.

Hall, Margaret E., ed. 1947. *Selected Writings of Benjamin Nathan Cardozo.* New Haven, CT: Yale University Press.

Kaufman, Andrew L. 1998. *Cardozo.* Cambridge, MA: Harvard University Press.

Kaufman, Andrew L. 2012. "Benjamin Cardozo and His Law Clerks." In Todd C. Peppers and Artemus Ward, eds. *In Chambers: Stories of Supreme Court Law Clerks and Their Justices.* Charlottesville: University of Virginia Press.

Levy, Beryl H. 2000. *Cardozo and Frontiers of Legal Thinking: With Selected Opinions.* Washington, D.C.: Beard Books.

Lewis, Neil A. 2009. "Was a Hispanic [Justice] on the Court in the '30s?" *New York Times,* May 26. https://www.nytimes.com/2009/05/27/us/27hispanic.html.

Polenberg, Richard. 1997. *The World of Benjamin Cardozo: Personal Values and the Judicial Process.* Cambridge, MA: Harvard University Press.

Pollard, Joseph P. 1970. *Mr. Justice Cardozo: A Liberal Mind in Action.* Westport, CT: Greenwood Press.

Posner, Richard A. 1993. *Cardozo: A Study in Reputation.* Chicago: University of Chicago Press.

Cartagena, Juan

1956–

Juan Cartagena is a civil rights and constitutional law attorney who was admitted to the New Jersey bar in 1981. Prior to joining LatinoJustice PRLDEF, he had been general counsel and vice-president for advocacy at the Community Service Society of New York, where he led the Mass Imprisonment & Reentry Initiative. One of his major accomplishments is his work on a national level with the Voting Rights Act, the National Voter Registration Act, and the Help America Vote Act, which led to invitations in 2005 to 2006 to testify before the U.S. House and Senate on the reauthorization of the Voting Rights Act and its effects on Latino communities in New York and New Jersey.

A New Jersey native of Puerto Rican descent, since 2011 Cartagena has been the president and general counsel of LatinoJustice, the former Puerto Rican Legal Defense and Education Fund. When he was appointed, he stated that,

> Our nation's largest minority group continues to face challenges that impede its ability to be accepted as equal partners in American society. Employing legal intervention strategies to ensure equal treatment under law and eliminating unfair stereotypes of the Latino community are the hallmarks of progressive lawyering. LatinoJustice PRLDEF has been doing just that for years and I'm excited and humbled to rejoin those efforts.

Cartagena litigated civil rights cases of Latinx and African American communities pertaining to employment, language, voting, public education financing, the environment, housing, and access to public health. In addition to his litigation experience, he is very active in effectuating social change within other branches of government. For example, in 2011, Cartagena participated with the

U.S. Department of Equal Employment Opportunity in examining arrest and conviction records as a hiring barrier to employment. He has also assisted state governments, such as when he was appointed by New York governor David Paterson to the Task Force on Transforming New York State's Juvenile Justice System and by New Jersey governor Jon Corzine to the Blue Ribbon Advisory Panel on Immigrant Policy.

Cartagena authored a number of articles regarding civil rights and constitutional laws. He writes about poor and marginalized communities—especially Puerto Rican and Latinx communities, as well as criminal justice and mass incarceration, voting and redistricting, and language rights. He is a lecturer in the Department of Arts and Sciences at Rutgers University in New Brunswick, where he teaches a senior seminar in Latino and Caribbean studies. He also writes a Spanish column for *El Diario NY* newspaper titled "Juan Cartagena Opina."

Born in Jersey City, New Jersey, Cartagena is a graduate of Dartmouth College and Columbia University School of Law. A former municipal court judge in Hoboken, New Jersey, he has also served as general counsel to the Hispanic Bar Association of New Jersey. He worked for the Commonwealth of Puerto Rico's Department of Puerto Rican Community Affairs in the United States, serving as its legal director from 1990 to 1991. He is married to Aramis Ayala and has two daughters.

Maria M. Pabón

See also: LatinoJustice PRLDEF

Further Reading

Cartagena, Juan. 2006. "Time to Walk the Walk: Vieques and Civil Disobedience in New York with Vicente 'Panama' Alba." *Centro Journal* 18, no. 1: 78–89.

Cartagena, Juan. 2007. "Latino/a Rights and Justice in the United States: Perspectives and Approaches." Review of "Latino/a Rights and Justice in the United States: Perspectives and Approaches" by José Luis Morín. *Centro Journal* 19, no. 1: 406–09.

Cartagena, Juan. 2016. "Will We Allow Trump to Undo Policing and Criminal Justice Reforms?" *New York Amsterdam News*, December 15. http://amsterdamnews.com/news/2016/dec/15/urban-agenda-sample-headline/

LatinoJustice. n.d. "President and General Counsel Juan Cartagena." https://latinojustice.org/about/staff/juan_cartagena.

New Jersey Hispanic Research and Information Center. n.d. "Juan Cartagena, Esq. President and General Counsel LatinoJusticePRLDEF." http://www.npl.org/Pages/Collections/njhric/Cartagena.html.

Castro, Julián

(1974–)

A Democratic politician, Julián Castro served as the U.S. secretary of Housing and Urban Development (HUD) under President Barack Obama from 2014 to 2017. Previously, Castro served as the mayor of San Antonio, Texas, from 2009 to 2014. He also was the youngest city councilman elected to serve in the history of San Antonio. Castro is married to Erica Lira and has two children.

On September 16, 1974, he was born to Jessie Guzman and Maria "Rosie" Castro in San Antonio, Texas. Castro is one minute older than his identical twin brother, Joaquín Castro, who currently serves in the House of Representatives for the San Antonio area in Texas's 20th congressional district (Kroll, 2015). Castro often credits his family, especially his mother, with sparking an early interest in politics. She was a Chicana activist who was defeated in her run for San Antonio City Council in 1971. However, Rosie Castro remained active in Latino politics and played a central role in the founding of La Raza Unida, a Chicano political party. Julián Castro attended Thomas Jefferson High School in San Antonio and then received undergraduate degrees in political science and communication from Stanford University. During his time at Stanford, Castro served as an intern for President Bill Clinton. Following his graduation, he studied law at Harvard University, where he graduated in 2000. He and his brother Joaquín attended the same schools throughout their life.

Immediately following law school, Castro began his political career in 2001 as the youngest city councilman to serve in San Antonio history. He was 26 at the time. The district he represented was composed of 115,000 residents and was 70 percent Hispanic (Milanese, 2001). Castro then ran for mayor of San Antonio in 2005, but was defeated. After a brief return to law following this defeat, Castro ran again for mayor in 2009 and was successful, earning 56 percent of the vote (Bexar County, 2005, 2009). He prioritized economic development, education, and downtown revitalization as major policy concerns during his tenure as mayor. In 2012, Castro gained mainstream political recognition for delivering a keynote address at the Democratic National Convention—becoming the first Latino to do so (Henderson, 2012).

In May 2014, Castro was selected by President Barack Obama to be the secretary of Housing and Urban Development. Castro accepted the position and subsequently resigned his position as mayor of San Antonio. He replaced Shaun Donovan at the agency. The mission of the department is "to create strong, sustainable, inclusive communities and quality affordable homes for all" (U.S. Department of HUD, 2018). During his tenure as secretary, Castro emphasized the importance of reducing veteran homelessness, connecting low-income Americans in public housing to broadband, and ensuring fair and equal opportunity in the housing market without discrimination (Kimura, 2017). One of Castro's major accomplishments during his time as secretary of Housing and Urban Development was the establishment of the HUD rule entitled "Affirmatively Furthering Fair Housing" (AFFR). AFFR sought to ensure that cities that receive federal housing funds actively screen for racial bias and other forms of discrimination. Additionally, cities were mandated to set goals to promote fair housing.

Castro continues to be viewed by many as a rising star within the Democratic Party. During the 2016 presidential election, he fervently campaigned for Democratic nominee Hillary Clinton and was seriously considered as a vice-presidential nominee by Clinton before she eventually selected Virginia senator Tim Kaine. Castro has expressed interest in running for president in 2020 and has been a vocal critic of the Trump administration.

Ryan Mundy

See also: La Raza Unida Party (LRU); Obama, Barack (1961–) and Latinos

Further Reading

Badger, Emily. 2015. "Obama Administration to Unveil Major New Rules Targeting Segregation Across U.S." *Washington Post,* July 8. https://www.washingtonpost.com/news/wonk/wp/2015/07/08/obama-administration-to-unveil-major-new-rules-targeting-segregation-across-u-s/?utm_term=.1d9af1445050.

Bexar County. 2005. "Past Election Reports." https://www.bexar.org/Archive.aspx?AMID=65.

Bexar County. 2009. "Past Election Reports." https://www.bexar.org/Archive.aspx?AMID=65.

Castro, Julián. n.d. "About Julián Castro." http://www.mayorcastro.com/bio.

Fernbach, Erika. 2013. *Rosie Castro: Trailblazer.* Biographies that Inspire. CreateSpace Independent Publishing Platform.

Griffin, Keri. 2005. "Interview with Julian Castro." *University of Texas at San Antonio,* November 9. http://digital.utsa.edu/cdm/ref/collection/p15125coll4/id/2016.

Henderson, Nia-Malika. 2012. "Latino Mayor to Keynote DNC Convention." *Washington Post*, July 31. https://www.washingtonpost.com/politics/latino-mayor-to-keynote-dnc-convention/2012/07/31/gJQA3fpqNX_story.html?utm_term=.1501bad2396c.

Kimura, Donna. 2017. "Castro Reflects on His Time at HUD." *Affordable Housing Finance,* January 17. http://www.housingfinance.com/policy-legislation/castro-reflects-on-his-time-at-hud_o.

Kroll, Andy. 2015. "The Power of Two: The Rise of the Castro Brothers." *The Atlantic*, January 23. https://www.theatlantic.com/politics/archive/2015/01/the-power-of-two-inside-the-rise-of-the-castro-brothers/440034.

Milanese, Marisa. 2001. "Spotlight: Julian Castro '96: 'Man on a Fast Track.'" *Stanford Alumni*, September/October. https://alumni.stanford.edu/get/page/magazine/article/?article_id=39260.

U.S. Dept. of Housing and Urban Development. 2018. https://www.hud.gov/about/mission.

Castro, Raúl Héctor

(1916–2015)

Raúl Castro was the first Mexican-born American to be elected governor of Arizona; he served as the state's 14th governor from 1975 to 1977. He was also ambassador to Argentina under President Jimmy Carter (1977–1980).

Castro was born in Cananea, Sonora, Mexico, on June 12, 1916. In the 1920s, the Castro family moved to Pirtleville, Arizona, a mining town near the U.S.–Mexico border. Being of Mexican descent, Castro experienced overt discrimination while growing up and maintained that many of these experiences shaped much of his political career. For instance, Castro was a miner when he was a teenager and would recount that the showers were segregated for white and Mexican workers. He also remembered that the public pool at the local YMCA could only be used by Mexican Americans on the day that it would later be cleaned. He also recounted that the schools he attended were inferior to those of Anglo students.

Castro graduated from high school and secured an athletic scholarship to the Arizona State Teachers College (now known as Northern Arizona University). During one of his summers in college, he returned home and worked in the smelter plants to help pay for school. Noticing that there was no labor union, Castro rallied his coworkers, later persuading a professional union organizer from Jerome to help establish a union. The Mine Mill Smelter Workers of America became the first smelter laborers' union, securing a contract with Phelps Dodge a year or so later in 1937.

By 1939, Castro had graduated from the Arizona State Teachers College with a Bachelor of Arts degree. Finding a teaching job proved impossible because Mexicans Americans were simply not hired as educators. He did, however, have success with boxing and laboring in agricultural fields. After several years Castro returned to Douglas, Arizona, where he was eventually hired at the American consulate in nearby Agua Prieta, Sonora, Mexico, for the U.S. State Department. For five years he worked on diplomatic issues between Mexico and the United States. He eventually moved to Tucson, Arizona, and secured a job teaching Spanish while attending the University of Arizona School of Law. Graduating in 1949, he was eventually elected a Pima County attorney and then Pima County Superior Court judge.

President Lyndon B. Johnson nominated Castro to be ambassador to El Salvador in 1964, which was later confirmed by the Senate. Later he was appointed by President Johnson ambassador to Bolivia in 1968. In the 1970s, he was a pivotal player, arranging a meeting between the presidents of five Central American countries. In the 1970s, Castro announced his campaign for governor of Arizona. He ran on a platform of pollution control, drug abuse prevention, and improved business and cultural relations between the United States and Mexico. He won the Democratic primary but lost the gubernatorial race to the incumbent governor by a narrow margin of 1.8 percent. He ran again in 1974, this time gaining support from the Native American community. Castro became the first and only Latino governor of Arizona in 1974. He later accepted President Jimmy Carter's offer to be ambassador to Argentina. In 1980, he stepped down as ambassador and returned to Phoenix to practice law. He died in 2015 at the age of 98.

Lisa Magaña

See also: Martinez, Susana (1959–); Richardson, William "Bill" (1947–)

Further Reading
August, J. L., & R. H. Castro. 2009. *Adversity Is My Angel: The Life and Career of Raúl H. Castro.* College Station: Texas A&M University Press.

Catholicism and Latino/a Politics

The majority of Latinos in the United States—55 percent—identify as Catholic (Funk and Martinez, 2014), in spite of increasingly rapid rates of conversion to other churches, and constitute more than 40 percent of the American Catholic population (CARA, 2014). Latino Catholics are not culturally cohesive: as a group they include both immigrant and established populations from a number of different countries with varying degrees of educational and economic success. Latino patterns in ideological and party affiliation do not conform to traditional expectations for U.S. voters, potentially as a result of their religious affiliation. The impact of Catholic devotion on Latino political preference and behavior is difficult to isolate because of the cultural aspect of Catholicism, a factor unaccounted for in the vast majority of studies on Catholicism and politics that traditionally only reference Anglo voters.

The mutually constitutive nature of Latino culture with Catholicism is witnessed by the (at least nominal) Catholic affiliation of the majority of all Latino countries. Catholicism has also been found to structure immigrant subcultures and aid in the maintenance of Latino culture, beliefs, and traditions. This results in a societal transference of Catholic values, but Catholic values that contain a different moral hierarchy from those that have developed in the United States. As such, Latinos demonstrate political preferences and priorities that diverge from the norm in the United States. Latinos are generally described as morally conservative but socially liberal. Their anti-abortion position is often cited as an opening for the Republican Party to woo Latino voters, but the Republican anti-immigration platform, combined with the Catholic Church's long history of immigrant advocacy, effectively retain Latinos as Democratic voters. The cultural component of Catholicism also negates the impact of devotion on political outcomes; the policy preferences of Latino Catholics who attend Mass weekly differ little from those of Latinos who never attend Mass at all. This challenges researchers' ability to effectively measure the influence of religion on Latino political preferences because the traditional political science models are predicated on the belief that increased religiosity or devotion, rather than culture itself, is what triggers religious political values.

This is not the case for Latinos, whose policy preferences are most clearly predicted by contemporary Catholic theology. Catholic social justice teaching (CSJT) is a set of principles based on a series of papal encyclicals that address how Catholic doctrine should be applied to contemporary society. Latino Catholic policy preferences (support for welfare and immigrant rights, opposition to abortion and same-sex marriage) clearly fall in line with CSJT. Vatican II also produced clear, though innovative, instructions for how Catholics should integrate faith and social action. Latin American leaders developed a specific plan ("see–judge–act") in response to Vatican II that emphasized a deductive rather than inductive approach to pastoral leadership. This philosophy is also evident in the expressed Catholicism of Latinos in the United States and encourages a more inclusive pastoral as well as political perspective that defies traditional U.S. political paradigms. These unique interactions between Catholicism, culture, and politics will hopefully become more clear as the Latino Catholic population continues to grow, both numerically and as a proportion of the American Catholic population.

Kiku E. Huckle

See also: Pope Francis (1936–) and Latinos; Religion and Latina/o Politics

Further Reading

Center for Applied Research in the Apostolate (CARA). 2014. "Fact Sheet: Hispanic Catholics in the U.S." Georgetown University.

DeSipio, Louis. 1996. *Counting on the Latino Vote.* Charlottesville: University Press of Virginia.

Funk, Cary, & Jessica Martinez. 2014. "Fewer Hispanics Are Catholic, So How Can More Catholics Be Hispanic?" *Pew Research Center*, May 7. http://www.pewresearch.org

/fact-tank/2014/05/07/fewer-hispanics-are-catholic-so-how-can-more-catholics-be-hispanic/.

Jones-Correa, Michael, & David Leal. 2001. "Political Participation: Does Religion Matter?" *Political Research Quarterly* 54, no. 4: 751–70.

Kelly, Nathan, & Jana Morgan. 2008. "Religious Traditionalism and Latino Politics in the United States." *American Politics Research* 36, no. 2: 236–63.

Matovina, Timothy. 2011. *Latino Catholicism: Transformation in America's Largest Church.* Princeton, NJ: Princeton University Press.

Cavazos, Jr., Dr. Lauro "Fred"

(1927–)

A Democratic educator and politician from Texas, Lauro Cavazos is the first Hispanic to serve in the U.S. cabinet. He was the fourth U.S. secretary of education, serving from 1988 to 1990 under Presidents Ronald Reagan and George H. W. Bush. He is also the former president of Texas Tech University, serving from 1980 to 1988. He is married to Peggy Murdock, with whom he has had 10 children.

Lauro Cavazos, Jr., was born in 1927 to Lauro Faustino Cavazos, Sr., and Tomasa Alvarez Quintanilla on King Ranch, located in south Texas. After graduating from high school, he enrolled in the U.S. Army in 1944. After his time in the military he earned his Bachelor of Arts and Master of Arts in zoology from Texas

Lauro Fred Cavazos, Jr., served as U.S. secretary of education (1988–1990), and was the first Hispanic to serve in the U.S. cabinet. Here he holds a press briefing at the White House, 1990. (Diana Walker//Time Life Pictures/Getty Images)

Tech University in 1949 and 1951, respectively. Three years later in 1954, he earned his doctoral degree in physiology from Iowa State University. For the next 26 years, from 1954 to 1980, he taught at the Medical College of Virginia and then served as both professor and dean of the Tufts School of Medicine in Boston, Massachusetts. During his tenure as a medical professor Cavazos also served as a consultant to the World Health Organization on national and international health issues, and through his involvement was awarded the Outstanding Leadership Award in the field of education from President Ronald Reagan (American President, 2005). In 1980 he returned to Texas Tech University as its president and became the university's first alumnus to hold that position, and the university became the largest American school to be overseen by a Hispanic.

On August 9, 1988, President Ronald Reagan announced his intention to nominate Cavazos to be the fourth secretary of education and succeed William J. Bennett (American Presidency Project, 1988). One month later, on September 20, 1988, Cavazos was sworn in to the office in the East Room at the White House (TAPP, 1988). During his two years in office Cavazos

> concentrated largely on reforming American [e]ducation by raising the expectations of students, teachers, and parents. He targeted federal resources to improve opportunities for those most in need and initiated special programs to combat drug and alcohol use. As a strong advocate of parental involvement in education, he provided leadership to encourage parental and community participation in education reform. (TAPP)

One of those resources aimed at helping parental involvement in the United States was the introduction of the book *Growing Up Drug Free: A Parent's Guide to Prevention,* written by the U.S. Department of Justice Drug Enforcement Administration and the U.S. Department of Education (TAPP, 1990). Other achievements of Cavazos during his term included assembling the Task Force on Hispanic Education, organizing a plan to combat loan defaults, calling for a national study of the problems plaguing Native American students, and advising President George H. W. Bush to order an Advisory Panel on Hispanic Education (Education Week, n.d.).

Cavazos ended his term in office on December 12, 1990, resigning as secretary of education and was preceded by the acting secretary of education Ted Sanders, chancellor for Illinois University (American Presidency Project, 1990). After Cavazos resigned, he returned to Tufts School of Medicine, where he continued to be involved with education (Education Week, n.d.).

In honor of his legacy the Texas Tech Alumni Association established the Lauro F. Cavazos Award in 1987, awarded to those who have "made a positive impact on the university through their generosity, professional accomplishments and acts of service" (Texas Tech Alumni Association, n.d.).

José E. Mendoza Vazquez

See also: Education and Latinos

Further Reading

The American Presidency Project. 1988. "Ronald Reagan: Remarks Announcing the Resignation of William J. Bennett as Secretary of Education and the Nomination of Lauro F. Cavazos." *The American Presidency Project*, August 9. http://www.presidency.ucsb.edu/ws/index.php?pid=36230&st=Cavazos&st1=education.

The American Presidency Project. 1988. "Ronald Reagan: Remarks at the Swearing-in Ceremony for Lauro F. Cavazos as Secretary of Education." *The American Presidency Project,* September 20. http://www.presidency.ucsb.edu/ws/index.php?pid =34867&st=Cavazos&st1=education.

The American Presidency Project. 1990. "George Bush: Remarks Announcing the Publication of 'Growing Up Drug Free: A Parent's Guide to Prevention." *The American Presidency Project*, February 26. http://www.presidency.ucsb.edu/ws/index.php?pid =18190&st=cavazos&st1=book.

"Issues A-Z: Lauro F. Cavazos, Fourth U.S. Education Secretary: Biography and Achievements." *Education Week*, August 18. http://www.edweek.org/ew/issues/secretary -of-education/lauro-f-cavazos.html.

"Lauro Fred Cavazos." 2017. *Prabook.com*. https://www.prabook.com/web/lauro.cavazos /326269.

"Lauro F. Cavazos, Jr. (1989–1991)." *University of Virginia, Miller Center.* https:// millercenter.org/president/essays/cavazos-1989-secretary-of-education.

"Lauro F. Cavazos Papers. 1943–1991." Southwest Collection/Special Collections Library. *Texas Tech University*. https://legacy.lib.utexas.edu/taro/ttusw/00035/tsw-00035 .html.

"Secretary of Education: Lauro F. Cavazos (1988–1989)." 2005. *American President*, January 9. http://www.americanpresident.org/history/ronaldreagan/cabinet/secretary ofeducation/laurocavazos/h–index.shtml.

Texas Tech Alumni Association. n.d. "Lauro F. Cavazos Award." http://www.texastech alumni.org/s/1422/alumni/index.aspx?sid=1422&gid=1&pgid=2035.

Central American Migration

Historically, analyses on Latinos in the United States have been limited to Mexican Americans, Puerto Ricans, and Cuban Americans because these were the largest Latino country-of-origin groups in the country. However, Latino communities have experienced significant diversity and changing demographics in recent years. Hispanics of Mexican, Puerto Rican, and Cuban origin or descent remain the nation's three largest Hispanic-country-of-origin groups, according to the 2010 U.S. Census. However, the next four Hispanic subgroups grew faster during the decade. Hispanics of Salvadoran origin, the fourth-largest Hispanic-country-of-origin group, grew by 152 percent since 2000. The Dominican population grew by 85 percent, the Guatemalan population by 180 percent, and the Colombian population by 93 percent.

Although Central American migration to the United States is not a new phenomenon, over time, distinct circumstances have led to the continued migration of Central Americans to the United States. For example, in 2015, Central American migrants represented 8 percent of the 43.3 million immigrants in the United States. Of the approximately 3.4 million Central Americans residing in the United States, 85 percent are from what is referred to as the "Northern Triangle"—El Salvador, Guatemala, and Honduras.

During the 19th century through World War II, Central America was incorporated into the world economy, specifically via one of its primary agricultural exports: coffee. Capitalist penetration into the region affected migration by creating cyclical migration patterns within countries in Central America as workers engaged in seasonal migration tied to the harvest of agricultural goods. As the United States became more involved in Central America, especially during the late 19th century, new patterns of international migration occurred. Banana plantations and the building of the Panama Canal brought Jamaican and other Caribbean workers into the region. Other development projects also led to groups such as Chinese workers settling in Central America. At the same time new emigration patterns emerged, such as Hondurans migrating to New Orleans as a consequence of the trading relationships of powerful fruit companies like the United Fruit Company. Yet, in essence, migration to the United States from Central America was fairly limited prior to the mid-1960s. In fact, as Hamilton and Chinchilla note, in places like California, now a major hub for Central American migration, "Central American immigrants came disproportionately from the upper educational and occupational segments of the population. . . . Most Central American migrants who arrived in the United States before 1975 presumably came for economic reasons" (1991: 94). It was not until the latter half of the 1970s that Central Americans began arriving in mass numbers in the United States desperately seeking to escape the rising violence, repression, and eventually full-scale civil wars that consumed El Salvador, Nicaragua, and Guatemala.

The civil conflicts that took place in Guatemala, Nicaragua, and El Salvador were devastating. Over 250,000 people were killed in the conflicts; over 1 million were internally displaced. Others chose to leave their countries, seeking refuge in neighboring Honduras or Costa Rica, choosing either to attempt to live as undocumented migrants in these countries or in United Nations–sponsored refugee camps. Others made the difficult decision to travel north to Mexico, the United States, or Canada. Over 2 million Central Americans eventually settled in North America (Hamilton and Chinchilla, 1991).

It was no secret that the United States backed Central American governments that engaged in violence against their own people. In fact, U.S. complicity in the Central American civil wars were the primary factor in the rise of a number of social movements both in Central America and among the Central American diaspora in the United States. Chief among those movements was the Central American Peace and Solidarity Movement, which tirelessly contested the Reagan administration's foreign policy toward Central America. Yet as these movements struggled to secure the rights of refugees fleeing the wars, the U.S. government maintained immigration policies that classified these refugees as economic migrants, rather than individuals escaping violent conflict, thus classifying them as "illegal aliens" subject to deportation and removal, rather than the protection afforded to refugees of war.

In the mid-1990s, as the civil conflicts in Guatemala, Nicaragua, and El Salvador drew to a close via peace treaties, the road toward restoring societies that had been trapped in violence, in the case of Guatemala for over 35 years, would be long and arduous. This process was compounded by the immigration policies of the United States, which continued to reject Central American migrants. In 1996, President Bill Clinton passed the Illegal Immigration Reform and Immigrant Responsibility Act. Among other things, this act enforced time limits on the number of years that undocumented immigrants would have to wait, once deported, to be able to re-enter the country. However, one particular aspect of this act would end up having long-standing and devastating effects on Central American countries.

One of the principal provisions of this bill was the deportation of "criminal aliens," those in jail or prison for felonies and nonviolent offenses, such as drug charges, back to their countries of origin. This led to the deportation of significant numbers of gang members back to Central America, some of which were brought to the United States as children during the war period. Central American countries that were emerging from civil war were completely unprepared to deal with the large-scale arrival of gang members, many of whom were rivals. Many of the young men who were deported back to Central America reconnected with their gangs once there, and once released back into society, the gang crisis erupted in Central America in uncontrollable proportions. Much of the violence currently facing Central American countries can be attributed to this irresponsible deportation of masses of young men to Central American systems that were underprepared, if prepared at all, to handle their arrival and subsequent reintegration into society.

From the mid-1990s forward, immigration to the United States was driven by the lack of economic opportunities and the continued violence that ensued in the Central American postwar context. In addition, another factor motivating migration from Central America to the United States was family reunification as families that had been divided by the wars sought to reunite.

Violence in Central America has not subsided. In fact, Northern Triangle countries have seen a marked increase in violence. Both Honduras and El Salvador have been classified by several government agencies and think tanks as the deadliest countries outside of a war zone due to their extremely high murder rates. Extra-legal groups and gangs, such as MS-13 and 18th Street, control large swaths of these countries with no apparent remedy in sight. The political instability and corruption of governments and the legitimization of antidemocratic practices such as the 2009 U.S.-backed coup of Manuel Zelaya in Honduras have only exacerbated issues in the region. It is this climate of constant insecurity and instability, coupled with limited economic opportunities, that continues to push migrants north.

In the spring and summer of 2014, record high levels of Central American unaccompanied minors (UACs) and families arrived at U.S. southern borders. Although there was a slight downturn in arrivals in 2015, in 2016 alone, U.S. Customs and Border Protection intercepted approximately 49,000 UACs and more than 70,000 family units from the Northern Triangle (Migration Policy Institute, 2017). Under the Trump administration, the U.S. political climate has become increasingly hostile and draconian toward undocumented Latin American migrants, which has led to a drop in Border Patrol apprehensions along the border (Customs and Border Protection, 2017); however, Central American migration has not been halted. The problems plaguing Central America have not disappeared; political instability, poor socioeconomic conditions, and widespread gang violence continue to drive outgoing migration.

Although the Trump administration has maintained a hardline stance on immigration, the real effects of a Trump-led increase in border enforcement have yet to be seen. As enforcement increases, one must question whether migrants will continue at previous rates to move north, and whether or not migrants will be forced into more dangerous terrain in an attempt to enter the United States. Yet the real question remains: Where should these migrants go? Caught between the xenophobia and discrimination present in the United States and Mexico, and the crises overwhelming their home countries, many ask where should migrants go for safety and security?

Linda Alvarez

See also: Asylum Seekers; Central American Peace and Solidarity Movement (CAPSM); Immigration as a Policy Issue; National Day Laborer Organizing Network (NDLON); National Security State and Latinos; Salvadoran Humanitarian Aid, Relief and Education Foundation (S.H.A.R.E.); Solis, Hilda (1957–); Trafficking, Issues of

Further Reading

Customs and Border Protection. 2017. "Southwest Border Migration." https://www.cbp.gov/newsroom/stats/sw-border-migration.

García, María Cristina. 2006. *Seeking Refuge: Central American Migration to Mexico, the United States, and Canada.* Berkeley and Los Angeles: University of California Press.

Hamilton, Norma, & Norma S. Chinchilla. 1991. "Central American Migration: A Framework for Analysis." *Latin American Research Review* 26, no. 1: 75–110.

Martínez, Óscar. 2013. *The Beast: Riding the Rails and Dodging Narcos on the Migrant Trail.* London: Verso.

Migration Policy Institute. 2017. https://www.migrationpolicy.org/research/strengthening-mexicos-protection-central-american-unaccompanied-minors-transit.

Central American Peace and Solidarity Movement (CAPSM)

The Central American Peace and Solidarity Movement (CAPSM) was a transnational movement formed in the 1970s and 1980s by Central American migrants and progressive organizations in the United States to halt the Reagan administration's foreign policy of low-intensity warfare in Central America. CAPSM mobilized to organize the Central American community and allies in the United States against the controversial, and at times illegal, foreign policy initiatives of the U.S. government. Although this movement has at times been conceptualized as a domestic U.S. movement, or a distant issue movement (DIM), initiated by North Americans who were appalled by the atrocities taking place in Central America (Nepstad, 2004; Smith, 1996), the CAPSM was an entirely transnational movement initiated by Central American immigrants, specifically revolutionaries, who fled the wars ravaging the region (Perla, 2008).

Upon their arrival in the United States revolutionary activists, primarily Salvadoran and Nicaraguan exiles, began organizing within their own communities to disseminate information and draw attention to the violent repression and economic injustice being carried out by Central American governments backed by the United States. Such revolutionaries were instrumental in launching the CAPSM.

Beginning in the 1970s in San Francisco, Nicaraguan exiles and migrants mobilized to protest against the rampant corruption of the Somoza regime. Marches and protests carried out by Nicaraguans captured the attention of Chicano activists who together formed El Comité Cívico pro Nicaragua en Los Estados Unidos (referred to as Comité Cívico; translation: the Pro-Nicaragua Civil Committee in the United States). In Nicaragua, a Sandinista unit had captured several of Somoza's top aides and had issued a communiqué to publish its demands, one of which called for the trading of Somoza's aides for Sandinista political prisoners. Working to support the Sandinistas in Nicaragua, the Comité Cívico had been charged with publishing and translating the Sandinistas' communiqué, as well as organizing a march to support the Sandinistas' demands. The Comité Cívico rose to action and published the communiqué in *La Gaceta Sandinista*, a newspaper publication, and organized a march in support of the Nicaraguan revolution. This was the first solidarity march in support of the Sandinistas and marked the beginning of the CAPSM (Perla, 2008). By drawing attention to the abuses of the Nicaraguan government and the United States' complicity in the Nicaraguan conflict, the Comité also succeeded in attracting the support of U.S. citizens. This led to the creation of the Non-Intervention in Nicaragua Committee, an organization that would help secure significant victories against the Somoza regime.

Simultaneously, Salvadoran migrants, also in San Francisco, were actively mobilizing solidarity groups to draw attention to the violence and human rights abuses taking place in El Salvador. By the mid-1970s, these migrants had formed El Comité de Salvadoreños Progresistas (Committee of Progressive Salvadorans), a student-led organization created as a response to the July 30, 1975, massacre of students at the National University of San Salvador. The Committee of Progressive Salvadorans successfully organized the first march in the United States aimed at exposing and denouncing U.S. support of the Salvadoran government's brutal human rights violations. Similar to the Comité Cívico, the Committee of Progressive Salvadorans also created a newspaper publication, *El Pulgarcito*, to disseminate information on the situation in El Salvador. By the late 1970s, the Committee had grown in number and was successful in launching several significant marches and protests, the most significant being the occupation of the Salvadoran consulate to expose the human rights violations of the Salvadoran government.

By the 1980s, Nicaraguans and Salvadorans were instrumental in founding solidarity organizations such as the National Network in Solidarity with the Nicaraguan People, the Committee in Solidarity with the People of El Salvador (CISPES), and the Salvadoran Humanitarian Aid, Relief and Education Foundation (S.H.A.R.E.), which coordinated campaigns against the United States' foreign policy toward Central America.

Through these initial CAPSM organizations, other significant solidarity groups emerged, such as the Sanctuary Movement, a primarily religious movement, that was organized to provide safety and sanctuary to Salvadoran refugees fleeing the war in an effort to assist in their settlement in the United States; Witness for Peace, whose members traveled to Nicaragua to serve as human shields in the conflict and to witness the ramifications of U.S.-sponsored terror against Nicaraguan communities; and The Pledge of Resistance, which organized approximately 80,000 U.S. citizens to pledge to protest or carry out acts of civil disobedience in event of "a major U.S. escalation in Central America" (Peace, 1981: 88).

Together these and other groups formed the broad umbrella of the CAPSM, which successfully launched a movement against the Regan administration's most contested foreign policy initiative. Ultimately, the CAPSM made significant strides in ending the conflicts in Central America, as well as securing the significant rights of Central Americans displaced by war in the United States.

Linda Alvarez

See also: Central American Resource Center (CARECEN); Salvadoran Humanitarian Aid, Relief and Education Foundation (S.H.A.R.E.)

Further Reading

Nepstad, Sharon Erickson. 2004. *Convictions of the Soul: Religion, Culture, and Agency in the Central America Solidarity Movement.* Oxford, UK: Oxford University Press.

Nepstad, Sharon E., & Christian Smith. 2001. "The Social Structure of Moral Outrage in Recruitment to the US-Central America Peace Movement." In Jeff Goodwin, James M. Jasper, and Francesca Polletta, eds. *Passionate Politics: Emotions and Social Movements.* Chicago: University of Chicago Press, pp. 158–74.

Peace, R. C. 1991. *A Just and Lasting Peace: The US Peace Movement from the Cold War to Desert Storm.* Ann Arbor: University of Michigan.

Perla, Hector, Jr. 2008. "Si Nicaragua venció, El Salvador vencerá: Central American Agency in the Creation of the US–Central American Peace and Solidarity Movement." *Latin American Research Review* 43, no. 2: 136–58.

Smith, C. 2010. *Resisting Reagan: The US-Central America Peace Movement.* Chicago: University of Chicago Press.

Central American Resource Center (CARECEN)

The Central American Resource Center (CARECEN) is a grassroots nonprofit organization that was established by Salvadoran refugees to assist Guatemalans, Nicaraguans, and Salvadoran refugees fleeing civil war during the 1980s and 1990s. It has since become the largest Central American organization in the United States, with offices in Houston, Los Angeles, New York, San Francisco, and Washington, D.C. Although it continues to provide important legal services to the immigrant community, CARECEN has adapted to the current local needs of the community it serves, engaging in advocacy work around immigration, education, health care, and workers' rights, while at the same time providing direct services and civic leadership training that seek to integrate immigrants economically, civically, and politically in the United States.

Washington, D.C., was the first city to establish a CARECEN center in 1981. Originally named the Central American Refugee Center, it started assisting Salvadorans who had left warn-torn El Salvador and were seeking refugee status in the United States. Los Angeles and New York CARECEN centers opened their doors in 1983, followed by Houston in 1985 and San Francisco in 1986. Established in key immigrant destination cities, CARECEN quickly began to service the immigrant community at large and expanded its services in order to better assist the growing population. In Washington, D.C., CARECEN was instrumental in the creation of La Clinica del Pueblo, a health clinic catering to the health needs of the growing immigrant community, as well playing a pivotal role in the founding of Casa de Maryland, a direct service organization that offered emergency clothing, food, and immigration assistance, as well as English instruction to new immigrants. More recently, CARECEN D.C. has been assisting immigrants with housing, employment, and consumer issues, all while continuing to provide low-cost legal service and advocating for just immigration laws at the local, state, and federal levels.

The Los Angeles CARECEN center changed its role from providing only legal services in the early 1990s, when the Salvadoran immigrant community that everyone expected would return home when the Salvadoran civil war ended decided to stay. In an interview for *La Opinión*, Martha Arevalo, the executive director of CARECEN in Los Angeles, stated that it was during this time that they expanded their services to assist all Latino immigrants and "started working not only on political asylum cases related to the war, but also on education reform, voter education, youth education, and in broader and more general problems" (Martinez Ortega, 2015). In 2004, CARECEN expanded its services into the Westlake neighborhood in the San Fernando Valley by opening a day labor center, where day laborers are trained, get service referrals, and are provided with opportunities to improve their economic standings.

With the recent announcement that the Temporary Protected Status (TPS)—a program that has provided quasi-legal status for some immigrants from El Salvador, Nicaragua, and Honduras for over two decades—will not be reauthorized after 2019, CARECEN is once again channeling its focus on immigration issues, mobilizing to assist the thousands of immigrants who will be applying for their last TPS renewal, providing immigration training for clients who might need to represent themselves in immigration court, and preparing to provide services to the children of TPS holders who might be separated from their parents.

CARECEN's ability to adapt its mission to the evolving needs of their respective community and its ability to mix social service with social justice work is the reason why it is the largest Central American organization in the country. Given the current immigrant debates, CARECEN's role in "changing unjust immigration policies, providing immigrant integration programs, delivering immigration legal services, and fostering community activism in immigration policy, education reform and workers' rights" (CARECEN, Los Angeles, n.d.) ensures that it will continue to play a vital role in the immigrant communities that it serves.

Yanira Rivas Pineda de Melendez

See also: Asylum Seekers; Central American Migration; Central American Peace and Solidarity Movement (CAPSM); *La Opinión*; Latino Political Power; Temporary Protected Status (TPS)

Further Reading

Berestein, Leslie Rojas. 2016. "Some Central American Asylum Seekers Learning to Represent Themselves in Court." *89.3 KPCC.* http://www.scpr.org/news/2016/07/19/62747/some-central-american-asylum-seekers-learning-to-r.

CARECEN. n.d. "About Us, History." http://carecendc.org/about/history

CARECEN, Los Angeles. n.d. http://www.carecen-la.org.

CARECEN, New York. n.d. http://www.carecenny.org.

CARECEN, San Francisco. n.d. https://carecensf.org.

Martínez Ortega, Araceli. 2015. "CARECEN: Por 32 años, un puerto seguro para los inmigrantes." *La Opinión.* https://laopinion.com/2015/05/20/carecen-por-32-anos-un-puerto-seguro-para-los-inmigrantes.

Melera, Yurina. 2015. "TPS: 25 25 años de protección pero sin camino a la legalización." *La Opinión.* https://laopinion.com/2015/12/14/tps-25-anos-de-proteccion-pero-sin-un-camino-a-la-legalizacion.

Taaffe, Lisa, & Robert Fisher. 1997. "Public Life in Gulfton: Multiple Publics and Models of Community Organization." *Journal of Community Practice* 4: 31–56.

Wick, Julia. 2018. "Salvadorans in L.A. Brace for Change." *City Lab.* https://www.citylab.com/equity/2018/01/salvadorans-in-la-brace-for-change/550586.

Chávez, César

(1927–1993)

César Chávez is considered one of the most influential public figures and civil rights leaders of the 20th century. His role as a labor activist and spokesman for farm workers' dignity and rights also makes Chávez one of the most notable Mexican Americans in U.S. history. Chávez is described as a community and political leader, spiritual mystic, labor activist, and advocate for social justice. He is often likened to Dr. Martin Luther King, Jr., and Mahatma Gandhi for his nonviolent campaign against California's largest agricultural growers in the 1960s, 1970s, and 1980s.

César Estrada Chávez was born on March 31, 1927, in Yuma, Arizona. His parents, Librado and Juana Chávez, emigrated from Chihuahua, Mexico, and owned

United Farm Workers union co-founder and leader César Chávez delivers a speech, July 1972. (National Archives)

a small ranch and general store. By the mid-1930s, the Great Depression and droughts devastated the family farm and business, forcing Chávez's family to move to California to survive. After settling in Delano, the Chávez family worked in agricultural fields in the San Joaquín Valley and migrated to harvest other crops throughout the year. Chávez saw thousands of Mexican, Mexican American, Anglo, black, and Filipino workers compete for work and meager wages to harvest crops. In some cases, the Chávez family and others walked off the fields in protest of low wages, poor working conditions, and abusive employers. These experiences profoundly shaped Chávez's role as a full-time labor organizer and community leader.

In 1943, Chávez met Helen Fabela and a year later joined the Navy. After the war, Chávez and Fabela married and settled in Delano, where Chávez worked the grape and cotton fields. By 1948, Chávez moved his family to San José, where he met Father Donald McDonnell, a farm labor activist who introduced him to Fred Ross, a Community Services Organization (CSO) organizer. In 1952, Ross invited Chávez to a CSO meeting and recruited him to help build CSO chapters. Under Ross's mentorship, Chávez learned the Saul Alinsky method of community organizing and helped register thousands of Mexican American voters, which increased their political awareness. By 1959 Chávez was an experienced organizer, community leader, and CSO director. He also met Dolores Huerta, who became a close friend and co-leader in the farmworker movement.

In 1962, Chávez and Huerta formed the National Farm Workers Association (NFWA) now known as the United Farm Workers (UFW). In 1965, the NFWA joined the Agricultural Workers Organizing Committee (AWOC), an AFL-CIO affiliate, in a strike against grape growers in the San Joaquín Valley. Chávez used nonviolent strategies that he learned from the works of Dr. Martin Luther King, Jr., Mahatma Gandhi, and St. Francis, such as boycotts, *perigrinaciónes* (penitent marches), fasts, and self-sacrifice to focus national attention on the plight of farm workers and garner support. For Chávez, fighting for farm workers' dignity, fair wages, and improved living and working conditions was more than fighting for a union; it was a social movement—one he called *El Movimiento* (the Movement) and *La Causa* (the Cause or struggle).

In 1968, Chávez captured the nation and gained widespread support for *La Causa* from youth, civil rights activists, religious leaders, and Robert Kennedy when he began a 25-day fast. By 1970 the grape boycott had spread throughout the Southwest, Midwest, and Europe, crippling the grape industry. The huge loss of profits compelled large growers such as Schenley, Giumarra, and Di Giorgio to sign union contracts with the UFW. Chávez continued his work to improve the lives and conditions for farmworkers until his death in 1993. Throughout his life, Chávez educated himself and others on organizing, leadership, civil rights, Catholic social teachings, and nonviolence. Ultimately, Chávez not only led one of the largest agricultural strikes in U.S. history, he also created a farm labor movement that raised public awareness about health, environmental, and civil rights issues that plagued farm workers and their families and communities. He is a national symbol of social justice, democracy, and civil rights for all Americans.

Maritza De La Trinidad

See also: Brown Power Movement/Chicano Civil Rights Movement; Community Service Organization (CSO); Delano Grape Strike (1965–1970); Huerta, Dolores (1930–); United Farm Workers (UFW)

Further Reading

Dalton, Frederick John. 2003. *The Moral Vision of César Chávez.* New York: Orbis Books.

Etulain, Richard W., ed. 2002. *Chávez: A Brief Biography with Documents.* The Bedford Series in History and Culture. Boston: Bedford/St. Martin's.

Ferriss, Susan, & Ricardo Sandoval. 1997. *The Fight in the Fields: César Chávez and the Farmworkers Movement.* New York: Harcourt Brace.

Ganz, Marshall. 2009. *Why David Sometimes Wins: Leadership, Organization, and Strategy in the California Farm Worker Movement.* Oxford: Oxford University Press.

García, Mario T., ed. 2007. *The Gospel of Chávez: My Faith in Action.* Lanham, MD: Sheed & Ward.

Griswold del Castillo, Richard, & Richard A. García. 1995. *Chávez: A Triumph of Spirit.* Norman: University of Oklahoma Press.

Mathiassen, Peter. 2000. *Sal si puedes: César Chávez and the New American Revolution.* With a Foreword by Illan Stavans and a Postscript by the Author. Berkeley: University of California Press.

Chavez-Thompson, Linda

(1944–)

A union leader and the grandchild of Mexican immigrants, Linda Chavez-Thompson went from picking cotton in a field and cleaning houses to becoming an influential labor leader. With over 48 years of activist experience, she was the first person of color elected to one of the American Federation of Labor–Congress of Industrial Organization's (AFL-CIO) highest offices, the then-newly created executive vice-president position, in 1995. After resigning from her post in 2007, Chavez-Thompson ran for lieutenant governor of Texas as the Democratic nominee in 2010. She was a member of the United Way of America board of trustees. In 2012, she stepped down as vice-chair of the Democratic National Convention (DNC).

Linda Chavez-Thompson was born on August 3, 1944, as one of eight children in Lubbock, Texas. Formerly named Lydia, Chavez changed it to Linda because one of her teachers claimed "Lydia" was difficult to pronounce. From a young age, she worked with her family as sharecroppers. Due to financial problems, Chavez-Thompson dropped out of high school to work full time. She would go on to marry Robert Thompson and work as a cleaning lady at the age of 19. In 1967, through her uncle's connections, she became a secretary at the Laborers' International Union in Lubbock. From there, she worked her way up as a union representative for Latino members and then worked at the American Federation of State, County and Municipal Employees Union (AFSCME) as the Austin Local international representative. She became the executive director of San Antonio Local 2399 in 1977, a responsibility that presented challenges including anti-union sentiment from Texas businesses and legislation banning government employees from forming unions. Despite these issues, she improved working conditions and saved jobs for thousands.

Chavez-Thompson has been widely recognized for these efforts and was elected the Labor Council for Latin American Advancement national vice-president in 1986 and vice-president of AFSCME in 1988. In 1995, she became the executive director of the AFSCME's Texas Council 42 and the first executive vice-president of the AFL-CIO and the first person of color to hold such a high position in the company. In her position, Chavez-Thompson promoted unionization through community engagement initiatives and partnerships with organizations such as the National Association for the Advancement of Colored People (NAACP), churches, and women's rights groups. She represented the AFL-CIO as a member of boards for the Congressional Hispanic Caucus Institute, Institute for Women's Policy Research, and National Interfaith Committee for Worker Justice.

She left her position in 2007 to pursue work in politics. In 2010 she ran as a Democrat against Republican incumbent David Dewhurst for lieutenant governor of Texas, focusing on education and jobs as her platform, but lost. The loss did not stop her from being a prominent advocate for workers. In 2011, she joined hundreds who were protesting the Grand Hyatt hotel chain for disregarding workers' rights. This support was especially important because of her role as a vice-chair of the DNC and the party's stance on this issue. At the protest, she took a stand against corporate interests by shouting that the Hyatt "thinks nothing of violating the law. [They] treat [their] employees in a way that is morally wrong" (Barajas, 2011). After holding the position for 15 years, Chavez-Thompson stepped down from the DNC in 2012.

Chavez-Thompson has received numerous accolades for her support of labor rights and the Latino community. In 2001, she received the National Mujer Award for her work as the executive vice-president of the AFL-CIO. She was also honored with an award from the American Association of People with Disabilities (AAPD) Leadership Gala in 2004 for her support for individuals with disabilities within the workers' rights movement.

Victoria Gonzalez and Marc Kirchner

See also: Congressional Hispanic Caucus Institute (CHCI); Moreno, Luisa (1907–1992)

Further Reading

Barajas, Michael. 2011. "Hyatt Protests Escalate with Hundreds on the Street and 11 Arrests." *San Antonio Current*, July 26. http://www.sacurrent.com/sanantonio/hyatt -protests-escalate-with-hundreds-on-the-street-and-11-arrests/Content?oid=2241985.

Gamboa, Suzanne. 2013. "Texas' Future as Swing State Could Be Tied to Latina State Senator's Political Plans." *NBC Latino*, November 22. http://nbclatino.com/2013/11/22 /texas-future-as-swing-state-could-be-tied-to-latina-state-senators-political-plans.

LaBalle, Candace. 2002. "Chavez-Thompson, Linda: 1944–: Labor Leader." In Ashyia N. Henderson, ed. *Contemporary Hispanic Biography.* Vol. 1. Detroit: Gale, pp. 47–49. *Gale Virtual Reference Library.* http://rlib.pace.edu/login?url=http://go.galegroup .com.rlib.pace.edu/ps/i.do?p=GVRL&sw=w&u=nysl_me_pace&v=2.1&it=r&id =GALE%7CCX3433700022&asid=ba1dafb21db863675c7516027e265b7c.

"Linda Chavez-Thompson." n.d. *AFL-CIO.* http://www.aflcio.org/index.php/About /Leadership/AFL-CIO-Top-Officers/AFL-CIO-Officers-Emeritus/Linda-Chavez -Thompson.

"Linda Chavez-Thompson Bio." 2010. *KVIA,* October 20. http://www.kvia.com/news/linda -chavez-thompson-bio/53130784.

Martin, Gary. 2012. "Longtime Labor Leader Stepping Down from Democratic Party."
  My San Antonio, September 6. http://www.mysanantonio.com/news/local_news
  /article/Longtime-labor-leader-stepping-down-from-3844627.php.

Nutter, Kathleen Banks, & Linda Chavez-Thompson. 2006. "Excerpts from the Voices of
  Feminism Oral History Project Interview with Linda Chavez-Thompson." *Meridi-
  ans: Feminism, Race, Transnationalism* no. 1: 191.

Taffet, David. 2010. "Lt. Governor Candidates Low Key on LGBT Issues." *DallasVoice
  .com,* September 16. http://m.dallasvoice.com/lt-governor-candidates-key-lgbtissues
  -1044487.html.

"2001 Mujer Award Recipients." n.d. National Hispana Leadership Institute. http://www
  .nhli.org/2001mujer_recipients.htm.

Chicano Civil Rights Movement. *See* Brown Power Movement/Chicano Civil Rights Movement

Chicano Moratorium

(1970)

The Chicano Moratorium, which occurred in East Los Angeles on August 29, 1970, became one of the most significant events regarding the escalating deaths among Chicanos during the Vietnam War. Indeed, it continues to be recognized annually. Some historical background information regarding the large gathering of Chicanas and Chicanos situates the significance of the Chicano Moratorium. The Vietnam conflict began as a military advisory role for the United States. It soon became evident that the conflict began to look more like an actual combative war situation. Indeed, Americans would be inundated each night through the national news of fallen Americans soldiers arriving home. Additionally, with the draft reinstated to ensure a steady supply of soldiers, Mexican American males had few economic job prospects, and military service was a common alternative. As a result, the death toll among Chicano soldiers was unusually higher than with other racial or ethnic groups. It became quite clear to the American public that the United States had committed itself to more than just a conflict in some far-away place in Southeast Asia. One of the criticisms of the Vietnam War was that most of the soldiers came from poor or working-class communities.

The Chicano Moratorium was organized by Chicana and Chicano activists to directly challenge the number of Chicano soldiers killed in Vietnam. Organized by groups such as the Brown Berets, the first National Chicano Moratorium demonstration occurred on December 1969. It attracted 2,000 concerned activists who felt the lives of Chicanos would be better served helping the Chicano community locally rather than in a foreign country. Antiwar activism among Chicanas and Chicanos further increased and eventually led to the Chicano Moratorium on August 29, 1970. The estimated number of participants ranged from 20,000 to 30,000. The march began in East Los Angeles and reached Laguna Park, where protesters listened to music and speeches from guests such as Rodolfo "Corky" Gonzales. Despite the high tensions between the local police force and the marchers, the gathering was peaceful. As the day wore on, a local liquor store robbery gave the sheriff's department an opportunity to enter the park to look for the suspects. Chicano activists were unable to deter the sheriff and deputies from entering the park, and the peaceful gathering soon turned hostile and violent. Although the park was filled with women and children, the sheriff's department did little to respect their rights. Using tear gas and their wooden batons, they entered the park and began hitting innocent bystanders.

Down the street from the park, *Los Angeles Times* reporter Ruben Salazar, who already had a combative relationship with L.A.'s police department, was sitting in the Silver Dollar Bar having a beer with two of his coworkers. Without any provocation, sheriff's officers looking for a gunman shot a 10-inch tear gas projectile into the room, striking Ruben Salazar in the head. Hours later Ruben Salazar's body was recovered. Despite evidence that shooting a tear gas projectile into a public bar was difficult to defend, none of the officers were convicted of killing Salazar.

The Chicano Moratorium would go down as one of the pivotal movements of the Chicano Movement. It would signify a turning point for Chicana and Chicano activists working toward a common goal: getting Chicanos to reconsider their support of the Vietnam War and calling for a re-evaluation of the loss of lives among Chicano GIs. Despite the many years since it occurred, the Chicano Moratorium continues to be a turning point toward the ending of the Vietnam War and is one of the most important events of the social activism of the 1960s.

Paul López

See also: Brown Berets; Gonzales, Rodolfo "Corky" (1928–2005); Salazar, Rubén (1928–1970)

Further Reading

Chavez, Ernesto. 2002. *"¡Mi Raza Primero!" (My People First): Nationalism, Identity, and Insurgency in the Chicano Movement in Los Angeles (1966–1978).* Berkeley: University of California Press.

Garcia, Mario T. 2015. *The Chicano Generation: Chicano Testimonios of the Movement.* Berkeley: University of California Press.

Rosales, Arturo. 1997. *Chicano! The History of the Mexican American Civil Rights Movement.* Hispanic Civil Rights Series. Houston: Arte Publico Press.

Cisneros, Henry G.

(1947–)

Henry G. Cisneros is a former mayor of San Antonio, Texas (1981–1989) and a former secretary of Housing and Urban Development (HUD) (1993–1997) under President Bill Clinton. He was only the second Latino mayor of a major U.S. city and the first Latino mayor of San Antonio since 1842. As mayor, Cisneros worked to rebuild the city's economic base and revitalized tourism in the area. Many speculated whether Henry Cisneros would become the first Mexican American U.S. senator or the first Mexican American governor of Texas. Urban revitalization became a hallmark of his time on the president's cabinet as well.

Cisneros was born into a political family. His maternal grandfather, José Romulo Munguia, was an immigrant fleeing the vicissitudes of the Mexican Revolution who immediately got involved in the politics of San Antonio. Whether his original intentions were to return to Mexico, as many Mexican Revolution political refugees did, once in San Antonio, Romulo established a print shop in the 1920s in the West Side barrio of San Antonio. His sons, Ruben and Romulo, continued that legacy through the print shop, which is still operating today. Cisneros's mother and his maternal grandmother continued the Munguia political tradition; both were active in civic affairs.

Cisneros graduated from Central Catholic High School and then entered Texas A&M University, where he was commander of the combined Texas A&M band—the first Mexican American to hold that position. He graduated from Texas A&M in 1968. In 1971, Cisneros became a White House Fellow. At age 21, Cisneros served as assistant director of the Model Cities Program in San Antonio. He did graduate work at Harvard and

Henry G. Cisneros served as mayor of San Antonio, Texas, from 1981–1989, and was the second Latino mayor of a major U.S. city. He was nominated to serve as U.S. secretary of Housing and Urban Development in 1992, and he held that office from 1993–1997. (U.S. Dept. of Housing and Urban Development)

MIT before earning a doctorate in metropolitan administration at George Washington University. While at George Washington University, Cisneros served as a White House intern in the Nixon administration, working for Elliot Richardson, the secretary of health, education, and welfare (HEW).

In 1974, Cisneros returned to San Antonio, where he aligned himself with the Good Government League (GGL), a nonpartisan group established by the economic elite of San Antonio to run slates of like-minded candidates in local elections. With GGL support, Cisneros won election to the San Antonio City Council in 1975. Just 27, Councilman Cisneros adopted various populist positions on labor, water, education, and housing issues, among others, endearing himself to the Mexican American community. When the city council split on the question of whether to accept an order by the Justice Department to devise an election plan to increase Mexican American access to office, Cisneros voted to accept the order (this was the swing vote). San Antonio thus moved to single-member districts in 1977.

Cisneros also supported economic development, which was the sole objective of the conservative GGL and its main constituent, the Greater Chamber of Commerce of San Antonio. By balancing these policy positions, Cisneros won the financial backing of the city's economic elite for his first run for mayor in 1981. He won the election with over 60 percent of the votes cast, becoming the first Mexican American mayor of San Antonio since Juan Seguin was alcalde (mayor) of San Antonio in the 1860s. Re-elected with over 90 percent of the vote in 1983, Cisneros served until 1989, when he declined to seek re-election. As mayor, Cisneros created a legacy of growth and expansion that was unmatched in the city's history. He was able to attract federal monies that allowed San Antonio to develop its downtown business district. His efforts brought investments to San Antonio like Sea World; he also convinced voters to support building the Alamo Dome, a city-financed sports arena.

Cisneros continued to take populist positions on issues that favored the poor and the working class. His business ties allowed him to establish an education partnership that paired the city with local colleges and universities, local businesses, and various community organizations. These partnerships provided financial aid for college for young people in San Antonio's poorest school districts.

With the election of Bill Clinton to the presidency in 1992, Cisneros accepted a position as Clinton's secretary of Housing and Urban Development. While at HUD, Cisneros took a more liberal position, likely because the more narrow focus of his department allowed him to do so. In 1995, Republican demands for an investigation into allegations that Cisneros had lied to the FBI during background checks arising from his appointment as HUD secretary led Attorney General Janet Reno to name an independent counsel to look into the matter. Cisneros was accused of being untruthful regarding payments that he had made to Linda Medlar, a former mistress. In December 1997, Cisneros was indicted on 18 counts of conspiracy, making false statements, and obstruction of justice. In 1999, Cisneros negotiated a plea agreement, which allowed him to plead guilty to a misdemeanor count of lying to the FBI and pay a fine of $10,000. He received no jail time or probation. President Clinton pardoned Cisneros in January 2001, just before leaving office. Cisneros then retired from political life and went on to another career in media and business.

Rodolfo Rosales

See also: Castro, Julián (1974–)

Further Reading

Cisneros, Henry G. 2009. *Twenty-First-Century Gateways: Immigrant Incorporation in Suburban America.* Washington, D.C.: Brookings Institution Press.

Munoz, C., & C. Henry. 1986. "Rainbow Coalitions in Four Big Cities: San Antonio, Denver, Chicago and Philadelphia." *PS: Political Science & Politics* 19, no. 3: 598–609.

Wolff, N. W., & H. Cisneros. 1997. *Mayor: An Inside View of San Antonio Politics, 1981–1995.* San Antonio: San Antonio Express-News.

Coalition for Humane Immigrant Rights of Los Angeles (CHIRLA)

The Coalition for Humane Immigrant Rights of Los Angles (CHIRLA) is a civil rights organization that was founded in 1986 to protect immigrant rights in the wake of the passage of the Immigration Reform and Control Act (IRCA). The organization is composed of individuals who seek to be agents of social change. Consequently, the organization seeks progressive social change by serving individuals, institutions, and coalitions in order to transform public opinion and change policies so they may achieve full human, civil, and labor rights. CHIRLA strives to be a multiethnic coalition of community organizations and individuals in order to foster a greater understanding of the issues affecting the immigrant community. Being that they are located in an area of Los Angeles that has served as an ethnic enclave for many Central Americans and Mexicans, much of the work that they do is with the Latinx community. However, as immigration continues to be a contentious issue with dire consequences of being jailed and deported, CHIRLA is being more intentional and reaching out to similar organizations who work with other immigrant communities of color.

For the immigrant community, the 1980s were tumultuous years socially and politically. The civil wars in Central America resulted in an increased number of refugee and asylum seekers. Thus, with the passage of IRCA the immigrant community in the United States became more alarmed, particularly because IRCA made it illegal to hire undocumented workers, and many feared that this would open the door to employee exploitation and abuse. Although the Catholic Church was serving as protective haven for some immigrants in cities such as Los Angeles, many immigrant activists felt that more formal organizations were needed in order to achieve any kind of protection for this vulnerable community. Consequently, CHIRLA was one of the organizations that was born in the wake of the immigration struggle that began in the 1980s. Furthermore, in the years after its formation, the issue of immigration and immigrant rights has not been resolved. This has resulted in the organization continuing to be at the forefront of protecting immigrants from discriminatory laws that came after the challenge with IRCA, laws such as Proposition 187 in 1994 and the Sensenbrenner Immigration Bill in 2006. Additionally, CHIRLA remains focused on working with California politicians to get sensible immigration reform passed that will not take advantage of those most vulnerable in society, as well as providing continued protection for the legally vulnerable immigrant community.

As part of their mission, the organization seeks to achieve a just society that is inclusive of immigrants. In their attempt to achieve this mission, the organization focuses on five general areas: civic engagement, community education, legal services, organizing, and policy and advocacy. They accomplish their work in these areas in a variety of ways. They conduct trainings for volunteers who are interested in helping people get registered to vote or learn about how all three levels of government work. They also hold workshops where community members can become informed about changes in immigration or social service laws and how the changes might affect them. They provide access to immigration attorneys and advice for no charge or small fees. Lastly, they work with local, state, and federal politicians in order to advocate for both worker and immigrant rights.

The general idea behind these five areas is to provide the immigrant community with education, community integration, and a means to participate politically. Under each of these five focal points CHIRLA's goal is to stay active and aware of political activity that will benefit the community they seek to assist. For example, under the civic engagement area, the organization hopes to help the voices of those who are low propensity, and new voters to be heard by helping to motivate them to become politically engaged. As a way to help immigrants integrate into their communities, CHIRLA provides community education so that there is an understanding of civil rights and human rights that everyone is afforded, regardless of their legal status. To ensure that low-income individuals who are encountering struggles with the legal system due to their immigration status have assistance, the organization provides low-cost immigration legal services. Under the last two focal areas of organizing and policy and advocacy, CHIRLA is looking to mobilize the community so that together they can develop strategies and tactics for the purpose of advocating and supporting policies that will bring positive systematic change to the area of immigration.

Ivy A. M. Cargile

See also: Asylum Seekers; Catholicism and Latino/a Politics; Immigration as a Policy Issue; Immigration Reform and Control Act (IRCA); Proposition 187 (1994)

Further Reading
Bermudez, Esmeralda. 2017. "Immigrant Advocates Spread the Word: Be Prepared, Be Self-Reliant, Know Your Rights." *Los Angeles Times*, March 23. http://www.latimes .com/local/california/la-me-know-your-rights-20170323-story.html.

CHIRLA. n.d. http://www.chirla.org.

"Coalition for Humane Immigrant Rights of Los Angeles." 2016. *Marguerite Casey Foundation.* http://caseygrants.org/grantees/coalition-for-humane-immigrant-rights-of -los-angeles.

Hamilton, Nora, & Nora Stoltz Chinchilla. 2001. *Seeking Community in a Global City: Guatemalans and El Salvadorans in Los Angeles.* Philadelphia: Temple University Press.

Ribeiro, Tatti. 2017. "How Is CHIRLA Educating L.A.'s Undocumented Community about Their Rights." *LAist*, March 7. http://laist.com/2017/03/07/chirla_rtv.php# photo-1.

Community Service Organization (CSO)

The Community Service Organization (CSO) is a civic-oriented, social action group formed in 1947 to encourage and mobilize a burgeoning, but disenfranchised, Mexican American community in East Los Angeles. The origins of CSO are tied to a committee formed to elect Edward Roybal as the first Mexican American to the Los Angeles City Council since the 1880s and to put an end to a long-standing political drought in local governance for Mexican Americans. Although the first attempt failed, the organizational machinery put into place resulted in a significant increase in Mexican American voter registration and turnout and a new optimism that political progress could be made. According to its constitution, the CSO sought to "extend democratic rights, provide education for citizens, encourage civic participation, coordinate community efforts for the common good, and promote improved relations among all races, nationalities and religions" (cited in Guzman, 1976: 139).

As a result of their successful voter turnout campaigns, CSO's accomplishments caught the attention of Fred Ross, an organizer for Saul Alinsky's Industrial Areas Foundation (IAF), who had been sent to organize Mexican and black areas in California's citrus belt. Ross and Ignacio López, editor of the Spanish newspaper *El Espectador*, first formed the Unity League, an endeavor to promote political activism and community engagement in the Pomona valley of Southern California through the use of grassroots activity and bloc voting. Because these strategies nicely paralleled CSO's efforts, the IAF eventually became its main source of funding and allowed CSO to expand its size and projects in California. In order to receive the grants, however, CSO was required to remain nonpartisan and service oriented in their mission; despite these restrictions, CSO activities enhanced Democratic Party support at the expense of the Republican Party.

At its apex, CSO had 34 chapters in California and Arizona and had 10,000 dues-paying members on their rolls. Their tactics included training and utilizing registrars to canvass the Mexican communities door to door and, in tandem, educating the public on germane social justice issues. In 1950, with the aid of 150 deputy registrars, it claimed 32,000 new Mexican Americans had been registered to vote, thus contributing to the elections of several Mexican American candidates into city council and state legislative posts. In its prime years, and despite its nonpartisan mission, there is little question that CSO's underlying objective was to obtain substantive political representation for the growing but marginalized Mexican community in L.A.'s East Side along with other Mexicano districts across California.

As CSO grew, it evolved into a quasi-service organization in the mutualista tradition and began expanding into practical social service functions. Notable achievements in these areas were the sponsorship of citizenship classes and the successful naturalization of 40,000 resident immigrants, involvement in the first successful police brutality cases, battling housing discrimination and indirectly helping bring down restrictive covenants in California, and the successful lobbying of the state legislature to make old-age pensions available to noncitizen residents. Other services offered by CSO included advisory offices for taxes, Social Security, English translations, consumer advocacy, and youth leadership. CSO is also acclaimed for being the training ground for a young César Chávez, who proved to be an able organizer for the group and who later went on to become its state director and, eventually, a world-renowned leader for the United Farmworkers movement.

As a testament to its successes, the CSO for some years received direct monies from the AFL-CIO; however, by the early to mid-1960s the organization began to wane due to a host of variables. As the composition of CSO membership changed from working class to middle class and from Mexicanos to whites, the organization transitioned from being barrio oriented to more accommodationist. Also, its advocacy function was eclipsed by more service-oriented functions, and fractures began to emerge within the membership and chapters, the most famous being César Chávez's departure when the CSO refused to take on the role of organizing farmworkers. Eventually union and community funding dried up and chapters began to disintegrate due to localism and parochialism. As the CSO abandoned agitation for services, in the eyes of many next-generation Mexicano and Chicano activists, it became outmoded in its mission. For a time, CSO survived as a purveyor of

President Johnson's War on Poverty, but it was never able to recoup its strong advocacy role on policy nor extend its influence in the electoral arena.

In conclusion, the CSO was an important landmark in the evolution of Mexican American politics in the Southwest and served as a training ground for future leaders in the electoral and civic arenas. Generally, the organization provided political education for a transplanted rural class and linked Mexican Americans with the political system for the very first time. "Its massive voter registration drives not only introduced thousands of new voters (mostly Democrats) to electoral politics, but it demonstrated that Mexicanos could win important localized elections" (Guzman, 1976: 142). This watershed would prove to be of critical importance to future electoral movements in other states, namely south Texas, where similar strategies succeeded. It was also one of the first organizations to depart from middle-class and assimilationist themes and incorporate noncitizens into its goals and membership, an important pivot from past Latino organizations, and it prefaced the formation of more politically independent organizations that promoted nationalism and self-determination as more effective ways to gain political capital in the U.S. system.

Daniel Gutierrez

See also: Chávez, César (1927–1993); Gonzales, Rodolfo "Corky" (1928–2005); Roybal, Edward R. (1916–2005); *Primary Documents:* Excerpt of an Oral History Interview of Congressman Edward Roybal (1975)

Further Reading

Acuña, Rodolfo F. 2007. *Occupied America: A History of Chicanos.* New York: Pearson Longman.

Gomez Quiñones, Juan. 1990. *Chicano Politics: Reality and Promise 1940–1990.* Albuquerque: University of New Mexico Press.

Gutiérrez, David G. 1995. *Walls and Mirrors: Mexican Americans, Mexican Immigrants and the Politics of Ethnicity.* Berkeley: University of California Press.

Guzmán, Ralph C. 1976. *The Political Socialization of the Mexican-American People.* New York: Arno Press.

Moore, Joan. 1966. "Mexican American Problems and Prospects." Institute for Research on Poverty Special Report. Madison: University of Wisconsin.

Navarro, Armando. 2005. *Mexicano Political Experience in Occupied Aztlán: Struggles and Change.* Walnut Creek, CA: AltaMira Press.

Servín, Manuel P. 1970. *The Mexican-Americans: An Awakening Minority.* Beverly Hills, CA: Glencoe Press.

Tirado, Miguel David. 1970. "Mexican-American Community Political Organizations: The Key to Chicano Political Power." *Aztlán* I (Spring): 53–78.

Vargas, Zaragosa. 2011. *Crucible of Struggle: A History of Mexican Americans from Colonial Times to the Present Era.* New York: Oxford University Press.

Vigil, Maurilio. 1978. *Chicano Politics.* Washington, D.C.: University Press of America.

Congressional Hispanic Caucus Institute (CHCI)

The Congressional Hispanic Caucus Institute (CHCI) is a nonpartisan 501(c)(3) educational organization that looks to transform opportunities for Latino youth and the nation, as well as educate, empower, and connect upcoming Latino leaders. U.S.

Domenika Lynch, president and CEO of the Congressional Hispanic Caucus Institute (CHCI), welcomes the audience to the 41st CHCI Awards Gala in Washington, D.C., 2018. (Shannon Finney/Getty Images)

representatives and Congressional Hispanic Caucus (CHC) members Edward Roybal, E. "Kika" de la Garza, and Baltasar Corrada del Rio created the Congressional Hispanic Caucus Institute in 1978 to provide educational opportunities and programs to the Hispanic community. Despite being founded at our nation's capital by congressional members, CHCI's board of directors now includes Hispanic leaders from different sectors. With the coupling of Hispanic leaders from a variety of sectors and Hispanic members of Congress, like current board of directors member U.S. representative Joaquín Castro (D-Texas 20th District), CHCI provides Congress and the Hispanic community with relevant policy information and opportunities in public service ranging from a local to a national level.

As the capacity of the organization continued to grow, so did the number of programs being offered by CHCI. During the 1980s, CHCI graduated its first Graduate Fellowship Program class, moved to a bigger office, started recognizing influential Hispanic leaders in communities across the country, and created its Summer Internship Program. During the 1990s and 2000s, CHCI launched a website, created additional resources for Latino students to facilitate access to higher education such as scholarships, and celebrated a number of program anniversaries that helped Latino youth develop their skills to better access career opportunities and which helped the organization ascend into one of the most respectable organizations in Washington, D.C., that seeks to foster Hispanic leadership in the government sector.

Since its inception, CHCI has fostered partnerships with companies and individual donors to provide sustainable educational and leadership development programs for young Latino students and professionals across the country and in

Washington, D.C. Today, the education and leadership development programs and resources that CHCI offers include databases for external resources, scholarships, internships, and fellowships. The programs at CHCI have a focus on one or many issues plaguing the Hispanic community and intersect the public policy sector. These programs are open to Latino students seeking to create change and start a career in the public service sector.

CHCI's mission is to create a transforming and lasting impact on Latino youth and the nation. As part of that mission, every year CHCI connects, empowers, and educates more than 1,600 Latino students and young professionals through scholarships and college access, internship, and fellowship programs that provide them with opportunities to explore public policy careers in Washington, D.C. CHCI provides their students, interns, and fellows with networking and mentoring opportunities with prominent Latino leaders, access to a pipeline of Latino talent and recruitment, and leadership development in our nation's capital. The variety of programs offered at CHCI are designed to prepare Latino youth and young professionals to become the next generation of Latino leaders in the United States.

Maria L. Ibarra Rodriguez

See also: de la Garza, Eligio "Kika" (1927–2017); Roybal, Edward R. (1916–2005)

Further Reading

Antelo, Cristina. "CHCI Is Leading the Way in Promoting Diversity on Capitol Hill." *The Huffington Post*, December 21. https://www.huffingtonpost.com/cristina-antelo/chci -is-leading-the-way-i_b_8855474.html.

The Congressional Hispanic Caucus Institute, Inc. (CHCI). n.d. "What We Do." *The Congressional Hispanic Caucus, Inc. (CHCI)*. https://chci.org/about/what_we_do.

The Congressional Hispanic Caucus, Inc. (CHCI) and Society for Human Resources (SHRM). 2016. *The Changing U.S. Workforce: The Growing Hispanic Demographic and the Workplace.* Washington, D.C.: The Congressional Hispanic Caucus, Inc. (CHCI) and Society for Human Resources (SHRM). https://www.shrm.org /hr-today/public-policy/hr-public-policy-issues/Documents/15-0746%20CHCI _Research_Report_FNL.pdf.

Corona, Humberto "Bert"

(1918–2001)

Born Humberto Noé Corona, Bert Corona was an American labor activist, educator, and civil rights leader. Corona has Mexican roots and was a passionate labor organizer who fought for the rights of many people, especially undocumented workers, Mexicans, and Latinos. Later in his life Corona became known as "El Viejo" (The Old Man), and with a career spanning more than seven decades, Corona's accomplishments are at times compared with those of César Chávez. He worked with numerous organizations and even founded his own organizations to help those in need.

Corona's main principle and belief was that undocumented workers should not be deported, but rather be organized. Based on this belief, he established the Hermandad Mexicana Nacional, or National Mexican Brotherhood, in 1951.

During the 1960s this organization began proactively organizing undocumented immigrants and working to improve their earning power and status in this country. They emerged as a major immigrant services provider, with numerous offices in Southern California, including offices in areas such as North Hollywood, Santa Ana, and Los Angeles. However, starting in 1992 with the cutbacks in federal grants, the organization became overburdened with debt.

Corona entered politics when he met Luisa Moreno, a labor organizer. Together they formed the League of Spanish-Speaking People in 1938. In the late 1940s, he became one of the principal organizers for the Community Service Organization (CSO) in California. As part of his CSO mission, Corona registered Mexican American voters. This work led to the successful election of Edward Roybal to the Los Angeles City Council in 1949. Through the 1950s, Corona served as the regional organizer for ANMA (National Association of Mexican Americans), an organization focused on preserving and safeguarding the cultural heritage of Mexican Americans.

As a member of the labor movement in 1959, Corona, along with numerous other activists, banded together and formed the Mexican American Political Association (MAPA). This organization fought to promote the interests of and provide representation for various Latinos in the United States. MAPA was the first Mexican American political group in California and was supported by both Democratic and Republican politicians during the 1960s and 1970s.

Corona came to be the organization's president in the early 1960s and used this position to highlight concerns and push for the fact that Mexican American issues need to have presidential cabinet-rank positions. In 1966, Corona purposely did not attend a White House conference in El Paso, Texas, on the topic of Mexican American affairs because he said he felt it was controlled by Anglos.

Although Corona had gotten an athletic scholarship to the University of Southern California, he devoted his energy and time to labor organizing and never earned a college degree. Yet later in his life, he lectured at prestigious universities such as Stanford and taught classes at California State University campuses at San Diego, Northridge, Fullerton, and Los Angeles.

In the 1980s, Corona and other professors at Cal State University, Los Angeles, wanted to leverage the Chicano Studies Department as a tool for social activism; this eventually led to a huge disturbance on campus when a fire was set outside of department head Louis Negrete's office and his car was set on fire in his garage at home. Corona, along with the other professors, was fired. Corona passed away from kidney failure at age 82 in 2001.

Zujaja Tehreem

See also: Brown Power Movement/Chicano Civil Rights Movement; Chávez, César (1927–1993); Community Service Organization (CSO); Mexican American Political Association (MAPA); Moreno, Luisa (1907–1992); Roybal, Edward R. (1916–2005)

Further Reading

"Bert Corona: 1918–2001: Labor Organizer—El Paso Childhood." http://biography.jrank .org/pages/3057/Corona-Bert-1918-2001-Labor-Organizer-El-Paso-Childhood .html.

"Corona, Bert N." n.d. *SNAC*. http://snaccooperative.org/ark:/99166/w67s7w3p.

Ramos, George. 2001. "From the Archives: Bert Corona; Labor Activist Backed Rights for Undocumented Workers." *Los Angeles Times*, January 17. http://www.latimes .com/local/obituaries/archives/la-me-bert-corona-20010117-story.html.

Crusade for Justice

Crusade for Justice was a Mexican American social and political organization founded by Rodolfo "Corky" Gonzales in Denver, Colorado, in 1966. Gonzales, a Mexican American poet and boxer with a passion for advancing the rights of people of Mexican descent in the United States, established the organization out of frustration with the perceived inability of the major two-party political system to bring about meaningful sociopolitical change. The Crusade for Justice is remembered as a social movement group that reflected often-held feelings by some members of racial/ethnic minority groups in the 1960s and 1970s—that urban organization and displays of group solidarity were more likely to advance minority causes than working with politicians to develop electoral coalitions. The sentiment that a third political party focused primarily on advancing the interests of Chicanos stems in part from beliefs expressed and actions taken by social movement groups like the Crusade for Justice.

The Crusade for Justice advocated for the establishment of alternative education and political institutions that would provide an avenue for Mexican Americans to achieve self-determination and advancement within the United States. In particular, Gonzales, at one time a frequent activist working for the Democratic Party in Denver, grew increasingly agitated at the seeming inability of the Democratic Party to address economic problems that many Mexican Americans faced (poverty, low opportunities for career development, etc.). Deciding to show active engagement with the Chicano community in Denver, Gonzales and the Crusade for Justice developed a newspaper covering Chicano interests and events, sponsored a conference for Chicano youth education and cultural advancement, and encouraged the development of a

More than 2,500 people registered for the second annual Chicano Youth Liberation Conference held in Denver, Colorado, in 1970. In this photo, conference participants watch a film at the Crusade for Justice headquarters, which served as an important resource for the community. (Denver Post via Getty Images) unique Chicano cultural independence movement known as El Plan Espiritual de Aztlán (The Spiritual Plan of Aztlan). With this movement, there would be the mass mobilization of Chicanos under a single identity (the Mestizo Nation), a distinct cultural identity established by uniform economic and political interests.

In the eyes of Gonzales, the Crusade for Justice needed to engage in advocacy efforts to increase the likelihood Mexican Americans would have direct influence over how policy decisions would be made and eventually implemented. While working with the Crusade for Justice in Denver, Gonzales opted to pursue leadership of the Raza Unida Party. As this was occurring, individual members of Crusade for Justice and their collective activities as an organization were put under significant surveillance by the Federal Bureau of Investigation and local police. This monitoring was a reaction to efforts by the Crusade to expand their political influence outside the confines of Denver, Colorado.

Tensions between the Crusade for Justice and the Denver police erupted on March 17, 1973. On this day, members of the Crusade and police officers engaged in a gun battle after the arrest of a man for jaywalking in front of the Crusade for Justice headquarters. An explosion occurred at the apartment building owned by the Crusade, resulting in 1 person being killed and 17 others left injured. The Denver police accused the Crusade of storing explosives in the building, while Gonzales claimed that the Denver police threw grenades into the apartment building in a deliberate strike on the headquarters for the group.

With the prosecution of members following the bombing, the recruitment of potential Crusade members into local gangs, and the suspicious deaths of prominent Mexican American activists in the area, there was a significant decline in the extent of influence the Crusade for Justice had in Denver. After the bombing incident, Gonzales opted for a reduced level of activity in advancing Mexican American sociopolitical causes until his death from liver disease in 2005.

Christopher Olds

See also: Gonzales, Rodolfo "Corky" (1928–2005)

Further Reading

Kaplowitz, Craig A. 2005. *LULAC, Mexican Americans, and National Policy.* College Station: Texas A&M University Press.

Lee, Michael A. 2012. "Forgotten Alliance: Jews, Chicanos, and the Dynamics of Class and Race in Denver, Colorado, 1967–1971." *Shofar: An Interdisciplinary Journal of Jewish Studies* 30, no. 2 (Winter): 1–25.

Orozco, Cynthia E. 2010. *No Mexicans, Women, or Dogs Allowed: The Rise of the Mexican American Civil Rights Movement.* Austin: University of Texas Press.

Vigil, Ernesto B. 1999. *The Crusade for Justice: Chicano Militancy and the Government's War on Dissent.* Madison: University of Wisconsin Press.

Cruz, Rafael Edward ("Ted")

(1970–)

The 34th U.S. senator from Texas, Ted Cruz was sworn into office on January 3, 2013. Cruz won the 2012 Texas general election with over 56 percent of the vote against Democrat and former congressman of Texas's 9th House District, Paul

Lindsey Sadler. He was also a Republican presidential candidate during the 2016 election. Born December 22, 1970, in Alberta, Canada, to an American mother and Cuban father, Cruz lived in Canada until 1974 when his family moved to Houston, Texas. Cruz graduated cum laude from Princeton University in 1992 with his bachelor's degree in public policy, and then went on to earn his juris doctorate from Harvard Law School in 1995. Cruz served in 1995 as a law clerk to Judge J. Michael Luttig of the U.S. Court of Appeals for the Fourth Circuit, in 1996 as a law clerk to Chief Justice William H. Rehnquist of the U.S. Supreme Court, and later worked for the private-sector law firm Cooper Carvin & Rosenthal. While at Cooper, Carvin & Rosenthal, Cruz worked on behalf of the National Rifle Association and on the Clinton impeachment proceedings.

In 1999, Cruz took a position as a domestic policy advisor to the George W. Bush presidential campaign, where he met his wife, Heidi Nelson. After Bush won the election, Cruz served as the Department of Justice coordinator, assisting in Bush's transition to the White House. Subsequently, Cruz was appointed associate deputy attorney general for the Department of Justice for six months until he was offered a senior appointment at the Federal Trade Commission (FTC). Cruz served as the director of the Office of Policy Planning at the FTC through January 2003, until he left to become the solicitor general of Texas.

As solicitor general of Texas from 2003 to 2008, Cruz became the first Hispanic in Texas to hold this position. He went before the U.S. Supreme Court for nine different cases, winning five and losing four. After his tenure as solicitor general, Cruz went back to privately practicing law in Texas until Senator Kay Bailey Hutchison's retirement announcement in 2012 (Toobin, 2014). Relying on Tea Party support, Cruz managed to best his Republican and Democrat competitors and thus became the first Latino elected to the Senate from Texas. In the first primary, Cruz only managed 34 percent of the vote compared to the establishment candidate David Dewhurst (45%). However, right-wing groups rallied behind Cruz in the runoff, as Cruz garnered 57 percent of the vote. In the general election—which was not considered competitive—Cruz received 57 percent of the vote compared to 41 percent for Democrat Paul Sadler.

As a senator, Cruz served on the Committee on Commerce, Science, and Transportation; the Committee on Armed Services; the Committee on the Judiciary; the Joint Economic Committee; and the Committee on Rules and Administration. Cruz is widely known for his attempted government shutdown of 2013, in which he attempted to filibuster provisions that would pay for the Affordable Care Act (ACA). On March 22, 2015, Cruz announced his candidacy for the 2016 presidential election. With his superlative debate skills, Cruz was a strong contender against and critic of presidential candidate Donald Trump. However, Cruz suspended his campaign on May 3, 2016, after losing the Republican primary in Indiana. In the end, Cruz managed 559 delegates to Trump's 1,543. As a senator and presidential candidate, Cruz's political stances are considered far-right. For instance, Cruz has come out in strong opposition to abortion, the ACA, bank bailouts, same-sex rights, diplomatic relations with Cuba, and a pathway to citizenship for undocumented immigrants.

Stephen Omar El-Khatib and Loren Collingwood

See also: Affordable Care Act of 2010 and Latinos; Election of 2016 and Latinos

Further Reading

"Cruz to Be Sworn in as First Hispanic U.S. Senator from Texas." 2013. *CBS Houston* http://houston.cbslocal.com/2013/01/03/cruz-to-be-sworn-in-as-first-hispanic-u-s-senator-from-texas/.

Dann, Carrie, Mark Murray, & Andrew Rafferty. 2015. "Ted Cruz Announces Presidential Bid." *NBC News*. http://www.nbcnews.com/politics/elections/ted-cruz-announce-presidential-bid-monday-n328051.

"Election 2016—Republican Delegate Count." 2016. *RealClear Politics*. http://www.realclearpolitics.com/epolls/2016/president/republican_delegate_count.html.

Geraghty, Jim. 2015. "Ted Cruz: The Bush Years." *National Review*. http://www.nationalreview.com/article/416074/ted-cruz-bush-years-jim-geraghty.

Markusoff, Jason, & Allen Abel. 2016. "Ted Cruz: Made in Canada." http://www.macleans.ca/politics/washington/ted-cruz-made-in-canada/.

Murse, Tom. 2017. "Ted Cruz Bio—2016 Republican Presidential Campaign." *ThoughtCo.* https://www.thoughtco.com/the-biography-of-ted-cruz-3368168.

"R. (Ted) Edward Cruz; Attorney Biography." 2017. https://web.archive.org/web/20100521123956/http://www.morganlewis.com/bios/tcruz.

"Ted Cruz Biography—Childhood, Life Achievements & Timeline." 2017. *The Famous People*. http://www.thefamouspeople.com/profiles/ted-cruz-6969.php.

"Ted Cruz Fast Facts." 2016. *CNN*. http://www.cnn.com/2015/03/26/us/ted-cruz-fast-facts/.

"Ted Cruz on the Issues." 2017. *On the Issues*. http://www.ontheissues.org/Senate/Ted_Cruz.htm.

"Ted Cruz Presidential Campaign, 2016." 2017. *Ballotpedia*. https://ballotpedia.org/Ted_Cruz_presidential_campaign,_2016.

"Ted Cruz's Biography." 2017. *Vote Smart*. http://votesmart.org/candidate/biography/135705/ted-cruz#.WQgKt_nytjE.

Toobin, Jeffrey. 2014. "Ted Cruz, The Absolutist." *The New Yorker*, June 30. http://www.newyorker.com/magazine/2014/06/30/the-absolutist-2.

Weiner, Rachel. 2012. "Who Is Ted Cruz?" *The Washington Post*, August 1. https://www.washingtonpost.com/blogs/the-fix/post/who-is-ted-cruz/2012/08/01/gJQAqql8OX_blog.html?utm_term=.82d85d054df0.

Cuban Adjustment Act of 1966

In 1959, Cuban president Fulgencio Batista was ousted by Fidel Castro and other revolutionaries, and the Batista government was replaced by a socialist state that after 1965 was controlled by the Cuban Communist Party. In 1966, President Lyndon Johnson signed into law the Cuban Adjustment Act (CAA), which allows any native or citizen of Cuba who entered the United States after January 1, 1959, to adjust their status to legal permanent resident (LPR) after being physically present in the United States for at least two years. This time period was later reduced to one year after the Immigration and Nationality Act Amendments of 1976. The CAA was not only thought of as a humanitarian mission but also a political one. "The US had underlying ideological motivations and foreign policy goals during the Cold War" (Henken, 2005: 396).

Between 1960 and 1970, the Cuban population in the United States grew six-fold, from 79,000 to 439,000. Most of these exiles settled in Miami, Los Angeles, and parts of New Jersey. Cuban migration by boat, or rafts, declined after the Mariel boatlift of 1980, which brought roughly 125,000 Cubans to the United States, or *marielitos,* as the Cuban refugees were labeled. However, Cubans migrating using boats and rafts increased from hundreds in 1989 to thousands in 1993 (Wasem, 2009: 1). According to the Congressional Research Service, "The number of Cubans intercepted by the U.S. Coast Guard or the U.S. Border Patrol reached a post-Mariel high of almost 40,000 in 1994" (Wasem, 2009: 1).

In September 1994, with the objective of "safe, legal, and orderly" immigration, the Clinton administration came to an agreement with Cuba (Clinton, 1995). This agreement relied on six points, including the United States' agreement to no longer permit Cubans intercepted at sea to come into the United States, instead placing them in a third location (Guantanamo Bay) and the admittance of no fewer than 20,000 immigrants from Cuba annually, not including the immediate relatives of U.S. citizens (Wasem, 2009: 1). On May 2, 1995, a second agreement was made adding two points to the 1994 agreement between the two countries. First, the second agreement resolved the dilemma of the 33,000 Cubans held in Guantanamo Bay by allowing most of them to enter the United States through the humanitarian parole provisions of the Immigration and Naturalization Act of 1952 (INA). Second, Cubans intercepted at sea will no longer be sent to a third location but repatriated back to Cuba. These two agreements comprise what is labeled the "wet foot, dry foot" policy. Additionally, special provisions make Cuban migrants in the United States eligible for federal assistance. The Refugee Education Assistance Act of 1980 defines the term "Cuban and Haitian entrant" for purposes of eligibility for federal assistance, and the Personal Responsibility and Work Opportunity Reconciliation Act (PRWORA) of 1996, as amended, makes Cuban and Haitian entrants eligible for certain federal public benefits (Bruno, 2016). However, the "wet foot, dry foot" policy was seen as controversial given the difference in policy for Cubans to that of Haitians.

On January 12, 2017, days before leaving office, the Obama administration ended the "wet foot, dry foot" policy established by the Clinton administration in 1995. In his press release, President Obama stated that Cuban nationals who do not qualify for humanitarian relief "will be subject to removal, consistent with U.S. law and enforcement priorities." He continued to say that by terminating this policy, the United States is "treating Cuban migrants the same way we treat migrants from other countries" (Obama, 2017). This policy change makes aspects of the CAA void because in 1996, wet foot/dry foot reduced the application of the CAA, and so without it, the CAA is even more reduced in application, given less Cuban migration and more removals/returns.

Jessica L. Lavariega Monforti and Yalidy Matos

See also: Immigration as a Policy Issue; Obama, Barack (1961–) and Latinos; Rubio, Marco (1971–)

Further Reading

Bruno, Andorra. 2016. "U.S. Policy on Cuban Migrants: In Brief." *Congressional Research Service.* https://fas.org/sgp/crs/row/R44714.pdf.

Clinton, Bill. 1995. "Joint Statement with the Republic of Cuba on Normalization of Migration." *The American Presidency Project,* May 2. http://www.presidency.ucsb.edu/ws/?pid=51305.

Henken, T. 2005. "Balseros, Boteros, and El Bombo: Post-1994 Cuban Immigration to the United States and the Persistence of Special Treatment." *Latino Studies* 3, no. 3: 393–416.

Obama, Barack. 2017. "Statement by the President on Cuban Immigration Policy." January 12. https://obamawhitehouse.archives.gov/the-press-office/2017/01/12/statement -president-cuban-immigration-policy.

Wasem, R. E. 2009. "Cuban Migration to the United States: Policy and Trends." *Congressional Research Service*. https://fas.org/sgp/crs/row/R40566.pdf.

DACA Sin Miedo

The campaign or hashtag "DACA Sin Miedo," or "DACA without fear," first surfaced in September 2015 when Pillsbury United Communities and advocates for human rights launched a campaign to encourage Deferred Action for Childhood Arrivals (DACA)–eligible youth to apply for the program. On June 15, 2012, President Barack Obama used his power to grant DREAMers, or youth who were brought to the United States without documentation at a young age, immigration relief by providing them with a two-year work permit and protection from deportation. The term "DACA Sin Miedo" took on a different meaning in 2017, as presidential candidate Donald Trump threaten to terminate the program.

The original meaning of the campaign was meant to motivate DACA-eligible youth to submit an application for the program and take advantage of the immigration relief it provides. The DACA program was expected to benefit about 1.5 million youth; however, barely half of the expected number of potential applicants had applied for the program. In 2016 on the fourth anniversary of the DACA program, United We Dream, the largest undocumented youth network, provided testimonies by DACA beneficiaries, or DACAmented youth, about what it meant to live without fear, "Sin Miedo." At the time, youth were being encouraged to continue applying for the program and use the DACA benefits to apply for scholarship, go to college, or continue with professional careers. Across the United States DACA success stories surfaced; even high school student Larissa Martinez took social media by surprise when in her valedictorian speech she told the world how she had benefited from the program. These stories of success raise the overall profile of the DACA program among conservative opposition.

Celebrations of DACA success stories came to an end when presidential candidate Donald Trump flip-flopped about the continuation of President Obama's DACA program. The threat to end the program reached a climax when in June 2017, the Texas attorney general asked newly elected president Trump to cease the program. The request caused confusion for DACAmented youth and DACA-eligible youth who had yet to apply for the program. A sense of fear and despair surfaced among the immigrant community. In September 2017, Cosecha Voces, a nonviolent immigration movement, planned a sit-in in Austin, Texas, as a way to protest the state of Texas's decision to encourage the termination of the DACA program. "DACA Sin Miedo" then became a phrase to give courage and inspiration to DACA beneficiaries or DACAmented youth who were being threatened by the Trump administration with the termination of the program. The program was ended in October 5, 2017, by President Trump, but immigration advocates took the termination of the program to the courts, where the legalities of the program's termination are being debated. At the time of termination, over 800,000 youth had benefited from the program. These youth would then face deportation at the end of their DACA protection. "DACA Sin Miedo" continued to be used and immigration activists also implemented phrases like "Sin DACA, Sin Miedo," meaning "without DACA, without fear." The statement was meant to provoke drive and desire to continue in the fight for immigration justice, regardless of the threats ahead.

Tania Chavez

See also: Deferred Action for Childhood Arrivals (DACA)/Deferred Action for Parents of Americans and Lawful Permanent Residents (DAPA); Immigration as a Policy Issue; Trump, Donald J. (1946–) and Latinos

Further Reading

Chavez, Maria, Jessica Lavariega Monforti, & Melissa Michelson. 2014. *Living the Dream: New Immigration Policies and the Lives of Undocumented Latino Youth.* New York: Paradigm Publishers.

Pallares, Amalia, & Nilda Flores-González, eds. 2010. *¡Marcha!: Latino Chicago and the Immigrant Rights Movement.* Vol. 28. Urbana: University of Illinois Press.

Ramos, Jorge. 2006. *Sin Miedo: Lecciones de Rebeldes* [Without Fear: Lessons of Rebels]. New York: Celebra.

Dawson, Rosario

(1979–)

Rosario Dawson is a well-known actor and political activist with a history of political advocacy and efforts to encourage Latinos throughout the United States to vote in federal, state, and local elections. In 2004, Dawson and MSNBC political pundit María Teresa Kumar cofounded Voto Latino, a political outreach organization that strives to increase Latino awareness on issues considered of extreme importance to the community, including immigration policy, education, racial discrimination and profiling, and health and wellness, among others.

Dawson was born on May 9, 1979, in Coney Island, Brooklyn, and grew up in the Lower East Side of Manhattan. She was raised by her mother and stepfather, who met Dawson's mother when she was eight months pregnant with her. Although she claims that she holds deep respect for her stepfather, Dawson also acknowledged in a 2008 interview with *Latina* magazine that she has longed to meet her biological father since her childhood. Dawson is of multiethnic heritage that includes Puerto Rican, Cuban, black, Irish, and American Indian descent and identifies as a Latina. Although she never attended college, Dawson established a successful acting career by her early twenties that included roles in films such as *Kids* (1995), *He Got Game* (1998), *The 25th Hour* (2002), and *Men in Black II* (2002). She also portrayed iconic United Farm Workers cofounder Dolores Huerta in the 2014 biopic *César Chávez*.

Today, however, Dawson generates as much, if not more, media attention for her social activism and political viewpoints as her acting skills. Her commitment to progressive issues and willingness to openly express her political opinions have at times resulted in arrest and provoked controversy. One such controversy occurred shortly after the 2016 Nevada Democratic Caucus in which Dawson wrote an open letter that

Rosario Dawson speaks at a campaign rally for Senator Bernie Sanders at St. Mary's Park in the Bronx, New York City, 2016. (scarletsails/iStockphoto.com)

sharply criticized statements made by Dolores Huerta, a staunch Hillary Clinton supporter, who had accused Bernie Sanders of not adequately fighting for Latino issues during his career in public office. Dawson also challenged allegations made by Huerta and fellow actress America Ferrera (also a Clinton supporter) that Sanders supporters shouted Huerta down with nativist cries of "English Only!" during the Nevada caucus. On April 16, 2016, Dawson was arrested during a protest staged at the U.S. Capitol in Washington, D.C., in opposition to the Supreme Court's controversial 2010 *Citizens United* decision that permits corporations and lobbying organizations to essentially contribute unlimited amounts of campaign donations to political candidates. Opposition to this decision remains one of Dawson's core political principles.

Dawson has openly expressed support for comprehensive immigration reform, the DREAM Act, and the Black Lives Matter movement, and she has been active in raising awareness of, and working against, domestic violence, fracking, and homelessness. During a 2014 interview with Black Entertainment Television (BET), Dawson revealed that she notices racism on a nearly daily basis throughout the United States and in various other nations. She has also sought to raise societal awareness of police mistreatment and violence toward Latinos, while calling for unity between African Americans and Latinos. California governor Jerry Brown awarded Dawson the California Latino Legislative Caucus's "Latino Spirit Award" for her social and political activism and philanthropy in May 2011.

Justin D. García

See also: Ferrera, America (1984–); Huerta, Dolores (1930–); Kumar, María Teresa (1974–); Voto Latino

Further Reading

Dawson, Rosario. 2016. "An Open Letter to Dolores Huerta." *HuffingtonPost.com*, March 24. http://www.huffingtonpost.com/rosario-dawson/an-open-letter-to-dolores -huerta_b_9538994.html.

"'It's a Revolution': Actress Rosario Dawson on Why She Supports Sanders for President Over Clinton." 2016. *DemocracyNow.org*, April 1. http://www.democracynow.org /2016/4/1/its_a_revolution_actress_rosario_dawson.

Malone, Noreen. 2013. "Why Washington Is so Sick of Rosario Dawson." *NewRepublic .com*, July 23. https://newrepublic.com/article/113990/rosario-dawson-and-politics -washington-dc-tired-her.

"Rosario Dawson: I See Racism 'Everywhere, Every Day.'" 2014. *BET.com*, March 24. http://www.bet.com/news/celebrities/2014/03/24/rosario-dawson-i-see-racism -everywhere-everyday.html.

Smundhra. 2008. "Cover Exclusive: Rosario Dawson." *Latina,* September 17. http://www .latina.com/entertainment/celebrity/cover-exclusive-rosario-dawson.

de la Garza, Eligio "Kika"

(1927–2017)

Kika de la Garza was a Mexican American Democrat from the Rio Grande Valley of Texas. He served in the U.S. House of Representatives for 32 years from 1965 to 1997. De la Garza devoted much of his political career to supporting farmers and agriculture, as many constituents in his district were Hispanics employed in the agricultural sector. After a career marked by a host of legislative accomplishments pertaining to agriculture as well as race and ethnic politics, today de la Garza enjoyed retirement.

Born in Mercedes, Texas, Hidalgo County, on September 22, 1927, to Darío de la Garza and Elisa Villarreal, de la Garza grew up in nearby Mission, Texas, and attended Mission High School. In 1945, at the age of 17, he enlisted in the Navy, serving until 1946. He went on to Edinburg Junior College, joined the U.S. Army Artillery School at Fort Sill, Oklahoma, and served in the Korean conflict. In 1952, de la Garza earned his law degree from St. Mary's University in San Antonio. That same year, he won a seat in the Texas House of Representatives in Hidalgo County District 38. De la Garza ran against Ramon P. Guerra in the Democratic primary, defeating the former city commissioner, and ran unopposed in the general election.

Among de la Garza's legislative accomplishments, he played a role in the incorporation of Pan American University (now known as University of Texas Rio Grande Valley) into the University of Texas system, in creating the Texas Water Commission, in constructing a coastal wetlands preserve, and in founding the first state-sponsored preschool English Language Learning program. De la Garza also sponsored a bill to allow Texas border cities and counties to build international bridges with towns south of the border.

In 1964, after serving six terms in the Texas House, de la Garza won a seat in the U.S. House of Representatives, representing Texas Congressional District 15. This district spans a thin strip in Deep South Texas and borders Mexico. Many residents in the area at the time were Mexican American farmhands employed by landowners. Competing for an open seat in the election, de la Garza first beat

Lindsey Rodriguez to win the Democratic Party nomination in the primary. He then defeated Republican Joe Coulter, a veterinarian from Brownsville, in the general election with 69 percent of the vote. De la Garza became the first Mexican American to represent the district in the U.S. House and the second Mexican American from Texas to ever win a seat in Congress. He never lost reelection, serving in the House until his retirement in 1997.

De la Garza joined the House Committee on Agriculture, became chairman of this committee's Departmental Operations Subcommittee in 1967, and served as the chairman of the entire committee from 1981 to 1995. He also served on the Merchant, Marine and Fisheries Committee (1971–1981) and the International Relations Committee (1977–1979). In Congress, de la Garza worked to pass the Sugar Act Amendments of 1971 and the Emergency Agricultural Act of 1978 (where both acts benefitted farmers), successfully opposed proposed agricultural spending cuts by the Ronald Reagan and George H. W. Bush administrations, worked on the reorganization of the U.S. Department of Agriculture (USDA), and lobbied in support of the North American Free Trade Agreement (NAFTA).

De la Garza also worked to strengthen Hispanic political clout and civil rights. He was a founding member of the Congressional Hispanic Caucus (CHC), formed in 1976. He was the chairman of the CHC from 1989 to 1991. He is an expert on U.S.–Mexico relations and worked to improve trade and dialogue between the two countries. In 1978, Mexican president José Portillo awarded de la Garza the Order of the Aztec Eagle, the highest honor Mexico grants foreigners. De la Garza voted in support of the Voting Rights Act of 1965 (and for extensions of the Act), the Elementary and Secondary Education Amendments of 1965, and the Civil Rights Restoration Act of 1987.

In December 1995, de la Garza announced his intent to retire at the end of the 104th Congress (in January 1997). His legacy in working to support the agricultural sector lives on through various honors. The USDA named a fellowship and its Subtropical Agricultural Research Center after de la Garza. He also received the Texas Agricultural Lifetime Achievement Award. He was married to Lucille de la Garza and had three children: Jorge, Michael, and Angela.

Lucila Figueroa

See also: Congressional Hispanic Caucus Institute (CHCI); Voting Rights Act of 1975

Further Reading

Enciso, Carmen E., & Tracy North, eds. 1996. *Hispanic Americans in Congress, 1822–1995*. Washington, D.C.: Government Printing Office.

History, Art & Archives: United States House of Representatives. n.d. "De la Garza, Eligio, II (Kika)." http://history.house.gov/People/Detail/12083.

"'Kika' de la Garza Elected Legislator While on Leave." 1952. *The Brownsville Herald*, September 21.

Schmal, John P. "The Tejano Struggle for Representation." *Houston Institute for Culture.* http://www.houstonculture.org/hispanic/tejanorepprint.html.

U.S. Census Bureau. n.d. "My Congressional District." https://www.census.gov/mycd.

Wasniewski, Matthew A., Albin Kowalewski, Laura Turner O'Hara, & Terrance Rucker, eds. 2013. *Hispanic Americans in Congress, 1822–2012*. Washington D.C.: Government Printing Office.

de León, Kevin

(1966–)

Having served as the 47th president pro tempore of the California Senate, Democratic senator Kevin de León was the most powerful Latino politician in the state of California and the first Latino to hold the position since 1883 (McGreevy, 2014a). As president pro tem, Senator de León was the leader of the state Senate and oversaw "the appointment of committee members, assignment of bills, progress of legislation through the house, confirmation of gubernatorial appointees, and overall direction of policy" (California Legislature, 2017). De León was also the chair of the Rules Committee, which has jurisdiction over matters related to the business of the legislature and all proposed amendments to the rules.

Born in Los Angeles on December 10, 1966, to Andres Leon, a Guatemalan cook of Chinese ancestry, and Carmen Osorio, a housekeeper from Guatemala, de León grew up with his single mom and half-siblings in the San Diego neighborhood of Logan Heights (Cadelago, 2017). The first and only member in his family to graduate from high school and college, de León attended the University of California Santa Barbara for two years, but the lack of college skills resulted in poor academic performance that ultimately led to an early dismissal (McGreevy, 2014a; Tinoco, 2017). It was this early college setback that quickly propelled de León into the world of political activism that eventually led him into public office.

Following the college dismissal, de León taught English and civics classes at the One-Stop Immigration and Education Center in Santa Barbara. Through this work,

Kevin de León served as the State Senate president pro tempore from October 15, 2014, to March 21, 2018. He was the first Latino to hold the former position in over 130 years. (Brphoto/Dreamstime.com)

he participated in the organization of the large rallies opposing Proposition 187 in Los Angeles (Aron, 2017; McGreevy, 2014b). Proposition 187 was a measure on California's 1994 ballot that made undocumented immigrants ineligible for public benefits (BallotPedia, 2017). Though it was approved by California voters, the measure was never implemented and was ultimately ruled unconstitutional. De León eventually returned to college and graduated with honors from Pitzer College in 2003.

It was another immigration law, one that banned undocumented immigrants from obtaining a driver's license in California, that impelled Kevin de León into elected office. Facing Christine Chávez, the granddaughter of the renowned labor leader and civil rights activist César Chávez, de León was elected to represent District 45 (the San Fernando Valley) to the California House of Representatives. He was reelected in 2008, and in 2010 he was elected to the state Senate representing District 22 (includes the cities of Alhambra, Los Angeles, San Marino, and Pasadena). In November 2014, he was elected senator for District 24, which encompasses, among others, the diverse neighborhoods of East Los Angeles, Little Armenia, Chinatown, Pico-Union, and the Civic Center (California State Senate Majority Caucus, 2017). That same year, de León was elected by his peers as the president pro tempore.

Since being elected into public office, Senator Kevin de León has been at the forefront on various policy issues. In 2013, de León used his political might to ensure the signage into law of Assembly Bill 60, which makes it possible for undocumented immigrants to obtain a driver's license (California State Senate Majority Caucus, 2017). De León has also spearheaded first-in-the-nation sexual assault legislation that requires affirmative consent—"conscious and voluntary agreement to engage in sexual activity" (De León and Jackson, 2015). In 2016, de León was also instrumental in negotiating California's increase of the minimum wage to $15 by 2022. In addition, the senator has been instrumental in California's leadership on environmental policies. Following President Donald Trump's election, Senator Kevin de León has been spearheading Senate Bill 54 ("sanctuary bill"), which would "prohibit state and local law enforcement agencies, including school police and security, from using resources to investigate, detain, report or arrest people for immigration enforcement" (Ulloa, 2017) and has vowed to protect all Californians, irrespective of their race, immigration status, religious creed, or sexual orientation.

Yanira Rivas Pineda de Melendez

See also: Chávez, César (1927–1993); Proposition 187 (1994)

Further Reading

Aron, Hillel. 2017. "Kevin de Leon Went from College Dropout to California's Senate President." *LA Weekly*, May 3. http://www.laweekly.com/news/kevin-de-leon-went-from -college-dropout-to-californias-senate-president-8175519.

BallotPedia. 2017. "California Proposition 187, Illegal Aliens Ineligible for Public Benefits (1994)." https://ballotpedia.org/California_Proposition_187_Illegal_Aliens _Ineligible_for_Public_Benefits_(1994).

Cadelago, Christopher. 2017. "The Untold Story of How Kevin Leon Became Kevin de León." *The Sacramento Bee*, February 21. http://www.sacbee.com/news/politics -government/capitol-alert/article133464794.html.

California Legislature. 2017. "Leadership." http://www.legislature.ca.gov/the_state_legisla ture/leadership_and_caucuses/leadership.html.

California State Senate Majority Caucus. 2017. "24th District Map." http://sd24.senate.ca .gov/sd24/map.

California State Senate Majority Caucus. 2018. "Senate President Pro Tempore Kevin de León Representing District 24." http://sd24.senate.ca.gov/biography.

De León, Kevin, & Hannah-Beth Jackson. 2015. "Why We Made 'Yes Means Yes' California Law." *The Washington Post*, October 13. https://www.washingtonpost.com /news/in-theory/wp/2015/10/13/why-we-made-yes-means-yes-california-law/ ?utm_term=.cee908e3cdf3.

McGreevy, Patrick. 2014a. "Kevin de León of Los Angeles Elected Leader of California Senate." *LA Times*, June 16. http://www.latimes.com/local/la-me-pol-legislature-de -leon-20140617-story.html.

McGreevy, Patrick. 2014b. "As Senate Head, Kevin de León Hopes to Wed Agenda with Leadership." *LA Times*, October 14. http://www.latimes.com/local/politics/la-me -pol-deleon-20141015-story.html.

Tinoco, Matt. 2017. "Kevin de León Is Building a Wall between California and Trump." *Mother Jones*, July/August. http://www.motherjones.com/politics/2017/06/kevin -deleon-california-democrat.

Ulloa, Jazmine. 2017. "L.A. Police Chief Charlie Beck Endorses 'Sanctuary State' Bill that Eric Holder Hails as 'Constitutional.'" *LA Times*, June 19. http://www.latimes.com /politics/la-pol-ca-eric-holder-charlie-beck-kevin-deleon-sanctuary-state-bill -20170619-story.html.

Deferred Action for Childhood Arrivals (DACA)/Deferred Action for Parents of Americans and Lawful Permanent Residents (DAPA)

Deferred Action for Childhood Arrivals (DACA) and Deferred Action for Parents of Americans and Lawful Permanent Residents (DAPA) are two related programs that aim to provide temporary relief from removal or deportation for undocumented immigrants in the United States. DACA was an active policy from 2012, when President Obama enacted it, until 2017, when President Trump ended the program. DAPA, another policy proposed by President Obama, was never implemented because of a court order that blocked Obama's executive action. In short, both programs were designed to provide undocumented immigrants with an opportunity to avoid deportation if they registered with the government and paid a fee. Participants were not given lawful immigration status or given a pathway to it; the programs were designed only to delay immigration enforcement activities. DACA was aimed at individuals brought to the United States as children, whereas DAPA was intended for the parents of such children. In contrast with the proposed DREAM Act, DACA and DAPA were not pieces of legislation. Rather, they were executive policies outlining the enforcement practices of the Department of Homeland Security, U.S. Citizenship and Immigration Services (USCIS).

DACA began in 2012, when President Obama put the policy in place. President Obama ordered DACA as an exercise of his prosecutorial discretion authority—in other words, the president's power as the chief law enforcement officer of the federal government to determine whether to take law enforcement action against individuals. Participants in DACA would be given relief from removal for two years, and they could renew their application and participate again before the two-year period expired. In 2014, the Obama administration attempted to expand DACA by eliminating the age requirement and expanding the relief period from two to three years. At the same time, the administration proposed the DAPA program, aimed at the parents of U.S. citizens and permanent residents. However, neither the DACA expansion nor DAPA were implemented. Both were blocked by an order from the Fifth Circuit Court of Appeals, following a lawsuit by a group of states. The order remained in force after an evenly divided 4–4 decision from the Supreme Court of the United States.

In 2017, President Trump issued an executive memorandum rescinding DACA. Under the new policy, the Department of Homeland Security would continue to accept DACA applications until the fall of 2017. In total, by September 2017, there were approximately 790,000 participants in DACA (Krogstad, 2017). After President Trump's revocation of the policy, members of Congress suggested several different legislative approaches to dealing with DACA beneficiaries. These included passing a version of the DREAM Act or other, less sweeping proposals to implement DACA legislatively rather than administratively. However, with the strong anti-immigrant position from the Republican Party and President Trump, the future of the program is unclear.

Collin Paschall and Gisela Sin

See also: DREAM Act; DREAM Act at the State Level

Further Reading

American Immigration Lawyers Association. 2017. "Resources on the Lawsuit Challenging DAPA and DACA Expansion." *American Immigration Lawyers Association,* September 8. http://www.aila.org/infonet/texas-et-al-v-us-documentation.

Bruno, Andorra. 2017a. "Deferred Action for Childhood Arrivals (DACA): Frequently Asked Questions." *Congressional Research Service,* September 6. https://fas.org/sgp/crs/homesec/R44764.pdf.

Bruno, Andorra. 2017b. "The DACA and DAPA Deferred Action Initiatives: Frequently Asked Questions." *Congressional Research Service,* February 15. http://trac.syr.edu/immigration/library/P13110.pdf.

Bruno, Andorra, Carla N. Argueta, Jerome P. Bjelopera, Michael John Garcia, William A. Kandel, Alison Siskin, & Ruth Ellen Wasem. 2016. "Immigration Legislation and Issues in the 114th Congress." *Congressional Research Service,* February 3. http://nationalaglawcenter.org/wp-content/uploads/assets/crs/R44230.pdf.

Congressional Research Service. 2016. "Frequently Asked Questions Regarding the Supreme Court's 4–4 Split on Immigration." *Congressional Research Service,* June 24. https://fas.org/sgp/crs/homesec/imm-faq.pdf.

Krogstad, Jens Manuel. 2017. "DACA Has Shielded 790,000 Young Unauthorized Immigrants from Deportation." *Pew Research Center,* September 1. http://www.pewresearch.org/fact-tank/2017/09/01/unauthorized-immigrants-covered-by-daca-face-uncertain-future.

Singer, Audrey, Nicola Prchal Svajlenka, & Jill H. Wilson. 2015. "Local Insights from DACA for Implementing Future Programs for Unauthorized Immigrants." *Brookings Institution,* June. https://www.brookings.edu/wp-content/uploads/2016/06/BMPP_Srvy_DACAImmigration_June3b.pdf.

Del Rio Independent School District v. Salvatierra

(1930)

Del Rio Independent School District v. Salvatierra is the first case heard in Texas courts that reviewed local school district decisions regarding the educational experience of children of Mexican descent. The Texas Court of Civil Appeals in San Antonio stated that the Del Rio Independent School District (DRISD) could separate the Mexican American students from other students into unique facilities, so long as it was not based on perceived color or race differences. Although this court decision could be viewed as a major loss for desegregation, in that it appeared to allow the segregation of Mexican American students in elementary grade levels, the decision helped to galvanize support for the civil rights organization League of United Latin American Citizens (LULAC). Following the decision, new LULAC chapters were created across Texas, and fundraising efforts to pursue legal actions against perceived segregation of Mexican American students were highly successful. The court decision helped to elicit increased support in attempts to curb perceived discriminatory treatment against students of Mexican descent in the United States.

In the 1930 court case, LULAC argued on behalf of parents of Mexican American students enrolled in Del Rio, Texas public schools. The lawsuit, filed in Texas district court, alleged that the DRISD was creating elementary school classroom and auditorium space where only Mexican American students in grades one through three would be assigned to attend. The parents believed this would mean their children were being segregated from other students. It had been common practice in recent years prior to the case for Texas school districts to establish segregated schools for students of Mexican descent.

LULAC made the claim that the act of segregating these students was not legal. Although it was the law in Texas at the time that "separate but equal schools" for Anglo/white and African American/black students were necessary, this was not a requirement for Mexican American students. In LULAC's view, if no state law was present that mandated separate school facilities needed to be used by Anglo/white and Mexican American students, the DRISD was violating the Equal Protection Clause of the Fourteenth Amendment. In DRISD's view, it was necessary to have separate school facilities to improve the educational performance of Mexican American students. The reason DRISD gave for separate facilities is that both the lack of adequate English-language skills and consistent class attendance exhibited by the Mexican American students required separating these students from others, and this was not due to any perception of color or race differences with Anglo/white students. Member of LULAC and practicing lawyer M. C. Gonzalez joined the lawyer originally hired by the parents of the children, John Dodson, to argue against the actions of DRISD.

Joseph Jones, the ruling district court judge, declared that the Mexican American students enrolled at DRISD could not be segregated from Anglo/white students because the Mexican American students were legally considered members of the "white race," so the school district could not separate them from other students of the same "white race."

The Texas Court of Civil Appeals in San Antonio overturned this ruling, saying that although it would be illegal for public schools to segregate Mexican American students because of their ethnicity or color, it is not at all illegal to classify students into particular groups to help bring about the most extensive amount of educational benefits to students, given their measurable aptitudes and needs. The judgment stated that the DRISD could separate the Mexican American students into unique facilities, so long as it was not done because of perceived color or race differences and that the school district did have the right to segregate on educational grounds if Mexican American students had unique language needs. The Supreme Court of the United States was asked to review the decision of the Court of Civil Appeals, but the Supreme Court declined to grant a review of the judgment.

Christopher Olds

See also: League of United Latin American Citizens (LULAC)

Further Reading

Donato, Rubén. 1997. *The Other Struggle for Equal Schools: Mexican Americans during the Civil Rights Era.* New York: SUNY Press.

Márquez, Benjamin. 1993. *LULAC: The Evolution of a Mexican American Political Organization.* Austin: University of Texas Press.

San Miguel, Guadalupe. 1983. "The Struggle against Separate and Unequal Schools: Middle Class Mexican Americans and the Desegregation Campaign in Texas, 1929–1957." *History of Education Quarterly* 23, no. 3 (October): 343–59.

San Miguel, Guadalupe. 1987. *"Let All of Them Take Heed": Mexican Americans and the Campaign for Educational Equality in Texas, 1910–1981.* Austin: University of Texas Press.

Valencia, Richard R. 2008. *Chicano Students and the Courts: The Mexican American Legal Struggle for Educational Equality.* New York: NYU Press.

Delano Grape Strike

(1965–1970)

In the 1960s, farm workers were among the few groups excluded from the National Relations Act of 1935, which guaranteed employees collective bargaining rights. As a result, farm laborers generally received below-subsistence wages, suffered from exposure to pesticides, and lived in inadequate housing. In California, these conditions had been exacerbated by the surplus of labor due to the importation of Mexican guest workers through the Bracero Program (1942–1964). Change came through the Delano grape strike (1965–1970), a five-year-long confrontation between farm workers and grape growers involving walkouts, marches, and consumer boycotts. The strike was the product of decades of worker organizing and earlier farmworker strikes. Farmworker leaders then acted because growers could no longer bring braceros into the United States to break strikes.

The grape strike started in Delano, California, when Filipino workers refused to work for the wages offered by the growers and asked Mexican American laborers to join them. This was the first major collaboration between Filipino and

Grape pickers carry U.S. flags and National Farm Workers Association banners as they march along a road from Delano to Sacramento to protest their low wages and poor working conditions. (Ted Streshinsky/Corbis via Getty Images)

Mexican American workers. Although César Chávez did not believe his newly founded National Farm Workers Association, with only $100 in its treasury, was ready for a long strike, he was aware of the growers' strategy of pitting one race against the other in the competition for jobs and encouraged his members instead to support the Filipinos. From then on, the struggle for farm workers would remain a multiethnic effort.

The first obstacle faced by the strikers was the ease with which they could be supplanted with scabs (non-union replacement workers). Their tactic was to stage picketers at the edge of vineyards where strikebreakers were working and exhort them to join them. On the pickets, however, they faced the growers' harassment, which included driving dangerously close to the demonstrators at high speed, spraying them with pesticides, and having them arrested by the local police on bogus charges. This campaign of intimidation, however, eventually gained the growers negative publicity when Senator Robert Kennedy came to Delano as a member of the Commission on Migratory Labor and ironically invited the local sheriff, who had arrested picketers because of rumors that the scabs in the fields would attack them, to read the Constitution of the United States.

The strike obtained further visibility through a 300-mile, 25-day march from Delano to the state capital of Sacramento in the spring of 1966. The march was both secular and religious. It was a protest against the California legislature for setting a minimum price on liquor while denying workers a minimum wage, but also a pilgrimage, a penance endured to pray for justice. For Chávez, as well as Dolores Huerta, Gilbert Padilla, and other Chicano leaders, it was a way to train union members in nonviolent tactics, as well as to bring the strike to workers outside of Delano. It was extremely successful: by the time they reached Stockton, the last stop before Sacramento, the crowd following the banner of the Virgin of Guadalupe and the black eagle of the union had swollen to several thousand and the marcher's primary target, the liquor company Schenley Corporation, had agreed to sign a contract rather than have its label tarnished by unfavorable press attention.

More effective than striking and marching, however, was boycotting. Realizing the difficulty of stopping the harvest, Chávez and his followers decided to block grapes at the consumer end by advocating a nationwide, and eventually international, boycott. Organizers, including, among others, Dolores Huerta and Eliseo Medina, were sent to all major American cities with $100, the name of a local sympathizer, and the task of persuading the American public not to eat grapes and not to patronize stores that carried them. Union members engaged in creative nonviolence: they demonstrated in front of supermarkets; flooded stores with helium-filled balloons reading "Don't eat grapes"; conducted pray-ins in the produce aisle, asking that growers would have their hearts turned from darkness to light; or, as in Boston, engaged in a Grape Party and dumped cartons of grapes into the Massachusetts Bay. By 1970, several major American retailers had stopped carrying grapes to retain their customers and sales were down by 25 percent. The growers' attempt to circumvent the boycott by redirecting shipments to Europe failed when dockworkers in England and Scandinavia refused to unload them.

Producer Lionel Steinberg was the first to capitulate, which effectively divided the market into union and nonunion grapes, creating a punishing price differential for those still holding out. Finally, on July 29, 1970, leading grower John Giumarra and 23 others agreed to a contract which granted a salary increase, union-controlled hiring halls, a health and welfare fund, and protection against pesticides. Social justice was thus achieved through peaceful collective action and the alliance of rural workers and urban consumers.

Paola Gemme

See also: Chávez, César (1927–1993); Huerta, Dolores (1930–); United Farm Workers (UFW); *Primary Documents:* Testimony of Dolores Huerta before the Subcommittee of Migratory Labor of the Senate Committee of Labor and Public Welfare (1966)

Further Reading

Garcia, Matt. 2012. *From the Jaws of Victory: The Triumph and Tragedy of César Chávez and the Farm Worker Union.* Berkeley: University of California Press.

Levy, Jacques E. 2007. *César Chávez: Autobiography of La Causa.* Minneapolis: University of Minnesota Press.

Pawel, Miriam. 2009. *The Union of Their Dreams: Power, Hope, and Struggle in César Chávez's Farm Worker Union.* New York: Bloomsbury Press.

Delgado v. Bastrop I.S.D., et al.

(1948)

Delgado v. Bastrop is the second civil rights case involving Mexican Americans and school segregation in Texas. It was also the first federal court desegregation case dealing with public schools in Texas. District court judge Ben H. Rice of the U.S. District Court, Western District of Texas (Austin division) held on June 15, 1948, that segregation of children of "Mexican extraction" was unconstitutional and in violation of the Fourteenth Amendment.

The case originated in a small town of Bastrop, Texas, 30 miles southeast of Austin. Up until the 1940s, it was not uncommon for Mexican Americans to be in segregated schools, called "Mexican schools," which were typically poorly equipped. Although there was no state law that legally segregated Mexican Americans at the time (unlike African Americans and Jim Crow laws), it was the common practice to separate Mexican American students, who were U.S. citizens, from white students. The first case that unsuccessfully challenged segregation in Texas in the courts was *Del Rio I.S.D. v. Salvatierra* in 1930. However, after the favorable ruling in *Méndez v. Westminster* in both the district court (1946) and the 9th Circuit Court (1947) in California, the Delgado case was initiated by LULAC and the American GI Forum (which had just formed in 1948 in Corpus Christi, Texas).

The case represented Minerva Delgado (who was six years old and in the first grade) and 19 other Mexican American children attending grades 1 through 5. The case was prompted when Delgado's grandfather was denied permission to allow his granddaughter to attend the white school, which was closer to their home. The class-action suit by the plaintiffs represented all students of "Mexican or other Latin American" descent. The plaintiffs filed suit against Bastrop I.S.D. (Independent School District) and three other districts (Elgin I.S.D., Martindale I.S.D., and Colorado Common School District) in central Texas, including the State Superintendent of Public Instruction L. A. Woods and others.

The legal team included lead counsel Gustavo García (a civil rights attorney from San Antonio), Carlos Cadena (who later became the first Mexican American hired as a law professor in the United States, when he accepted a position at St. Mary's University School of Law in San Antonio, Texas), A. L. Wirlin (who served as co-counsel in the Méndez case), and Professor George I. Sánchez of the University of Texas and Dr. Hector García (founder of the GI Forum), who assisted in the case.

There were two central issues in the case. The first issue was whether segregation was illegal because there were no state laws or constitutional provisions expressly authorizing it for Mexican Americans. The second issue was whether the application of existing cases upholding the segregation of black students applied to Mexican Americans was unconstitutional because they were considered white and not a different race.

The district judge ultimately held that the "regulations, customs, usages and practices" by the school districts were "arbitrary and discriminatory," and thereby unconstitutional and illegal. The judge also "permanently restrained and enjoined from segregating Mexican American pupils." Thus, school officials could be held legally responsible for approving or maintaining segregation. However, unlike the *Méndez* case that struck down segregation in the schools for Mexican American students, the ruling in the *Delgado* case did allow separate classes for students with language deficiencies as identified by "scientific and standardized tests" applied to all students. The ruling also allowed segregation of non–English-speaking students, but only for those entering the first grade.

Comprehensive desegregation for Mexican American children, however, never took place. Research indicates noncompliance by many school administrators and the state legislature with a variety of delaying tactics or practices that undermined integration, such as offering school choice for white students. Nevertheless, both the *Méndez* case and the *Delgado* case served as precursors for the landmark case, *Brown v. Board of Education*, which struck down racial segregation in public schools in the country.

Sonia R. García

See also: American GI Forum; *Del Rio Independent School District v. Salvatierra* (1930)*; Hernández v. Texas* (1954); League of United Latin American Citizens (LULAC); Méndez, Sylvia (1936–); Pérez García, Héctor (1914–1996)

Further Reading

Castillo, Richard. 2017. "Bastrop Revives Undertold Story of 'Mexican' Schools." *Austin-American Statesman*, September 23.

"Delgado v. Bastrop ISD." *Texas State Historical Association.* http://www.tshaonline.org.

Rice, Ben H. 1948. [Judgment, Minerva Delgado et al vs. Bastrop Independent School District—1948-06-15], legal document, June 15, 1948; https://texashistory.unt.edu/ark:/67531/metapth248859. University of North Texas Libraries, The Portal to Texas History, texashistory.unt.edu; credited Houston Metropolitan Research Center at Houston Public Library.

San Miguel, Guadalupe. 1987. *"Let Them All Take Heed:" Mexican Americans and the Campaign for Educational Equality in Texas, 1910–1980.* Austin: University of Texas Press.

Valencia, Reynaldo, Sonia R. García, Henry Flores, & José R. Juárez. 2004. "Educational Equality." In *Mexican Americans and the Law: El Pueblo Unido Jamás Será Vencido.* Tucson: University of Arizona Press.

Valencia, Richard. 2008. *Chicano Students in the Court: The Mexican American Struggle for Educational Equality.* New York: New York University Press.

Depression-Era Repatriation of Mexicans

The Great Mexican Repatriation refers to the extraordinary number of Mexicans who returned to Mexico from the United States during the economic slowdown of the Great Depression. Mexican migration offices recorded over 458,000 repatriations from 1929 to 1937. In 1931, during the peak of repatriation, over 138,000 individuals entered Mexico. The numbers might be higher to account for entries not done through government entry points.

The repatriation affected all Mexicans, but most left from California and Texas, as well as the Great Lakes region and the rest of the American Southwest, which had only become part of the United States 80 years earlier. The repatriation was both voluntary and involuntary, although their proportions remain unknown. Mexicans of all political statuses were targeted: American born, naturalized, legal residents, and undocumented.

In the United States, the prolonged economic downturn of the Great Depression in the 1930s and discrimination toward Mexicans fueled the exodus. Contributors to the repatriation included federal agencies and officials, as well as local and state politicians and organizations. At the top was President Herbert Hoover, who blamed

A Depression-era Mexican migrant family stands near their broken-down car. Migrant families worked on farms as fruit and vegetable pickers during the Depression. Some were eventually repatriated to Mexico when the Depression era came to an end. (Library of Congress)

immigrants for the country's dire economic situation. Hoover instructed Secretary of Labor William Doak to deport half a million foreigners to open jobs and reduce relief expenditures, a policy that was legitimized by labeling foreigners "radicals" and "subversives." Furthermore, federal agencies passed relief measures for U.S. citizens while simultaneously excluding immigrants. Under President Franklin D. Roosevelt, H.R. Bill 3472 sought to deport individuals who were considered public charges and H.R. Bill 5921 would have made it easier to deport unwanted individuals.

During the repatriation, immigration agents raided homes of Mexicans without warrants, and newspapers and magazines called to get rid of Mexicans. To intensify and coordinate deportation efforts, the Department of Labor reorganized and strengthened the Immigration Services in 1930. If individuals asked for a formal hearing and were denied, they were barred from re-entering the United States. However, if they left voluntarily, no legal record was kept and they could legally re-enter in the future.

The Mexican government played a dual role. To protect their countrymen, the Mexican embassy in Washington, D.C., ordered its consuls to take steps to protect the interests of Mexicans. However, the Mexican government also lured back its citizens as early as 1932 by providing transportation, free land, education, and work to returning Mexicans.

The new stability in Mexico was important because from 1910 to 1920, up to 2 million people died in ongoing conflicts throughout Mexico, including the Mexican Revolution and the Cristero Wars—the Mexican government's antireligious campaign. After these conflicts, the new Mexican ruling party (National

Revolutionary Party, PNR, later renamed the Revolutionary Institutional Party, PRI) implemented programs including the provision of land and colonization projects to sustain new massive irrigation projects in many regions as well as road development. New agricultural projects in the states of Aguascalientes, Durango, Hidalgo, Coahuila, Chihuahua, and Sonora also promised to revitalize and industrialize Mexico.

The actions of the Mexican consulates were a result of the ideology of Mexican revolutionary nationalism, which intensified in the 1920s and early 1930s. Material assistance, protection of nationals, and maintaining the loyalty of Mexican citizens in the United States—as well as helping them repatriate—were consistent with the revolutionary nationalist ideas. Government officials, intellectuals, and artists like Diego Rivera argued that Mexican workers should have never left in the first place. To increase repatriations, Mexican media emphasized U.S. discrimination in employment, housing, and the judicial system.

Juve J. Cortes

See also: Mexican Repatriation; Operation Gatekeeper (1994); Operation Hold the Line/ Blockade (1993)

Further Reading

Balderrama, Francisco E., & Raymond Rodríguez. 2006. *Decade of Betrayal: Mexican Repatriation in the 1930s.* Albuquerque: University of New Mexico Press.

Hoffman, Abraham. 1974. *Unwanted Mexican Americans in the Great Depression: Repatriation Pressures, 1929–1939.* Tucson: University of Arizona Press.

Kiser, George C., & David Silverman. 1973. "Mexican Repatriation during the Great Depression." *Journal of Mexican American History* 3: 139–64.

McKay, Robert Reynolds. 1982. *Texas Mexican Repatriation during the Great Depression.* Norman: University of Oklahoma.

Development, Relief, and Education for Alien Minors Act. See DREAM Act; DREAM Act at the State Level

Díaz, Rubén, Jr.

(1973–)

A politician and member of the Democratic Party from the Bronx, New York, Rubén Díaz, Jr., is currently president of the borough of the Bronx in New York City and previously served as a representative in the New York State Assembly for District 85. At age 23, Díaz was elected to the New York State Assembly, where he served from January 1, 1997, to April 22, 2009, which made him the youngest person elected to the legislative body since Theodore Roosevelt.

During his tenure in the New York State Assembly, Díaz represented District 85, which covers the Soundview and Hunts Point sections of the Bronx. Díaz supported an expansion of the state health care system and increased funding for schools. He gained greater notoriety after the February 1999 shooting of an unarmed African immigrant named Amadou Diallo. Díaz was critical of the police and called for a federal investigation into the shooting, which earned him support from Reverend Al

Sharpton. Díaz was a part of the Rainbow Rebels, a multiethnic group of individuals who opposed the long-time political establishment in the Bronx. They were successful in their goal of ousting Bronx Democratic County leader José Rivera.

In April 2009, Díaz won a special election for the position of Bronx Borough president. He replaced Adolfo Carrión, Jr., after Barack Obama appointed Carrión to the position of director of the White House Office of Urban Affairs. As borough president, Díaz attempted to expand the economic position of the Bronx. He has consistently supported environmentally friendly infrastructure and business expansion projects for the Bronx. He supported living wage legislation in 2010, specifically the Fair Wages for New Yorkers Act, which passed in 2012. This Act mandates a $10 minimum wage that increases with inflation and is supplemented by additional wages if the worker does not receive health insurance.

Díaz ran for re-election in 2013 where he faced a Democratic primary challenge from Mark Escoffery-Bey. Díaz won with 85 percent of the vote. He proceeded to win the general election with 89 percent of the vote. Díaz focused his campaign on business expansion and job creation. He also supported the expansion of Metro North service in the Bronx, greater funding for public schools, and environmental initiatives.

During the 2016 Democratic presidential primary, Díaz supported Hillary Clinton. He continued to support Clinton during the 2016 general election. He is critical of New York City mayor Bill de Blasio, which led to widespread speculation that Díaz would challenge de Blasio in the 2017 Democratic primary election. However, in April 2017, Díaz stated that he would not run a primary campaign against the mayor after an investigation into de Blasio's fundraising ended without charges. Díaz is expected to run in 2021.

Díaz has been critical of President Trump's immigration proposal and policies. During Trump's presidential campaign, Díaz called Trump's comments about Latinos "disgusting" (Coleman, 2015). Díaz stated that he will boycott Trump's golf course located at Ferry Point Park in the Throgs Neck section of the Bronx, despite Díaz's initial praise for the project. He has also been critical of the funding cuts that Trump has proposed in response to New York City's refusal to cooperate with federal immigration enforcement.

Díaz's family is heavily involved in New York City politics. His father, Rubén Díaz, Sr., is an evangelical pastor and current Democratic New York state senator and represents the 32nd District. His two siblings both work as civil servants in New York City. Díaz's father has been a vocal opponent of same-sex marriage and abortion, despite his Democratic affiliation. As a result, Díaz, Jr.'s decision to support marriage equality in 2013 was widely reported.

Díaz was born in Puerto Rico. His parents moved to the Soundview section of the Bronx when Díaz was young. He attended Bronx public schools for primary and secondary education and later attended LaGuardia Community College and City University of New York, Lehman College, where he earned a degree in political science.

Nathan Angelo

See also: Mark-Viverito, Melissa (1969–); Trump, Donald J. (1946–) and Latinos

Further Reading

Bredderman, Will. 2015. "Boogie Down Production: Is Díaz, Jr., on Track to Become the Next Mayor?" *New York Observer,* August 5. http://observer.com/2015/08/boogie -down-production-is-ruben-diaz-jr-on-track-to-become-the-next-mayor/.

Bredderman, Will. 2017. "Bronx Borough President Will Not Challenge NYC Mayor Bill de Blasio." *New York Observer,* April 27. http://observer.com/2017/04/bronx -borough-president-ruben-diaz-jr-bill-de-blasio-mayor-challenge.

Coleman, Oli. 2015. "Bronx Borough Prez Ruben Diaz, Jr., Blasts Trump's 'Disgusting' Comments about Mexicans, Just Weeks after Offering Praise." *New York Daily News,* July 6.

Halbfinger, David. 2009. "Díaz Unites Bronx Democrats in Race for Borough President." *New York Times,* April 20. http://www.nytimes.com/2009/04/21/nyregion/21bronx .html.

Hicks, Jonathan. 1999. "After Fatal Shooting, Bronx Assemblyman Emerges as a Critic of the Police." *New York Times,* February 16. http://www.nytimes.com/1999/02/16 /nyregion/after-fatal-shooting-bronx-assemblyman-emerges-as-a-critic-of-the -police.html.

Jones-Correa, Michael. 1998. *Between Two Nations: The Political Predicament of Latinos in New York City.* Ithaca, NY: Cornell University Press.

Living Wage NYC. 2010. "Living Wage NYC Campaign Begins." May 25. http://www .livingwagenyc.org/releases/detail.php?id=1.

Terris, Ben. 2016. "Two Bronx Politicians, Father and Son, Find Themselves at Odds in the 2016 Race." *Washington Post,* April 18. https://www.washingtonpost.com /lifestyle/style/two-bronx-politicians-father-and-son-find-themselves-at-odds-in -the-2016-race/2016/04/18/dc258216-033e-11e6-9203-7b8670959b88_story.html.

Díaz-Balart, Lincoln

(1954–)

From 1993 to 2011, Lincoln Díaz-Balart was a Republican member of the U.S. House of Representatives from Florida's 21st District, which covers parts of Miami-Dade County. As a representative, Díaz-Balart was the first Cuban American Republican man to represent Florida in Congress.

Lincoln Díaz-Balart was born to Rafael Lincoln and Hilda Caballero Díaz-Balart in Havana, Cuba, on August 13, 1954. Díaz-Balart's father was deeply involved in Cuban politics, serving as president of the Senate in Cuba during the government of Fulgencio Batista. Díaz-Balart and his family left Cuba in 1959 when their house was destroyed by revolutionary forces. They appealed to New York Congressman Victor Anfuso for help in securing their legal entry into the United States. Once in the United States, Díaz-Balart obtained a degree in international relations from the University of South Florida in 1976 and a law degree from Case Western University in 1979. Díaz-Balart worked as a lawyer both in private practice and as an assistant state's attorney.

Díaz-Balart's first foray into politics took the form of his membership in the Florida Young Democrats in the late 1970s and early 1980s. He ran for the Florida legislature in 1982 against Republican Humberto Cortina but failed. While initially supporting the Democratic Party because of John F. Kennedy's tough stance against

Congressman Mario Díaz-Balart is a Republican representative for Florida's 25th congressional district. Elected in 2002, his current district includes much of southwestern Miami-Dade County. (mariodiazbalart.house.gov)

the Castro regime, Díaz-Balart began identifying more with the Republican Party in the early to mid-1980s. During the 1984 presidential election, he co-chaired the Democrats for Reagan organization. In 1985, he formally switched his party affiliation to Republican, citing his dissatisfaction with the Democratic Party's stance toward communism in Central America. Díaz-Balart was elected to the Florida House of Representatives in 1986 and the Florida Senate in a special election in 1989. He was then re-elected to the House of Representatives in 1992.

During his time in Congress, Díaz-Balart championed protections for immigrants and took a tough posture against communism abroad, particularly in Cuba. In 1997, Díaz-Balart helped the Nicaraguan Adjustment and Central American Relief Act (NACARA) become law. In the late 1970s and 1980s, Nicaraguan immigrants began entering the United States, specifically South Florida, an area Díaz-Balart represented. By the 1990s, they feared deportation. Díaz-Balart met with then-chairperson of the Immigration Subcommittee, Lamar Smith (R-Texas), and convinced him to push his bill through. With respect to Cuba, Díaz-Balart used his position in Congress to advocate for maintaining and strengthening sanctions against Cuba, with the ultimate goal of transforming Cuba into a democratic state. He formed the Cuba Democracy Group and in 1996 he co-sponsored a bill that codified the trade embargo that been in place against Cuba since the beginning of Fidel Castro's regime.

In total, Lincoln Díaz-Balart served in Congress for 18 years from the 103rd to the 111th Congress. He announced his retirement from the House of Representatives in the middle of his final term, stating he would not seek re-election. In 2010, Díaz-Balart's brother, Mario Díaz-Balart, ran for Congress in his former district and won. Díaz-Balart and his wife Cristina raised two sons, Daniel and Lincoln, Jr. The latter son died in 2013.

Jack Rockwood

See also: Díaz-Balart, Mario (1961–); Immigration as a Policy Issue; Nicaraguan Adjustment and Central American Relief Act (NACARA); United States–Cuban Relations

Further Reading

"Díaz-Balart, Lincoln." U.S. House of Representatives: History, Art & Archives. http://history.house.gov/People/Detail/12198.

MacManus, Susan. 2016. *Florida's Minority Trailblazers: The Men and Women Who Changed the Face of Florida Government.* Florida Government and Politics. Gainesville: University Press of Florida.

Moreno, Dario, & Nicol Rae. 1992. "Ethnicity and Partnership: The Eighteenth Congressional District In Miami." In Guillermo Grenier and Alex Stepick, eds. *Miami Now! Immigration, Ethnicity, and Social Change.* Gainesville: University Press of Florida, pp. 186–204.

Vanderbush, Walt, & Patrick J. Haney. 1999. "Policy toward Cuba in the Clinton Administration." *Political Science Quarterly* 114, no. 3: 387–408.

Díaz-Balart, Mario

(1961–)

Of Cuban descent, Mario Díaz-Balart is a Republican member of the U.S. House of Representatives representing the 25th congressional district of Florida. His congressional district is located in South Florida and encompasses parts of Miami-Dade, Collier, Lee, and Hendry counties and includes a sizeable Latino population, particularly Cuban Americans. He was first elected to this position in 2002 after serving 14 years as a representative and senator in the Florida state legislature.

Díaz-Balart was born in Fort Lauderdale, Florida, and studied political science at the University of South Florida. He is the son of immigrants from Cuba who fled the country due to the anti-Castro stance taken by his father during the Cuban Revolution. Members of Díaz-Balart's family have served in political office in both Cuba and the United States. Most notably, his father, Rafael, was the majority leader of the Cuban House of Representatives before the revolution and was later elected to the Cuban Senate but was not allowed to assume the position due to the revolution. In the United States, Diaz-Balart's brother, Lincoln, served as a Republican member of the House of Representatives for the 21st congressional district of Florida from 1993 to 2011. This marks one of the few instances in which brothers have served in Congress at the same time.

During his eight terms in Congress, Diaz-Balart has served on several committees and is currently the chairman of the Subcommittee on Transportation, Housing, and Urban Development along with being a member of the House Appropriations Committee; the State, Foreign Operations, and Related Programs; the House Committee on the Budget; and Defense subcommittees. He is also a founding member and chairman of the Congressional Hispanic Conference, which focuses on issues affecting the Hispanic community in the United States and abroad.

Diaz-Balart is also known for his conservative stance across both social and economic issues and has a strong record of voting with the Republican Party. In fact, Diaz-Balart currently has a 100 percent record of voting in favor of positions espoused by the current administration (FiveThirtyEight, 2017). In terms of his more conservative stance, Diaz-Balart is pro-life and has voiced opposition to same-sex marriage. He also favors the repeal of Obamacare and has expressed doubts about global warming. In addition, Diaz-Balart is fiscally conservative and argues for more efficiency in government programs and more responsible spending by the federal government. He was even chosen to share the conservative stance of the Republican Party in the Spanish-language response to the State of the Union address.

However, although Diaz-Balart recently praised President Trump's stance on securing the nation's southern border, he diverges from many Republicans in his desire to enact immigration reform that will allow those who are in the country without documentation to stay and gain legal status if they meet certain requirements. This plan has received resistance from many within the Republican Party who view the granting of legal status as amnesty. Yet Diaz-Balart has responded to recent calls for immigration reform by reiterating that there needed to be a "humane solution to those living in the shadows" (U.S. House of Representatives, 2017).

As a representative of Florida, Diaz-Balart has likewise championed legislation geared more specifically to his district and his constituency. In particular, he has focused on minimizing property damage and loss of life in areas vulnerable to hurricanes and other natural disasters. This led Diaz-Balart to introduce legislation that provides incentives for utilizing resilient building materials, which has resulted in buildings that are better able to withstand such disasters. Furthermore, he has focused on preservation of the Everglades in South Florida and founded the Everglades Caucus in Congress to fight for greater funding for restoration of this ecosystem. Also, in keeping with his Cuban constituents who fled the revolution, Diaz-Balart has staunchly opposed President Obama's executive order to lift the economic embargo on Cuba due to the communist government still existing in that country. Although he has received no guarantees from the current administration, Díaz-Balart continues to advocate for the embargo to be reinstated until either the current regime is no longer in power or human rights issues in Cuba are addressed.

Amy Stringer

See also: Díaz-Balart, Lincoln (1954–)

Further Reading

Chen, Elaine. 2014. "The Power of the Díaz-Balart Name, from Cuba to Miami." *WLRN*, July 10. http://wlrn.org/post/power-diaz-balart-name-cuba-miami.

FiveThirtyEight. 2017. "Mario Diaz-Balart." https://projects.fivethirtyeight.com/congress -trump-score/mario-diaz-balart.

House Republicans. 2016. "Mario Diaz-Balart." https://www.gop.gov/member/mario-diaz -balart.

Iannelli, Jerry. 2017. "Miami Rep. Mario Diaz-Balart Denies He's Trading Health-Care Vote for Cuba Concessions." *Miami New Times,* March 24. http://www.miaminew times.com/news/miami-rep-mario-diaz-balart-supports-ahca-denies-hes-trading -vote-for-cuba-change-9228317.

Mario Diaz-Balart for Congress. 2014. "About Mario." http://www.mariodiazbalart.com /about-mario-diaz-balart.

U.S. House of Representatives. 2017. "Mario Diaz-Balart." http://mariodiazbalart.house .gov.

Dickerson Montemayor, Alicia

(1902–1989)

A 20th-century civil rights activist, feminist, and folk artist, Alicia Dickerson Montemayor was a lifelong advocate for the descriptive and substantive representation of women and youth in politics generally, and in the League of United Latin American Citizens (LULAC) in particular. Montemayor remains a key political figure in Latinx politics and Mexican American history, and is viewed as being important to the 20th-century struggle for gender equality.

Montemayor was born on August 6, 1902, in Laredo, Texas, to John Randolph and Manuela Dickerson. She grew up in a bilingual household with a "Mexico Texano identity"; however, she also acknowledged and celebrated her indigenous and Irish heritage (Orozco, 1996). She graduated from high school in 1924 and attended Laredo Business School during the evenings for a year. After the untimely death of her father, Montemayor remained in Laredo with family, despite her desire to study law. Between 1934 and 1949, Montemayor, working as a social worker, investigated Mexican American welfare cases in Webb County, Texas.

Montemayor joined LULAC—one of the leading Mexican American civil rights organizations in the United States—as a charter member in 1936. She quickly rose through the ranks, eventually serving as secretary (1936–1937) and president (1938–1939). In her charter, the Laredo Ladies LULAC, women were encouraged to vote, hold citizenship classes, and be active in politics and in the community. Montemayor was selected to serve as a national delegate at the 1937 LULAC National Convention and Exposition. At the convention, she was elected to the position of second national vice-president general, making her the first woman in LULAC to be elected to a national office not expressly designated for a woman.

Between 1937 and 1940, Montemayor served as associate editor of LULAC News, director general of Junior LULAC, and second national vice-president general. In her role as vice-president, Montemayor became a leading voice for women in the organization. She promoted the creation of more Ladies LULAC chapters. She also wrote numerous articles and editorials on women's rights and patriarchal ideology in LULAC. In her first essay, titled "We Need More Ladies Councils," Montemayor pushed for a more active role for women in LULAC. She denounced patriarchy and notions of male superiority in her legendary 1938 editorial, titled "Son Muy Hombres?" And in "A Message from Our Second Vice-President General," Montemayor called for more women to join LULAC. Beyond being a voice for women in LULAC, Montemayor was a voice for the youth. She organized a coed Junior LULAC youth chapter, wrote its charter, and served as its director general between 1939 and 1940. Montemayor left LULAC in 1940. Throughout her time as a LULAC member, Montemayor continuously empowered, advocated for, and substantively represented the interests of women, youth, and middle-class Mexican Americans.

In 1947, Montemayor enrolled in Laredo Junior College and took classes for two years in the evenings. She also worked as a business owner of several dress shops in the 1930s and 1950s; as organist, teacher, and organizer with Our Lady of Guadalupe Catholic Church; and as a school registrar in the Laredo school district between

1956 and 1972. After retiring as school registrar, Montemayor began painting and eventually established herself as a folk artist. Although starting with gourds in 1973, Montemayor was painting on a number of surfaces, including tin and Masonite, by 1976. By 1978, she was painting on frames she had personally designed. In her paintings, Montemayor often depicted family, women, and nature and used bright primary colors. Her work, which many consider to be "authentically Mexican," has been displayed both in the United States and in Mexico, including an exhibition in 1978 sponsored by The League of United Chicano Artists of Austin, and an exhibition in 1970 sponsored by The Instituto Cultural Mexicano in San Antonio.

On September 8, 1927, she married Francisco Montemayor, and they had two sons: Francisco and Aurelio Montemayor. Montemayor died on May 13, 1989, and is buried in the Catholic cemetery in Laredo, Texas. Montemayor's materials, including her photographs, artwork, and correspondence, are archived in The Nettie Lee Benson Latin American Collection at the University of Texas, Austin.

Taneisha N. Means

See also: League of United Latin American Citizens (LULAC)

Further Reading

Alice Dickerson Montemayor Papers, Benson Latin American Collection, University of Texas Libraries, the University of Texas at Austin.

Orozco, Cynthia E. n.d. "Alice Dickerson Montemayor." *Texas State Historical Association.* http://www.tshaonline.org/handbook/online/articles/fmobl.

Orozco, Cynthia E. 1996. "Alice Dickerson Montemayor's: Feminist Challenge to LULAC in the 1930s." https://www.idra.org/resource-center/alice-dickerson-montemayors-feminist-challenge-to-lulac-in-the-1930s/.

Orozco, Cynthia E. 1997. "Alice Dickerson Montemayor: Feminism and Mexican American Politics in the 1930s." In Elizabeth Jameson and Susan Armitage, eds. *Writing the Range: Race, Class, and Culture in the Women's West.* Norman: University of Oklahoma Press, pp. 435–57.

Orozco, Cynthia E. 2009. *No Mexicans, Women, or Dogs Allowed: The Rise of the Mexican American Civil Rights Movement.* Austin: University of Texas Press.

Quiroz, Anthony. 2015. *Leaders of the Mexican American Generation: Biographical Essays.* Boulder: University Press of Colorado.

Ruiz, Vicki L. 2008. *From Out of the Shadows: Mexican Women in Twentieth-Century America.* 10th ed. Oxford, UK: Oxford University Press.

San Miguel, Guadalupe, Jr. 1987. *"Let All of Them Take Heed": Mexican Americans and the Campaign for Educational Equality in Texas, 1910–1981.* Austin: University of Texas Press.

Discrimination against Latinas/os

Over time, scholars have shown how racial discrimination has become embedded in the criminal justice, health care, and education systems of the United States, as well as in its housing and hiring practices. Racial discrimination is typically perpetuated by racialized policies with redistributive and punitive undertones (i.e., drug sentencing laws, mass incarceration, welfare policy, inequitable public school funding, redlining, and gerrymandering) (Alexander, 2012; Citrin, Green, and

Sears, 1990). Most research concerning discrimination tends focuses on white attitudes of discrimination, the black–white binary, or the significance of individual factors such as income or ideology. Rarely do studies consider experiences and perceptions of discrimination against Latinas/os.

The relationship between political engagement, local socioeconomic conditions, and perceptions of Latino discrimination is important for two reasons. First is the changing nature of racial discrimination over time, the gradual broad shift away from overt racism to new or institutional racism. When examining perceptions of discrimination, it is often hard to disentangle the perpetrator, people, and institutions. Second, localities have become increasingly divergent in terms of housing, education, and employment opportunities for Latinas/os, sparking dynamic migration patterns. Thus, in addition to individual differences in experiences of discrimination, historical analysis suggests varying experiences of institutional discrimination by place. The movement of Latinos potentially further complicates the Latino mobilization conundrum.

WHAT IS DISCRIMINATION AGAINST LATINAS/OS?

To be clear, racial discrimination occurs when someone is treated unfavorably due to their race or personal characteristics associated with race (such as hair texture, skin color, or certain facial features). Related to racial discrimination is color discrimination, which involves unfair treatment because of skin color complexion. In interracial marriages, someone may experience racial/color discrimination due to the race or color of their spouse. It is also possible for the victim and the individual who inflicts discrimination to be the same race or color. Great diversity within the Latina/o community leads to varying experiences of race/color discrimination.

WHY LATINO DISCRIMINATION IS A PRESSING POLITICAL ECONOMY ISSUE

An often overlooked but enduring paradox in American political economy is that Latinos are both desired and viewed as a threat in U.S. society. The racial threat theory suggests that Latinas/os are viewed as a threat, raising feelings of fear and economic anxiety among mostly middle-class and poor whites and some blacks, possibly leading to racial discriminatory behavior. Contrastingly, Latinas/os are simultaneously desired by a segment of the business class for their labor and/or skills. In the American economic system there are elements of racial capitalism, which connects a cycle of low-wage expendable labor and residential segregation among Latinas/os to a history of racism and colonialism/conquest. In addition to being desired economically by the elite business class, Latinos are desired by the political elite for votes. Politicians often walk a fine line attempting to engage Latino voters while also not wanting to alienate those who discriminate against them. Ironically, similar to the way economic anxiety triggers feelings of being under threat for whites, so racial discrimination triggers feelings of being under threat for Latinos.

The prevalence of racial discrimination against Latinos despite U.S. society's principled commitment to racial equality has societal consequences. Based on polling, the majority of Latinos have experienced both individual and institutional racism, particularly in regard to issues of employment. Widespread experiences of individual and institutional discrimination heighten feelings of group threat. As individuals begin to feel like a core part of their identity is being attacked, whether real or perceived, they are most likely to turn to their in-group for support. Perceptions of discrimination against one's self or one's group are used as a measure of marginalized status. Group threat can activate greater group unity and group consciousness, while simultaneously fostering increasing political distrust and alienation.

However, not all Latinos experience racial discrimination. Those who feel as though they have not been treated unfairly because of their race may not feel like their group is being threatened or have any sense of group consciousness. While organizations work to increase the political incorporation of Latinos, intragroup diversity complicates mobilization efforts, particularly around issues of economic justice. Latinos of different country-of-origin groups across the United States are linked through common experiences of discrimination. As grassroots groups attempt to mobilize from a community perspective, it becomes clearer that there may not be a unified Latino community perspective. There remain segments of the Latino community who either support race-neutral politics, are ignorant of interracial dynamics, or have not experienced racial discrimination. Varying experiences of discrimination within the Latino community make some linkages stronger than others, which negatively affects the conceptualization of a pan-ethnic Latino identity and the possibility of a national Latino political agenda, particularly if centered on economic justice.

UNDERSTANDING LATINOS' VIEWS ON DISCRIMINATION: FOUR EXISTING PERSPECTIVES

Colorism. Colorism is a form of within-group racial discrimination that highlights systems of ethnic and racial stratification established over the course of three distinct historical eras: conquest, colonization, and post-colonization. Though American society has adopted color-blind rhetoric as a strategy to deny and minimize skin-color privilege, today and historically, at the individual level colorism has been a contributing factor in experiences of discrimination. Colorism has led scholars to warn against the use of a pan-ethnic label, such as Latinos/as because it obscures within-group diverging realities and inequities. Darker Latino individuals are more likely to experience racial discrimination than lighter-skinned Latinos, which confers a racialized privilege to Latinos with European phenotypes. The privilege conferred to lighter-skinned Latinos/as is rarely acknowledged but reflected in their higher socioeconomic status compared to darker Latinos/as.

A New Type of Ideology: Color-Blind Conservatism. Color-blind conservatism theorists contend that color-blindness is used to dismiss contemporary instances of racism and retreat from targeted institutional approaches to combating racial discrimination. Embedded in color-blind conservatism is racial resentment theory, which suggests some Americans believe racial progress has been made, racism no longer exists, and racial discrimination is no longer a major problem. Though typically thought of from a white American perspective, a growing group of scholars is addressing the impact of color-blind conservatism and an increasingly conservative political context on Latino's perceptions of whether racial discrimination is a present problem.

Increasing Intragroup Socioeconomic Inequality. Recognizing increasing socioeconomic polarization, intragroup socioeconomic inequality theory suggests higher-income Latinos may underestimate the current prevalence of racial discrimination, given their privileged position. Others argue racial and economic oppression across income and education levels strengthens Latino identity, shared group interests, and a belief in linked fate. For example, based on Lichter, Parisi, and Taquino's (2015) study of Latino segregation, economic mobility is no guarantee of residential integration. High-income and highly educated Latinos continue to personally experience discrimination in higher education and senior management. Given that most elites of color come from humble roots, they are also exposed to experiences of marginalization through interactions with family members.

Age-Cohort Theory. Another theory, age-cohort theory, holds that individuals may vary in their perceptions of racial discrimination based on varying collective memories/reference points. Some scholars have suggested that young Latinos, though aware of educational and economic inequities, are less likely than older generations to connect current racial disparities to a legacy of racial discrimination. Today the Dreamers movement and fast-food worker protests suggest otherwise. Young Latinos continue to invoke the grievances of Chicano social justice icons like César Chávez and Dolores Huerta, pointing to a sustained awareness of economic exploitation and racial discrimination across generations.

Colorism, color-blind conservatism, intragroup socioeconomic inequality, and age-cohort theorists have yet to address the role of local distinctions in shaping perceptions of discrimination within racial groups. These existing theories must be revisited to account for the changing American landscape of economic and educational opportunities.

A NEW APPROACH: THE INCREASING IMPORTANCE OF PLACE AND DIVERGING DISCRIMINATION ATTITUDES

Given recent migration patterns and changes in the American political economy, increased attention to how local socioeconomic conditions help explain divided Latino views on racial discrimination is needed. Neoclassical economists in the 1980s hypothesized that competitive market forces would eventually lead to the demise of discrimination. Instead it seems as though competitive market forces have continued to exacerbate economic inequality, increased intragroup inequality, and precipitated a stark increase in racial tension due to economic anxiety. Less is known about how the feedback effects of local economic restructuring and structural racism, such as increasing concentrations of poverty and low homeownership rates, affect views of racial discrimination in comparison to individual-level factors. Examining Latino perceptions of discrimination from a political economy perspective helps illuminate the types of local conditions where racial tension is particularly high and who is most affected.

A majority of Latinos no longer live in inner-city ethnic enclaves on the West Side of Chicago or the East Side of Los Angeles. Now the Latino individual lived experience varies more by place. Today, in comparison to the 1970s, a substantial portion of Latinos live in rural areas in states like Utah, Idaho, and Nevada. Similar to African Americans, changes in Latino population and poverty levels can vary drastically from county to county. For example, in 1970 Los Angeles County had a total of 417,065 Spanish families, of which 14 percent lived below poverty. In 2013, 4.5 million Latinos lived in Los Angeles, of which 23.7 percent lived below poverty. In 1970 Washoe County, Nevada, which includes Reno, had 2,091 Spanish families, and 9.13 percent of those families lived below poverty. In 2013, about 98,000 Latinos lived in Washoe County, and 25.04 percent lived below poverty. Economic conditions for Latinos are now the most bleak in traditional "gateway cities" such as Los Angeles and New York. For example, New York City has one of the lowest rates of Latino homeownership in the country at 26.5 percent and in the Bronx, where the population is 55 percent Latino, roughly 30 percent of households are below the poverty line (Kotkin, 2015). According to the 2012 Collaborative Multi-Racial Post-Election Survey (CMPS), the largest perceptual gap between blacks, Latinos, and whites in regard to discrimination is in the Northeast, where 90 percent of blacks and Latinos believe discrimination is a problem (major or minor), compared to 47 percent of white Americans. For Latinos there is greater regional variability in perceptions of discrimination than seen with white Americans, which confirms the need for further exploration of spatial distinctions in racial attitudes beyond a South/non-South dichotomy.

FUTURE RESEARCH, DISCUSSION, AND CONCLUSION

Though some may claim rapid Latino population growth is a trend to be feared, it may be in U.S. society's best interest to seek understanding by further researching the intricacies of Latino public opinion. This essay has discussed both the individual and contextual dynamics of how Latinos perceive racial discrimination, highlighting sources of disagreement within the Latino community due to generational, socioeconomic, and skin color differences. Future studies must continue to focus on intragroup disagreements over racial discrimination through a spatial and political economy lens. By moving beyond use of a black–white binary in a national framework, existing theories can evolve along with changing American neighborhoods in a new economy. Researchers must also continue to shed light on the connection between employment opportunity, economic anxiety, and Latino discrimination, a web of conflict due to a long history of Latino labor being racialized.

Jessica Lynn Stewart

Further Reading

Alcoff, Linda Martin. 2003. "Latino/as, Asian Americans, and the Black–White Binary." *The Journal of Ethics* 7, no. 1: 5–27.

Alexander, Michelle. *The New Jim Crow: Mass Incarceration in the Age of Colorblindness.* New York: The New Press, 2012.

Bonilla-Silva, Eduardo. 2006. *Racism without Racists: Color-Blind Racism and the Persistence of Racial Inequality in the United States.* Lanham, MD: Rowman & Littlefield Publishers.

Citrin, Jack, Donald Philip Green, & David O. Sears. 1990. "White Reactions to Black Candidates: When Does Race Matter?" *Public Opinion Quarterly* 54, no. 1: 74–96.

Cobas, José A., Jorge Duany, & Joe R. Feagin. 2009. *How the United States Racializes Latinos: White Hegemony and Its Consequences.* London: Paradigm.

Crowley, Martha, Daniel T. Lichter, & Richard N. Turner. 2015. "Diverging Fortunes? Economic Well-Being of Latinos and African Americans in New Rural Destinations." *Social Science Research* 51: 77–92.

Escobar, Edward. 1993. "The Dialectics of Repression: The Los Angeles Police Department and the Chicano Movement, 1968–1971." *Journal of American History* 79, no. 4: 1483.

Henry, Patrick J., & David O. Sears. 2002. "The Symbolic Racism 2000 Scale." *Political Psychology* 23, no. 2: 253–83.

Hernández-Léon, Rubén, & Victor Zúniga. 2000. "'Making Carpet by the Mile': The Emergence of a Latino Immigrant Community in an Industrial Region of the U.S. Historic South." *Social Science Quarterly* 81: 49–66.

Hochschild, Jennifer L., Vesla M. Weaver, & Traci R. Burch. 2012. *Creating a New Racial Order: How Immigration, Multiracialism, Genomics, and the Young Can Remake Race in America.* Princeton, NJ: Princeton University Press.

Kotkin, Joel. 2016. *The Human City: Urbanism for the Rest of Us.* Chicago: Agate Publishing.

Lichter, Daniel T., & Kenneth M. Johnson. 2009. "Immigrant Gateways and Hispanic Migration in New Destinations." *International Migration Review* 43: 496–518.

Lichter, Daniel T., Domenico Parisi, & Michael C. Taquino. 2015. "Spatial Assimilation in U.S. Cities and Communities? Emerging Patterns of Hispanic Segregation from Blacks and Whites." *The Annals of the American Academy of Political and Social Science* 660, no. 1: 36–56.

Logan, John R. 2011. "Separate and Unequal: The Neighborhood Gap for Blacks, Hispanics and Asians in Metropolitan America." *Project US2010 Report*, pp. 1–22.

Parks, Virginia. 2012. "The Uneven Geography of Racial and Ethnic Wage Inequality: Specifying Local Labor Market Effects." *Annals of the Association of American Geographers* 102, no. 3: 700–25.

Pérez, Debra Joy, Lisa Fortuna, & Margarita Alegria. 2008. "Prevalence and Correlates of Everyday Discrimination among US Latinos." *Journal of Community Psychology* 36, no. 4: 421–33.

Rodriguez, Nestor P. 1993. "Economic Restructuring and Latino Growth in Houston." In Joan Moore and Raquel Pinderhughes, eds. *The Barrio: Latinos and the Underclass Debate.* New York: Russell Sage Foundation, pp. 101–28.

Sanchez, Gabriel R. 2006. "The Role of Group Consciousness in Latino Public Opinion." *Political Research Quarterly* 59, no. 3: 435–46.

Sullivan, Mercer L. 1993. "Puerto Ricans in Sunset Park, Brooklyn: Poverty amidst Ethnic and Economic Diversity." In Joan Moore and Raquel Pinderhughes, eds. *The Barrios: Latinos and the Underclass Debate.* New York: Russell Sage Foundation, pp. 1–25.

Telles, Edward M., & Vilma Ortiz. 2008. *Generations of Exclusion: Mexican-Americans, Assimilation, and Race.* New York: Russell Sage Foundation.

Tesler, Michael, & David O. Sears. 2010. *Obama's Race: The 2008 Election and the Dream of a Post-Racial America.* Chicago: University of Chicago Press.

Tuch, Steven A., & Michael Hughes. 2011. "Whites' Racial Policy Attitudes in the Twenty-First Century: The Continuing Significance of Racial Resentment." *The Annals of the American Academy of Political and Social Science* 634, no. 1: 134–52.

Zúniga, Victor, & Rubén Hernández-Léon. 2005. *New Destinations: Mexican Immigration in the United States.* New York: Russell Sage Foundation.

DREAM Act

The "DREAM Act" refers to a number of pieces of legislation proposed in Congress and designed to grant legal status to undocumented immigrants, particularly those who arrived in the United States as children and pursued higher education or military service. It takes its name from the title of a Senate bill introduced in 2001, the "Development, Relief, and Education for Alien Minors Act." Potential beneficiaries of such legislation are commonly referred to as "DREAMers." As of January 2018, the legislation remains unenacted, though it continues to be a contentious political issue.

The legislative history of the DREAM Act begins in the 107th Congress, in 2001. In response to the growing questions around the status of young, undocumented immigrants, Luis Gutierrez (D-IL) introduced a bill in the House designed to protect alien school-age and college students from removal from the United States. In the same term of Congress, Orrin Hatch (R-UT) and Dick Durbin (D-IL) introduced a similar bill in the Senate; the Senate bill was the first to be called the

The reflection of demonstrators on a shop window. A woman carries a poster with the image of Dr. King and the slogan "We Too Have a Dream" in reference to DREAMer rights, Washington, D.C., 2011. (Montes-Bradley/iStockphoto.com)

DREAM Act. The bill had two purposes: first, to extend higher education benefits (including federal student loan programs) to children of immigrants, and, second, to give permanent resident status to children of immigrants if they filed an application with the government and met a series of conditions. The conditions for permanent resident status included earning a high school diploma, being of "good moral character," and, for students no longer in high school, enrolling or having graduated from an institution of higher education. Beneficiaries of the DREAM Act would not be given citizenship, but they would be able to live in the United States permanently and work legally. It is possible that, once given legal status, "DREAMers" could apply for citizenship under the traditional naturalization process.

The DREAM Act and subsequent related legislation have garnered varying degrees of bipartisan support but have never become law. The various versions of the DREAM Act have modified the requirements for applicants, but the central feature of all the proposed legislation has been the award of permanent, legal status based on satisfying a set of conditions similar to the original act. The closest the legislation has come to passage was in 2010, when the House of Representatives passed a version of the DREAM Act, but the bill failed to garner the 60 votes in the Senate necessary to overcome a filibuster.

Notably, the original sponsor of the DREAM Act, Senator Orrin Hatch, voted against the measure in 2010, an indication of how politically contentious the issue had become in the previous decade. Critics of the DREAM Act, often conservative Republicans, frame it as an "amnesty" bill that rewards undocumented immigrants who did not follow the procedures of the immigration system. On the other hand, advocates for the legislation argue that it is a solution to the perceived unfairness of deporting a person who was brought to the United States through the action of his or her parents. Advocates also argue that clarifying these immigrants' legal status would have economic benefits, as they would be able to pursue educational opportunities and openly contribute to the workforce.

As of January 2018, the prospects for the DREAM Act becoming law are dim. In July 2017, Senators Lindsey Graham (R-SC) and Richard Durbin (D-IL) introduced a version in the Senate, while Representatives Lucille Roybal-Allard (D-CA) and Ileana Ros-Lehtinen (R-FL) did so in the House. Other House members of both parties have also introduced related legislation. However, President Trump's strongly anti-immigrant rhetoric, as well as his cancellation of President Obama's DACA policy, suggest that the DREAM Act is unlikely to become law in the near future.

Collin Paschall and Gisela Sin

See also: Deferred Action for Childhood Arrivals (DACA)/Deferred Action for Parents of Americans and Lawful Permanent Residents (DAPA); DREAM Act at the State Level

Further Reading

American Immigration Council. 2017. "The Dream Act, DACA, and Other Policies Designed to Protect Dreamers." *American Immigration Council,* September 6. https://www.americanimmigrationcouncil.org/research/dream-act-daca-and -other-policies-designed-protect-dreamers.

Barron, Elisha. 2011. "The Development, Relief, and Education for Alien Minors (DREAM) Act." *Harvard Journal on Legislation* 48, no. 2: 623–56.

Bruno, Andorra, Karma Ester, Margaret Mikyung Lee, Alison Siskin, & Ruth Ellen Wasem. 2011. "Immigration Legislation and Issues in the 111th Congress." *Congressional Research Service,* January 18. https://fas.org/sgp/crs/homesec/R40848 .pdf.

Conger, Cristen. 2011. "What Is the DREAM Act?" *HowStuffWorks.com,* July 21. https:// people.howstuffworks.com/dream-act.htm.

Congressional Research Service. 2015. "Unauthorized Alien Students: Issues and 'DREAM Act' Legislation." *Congressional Research Service,* January 20. https://www .everycrsreport.com/files/20150120_RL33863_1971a9bbe615665b6ffd96d271d6c 6fbe2edd307.pdf.

"DACA and the DREAM Act." *Georgetown Law Library.* http://guides.ll.georgetown.edu /c.php?g=592919&p=4170929.

Edwards, Ryan D., Francesca Ortega, & Philip E. Wolgin. 2017. "The State-by-State Economic Benefits of Passing the Dream Act." *Center for American Progress,* October 26. https://www.americanprogress.org/issues/immigration/news/2017/10/26 /441298/the-state-by-state-economic-benefits-of-passing-the-dream-act/.

Fuchs, Chris. 2017. "'Original Dreamer' Still Fights for Undocumented Immigrants 16 Years after First Dream Act." *NBC News,* March 30. https://www.nbcnews.com /news/asian-america/original-dreamer-still-fights-undocumented-immigrants-16 -years-after-first-n740491.

Jaggers, Jeremiah, W. Jay Gabbard, & Shanna J. Jaggers. 2014. "The Devolution of U.S. Immigration Policy: An Examination of the History and Future of Immigration Policy." *Journal of Policy Practice* 13: 3–15.

Olivares, Mariela. 2013. "Renewing the Dream: Dream Act Redux and Immigration Reform." *Harvard Latino Law Review* 16: 79–126.

Wong, Scott. 2010. "GOP Rises, DREAM Act Falters." *Politico,* December 7. https://www .politico.com/story/2010/12/gop-rises-dream-act-falters-046052.

Wong, Tom K., Greisa Martinez Rosas, Adrian Reyna, Ignacia Rodriguez, Patrick O'Shea, Tom Jawetz, & Philip E. Wolgin. 2016. "New Study of DACA Beneficiaries Shows Positive Economic and Educational Outcomes." *Center for American Progress,* October 18. https://www.americanprogress.org/issues/immigration/news/2016/10 /18/146290/new-study-of-daca-beneficiaries-shows-positive-economic-and -educational-outcomes.

DREAM Act at the State Level

The Development, Relief, and Education for Alien Minors Act, commonly referred to as the DREAM Act, is a congressional legislative proposal to create educational opportunities for undocumented students at the state and federal levels. All proposals called "Dream Acts" improve access to higher education opportunities for undocumented immigrants who arrived as children, often called "DREAMers." Many DREAMers have spent the majority of their lives within the United States and are, or will be, graduates of U.S. secondary schools. Although federal action has stalled, several states have implemented various state-level reforms. As of 2016, 21 states have created policies aimed at increasing access to higher education for DREAMers, while others have created policies aimed at limiting access for undocumented students.

The DREAM Act was first introduced in Congress in 2001 and has seen frequent reintroductions in both the House and Senate by both Republican and Democratic sponsors. The various reintroductions vary in the extent of benefits ranging from access to in-state tuition or financial aid to pathways for permanent legal status or citizenship. The DREAM Act has been acted on in both chambers, having passed the U.S. House of Representatives in 2010 and the Senate in 2013. However, the bill has never succeeded in passing both chambers during the same Congress and remains a source of political contention. With federal action deadlocked, many states have opted to address the issue themselves. Much like the federal DREAM Act, state policies are sources of deep political division. Advocates and support organizations, such as United We Dream, argue that placing obstacles in the way of people who arrived as children—through no fault of their own—is counter to American values and decreases the competitiveness of the U.S. workforce and economy. Opponents argue that the DREAM Act would incentivize undocumented immigration and benefit undocumented immigrants at the expense of citizens and legal residents.

State policies also vary in the extent of benefits. The spectrum of state policies ranges from states like California, New Mexico, and Washington, which have passed laws to make undocumented students eligible for in-state tuition rates and state financial aid, to states such as Georgia and Montana, where some college systems ban undocumented student enrollment (DEEP, 2015; Perez, 2014). The 2012 Deferred Action for Childhood Arrivals (DACA) policy, established by executive order by President Obama, provides some students in-roads to higher education. Some states, such as South Carolina and Alabama, ban enrollment of undocumented students but may enroll DACA students (DEEP, 2015; NILC.org, 2017). Policies that permit undocumented students to be eligible for in-state tuition prices, often called "tuition equity," are available at all or some public colleges in 21 states (Gordon, 2016). California, Hawaii, Illinois, Minnesota, New Mexico, Oklahoma, Texas, and Washington provide both tuition equity and some form of access to state financial aid or scholarships (DEEP, 2015).

The range of policies on tuition equity, financial aid, and eligibility creates widespread variation in educational opportunity for undocumented students. As diverse as the policies themselves are the times and methods by which DREAM Act provisions (and their antitheses) are implemented. Provisions have been created by state legislatures, ballot propositions, and decisions issued by boards of regents. Some states, like Texas, the first to pass a state-level DREAM Act in 2001, established tuition equity at the same time as access to financial aid, while other states, like California, implemented tuition equity (2001) and financial aid (2013) separately. The Colorado tuition equity policy, or Colorado ASSET, became law in 2013, but had been introduced and debated for 10 years before succeeding. Even after a policy is implemented, challenges are not uncommon. Kansas's 2004 tuition equity law faced two legislative challenges and a lawsuit aimed at rolling back tuition benefits. Until action from Congress brings a nationwide policy, access to higher education for DREAMers will likely continue to vary greatly according to their state of residence.

Angelina L. Gonzalez-Aller

See also: Deferred Action for Childhood Arrivals (DACA)/Deferred Action for Parents of Americans and Lawful Permanent Residents (DAPA); DREAM Act; United We Dream

Further Reading

Chávez, Maria, Jessica Lavariega Monforti, & Melissa R. Michelson. 2014. *Living the Dream: New Immigration Policies and the Lives of Undocumented Latino Youth.* Boulder, CO: Paradigm Publishers.

DEEP. 2015. "Tuition and State Aid for Undocumented Students and DACA Grantees: Access by State." http://unitedwedream.org/wp-content/uploads/2014/05/DEEP_TuitionAidMap_June2015.pdf; http://unitedwedream.org/wp-content/uploads/2014/05/DEEP_TuitionAidMap_June2015.pdf.

Gordon, L. 2016. "Some States Bypass Congress, Create Their Own Versions of the DREAM Act." *The Hechinger Report*, April 7. http://www.pbs.org/newshour/rundown/some-states-bypass-congress-create-their-own-versions-of-the-dream-act/.

NCSL. 2015. "Undocumented Student Tuition." *National Conference of State Legislatures.* http://www.ncsl.org/research/education/undocumented-student-tuition-overview.aspx.

NILC.org. 2017. "Toolkit: Access to Postsecondary Education." https://www.nilc.org/issues/education/eduaccesstoolkit/eduaccesstoolkit2/—maps.

Perez, Z. J. 2014. "Removing Barriers to Higher Education for Undocumented Students." https://cdn.americanprogress.org/wp-content/uploads/2014/12/UndocHigherEd-report2.pdf.

TheDream.US. 2017. "Education Resources." http://www.thedream.us/resources/education/.

E

Echaveste, Maria

(1954–)

A former advisor to President Bill Clinton, Maria Echaveste is the only Latina to have held the title of White house deputy chief of staff; this makes her the highest-ranking Latinx to have ever served in a presidential administration.

Born in 1954 to Mexican immigrant parents in Harlingen, Texas, she grew up the eldest of seven. Her father had come to the United States under the Bracero Program, an initiative that brought guest workers from Mexico to deal with agricultural labor shortages exacerbated by World War II. When Maria was a year old, her parents, along with several other families, made the long trek to California's central valley, the agricultural "bread basket" of the West. Her parents toiled in the fields and, like other children of farmworkers, Maria helped her parents by picking grapes, stone fruit, and cotton. At age 12, she and her family moved to Oxnard, California, the strawberry capital of California, again in the never-ending search for better wages and living conditions. Although her parents had little education, Maria excelled in California public schools. She recalls finding refuge in her local and school libraries, "I would just go through the stacks . . . . books revealed another world of places and possibilities to me" (Interview with author, May 2017).

Echaveste entered Stanford in 1972. She recalls the culture shock of being a Chicana on the elite campus during a time when women's and civil rights discourse, Chicano politics, and the issue of farmworker rights were heightened across California. She majored in anthropology and was active in M.E.Ch.A. and Third World coalition politics. There she thought about the larger questions of inequality, culture, and social change. After a year working in Washington, D.C., Echaveste went to the University of California, Berkeley to receive her JD in 1980.

After a decade working as a corporate attorney, Echaveste joined the Clinton/Gore presidential campaign in 1992 as the national Latino coordinator. She worked on transition, then at the Department of Labor, and finally the White House. Over eight years, Echaveste worked on issues as diverse as civil rights, labor, family and medical leave policy bankruptcy, Latin America, and immigration. From 1998 to 2001 Echaveste served as deputy chief of staff. In that capacity, she coordinated the development of a range of policy initiatives, including education, economic development, and disaster relief. She also oversaw the development of President Clinton's State of the Union addresses for 1999 and 2000, and participated in many of the president's foreign and domestic trips.

Upon leaving the White House, Echaveste became a founding partner of Nueva Vista Group (now NVG), a Washington, D.C.–based consulting group whose clients have included the Service Employees International Union (SEIU), the United

Farmworkers Union of America, and the National Latina Institute for Reproductive Health. The firm provides legislative and policy strategies to a variety of clients and helps them to diversify their outreach efforts. Echaveste currently remains as counsel to the firm. Since 2007 Echaveste has taught immigration and education reform at the Berkeley School of Law. She has also taught undergraduate courses in legal studies and ethnic studies. In 2012, Echaveste helped to launch the UC Berkeley Food Institute, a multidisciplinary research center focused on food production and consumption with a focus on sustainability. One research project Echaveste worked on with her colleagues looked at building the business case for worker-friendly standards. To date Echaveste continues to work on behalf of Latinx immigration causes both at the state and national level, as well as increasing Latinx civic engagement. Her passion is to connect research to policy battles focused on creating a more equitable nation for all.

G. Cristina Mora

See also: United Farm Workers (UFW)

Further Reading

Echaveste, Maria. 2002. "Brown to Black: The Politics of Judicial Appointments for Latinos." *Berkeley La Raza Law Journal* 13: 39.

Echaveste, Maria. 2009. "Invisible Yet Essential: Immigrant Women in America." In Maria Shriver, ed. *Invisible Yet Essential: Immigrant Women in America.* Washington, D.C.: Center for American Progress, pp. 114–19.

Green, Mark J., & Michele Jolin, eds. 2009. *Change for America: A Progressive Blueprint for the 44th President.* New York: Basic Books.

Education and Latinos

Public education is a vehicle for Latino political incorporation. Although education is often regarded as a matter of public policy and less as an arena of democratic politics, many of the most critical outcomes in education are inherently political. This includes the outcomes of local elections and the influence of ethnoracial attachments on the performance of governmental services. Indeed, the politics of public education help to set the stage for Latinos' incorporation in other spheres of politics. Education is understood to be among the key predictors of one's social, economic, and political standing. Like other ethnoracial groups, Latinos have long been in pursuit of access to educational experiences that can help close the gap between their numeric presence in the polity and their substantive influence in the political sphere. Against the backdrop of the K–12 education system, this essay discusses how the success of this pursuit has itself been a function of political forces that are present throughout the education system.

To date, much of the discussion surrounding Latinos in the U.S. political system has focused on what their increasing share of the electorate implies for the national political landscape. But like their growing presence in the electorate, Latinos occupy a formidable presence in public education. Indeed, a considerable source of Latinos' political influence is nested within the governance of U.S. school districts (Leal, Martinez-Ebers, and Meier, 2004). The National Association of

Latino Elected and Appointed Officials (NALEO) reported that as recently as 2016, approximately 38 percent of all Latino elected officials in the United States were elected school board members. It is therefore important to understand education through a political lens because politics in this arena has the potential to shape Latinos' incorporation within their larger sociopolitical setting. If Latinos are not welcomed into the politics of education within a democratic state, there is reason to believe that the long-term outlook for Latino incorporation in other political arenas is dim.

Latinos' place in U.S. education is the result of a process that allows for influence over school governance. Indeed, a lack of influence over school governance helps to explain many of the educational inequities that Latino communities face. In their extensive analysis of Latino focus groups, Fraga, et al. (2010: 64) find that "Latinos . . . indicated that they valued education as a means to facilitate securing gainful employment and achieving upward mobility in the United States generally." Education is among Latinos' most salient policy concerns, suggesting that their preferences for systems that create pathways to academic advancement are concrete. However, creating the foundation for such gains requires the translation of education preferences into a formal voice at the education policy-making table. Meier, Stewart, and England (1989: 12) argue that "determining overall policy, translating overall policy into administrative rules and procedures, and implementing rules and procedures by applying them to individuals" are three decision areas that shape local education politics. In order to influence these critical decision points, Latinos must overcome an initial hurdle by gaining access to school board seats.

As with electoral arenas, Latinos' ethnic identification matters for representation in the education system. Similar to patterns of ethnic identification and political behavior, ethnic attachments are thought to influence Latino school board representatives to make decisions that benefit Latino students. According to Barreto (2010), the presence of a Latino candidate creates an ethnic political context wherein Latino communities exhibit a greater interest in elections. Shared ethnic identification between Latino communities and their political aspirants bears important implications for the outcomes of school board elections. Controlling for a variety of other factors, studies of Latino representation on school boards consistently find a strong association between measures of Latino population size and the presence of Latinos on elected school boards (Fraga and Elis, 2009; Leal, et al., 2004; Meier and Stewart, 1991). Latino communities favor co-ethnic school board candidates, as these representatives are likely to advance a policy agenda oriented toward the needs of Latino students and the preferences of the broader Latino community. Without representation on school boards, Latinos' prospects for inclusion in the education system are compromised.

Latino group size is correlated with their political influence and is a necessary condition for occupying positions of influence in the education system. Still, numbers alone are not enough. At the top level of many local public school systems, the election of Latinos to school boards is subject to the structure of school board elections (Molina and Meier, 2016). Meier (2002) notes that institutional reforms designed to shield schools from political influences have often had the opposite effect, resulting in greater disparities between the various groups relying on public schools. Institutional features of local school systems must in turn be conducive to the representation of minorities in surrounding communities before Latinos' numbers in the population are converted into policy-making roles.

Of the discussion concerning the institutional determinants of Latino power in public education, at-large elections have long been an important issue. At-large elections are the most prevalent system of local election in the U.S. federal system. The at-large design allows an entire body of eligible voters in a particular location such as a county or school district to cast their vote for various candidates. However, they are thought to limit the prospects for minority political representation because they require minority candidates to secure political support from a broad body of voters where minority constituents are concentrated within specific areas of a larger jurisdiction. Evaluations of these election systems often conclude that their implementation poses an institutional barrier that suppresses the representation of racial and ethnic minority communities in elected offices (Marschall, Ruhil, and Shah, 2010; Meier, et al., 1989; Trounstine and Valdini, 2008).

Leal, et al. (2004) examine how different election systems affect Latino representation within a sample of the nation's largest school districts. Although their analysis demonstrates that Latino group size is a powerful predictor of school board representation, results also indicate at-large elections are a detriment to Latinos' political in-roads. In their study of California school districts, Fraga and Elis (2009) find that Latinos are underrepresented in areas where they comprise a minority, whereas district-based elections did not significantly enhance representation relative to the impact of at-large systems. In a separate analysis of school board representation in California, Reyes and Neiman (2011) find that although ward elections greatly increase the chances of a Latino being elected to serve when Latino students comprise a minority of the student population, the effect is even greater in districts whose student population is majority Latino. The system of election, although an important determinant of minority access to school board seats in general, is not the only institutional element of local elections that can affect Latinos' access to import decision-making points. The timing of local elections can also have a significant impact on election outcomes, as does the removal of partisan politics from local elections. More than just a matter of who becomes elected, these institutional components are also important because they have the potential to influence whether school outputs and policy outcomes align with Latino group preferences.

The increased presence of Latinos in the general population has also shaped the politics of intergroup dynamics between members of different racial cleavages. One result of this has been the need for Latino school candidates to campaign within multiracial settings. In their discussion of the politics that underlie conflict among different racial groups in the United States, Bowler and Segura (2012) emphasize that Latino population increase has brought with it a greater degree of conflict between whites and Latinos. The manifestation of this conflict has important political implications for Latinos, as it can result in white support for anti-Latino policy (Branton and Jones, 2005). As an illustration of this, in their study of county-level support for California's Proposition 187, which aimed to deny public services to illegal immigrants, Tolbert and Hero (1996) find that white support for the initiative was particularly high in areas where they resided alongside high proportions of Latinos. In education, Latino group size also influences white opposition to education policies that produce benefits for Latino students (Hempel, Dowling, Boardman, and Ellison, 2013).

Social status can also influence whether or not a Latino is elected to school boards, because members of the Latino population are more likely to become competitive political candidates when they have ascended into the ranks of America's middle class (Garcia and Arce, 1988). Yet it may also mitigate intergroup tensions in a manner that influences whether or not Latinos gain support from white members of the community. The *power thesis* perspective of group interactions argues that different racial groups in society are competing for control of various structures that are economic, social, and political in nature (Giles and Evans, 1986). This competition shapes group interactions as ethnic minority communities also engage in a process of group formation for the purpose of gaining access to resources traditionally controlled by members of the dominant class. In their investigation of the factors that affect Latino school board representation, Meier and Stewart (1991) use the power thesis to advance the argument that middle-class whites favor Latinos of similar socioeconomic status over other minorities. The same study also uncovered a positive relationship between the percentage of whites below the poverty line and the presence of Latino school board officials, while finding empirical support that socioeconomic status determines whether Latinos are thought to pose less of threat to the white dominant group than other minorities.

Access to education governance is not just a matter of academic outcomes. It is, in a much broader sense, a matter of determining where groups in a democracy are positioned in relation to each other. The future of the Latino demographic, and the degree to which their population numbers are converted into formal political power, is in many ways contingent upon what happens in the education system. Education, to be sure, is an area of policy where the outcomes are determined by myriad forces. What's more, education occurs across different systems, namely primary, secondary, and postsecondary.

Angel Luis Molina, Jr.

See also: Bilingual Education; Méndez, Sylvia (1936–); National Association of Latino Elected and Appointed Officials (NALEO) Educational Fund

Further Reading

Barreto, Matt A. 2010. *Ethnic Cues: The Role of Shared Ethnicity in Latino Political Participation.* Ann Arbor: University of Michigan Press.

Bowler, Shaun, & Gary M. Segura. 2012. *The Future Is Ours: Minority Politics, Political Behavior, and the Multiracial Era of American Politics.* Thousand Oaks, CA: SAGE.

Branton, Regina P., & Bradford S. Jones. 2005. "Reexamining Racial Attitudes: The Conditional Relationship between Diversity and Socioeconomic Environment." *American Journal of Political Science* 49: 359–72.

Fraga, Luis, & Roy Elis. 2009. "Interests and Representation: Ethnic Advocacy on California School Boards." *The Teachers College Record* 111: 659–82.

Fraga, Luis R., John A. Garcia, Rodney E. Hero, Michael Jones-Correa, Valerie Martinez-Ebers, & Gary M. Segura. 2012. *Latinos in the New Millennium: An Almanac of*

Opinion, Behavior, and Policy Preferences. New York: Cambridge University Press.

Fraga, Luis, John A. Garcia, Gary M. Segura, Michael Jones-Correa, Rodney Hero, & Valerie Martinez-Ebers. 2010. *Latino Lives in America: Making It Home.* Philadelphia: Temple University Press.

Garcia, John A., & Carlos H. Arce. 1988. *Political Orientations and Behaviors of Chicanos: Trying to Make Sense Out of Attitudes and Participation.* South Bend, IN: University of Notre Dame Press.

Giles, Michael W., & Arthur Evans. 1986. "The Power Approach to Intergroup Hostility." *Journal of Conflict Resolution* 30: 469–86.

Hempel, Lynn M., Julie A. Dowling, Jason D. Boardman, & Christopher G. Ellison. 2013. "Racial Threat and White Opposition to Bilingual Education in Texas." *Hispanic Journal of Behavioral Sciences* 35: 85–102.

Leal, David L., Valerie Martinez-Ebers, & Kenneth J. Meier. 2004. "The Politics of Latino Education: The Biases of At-Large Elections." *Journal of Politics* 66: 1224–44.

Marschall, Melissa J., Anirudh V. S. Ruhil, & Paru R. Shah. 2010. "The New Racial Calculus: Electoral Institutions and Black Representation in Local Legislatures." *American Journal of Political Science* 54: 107–24.

Meier, Kenneth J. 2002. "A Research Agenda on Elections and Education." *Educational Policy* 16: 219–30.

Meier, Kenneth J., & Joseph Stewart. 1991. *The Politics of Hispanic Education: Un Paso Pa'Lante y Dos Pa'Tras.* Albany: SUNY Press.

Meier, Kenneth J., Joseph Stewart, & Robert E. England. 1989. *Race, Class, and Education: The Politics of Second-Generation Discrimination.* Madison: University of Wisconsin Press.

Molina, Angel Luis, Jr., & Kenneth J. Meier. 2018. "Demographic Dreams, Institutional Realities: Election Design and Latino Representation in American Education." *Politics, Groups, and Identities* 6, no. 1: 77–94. doi: 10.1080/21565503.2016.1182931.: 1–18.

Molina, Angel Luis, Jr., & Francisco I. Pedraza. 2017. "Judging Dream Keepers: Latino Assessments of Schools and Educators." *Politics, Groups, and Identities* 5, no. 2: 1–21.

Reyes, Belinda I., & Max Neiman. 2011. "System of Elections, Latino Representation, and School Policy in Central California Schools." In David Leal and Stephen Trejo, eds. *Latinos and the Economy: Integration and Impact in Schools, Labor Markets, and Beyond.* New York: Springer, pp. 37–60.

Tolbert, Caroline J., & Rodney E. Hero. 1996. "Race/Ethnicity and Direct Democracy: An Analysis of California's Illegal Immigration Initiative." *Journal of Politics* 58: 806–18.

Trounstine, Jessica, & Melody E. Valdini. 2008. "The Context Matters: The Effects of Single-Member Versus At-Large Districts on City Council Diversity." *American Journal of Political Science* 52: 554–69.

El Especialito

El Especialito is a newspaper founded in Union City, New Jersey, in 1985 by Antonio Ibarria, an immigrant from Cuba who arrived in 1955. Initially, when Ibarria arrived to the United States, he was involved in several other businesses before creating *El Especialito*, such as a barbershop, a series of dry cleaners, bakeries, restaurants, and a furniture store. However, in the 1980s, Ibarria began to shift into media, when he became frustrated with maintaining relationships with revolving executives in the media industry. In the 1970s, he developed the newspaper *El Clarin*, and in 1998, a newspaper named *Hoy*. Eventually, Ibarria decided to develop his own media group. Since then, Ibarria has been recognized for his business, humanitarian, and philanthropic efforts in the community of Union City. On June 1, 2015, the city recognized Ibarria by naming a street post after him (Sandoval and Hutchinson, 2015). It is located on the corner of 38th Street, in front of *El Especialito's* headquarters. In addition to creating *El Especialito*, Ibarria founded an organization, Save Latin America, also located in Union City, that serves the Latino population through a series of health, medical, law, and educational services.

Ibarria's newspaper, *El Especialito*, has become an important medium in the Latino community, initially reaching only one zone in Hudson County, New Jersey, and expanding into 13 zones in the New York–New Jersey–Connecticut area. Ibarria stated that he developed the newspaper in order to inspire, as well as inform the Latino community in the United States. The newspaper is run as a family business by Ibarria and his two sons, Anthony and Joseph, as well as 90 employees located in the Union City, New Jersey headquarters and the South Florida office. The newspaper is currently available in New York, New Jersey, and Miami, areas considered to have a high Latino presence. In these areas, *El Especialito* is the most popular weekly newspaper. Most familiar to the residents of New York and New Jersey is *El Especialito*'s iconic yellow boxes that contain the newspaper. These yellow boxes are located on several street corners and intersections in the Latino community. Presently, there are over 5,000 in the Tri-State area (Ibarria, personal communication). *El Especialito* reaches over 1 million readers a week, including 500,000 in New Jersey and 650,000 in the New York area (Ibarria Media Group and Western Publication Research, 2015). More specifically, the newspaper targets areas in New York where there is a high Latino presence, such as Washington Heights, the Bronx, Spanish Harlem, Jackson Heights, Brooklyn, Lower East Side, and the West Side (Ibarria Media Group and Western Publication Research, 2015). In New Jersey, the newspaper caters specifically to the counties of Hudson, Bergen, Passaic, Essex, Union, and Middlesex (Ibarria Media Group and Western Publication Research, 2015).

El Especialito focuses on entertainment news, celebrity interviews, beauty and fashion, lifestyle, health, sports, travel, business, science, and technology (Ibarria Media Group and Western Publication Research, 2015). The newspaper also contains a section that provides information on various types of immigration services offered in the area. It caters to all Latino subgroups, cultivating a pan-ethnic ethos among its readership. Demographics demonstrate the diversity of Latinos who read *El Especialito*. Its readership is made up of South Americans (34%), Dominicans (23%), Puerto Ricans (14%), Mexicans (11%), Central Americans (7%), Cubans (5%), and other Hispanic/Latino-identified persons (6%) (Ibarria Media Group and Western Publication Research, 2015). The newspaper is also written in Spanish, which is the language of choice for its readers. *El Especialito* relies on advertising as well as co-sponsorships to thrive in the Latino community, and it is also involved in several events that cater to the population. In 2016, *El Especialito* hosted its first beauty contest, "Nuestra Reina Latina USA." Recently, the newspaper has moved from print to digital under the website www.elespecial.com. The newspaper has maintained its relevance to its readership by continuing to resonate with the diverse Latino population through its print and online platform.

Melanie Z. Plasencia

See also: *La Opinión*; *La Voz de Houston*

Further Reading

Ibarria, Antonio. April 25, 2017. E-mail message to Melanie Plasencia.

Ibarria Media Group and Western Publication Research. 2015. "El Especialito Media Kit." http://www.elespecialitomk.com/.

Lopez, Erica Y. 2016. "N.J. Businessman, Publisher of Largest Spanish-Language Weekly Newspaper, Master of Reinvention." *Daily News*, October 30. http://www .nydailynews.com/news/national/n-publisher-spanish-weekly-paper-master -reinvention-article-1.2850581.

Sandoval, Edgar, & Bill Hutchinson. 2015. "Owner of Spanish-Language Newspaper *El Especialito*, Antonio Ibarria, Gets Street Named after Him in Union City, N.J." *Daily News*, June 2. http://www.nydailynews.com/new-york/owner-spanish -language-newspaper-street-named-article-1.2243258.

El Nuevo Herald

As one of the biggest Spanish-language papers in the United States, *El Nuevo Herald* has been a very influential news publication, bringing investigative and breaking news to Miami-area readers. The paper began in 1977 as *El Herald*, a weekly insert in the *Miami Daily News* that was mostly a Spanish translation of *Miami Herald* stories. In 1987, the Miami Herald Media Company launched *El Nuevo Herald* (*ENH*) to bring original content and news to its large Spanish-speaking population that included primarily Cuban Americans initially, but grew to include a growing immigrant community from Latin America.

By the turn of the 21st century, Miami's population went from majority Anglo to majority Hispanic. In the early 1990s, *ENH* developed a reputation as a primarily "Cuban newspaper," and as the non-Cuban Latino community grew, it began to resent the narrow focus. Under Alberto Ibargüen, the new publisher hired in 1996 who had both Puerto Rican and Cuban parents, *ENH* expanded its Latin American news coverage, going in greater depth than even its parent publication, the *Miami Herald*. After working as publisher of *Nuevo Herald* and serving as vice-president for the *Miami Herald* international edition for two years, Ibargüen became publisher of both newspapers in 1998. Ibargüen's biggest strength was in recognizing Miami's unique blend of native Floridians as well as emigres—first coming from Nicaragua in the 1950s and later from Cuba in the 1960s—and insisting that *El Nuevo Herald* have its own identity separate from the *Miami Herald* in order to reach this unique readership.

Ibargüen reinvented the *El Nuevo Herald* in 1998 when he hired Carlos Castañeda, who had helped the Puerto Rican *El Nuevo Día* grow its circulation 10-fold. With a staff of 84, including 11 general assignment reporters (compared to more than 400 at the *Miami Herald*), *El Nuevo Herald* aimed to cover its community in depth while also running signed opinion pieces every day. With Castañeda at the helm of *ENH*, revenue grew and circulation climbed to nearly 98,000 on Sunday from 90,000 in 1999, and 91,000 daily from 76,000 (Roth, 2001). The paper also began to gain international attention, winning the prestigious Ortega y Gasset Journalism Award in 2002 for best Spanish-language newspaper in the world. But *El Nuevo Herald* also began to separate from its sister publication, the *Miami Herald*, with splashier coverage, livelier headlines, and more graphic photos.

El Nuevo Herald's journalistic integrity came into question in 2006 when a *Miami Herald* investigative reporter discovered that three *ENH* reporters were among 10 local journalists taking money from a U.S. federal government agency for reporting on Cuban affairs—specifically with a pro-U.S./anti-Fidel Castro leaning—on government-run broadcast stations. Within days of the story being published in the *Miami Herald*, the *ENH* reporters were fired, leading to discord within the *El Nuevo Herald* newsroom—some campaigned to get the reporters reinstated, calling the report sensationalized and a witch hunt against reporters working at the Spanish-language newspaper, while others at *ENH* supported the firings and the attempt to rid the newsroom of any corruption. Because *ENH* reporters were often encouraged to appear on national news media outlets such as CNN and Fox, many saw the appearance on the state-run media to be no different even though pay was involved. The situation made it clear that the two newsrooms operated under different ethics. After consultation with executives of the newspaper company's new owner, McClatchy Media, which had purchased the Miami Herald Media Company from Knight Ridder just a few months before the investigative story broke, two of three fired *ENH* reporters were reinstated as part of its attempt to smooth things over with the Cuban exile community that had cancelled nearly 2,000 subscriptions to *ENH* over a controversial editorial that was published (Hanks, 2006).

Today the *El Nuevo Herald* continues to flourish and has maintained a strong reputation for journalistic integrity in the midst of turbulent times—both in South Florida and among Latin American countries. Daily circulation has remained steady around 42,000, while Sunday circulation is just under 60,000. Digital traffic to the *El Nuevo Herald* has averaged more than 3 million unique visitors and more than 15 million page views each month. In addition, the *El Nuevo Herald* staff contributed to a joint *Miami Herald–El Nuevo Herald* "Breaking News" entry that was a finalist for the 2011 Pulitzer Prize awards. The two publications also won the 2011 James Batten Public Service Award from the Florida Society of Professional Journalists for their joint reporting on the Haiti crisis. Since the Florida Society of Professional Journalists recently added a separate awards category for Spanish-language newspapers to their annual Sunshine State Awards, *El Nuevo Herald* reporters have won "journalist of the year" in 2015 and 2017.

Laurie Lattimore-Volkmann

See also: El Especialito; La Opinión; La Voz de Houston

Further Reading

Corral, Oscar. 2006. "10 Miami Journalists Take U.S. Pay." *Miami Herald*, September 8. https://corpwatch.org/article/us-10-miami-journalists-take-us-pay.

Hanks, Douglas. 2006. "A Column, a Quarrel—and Change at the Top." *Miami Herald*, October 4.

Lundberg, Kirsten. "When the Story Is Us: *Miami Herald, Nuevo Herald* and Radio Martí." *Knight Case Studies Initiative, Columbia University.* http://ccnmtl.columbia.edu /projects/caseconsortium/casestudies/43/casestudy/www/layout/case_id_43.html.

McClatchey Company. n.d. "*El Nuevo Herald.*" http://www.mcclatchy.com/our-impact /markets/el-nuevo-herald.

Roth, Daniel Shoer. 2001. "Nombran a Humberto Castelló director de El Nuevo Herald." *El Nuevo Herald*, December 6.

Society of Professional Journalists, Florida Chapter. n.d. "Sunshine State Awards Archive." https://spjflorida.com/sunshine-state-awards/winners-archive.

El Teatro Campesino

El Teatro Campesino, or Farmworkers Theater, was launched in 1965 when Luis Valdez, a member of the San Francisco Mime Troupe, met labor organizer César Chávez and followed him to Delano, California, where the United Farm Workers union was conducting a strike against grape growers. Valdez published a flyer announcing the creation of a farm workers' theater project and inviting volunteers to join to express their grievances and their hopes—no acting experience needed. The first *actos*, as the brief performances were called, were staged by the picket lines and dramatized the farmers' inequitable working conditions and the need for collective action. It was a militant, bilingual theater aimed at persuading those still in the fields to join the strike and to reassure union members that they would succeed.

Although Valdez was the initiator of the group and functioned as its artistic director, the pieces were created collectively during rehearsals and performance was improvisational, often in response to audience participation, which, unlike in traditional Western theater, was a desired feature of the show. Performances of the same *acto* could never be identical and were instead committed to memory. A written text would have been reductive as well as inaccurate because the acting was heavily

Luis Valdez attends the Academy Museum of Motion Pictures screening of his critically acclaimed film *Zoot Suit* in Beverly Hills, California, 2017. (Matt Winkelmeyer/Getty Images)

mimic, based on exaggerated facial expressions and gestures to externalize the characters' psychological state. Although Valdez later did transcribe the early *actos, Teatro Campesino* was more visual art than language-based theater, a performance to watch and respond to, not to read.

The cultural origins of *Teatro Campesino* are geographically and chronologically diverse: it was inspired as much by the sociopolitical drama of 20th-century German playwright Bertold Brecht as by the improvisational style of the 16th-century Italian *Commedia dell'arte.* Closer to home, a central source was the Mexican oral performance tradition of the *carpa,* or tent show, from which *Teatro Campesino* derived the archetypal character of the *pelado,* the underdog trickster, which it reinvented as the exploited but resourceful migrant worker, Don Sotaco. Other stock characters included the despised labor contractor, El Coyote; the greedy grower, El Patroncito; and the cowardly scab, El Esquirol. The plot invariably featured the victory of the underdog and often a reversal of power differentials. In *Las Dos Caras del Patroncito* (1965), for instance, the farm worker, who has been persuaded to trade places with his employer, eager to experience the allegedly carefree life of the worker, refuses to let go of his new authority. In the closing scene, a disabused Patroncito screams for help from César Chávez and his union, now acknowledged as the only recourse for the oppressed.

The genesis of *Teatro Campesino* is inseparable from the farm workers' cause. However, a desire for artistic development soon led the cooperative to explore different social issues, and especially so after the UFW's victory in 1970, when all major Delano growers signed union contracts. Among others, *Los Vendidos* (1967) criticizes Mexican Americans who assimilate into white culture; *La Conquista de México* (1968) retells the Western narrative of colonization as Christianization as one instead of unredeemable plunder; *No Saco Nada de la Escuela* (1969) condemns instructional policies that amount to cultural genocide; and *Vietnam Campesino* (1970) denounces the collaboration of agribusiness and military, as in the practice of feeding soldiers scab produce or testing chemical weapons on food crops. Eventually, the intended audience for the plays changed too. Whereas the early performances had been created for farmworkers, *Teatro Campesino* later moved to the mainstream and aimed at acquainting middle-class, Euro-American spectators with Chicano culture. This shift was signaled by the 1979 Broadway production of *Zoot Suit,* a play about the unjust conviction of a group of Mexican American youth in the Sleepy Lagoon murder trial of 1943. With this performance, *Teatro Campesino* officially switched from the original collective, oral mode of production to individual authorship and print culture, and from agitational theater to for-profit theater.

While the conversion to commercial theater had the advantage of reaching a larger public, commentators agree that *Teatro Campesino*'s most powerful productions are linked to the farmworkers' struggle. Today, *Teatro Campesino* still exists in its historical location in San Juan Bautista, California, and is directed by Luis Valdez's son, Kinan. It focuses its energy on culturally relevant art education for Latino students.

Paola Gemme

See also: Chávez, César (1927–1993); Sleepy Lagoon (1942); United Farm Workers (UFW); Zoot Suit Riots (1943)

Further Reading

Broyles-Gonzáles, Yolanda. 1994. *El Teatro Campesino: Theater in the Chicano Movement.* Austin: University of Texas Press.

Elam, Harry J., Jr. 2001. *Taking It to the Streets: The Social Protest Theater of Luis Valdez and Amiri Baraka.* Ann Arbor: The University of Michigan Press.

Ontiveros, Randy J. 2013. *In the Spirit of a New People: The Cultural Politics of the Chicano Movement.* New York: New York University Press.

Valdez, Luis. 1990. *Early Works: Actos, Bernabé and Pensamiento Serpentino.* Houston: Arte Publico Press.

Election of 2016 and Latinos

Latinos made up approximately 11 percent of the total vote in the 2016 presidential election, which is about equal to their 2012 vote share; however, only 34 percent of Latinos said they were mobilized to vote. Although Get Out the Vote (GOTV) campaigns typically do not target the Latino community, the majority of these campaigns come from the Democratic Party. Among the Latinos who received GOTV messaging, an overwhelming majority reported that the messages came from the Democrats. For comparison, in 2008, 67 percent of the Latino community voted for the Democratic candidate, Barack Obama, in the general election, and 75 percent supported him in 2012. Again, the majority of the vote went to the Democratic candidate in 2016. Almost half (44%) of the Latino eligible voters were millennials, and about 20 percent were voting for the first time. An astonishing 79 percent of Latinos voted for Hillary Clinton (D), whereas Donald Trump (R) only received 18 percent of the vote. This 18 percent has been interpreted as the religious vote of conservative Latino Christians and evangelicals. The larger percentage is easily explained, as at least 57 percent of Latinos reported that they felt Clinton cared about them, whereas just 13 percent thought that Trump cared about them. About 75 percent of registered Latino voters said that they have discussed comments made by Trump with peers or family members. Of the issues that Latinos cared most about, immigration ranked as the number one concern for Latino voters, with 39 percent citing it as such. The second most important issue ranked by Latino voters was the economy, at 33 percent, and falling in third place was education with 15 percent of Latinos citing it as their most important issue.

These statistics are not at all surprising, considering that while on the campaign trail, then presidential candidate Donald Trump gave speeches in which he called Mexican immigrants names, stating that they were both "thieves" and "rapists." He is also known to have publicly called Latinos "bad hombres" (Ross, 2016). This may be one reason about half of Latinos voted *against* Donald Trump instead of *for* Hillary Clinton. This percentage of anti-Trump sentiment jumped to 64 percent for millennial voters. While Trump acknowledged "some of them [Mexicans] are good people," his statements, as a whole, gave a "Trump bump" to the Democratic candidate. Again, Latinos may not have supported Clinton outright, but many fearfully voted to avoid a Trump victory (Sanchez and Barreto, 2017). In general, Latino voters expressed the same sentiment as the general population of registered voters.

Comments made by both candidates resonated within Hispanic communities across the country. Statements made by the Republican candidate that Mexico had not been "sending their best" and that immigrants brought their problems to the United States, along with a variety of crimes and drugs, influenced discussions had by the Latino community at home, among friends, and even in the workplace. In fact, about 7 in 10 Hispanics reported that they had been holding conversations about Trump's statements. Although these comments seem to be directed at Mexico and Mexicans here and abroad, Latinos of Mexican descent do not actually talk any more about these comments than the Latino community at large.

Although campaign rhetoric started quite a buzz domestically, Mexican president Enrique Peña Nieto expressed support for and a deep friendship with both U.S. candidates. Trump then famously promised the American people that Mexico would be paying for the 30-foot-high U.S.–Mexico Border Wall. In addition to the wall, Trump promised to triple the number of Immigration and Customs Enforcement agents. In the same policy proposal he stated that all "illegal aliens in gangs should be apprehended and deported." Furthermore, he said in speeches that the 11.3 million undocumented immigrants in the United States "have to go" and promised not only an uptick in deportation, but that every one of them would be deported. He also talked about rescinding President Obama's immigration accountability executive orders. This would result in the elimination of Deferred Action for Parents of Americans and Lawful Permanent Residents (DAPA) and would remove the extension of Deferred Action for Childhood Arrivals (DACA), both of which were enacted by the former president without support from Congress. When it came to foreign policy, Trump promised to undo the controversial changes President Obama made with regard to diplomacy and trade with Cuba.

Social media has been playing an increasingly large role in campaigns and elections. Trump posted a photo on Twitter posing with a Trump Tower taco bowl, with the caption, "Happy #CincoDeMayo! The best taco bowls are made in Trump Tower Grill. I love Hispanics!" (Kopan, 2016). He has also published tweets throughout his campaign that include the hashtag "#BuildTheWall," which is directed toward the southern Border Wall. Meanwhile, Clinton took a different approach. She pointed out the caveat in Trump's statements by publishing "I'm with you*"—@realDonaldTrump *Not included: women, African Americans, LGBT people, Muslims, Latinos, immigrants." She not only used social media to combat her competitor directly, she brought economics into the picture by drawing the comparison between taxes and the role undocumented immigrants play in our economy. Before a debate, Clinton tweeted that there are "undocumented immigrants in America who are paying more federal income tax than a so-called billionaire. #DebateNight" (Clinton, 2016). Anthony Suarez, a Latino Republican, even said that "I thought that the rhetoric coming out of Donald Trump was so toxic, that it would eventually turn off the Hispanic community as Barry Goldwater turned off the African-American community" (Khalid, 2016). Instead, Latinos turned out in the same strength as they did for 2012 candidate Mitt Romney. When asked directly, Latino Trump supporters either said that they did not take the candidate's comments personally, that they saw Hillary as the same old politician, or that they supported Trump's emphasis on family values or his stance on increasing the size of the military.

Hillary Clinton appeared to court the Latino vote early on in her campaign, directly speaking to the community. Even before she accepted the presidential nomination, she told the Latino community at the League of United Latin American Citizens that "[y]ou are not intruders. You are our neighbors, our colleagues, our friends, our families. You make our nation stronger, smarter, more creative" (Gamboa, 2016). Clinton promised on the campaign trail to pass comprehensive immigration "that kept families together" and would have included a pathway to citizenship and increased immigration enforcement (Carroll, 2016). She also supported increasing border security, but rather than focus on physical barriers, she supported an increase in Border Patrol agents. Clinton also supported Obama's executive orders on DACA and DAPA and said that although she would continue to deport violent criminals, she would limit immigration raids (Peoples, 2016). Clinton was successful in garnering the Latino vote; however, to ascertain exactly what that vote was, more analysis needs to be conducted.

Maricruz Ariana Osorio and Stephanie L. DeMora

See also: Deferred Action for Childhood Arrivals (DACA)/Deferred Action for Parents of Americans and Lawful Permanent Residents (DAPA); Immigration as a Policy Issue; Trump, Donald J. (1946–) and Latinos

Further Reading

Barreto, Matt A., & Loren Collingwood. 2015. "Group-Based Appeals and the Latino Vote in 2012: How Immigration Became a Mobilizing Issue." *Electoral Studies* 40: 490–99.

BBC. 2017. "Trump Promises Before and After the Election." September 19. http://www.bbc.com/news/world-us-canada-37982000.

Carroll, Lauren. 2016. "Hillary Clinton's Top 10 Campaign Promises." July 22. http://www.politifact.com/truth-o-meter/article/2016/jul/22/hillary-clintons-top-10-campaign-promises.

Clinton, Hillary. 2016. "@HillaryClinton." https://twitter.com/HillaryClinton.

Gamboa, Suzanne. 2016. "Clinton to Latinos at LULAC: You Are Not Intruders." *NBC News*, July 14. https://www.nbcnews.com/news/latino/clinton-latinos-lulac-you-are-not-intruders-n609476.

Khalid, Asma. 2016. "Latinos Will Never Vote for a Republican, and Other Myths about Hispanics from 2016." *NPR*, December 22. http://www.npr.org/2016/12/22/506347254/latinos-will-never-vote-for-a-republican-and-other-myths-about-hispanics-from-20.

Kopan, Tal. 2016. "What Donald Trump Has Said about Mexico and Vice Versa." August 31. http://www.cnn.com/2016/08/31/politics/donald-trump-mexico-statements/index.html.

Krogstad, Jens Manuel. 2016. "Key Facts about the Latino Vote in 2016." October 14. http://www.pewresearch.org/fact-tank/2016/10/14/key-facts-about-the-latino-vote-in-2016.

Latino Decisions. 2016. "Latino Decisions 2016 Election Eve Poll." November 7. http://www.latinovote2016.com/app/#all-national-all.

Lopez, Mark Hugo. 2008. "The Hispanic Vote in the 2008 Election." *Pew Hispanic,* November 7. http://www.pewhispanic.org/2008/11/05/the-hispanic-vote-in-the-2008-election.

Lopez, Mark Hugo, Ana Gonzalez-Barrera, Jens Manuel Krogstad, & Gustavo Lopez. 2016. "The Latino Vote in the 2016 Presidential Election." *Pew Hispanic*, October 11. http://www.pewhispanic.org/2016/10/11/the-latino-vote-in-the-2016-presidential-election.

Pedraza, Francisco I., & Bryan Wilcox-Archuleta. 2017. "Did Latino Voters Actually Turn Out for Trump in the Election? Not Really." *LA Times*, January 11. http://www .latimes.com/opinion/op-ed/la-oe-pedraza-latino-vote-20170111-story.html.

Peoples, Steve. 2016. "Here's What Clinton and Trump Plan on Immigration." September 3. https://www.pbs.org/newshour/politics/trump-clinton-immigration-plans.

Ross, Janell. 2016. "From Mexican Rapists to Bad Hombres, the Trump Campaign in Two Moments." *Washington Post,* October 20. https://www.washingtonpost.com/news /the-fix/wp/2016/10/20/from-mexican-rapists-to-bad-hombres-the-trump-campaign -in-two-moments/?utm_term=.e09be3199a81.

Sanchez, Gabriel, & Matt Barreto. 2016. "In Record Numbers, Latinos Voted Overwhelmingly against Trump. We Did the Research." *The Washington Post*, November 11. https://www.washingtonpost.com/news/monkey-cage/wp/2016/11/11/in-record -numbers-latinos-voted-overwhelmingly-against-trump-we-did-the-research/?utm _term=.a739b2f1b40e.

Suro, Roberto. 2016. "Here's What Happened with the Latino Vote." *New York Times.* https://www.nytimes.com/interactive/projects/cp/opinion/election-night-2016 /heres-what-happened-with-the-latino-vote.

Trump, Donald. 2016. "@realDonaldTrump." https://twitter.com/realDonaldTrump.

English-Only Policy. *See* Official English Movement

Environmental Justice and Latinos

The Environmental Protection Agency (EPA) defines the term "environmental justice" as "the fair treatment and meaningful involvement of all people regardless of race, color, national origin, or income, with respect to the development, implementation, and enforcement of environmental laws, regulations, and policies" (Environmental Protection Agency, 2016). Concern with environmental issues has a long history in Latino politics reaching as far back as the 1960s. Environmental justice organizing is different from the more typical interest-group advocacy or electoral campaigning typically claiming to represent Latinos. Latino environmental justice organizations see themselves as part of a larger movement to restructure social and economic relations and trace their lineage to the Chicano Movement of the 1960s. Groups like the Black Berets of New Mexico and Puerto Rican civil rights groups like the Young Lords drew connections between the environment and social and economic issues like police brutality, lack of affordable health care, low-quality education, poverty, and cultural survival. The premise of their activism was that all the ills suffered by Latino communities were interwoven. Hence, the criticism of mainstream environmental organizations is a critique of racial and economic stratification. It is a call for the redistribution of power, investment in community infrastructure, and a redistribution of profits to the local community, in addition to well-paying jobs and a clean and safe workplace (Marquez, 2003).

The best-documented episodes of environmental justice activism in Latino communities occurred in the 1980s and 1990s. Activists in Los Angeles, Dallas, Phoenix, Albuquerque, and New York protested the exposure of their communities to pollution in the air, water, and soil. They argued that not only were environmental problems in Latino neighborhoods numerous, but they constituted a disturbing pattern of neglect and intent to target minority communities. Latino and other ethnoracial groups were not only residentially segregated, their neighborhoods were contaminated in numerous ways, and sometimes dangerously so. They called for a more equal distribution of environmental hazards so that all groups bear the burdens of environmental hazards, full participation in environmental policy making, and a more equitable distribution of society's wealth and opportunities (Harrison, 2014; Schlosberg, 2013; Schlosberg and Carruthers, 2010; Sze, 2007). Environmental injustices include inadequate garbage disposal services, poor enforcement of sanitation codes, pesticide use on farms, and illegal dumping in neighborhoods. The list also includes the addition of new environmental hazards in Latino communities like garbage incinerators, recycling centers, oil pipelines, power plants, and landfills in or near minority neighborhoods. Activist groups also grappled with the legacy of past hazardous waste disposal practices. In some areas, the refuse from mining and smelting factories exposed communities to deposits of hazardous waste, fuel storage facilities constituted a groundwater and soil hazard, and lead paint in old housing units threatened the health of the young and old alike.

Environmental justice activists perceive few similarities between themselves and the mainstream environmental movement. In 1990 Latino environmental justice groups accused Anglo-dominated environmental organizations of contributing to environmental inequalities by accepting monetary support from some of the country's worst polluters. They charged the Sierra Club, the National Wildlife Federation, Audubon Society, Wilderness Society, and the National Resources Defense Council with racism for refusing to recognize the environmental problems faced by people of color in urban areas. They see the Anglo environmentalist emphasis on forests, lakes, streams, and wildlife as nothing less than the preservation of the recreational areas of the middle and upper classes. Latino environmental activists fought to undo the damage done by the free market and public policy to create safe and sustainable communities. They also link the state of the environment to the integrity of their culture, a world view that oftentimes put them in conflict with business interests, local growth coalitions, and other Latinos hoping to increase employment opportunities for the community (Marquez, 2012).

For example, in the 1990s when high-tech firms began relocating in New Mexico, environmental activists called the development an assault on New Mexican culture. Computer chip production required large amounts of water, a highly symbolic resource. Water is scarce in New Mexico, and the cooperative management of this resource has deep roots in the state's history and culture. The computer chip industry's demand for large amounts of water angered activists, who argued that it would be squandered at the expense of small farmers and ranchers. They likened the arrival of the computer industry as a continuation of the colonization process begun by the Spanish conquest of New Mexico. The search for cheap land, resources, and labor had brought electronics firms to New Mexico.

A large body of quantitative research grew around the environmental justice movement and its contentious assertions (Noonan, 2008). The most difficult claim to substantiate is that of overt racism driving the placement of environmental hazards in or adjacent to minority neighborhoods. As in other instances of racial disparities, finding the "smoking gun" of racist intent behind the location of environmental pollutants is extraordinarily difficult. Still, there is strong and consistent evidence of a disproportionate exposure to environmental hazards by race and the negative health impact of race-neutral environmental policies (Pastor, Sadd, and Hipp, 2001; Pastor, Sadd, and Morello-Frosch, 2004). The correlation between the worst environmental practices and race is found in the lax enforcement of existing laws, proximity of environmental hazards, soil and water pollution, location of polluting industries, and other forms of environmental risks. The relationship between race and pollution is strongest in areas of the country with a history of racial conflict and discrimination (Wilson, Joseph, and Williams, 2010).

Historians and social movement researchers have documented the environmental justice movement's complex history (Pellow, 2002). The issue of community organizing and the exercise of power has received scholarly attention. Latino environmental justice mobilization in the 1990s forced large corporations to change their manufacturing practices, move polluting facilities, and clean contaminated soil and water. The successes of the era captured headlines and sparked an interest in academia, but Latino environmental politics dates back much further.

There have been few of the high-profile campaigns and victories in the new millennia that characterized the environmental justice movement of the 1990s. Hardened resistance by polluters and avoidance of the mistakes that rendered some businesses vulnerable to environmental justice demands have made protest and disruption less effective. The task is made even more difficult because polluting industries use their resources to map out strategies that can wear down activists in long-term struggles and avoid the political and public relations pitfalls that exposed previous businesses to environmental justice claims.

The courts, which were key to gaining redress or compensation in the 1990s, now provide few effective tools for fighting environmental inequalities (Sassman, 2014). In 2001 the Supreme Court ruled that Title VI prohibits discrimination but does not give individuals the right to challenge policies that are neutral on their face but have disparate impact by color, race, or national origin.

The Supreme Court upheld the Third Circuit Court of Appeals reasoning to strike down almost 30 years of Environmental Protection Agency disparate impact regulations (McNamara, 2002; Montag and Trinkle, 2002). Existing civil rights law only recognizes disproportionate exposure to toxics as racism when a clear intent to harm based on race can be demonstrated—an almost insurmountable barrier. Although some environmental justice lawsuits have resulted in a negotiated settlement, as of 2015, almost all legal actions have failed to establish discriminatory intent (Foster, 2016). Civil rights legislation can be used to prevent actions such as the granting of a construction permit or prevent permit renewal, but it cannot be used to compensate communities for past injuries caused by exposure to pollutants. Minority communities suffering from a history of exposure to environmental hazards will have to pursue the difficult and time-consuming use of common law claims of negligence and nuisance. However, as environmental regulations are weakened, activists have fewer tools with which to work and find that regulatory agencies and their officials are increasingly uncooperative or hostile (Switzer and Teodoro, 2017).

One positive development on the horizon is the increased number and leadership of Latino elected officials. Congressional representatives Raúl M. Grijalva (D-AZ), Ruben Gallego (D-AZ), Linda Sánchez (D-CA), and Raul Ruiz (D-CA) have advocated policies that advance clean energy, public health, and the environment (Allen, 2016). In California, Latino legislators are leading members of an environmental coalition that makes the state a leader in clean energy policies and protection of communities of color. The California Environmental Justice Alliance praises Latino legislators for their support of innovative legislation and the oversight of regulatory agencies (CEJA, 2015, 2016). In this way, the state of California offers a model for the way that elected officials and community groups can work together to advance the cause of environmental justice.

Benjamin Marquez

See also: Brown Berets; Brown Power Movement/Chicano Civil Rights Movement; Gallego, Ruben (1979–); Grijalva, Raúl M. (1948–); Ruiz, Raul (1972–); Sánchez, Linda (1969–)

Further Reading

Allen, Jennifer. 2016. "Latinos in Congress Are Leading on Climate and Environmental Justice." *The Hill,* October 28.

California Environmental Justice Alliance. 2015. "Environmental Justice Scorecard. Oakland, CA." *California Environmental Justice Alliance.* http://caleja.org/resources /reports/.

California Environmental Justice Alliance. 2016. "Environmental Justice Scorecard. Oakland, CA." *California Environmental Justice Alliance.* http://caleja.org/resources /reports/.

Cole, Luke W., & Sheila R. Foster. 2001. *From the Ground Up: Environmental Racism and the Rise of the Environmental Movement.* New York: New York University Press.

Environmental Protection Agency (EPA). 2016. https://www.epa.gov/environmentaljustice.

Foster, Sheila. 2016. "Vulnerability, Equality, and Environmental Justice: The Potential and Limits of Law." June 5. *Handbook of Environmental Justice.* 2018. Fordham Law Legal Studies Research Paper No. 2790584. https://ssrn.com/abstract=2790584.

Galalis, David J. 2004. "Environmental Justice and Title VI in the Wake of Alexander v. Sandoval: Disparate-Impact Regulations Still Valid Under Chevron." *Boston College Environmental Affairs Law Review* 31. http://lawdigitalcommons.bc.edu/ealr/vol31 /iss1/4.

Harrison, Jill Lindsey. 2014. "Neoliberal Environmental Justice: Mainstream Ideas of Justice in Political Conflict over Agricultural Pesticides in the United States." *Environmental Politics* 23, no. 4: 650–69.

Marquez, Benjamin. 2003. *Constructing Identities in Mexican American Political Organizations: Choosing Issues, Taking Sides.* Austin: University of Texas Press.

Marquez, Benjamin. 2012. "Mexican Americans and Environmental Justice: Change and Continuity in Mexican American Politics." In Ralph David Diaz and Rodolfo D. Torres, eds. *Latino Urbanism: The Politics of Planning, Policy, and Redevelopment.* New York: New York University Press, pp. 163–80.

McNamara, Patrick J. 2002. "Environmental Justice: Injunction Stopping Issuance of Air Permit Thrown Out on Title VI Grounds." *Environmental Compliance and Litigation* 17, no. 8 (January): 1.

Minkler, M., A. P. Garcia, J. Williams, T. LoPresti, & J. Lilly. 2010. "Si Se Puede: Using Participatory Research to Promote Environmental Justice in a Latino Community in San Diego, California. *Journal of Urban Health* 87, no. 5: 796–812.

Montag, Brian S., & Catherine A. Trinkle. 2002. "Environmental Justice at a Crossroads: Third Circuit Eliminates the Right of Private Plaintiffs to Enforce Title VI Disparate Impact Regulations in Federal Court." *New Jersey Law Journal* 14, no. 1 (February).

Noonan, Douglas S. 2008. "Evidence of Environmental Justice: A Critical Perspective on the Practice of EJ Research and Lessons for Policy Design." *Social Science Quarterly* 89, no. 5: 1153–74.

Pastor, Manuel, Jr., Jim Sadd, & John Hipp. 2001. "Which Came First? Toxic Facilities Minority Move-In and Environmental Justice." *Journal of Urban Affairs* 23, no. 1: 1–21.

Pastor, Manuel, Jr., James L. Sadd, & Rachel Morello-Frosch. 2004. "Waiting to Inhale: The Demographics of Toxic Air Release Facilities in 21st Century California." *Social Science Quarterly* 85, no. 2 (June): 420–40.

Pellow, David Naguib. 2002. *Garbage Wars: The Struggle for Environmental Justice in Chicago.* Cambridge, MA: The MIT Press.

Pulido, Laura. 2006. *Black, Brown, Yellow, and Left Radical Activism in Los Angeles.* Berkeley: University of California Press.

Sassman, Wyatt. G. 2014. "Environmental Justice as Civil Rights." *Richmond Journal of Law and Public Interest* 18: 441.

Schlosberg, David. 2013. "Theorizing Environmental Justice: The Expanding Sphere of a Discourse." *Environmental Politics* 22, no. 1: 37–55.

Schlosberg, David, & David Carruthers. 2010. "Indigenous Struggles, Environmental Justice, and Community Capabilities." *Global Environmental Politics* 10, no. 4: 12–35.

Switzer, David, & Manuel P. Teodoro. 2018. "Class, Race, Ethnicity, and Justice in Safe Drinking Water Compliance." *Social Science Quarterly* 99, no. 2: 524–35.

Sze, Julie. 2007. *Noxious New York: The Racial Politics of Urban Health and Environmental Justice.* Cambridge, MA: MIT Press.

Wilson, Sacoby M., R. Richard, L. Joseph, & E. Williams. 2010. "Climate Change, Environmental Justice, and Vulnerability: An Exploratory Spatial Analysis." *Environmental Justice* 3, no. 1: 13–19.

Equal Voice Network (EVN)

The Equal Voice for America's Families Campaign is the coalition movement arm of a family-based grant-making entity called the Marguerite Casey Foundation (MCF). In 2008, the foundation decided to call to action over 30,000 families who were affiliated with Marguerite Casey Foundation grantees. Over 225 nonprofit groups organized 40 town hall meetings across the United States on September 6, 2008. The gathering was intended to bring about a platform to help families in the United States fight poverty and form a strategic plan for sustainable social and economic justice. At the gathering, a national platform was created to address specific topics. In order to carry out the work, each region was to create a network of organizations (MCF-funded groups) to tailor and implement proposed strategies to meet local needs. Each group of organizations would then be known as the Equal Voice Network (EVN).

The Marguerite Casey Foundation takes great pride in the Equal Voice Network planning town halls because for many of the attendees, this was the first time individuals felt like their voice was being heard. Moreover, it was the first time they realized their voice had power. The 2008 platform identified over 98 policy needs in the following areas: immigration, education, health care, child care, criminal justice reform, employment/jobs, housing, and safe communities. Although these were overarching policy platforms, the various networks across the nation were tasked with creating their regional/local strategies to be able to affect policy change in their communities and local movement entities.

Since the first gathering in 2008, organizations from across the country have come together at conventions to update the national platform goals. Shortly after the initial gathering, civic engagement was added to the platform, and in the 2012 gathering, community members leading the various Equal Voice Networks decided to include LGBTQ issues as a key policy issue to tackle in their communities. Although there are various topics for the overall EVN agenda, local networks are not bound to work on every issue, but only those that matter the most to their specific region or local community.

The local networks carry out the work by having staff or community members represent the various MCF foundation grantees at working-group meetings. Each area of interest has a working group, with meetings facilitated by a volunteer chair or co-chair. In order to coordinate the overall regional strategy, the MCF provides funding for a local network weaver to facilitate relationships among local partner organizations and movement-based initiatives. Although the funded partners are the only ones who can make major decisions on the overall direction and strategy of the coalition, nonfunded partners are welcome to take part in work groups to carry out topic-specific initiatives. To help subsidize incurred expenses, the MCF provides general funding support to Equal Voice Network organizations.

Tania Chavez

See also: Education and Latinos; Immigration as a Policy Issue; Politics of a Latinx Lesbian, Gay, Bisexual, and Transgender Identity

Further Reading

Cortes, Michael, William A. Díaz, & Henry A. J. Ramos. 1999. "A Statistical Profile of Latino Nonprofit Organizations in the United States." *Nuevos Senderos: Reflections on Hispanics and Philanthropy*: 17–54.

Hung, Chi-Kan Richard. 2007. "Immigrant Nonprofit Organizations in US Metropolitan Areas." *Nonprofit and Voluntary Sector Quarterly* 36, no. 4: 707–29.

"A National Family Platform: Equal Voice for America's Families." 2016. http://www.poli cylink.org/blog/equal-voice.

Espaillat, Adriano

(1954–)

On January 3, 2017, Adriano Espaillat made history when he was sworn in as a U.S. House representative for New York's 13th congressional district for the

115th Congress. After two unsuccessful campaigns for the congressional seat, Espaillat won the seat to replace Representative Charles Rangel, who had decided to retire after 46 years in Congress. Espaillat's victory made him the first Dominican American and first "formerly undocumented immigrant" to be elected to Congress (Latimer, 2016). Congressman Espaillat's election marked the first time in over 70 years that the 13th congressional district would not be represented by an African American. However, as an Afro-Latino, Congressman Espaillat has stated, "I am a Latino of African descent. It doesn't matter if you're from Cuba or the Dominican Republic or South Carolina or Alabama, the roots are the same and I hope we can build upon that" (Joseph, 2017).

At the age of nine, Congressman Adriano Espaillat's family migrated to New York City from the Dominican Republic (U.S. House of Representatives, 2017). Espaillat arrived in New York

Adriano Espaillat is a Dominican American politician. He is the representative for New York's 13th congressional district and the first formerly undocumented immigrant to ever serve in Congress. (JP PULLOS/Patrick McMullan via Getty Images)

with his parents and siblings on a temporary visa, which they later overstayed. The Espaillat family had to leave the country in order to obtain a green card that would enable them to re-enter the country legally (Joseph, 2017). Congressman Espaillat has described his immigration experience as traumatic because of the fear of being separated from his family.

Prior to becoming a member of Congress, Representative Espaillat worked for various community organizations. He served as director of Project Right Start, an organization that worked to combat substance abuse. He was also director of the Washington Heights Victims' Services Community Office, which provided services to families of victims of homicides and other crimes (U.S. House of Representatives, 2017). In 1996 Espaillat became the first Dominican American to be elected to the New York State Assembly, and in 2010 he was elected to the New York State Senate. In 2002, he was elected chair of the New York State Black, Puerto Rican, Hispanic, and Asian Legislative Caucus (U.S. House of Representatives, 2017).

In his campaign for Congress, Representative Espaillat focused on issues that affected his mostly African American and Latina/o congressional district, including education and affordable housing, in particular, issues with gentrification. Following his swearing in, Espaillat joined the Congressional Hispanic Caucus, and as a Latino of African descent, attempted to join the Congressional Black Caucus (CBC) as well. However, members of the CBC debated whether an Afro-Latino can be part of the Caucus, and as of June 2017, Espaillat was not a member of the CBC.

In the 115th Congress, Representative Espaillat serves as a member of the U.S. House Foreign Affairs Committee, House Committee on Education and Workforce, House Select Committee on Small Business, and Congressional Hispanic Caucus. Congressman Espaillat also serves as chairman of the Congressional Hispanic Caucus Task Force for Transportation, Infrastructure, and Housing (U.S. House of Representatives, 2017). During his first term in Congress, Representative Espaillat emerged as a staunch critic of President Donald Trump's policies, particularly on issues of immigration. Espaillat, a formerly undocumented immigrant, has said that his story as an immigrant who arrived to New York City from the Dominican Republic "is an American story" (Neuman, 2016) and has argued that Trump's rhetoric about building a wall on the U.S.–Mexico border and the administration's deportation policies contradict the idea of the United States as a "country of aspirations" (Scott, 2017).

Domingo Morel

See also: Taveras, Angel (1970–)

Further Reading

Joseph, Cameron. 2017. "New York's Newest Congressman Adriano Espaillat to Make History." *New York Daily News*, January 3. http://www.nydailynews.com/news/politics/new-york newest-congressman-adriano-espaillat-history-article-1.2932252.

Latimer, Brian. 2016. "Adriano Espaillat Elected First Dominican-American to US Congress." *NBC News*, November 8. http://www.nbcnews.com/news/latino/adriano-espaillatelected-first-dominican-american-us-congress-n680806.

Neuman, William. 2016. "Adriano Espaillat Is in Position to Replace Rangel and Become First Dominican in Congress." *New York Times*, June 29. https://www.nytimes.com/2016/06/29/nyregion/adriano-espaillat-charles-rangel-first-dominican-in-congress.html?_r=0.

Scott, Eugene. 2017. "Espaillat: 'Are We a Country of Deportation or a Country of Aspirations?'" *CNN News*, February 22. http://www.cnn.com/2017/02/22/politics/adriano-espaillat-donald-trump-immigration/index.html.

U.S. House of Representatives. 2017. "About Adriano Espaillat." https://espaillat.house.gov/about.

Espinoza v. Farah

(1973)

Pivotal to litigation concerning Latino workers, *Espinoza v. Farah* (414 U.S. 86) pushed the U.S. Supreme Court to decide whether Title VII of the Civil Rights Act of 1964 afforded protections to citizens and noncitizens alike. Centralizing issues of citizenship, immigration, and alienage status, this court case tested the strength of Title VII protections against national-origin discrimination and highlighted the complexity of citizenship and national origin for Latino, transnational, and immigrant workers.

In 1973, Cecilia Espinoza sued the Farah Manufacturing Company on the basis of discrimination. Claiming protection under Title VII of the Civil Rights Act of 1964, Espinoza argued that the Farah Manufacturing Company violated national law when it refused to hire her due to her national origin. Title VII of the Civil Rights Act of 1964 prohibited employers from discriminating against "any individual on the basis of race, color, religion, sex or national origin" (Bendremer and Heiden, 1987: 1033). Espinoza, a legal resident alien married to a U.S. citizen and living in San Antonio, Texas, challenged the Farah Manufacturing Company policy of only hiring U.S. citizens. She claimed that even though she was legally able to work in the United States, Farah discriminated against her because she was a Mexican citizen.

The Supreme Court ruled in favor of the Farah Manufacturing Company and concluded that Title VII did not deal with citizenship status. Opposing the Equal Employment Opportunity Commission (EEOC), the Supreme Court determined that even though Title VII protected individuals, citizens and noncitizens, from employment-based discrimination due to race, color, religion, sex, or national origin, citizenship status was not included in the protections. Though national origin was protected, national origin was markedly different from an individual's citizenship. Thus, Farah, as a private employer, had the right to distinguish between citizens and noncitizens in hiring decisions. The Court ruled that Farah did not discriminate against Espinoza because of her national origin or because she was from Mexico, her nation of birth, but because of her alienage or citizenship status. In fact, the Farah Manufacturing labor force was 92 percent Mexican American. National origin and citizenship, in this case, should be considered two distinct categories.

Espinoza v. Farah allowed employers to legally refuse to hire lawfully admitted noncitizen workers because of their lack of U.S. citizenship. It essentially allowed for a two-tiered rights system between citizens and noncitizens, often intersecting with immigrant rights. Latino workers, often part of transnational communities, as in the case of the Espinoza family, experienced different sets of rights, responsibilities, and access to jobs within their own families due to their citizenship status.

In 1980, the EEOC issued new guidelines on the definition of national origin discrimination. The United States' continual need for immigrant labor, immigrant rights' movements, and federal and state governments' role in shaping employment practices resulted in the EEOC's clarification and revision of the earlier 1970s approach to national origin discrimination. In 2002, the EEOC again established new guidelines that elaborated on the definition of national origin and citizenship status. To date, the EEOC guideline on citizenship status reads, "Employment discrimination based on citizenship status if it has the purpose or effect of discriminating based on national origin" is prohibited (EEOC, 2017).

Jennifer R. Mata

See also: Immigration as a Policy Issue

Further Reading

Bendremer, Fedric, & Lisa A. Heiden. 1987. "The Unfair Immigration-Related Employment Practices Provision: A Modicum of Protection against National Origin and Citizenship Status Discrimination." *University of Miami Law Review* 41: 1025. http://repository.law.miami.edu/umlr/vol41/iss5/6.

EEOC. 2016. https://www.eeoc.gov/eeoc/publications/immigrants-facts.cfm.

Espinoza v. Farah Mfg. Co., Inc. 1973. Supreme Court Case Files Collection. Box 13. Powell Papers. Lewis F. Powell Jr. Archives, Washington & Lee University of Law, Virginia. http://scholarlycommons.law.wlu.edu/casefiles/257.

López, María Pabón. 2008. "The Intersection of Immigration Law and Civil Rights Law: Noncitizen Workers and the International Human Rights Paradigm." *Brandeis Law Journal* 44, no. 3: 611. https://ssrn.com/abstract=1199742.

Ornati, Oscar A. 1981. "Arbitrators and National Origin Discrimination." *The Arbitration Journal* 36, no. 2: 30–34 (June).

Saucedo, Leticia M. 2010. "National Origin, Immigrants, and the Workplace: The Employment Cases in Latinos and the Law and the Advocates' Perspective." *Harvard Latino Law Review* 12: 53; UNLV William S. Boyd School of Law Legal Studies Research Paper No. 10–10 (2009). https://ssrn.com/abstract=1578940.

Evenwel v. Abbott

(2016)

Evenwel v. Abbott is a U.S. Supreme Court case concerning how state legislative districts in Texas were to be apportioned (i.e., the process of deciding what population metric would be used when drawing electoral districts). The plaintiffs in the case alleged that the current practice of drawing state legislative boundaries based on total population instead of the voting-eligible population was a violation of the Equal Protection Clause of the Fourteenth Amendment. The Supreme Court ruled in an 8–0 decision that states may use total population when it comes to drawing state legislative districts, therefore supporting the "one person, one vote" principle under the Equal Protection Clause of the Fourteenth Amendment. This case was significant because it would have diluted Latino voting power as districts apportioned based on voting-eligible population would lead to fewer Latino-majority districts (electoral districts where a majority of residents are Latino) and such districts tend to feature more noncitizen immigrants and children.

The plaintiffs in *Evenwel v. Abbott* were Texas voters Sue Evenwel and Edward Pfenninger, who argued that apportioned legislative districts based on total population violated the principle of "one man, one vote" (the belief that everyone's vote is equal and proportionate in the selection of elected officials) because their vote was diluted by the fact that they lived in districts with more eligible voters than other districts. They sued the state of Texas (the defendant was Texas governor Greg Abbott) with the help of the conservative advocacy organization Project on Fair Representation. The plaintiffs argued that Texas should be allowed to draft an apportionment plan based on voter-eligible population and that such a plan would be able to satisfy the requirement of the Supreme Court case *Reynolds v. Sims* (1964) that all legislative districts across the country be of roughly equal population. The defendant, Governor Abbott, argued that by using total population as the metric for apportionment, the state of Texas was abiding by the constitutional principle of one man, one vote as actualized by the Supreme Court for nearly 50 years.

The U.S. District Court for the Western District of Texas, which ruled against the plaintiffs' wishes, originally heard the case. The U.S. District Court ruled in 2014 that the case concerned a solely political question, not a judicial question that the court could review. The court found that determining the appropriate population base for apportionment should lie with the states. The plaintiffs then appealed to the Supreme Court, which agreed to hear the case in 2014. Oral arguments began in 2015.

In 2016, the Supreme Court ruled unanimously that states could draw legislative boundaries based on total population. The opinion of the Court (an explanation of the Court's rationale for its final decision on a case as supported by a majority of the justices) was written by Justice Ruth Bader Ginsburg and supported by Chief Justice John Roberts and Justices Anthony Kennedy, Stephen Breyer, Sonia Sotomayor, and Elena Kagan. Justices Clarence Thomas and Samuel Alito did not sign on to the majority opinion. The majority opinion of the Court argued that by using the total population metric, states were guaranteeing that nonvoters would receive equitable representation on par with voters by ensuring that all elected officials had roughly the same number of constituents. This was necessary due to the fact that nonvoters had as much at stake in government policies as voters.

The Supreme Court's decision did not say that states could not use another population metric other than total population in drawing legislative boundaries. The opinion was clear that this was a question they would not address in this case. In his concurrence (an opinion written by a justice that states a different rationale for the decision made on the case), Justice Thomas argued that the states should have the right to draw legislative boundaries however they see fit, as the U.S. Constitution does not address how states should apportion their own legislative districts.

Matthew S. Mendez

See also: Voting Rights Act of 1975

Further Reading

Barnes, Robert. 2016. "Supreme Court Rejects Conservative Challenge to 'One Person, One Vote.'" *Washington Post,* April 4. https://www.washingtonpost.com/politics /courts_law/supreme-court-rejectsconservative-bid-to-count-only-eligible-voters -for-districts/2016/04/04/67393e52-fa6f-11e5-9140e61d062438bb_story.html?utm _term=.701002d1df90&wpisrc=nl_headlines&wpmm=1.

Cain, Bruce E., & Emily R. Zhang. 2016. "Blurred Lines: Conjoined Polarization and Voting Rights." *Ohio State Law Journal* 77, no. 4: 867–904.

Collingwood, Lauren, Matt A. Barreto, & Sergio I. Garcia-Rios. 2014. "Revisiting Latino Voting: Cross-Racial Mobilization in the 2012 Election." *Political Research Quarterly* 67, no. 3: 632–45.

Liptak, Adam. 2016. "Supreme Court Rejects Challenge on 'One Person, One Vote.'" *New York Times,* April 4. https://www.nytimes.com/2016/04/05/us/politics/supreme -court-one-person-onevote.html.

Michelson, Melissa R. 2016. "Majority-Latino Districts and Latino Political Power." *Duke Journal of Constitutional Law and Public Policy* 5: 159–75.

Reynolds v. Sims, 377, U.S. 533 (1964).

F

Family Leave and Reproductive Policy

Policies related to family leave and reproductive rights are of special interest to Latinos/as for at least two reasons. First, the Latino/a population is very young in terms of average age (the median age for Hispanics is 27 years, whereas the median age for the U.S. population is 37 years), and many in this population are part of the labor force these childbearing years. This means that family planning and flexibility at work to handle, for example, health emergencies, are everyday issues many Latinos/as deal with (see U.S. Bureau of Labor Statistics, 2015 for labor force information). Second, Latinos/as tend to disproportionately work in areas of the economy such as services, agriculture, and production, and in these types of jobs employers are less likely to offer family leave benefits as well as health benefits that offer family planning. Even though the topic of family leave and reproductive policy is of importance for Latinos/as currently, this is a much more complex topic. Latinas' right to decide over their bodies has been marked by events like forced sterilization at the moment of the delivery of their babies, such as the case of Mexican American women in California in the 1960s and 1970s and Puerto Rican women in the island and in New York. Latinos/as navigate a society where they are accused of burdening the U.S. welfare system (as if there was a comprehensive one in the United States) and using their children to benefit their migratory status. The constant stigmatization of Latinos/as adds a barrier that prevents the success of policies related to family leave and reproductive rights that aim to benefit people of color. The intersection of race, gender, and class should be taken into account when studying and advancing policies related to family leave and reproductive rights.

ABORTION AND REPRODUCTIVE RIGHTS

In the United States, one's opinion on abortion is influenced by a person's party affiliation, political ideology, and religious beliefs. Conservatives tend to oppose abortion rights, whereas liberals are more likely to favor abortion rights. Although most Latinos identify as Democrats politically, their views on abortion are not fully aligned with the party's mainstream. This makes sense because most Latinos simultaneously identify with religious groups that oppose abortion and with the political party that favors its legality. Moreover, Roman Catholic and evangelical Christian believers are less likely to support abortion. Latinos/as, despite being overwhelmingly Catholic and Christian in their religious outlook, tend to have mixed opinions on abortion. For example, a Public Religion Research Institute

(PRRI) survey among millennials found that about 55 percent of Latino Catholics and about 6 out of 10 (61%) Latino Protestant millennials said abortion should be illegal. However, Latinos have a split position on "whether having an abortion can be the most responsible decision or not (51% vs. 46%, respectively)" (Cox and Jones, 2015). These mixed findings are consistent with scholarship finding that Latinos/as hold liberal positions on social issues despite their religious beliefs (Bejarano, Manzano, and Montoya, 2011). Latinos' views on family and reproductive policies are shaped by their religious values and their experiences.

FAMILY LEAVE POLICY

According to data compiled by the Organisation for Economic Co-operation and Development (OECD), the United States is the only country among 41 similarly situated nations that does not mandate any paid leave for new parents. Most Americans, Latinos included, overwhelmingly support both paid parental leave and paid sick leave to use in case of illness or to take care of sick relatives. Research by the Public Religion Research Institute (Cox, Navarro-Rivera, and Jones, 2014) shows that 80 percent of Latinos support paid parental leave to take care of a newborn or adopted child. Likewise, 89 percent of Latinos also want the government to enact sick pay leave that allows them to rest from work when sick without fear of losing their job or losing pay.

Latinos' views on family leave policy and their preferences for fairer sick and parental leave policies are shaped by their experiences in the labor force. Latino voters want to have the right to take care of themselves, their children, and their families without fear of employer retribution. Candidates and politicians who support and propose these types of employee benefits will certainly gain the goodwill of Latino voters.

FORCED STERILIZATION

Some of the stereotypes that Latinas/os encounter in the United States is related to having large families that in turn deplete the U.S. welfare system. This stereotype gets more complicated when there is also a belief that undocumented Latinas/os use their U.S.-born children to take advantage of the immigration system. As Deeb-Sossa (2016) explains in her review of the documentary *No más bebés* [*No More Babies*], population control and a family planning discourse in the 1970s was often the logic used to justify forced sterilization and avoid any "abuse" to the welfare and immigration systems. The film is based on the *Madrigal v. Quilligan* case in which women of Mexican origin in Los Angeles sued their practitioners for forcibly sterilizing them through coercion or without their knowledge. Although the court ruled in favor of the practitioners, the women became heroes on reproductive rights for the Chicana activists defending reproductive rights. This was unfortunately not an isolated case in the United States, as women in Puerto Rico went through a mass sterilization campaign in the 1950s and 1960s promoted by the state. The implications of this campaign have placed Puerto Rican women as having "one of the highest documented rates of sterilization in the world" (López, 1997). Forced sterilization may seem as something that only happened in the past. However, this perspective keeps appearing and targets vulnerable populations. For instance, recent news reported on a Tennessee judge who created a program of prison sentence reduction in exchange for vasectomies and implants preventing pregnancies (Hawkins, 2017). It is not surprising that such programs specifically target people of color who happen to be overrepresented in the U.S. prison system. The study of family leave and reproductive rights among Latinas/os should therefore include the intersection of gender, race, and class to fully understand its past, present, and future implications.

Yazmín A. García Trejo

See also: Catholicism and Latino/a Politics; Latina/o Gender Gap; National Latina Institute for Reproductive Health (NLIRH)

Further Reading

Bejarano, Christina E., Sylvia Manzano, & Celeste Montoya. 2011. "Tracking the Latino Gender Gap: Gender Attitudes across Sex, Borders, and Generations." *Politics & Gender* 7: 521–49.

Briggs, Laura. 1998. "Discourses of 'Forced Sterilization in Puerto Rico: The Problem with the Speaking Subaltern." *Differences: A Journal of Feminist Cultural Studies* 10 (Summer): 30–66.

Cox, Daniel, & Robert P. Jones. 2015. "How Race and Religion Shape Millennial Attitudes on Sexuality and Reproductive Health." *Public Religion Research Institute (PRRI)*. https://www.prri.org/wp-content/uploads/2015/03/PRRI-Millennials-Web-FINAL-1.pdf.

Cox, Daniel, Juhem Navarro-Rivera, & Robert P. Jones. 2014. "Economic Insecurity, Rising Inequality, and Doubts about the Future (Dataset)." *Public Religion Research Institute (PRRI)*. https://www.prri.org/research/survey-economic-insecurity-rising-inequality-and-doubts-about-the-future-findings-from-the-2014-american-values-survey.

Deeb-Sossa, Natalia. 2016. "Review of the Film No Más Bebés (No More Babies)." *Journal of Latinos and Education* 16, no. 2: 164–66.

Hawkins, Derek. 2017. "Tenn. Judge Reprimanded for Offering Reduced Jail Time in Exchange for Sterilization." *Washington Post*, November 21. https://www.washingtonpost.com/news/morning-mix/wp/2017/11/21/tenn-judge-reprimanded-for-offering-reduced-jail-time-in-exchange-for-sterilization/?utm_term=.171a7e77ea34.

Livingston, Gretchen. 2016. "Among 41 Nations, U.S. Is the Outlier When It Comes to Paid Parental Leave." *Pew Research Center.* http://www.pewresearch.org/fact-tank/2016/09/26/u-s-lacks-mandated-paid-parental-leave.

López, Iris. 1997. "Agency and Constraint: Sterilization and Reproductive Freedom among Puerto Rican Women in New York City." In Louise Lamphere, Helena Ragone, and Patricia Zavella, eds. *Situated Lives: Gender and Culture in Everyday Lives.* New York: Routledge, pp. 157–74.

McLanahan, Sara, & Christine Percheski. 2008. "Family Structure and the Reproduction of Inequalities." *Annual Review of Sociology* 34: 257–76.

O'Connor, Julia S., Ann Shola Orloff, & Sheila Shaver. 1999. *States, Markets, Families: Gender, Liberalism and Social Policy in Australia, Canada, Great Britain and the United States.* New York: Cambridge University Press.

Pattatucci-Aragón, Angela. 2002. "Hispanic/Latina Women and Reproductive Rights." In Judith A. Baer, ed. *Historical and Multicultural Encyclopedia of Women's Reproductive Rights in the United States*. Westport, CT: Greenwood Press, pp. 103–06.

U.S. Bureau of Labor Statistics. 2015. *Labor Force Characteristics by Race and Ethnicity*. https://www.bls.gov/opub/reports/race-and-ethnicity/2015/home.htm.

Fariña, Carmen

(1943–)

Carmen Fariña became chancellor of the New York City Department of Education, the largest public school district in the United States, in January 2014. Her chancellorship was the culmination of 50 years of service in New York City education, including 22 years as an English teacher at P.S. (Public School) 29 in Brooklyn, serving as principal of P.S. 6 in Manhattan and the elected community superintendent of Brooklyn's District 15. She also served as superintendent of Region 8 and was the deputy chancellor for Teaching and Learning from 2004 to 2006.

A daughter of Spanish immigrants and an immigrant herself, Fariña was the first person in her family to graduate from college. Fariña has a bachelor's degree from New York University and earned three master's degrees from Brooklyn College, Fordham University, and Pace University. In a speech at Columbia University, Fariña reflected on her own experiences growing up and how that has affected her career as an educator, telling the audience "As a child of Spanish immigrants, I entered school unable to even speak English. My teacher marked me absent every day because I never answered during roll call. Why would I? I never heard my name called. My father eventually discovered that my teacher had been mispronouncing it for weeks" (Fariña, 2014b).

Fariña was chosen as chancellor by Mayor Bill de Blasio, with whom she had worked previously in District 15 when de Blasio was a city councilman. Of Fariña's work in District 15 de Blasio said, "She gained respect immediately. This is one of her great characteristics. She really gives people a sense of what the mission is for all of us" (Herszenhorn, 2004).

During her first year in office, Fariña implemented several significant programs and policy changes, including an expansion of the pre–K program by over 50,000 students, a new after-school program for middle school students, an end to the use of standardized test scores as the primary factor in deciding grade-level promotions and eliminating the practice of assigning letter grades to city schools. Fariña's tenure demonstrated a departure from the principles of the Department of Education during Mayor Michael Bloomberg's tenure, which featured a focus on accountability through test scores. Fariña stated that there are four pillars upon which she bases all of her actions as chancellor, which are "to return dignity and respect to our work force . . . to improve student achievement by aligning Common Core strategies with everything we do . . . to engage parents in every aspect of school life . . . to create new collaborative and innovative models within our City and schools" (Fariña, 2014a).

Fariña's tenure has seen reductions in school crime and incremental improvements in the city's lowest-performing schools with the adoption of the Renewal School program that provided $582 million in additional funding for those buildings to improve academic performance. In an effort to address concerns over teacher contracts limiting innovation in city schools, the United Federation of Teachers and Chancellor Fariña implemented the Progressive Redesign Opportunity Schools for Excellence Program (PROSE), which provided individual schools with the flexibility to adjust teacher schedules, class sizes, school calendars, and professional development to improve student achievement. Additional new programming under Fariña has included an elementary literacy program, a college awareness program for middle school students, a universal free lunch program, and additional access to Advanced Placement (AP) courses in the city's high schools. Chancellor Fariña has also prioritized increasing parental involvement in New York City schools by reorganizing the Education Department's Division of Family and Community Engagement, offering more parent workshops on topics including financial literacy and college awareness, and retraining the city's 1,400 parent coordinators who are responsible for increasing parental involvement in each school. As of 2016, these initiatives have been highly successful, with parent attendance at workshops up 59 percent and parent–teacher conference attendance up 38 percent (Chapman, 2016).

Adam McGlynn

See also: Education and Latinos

Further Reading

Chapman, Ben. 2016. "New York City Parents Are Getting More Involved in the Education of Their Kids." *New York Daily News*, February 4, http://www.nydailynews.com/new-york/education/exclusive-nyc-schools-parents-involved-article-1.2520735.

Fariña, Carmen. 2014a. "The Answer Is in the Room." Presentation at Teachers College, Columbia University, New York, NY, April 12.

Fariña, Carmen. 2014b. "Change in Climate of Education." *Education Update Online*, May/June. http://www.educationupdate.com/archives/2014/MAY/HTML/edit.html#.WsKu3tIm7MA.

Herszenhorn, David. 2004. "A Troubleshooter with a Passion for Schools." *The New York Times*, March 12. http://www.nytimes.com/2004/03/12/nyregion/a-troubleshooter-with-a-passion-for-schools.html.

New York City Department of Education. 2016. "Chancellor Fariña, UFT & CSA Announce New PROSE Schools for 2016–2017 School Year." http://schools.nyc.gov/Offices/mediarelations/NewsandSpeeches/2016-2017/Chancellor+Fariña+UFT+CSA+Announce+New+Prose+Schools+for+2016-2017+School+Year.htm.

New York City Department of Education. 2017. "Chancellor Fariña and the Leadership Team." http://schools.nyc.gov/AboutUs/leadership/leadershipteam/Chancellor+Fari%C3%B1a.htm.

Superville, Denisa R. 2014. "N.Y.C. Chancellor Carmen Fariña Forges a New Schooling Era." *Education Week*, October 22.

Taylor, Kate. 2017. "Struggling Schools Improve on Test Score, But Not All Are Safe." *The New York Times*, August 22. https://www.nytimes.com/2017/08/22/nyregion/renewal-schools-test-scores-math-reading.html.

Ferrera, America

(1984–)

Latina actor and activist America Ferrera was born in Los Angeles on April 18, 1984, the daughter of Honduran immigrants. Appearing in more than 20 films, she has acted in many roles that relate to her experiences as a Latina in the United States. In addition to her acting, Ferrera has gained notoriety for her social and political activism in recent years—particularly in regard to women's rights and immigrants' rights issues. She has also been an active participant in Voto Latino, a nonprofit organization that seeks to increase Latinx voter engagement in the electoral process and appears in various programs on their behalf. She attended the 2012 Democratic National Convention in Charlotte, North Carolina, pledging her support for President Barack Obama's re-election campaign. Ferrera spoke at the 2016 Democratic National Convention in Philadelphia. She was also the opening speaker for the Women's March on Washington, D.C., on January 21, 2017.

Since 2012, Ferrera has become increasingly vocal in U.S. politics. She claims that she first became politically conscious around the age of nine, when Proposition 187 (a voter referendum aiming to crack down on undocumented immigrants) appeared on California's ballot (her home state). As a child growing up in Los Angeles, Ferrera acknowledges that she felt like an "other" and an "outsider." Her mother directly addressed the mounting nativism and anti-Latinx sentiments by telling a young America, "Someone may ask you what you are and where you are from. Don't let anyone scare you. You are an American. You have every right to be heard. Don't be intimidated. Don't be afraid." In 2011, President Barack Obama met with Ferrera, fellow Latinx actor Eva Longoria, and other prominent Latinx figures at the White House to discuss immigration policy and outreach efforts to Latinx voters for the 2012 presidential election. That same year, Ferrera established the website America4America.com, which registered Latinx voters and encouraged Latinx to participate in the political process.

Actor America Ferrera speaks to attendees during a 2016 Hillary Clinton campaign rally at the Clark County Government Center Amphitheater in Las Vegas, Nevada. (Joe Sohm /Dreamstime.com)

Ferrera was an outspoken supporter and surrogate for Democratic candidate Hillary Clinton during the 2016 primary and presidential campaign seasons. Ferrera repeatedly emphasized the tremendous personal importance that the 2016 election held for her as a Latinx woman, a committed feminist, and the daughter of immigrants. Appearing as a guest on HBO's political talk show *Real Time with Bill Maher* on July 22, 2016, Ferrera remarked, "I'm not here as a celebrity. I'm here as a person who has a lot to lose in this election—as a woman, as a Latina." Ferrera spoke at the 2016 Democratic National Convention in Philadelphia on the event's second day, where she heavily criticized Republican presidential nominee Donald Trump's harsh rhetoric and stringent policy proposals targeting undocumented immigrants. In perhaps the most famous line of her speech, Ferrera opened her remarks by mockingly stating, "I am America Ferrera, and according to Donald Trump, I am probably a rapist," in reference to Trump's previous comments equating Mexicans with drug trafficking, rape, and other crimes. During the Women's March in Washington, D.C., on January 21, 2016, which occurred the day after Trump's inauguration, Ferrera delivered a powerful emotional condemnation of Trump's policy agenda and political rhetoric. Speaking to an audience of 400,000 protestors, Ferrera declared, "It's been a heart-wrenching time to be a woman and an immigrant in this country—a platform of hate and division assumed power yesterday. But the president is not America. His cabinet is not America. Congress is not America. We are America!"

Justin D. García

See also: Dawson, Rosario (1979–); Kumar, María Teresa (1974–); Longoria, Eva (1975–); Obama, Barack (1961–) and Latinos; Proposition 187 (1994); Voto Latino

Further Reading

Bacon, Perry, Jr. 2011. "Obama Sits Down with Eva Longoria and Other Latinos to Discuss Immigration." *Washington Post*, April 28. https://www.washingtonpost.com/blogs/44/post/obama-meets-with-eva-longoria-and-other-latinos-on-immigration-reform/2011/04/28/AFKZUM8E_blog.html?utm_term=.4105e6513e77.

Hung, Kineta. 2014. "Why Celebrity Sells: A Dual Entertainment Path Model of Brand Endorsement." *Journal of Advertising* 43, no. 2: 155–66.

Lynch, John. 2016. "Lena Dunham and America Ferrera Slammed Donald Trump in a DNC Speech: 'He's Making America Hate Again.'" *Business Insider*, July 27. http://www.businessinsider.com/lena-dunham-and-america-ferrera-mock-donald-trump-in-a-dnc-speech-2016-7.

Molloy, Parker. 2017. "America Ferrera's Speech at the Women's March Sends a Powerful Message Against Hate." *Upworthy.com*, January 21. http://www.upworthy.com/america-ferreras-speech-at-the-womens-march-sends-a-powerful-message-against-hate.

Ross, Janell. 2012. "America Ferrera's Message to Latino Voters: 'Don't Let Anyone Scare You.'" *Huffington Post*, May 31. http://www.huffingtonpost.com/2012/05/31/america-ferrera-america4america_n_1559941.html.

Shadid, Aliyah. 2013. "America Ferrera: Racist Immigration Laws Make It Critical for Latinos to Vote." *MSNBC.com*, September 6. http://www.msnbc.com/msnbc/america-ferrera-racist-immigration-laws.

Ferreras-Copeland, Julissa

(1976–)

Julissa Ferreras-Copeland is a New York City council member. In 2000, she began her career in politics when Assemblyman Ivan Lafayette nominated her to be a delegate to the Democratic National Convention. She went on to join Councilman Hiram Monserrate as his chief of staff and campaign manager and serve as the New York director of the National Association of Latino Elected and Appointed Officials (NALEO), an organization that she still sits on the board of directors of today. As a New York City council member, she was appointed to chair the council's Committee on Finance, the first Latina, person of color, and woman to do so in 2014.

In 2009, Ferreras-Copeland won her New York City councilor race for District 21, making her the first Latina ever elected to represent Queens. The special election for the 2009 election had four competitors, three of which were Democrats and the other had no party affiliation. Ferreras-Copeland won the special election with 45.66 percent of the vote. Her district encompasses Corona, LeFrak City, East Elmhurst, Elmhurst, and sections of Jackson Heights. In 2014, Ferreras-Copeland ran for reelection in District 21, winning 99.72 percent of the general election vote. In her position, Ferreras-Copeland manages New York City's budget of $75.3 billion. She also oversees the Independent Budget Office, the Department of Design and Construction, the Comptroller's Office, the Tax Commission, the Banking Commission, and the Department of Finance. Ferreras-Copeland also serves on the council's Budget Negotiating Team and Committees on Public Safety, Cultural Affairs, Consumer Affairs, Standards and Ethics, and Economic Development. Ferreras-Copeland co-chairs the council's Progressive Caucus in addition to being a member of the Black, Latino, Asian, and Women's Caucus.

Councilwoman Ferreras-Copeland was born in the Corona neighborhood of the borough of Queens in New York City to two immigrants from the Dominican Republic. Her mother, Josefina Ferreras-Palaez, worked as an office aid in New York City's Human Resource Administration, while her father, Julio Alejandro Ferreras, worked as a subway car inspector. At 14 years old, Julissa was appointed to serve on the Corona Youth Council by then Queens borough president Helen Marshall. It was on the Corona Youth Council that she championed a youth employment program for her community and was then selected for the role of NAACP Youth Council president for the neighborhoods of Corona and East Elmhurst, which she performed for three years. Upon graduating high school at age 19, she joined the workforce serving as the assistant director of the Corona Community Conciliation Network. Ferreras-Copeland quickly transitioned into a new position as the beacon director of P.S. 19, the most overcrowded school in the United States. As beacon director, she piloted programs such as mentoring, homework help, and after-school programs to get at-risk youth off the street.

Ferreras-Copeland's work in her community has greatly benefited numerous New York City residents. Due to her work, Julissa has received numerous awards and recognitions. In 2011, she won the City University of New York's (CUNY) Educational Leadership Award for her dedicated support of CUNY schools, and she also won the Queen's Courier Rising Star Award. In 2014, she was awarded Crain's Rising Star 40 Under 40 Award, was the 62nd recipient of the Corona East Elmhurst NAACP Annual Freedom Fund's Political Service Award, and received the Statewide Associate of Minority Business PAC's Business Leadership Award. Most recently, Ferreras-Copeland has received recognition for spearheading the city council movement to provide free tampons to New York City public schools, jails, and homeless shelters. In addition to her work as a New York City council member, Julissa serves her local community through her position on the board of directors of the 82nd Street Business Improvement District and on the board of directors of Elmcor. Julissa currently lives in East Elmhurst with her husband, Aaron Copeland, and son, Julian.

Ryan K. O'Neill

See also: Espaillat, Adriano (1954–); Mark-Viverito, Melissa (1969–)

Further Reading

Marvilli, Joe. 2014. "Education: Corona Schools Suffer from Overcrowding." *Queens Tribune,* June 26. http://queenstribune.com/education-corona-schools-suffer-from -overcrowding.

National Association for the Advancement of Colored People (NAACP). 2016. "Oldest and Boldest." https://live-naacp-site.pantheonsite.io/oldest-and-boldest/.

National Association of Latino Elected and Appointed Officials (NALEO). 2016. "NALEO Educational Fund." http://www.naleo.org.

Ruiz-Grossman, Sarah. 2016. "NYC Mayor Signs Free Tampons for Schools, Jails, Shelters into Law." *The Huffington Post,* July 14. http://www.huffingtonpost.com/entry /new-york-city-mayor-bill-de-blasio-signs-tampons-free-law_us_5787bc57e4b08 608d3336b27.

Fierro de Bright, Josefina

(1914–1998)

An American civil rights leader who was most active between 1930 and 1960, Josefina Fierro de Bright is most noted for her leadership and activism on behalf of Mexican-origin and other Spanish-speaking people. She played key roles in El Congreso del Pueblo de Habla Española (Congress of Spanish-Speaking Peoples, aka El Congreso), Asociación Nacional México Americana (ANMA) (National Association of Mexican Americans), and the Sleepy Lagoon Defense Committee. She was one of the most ardent organizers and dynamic political activists of her day. As an activist during the World War II and postwar eras, Fierro de Bright fought for fair wages, labor and employment rights, and equality in housing, education, and the legal system. Her contemporaries include Chicana/Latina labor leaders such as Manuela Solis Sager and Emma Tenayuca from Texas, and Luisa Moreno from Guatemala and New York.

Josefina Fierro (de Bright is her married name) was born in Calexico, California, in either 1913, 1914, or 1920 (sources indicate the correct date is unclear) to Josefa and Plumo Fierro of Sinaloa, Mexico. Both parents supported the cause of the Mexican Revolution; Josefa supported the revolutionary leader Ricardo Flores Magón, and Plumo joined Pancho Villa's army on the Mexican side and later became involved in Mexican politics in the 1930s. After her parents separated, she and her brother moved to Los Angeles with their mother. To support her family, Josefa opened a restaurant in downtown Los Angeles. During the 1930s, Fierro witnessed the Mexican Repatriations and learned about the plight of migrant farmworkers through her mother, who provided them with food from a converted-trailer-restaurant as she traveled throughout California. Josefina learned to challenge discrimination, organize, and be proud of her Mexican heritage from her mother.

After graduating from a high school in Madero, California, Fierro returned to Los Angeles to attend the University of California, Los Angeles (UCLA) in hopes of studying medicine and becoming a doctor. While in Los Angeles, Fierro met notable Hollywood actors, entertainers, and celebrities such as Lupe Velez, Carmen Miranda, and Dolores del Rio through her aunt who sang in a nightclub. In 1938 Fierro met and married John Bright, a left-leaning Hollywood screenwriter and founder of the Writers Guild of America. After they married, Fierro de Bright left the university and shifted her focus to organizing the Mexican American community full time. In 1939, she became involved in El Congreso del Pueblo de Habla Española, a leftist organization founded by labor leaders Luisa Moreno and Bert Corona. Modeled after the National Negro Congress, El Congreso was founded as a coalition of organizations with a pro-labor agenda to fight for Mexican and Mexican American workers' rights. As El Congreso's treasurer and executive secretary, Fierro de Bright worked with President Eduardo Quevedo to sustain the organization's daily operations. Because many of El Congreso members were women who worked in California's canneries, Fierro de Bright also advocated for women's equality in the workplace, education, and society.

Through her work and personal connections in Hollywood, Fierro de Bright rallied support for Mexican American causes and funds for the civil rights work to address social and economic inequalities and discrimination in housing, wages, health care, education, immigration, and labor unions. Working with Moreno, she also pushed for union membership among Mexican-origin workers, especially in the Congress of Industrial Organizations (CIO); the United Cannery, Agricultural, Packing and Allied Workers of America (UCAPAWA); and International Mine, Mill, and Smelter Workers Union (Mine Mill). In 1943, Fierro de Bright helped create the Sleepy Lagoon Defense Committee and organized a legal team to provide representation for 17 Mexican American male youth who were wrongfully convicted of second-degree murder and other charges in connection with the mysterious death of José Gallardo Díaz in Los Angeles. Again, Fierro de Bright used her Hollywood contacts to rally support for the case and raise funds for the appeal. In May 1944, the Second District Court of Appeals overturned the men's convictions for insufficient evidence and ordered their release.

Fierro de Bright was also a member and leader in the Asociación Nacional Mexico Americana (ANMA), a national organization created in 1949 in Grant County, New Mexico. Members of the ANMA's 30 chapters fought discrimination in labor unions, housing, immigration policies, police brutality, and negative media images of Spanish-speaking people; supported progressive candidates for public office; and opposed U.S. intervention in Korea, Latin America, and the Middle East. In 1951, Fierro de Bright ran for Congress as a progressive to advance the cause of Spanish-speaking peoples. During the 1950s, the ANMA was red-baited and fell under federal investigation, resulting in its demise. Throughout her career as an activist, Fierro de Bright remained steadfast to fighting injustices suffered by Mexican-origin and other Latino communities. Her skills as an organizer, administrator, astute negotiator, and politician combined with her personal connections enabled her to champion the Latina/o cause for civil rights and social justice. Fierro de Bright passed away March 2, 1998.

Maritza De La Trinidad

See also: Depression-Era Repatriation of Mexicans; Mexican Repatriation; Moreno, Luisa (1907–1992); Sleepy Lagoon (1942); Tenayuca, Emma (1916–1999)

Further Reading

Camarillo, Albert M. 2016. "Fierro de Bright, Josefina." *American National Biography Online.* http://www.anb.org/articles/15/15-01405.html.

Garcia, Mario T. 1989. *Mexican Americans: Leadership, Ideology & Identity, 1930–1960.* New Haven, CT: Yale University Press.

Gómez Quiñonez, Juan. 1990. *Chicano Politics: Reality & Promise, 1940–1990.* Albuquerque: University of New Mexico Press.

Larralde, Carlos. 2010. "Josefina Fierro and the Sleepy Lagoon Crusade, 1942–1945." *Southern California Quarterly* 92, no. 2: 117–60.

Ruiz, Vicki L., 2004. "Una Mujer Sin Fronteras." *Pacific Historical Review* 73, no. 1: 1–20.

Ruiz, Vicki L. 2008. *From Out of the Shadows: Mexican Women in Twentieth-Century America.* New York: Oxford University Press.

Vargas, Z. 2005. *Labor Rights Are Civil Rights: Mexican American Workers in Twentieth-Century America.* Princeton, NJ: Princeton University Press.

G

Gallego, Ruben

(1979–)

Ruben Gallego is the U.S. representative for Arizona's 7th congressional district, which includes parts of the city of Glendale, as well as the western, southern, and downtown areas of Phoenix. Prior to becoming a member of Congress, Gallego, a Democrat, was a member of the Arizona House of Representatives from 2011 to 2014, where he served as an assistant minority leader. Gallego was first elected to Congress in 2014, and in 2016 he won re-election. Both in the Arizona legislature and in Congress, Gallego has been a champion of veterans issues, higher education, job creation and immigration reform.

Congressman Gallego was born in 1979 in Chicago to Mexican and Colombian low-income immigrants. Gallego, along with his three sisters, were raised by his single mother. Gallego's mother worked as a secretary and often times would take Gallego to work with her. This is where Ruben Gallego would be inspired to one day become a professional. As a first-generation college student, Gallego attended Harvard University and earned a bachelor's degree in international relations in 2004. Gallego later joined the U.S. Marine Corps, and in 2005 he was deployed to Iraq. As a Marine, he would serve one tour with the Lima Company, 3rd Battalion, 25th Marine Regiment. Gallego lost his best friend to an improvised explosive device (IED) attack in 2005. The incident was precipitated by limited armor and poor equipment. Upon return from his tour in Iraq, Gallego witnessed the difficulties that veterans faced with GI Bills and access to health care. These experiences, coupled with the challenges he faced during his upbringing, propelled Gallego to become active in politics.

Gallego began his career in politics as a consultant and soon became active in the Arizona Democratic Party. In 2009 he served as a delegate to the Democratic National Convention and was also elected to be vice-chair of the party. In 2010, Gallego was elected to the Arizona House of Representatives along with Representative Catherine Miranda. He served as a state representative until 2014 and represented the 27th District.

As an Arizona state representative, Gallego served on the Agricultural and Water Committee, the Military Affairs and Public Safety Committee, and the Ways and Means Committee. Gallego became assistant minority leader and was a strong advocate of veterans issues, in particular Medicaid and in-state tuition for veterans.

In 2014, Congressman Ed Pastor announced his retirement after 23 years in Congress. Pastor's retirement left open the U.S. House of Representatives seat for Arizona's 7th congressional district. Gallego announced his candidacy for this seat and was elected to represent this district in November 2014.

Congressman Gallego sits on the House Committee on Armed Services and the Committee on Natural Resources. Throughout his time in Congress, Gallego has

Ruben Gallego is a Democrat who serves as the representative for Arizona's 7th congressional district. He has held that position since 2015. He is a Marine Corps veteran. (U.S. House Office of Photography)

worked on issues of immigration, armed forces, and crime and law enforcement. More specifically, he has authored and sponsored legislation that decreases student loan debt on veterans and provides additional support and benefits to injured and deceased veterans and their families. He has also advocated for the restoring of the Voting Rights Act to ensure that all Americans have equal access to exercising their right to vote.

He currently serves as a senior whip for the Democratic Caucus, a vice-chair for the Congressional Progressive Caucus, the second vice-chair of the Congressional Hispanic Caucus, and vice-chair of the Equality Caucus.

Angela X. Ocampo

See also: Congressional Hispanic Caucus Institute (CHCI)

Further Reading

Berman, David R. 1998. *Arizona Politics & Government: The Quest for Autonomy, Democracy, and Development.* Lincoln: University of Nebraska Press.

Casellas, Jason P. 2010. *Latino Representation in State Houses and Congress.* Cambridge, UK: Cambridge University Press.

Nevares, Griselda. 2015. "Memorial Day: Ruben Gallego Remembers Best Friend, Fellow Marine." *NBC News,* May 24. http://www.nbcnews.com/news/latino/memorial-day -rep-ruben-gallego-remembers-best-friend-fellow-marine-n363966.

Parker, Ashely. 2015. "For Ruben Gallego, a Ride on Air Force One and a Presidential Aside." *The New York Times,* March 16. https://www.nytimes.com/2015/03/17/us /politics/for-ruben-gallego-a-ride-on-air-force-one-and-a-presidential-aside .html.

United States Representative Ruben Gallego. 2017. "Ruben Gallego Biography." https:// rubengallego.house.gov/about/full-biography.

Gay Identity. *See* Politics of a Latinx Lesbian, Gay, Bisexual, and Transgender Identity

Giménez, Carlos

(1954–)

As mayor of Miami-Dade County since 2011, Carlos Giménez is arguably the second most powerful executive in Florida after the governor. Mayor Giménez is responsible for over 2.7 million residents, over 2,000 square miles of land, nearly 25,000 county employees, and a governmental budget of nearly $7.5 billion. Miami-Dade is not only large but also complex and diverse. It is the largest county in the United States with a Hispanic-majority population. Nearly two-thirds of all residents of Miami-Dade are Hispanic.

Born in Cuba, Mayor Giménez and his family moved to the United States in 1960. He has been a Miami-Dade County resident ever since. He graduated from Christopher Columbus High School and earned his bachelor's degree in public administration from Barry University.

Giménez, who came to office in 2011 in the wake of a taxpayer revolt, has restored voter trust in county government after it was badly tarnished by his predecessors. Giménez's term has been characterized by fiscal austerity, low taxes, good administration, and lack of major scandals. His top priority has been to protect Miami-Dade taxpayers. Giménez's first major policy initiative after his election was to champion and secure approval for the largest tax cut in county history. Between 2011 and 2017 the average homeowner has saved approximately $1,400 in property taxes, and collectively Miami-Dade taxpayers have saved approximately $2 billion during his tenure.

Prior to becoming mayor, the Cuban-born Giménez served on the board of county commissioners for seven years. As a commissioner, Giménez opposed both the 2010 Marlin Stadium deal and the 2010 county property tax increase—the largest increase in county history and one that was widely unpopular. Public anger at the issue spilled over and a movement led by Miami billionaire Norman Braman to recall Mayor Alvarez began in earnest. It took Braman less than two weeks to gathered 100,000 signatures, more than enough for the recall to qualify for the ballot. The county establishment, consisting of public employee unions, the lobbying corps, and a majority of the bureaucracy, all lined up against the recall. The only commissioner to publicly support the recall was Carlos Giménez. Despite the strong opposition from the establishment, the public anger was too much to overcome. Alvarez was recalled on March 11, 2011, with 88 percent of the vote. The recall and Giménez's support for it allowed him to win the special election for mayor on June 28, 2011. Voters have rewarded Giménez for his tough antitax stance, re-electing him in 2012 and again in 2016.

The mayor's focus on austerity has frustrated different interest groups in the county that advocated for increased government spending. Giménez's string of austerity budgets has led to very public clashes with the public services unions that represent county workers. The mayor has an especially contentious relationship with John Rivera, the president of the Miami-Dade Police Benevolent Association (PBA). Rivera has compared the mayor to both herpes and a terrorist over various disputes about police funding and contract provisions. The relationship was so bad that members of the PBA ousted Rivera in November 2017 to improve relations with county hall.

The major capital project during Giménez's tenure is a $12.6 billion infrastructure project for the Water and Sewer Department. The 20-year-long project includes utilizing state-of-the-art technologies that will improve the reliability and sustainability of the water and sewer system. This project will also contribute over 16,000 new jobs to the community over the course of the next 10 years.

Giménez has spent most of his adult life in public life. From May 2000 to January 2003, Mayor Giménez was Miami's city manager. During that time, he helped restore the city's financial stability and integrity. During his time as city manager, Miami's bond rating rose from "junk" status to investment grade; the city's tax rate also dropped to its lowest level in 50 years. Miami was able to establish more than $140 million in reserves during his tenure as well.

Mayor Giménez spent 25 years with the Miami Fire-Rescue Department before becoming city manager. The last nine years with the department, he served as the first Hispanic chief, during which time he was credited with modernizing the department and overseeing the largest reorganization in the department's history.

Dario Moreno

See also: Essays: Latina/o Mayors

Further Reading

Hill, Kevin A., Dario V. Moreno, & Lourdes Cue. 2001. "Racial and Partisan Voting in a Tri-Ethnic City: The 1996 Dade County Mayoral Election." *Journal of Urban Affairs* 23, no. 3–4: 291–307.

Lavariega Monforti, Jessica. 2015. "Inevitable Change: A New Look at Cubans and Cuban Americans." In Tom Baldino and Kyle Krieder, eds. *Minority Voting in the United States.* Santa Barbara, CA: Praeger, pp. 270–91.

Portes, Alejandro, & Alex Stepick. 1993. *City on the Edge: The Transformation of Miami.* Berkeley: University of California Press.

Gómez, Cruz

(1941–)

Born Dolores Cruz Gómez in Goleta, California, in October 1941, Cruz Gómez is a community organizer, teacher, social service provider, writer, and activist. She is also one of the most prominent political activists in the history of the Chicano worker's rights movement. Cruz Gómez organized cannery workers along the central coast of California, where she fought for the provision of community health care. She was also instrumental in the historic redistricting of Watsonville, California, which set a pattern for how to achieve Latino electoral success in American cities with significant Latino populations, including Los Angeles.

The daughter of farmworkers from Jalisco, México, Gómez experienced first-hand how few rights and privileges were extended to farmworkers. She attended high schools in Santa Barbara and in Stockton, as well as Santa Barbara City College and the University of California at Santa Barbara. Gómez put herself through school as a single mom, and she later worked as an elementary school teacher and social worker during her twenties and thirties. She moved to Watsonville, California, and worked as an often-unpaid political activist for 19 years, from 1978 to 1997.

She was instrumental in establishing health centers like Salud Para la Gente in Watsonville, focusing on the needs of the poor, immigrants, migrant workers, and the undocumented and underserved populations of Santa Cruz County and of Pajaro, an impoverished town south of Watsonville in Monterey County. Today, Salud Para La Gente provides community-based medical, optical, and dental care, including focuses on women's health, family planning, counseling, farmworker outreach, and school clinics. Gómez influenced many social service agencies in Santa Cruz County to better serve Mexican American communities of the central coast that had been historically ignored by mainstream society.

Gómez also supported the historical Teamsters strike in which the workers won the strike that occurred from 1985 to 1987. This is widely recognized as a national triumph for cannery workers in the United States, one of their points of contention being a large reduction in salary for the workers, who were established in Watsonville with seniority and mortgages. Watsonville Canning lost this battle, in large part thanks to the organizing efforts of Cruz Gómez among the working-class Mexican women and Chicana/o workers, who trusted her judgment in mobilizing the 18-month nonviolent strike with fairness while securing better wages and benefits for the workers. People like Jesse Jackson and many other political celebrities were able to support the strike thanks to Gómez, the community, and academic support from University of California, Santa Cruz.

In 1983, Cruz Gómez symbolically ran for city council in what was then a town of about 30,000 inhabitants in the Salinas Valley: Watsonville, California. Although she and three other Latinos lost the election, Gómez, along with Patricia Leal and Waldo Rodriguez, filed a lawsuit in 1986, challenging a violation of the Voting Rights Act of 1965. The Mexican American Legal Defense and Educational Fund (MALDEF), together with the Southwest Voter Registration Project and two Bay Area civil rights law firms, went on to prove that there was unequal representation of Latinos in at-large elections. Joaquin G. Avila, a Bay Area civil rights lawyer then went on to become a MacArthur Fellow as a result of his involvement in redistricting law. Watsonville did not have representation by Latinos in the city council until 1987, after the Cruz Gómez–inspired lawsuit was victorious.

Cruz Gómez must remain a central name, as the names of others involved in redistricting cases have become household names in the political arena, including, for example, Joaquin Avila. Watsonville, California, remains a small city that set a redistricting precedent for many other small and large cities in the United States, such as Los Angeles. In the 21st century, Cruz Gómez continues her social justice brigade. She continued to do health outreach in Maine's migrant community for some time. She has also been known to work in Baja California, Mexico, supporting the elderly and poor communities there. In 2008, Gómez told *The Santa Cruz Sentinel*, "Everything's political, the air you breathe, the gasoline you buy, the food you buy. I'm addressing political issues every day, but at the individual or family level" (Jones, 2008).

Gabriella Gutiérrez y Muhs and Veronica Eldredge

See also: Avila, Joaquín (1954–2018); Brown Power Movement/Chicano Civil Rights Movement; Huerta, Dolores (1930–); Mexican American Legal Defense and Educational Fund (MALDEF); Voting Rights Act of 1975

Further Reading

Garcia, Rebecca. 2013. "Voting Rights Act, 1965." *Watsonville Patch*, July 8. https://patch
.com/california/watsonville/voting-rights-act-1965.

Jones, Donna. 2008. "Celebration Honors Voting Rights Advocate Who Opened Doors for
Watsonville's Latino Politicians." *Santa Cruz Sentinel*, August 20. http://www
.santacruzsentinel.com/article/ZZ/20080820/NEWS/808209869.

Leagle. 2013. "No. 87-1751: Gomez v. City of Watsonville." *Leagle.com*. http://www.leagle
.com/decision/19882270863F2d1407_12072.xml/GOMEZ%20v.%20CITY%20
OF%20WATSONVILLE.

Reich, Kenneth. 1989. "Watsonville Loss on Election Issue Could Be Victory for State Latinos." *Los Angeles Times*, May 1. http://articles.latimes.com/1989-05-01/news/mn
-2216_1_watsonville-case-tony-campos-latino-political-power/2.

Gonzales, Alberto

(1955–)

Alberto Gonzales served as the 80th attorney general of the United States from
2005 to 2007. Upon his appointment by President George W. Bush, he became the
highest-ranking Latino to serve in the executive branch of the U.S. government.
Prior to his service as the U.S. attorney general, Gonzales was the first Hispanic to
serve as White House counsel, as an associate justice on the Texas Supreme Court,
and as the 100th secretary of state for Texas. Gonzales's tenure as White House
counsel and as U.S. attorney general were marked by controversies surrounding
legal opinions he wrote or oversaw dealing with the use of torture on enemy
combatants during the War on Terror, the constitutional right of individuals to
habeas corpus, and the improper firing of several U.S. attorneys.

Born to parents of Mexican descent in San Antonio, Texas, Gonzales has
acknowledged that three of his grandparents may have entered the United States
without documentation. Though neither parent had more than an elementary school
education, Gonzales earned a bachelor's degree with honors in political science
from Rice University in 1979. He then went on to earn a juris doctorate from Harvard Law School in 1982. Gonzales worked in private practice from 1982 to 1994.
He primarily served corporate clients at the Houston-based firm Vinson and Elkins
(Department of Justice, 2017). He also served in the U.S. Air Force in the 1970s.

In 1994, George W. Bush, then governor of Texas, appointed Gonzales to be his
general counsel. This appointment marked the beginning of a working relationship
between Gonzales and Bush. Gonzales was subsequently named the secretary of
state for Texas and to the Texas Supreme Court. Both appointments were made by
Governor Bush. Though elected in November to serve a six-year term on the state
Supreme Court, Gonzales left on January 20, 2001, to serve as White House counsel to George W. Bush upon his inauguration as president of the United States.

After the 9/11 attacks, Gonzales, as White House counsel, played a key role in
crafting legal arguments justifying some of the tactics used by the U.S. government in the War on Terror. In January 2002 he helped author a brief justifying the
denial of the writ of habeas corpus and trial by military tribunals of noncitizen individuals deemed by the president to be "enemy combatants" (ABA Task Force on
Terrorism, 2002). Three subsequent Supreme Court decisions, *Rasul v. Bush*, *Ham-
dan v. Rumsfeld*, and *Boumediene v. Bush,* contradicted Gonzales's position and
granted habeas corpus to detained individuals.

Gonzales also authored a memorandum for the president in January 2002 that
provided some legal justification for the use of "enhanced interrogation techniques"
on individuals detained as enemy combatants. The memo, entitled "Decision Re

Application of the Geneva Convention on Prisoners of War to the Conflict with Al Qaeda and the Taliban," argued that Article III of the Geneva Convention pertaining to the treatment of prisoners of war was outdated and ill suited to guiding treatment of enemy combatants (Greenberg and Dratel, 2005). The memo drew strong criticism from politicians, journalists, and academics, who argued that it justified the use of torture. The memo remained an influential justification for "enhanced interrogation techniques" until the Obama administration stated its intention to abide by Article III of the Geneva Convention in 2009.

In 2005, President Bush appointed Gonzales as the 80th U.S. attorney general of the United States. He served until September 2007. Gonzales resigned under pressure from several members of the U.S. Senate, both Democrat and Republican, over improper firings of several U.S. attorneys. Since resigning, Gonzales has held a variety of academic posts. He taught political science and worked as a diversity recruiter at Texas Tech University. He is currently dean of Belmont University College of Law in Nashville, Tennessee, and works in private practice.

Richard M. Neve

See also: Military Participation and Latinos

Further Reading

American Bar Association Task Force. 2002. "American Bar Association Task Force on Terrorism and the Law Report and Recommendations on Military Tribunals." *American Bar Association.* https://www.americanbar.org/content/dam/aba/migrated/leadership/military.authcheckdam.pdf.

Department of Justice. 2017. "Attorney General: Alberto Gonzales." https://www.justice.gov/ag/bio/gonzales-alberto-r.

Greenberg, Karen, & Daniel Dratel. 2005. *The Torture Papers: The Road to Abu Ghraib.* Cambridge, UK: Cambridge University Press.

Gonzales, Rodolfo "Corky"

(1928–2005)

Rodolfo "Corky" Gonzales was a professional boxer, businessman, politician, civic leader, poet, family man, and a major leader of the Chicano Movement of the 1960s and 1970s.

He was born on June 18, 1928, in Denver, Colorado, as the youngest of eight children born to Federico and Indalesia Gonzáles. His father, originally from Buena Ventura, Chihuahua, Mexico, immigrated to the United States early in life, but told his children accounts of Mexico's struggles for independence and, later, against Mexico's dictator, Porfirio Diaz. His mother, who was from southern Colorado, died when he was two years old. The family was a seasonal agricultural family that followed the crops, often working in the beet fields of northern Colorado. At the age of 10, Rodolfo began working alongside his father in the beet fields. Rodolfo's family lived in Denver's Eastside Barrio and in many of Denver's other barrios, or Mexican American neighborhoods, where he grew up during the Great Depression.

Inspired by the stories told by his father, Rodolfo became an avid reader, especially of the histories of Mexican Americans, Mexico, and the United States. Given

Rodolfo "Corky" Gonzales speaks during a Chicano conference at Colorado State Penitentiary, ca. 1972. Gonzales founded the Crusade for Justice and wrote the epic poem "Yo Soy Joaquin." (Bettmann/Getty Images)

the migrant lifestyle, Rodolfo, who acquired the nickname "Corky" from an uncle who saw him as "always popping off like a cork," attended many schools and graduated from Manual High School in Denver in 1944 at the age of 16. His grades were good, and he enrolled at the University of Denver for one semester but left due to financial challenges. Gonzales continued reading, including the works of John Steinbeck, Ernest Hemingway, Pablo Neruda, and many other authors, but he also turned his attention to boxing, the sport that propelled him to national status.

Gonzales began his boxing career as a flyweight (112 lb) and later fought as a bantamweight (118 lb) and a featherweight (126 lb). Gonzales began his amateur career in 1944, fighting out of a Veterans' Athletic Club Smoker in Denver. He went on to win numerous championships, finishing his amateur career with 47 wins and 3 losses. In 1947, Gonzales turned professional, rising rapidly to the rank of third in the world in the featherweight division. His professional record was 65 wins, 9 losses, and 1 draw. Most of his fights were outside of Denver, forcing him to live for short periods in Omaha, Nebraska, and St. Paul, Minneapolis. In 1952 he fought a professional bout in Denver as a benefit for the Latin American Education Fund. Boxing continued to be part of his life as a coach and as a trainer at the Crusade for Justice in Denver.

Early in his boxing career Gonzales showed an interest in politics, campaigning for Quigg Newton for mayor of Denver in 1947. He later became a district captain for the Democratic Party in Denver County, organizing Mexican American support for the party in the 1950s. In 1955 he ran unsuccessfully for a position on

Denver's city council. In 1960, Corky headed the "Viva Kennedy" campaign in Colorado, where police brutality, segregated schools, and discrimination were simmering concerns in Denver's Mexican American neighborhoods. In 1963, Corky organized Los Voluntarios, an advocacy group of Mexican Americans that engaged in voter registration drives and demonstrated against police brutality. Los Voluntarios became the precursor to the Crusade for Justice, the civil rights organization that served as his base of operations. In 1964 Gonzales made an unsuccessful bid for the Colorado House of Representatives, and in 1967 for the position of mayor in Denver. In 1965 he was appointed director of Denver's War on Poverty, only to be fired a year later for participating in a walkout of the Equal Employment Opportunity Commission (EEOC) in Albuquerque, New Mexico. Corky then moved away from mainstream politics and founded the Crusade for Justice, a civil rights organization that promoted economic and cultural empowerment. In 1967, the year that he published his epic poem, *Yo Soy Joaquin*, he resigned from the Democratic Party. The poem was adapted to film by the Teatro Campesino in 1969.

The poem galvanized a nationalist movement among the increasingly frustrated Mexican Americans across the Southwest. Concerned with ethnic identity, Gonzales articulated a historically based identity that synthesized the various roots of Chicanismo. In 1968, the Crusade participated in the Poor People's March in Washington, D.C., which emphasized economic justice for poor people. There, Corky delivered the "Plan del Barrio" speech in which he called for reforms in housing, education, law enforcement, land, agriculture, and the economy. In 1969, the Crusade hosted the first National Chicano Youth Liberation Conference in Denver. The conference brought together hundreds of Chicanos, Puerto Ricans, and other communities.

Moreover, the conference produced the proclamation titled "El Plan Espiritual de Aztlan," which declared Chicanos a "free and sovereign" people and articulated steps for self-determination. The Plan would further galvanize Chicano and Chicana activism across the Southwest. By this time, Gonzales was recognized as one of the major leaders of the Chicano Movement, giving speeches on college campuses and other venues across the country. In 1970, he established an alternative school, Esquela Tlatelolco, in Denver, as well as the Colorado Raza Unida Party, a third party dedicated to Chicano political empowerment.

By 1975, the Crusade was peaking in influence, and by the early 1980s its decline was evident. Corky Gonzales died on April 12, 2005, at the age of 76. He had suffered a heart attack in 1987 that left him debilitated. In 1988, Corky was inducted to the Colorado Sports Hall of Fame, and in 1990 he received the Humanitarian Award from the Martin Luther King, Jr., Colorado Holiday Commission.

Rubén O. Martinez

See also: Crusade for Justice; *El Teatro Campesino;* La Raza Unida Party (LRU)

Further Reading

Gonzales, Rodolfo. 1972. *Yo Soy Joaquin: An Epic Poem.* New York: Bantam Books.

Gonzales, Rodolfo "Corky." 2001. *Message to Aztlan: Selected Writings.* Edited by Antonio Esquivel. Houston: Art Publíco Press.

Vigil, Ernesto B. 1999. *The Crusade for Justice: Chicano Militancy and the Government War on Dissent.* Madison: University of Wisconsin Press.

González, Charles Augustine "Charlie"

(1945–)

Charlie González served as the representative for the 20th U.S. congressional district in San Antonio, Texas. González first ran for Congress in the Democratic primary in 1998 when his father, long-time congressman, civil rights advocate, and the first Mexican American elected to the U.S. Congress from Texas, Henry B. González, decided not to run for his 19th term.

Born in San Antonio, González is the eldest of eight children to Henry B. González and Bertha M. Cuellar, both born in Texas. González's paternal grandparents fled to San Antonio from the state of Durango in northern Mexico during the Mexican Revolution in 1911. González graduated from Edison High School in San Antonio. He then completed his bachelor's of arts in government from the University of Texas at Austin in 1969. He furthered his education by receiving his law degree in 1972 from St. Mary's University School of Law in San Antonio—the same law school where his father earned his law degree. During this time, González also served as a technical sergeant in the Texas Air National Guard from 1969 to 1972. After graduating from law school, González practiced law in San Antonio until 1982. He began his political career within the judicial court system in San Antonio, first as a municipal court judge, then elected as a county judge in 1983 until 1987. Afterwards, he ran for a district court position and won in 1989. González was re-elected unopposed and served in this position for several terms of office until 1997.

Groomed to follow in his father's footsteps for political office, González ran for Congress in an open seat, which was the first time since his father first served in this office in the 1960s. González was among a number of candidates who ran in the Democratic primary in 1999. Although González had the name recognition and legacy, he finished first in a seven-person primary but was unable to win the required 50 percent threshold of voters. In a run-off election, González faced former city councilwoman and the first Mexican American woman to hold a position in San Antonio's city council, Maria Berriozábal, in June. He successfully won the nomination with 62 percent of the vote and later defeated the Republican candidate in the general election by 63 percentage points. The 20th congressional district, created in 1934, is a predominately Democrat and majority-Latino district, based in San Antonio's downtown. González was re-elected for seven terms until 2012, when he decided not to run for re-election. His successor is Joaquin Castro, twin brother to former mayor of San Antonio and former secretary of Housing and Urban Development under the Obama administration, Julián Castro.

While in Congress, González served in multiple committees such as the Committee on Energy and Commerce, the Judiciary, and House Administration. He also served as chair of the Housing Banking Committee. Some of his most historic votes include opposing the Bush administration's decision to invade Iraq and supporting the Affordable Health Care Act under the Obama administration. He also played an active role as chair and vice-chair on the Congressional Hispanic Caucus, which his father and four other Latino congressmen founded in 1976. González also belonged to the Congressional LGBT Equality Caucus, which was established in

2008. Considered a moderate, ideologically, González was a member of the New Democrat Coalition. He championed causes, such as civil rights, immigrant rights, judicial selection, and election reform. A strong and early supporter of Obama's presidential nomination, he served as chairman of Latinos for Obama in 2008. Later, he served as national co-chair of President Obama's 2012 re-election campaign.

Sonia R. García

See also: González, Henry B. (1916–2000); Obama, Barack (1961–) and Latinos

Further Reading

Casellas, Jason P. 2007. "Latino Representation in Congress: To What Extent Are Latinos Substantively Represented." In Rodolfo Espino, David L. Leal, and Kenneth J. Meier, eds. *Latino Politics: Identity, Mobilization and Representation*. Charlottesville: University of Virginia Press, pp. 219–31.

"Gonzalez, Charles." n.d. *Congressional Record*. http://www.congress.gov/member/charles-gonzalez/G000544.

"Gonzalez, Charles." n.d. *History, Art and Archives: United States House of Representatives*. http://history.house.gov/People/Detail/14247.

"Gonzalez, Charles." 2013. In *Hispanic Americans in Congress, 1822–2012*. Office of the Historian and the Office of the Clerk, U.S. House of Representatives. Washington, D.C.: Government Printing Office.

Hero, Rodney E., & Caroline J. Tolbert. 1995. "Latinos and Substantive Representation in the U.S. House of Representatives: Direct, Indirect, or Nonexistent?" *American Journal of Political Science* 39, no. 3: 640–52.

Rocca, Michael S., Gabriel R. Sanchez, & Joseph Uscinski. 2008. "Personal Attributes and Latino Voting Behavior in Congress." *Social Science Quarterly* 89, no. 2: 392–405.

González, Henry B.

(1916–2000)

Henry González, a Democratic congressman from Texas, began his lifelong political career in his hometown of San Antonio in the mid-1950s. González spent the bulk of his adult life as a public servant who held multiple civil service positions and public office at the local, state, and national levels. González was a trailblazer as the first Mexican American to be elected to the San Antonio City Council, state Senate and Congress. As an outspoken advocate for civil rights, equality, and social justice, he fought controversial issues of the day, many of which were unpopular in Texas politics, such as juvenile justice and ending segregation; poverty; homelessness; the poll tax; and discrimination in housing, employment, and public accommodations, which he viewed as immoral and antithetical to American ideals of democracy.

Enrique (Henry) Barbosa González was born on May 3, 1916, to Leonides González Cigarroa and Genoveva Barbosa Prince de González. His parents immigrated to San Antonio in 1911 after fleeing their home in Mapimí, Durango, Mexico, during the Mexican Revolution. His father, Leonides, had operated a silver mine and was the mayor of Mapimí when he was forced to leave for political reasons. Leonides was hired as the managing editor of *La Prensa*, a new Spanish-language newspaper that quickly became the voice of Mexican intellectuals and politicos in San Antonio, earning a modest wage. After studying pre-engineering, Henry González transferred to the University of Texas to complete his education. He enrolled at St. Mary's University School of Law and graduated in 1940. That same year, he married Bertha Cuellar and started a family.

After working for two years in civil service, González accepted a position as a juvenile probation officer. He worked to reform the injustices in the system and by 1946 became the chief juvenile probation officer. By 1950, his interest in politics had grown and he had an unsuccessful run for the Texas House of Representatives in the Democratic primary. In 1953, González successfully ran for a seat on the San Antonio City Council. González used this position to advocate for equality, fairness, and an end to segregation by pushing through ordinances to desegregate all city facilities. His achievements in city council and discontent with state political leaders compelled him to run for the Texas State Senate in 1956; he won the election.

As a state senator, González proposed and supported bills to promote economic development, fair housing projects, a medical school, a minimum wage, a public defender's office for Bexar County, and urban renewal. He also continued to speak out against segregation and opposed several segregation bills aimed at circumventing the U.S. Supreme Court decision in *Brown v. Board of Education*. In 1957, he gained notoriety when he and fellow state senator Abraham "Chick" Kazen from Laredo filibustered a bill that would have allowed school segregation through discriminatory placement policies; the filibuster lasted 36 hours, the longest in Texas history, and was successful in killing the bill. A year later, in 1958, González ran for governor against Price Danie but lost and returned to the state Senate. By 1960, González was the best-known politician in San Antonio when he ran for reelection for the state Senate. During his campaign, he caught the attention of presidential candidate John F. Kennedy, who asked him to co-chair the Viva Kennedy Clubs with U.S. senator Dennis Chávez. Kennedy's election also put Texas senator Lyndon B. Johnson in office as vice-president, leaving his U.S. Senate seat open. This important vacancy provided an opportunity for González to run for national office.

On November 4, 1961, Henry González was elected U.S. representative for the 20th congressional district of Texas. As a member of Congress, González continued to push for civil rights and antipoverty legislation. He also worked to end the Bracero Program, a binational agreement between the United States and Mexico that allowed Mexican workers into the United States to work in the agricultural and railroad industry, because of the abuses that relegated workers to harsh working and living conditions and left them in poverty.

Despite his popularity and reputation for fairness and integrity, González faced opposition from Republican and Democratic political foes, as well as from some Mexican American community leaders, especially youth, who did not believe he was doing enough to combat discrimination against Mexican Americans or improve poverty-stricken conditions in the barrios of San Antonio, which persisted in the 1960s. Despite economic growth and development in the city and state, many Mexican Americans remained poor, segregated, poorly educated, and lacked health care. Youth leaders and members of the Mexican American Youth Organization (MAYO) were especially critical of González for not doing more for the Mexican American community, his accommodationist politics, and his lack of support for the farmworkers strike in the Rio Grande Valley and the student walkouts in protest of educational discrimination and unequal education. Despite these criticisms, González continued to represent his constituency in San Antonio and Texas and remained a loyal Democrat and public servant.

Throughout his long career, González was recognized for his civil rights work and achievements to improve the lives of ordinary citizens. He received numerous awards, and in 1998 he served his last term in office and died on November 28, 2000, at the age of 84.

Maritza De La Trinidad

See also: González, Charles Augustine "Charlie" (1945–); Mexican American Youth Organization (MAYO); Viva Kennedy! Clubs

Further Reading

Haugen, Brenda. 2006. *Henry B. González: Congressman of the People.* Minneapolis: Compass Point Books.

Montejano, David. 2010. *Quixote's Soldiers: A Local History of the Chicano Movement, 1966–1981.* Austin: University of Texas Press.

Quiñones, Juan Gómez. 1990. *Chicano Politics: Reality & Promise, 1940–1990.* Albuquerque: University of New Mexico Press.

Rodríguez, Eugene, Jr. 1976. *Henry B. González: A Political Profile.* New York: Arno Press.

Sloane, Todd A. 1996. *González of Texas: A Congressman for the People.* Evanston, IL: John Gordon Burke Publisher.

United States House of Representatives. 1997. "González, Henry Barbosa." http://history.house.gov/Collection/Detail/29010?ret=True.

Great Mexican Repatriation. *See* Depression-Era Repatriation of Mexicans

Grijalva, Raúl M.

(1948–)

A Democrat, Raúl Grijalva has represented Arizona's southernmost 3rd District in the U.S. House of Representatives since 2003. Grijalva is an outspoken critic of President Trump, especially the Trump administration's immigration policies that hold DREAMers hostage by requiring funding for a Border Wall and the restriction of family reunion–based immigration in exchange for DACA renewal. Grijalva's voting record in the House positions him as one of the most progressive members of Congress due to his persistent calls for immigration reform, government regulation, environmental protection, and tribal sovereignty.

Raúl M. Grijalva is deeply rooted in the district he represents. He was born in Tucson, Arizona, in 1948 to a father who migrated to southern Arizona from Mexico as part of the Bracero Guest Worker Program. His close ties to public education in Tucson span his years as a K–12 student in the Sunnyside district, as a college student at the University of Arizona (BA in sociology), and as a member of the Tucson Unified School Board, where he served from 1974 to 1986 while simultaneously heading the El Pueblo Neighborhood Center. Grijalva was a leader in

M.E.Ch.A. and the Raza Unida Party in Arizona and in 1989 was elected to the Pima County board of supervisors. In 2002 Grijalva entered a crowded field of Democrats running in the primary campaign for what was then Arizona's newly renumbered 7th District for the U.S. House (now District 3). Grijalva won the election and easily won the following three re-elections, but in 2010, his controversial call for a boycott of Arizona in opposition to SB 1070, Arizona's "Show Me Your Papers" Law, led to the closest election of his political career against Republican Ruth McClung, even though his district is heavily Democrat and Latino. Grijalva has won re-election seven times while establishing a consistent record of voting with the Democratic Party.

Immigration is a focal issue for Grijalva; he took a strong stance against SB 1070 and has been a staunch and vocal supporter of the DREAM Act since its inception. Grijalva vehemently opposes the Border Wall, insisting that it will not enhance security but will be damaging to the environment and to tribal interests and sovereignty. He makes repeated references to the Border Wall as a "monumental waste of money" on Twitter; in a tweet on February 16, 2018, Grijalva blamed Donald Trump and congressional Republicans for shamefully using DREAMers as "a bargaining chip for far-right immigration policies" and called for a vote on a "Clean DREAM Act" in an effort to disconnect the issues of DACA renewal from other immigration enforcement policies (Grijalva, 2018). Grijalva voted in opposition to the draconian H.R. 4437 in 2005 and the Secure Fence Act in 2006; he supports the Comprehensive Immigration Reform for America's Security and Prosperity Act, which features alternatives to heavy-handed enforcement and seeks instead to further monitor the border through cameras and other technologically advanced techniques.

Grijalva is active in a large number of congressional caucuses, most notably the Progressive Caucus and the Hispanic Caucus. As co-chair of the Progressive Caucus, Grijalva drafted an alternative "People's Budget" in 2011 and then the "Budget for All" of 2012, designed to achieve a balanced budget without massive cuts in services. Grijalva supports a variety of progressive issues, including single-payer health care, stronger environmental regulation, gun control, net neutrality to ensure a free and open Internet, tribal sovereignty, educational equity, and financial protections against payday lenders.

Adelita Grijalva, one of Grijalva's three daughters, is a member of the Tucson Unified School Board. Raul Grijalva began his life of public service as a community organizer, and those grassroots origins are evident to this day. In honor of this legacy, the Tucson Unified School District named Grijalva School in his honor.

Teresa Carrillo

See also: DREAM Act; DREAM Act at the State Level; Environmental Justice and Latinos; Immigration as a Policy Issue; La Raza Unida Party (LRU); Movimiento Estudiantil Chicanx de Aztlan (M.E.Ch.A.); National Security State and Latinos; SB 1070 (2010); Trump, Donald J. (1946–) and Latinos

Further Reading

Espino, Rodolfo. 2013. "Immigration Politicking and the Perceptions of Latino Voters in Arizona." In *Latino Politics and Arizona's Immigration Law SB 1070*. New York: Springer, pp. 27–41.

Garrett, Terence M. 2010. "The Border Fence, Immigration Policy, and the Obama Administration: A Cautionary Note." *Administrative Theory & Praxis* 32, no. 1: 129–33.

Grijalva, Raul. 2011. "Political Fight over Ethnic Studies Should Never Have Been Ignited at All." *Arizona Daily Star.*

Grijalva, Raul. 2018. Twitter Account. https://twitter.com/RepRaulGrijalva/status /964634276959485959.

Gutiérrez, José Ángel

(1944–)

José Ángel Gutiérrez is an attorney, retired professor, former judge, and long-time Chicano political activist and civil rights leader who cofounded the Mexican American Youth Organization and La Raza Unida.

He was born on October 25, 1944, in Crystal City, Texas, as the only child of Ángel and Concepción Gutiérrez. His father was a Mexican medical doctor who served Mexican and Mexican Americans in a small south Texas town in which the majority of residents were migrant farmworkers. His father died when Gutiérrez was 12 years old, and when local business owners turned their backs on his mother and him, the forms of racial oppression became increasingly evident. Gutiérrez came of age adapting to downward mobility within the racially hostile environment of south Texas, forced to abide as a "Mexican" by the racial norms of everyday life and educated in a segregated school system. Growing up he had several jobs, including as a migrant farmworker.

His mother had family ties in the Midwest, and Gutiérrez and his mother lived for a period in Chicago, but he returned to Crystal City and graduated from Crystal City High School in 1962 and enrolled at Southwest Texas Junior College in nearby Uvalde. At that time he took an interest in local politics and actively canvassed for "los cinco candidados" of Crystal City. Los Cinco comprised a slate of Mexican Americans who in 1963 swept the elections for city council positions. They were organized and supported by the Political Association of Spanish-Speaking Organizations (PASSO), which was based in Bexar County, and the local Teamsters Union.

That year, José Ángel took a job in Los Angeles, California, but returned to Texas, making occasional employment excursions to the Midwest. He enrolled in what was then Texas Arts and Industries University at Kingsville, Texas, where he led the formation of a PASSO group. He obtained a bachelor's degree in 1966, in government, from Texas A&I, Kingsville. He then enrolled at St. Mary's University in San Antonio, where he earned a master's degree, again in government, in 1967. While at St. Mary's, Gutiérrez, along with Willie (William) C. Velásquez, Mario Compean, Ignacio Pérez, and Juan Patlán, formed the Mexican American Youth Organization (MAYO), which became the precursor to La Raza Unida Party (LRU), which was formed in 1970.

MAYO was a statewide nonprofit organization that was initially active in San Antonio, but chapters were soon established at other colleges and universities. MAYO was active in the student walkouts across the state in 1968, and particularly in those that occurred in Crystal City in 1969. After successful negotiations in Crystal City, and in 1970, following the formation of La Raza Unida Party (LRU),

Mexican Americans began to organize for the elections of 1971, when several LRU candidates were elected to local school boards and city councils. LRU was dedicated to the empowerment of Chicanos and the betterment of their well-being. It spread to other states and, in 1972, held its first national convention in El Paso, Texas, where José Ángel was elected national chairperson over Rodolfo "Corky" Gonzales. Experiencing heavy losses in 1974 and 1978, LRU lost its influence as a political party. However, during its time it challenged the mainstream parties to court Chicano voters and showed that the Chicano electorate could be mobilized.

In the 1970s José Ángel worked on obtaining his doctorate degree and at the same time was elected to several positions, including trustee and president of the Crystal City Independent School District, urban renewal commissioner for Crystal City, and county judge for Zavala County. Throughout this period he taught courses at different colleges and universities. In 1976, he completed his dissertation on developing a theory of community organization based on what had occurred in Crystal City and the work of the La Raza Unity Party. With a doctoral degree in hand, he began teaching at the University of Houston, and did so until 1979. In 1980, Gutiérrez left Texas for Oregon, where he assumed the position of director of the International Education Studies Department at Colegio César Chávez in Mt. Angel and was active in Oregon politics. In 1985, he obtained the status of associate professor at Western Oregon State College, only to lose the position due to reductions in force. The following year he returned to Texas, enrolled at the University of Texas Law Center, and earned his law degree in 1988. He then became an executive with the Greater Dallas Legal and Community Development Foundation, Inc., and began practicing law in Dallas. He also served as an administrative law judge for the city of Dallas. In 1993, he ran as a Democratic candidate for the U.S. Senate seat vacated by Senator Lloyd Bentsen, Jr., and lost in the primary election.

In 1991, he began teaching courses at the University of Texas at Arlington, and in 1993 he joined the Department of Political Science as an associate professor. In 1994, Gutiérrez led the establishment of the Mexican American Studies Center there, and was its founding director through the end of 1996. He then took a series of visiting professorships at different universities as he continued his research on Latino issues. In 2005, he was promoted to full professor at the University of Texas, a position he held until he retired in 2015. Throughout his career José Ángel has been an active public speaker and author, writing and publishing several books. His most recent volume focuses on the political activities of Albert Peña, who was a leading political figure in Mexican American and Chicano politics throughout the second half of the 20th century. Today, he continues as the executive director of the Greater Dallas Legal and Community Development Foundation, Inc., as well as continues to practice law.

Rubén Martinez

See also: Gonzales, Rodolfo "Corky" (1928–2005); La Raza Unida Party (LRU); Mexican American Youth Organization (MAYO); Political Association of Spanish-Speaking Organizations (PASSO)

Further Reading

Gutiérrez, José. A. 1973. *A Gringo Manual on How to Handle Mexicans*. Crystal City, TX: Wintergarden Publishing House.

Gutiérrez, J. A. 1998. *The Making of a Chicano Militant: Lessons from Cristal.* Madison: University of Wisconsin Press.

Gutiérrez, J. A. 2017. *Albert A. Peña Jr.: Dean of Chicano Politics.* Latinos in the United States Series. East Lansing: Michigan State University Press.

Gutiérrez, Luis

(1953–)

First elected to Congress in 1992 and since re-elected 11 times, Luis Gutiérrez is a Democrat from Illinois. He is of Puerto Rican descent and is one of the first Latinos elected to Congress from the Midwest. He is an advocate for defending immigrants' rights as well as supporting the path to citizenship for unauthorized immigrants. Interestingly although his family is from Puerto Rico and never personally dealt with issues of immigration and citizenship, Gutiérrez contends that he became engaged with the agenda because of problems that friends and colleagues confronted.

In 1993, Gutiérrez established workshops to help Latinos gain citizenship in his home district, Chicago. According to his website, "[A]s of 2014, more than 55,000 constituents had received assistance . . . to make the transition from legal permanent resident to citizen of the United States." Representative Gutiérrez also introduced legislation that would later become the DREAM Act. His proposed bill, the Immigrant Children's Educational Advantage and Dropout Prevention Act (H.R. 1582), would grant legal status for all minors who have lived in America for at least five years and who are currently a student of some kind.

Although the House failed to vote on much of his legislation, Gutiérrez continues to be the most vocal advocate for immigration. He also pushed for legislation that would prevent the separation of families after President Obama announced the Deferred Action for Childhood Arrivals (DACA) Act. In a famous speech made to the House on June 27, 2012, "Pick Out the Immigrant," Gutiérrez

Luis Gutiérrez is a Democrat serving as the U.S. representative for Illinois's 4th congressional district since 1993; he recently announced his retirement from this position. From 1986 until his election to Congress, he served as a member of the Chicago City Council representing the 26th Ward. (U.S. House of Representatives)

compared well-known figures like Justin Bieber and Selena Gomez, Jeremy Lin and Tony Parker, and Supreme Court justices Antonin Scalia and Sonia Sotomayor to make the point that these individuals were most likely immigrants or children of immigrants. He noted, "[M]aybe with practice, we can become like Arizona politicians and police officers who are able to telepathically determine who to accuse of not belonging in America" (Gutiérrez, 2015).

Finally, Representative Gutierrez has been outspoken about Republicans' stagnancy on immigration reform and at times even about President Obama's silence on the matter. In his autobiography, *Still Dreaming: My Journey from the Barrio to Capitol Hill*, Gutiérrez criticizes the president for not fulfilling his campaign promises of reforming immigration. He wrote that Obama "hadn't lifted a finger" toward reform six months into his first term. In 2010, he and other Latino lawmakers considered blocking Obamacare to coerce the president into backing immigration reform.

Frustrated over the lack of progress on immigration reform, Gutierrez and seven other members of Congress participated in the "Camino Americano: March for Immigration Reform." Led by the National Hispanic Foundation for the Arts, CASA de Maryland, and other organizations, the protest led thousands of participants to Capitol Hill on October 8, 2013. Gutiérrez stated: "Our communities and our families do not have the luxury to rest or relax. 1,100 people will be deported today, 1,100 people will be deported tomorrow, and the next day." Representatives John Lewis (D-GA), Charlie Rangel (D-NY), Raul Grijalva (D-AZ), Joe Crowley (D-NY), Jan Schakowsky (D-IL), Keith Ellison (D-MN), and Al Green (D-TX), as well as Representative Gutierrez (D-IL), were all arrested as a result of the protest. In 2017, Gutierrez announced his retirement from Congress. Many speculate that he will support Jesus "Chuy" Garcia to replace him and that Gutierrez will run for another office.

Lisa Magaña

See also: DREAM Act; DREAM Act at the State Level

Further Reading

Casellas, Jason. 2007. "Latino Representation in Congress: To What Extent Are Latinos Substantively Represented?" In Rodolfo Espino, David L. Leal, and Kenneth J. Meier, eds. *Latino Politics: Identity, Mobilization and Representation*. Charlottesville: University of Virginia Press, pp. 219–31.

Gutierrez, Luis. 2013. *Still Dreaming: My Journey from the Barrio to Capitol Hill*. New York: W. W. Norton Company.

Luis Gutierrez Website. http://gutierrez.house.gov.

Rocca, M. S., G. R. Sanchez, & J. Uscinski. 2008. "Personal Attributes and Latino Voting Behavior in Congress." *Social Science Quarterly* 89, no. 2: 392–405.

H

Hernandez v. New York

(1991)

Hernandez v. New York is a Supreme Court case regarding the right to an impartial jury as guaranteed by the Sixth Amendment of the U.S. Constitution. Previous court decisions had dealt with the discriminatory practice of excluding potential jurors based on race, ethnicity, or gender. *Hernandez*, however, dealt with the exclusion of jurors because they were bilingual; raising the question of whether fluency in Spanish can be used as a proxy for ethnicity.

When selecting a jury, attorneys understandably attempt to select people they believe will be sympathetic to their client. To this end, attorneys ask potential jurors questions to determine if they have any experiences or characteristics that might affect their judgment. If so, the person can be struck off the jury for cause. For example, an attorney may strike off a potential juror who has been the victim of the type of crime being tried. This experience may have no impact on the potential juror's ability to fairly decide the case. However, it is reasonable to assume that it might, and the attorney is therefore justified in excluding that person from the jury. In addition to striking off individuals for cause, attorneys have a set amount of preemptory challenges. When using a preemptory challenge, the attorney does not have to explain why that person is being dismissed. As a result of this lack of transparency, attorneys were using peremptory challenges to exclude nonwhites from juries. The Supreme Court addressed this issue in *Batson v. Kentucky* (1986) by creating the Batson challenge. A Batson challenge can be raised if an attorney suspects that her opposing counsel is using peremptory challenges in a racially discriminatory manner. The accused counsel must then offer a race-neutral explanation for excluding certain individuals, leaving the judge to determine whether the race-neutral explanations are credible. If the challenges are deemed discriminatory, the process violates the right to be tried by an impartial jury.

During Dionisio Hernandez's trial for attempted murder and criminal possession of a weapon, the prosecutor used peremptory challenges to dismiss potential jurors who were bilingual. Hernandez challenged these exclusions, claiming it was a case of racial discrimination as understood under *Batson*. In response to the Batson challenge, the prosecutor claimed that he struck the jurors because they hesitated to answer when asked if they would accept the translator's version of witness statements. The concern in this situation is that someone fluent in Spanish could not help but listen to and understand testimony given by Spanish-speaking witnesses. If the translator's interpretation of the answers was different from the bilingual juror's understanding of what was said, the juror is instructed to accept the translator's version as the final word so that all jurors receive the same information.

The prosecutor claimed that the bilingual jurors in this case were hesitant to do so. The judge accepted this justification as race-neutral and allowed the trial to go forward. The case was appealed to the Supreme Court with the argument that fluency in Spanish is closely related to ethnicity; therefore, bilingualism is not a race-neutral justification. The Court found no clear case of discriminatory intent and deferred to the trial judge's decision. They did, however, note that their decision should not be read as condoning the exclusion of bilingual jurors, as, in some cases, it may be a proxy for discrimination based on ethnicity. Thus, *Hernandez* was not the final word, but did allow the singling out and exclusion of Spanish-speaking individuals in this trial.

Mary McThomas

See also: Official English Movement

Further Reading

Batson v. Kentucky, 476 U.S. 79 (1986).

Clasby, Sarah B. 1991/1992. "Understanding Testimony: Official Translation and Bilingual Jurors in Hernandez v. New York." *The University of Miami Inter-American Law Review* 23, no. 2 (Winter): 515–39.

Hernandez v. New York, 500 U.S. 352 (1991).

Hurwitz, Mark S. 2008. "Peremptory Challenges and National Origin: Watson v. Ricks." *The Justice System Journal* 29, no. 2: 210–12.

Sheridan, Clare. 2003. "'Another White Race:' Mexican Americans and the Paradox of Whiteness in Jury Selection." *Law and History Review* 21, no. 1: 109–44.

Hernández v. Texas

(1954)

Hernández v. Texas is the first civil rights case involving Mexican Americans and jury selection. This landmark case was also the first to be tried by Mexican American lawyers before the U.S. Supreme Court, Gustavo García and Carlos Cadena. The Court held for the first time that Mexican Americans were constitutionally protected under the 14th Amendment of the U.S. Constitution.

The case originated in a small town of Edna, Texas, in Jackson County in 1950. Pete Hernández, an agricultural worker, was accused of murdering Joe Espinoza. During the trial, Hernández was tried by an all-white jury in a town where Mexican Americans had not served on a jury for at least 25 years. Although convicted, Hernández appealed the decision to the Texas Court of Appeals, where the decision was upheld. García, a seasoned civil rights attorney from San Antonio, Texas, agreed to represent Hernández without a legal fee (pro bono). He viewed this case as an opportunity to challenge the systematic exclusion of Mexican Americans from all types of jury duty in at least 70 counties in Texas, in violation of the Equal Protection Clause of the Fourteenth Amendment. They appealed the case to the U.S. Supreme Court. The legal team included García, John J. Herrera, and Carlos Cadena of LULAC (League of United Latin American Citizens). (Cadena later became the first Mexican American hired as a law professor in the United States, when he accepted a position at St. Mary's University School of Law in San

Antonio, Texas.) The team also included members of the GI Forum, James DeAnda, and Cris Alderete.

The Court heard arguments on January 11, 1954. In their oral arguments, García and Cadena argued that Mexican Americans were considered white, yet Anglos identified them as separate, a class apart. He showed a historical pattern of discrimination and segregation of Mexican Americans by Anglos. Essentially, they proposed that Mexican Americans constituted a "distinct class" for purposes of applying the Fourteenth Amendment. The state, in contrast, argued that the Fourteenth Amendment applied to only whites and blacks, and Mexican Americans were considered white. Moreover, they denied any systematic exclusion of Mexican Americans in jury duty.

The case was decided on May 3, 1954. Chief Justice Earl Warren, writing the opinion for the Court in a unanimous decision, held that Mexican Americans had been historically discriminated against and constituted an "identifiable class" protected under the Equal Protection Clause of the Fourteenth Amendment. For the first time, the U.S. Supreme Court had extended constitutional protections to Mexican Americans. The case was decided in the same year as the landmark case, *Brown v. Board of Education*, which struck down segregation in public schools.

Sonia R. García

See also: America GI Forum; *Delgado v. Bastrop I.S.D., et al.* (1948); Méndez, Sylvia (1936–); *Plyler v. Doe* (1982); *Primary Documents:* U.S. Supreme Court Decision in *Hernández v. the State of Texas* (1954)

Further Reading

García, Ignacio. 2008. *White But Not Equal: Mexican Americans, Jury Discrimination, and the Supreme Court.* Tucson: University of Arizona Press.

Hernández v. Texas, 347 U.S. 475 (1954).

"Hernández v. Texas." *Oyez Oyez.* http://www.oyez.org/cases/1940-1955/347us475.

Olivas, Michael A. 2006. *Colored Men and Hombres Aqui: Hernandez v. Texas and the Emergence of Mexican American Lawyering.* Houston: Arté Publico Press.

Sandoval, Carlos. 2009. *A Class Apart.* A PBS American Experience Documentary.

Soltero, Carlos. 2006. *Latinos and American Law: Landmark Supreme Court Cases.* Austin: University of Texas Press.

Valencia, Reynaldo, Sonia R. García, Henry Flores, & José R. Juárez. 2004. "Mexican Americans and the Law." In *Mexican Americans and the Law: El Pueblo Unido Jamás Será Vencido.* Tucson: University of Arizona Press.

Herrera Beutler, Jaime

(1978–)

Jaime Herrera is a Republican member of Congress representing Washington's 3rd district, which covers the southwestern portion of the state. She was the first Latino to represent Washington in the U.S. House of Representatives. She is also a former Washington state legislator. She is married to Daniel Beutler; the couple has two children, Abigail and Ethan, and reside in Battle Ground, Washington.

Jaime Herrera was born in 1978 in Glendale, California, but was raised since childhood in southwestern Washington. Her father is a second-generation Mexican American who grew up in Southern California. Beutler was raised alongside her two siblings and three cousins, whom her parents adopted in an effort to protect them from the influence of drugs and gangs. She was homeschooled until high school when she attended Prairie High School in Vancouver, Washington. Herrera graduated from the University of Washington in 2004, where she majored in communication. After college, Beutler interned with the Washington State Senator, Republican Joe Zarelli and then earned a prestigious White House political affairs internship.

After her White House internship, Beutler stayed in Washington to serve as a senior legislative aide for Congresswoman Cathy McMorris Rodgers (R-Spokane). In this position she specialized in health care, education, and veterans' issues. In 2007, she returned to Washington after seizing an opportunity for appointment to an open seat to the state legislature's 18th district by the Clark and Cowlitz county commissioners. She was appointed to the House Transportation Committee and worked to resume a highway project that had been indefinitely delayed. She was re-elected by 60 percent of voters in 2008.

Beutler decided to run for Congress after Brian Baird of Washington's 3rd district announced his retirement in late 2009. In the coming year, she ran her campaign for Congress while serving in the state legislature. In early 2010, Beutler received criticism as a state representative for fundraising in Washington, D.C., while the state legislature was in session. In August 2010, she placed second in the nonpartisan primary with 28 percent of the vote. By the time of the general election, Beutler raised $1,493,260 compared to her opponent, Denny Heck, who raised $1,605,250; he also outspent her by nearly $500,000 (*The New York Times*, 2010). On November 2, 2010, she was elected to Washington's 3rd district as the first Latina member of Congress from Washington State, with 53 percent of the vote.

Elected at the age of 31, Beutler was one of the youngest members of Congress at the time of her election. In her tenure, Beutler has served on the House Committees for Small Business, Transportation, and Appropriations. She is considered a moderate Republican, although she generally falls in line with many Republican issues, including her stance on abortion and government spending. She caucuses with the Congressional Hispanic Conference, the Congressional Caucus for Women's Issues, and the Congressional Caucus on Maternity Care.

In 2013, Beutler gave birth to her daughter, Abigail, who was diagnosed with Potter's syndrome (an often-fatal disease resulting in underdeveloped lungs and kidneys). After undergoing experimental treatment and a kidney transplant, Abigail survived the disease. Upon becoming a mother, Beutler has sponsored legislation aimed at improving lives for parents, including legislation such as the Bottles and Breastfeeding Equipment Screening Act (BABES Act) and the Safe Medication for Moms and Babies Act.

In October 2016, following the release of lewd comments regarding women by then-Republican presidential nominee Donald Trump, Beutler announced she would not vote for her party's candidate and would instead write in House Speaker Paul Ryan's name.

Julia Marin Hellwege

See also: Congressional Hispanic Caucus Institute (CHCI)

Further Reading
Bejarano, Christina E. 2013. *The Latina Advantage: Gender, Race, and Political Success.* Austin: University of Texas Press.

Dake, Lauren. 2016. "Herrera Beutler Rejects Trump for President; Will Write in Ryan." *The Columbian,* October 8. https://www.sos.wa.gov/elections/research/Election -Results-and-Voters-Pamphlets.aspx.

Durbin, Kathie. 2010. "Jaime Herrera: Staying 'True to the Principles' Republican State Legislator Doesn't Hesitate to Criticize Both Parties." *The Columbian*, July 23. http://www.columbian.com/news/2010/jul/23/3rd-congressional-district-jaime -herrera-staying-t/.

GovTrack.us. 2013. "Ideology Analysis of Members of Congress: Rep. Jaime Herrera Beutler." https://www.govtrack.us/congress/members/jaime_herrera_beutler/412486.

Hardy-Fanta, Carol, Pei-te Lien, Dianne Pinderhughes, & Christine Marie Sierra. 2016. *Contested Transformation: Race, and Political Leadership in 21st Century America.* New York: Cambridge University Press.

Herrera Beutler, Jaime. n.d. "Jaime Herrera Beutler-Congress." https://www.votejaime.com.

Herrera Beutler, Jaime. n.d. "U.S. Congresswoman Jaime Herrera Beutler." http:// herrerabeutler.house.gov/.

National Association of Latino Elected and Appointed Officials (NALEO). n.d. "National Directory of Latino Elected Officials." http://www.naleo.org/at_a_glance.

Navarro, Sharon A., Samantha L. Hernandez, & Leslie A. Navarro, eds. 2016. *Latinas in American Politics: Changing and Embracing Political Tradition.* Lanham, MD: Lexington Press.

The New York Times. 2010. "Washington 3rd District Profile." *The New York Times*, December 10. http://www.nytimes.com/elections/2010/house/washington/3.html.

Washington Secretary of State, Elections Division. 2007–2016. "Election Results and Voters Pamphlets." https://www.sos.wa.gov/elections/research/Election-Results-and -Voters-Pamphlets.aspx.

Wasniewski, Matthew A., Albin Kowalewski, Laura Turner O'Hara, & Terrance Rucker. 2013. *Hispanic Americans in Congress 1822–2012.* Washington, D.C.: Office of the Historian and Office of the Clerk U.S. House of Representatives.

Weisensee Egan, Nicole. 2016. "Congresswoman's 'Miracle Baby' Born without Kidneys Finally Gets One—from Her Dad: 'We Are Blessed.'" *People Magazine,* April 15. http://people.com/celebrity/congresswomans-miracle-baby-gets-a-kidney-from -her-dad.

Hinojosa, Maria

(1961–)

Maria Hinojosa is a Mexican American journalist who came to prominence as the host and executive director of NPR's *Latino USA*. She is also the founder of Futuro Media Group, a nonprofit multimedia organization dedicated to giving voice to people of color and other groups underrepresented in media.

Hinojosa began her work in journalism in 1985 as a production assistant at the Washington, D.C., office of National Public Radio (NPR). It took five years for Hinojosa to work her way into the reporter job she had aspired to. In her 1999 memoir Hinojosa explained, "I wanted to tell stories about the America that I had grown up in but that I never saw in the media." Working as a correspondent for NPR from 1990 to 1996, Hinojosa developed a style of reporting that went right to the heart of the many untold stories of Latinos and people of color in the United States. Her unique coverage attracted the attention of CNN, who hired her as an urban affairs correspondent where she covered New York City for eight years. Hinojosa began to branch out into various public affairs shows and became a senior correspondent for PBS. She hosted the *NOW* series and *One on One* for PBS and *Visiones*, a Spanish-language public affairs show, on WNBC. In 1992, Maria Hinojosa and Maria Martin launched *Latino USA*, a weekly NPR show focused on Latinos with Hinojosa as the host. In 2010 Hinojosa created the Futuro Media Group, an entity that became the exclusive producer of *Latino USA* with Hinojosa in full control as anchor and executive producer. *Latino USA* is still going strong with an hour-long format and a large and devoted national audience.

Hinojosa is founder, president, and CEO of Futuro Media Group, whose mission is to increase visibility of Latinos and others in media in order to empower communities of color. Futuro Media has developed a number of productions in addition to its flagship *Latino USA* radio show. *America by the Numbers with Maria Hinojosa* is a documentary series on PBS that explores how demographic change in the United States is reconstituting what Hinojosa calls "America's new mainstream." Hinojosa focuses on the voices of "the new deciders," Latinos, Asians, African Americans, immigrants, young people, and LGBT, as these growing populations become more influential in U.S. politics and culture. As of 2018, nine episodes have aired on the WORLD channel and on PBS. Hinojosa has also hosted nearly 100 podcasts of *In the Thick*, a 20- to 30-minute political podcast supplemented with occasional shorter podcasts on timely topics referred to as *In the Thick FYIs. Humanizing America* is a series of short documentaries that tell the stories of people from the forgotten corners of America's emerging electorate.

Hinojosa's journalistic work has won many awards, including, among others, a Peabody Award for *Latino USA*, an Emmy for her talk show *Maria Hinojosa: One on One,* the John Chancellor Award for Excellence in Journalism, the Robert F. Kennedy Journalism Award for reporting on disadvantaged people, the National Association of Hispanic Journalists' Radio Award, an Associated Press Award, and the National Council of La Raza's Rubén Salazar Lifetime Achievement Award. Hinojosa has authored two books, one a collection of interviews with gang or "crew" members, and a second on becoming a mother.

Hinojosa was born in 1961 in Mexico City but grew up in the Hyde Park area of Chicago. She graduated from Barnard University with a BA in Latin American studies and received an honorary doctorate from De Paul University, where she presently occupies the Sor Juana Ines de la Cruz Chair of Latin American and Latino Studies. Maria Hinojosa lives in Harlem with her two children and German Perez, her Dominican artist husband.

Teresa Carrillo

See also: Ramos, Jorge (1958–); Salazar, Rubén (1928–1970); Salinas, Maria Elena (1954–)

Further Reading

Hinojosa, Maria. 1995. *Crews: Gang Members Talk with Maria Hinojosa.* Orlando, FL: Harcourt Brace Company.

Hinojosa, Maria. 1999. *Raising Raul: Adventures Raising Myself and My Son.* New York: Penguin Books.

Hinojosa, Rubén

(1940–)

A Mexican American Democrat from Texas, Rubén Hinojosa served in the U.S. House of Representatives for 20 years, from 1997 to 2017. Hinojosa's legislative accomplishments center on education. He is also a vocal supporter of immigrants in the United States. He recently retired from the House and has mentioned that he might explore opportunities to work as a distinguished visiting professor or as a vice-chancellor in a university system.

Born on August 20, 1940, in Edcouch, Texas, Hinojosa received a bachelor's in business administration from the University of Texas in Austin in 1962 and a master's in business administration from the University of Texas-Pan American (now called the University of Texas Rio Grande Valley) in Edinburg in 1980. He was the president and chief financial officer of his family-owned business, H&H Foods, for 20 years.

Hinojosa's political career began when he became a local school board member in 1972. He was also a South Texas Community College board member and a Texas State Board of Education member from 1974 to 1984. Hinojosa was instrumental in creating the South Texas Independent School District magnet high school system and the South Texas Community College. The community college, founded in 1993, opened its doors with only 876 enrolled students. Today, it is one of Texas's largest community colleges with about 34,000 students.

In 1996, Hinojosa ran for the U.S. House of Representatives in Texas District 15 after the previous representative, Kika de la Garza, decided to retire. Hinojosa won the election with 62 percent of the vote. He

Democrat Rubén Hinojosa is a former U.S. representative for Texas's 15th congressional district, serving from 1997 to 2017. The district stretches from Seguin to McAllen on the Mexican border. (U.S. House of Representatives)

continued working to enhance educational opportunities. Hinojosa played a pivotal role in creating the Developing Hispanic-Serving Institutions (HSIs) Program in 1998. This program provides grants for HSIs (an HSI is a nonprofit college or university with a Hispanic population of at least 25%). Hinojosa also co-sponsored the College Cost Reduction and Access Act of 2007, which provided the single largest increase in student financial aid since 1944.

Hinojosa is also an advocate for undocumented immigrants. A vocal supporter of the DREAM Act, he penned an article in 2010 in *The Hill* urging colleagues to vote for the Act. He was also among the 111 members of Congress who sent a letter to Obama, urging the president to prevent the use of information collected on undocumented individuals as part of the Deferred Action for Childhood Arrivals (DACA) program for any purpose other than the program's original intent. This letter was a response to the anti-immigrant rhetoric and deportation threats made by Donald Trump, a former reality television personality, during the 2016 presidential election. Finally, Hinojosa was the chairman of the Congressional Hispanic Caucus in 2013 and 2014.

Hinojosa's career was not without controversy. In 2010, he filed for bankruptcy. In 2015, Hinojosa and nine other lawmakers were investigated for ethics violations after the legislators attended a conference in Azerbaijan that was paid for by the state oil company of Azerbaijan (SOCAR). Not only did SOCAR pay for a lavish trip, costing hundreds of thousands of dollars, but lawmakers also received extravagant gifts, like rugs valued between $2,500 and $10,000 (House members are not supposed to accept gifts from foreign governments). The House Ethics Committee conducted an investigation, concluded that the lawmakers were unaware that the trip was sponsored by SOCAR, and ruled that the legislators acted in good faith.

In November 2015, at the age of 75, Hinojosa announced that he would retire at the end of his 10th term in January 2017. He leaves office with multiple honors under his belt. There is a highway, two elementary schools, and a Regents Endowment Professorship in perpetuity at the University of Texas in Austin named after him. He also received a Hispanic Heritage Award from the Hispanic Heritage Foundation and the Mexican American Legal Defense and Education Fund (MALDEF) Award for Lifetime Achievement, Excellence in Government. Hinojosa and his wife, Martha, have five children: Rubén, Jr., Laura, Iliana, Kaitlin, and Karén.

Lucila Figueroa

See also: de la Garza, Eligio "Kika" (1927–2017); DREAM Act; DREAM Act at the State Level; Immigration as a Policy Issue; Mexican American Legal Defense and Educational Fund (MALDEF)

Further Reading

Bresnahan, John. 2011. "House Dem Files for Bankruptcy." *Politico*, February 6. http://www.politico.com/story/2011/02/house-dem-files-for-bankruptcy-048799.

Cohen, Richard E., & James A. Barnes. 2015. *The Almanac of American Politics*. Bethesda, MD: Columbia Books & Information Services.

Diaz, Kevin. 2017. "Ethics Office in GOP Sights Probed Houston Lawmakers." *Houston Chronicle*, January 3. http://www.houstonchronicle.com/news/politics/us/article/Ethics-office-in-GOP-sights-probed-Houston-10833290.php.

Excelencia in Education. n.d. "Causes Need Champions." http://www.edexcelencia.org /hinojosa.

Helton, John. 2015. "Hinojosa Announces Retirement after Nine Terms." *Roll Call*, November 12. http://www.rollcall.com/news/home/report-hinojosa-expected-to-announce -retirement-friday.

Higham, Scott, Steven Rich, & Alice Crites. 2015. "10 Members of Congress Took Trip Secretly Funded by Foreign Government." *The Washington Post*, May 13. https:// www.washingtonpost.com/investigations/10-members-of-congress-took-trip -secretly-funded-by-foreign-government/2015/05/13/76b55332-f720-11e4-9030 -b4732caefe81_story.html?utm_term=.0288403d8581.

"Hinojosa, Rubén, (1940–)." *Biographical Directory of the United States Congress*. http:// bioguide.congress.gov/scripts/biodisplay.pl?index=H000636.

Hinojosa, Rubén. 2010. "The DREAM Act Offers Hard-Working Students a Path to Citizenship (Rep. Rubén Hinojosa)." *The Hill*, September 21. http://64.147.104.30/blogs /congress-blog/homeland-security/119935-the-dream-act-offers-hard-working -students-a-path-to-citizenship-rep-ruben-hinojosa.

"HR 2669—College Cost Reduction and Access Act." *Congress.gov*. https://www.congress .gov/bill/110th-congress/house-bill/2669/cosponsors.

National Clearinghouse for English Language Acquisition. n.d. "High Quality STEM Education for English Learners: Current Challenges and Effective Practices, Invited Guests." http://www.ncela.us/files/uploads/36/STEM_forum_bios.pdf.

Nelsen, Aaron. 2015. "Hinojosa Emotional Announcing Retirement." *San Antonio Express-News*, November 13. http://www.expressnews.com/news/local/article/U-S-Rep -Ruben-Hinojosa-ends-two-decade-6630339.php.

Pablos, Roland. n.d. "Office of the Secretary of State Race Summary Report: 1996 General Election." http://elections.sos.state.tx.us/elchist56_state.htm.

Perez-Hernandez, Danya. 2017a. "Rubén Hinojosa's Retirement Begins after 20 Years in Congress." *Valley Morning Star*, January 3. http://www.valleymorningstar.com /news/local_news/article_3a06cbb4-d234-11e6-ba2e-772714825129.html.

Perez-Hernandez, Danya. 2017b. "DHS: Dreamers' Info Shouldn't Be Used for Deportation." *The Monitor*, January 5. http://www.themonitor.com/news/local/dhs-dreamers -info-shouldn-t-be-used-for-deportation/article_79bbc207-b065-50e7-be55 -942a90b6f843.html.

Santiago, Deborah A. 2006. *Inventing Hispanic-Serving Institutions (HSIs): The Basics.* Washington, D.C.: Excelencia in Education Publications. http://files.eric.ed.gov /fulltext/ED506052.pdf.

South Texas College. n.d. "About South Texas College." http://www.southtexascollege.edu /about.

U.S. Department of Education. n.d. "Programs: Developing Hispanic-Serving Institutions Program—Title V." https://ed.gov/programs/idueshsi/index.html?src=rt.

U.S. House of Representatives Committee on Ethics. "House Ethics Manual: Committee on Standards of Official Conduct, 110th Congress, 2d Session." https://ethics.house .gov/sites/ethics.house.gov/files/documents/2008_House_Ethics_Manual.pdf.

Vote Smart. n.d. "Rubén Hinojosa, Sr.'s Biography." https://votesmart.org/candidate /biography/291/ruben-hinojosa-sr#.

Wasniewski, Matthew A., Albin Kowalewski, Laura Turner O'Hara, & Terrance Rucker, eds. 2013. *Hispanic Americans in Congress, 1822–2012.* Washington, D.C.: Government Printing Office.

Hispanic Association of Colleges and Universities (HACU)

Established in 1986, the Hispanic Association of Colleges and Universities (HACU) is an association of colleges and universities that assists in the development of member institutions; looks to improve the educational opportunities of Hispanic students; and addresses the needs of business, industry, and government. The HACU was created after Dr. Antonio Rigual, vice-president for institutional advancement at Our Lady of the Lake University (OLLU), and Sister Elizabeth Anne Sueltenfuss, OLLU president at the time, started conversations with the Xerox Corporation regarding funding to establish a "Center for Hispanic Higher Education." Through the creation of the center, Rigual and Sueltenfuss sought to enhance opportunities for Hispanic students at OLLU. Their quest started a conversation that spawned beyond OLLU. In May 23–24, 1986, at a meeting with other administrators from Hispanic-serving institutions (HSIs), HACU was created with the mission to engage corporations, foundations, government agencies, and colleges and universities in activities that increased educational opportunities for Hispanics.

HACU's headquarters are in San Antonio, Texas, and it has a regional office in Sacramento, California. HACU's Office of Government Relations, located in Washington, D.C., enables the association to effectively lead advocacy efforts, maintain relations with Congress, conduct public policy research regarding the Hispanic population, and offer educational opportunities for Hispanic youth looking for professional experience to enter careers and become leaders in the federal government. Despite offering many of the opportunities in our nation's capital, HACU is present in 37 states, Puerto Rico, Washington, D.C., and nine countries in Latin America. In those geographic locations, HACU's membership today includes 481 colleges and universities, 23 Hispanic-serving school districts, 62 faculty and staff, and 32 students (HACU, 2016).

As part of its mission to assist in the development of HSIs, and in order to provide sustainable opportunities for students, in 1992 HACU embarked on an advocacy campaign seeking recognition and federal funding for HSIs. This advocacy campaign was successful after Congress agreed to recognize colleges and universities with a high enrollment of Hispanic students as "HSIs" and started conversations to appropriate federal money to HSIs. HACU's efforts to secure federal funding for HSIs were successful when it secured $12 million in funding in 1995 (HACU, 2012: 4). Securing federal funds for HSIs was crucial to the mission of HACU, but in order to also support the programs designed to develop Hispanic youth, HACU began to foster relationships with sponsors and partners to ensure program sustainability. HACU's resources support scholarships, internships, and leadership development for Hispanic students across the country.

HACU views educational opportunities such as internships as the key to helping the largest minority group, Hispanics, close the gap that exists in their economic and social success. More than 11,000 Hispanic students have already benefitted from programs offered by HACU (HACU, 2017). Through the use of its resources, HACU and its partner colleges and universities host training workshops across the country to develop the leadership and work skills of Hispanic students in communities across the nation. The skills acquired through the trainings enable Hispanic students to have the tools to access opportunities to enhance their career outcomes. In addition to trainings, HACU partners with 40 federal agencies to provide paid internships to undergraduate and graduate Hispanic students seeking to gain work experience to enhance their resumes and work opportunities after graduation (HACU, 2017). HACU's internship experience also includes networking opportunities and mentorship and leadership development to enhance the intern's experience and increase the opportunities to become prominent Hispanic leaders in their chosen sectors or the federal government. HACU also offers scholarships that enable Hispanic students to access and afford higher education. Through all these avenues, HACU seeks to enhance opportunities for the Hispanic population and champion their success in higher education to create the next generation of Hispanic leaders in the United States.

Maria L. Ibarra Rodriguez

See also: Education and Latinos

Further Reading

The Hispanic Association of Colleges and Universities (HACU). 2012. "1986–2011: 25 Years of Championing Hispanic Higher Education, A Historical Review and a Glimpse into the Future." *The Hispanic Association of Colleges and Universities (HACU)*. https://www.hacu.net/images/hacu/about/HACU_History_1986-2011F.pdf.

The Hispanic Association of Colleges and Universities (HACU). 2016. *2016 HACU Annual Report*. Washington, D.C.: The Hispanic Association of Colleges and Universities (HACU). http://www.hacu.net/images/hacu/annualreports/2016/#page/1.

The Hispanic Association of Colleges and Universities (HACU). 2017a. "HACU 101." *The University of Association of Colleges and Universities (HACU),* January 9. https://www.hacu.net/hacu/HACU_101.asp.

The Hispanic Association of Colleges and Universities (HACU). 2017b. "The HACU Alumni Association (HAA)." *The Hispanic Association of Colleges and Universities (HACU)*, January 10. https://www.hacu.net/hacu/Federal_MOUs.asp.

The Hispanic Association of Colleges and Universities (HACU). 2017c. "Memoranda of Understanding with Federal Agencies" *The Hispanic Association of Colleges and Universities*, January 10. https://www.hacu.net/hacu/Federal_MOUs.asp.

Núñez, Anne-Marie, Sylvia Hurtado, & Emily Calderón Galdeano. 2015. *Hispanic-Serving Institutions: Advancing Research and Transformative Practice*. New York: Routledge.

Huerta, Dolores

(1930–)

Perhaps the most well-known Mexican American woman in U.S. history, Dolores Huerta is a long-time labor organizer, civil rights leader, and political activist who continues to advocate for social equality and justice for all Americans. Huerta is most notable for her role as the cofounder of the Farm Workers Association (FWA) with César Chávez in 1962, which evolved into the National Farm Workers Association (NFWA) and is now known as the United Farm Workers (UFW). Huerta

Dolores Huerta, co-founder of UFW, labor leader, and civil rights activist, with a union flag that reads "Viva La Causa," ca. 1975. (Cathy Murphy/Getty Images)

dedicated much of her life to organizing and developing the UFW as a co-leader, policy maker, administrator, and principal negotiator. She was also a successful lobbyist who helped end the national Bracero Program in 1964 and pass the Agricultural Labor Relations Act of 1975 in California. At 88, Huerta continues her humanitarianism work as a tireless advocate for fair treatment for workers, immigrants, women, and marginalized communities. In 1998, she was honored with the Eleanor Roosevelt Human Rights Award, and in 2012 President Obama awarded her the Presidential Medal of Freedom.

Dolores Clara Fernández Huerta was born on April 10, 1930, in Dawson, New Mexico, a small mining town in northern New Mexico. Her mother, Alicia Chávez, hailed from a long line of New Mexican Hispanos, and her father, Juan Fernández, was the son of Mexican immigrants. After her parents divorced in 1935, Huerta's mother took her and two brothers to Stockton, California, to start a new life. For the most part, Huerta was raised by her independent mother and grandfather and had a middle-class, Catholic, multicultural, urban upbringing. After graduating high school, Huerta started college and at age 20 married her high school sweetheart, Ralph Head, and had two daughters. After the marriage failed, Huerta went back to school and completed her associate's degree in education in preparation for a career in teaching. She taught elementary school for a short time, but desired to do more with her life beyond teaching. She volunteered in her community through organizations such as Catholic Relief Services and Club Azul y Oro (Blue and Gold Club). Through her social activism she became involved in political activism when she and her mother became members of the Community Service Organization (CSO) in 1955.

While working for the CSO, Huerta met and married fellow CSO organizer, Ventura Huerta, and had five more children. She continued her work at the CSO as a lobbyist and organizer alongside Chávez. Chávez encouraged the CSO to take up the cause of organizing farmworkers as part of the CSO's mission to empower and organize poor people in the political sphere. Huerta shared Chavez's desire to organize farm workers because she saw her mother help farm workers and braceros and taught the children of farm workers as a teacher. Her empathy and critical awareness of the economic inequalities, racism, and injustices workers suffered at the hands of employers motivated Huerta to advocate for the poor, working class, and oppressed.

By the late 1950s, Huerta had become more actively involved in organizing farm workers through the CSO and the Agricultural Workers Organizing Committee (AWOC) where she held leadership roles. She continued her political activism as an ardent lobbyist and advocated for the interests of farmworkers and working-class people. By 1962, Huerta left the AWOC and joined Chávez to organize farmworkers and form the Farm Workers Association (FWA). Between 1962 and 1965 Huerta held various leadership positions in the FWA, the National Farm Workers Association (NFWA), United Farm Workers Organizing Committee (UFWOC), and United Farm Workers (UFW). As vice-president and chief contract negotiator of the UFW, she was instrumental in organizing and carrying out the five-year table grape boycott, one of the most successful strikes in U.S. labor history. From the 1970s through the 1980s, Huerta worked with Chávez to build the UFW as a solid labor organization to improve wages, working and living conditions, and standard of living for farmworkers and the working poor. After being arrested and suffering a serious injury during a nonviolent protest in 1988, Huerta took a leave of absence to advocate for women's issues and encourage women to enter electoral politics through the Feminist Majority's Feminization of Power campaign. Although she continued to support and promote the cause of farm workers, the working class, and labor reform after Chávez's death in 1992, she also advocated for health care reform, environmental justice, political representation, women's rights, and human rights. To date, Huerta remains one of the most influential and inspirational women in the United States and a positive role model for all Americans, especially for Mexican American/Chicana/Latina women.

Maritza De La Trinidad

See also: Brown Power Movement/Chicano Civil Rights Movement; Chávez, César (1927–1993); Community Service Organization (CSO); Obama, Barack (1961–) and Latinos; United Farm Workers (UFW)

Further Reading

Chávez, Alicia. 2005. "Dolores Huerta and the United Farm Workers." In Vicki L. Ruiz and Virginia Sánchez Korrol, eds. *Latina Legacies: Identity, Biography, and Community*. New York: Oxford University Press.

De Ruiz, Dana Catherine, & Richard Larios. 1992. *La Causa: The Migrant Farmworkers' Story.* Minneapolis: Steck-Vaughn.

"Dolores Huerta." *Dolores Huerta Foundation.* http://doloreshuerta.org/dolores-huerta.

Etulain, Richard W., ed. 2002. *Chávez: A Brief Biography with Documents.* The Bedford Series in History and Culture. Boston: Bedford/St. Martin's.

Ferriss, Susan, & Ricardo Sandoval. 1997. *The Fight in the Fields USA.* New York: W. W. Norton.

García, Mario T., ed. 2008. *A Dolores Huerta Reader.* Albuquerque: University of New Mexico Press.

Garcia, Richard A. 1993. "Dolores Huerta: Woman, Organizer and Symbol." *California History* 72, no. 1: 56–71.

Michals, Debra. 2015. "Dolores Huerta." *National Women's History Museum.* https://www.nwhm.org/education-resources/biography/biographies/dolores-fernandez-huerta.

Immigrant Youth Justice League (IYJL)

The Immigrant Youth Justice League (IYJL) was a Chicago-based nonprofit organization founded and led by undocumented youth. The founders of IYJL wanted to mobilize on behalf of their rights in the face of their vulnerability to deportation and the detrimental impact that their legal status had on their social, economic, and emotional well-being. The organization was created in October 2009 by a group of undocumented youth and allies who were working on stopping the deportation of one of their peers, a student at the University of Illinois at Chicago. Politicians and immigrant rights organizations had been reluctant to advocate for his case, so the youths initiated a campaign that included a massive national petition drive and local outreach, recruiting many individual and institutional allies. The student's deportation was halted, and IYJL continued to organize with the vision of using their own voices, as undocumented youth directly affected by immigration policies, in creating transformative change so that individual antideportation campaigns would not be necessary. They emphasized the importance of undocumented immigrant voices being at the forefront and organizing for their own rights, a novel position in a period when most organizing for immigrant rights had been led by individuals who were not undocumented. Raised in the United States for most of their lives, their fluency in English and familiarity with U.S. society enable them to position themselves in the public discourse in novel and unprecedented ways.

IYJL held some closed "coming out" meetings as they recruited more undocumented youth and became a member of United We Dream in their early phase. They planned a Coming Out of the Shadows event and proposed that other undocumented youth organizations in United We Dream do the same. On March 10, 2010, hundreds of youth and their allies marched to the Federal Plaza in Chicago, carrying a banner with a slogan their IYJL members had created: "Undocumented and Unafraid." Five youth came out as undocumented in the square, sharing their individual and family stories and calling for immigration reform. This was the first Coming Out of the Shadows event held in the nation. Adapting IYJL's slogan, several undocumented youth organizations throughout the nation came out of the shadows in the following weeks, stating that they, too, were "undocumented and unafraid."

In subsequent months IYJL joined other youth organizations in calling for the DREAM Act in Congress, a bill that would have provided undocumented youth who arrived in the United States before age 16 a path to citizenship. This was not initially supported by many immigrant rights organizations that feared passing the DREAM Act might impede the passage of comprehensive immigration reform in the future. Having disaffiliated from United We Dream, IYJL coordinated with other organizations and groups under the National Immigrant Youth Alliance

(NIYA) to stage the first civil disobedience of undocumented youth in the nation in Senator John McCain's office in Tucson, Arizona, in May 2013. As the campaign for the DREAM Act intensified, IYJL also participated actively in a national civil disobedience of undocumented youth held in Washington, D.C., in July 2010. Increased mobilization led to several organizations to switch their position and support the DREAM Act. Although the DREAM Act passed in the House of Representatives, it failed to achieve closure in the Senate in December 2010.

This disappointment in Congress led IYJL to shift its strategy in a few key ways. First, its members modified their slogan, claiming to be "undocumented, unafraid and unapologetic." This slogan reflected a new direction in which they would lay responsibility on the U.S. immigration system, and not on their parents or themselves, for the restrictions affecting their lives. They moved away from an idealized "DREAMER" narrative, which had emphasized their exceptional status as model students and proto-citizens, to one that emphasized the diversity among undocumented youth, as well as their strong connection to undocumented immigrants who did not come as youth. Still linked with NIYA, IYJL youth engaged in a two-tier strategy of working on individual antideportation cases and continued participation in civil disobedience against state enforcement policies, while continuing their annual Coming Out of the Shadows event. The target of these strategies switched from Congress to President Barack Obama and Immigration and Custom Enforcement (ICE), under the Department of Homeland Security. In 2012, IYJL was disaffiliated from NIYA and became independent and focused primarily on antideportation campaigns and building bridges with other undocumented youth organizations in Illinois colleges and communities outside Chicago. In spring 2012 several members of IYJL joined forces with the Latin@ Youth Action League in DuPage, Undocumented Students and Allies at IIT, Elgin Dreamers, and undocumented students at Dominican University to create Undocumented Illinois, a coalition organization. By 2013 IYJL was no longer an active organization, though several of its members remained active in Undocumented Illinois.

Amalia Pallares

See also: DREAM Act; DREAM Act at the State Level; Immigration as a Policy Issue; United We Dream

Further Reading

Mena Robles, J., & R. Gomberg-Muñoz. 2016. "Activism after DACA: Lessons from Chicago's Immigrant Youth Justice League." *North American Dialogue* 19: 46–54. doi:10.1111/nad.12036.

Unzueta Carrasco, Tania, & Hinda Seif. 2014. "Disrupting the Dream: Undocumented Youth Reframe Citizenship and Deportability through Anti-Deportation Activism." *Latino Studies* 12, no. 2 (June): 279–299.

Immigration and Customs Enforcement (ICE), Expanded Powers of (2000s)

In March 2003, the U.S. Department of Defense created the new Department of Homeland Security (DHS) in response to the tragic events of September 11, 2001.

Immigration and Customs Enforcement (ICE) arrests 16 people during the two-day Operation SOAR in the New York City metropolitan area, September 2018. (U.S. Immigration and Customs Enforcement)

One of three DHS investigative agencies, Immigration and Customs Enforcement (ICE) was created as a merger of the Immigration and Naturalization Service and the U.S. Customs Service. ICE operates in all 50 U.S. states and 48 foreign countries. It has more than 20,000 employees charged with enforcing border control, customs, and migration. Executive orders and policies by the Donald J. Trump administration are expanding the power and reach of ICE to manage immigration issues.

Four major divisions compose ICE: Homeland Security Investigations (HSI), Enforcement and Removal Operations (ERO), Office of the Principal Legal Advisor (OPLA), and Management and Administration (M&A). All divisions are granted civil and criminal authority to protect national security, but ERO's focus is to arrest, detain, and remove criminals and undocumented individuals from the United States.

A significant policy shift occurred in November 2014 when U.S. Department of Homeland Security secretary Jeh Charles Johnson issued a memorandum to revise department-wide immigration enforcement priorities. The memorandum, titled *Policies for the Apprehension, Detention, and Removal of Undocumented Immigrants,* intensified ICE's actions to remove individuals convicted of serious crimes, those who pose a threat to public safety and national security, and recent border entrants. Specifically, the memorandum created the Priority Enforcement Program (PEP), which enabled DHS to work with state and local law enforcement agencies to increase efforts to detain individuals. The creation of PEP signified an expansion of ICE power and was an attempt to increase cooperation from state and local law agencies. Since the creation of ICE, several state statutes and local ordinances reduced or prevented cooperation with ICE, and several court decisions created liability concerns for cooperating law enforcement agencies. This result was an increasing number of jurisdictions that declined to honor ICE's demands. The implementation of PEP in 2015 improved implementation of ICE ERO goals by law agencies at all levels of government.

As part of PEP, DHS and ICE officials regularly engage with state and local law enforcement officials, including in counties like Los Angeles and Miami-Dade. Today, many law enforcement agencies—even those previously unwilling to cooperate—now collaborate with ICE through PEP. The PEP priorities took effect during fiscal year (FY) 2015, and FY 2016 was the first full year of implementation. In FY 2016, ICE ERO removed 240,255 individuals—a 2 percent increase over FY 2015—originating from 185 countries. The top four countries of origin for removals were Mexico (150,000), Guatemala (34,000), Honduras (22,000), and El Salvador (20,500). Removals, however, have been in steady decline since 2012 when over 409,000 individuals were removed.

Under President Donald J. Trump, the power of ICE has and is likely to continue to grow. Executive order 13767—signed on January 25, 2017—will hire 10,000 more immigration officers to help ICE carry out its functions. Since then, ICE ERO has arrested more than 41,000 individuals who are known or suspected of residing in the United States without documents. This is an increase of 37 percent over the same period in 2016. These realities reflect the increase in funding for ICE; the budget for ICE for FY 2016 was over $6.2 billion—a significant increase from an average of about $3 billion from 2010 to 2015.

Juve J. Cortes

See also: DACA Sin Miedo; Immigration Reform and Control Act (IRCA); National Immigration Law Center (NILC); National Security State and Latinos; Operation Gatekeeper (1994); Operation Hold the Line/Blockade (1993)

Further Reading

DeSipio, Louis, & Rodolfo O. de la Garza. 2015. *U.S. Immigration in the Twenty-First Century: Making Americans, Remaking America.* Boulder, CO: Westview Press.

Golash-Boza, Tanya Maria. 2016. *Immigration Nation: Raids, Detentions, and Deportations in Post-9/11 America.* New York: Routledge.

Hartelius, E. Johanna, ed. 2015. *The Rhetoric of US Immigration: Identity, Community, Otherness.* University Park: The Pennsylvania State University Press.

Wang, Lisa Y. 2017. "Undocumented: How Immigration Became Illegal by Aviva Chomsky." *Yale Human Rights and Development Journal* 18: 117–22.

Immigration and Naturalization Service (INS) v. Cardoza-Fonseca

(1987)

Immigration and Naturalization Service (INS) v. Cardoza-Fonseca is a 1987 U.S. Supreme Court case that deals with the question of the appropriate statutory standard to be used when assessing claims for withholding of deportation under INA §243(h) and claims for asylum as a refugee under INA §208(a). This legal issue arose largely due to the recent passage of the Refugee Act of 1980, which created the category of asylum within U.S. immigration law (Johnson and Salinas, 2012: 1043).

Luz Cardoza-Fonseca was, at the time the Court heard the case, a 38-year-old immigrant from Nicaragua who entered the United States in 1979 with a visitor's visa (*INS v. Cardoza-Fonseca*, 1987). She then overstayed her visa and was offered to take part in the Immigration and Naturalization Service's voluntary departure program, but instead requested that deportation proceedings against her be halted due to fear for her life if she returned to Nicaragua. The fear that Cardoza-Fonseca held was based on the experiences of her brother who was "tortured and imprisoned because of his political activities in Nicaragua" (*INS v. Cardoza-Fonseca*, 1987).

As leading legal scholars have noted, this case has been particularly notable, as it was the second case following *INS v. Stefanic*, decided with the new provisions outlined in the Refugee Act of 1980 (Helton, 1987). Pointing to the enduring importance of the case for immigration and refugee law matters, legal scholars Kevin Johnson and Serena Faye Salinas write, "After a quarter century, the Supreme Court's seminal decision in *INS v. Cardoza-Fonseca* remains at the heart of modern asylum and refugee law. It almost unquestionably is the leading American decision in the field" (Johnson and Salinas, 2012: 1043).

Whereas the immigration judge in the case "applied a 'clear probability of persecution' standard to both the claim for withholding of deportation and the claim for asylum," the Supreme Court held that "the 'well-founded fear' standard for asylum was different from the 'would be threatened' test for withholding of deportation because of the broader class of persons eligible for asylum as opposed to [those] eligible for withholding" (Munley, 2013: 815–816). As a result, the Court's decision that "the burden of proof in asylum cases was a 'well-founded fear' of persecution, a standard . . . more generous than the 'clear probability' standard" previously used was seen by advocates as a shift toward potentially increasing the strength of arguments by those seeking asylum (Anker, 1988: 120).

Though one may assume that the Court's ruling in *Cardoza-Fonseca* would have increased opportunities for credible asylum claims to be processed, further empirical research is needed to examine this claim. However, there have been some calls for greater examination of the relationship between the Board of Immigration Appeals' interpretations of the law and human rights discourse globally (Anker, 1988: 120). Yet the Court has, with minor revisions, kept the standard established in *INS v. Cardoza-Fonseca* intact. This is particularly important for Latinas/os in the United States today in light of the recent end of Temporary Protected Status for migrants from El Salvador (Jordan, 2018). Like other Central American migrants, many Salvadorans migrated to the United States as a result of U.S. military intervention. Thus, greater numbers of Central American migrants may once again be looking to asylum as a viable path to citizenship after having spent so many years in legal limbo.

Kevin Escudero

See also: Asylum Seekers

Further Reading

Anker, Deborah. 1988. "INS v. Cardoza-Fonseca, One Year Later: Discretion, Credibility and Political Opinion." *In Defense of the Alien* 11: 120.

D'Haeseleer, Brian. 2017. *The Salvadoran Crucible: The Failure of U.S. Counterinsurgency in El Salvador, 1979–1992*. Lawrence: University of Kansas Press.

Helton, Arthur, C. 1987. "INS v. Cardoza-Fonseca: The Decision and Its Implications." *NYU Review of Law and Social Change* 16: 35.

Immigration and Naturalization Service (INS) v. Cardoza-Fonseca, 480 U.S. 421 (1987).

Johnson, Kevin, & Serena Faye Salinas. 2012. "Judicial Remands of Immigration Cases: Lessons in Administrative Discretion from *INS v. Cardoza-Fonseca*." *Arizona State Law Journal* 44: 1041.

Jordan, Miriam. 2018. "Trump Administration Says that Nearly 200,000 Salvadorans Must Leave." *The New York Times*, January 8. https://www.nytimes.com/2018/01/08/us/salvadorans-tps-end.html.

Menjívar, Cecilia. 2000. *Fragmented Ties: Salvadoran Immigrant Networks in America*. Berkeley: University of California Press.

Munley, Caitlin B. 2013. "The Refugee Act of 1980 and INS v. Cardoza-Fonseca." *Georgetown Immigration Law Journal* 27: 809.

Immigration as a Policy Issue

Not all Latinos are immigrants, and not all immigrants are Latino, but the terms "immigrant" and "Latino" have become nearly synonymous in the eyes of many Americans, according to the Latino Policy Forum. Immigration is an important policy issue for Latinos because as the United States implements policy to control and limit migration, there are economic, political, and social costs to bear along with benefits to reap for Hispanic populations. Data from a Pew Research Center poll shows that about half (47%) of Hispanic adults, regardless of their immigration status, say they worry "a lot" or "some" that they themselves, a family member, or a close friend could be deported, whereas 52 percent say they are worried "not at all" or "not much."

The U.S. Hispanic population stood at 57 million in 2015 and is among the nation's fastest-growing groups. It is also a largely U.S.-born population—66 percent were born in the United States. Among Hispanics who are foreign-born, roughly 3 in 10 are lawful permanent residents and about 4 in 10 are unauthorized immigrants. At the same time, the group's population growth has slowed in recent years and is now driven more by births in the United States than the arrival of new immigrants, driving down the group's foreign-born share in recent years.

MIXED-STATUS FAMILIES

One reason that many Latinos are concerned about immigration policy is because many are part of mixed-status families. Demographers estimate that for "every two immigrants deported, one citizen-child is affected" (Zayas and Bradlee, 2014). When members of a family vary in legal status, they are known as mixed-status families. If an undocumented parent is deported, they are faced with leaving their

A girl and her family stand with some 200,000 immigrants' rights activists flooding the National Mall on March 21, 2010, to demand comprehensive immigration reform in Washington, D.C. (Rrodrickbeiler/Dreamstime.com)

young dependent citizen-children with a caretaker or bringing their children with them to an unfamiliar country. In June 2012 former president Obama used his executive order to provide deferred action for at least two years to immigrants aged 15 to 30 that were brought to the United States as children, while allowing them the opportunity to apply for a work permit. The Deferred Action for Childhood Arrivals (DACA) was rescinded by the Trump administration in 2017.

NATIONAL U.S. IMMIGRATION LAWS, PROGRAMS, AND POLICIES

Contemporary immigration patterns emerged as a result of the 1965 Immigration and Nationality Act, which was known as the Hart-Celler Act for its congressional sponsors. The law took race and ethnicity out of U.S. admissions policy for immigrants and led to large-scale immigration, both legal and unauthorized. The law achieved this by abolishing the national-origins quota system in favor of a preference system that was based on an immigrant's family relationships with U.S. citizens or permanent legal residents and, to a lesser degree, the immigrant's skills. The law limited the number of visas for immigrants from the Eastern Hemisphere to 170,000, with no one country allowed more than 20,000 visas. And, for the first time, the Act capped visas for immigrants from the Western Hemisphere at 120,000. The statute reserved three-quarters of admissions for immigrants in family categories. Immediate relatives (e.g., spouses, minor children, and parents of adult U.S. citizens) were exempt from the caps; 24 percent of family visas were assigned to siblings of U.S.

citizens. In 1976, Congress extended the 20,000 per country cap to the Western Hemisphere. In conjunction with the end of the Bracero Program in 1964, these limits on legal immigration from the Western Hemisphere fueled the growth of undocumented immigration. Since 1965, the flow of immigrants into the United States has been more than half Latin American and one-quarter Asian. The largest share of today's immigrant population, about 11.6 million people, is from Mexico.

The Immigration Reform and Control Act of 1986 is the overarching policy that has been established to deter illegal immigration and to regulate the process of allowing immigrants to become eligible to work in the United States. The Anti-Drug Abuse Act of 1988 allowed for an immigration offense to be considered an "aggravated felony." The Illegal Immigration Reform and Immigrant Responsibility Act of 1996 (IIRIRA) and the Antiterrorism and Effective Death Penalty Act of 1996 expanded the list of aggravated felonies, and therefore deportable offenses, to include not only the more serious crimes of murder and drug trafficking but to also include misdemeanors and civil offenses such as tax evasion, check fraud, and failure to appear in court (Armenta and Verga, 2017).

Employment authorization in the United States is verified by the employer upon hiring an employee through the completion of an I9 Employment Eligibility Verification form, where the employer records and retains information from the approved governmental documents that the employee provides.

The E-Verify program is authorized by IIRIRA. The program is jointly administered by the U.S. Citizenship and Immigration Services (USCIS), U.S. Department of Homeland Security (DHHS) and Social Security Administration (SSA). With an automated link to federal databases, this free electronic program verifies new employees' eligibility to work in the United States. Although its usage is voluntary, some states have required its usage for specific employers (NCSL, 2015). The Trump administration has suggested mandating E-Verify usage for all employers; however, there is a significant cost to expanding the program.

The H1B visa program began in 1990 and is administered by the USCIS and allows for employers to temporarily hire highly skilled immigrant workers with a bachelor's degree or higher. H1B visa holders are selected by a lottery, which allows applicants the equal opportunity to gain one of 65,000 positions annually; a limit set by Congress. Applicants are exempt from the regular congressionally mandated cap if they hold a U.S. master's degree or higher until the number qualifying reaches 20,000. President Trump has stated his intentions to dismantle the lottery system. Although employers rely on the H1B visa program to recruit workers with specialized skills and education, especially in the tech and STEM (science, technology, engineering, and mathematics) fields, critics assert that the program can be exploited by employers who seek to depress wages by offering H1B visa holders lower than industry standard wages, and the program may also discourage the hiring of U.S. workers (Ainsley, 2017; USCIS, 2017b).

UNAUTHORIZED IMMIGRATION

In mid-June 2012, President Barack Obama announced a new program that would shield young unauthorized immigrants from deportation and allow them to apply for temporary but renewable work permits. The program, known as Deferred

Action for Childhood Arrivals (DACA), provides relief from deportation for unauthorized immigrants younger than 30 who were brought into the country as children and who are currently enrolled in school or have obtained a high school diploma or GED. Nearly 790,000 young unauthorized immigrants have received work permits and deportation relief through this program, many of whom are Latino. Unauthorized immigrants from Mexico make up more than three-quarters of all DACA recipients. Obama also set up a new program to offer similar benefits to some unauthorized-immigrant parents of U.S.-born children. The DACA expansion and the new program (Deferred Action for Parents of Americans and Lawful Permanent Residents, or DAPA) are on hold because of a legal challenge by 26 states. President Trump repealed this program in 2017, leaving the future of these people in limbo.

The number of unauthorized immigrants in 2015 was 11 million, down from 11.3 million in 2009 during the Great Recession. Of these unauthorized immigrants, Mexicans make up approximately half. Yet in 2016, non-Mexicans were estimated to make up 5.6 million unauthorized immigrants compared to 5.4 million unauthorized Mexicans (Krogstad, Passel, and Cohn, 2017). In 2015 there were 462,388 undocumented immigrants apprehended from all regions of the world, down from 1,206,488 in 2006. Of the 462,388 apprehended in 2015, the largest number of all regions, 267,885, were apprehended from Mexico. Other undocumented immigrants deriving from Latin American countries that were apprehended at high numbers were 66,982 from Guatemala, 51,200 from El Salvador, and 42,433 from Honduras (U.S. DHHS, 2016).

INCREASED FOCUS ON THE SOUTHERN BORDER

Since 1965, the United States has engaged in a buildup of border security. Starting in 1994, three larger "Operations"—Operation Gatekeeper in California, Operation Hold the Line in Texas, and Operation Safeguard in Arizona—led to the building of physical barriers (walls) to cut the flow of both illegal drugs and undocumented immigrants from Latin America. On September 14, 2006, one day after it was introduced, the U.S. House of Representatives passed H.R. 6061, the "Secure Fence Act of 2006," by a vote of 283–138.

The U.S. Senate confirmed H.R. 6061 on September 29, 2006, by a vote of 80–19. The measure authorized and partially funded the "possible" construction of 700 miles of fences and physical barriers along the U.S. southern border. During the 2016 presidential campaign, Donald Trump, the Republican candidate, called for construction of a much larger and fortified wall. Trump declared that Mexico would pay for construction of the wall. Such a wall was estimated to cost between $8 and $12 billion, although the many uncertainties that would accompany such a project led to other estimates of between $15 and $25 billion. In January 2017, President Enrique Peña Nieto of Mexico said that his country would not pay for such a wall. On January 25, 2017, President Trump signed an executive order on Border Security and Immigration Enforcement Improvements (Executive Order 13767), which commenced the extension of the Border Wall. Between 1998 and 2004, 1,954 persons were officially reported as having died along the U.S.–Mexico border. Since 2004, the bodies of 1,086 migrants have been recovered in the southern Arizona desert.

In addition to physical and technological barriers, there has been an increase in boots on the ground at the southern border. According to a March 2010 analysis of border security by the Congressional Research Service,

> Border Patrol agent manpower assigned to the southwest border has been increasing steadily since the early 1990s. In 1992, there were 3,555 agents assigned to the southern border, by 2000 that number had increased by 141 percent to 8,580. Since 2000, the number of agents assigned to the southern border has continued to increase, more than doubling once more to 20,119 agents at the end of FY2009. The rapid and steady increase of Border Patrol agents assigned to the southern border reflects the ongoing interest in Congress in stemming the tide of illegal immigration.

President Trump is requesting further expansion on manpower along the southern U.S. border.

DEPORTATIONS

U.S. deportation laws have changed little since 1996, and the volume of immigration has been relatively stable in the 2010s. A large increase in deportations has been related to significant growth in the size of the Department of Homeland Security budget. In fiscal year 2011 Homeland Security had a budget of $56 billion, between a third and a half of which was marked for border security and immigration enforcement. The 2011 budget of the Department of Education was $77.8 billion, and the Department of Justice budget was $29.2 billion.

Decisions by the executive branch have made immigration enforcement a growing part of the War on Terror, which was launched after 2001. The budget of Immigration and Customs Enforcement—now $6 billion—is larger than the entire final budget of its predecessor, the Immigration and Naturalization Service; the Customs and Border Patrol has also seen a twofold increase in its budget.

With the cooperation of local police, federal authorities have been able to deport more people from the U.S. interior. Under President Obama, Homeland Security deported 2.7 million people—an average of about 1,000 immigrants a day, for eight years. These numbers earned Obama the title "Deporter in Chief." In early 2017, U.S. immigration arrests increased nearly 40 percent as immigration agents emboldened by the rhetoric of the Trump administration detained more than 40,000 people suspected of being in the country illegally—with a renewed focus on immigrants without criminal convictions.

In April 2012, 3,100 arrests were made in nationwide raids dubbed "Operation Cross Check." These broad immigrant sweeps have been led by the U.S. Immigration and Custom Enforcement's (ICE) Enforcement and Removal Operations (ERO) division. In March 2015, 2,059 more immigrants were arrested. According to the Department of Homeland Security (DHS), of the 2,059 arrested, 1,000 had felony convictions, 58 were known gang members or affiliates, 89 were sex offenders, and 476 were charged with attempting to re-enter the country illegally.

In February 2017, continued raids took place across the United States in Los Angeles and surrounding areas, Illinois, Indiana, Wisconsin, Kentucky, Kansas, Missouri, Georgia, North Carolina, South Carolina, New York, and San Antonio, netting 655 arrests of foreign nationals, many of which ICE contends have criminal records. However, there have been reports that immigrants have been captured on their way to obtain day laborer work or while on the job and that a number of those captured in the sweeps possess low-level misdemeanor charges or lack any criminal convictions (Tafani, 2015). The increase in arrests and raids has caused fear in Latino immigrant communities.

LaTasha Y. Chaffin

See also: Asylum Seekers; Border Wall; Deferred Action for Childhood Arrivals (DACA)/ Deferred Action for Parents of Americans and Lawful Permanent Residents (DAPA); Immigration Reform and Control Act (IRCA); Minors, Unaccompanied and Undocumented (2010s); Operation Gatekeeper (1994); Operation Hold the Line/Blockade (1993); SB 1070 (2010); Secure Communities Program

Further Reading

Ainsley, Julia Edwards. 2017. "HB Visa Fraud Getting New Scrutiny." *U.S. News & World Report*, April 3. https://www.usnews.com/news/top-news/articles/2017-04-03/us -homeland-security-announces-steps-against-h1b-visa-fraud.

Armenta, Amada, & Irene I. Verga. 2017. "Latinos and the Crimmigration System." In Mathieu Deflem, ed. *Race, Ethnicity and the Law*. Bingley, UK: Emerald Publishing Limited, pp. 221–36.

Epi. 2016. "People of Color Will Be the Majority of the Working Class by 2032." http://www .epi.org/press/people-of-color-will-be-the-majority-of-the-working-class-by-2032.

Flores, Antonio. 2017. "Facts on U.S. Latinos, 2015." *Pew Research Center, Hispanic Trends*. http://www.pewhispanic.org/2017/09/18/facts-on-u-s-latinos/#share-foreign-born.

Krogstad, Jens Manuel, Jeffrey S. Passel, & D'Vera Cohn. 2017. "5 Facts about Illegal Immigration in the U.S." *Pew Research Center*. http://www.pewresearch.org/fact -tank/2017/04/27/5-facts-about-illegal-immigration-in-the-u-s.

NCSL. 2015. http://www.ncsl.org/research/immigration/report-on-2015-state-immigration -laws.aspx.

Tafani, Joseph. 2015. "U.S. Immigration Officials Announce 2,000 Arrests in Nationwide Raids." *Los Angeles Times*, March 9. http://www.latimes.com/nation/la-na -immigration-arrests-deportations-20150309-story.html.

Terrio, Susan J. 2015. *Who's Child Am I? Unaccompanied, Undocumented Children in U.S. Immigration Custody*. Oakland: University of California Press.

USCIS. 2017a. "H-1B Fiscal Year (FY) 2018 Cap Season." https://www.uscis.gov/working -united-states/temporary-workers/h-1b-specialty-occupations-and-fashion -models/h-1b-fiscal-year-fy-2018-cap-season.

USCIS. 2017b. "Immigration Reform and Control Act of 1986." (IRCA). https://www.uscis .gov/tools/glossary/immigration-reform-and-control-act-1986-irca.

U.S. DHHS. 2016. "2015 Yearbook of Immigration Statistics." *Department of Homeland Security. Office of Immigration Statistics*. https://www.dhs.gov/sites/default/files /publications/Yearbook_Immigration_Statistics_2015.pdf.

Zayas, Luis H., & Mollie H. Bradlee. 2014. "Exiling Children, Creating Orphans: When Immigration Policies Hurt Citizens." *Social Work* 59, no. 2: 167–75.

Immigration Reform and Control Act (IRCA)

Republican president Ronald Reagan signed the Immigration Reform and Control Act (IRCA) into law on November 6, 1986. The legislation resulted from years of immigration debates in the U.S. Congress and remains among the most frequently cited U.S. immigration legislative actions of modern times. This law was intended to control unauthorized immigration to the United States while at the same time allowing some undocumented immigrants who met certain criteria to apply for legal status. By most estimates, the legislation awarded legal status to approximately 2.7 million immigrants. Despite these numbers, it is believed that many eligible undocumented immigrants did not apply for legal status for fear of being deported, not understanding the policy, the inability to pay the application fees, and a variety of other reasons. The legislation was sponsored by Senator Alan Simpson (R-WY) and with bipartisan support passed the Senate by a vote of 69–21 but faced a greater challenge in the House where it passed by only four votes.

The legislation contained numerous programs and ways through which individuals could qualify for legal status. The Legal Authorized Worker (LAW) program allowed individuals who had been in the United States before January 1, 1982, to apply for temporary legal status. The filing period for this program was from May 5, 1987, to May 4, 1988. It is estimated that approximately 1.7 million individuals were granted legal status under this program. The Special Agricultural Worker (SAW) program required applicants to have worked in the U.S. agricultural industry for a minimum of 90 days in each of the three years prior to the enacting of the legislation. The filing period for this program was from May 5, 1987, to November 8, 1988. It is estimated that approximately 1 million individuals were granted legal status under this program. Beyond these two programs, the law also allowed undocumented immigrants who had lived continuously in the United States since January 1, 1972, to apply for legal status (Orrenius and Zavodny, 2003).

A central aim of this legislation was to curb unauthorized entries into the country. To that end, the law called for an increase in Border Patrol personnel of 50 percent. It also called for an increased budget of 75 percent for that year and the following one. It further instituted civil and criminal penalties for employers who knowingly hired undocumented workers. However, largely at the insistence of Latino advocates, the legislation also included a clause that outlawed the discrimination of employees based on national origin. Latino advocates wanted to ensure that employees were not discriminated against because of this legislation.

As studies continue to examine the long-term impact of IRCA on immigration, a primary challenge to any assessment is the lack of accurate information regarding undocumented individuals in this country. The best estimates about border crossings are based on border apprehension data collected by INS. Proponents of the legislation argued that immigrants often take on jobs that many U.S. citizens are unwilling to do. They cited the garment industry, agriculture work, and many service industry occupations that few U.S. citizens are willing to undertake. Opponents of the legislation argued that IRCA would encourage further immigration by setting the precedent for the legalization of millions. Several studies have concluded that the impacts of IRCA on undocumented immigration were most visible immediately following its enacting, with drops in unauthorized crossings but that immigration numbers returned to their normal levels several years after. Studies also suggest that the penalties implemented by this legislation have done little to curb the hiring of undocumented workers in many sectors of the economy. One of the primary reasons cited for such a small impact due to employer penalties was the difficulty of regulation when 600 investigators were charged with overseeing 7 million employers.

José L. Martínez

See also: DREAM Act; DREAM Act at the State Level

Further Reading

Donato, Katherine M., Jorge Durand, & Douglas S. Massey. 1992. "Stemming the Tide? Assessing the Deterrent Effects of the Immigration Reform and Control Act." *Demography* 29: 139–57.

Finch, Wilbur A., Jr. 1990. "The Immigration Reform and Control Act of 1986: A Preliminary Assessment." *Social Service Review* 64: 244–60.

Gonzalez Baker, Susan. 1997. "The 'Amnesty' Aftermath: Current Policy Issues Stemming from the Legalization Programs of the 1986 Immigration Reform and Control Act." *The International Migration Review* 31: 5–27.

Immigration Reform and Control Act of 1986, Public Law 99-603, S 1200 (1986).

Orrenius, Pia M., & Madeline Zavodny. 2003. "Do Amnesty Programs Reduce Undocumented Immigration? Evidence from IRCA." *Demography* 40: 437–50.

J

Johnson v. De Grandy

(1994)

One of the U.S. Supreme Court's first voting rights cases after *Shaw v. Reno* (1993), *Johnson v. De Grandy* (1994) involved a challenge by groups of Hispanic and African American voters to Florida's redistricting of Miami-Dade County's state legislative districts after the 1990 census. The plaintiffs argued that the redistricting plan violated Section 2 of the Voting Rights Act of 1965 by watering down minority voting strength. Yet the plan yielded functional proportionality in Dade County by providing a proportion of majority–minority districts that roughly equaled the proportion of the minority voting-age population. This case followed the population boom in Florida during the 1980s, when Florida's population increased by over 3.2 million people. The 1990 census reported Florida's population to be 12,937,926. This presented the state's 40 Senate districts with 323,448 persons each. In addition, the 120 House of Representative districts held approximately 107,816 persons each.

Miguel De Grandy (at the time, a member of the Florida House of Representatives), a group of Hispanic voters, a group of black voters, and a federal agency claimed that these districts unlawfully diluted the voting strength of Hispanics and blacks in the Dade County area, in violation of Section 2 of the Voting Rights Act.

Initially, De Grandy and other plaintiffs found their claim reviewed by the U.S. District Court for the Northern District of Florida. The three-judge panel found that the districts, as redrawn, diluted Hispanic and black voting strength. Specifically, the federal court held that Hispanics in the Dade County area could occupy a majority in 11 House and four Senate districts. However, Florida's reappointment plan only created nine House and three Senate districts with Hispanic majorities. The federal court proposed a remedial plan with 11 majority-Hispanic House of Representative districts.

Bolley Johnson, Speaker of the Florida House of Representatives, led appeal efforts challenging the Northern District of Florida's decision. On October 4, 1993, the U.S. Supreme Court listened to oral arguments on three consolidated cases: *Johnson v. De Grandy, De Grandy v. Johnson*, and the *United States v. State of Florida*. The Supreme Court reviewed whether the totality of the circumstances supported a finding of vote dilution.

In the Supreme Court's 7–2 decision in favor of Johnson, Justice David Souter wrote, "[W]hile proportionality in the sense used here is obviously an indication that minority voters have an equal opportunity, in spite of racial polarization, 'to participate in the political process and to elect representatives of their choice,' 42 U.S.C. §1973(b), the degree of probative value assigned to proportionality may vary with other facts." Otherwise stated, even under continued discrimination and racial bloc voting, no violation of the Act occurs when minority voters form effective (or ineffective) voting majorities. The Supreme Court held that dilution cannot be inferred by mere failure to guarantee minority voters a maximum political influence.

The Supreme Court emphasized the importance of reviewing the Gingles factors when considering liability under the Voting Rights Act. Under *Thornburg v. Gingles*, 478 U.S. 30, (1986), the U.S. Supreme Court outlined a series of nonexhaustive factors to consider in evaluating alleged violations under the Act. As the Supreme Court noted in *Gingles*, "[T]he most important . . . factors bearing Section 2 challenges to multi-member districts are the 'extent to which minority group members have been elected to public office in the jurisdiction' and the 'extent to which voting in the elections of the state or political subdivision is racially polarized.'"

Referring back to the *Johnson v. De Grandy* case, the Supreme Court arrived at a similar decision: "[T]he District Court's finding of dilution did not address the statutory standard of unequal political and electoral opportunity, and reflected instead a misconstruction of section 2 that equated dilution with failure to maximize the number of reasonably compact majority-minority districts." The Supreme Court reversed the Northern District Court's decision and the remedial plan as presented.

Victor A. Flores

See also: Voting Rights Act of 1975

Further Reading

Bierstein, Andrea. 1994. "Millennium Approaches: The Future of the Voting Rights Act after Shaw, De Grandy, and Holder." *Hastings Law Journal* 46: 1457.

De Grandy v. Wetherell, 815 F.Supp. 1550, 1554 (1992).

Dietz, Matthew W. 1994. "Equal Electoral Opportunity: The Supreme Court Reevaluates the Use of Race in Redistricting in Johnson v. De Grandy." *Journal of Law and Policy* 3: 497.

Guinier, Lani. 1994. "[E]racing Democracy: The Voting Rights Cases." *Harvard Law Review* 108: 109.

Johnson v. De Grandy, 512 U.S. 997 (1994).

Jones Act

(1917)

The Jones Act extended U.S. citizenship to the residents of Puerto Rico and to anyone born on the island after the U.S. invasion of 1898. The Act—signed into law on March 2, 1917, by President Woodrow Wilson—also introduced limited forms of representation. Notably, the Jones Act created an elected bicameral legislative body in Puerto Rico, instituted individual civil rights, and allowed for the election of a resident commissioner as a nonvoting member of the U.S. House of Representatives. Nonetheless, the U.S. government continued to appoint the governor and most public officials, as well as retained veto power over legislative decisions.

After the U.S. invasion of Puerto Rico in the aftermath of the Spanish-American War in 1898, residents of the island were left in a state of political ambiguity—neither citizens nor aliens to the United States. By virtue of the Foraker Act, they were "Citizens of Porto Rico [sic]"—yet they resided in what the U.S. Supreme Court deemed a "non-incorporated territory" (Whalen, 2005). During that period, members of the U.S. Congress introduced dozens of bills to assign American citizenship to Puerto Ricans (Torruella, 2013). However, these efforts were not successful until 1917, when Congress finally passed the Jones Act. Despite dissent from Puerto Rican leaders, the bill effectively eliminated Puerto Rican citizenship and extended U.S. citizenship to the residents of the island.

It should be noted that the passage of the Jones Act did not represent any real interest from the U.S. government to fully incorporate Puerto Rico as a state. Much to the contrary, key figures in the citizenship debate, such as President Taft (and later Chief Justice Taft), were adamant that the move to grant U.S. citizenship was not to be thought of as a pathway to statehood. Instead, the motivation behind the passage of the Jones Act was largely rooted in America's economic and political interests. On the one hand, the geographic location of Puerto Rico was deemed necessary to protect the Panama Canal, which served the economic interests of the nation. And on the other hand, the Jones Act passed in anticipation of U.S. entry into World War I. Citizenship in the island allowed for the extension of the draft to its residents. Indeed, soon after the United States declared war on Germany, Puerto Ricans became eligible for the draft.

Beyond assigning U.S. citizenship to Puerto Ricans, the Jones Act instituted the first form of an elected bicameral legislative body in the territory. That said, the powers of the elected assembly were significantly limited in both scope and independence. Notably, the Jones Act allowed for the governor to hold veto power and for the U.S. Congress to retain its discretion to override and pass legislation pertaining to the island. Moreover, under the Jones Act of 1917, the United States continued to appoint the governor of Puerto Rico, Supreme Court justices, and most government officials. Most of these appointed officials were not Puerto Rican until well into the 1940s. In practice, then, the political and administrative power achieved by the creation of a local legislative assembly was offset by strong supervision from the U.S. federal government.

In the end, the Jones Act of 1917 did not resolve the political uncertainty of Puerto Ricans vis-à-vis Americans in the U.S. mainland. Those who argued in favor of the bill in Congress did so with an understanding that it was in the interest of the United States to retain Puerto Rico as a territory. That said, the Jones Act did have long-lasting effects on Puerto Rican–U.S. migration. Indeed, citizenship afforded Puerto Ricans ease of movement from the island to the mainland. Today—100 years after the passage of the Jones Act—the size of the Puerto Rican diaspora in the 50 states surpasses the number of Puerto Ricans on the island.

Aileen Cardona-Arroyo

See also: Primary Documents: The Preamble and Articles I and II of Constitution of the Commonwealth of Puerto Rico (1952) [in English and Spanish]

Further Reading

Ayala, César J., & Rafael Bernabe. 2009. *Puerto Rico in the American Century: A History since 1898*. Chapel Hill: University of North Carolina Press.

Duany, Jorge. 2017. *Puerto Rico: What Everyone Needs to Know.* New York: Oxford University Press.

Monge, José Trías. 1999. *Puerto Rico: The Trials of the Oldest Colony in the World.* New Haven, CT: Yale University Press.

Torruella, Juan R. 2013. "Ruling America's Colonies: The Insular Cases." *Yale Law and Policy Review* 32: 57.

Whalen, Carmen Teresa. 2005. "Colonialism, Citizenship, and the Making of the Puerto Rican Diaspora: An Introduction." *The Puerto Rican Diaspora: Historical Perspectives*: 1–42.

K

Kumar, María Teresa

(1974–)

María Teresa Kumar is the founding president and CEO of the nonpartisan civic engagement organization Voto Latino. Cofounded with Rosario Dawson in 2004, Voto Latino promotes civic engagement among U.S. Latinos. Kumar has received multiple accolades for her work at Voto Latino. In 2013, *Elle* magazine included her in the list of the top 10 most influential women in Washington, D.C., and *Hispanic Business* named her one of most influential Latinos in America. Kumar was named by *PODER Magazine* among one of the 20 most influential Latinos under 40, by *Hispanic Magazine* as one of the top Latinas in government and politics, and Fast Company named her one of the top 100 creative minds. She is also an Ambassador Swanee Hunt Prime Mover Fellow, a Women's Media Center Fellow, and a Woodrow Wilson Public Policy International Affairs Fellow. She has received various leadership awards from The White House Project, Imagen Foundation, and the New York legislature. In 2017, *Washington Life* magazine named her one of the most influential residents of Washington, D.C.

Kumar launched her career in the late 1990s as a legislative aide for former Democratic Caucus chairman Vic Fazio (D-CA), where she credits her love for U.S. politics by interning in the nation's capital as an undergraduate. Since then she has served as a political strategy consultant for Fortune 500 companies. During the 2008 election cycle, Kumar was not only a regular commentator on MSNBC, but also on CNN, American-morning, and Spanish-language TV channels like Telemundo.

Under her leadership, Voto Latino has registered over 250,000 new voters and reaches out to millions through mass media campaigns, often featuring famous Latino figures. There was a 5 percent increase in Latino turnout in battleground states during the 2008 presidential elections because of her work with the organization. In 2010, Kumar helped create *Beyond Borderlines*, the first televised English-language town hall to focus on the emerging role of Latinos in U.S. society and politics. Kumar believes that Latino issues are American issues, noting in particular the lack of access to education, health care, and economic opportunities. The two-hour special hosted by Kumar on MSNBC earned her an Emmy nomination this year in the Outstanding News Discussion and Analysis category.

Kumar recently cofounded boutique social media strategy firm FastFWD Group and also serves on the national boards of EMILY's List, Planned Parenthood Federation, and the Latino Leaders Network, and is a member of the Council on Foreign Relations. She is also the author of several national media outlet opinion pieces, where she writes about the Trump administration, voter restriction and disenfranchisement, and immigration policies and their consequences for racial

Colombian-born María Teresa Kumar, founding executive director of Voto Latino, speaks during the Voto Latino In Conversation event in Washington, D.C., 2012. (Kris Connor/Getty Images)

profiling for the Latino community, as well as the importance of immigration reform, the role that Latinas play in politics and Latina health, and the significance of the Latino vote.

A frequent guest analyst on NPR and PBS and a coveted public speaker, Kumar has been featured at Harvard Law School, Personal Democracy Forum, NetRoots Nation, Intel, GE, Prudential, and TEDx to speak on issues such as social entrepreneurship and business strategies, technology, and politics. Kumar often credits her Colombian mother and grandmother for inspiring her work.

Kumar was born in Bogotá, Colombia, in 1974 to an American father and a Colombian mother, but grew up in Sonoma, California, and is now based in Washington, D.C. She earned her bachelor's degree in international relations from University of California, Davis and her master's degree in public policy from the Kennedy School of Government at Harvard University. She is married to Raj Kumar and has two children.

Kimberly Cárdenas

See also: Dawson, Rosario (1979–); Ferrera, America (1984–); Voto Latino

Further Reading

Brown, Heath A. 2011. "Immigrants and Electoral Politics: Nonprofit Organizing in a Time of Demographic Change: Innovators and Innovations in the Hemisphere." *Americas Quarterly* 5, no. 4: 30–3.

McGrath, Michael. 2011. "Technology, Media, and Political Participation." *National Civic Review* 100, no. 3: 41–4.

L

La Opinión

A leading Spanish-language daily newspaper, *La Opinión* has been informing the Latino community in Southern California for more than 90 years. According to its founder, Ignacio Eugenio Lozano, Sr., from its very beginning, *La Opinión* sought to "unite two nations: the U.S. and Mexico" while at the same time being a trusted source of information to the Mexican community (Bran, 2016). It has since expanded its coverage to include the larger Latino community, focusing on issues that directly affect them, such as immigration, the economy, health, education, and politics.

La Opinión was founded on September 16, 1926, which happens to coincide with Mexican Independence Day. Its founder, Ignacio E. Lozano, Sr., was born in Marín, Nuevo León, Mexico, in 1886. He was 22 years old when the political instability that eventually led to the Mexican Revolution forced his family to migrate to the United States in 1908. Lozano, Sr., his mother, and five sisters settled in San Antonio, Texas, and in 1913, he founded *La Prensa,* a Spanish-speaking newspaper directed at the Mexican community. Eventually, as the Mexican population of Los Angeles, California, grew, Lozano, Sr., founded *La Opinión* in 1926 and put his son, Ignacio E. Lozano, Jr., in charge while he continued to oversee *La Prensa.* Though *La Opinión* was not the first Spanish-speaking newspaper in Los Angeles, within a year of its first publication, it was able to eliminate all its competitors.

At *La Opinión*'s 88th anniversary, then publisher and chief executive officer Monica Lozano stated that "the mission of *La Opinión* is to inform, educate, and make Hispanics in the United States acquire enough power to take informed decisions that could motivate their lives" (Martínez Ortega, 2009). Furthermore, it has also been instrumental in encouraging its readers to be proud of being Latino, of speaking Spanish, and of being an important part of the American society. As Ignacio E. Lozano, Sr., stated in the first editorial in 1926, "[W]e want to show that our people are educated and civilized people who know how to sustain their newspapers" (Bran, 2016). In 2006, the Lozano family was awarded the Ortega y Gasset Award for their ability to not only create but maintain a means of communication for the Hispanic community in the United States. The Ortega y Gasset Award highlights only the best journalistic works in the Hispanic field (Premios Ortega y Gasset). Similarly, in 2012, according to the paper's website, "*La Opinión* was awarded Gold for Outstanding Spanish Daily by the National Association of Hispanic Publications' 2012 José Martí Publishing Awards."

For more than 90 years, *La Opinión* has been able to cover stories that directly affect the Latino community. These stories include the massive deportations that took place during the Great Depression, the Zoot Suit Riots of 1943, and the many times the Latino community has had to face immigration policies that directly target them. At the same time, *La Opinión* has provided vital immigration information that encourages its readership to apply for permanent residency status, to become U.S. citizens, to register to vote, and to vote on Election Day.

La Opinión had been a family-owned business up until 1990, when Times Mirror Company purchased a 50 percent stake in the newspaper. Times Mirror Company was later purchased by Tribune Company in 2000, and in 2004 with the help of CPK Media, the Lozano family was able to regain full control of the newspaper. That same year, *La Opinión* joined forces with CPK Media to create ImpreMedia LLC, the first national company of Spanish-language newspapers in the United States.

According to ImpreMedia, *La Opinión* has 2 million readers every month (online and in print), continuing to be the leading daily Spanish-language newspaper in the country and the second most-read newspaper in Los Angeles (with the *Los Angeles Times* being number one). Although based out of Los Angeles, *La Opinión* is sold in six Southern California counties, Monday through Sunday, and is accessible online for readers all around the country and the world. *La Opinión* is currently headed by Gabriel Lerner (publishing editor) and Javier Casas (CEO).

Yanira Rivas Pineda de Melendez

See also: *El Nuevo Herald*; *La Voz de Houston*; Zoot Suit Riots (1943)

Further Reading

Bran, Josue. 2016. "La Opinión, un diario joven de 90 años de edad: La primera edición de La Opinión fue publicada el 16 de septiembre de 1926." https://laopinion.com /2016/09/19/la-opinion-un-diario-joven-de-90-anos-de-edad.

Goldman, Abigail, & José Cardenas. 2004. "Spanish-Language Newspapers La Opinion, El Diario to Merge." http://articles.latimes.com/2004/jan/16/business/fi -opinion16.

La Opinión Online. n.d. https://laopinion.com.

La Opinión Website. n.d. http://www.impremedia.com/#brands.

Lopez, J. Gerardo. 2006. "El legado de La Opinión: una gran institución de la comunidad latina en EEUU." https://laopinion.com/2016/11/04/el-legado-de-la-opinion-una -gran-institucion-de-la-comunidad-latina-en-eeuu.

Martínez Ortega, Elsa Araceli. 2009. "La corresponsalía del periódico *La Opinion* en Sacramento, California (2002–2007)." Bachelor's thesis. Universidad Nacional Autónoma De Mexico. http://premiosortegaygasset.com/ediciones-anteriores.html#.

"Times Mirror Buys 50% of La Opinión." 1990. *Los Angeles Times*, August 30. http:// articles.latimes.com/1990-08-30/news/ti-681_1_la-opinion.

La Raza Unida Party (LRU)

La Raza Unida (LRU) was a political party centered on Chicano (Mexican American) nationalism; it started in 1970 as a regional political movement in Texas where Chicanxs had historically faced electoral disenfranchisement. The party was primarily organized by MAYO (Mexican American Youth Organization) members. It went statewide in 1971 and began developing a party structure and platform, which included radical stances on race, gender, and class reflecting the sociopolitical dynamics of the times. LRU would eventually launch political campaigns across Texas and then nationally after the 1972 national convention in El Paso. However, factionalism inhibited the party's growth and the movement lost steam in the 1980s. Currently, there are a handful of local chapters of LRU across the Southwest, including a branch in Albuquerque, New Mexico, still active in local politics.

La Raza Unida Party was founded in 1970 by prominent Chicanx organizers, including José Ángel Gutiérrez and Mario Compean, who were also founders of MAYO. The founding of LRU occurred during a mass gathering of over 300 Mexican American activists and community members in Crystal City, Texas. The Chicanx organizers viewed LRU as a party that could take on issues of social, economic, and political inequality among Chicanxs in Texas, with a specific focus on addressing the disenfranchisement felt with the Democratic Party. Its initial members also included journalist Bidel Aguero, who headed the youth organization in Lubbock.

The party had initial success in Texas, winning prominent political offices across the state. Alfredo Zamora, Jr., for example, was the first Chicano mayor of Cotulla, Texas. Following Zamora, Arcenio A. Garcia then became the youngest mayor to be elected in Texas at age 24. These two LRU candidates became the first Chicanos elected as mayors in LaSalle County history. Following these victories, the party spread across the Southwest and into Colorado, where dissatisfaction with the Democratic Party also created political tensions among the Mexican American communities. In Colorado, the LRU worked closely with Rodolfo "Corky" Gonzales and the Crusade for Justice. In California, dozens of chapters were formed, especially in Los Angeles County and the southern part of the state.

LRU differed from the dominant political parties in that its platform directly sought to embrace cultural values and ethnic ties of Mexican Americans, its primary constituency. Additionally, LRU and its leadership were explicit in naming racism and capitalism as direct sources of oppression against people of color in the United States. An important part of LRU's platform was to highlight the socioeconomic and political inequalities experienced between Mexican Americans and whites. LRU also put special emphasis on the education of Mexican American youth by championing bilingual and culturally relevant education and holding school board positions in primarily Mexican American school districts.

Another key facet of the LRU to note was the role women played in the organization. Women were not only involved in day-to-day administrative roles, they were central organizers and part of the political leadership. One of their most notable women organizers was María Elena Martinez, a bilingual educator in the state of Texas and the last chair of the LRU in Texas from 1974 to 1976. LRU also launched multiple female candidates, including Alma Canales, who ran for lieutenant governor of Texas in 1972.

By 1975, LRU's national influence began to decline due to internal conflicts, outside pressures from the U.S. political system, and controversies played out in the media. LRU's split with more leftist contingencies of the Chicano Movement lost them the ability to cater to different sections of the community, particularly those with lower economic status, from which they drew a lot of their support in the past. Although LRU continued to be active in local Texas politics, the final blow to the party came in 1978 during the gubernatorial race. Much of the support from the Mexican American community went to the Democratic Party, leaving the LRU with insufficient political and economic support to challenge the two-party system.

Melina Juárez and Moises Santos

See also: Crusade for Justice; Gonzales, Rodolfo "Corky" (1928–2005); Mexican American Youth Organization (MAYO)

Further Reading

Espinoza, Dionne. 2011. "'The Partido Belongs to Those Who Will Work for It': Chicana Organizing and Leadership in the Texas Raza Unida Party, 1970–1980." *Aztlan: A Journal of Chicano Studies* 36, no. 1: 191–210.

Garciá, Ignacio M. 1989. *United We Win: The Rise and Fall of La Raza Unida Party.* Tucson: University of Arizona Press.

Gutiérrez, José Angel. 1998. *The Making of a Chicano Militant: Lessons from Cristal.* Madison: University of Wisconsin Press.

Navarro, Armando. 2000. *La Raza Unida Party: A Chicano Challenge to the U.S. Two-Party Dictatorship.* Philadelphia: Temple University Press.

La Voz de Houston

Established in 1979, *La Voz de Houston* is a Spanish-language newspaper in the Houston-metro area. Having begun in a small home by two Cuban immigrants in the late 1970s, *La Voz* expanded even during a downturn among the newspaper industry, bringing their growing Hispanic audience important local, state, national, and international news. With a weekly circulation of over 400,000, *La Voz* is published two times a week as a complement to its flagship, the *Houston Chronicle*, providing enterprising stories on compelling issues to the Latino community, exclusive sports and entertainment content, plus in-depth series and opinions.

Owned by the *Houston Chronicle*, the second largest daily newspaper in Texas, since 2004, *La Voz* began in 1979 as a self-published weekly founded by two Cuban refugees, Armando and Olga Ordóñez. Armando, a chemical engineer, had owned a soup company in Havana before he and his wife Olga fled the Castro regime in 1962. The couple moved to Texas, where Armando worked as a chemical engineer before later becoming a general manager at La Tremenda, a Spanish radio station in Houston. Armando had always wanted to publish a newspaper for the Hispanic community, so the couple started the publication in a small house they used as an office in the late 1970s, with the help of their children, Carlos and Laura. When Armando died five years later in 1984, Olga took over, ultimately expanding the staff to 14 and the newspaper's circulation to 100,000 over the next 20 years.

Although their English-language counterparts hit their circulation peaks in the early 1990s, Spanish-language newspapers continued to experience growth and often increased their circulation. This was certainly true for *La Voz* as it added a Wednesday delivery in November 2012, moving publication to twice weekly and quadrupling circulation to more than 400,000—reflecting a commitment from the *Chronicle* to expand its Hispanic-oriented publications.

"*La Voz* is Houston's most-read Spanish-language newspaper and the only one delivering local, national and international news twice a week," said *La Voz de Houston*'s publisher, Alejandro "Alex" Sanchez in 2012 after the increase in publication days. "Our Wednesday and weekend issues each reach 165,000 hand-selected Spanish-speaking households, with an additional 75,000 copies of the weekender distributed within targeted retail outlets in high-traffic areas" (Britton, 2012).

Despite the growing Latino population in Texas, the downturn in the newspaper industry overall eventually took its toll on Spanish-language newspapers as well. It caught up to *La Voz* in April 2016 when *Chronicle* announced layoffs of four *La Voz* reporters. *La Voz* also cut down on original content and moved to primarily translating *Chronicle* stories.

Today *La Voz* remains a primary source of news and information for Houston's large Hispanic community—which equals just over 40 percent of the city's total population. With a regularly updated digital version in addition to its twice-weekly printing, *La Voz* is also active on Facebook as La Voz de Houston.

Among a growing number of Spanish-language newspapers, *La Voz* has maintained a strong editorial reputation—often earning recognition at the Texas Associated Press Managing Editors annual awards competition. *La Voz* reporter Jorge Luis Sierra won two first-place awards for News and Features in 2009, and Héctor Pina won the first-place award for opinion writing in 2010. Germán Fernández Moores won a sports writing award in the Spanish-language division in 2016.

Laurie Lattimore-Volkmann

See also: El Nuevo Herald; La Opinión

Further Reading

Agility PR Solutions. 2016. "Top 10 Texas Daily Newspapers by Circulation." https://www .agilitypr.com/resources/top-media-outlets/top-10-texas-daily-newspapers -circulation.

Britton, Nicki. 2012. "La Voz de Houston Adds Wednesday Edition, Quadruples Circulation." *Houston Chronicle*, November 14. https://www.prnewswire.com/news -releases/la-voz-de-houston-adds-wednesday-edition-quadruples-circulation -179340961.html.

Moreno, Jenalia. 2004. "*Chronicle* Adds La Voz to Its Family." *Houston Chronicle*, December 2. http://www.chron.com/business/article/Chronicle-adds-La-Voz-to-its-family -1512934.php.

"Newspaper Circulation Increases? Yep, in Hispanic Markets." 2013. *Portada Online*, May 13. https://www.portada-online.com/2013/05/13/newspaper-circulation -increases-yes-in-the-hispanic-market.

"Race and Ethnicity in Texas (City)." *Statistical Atlas*. https://statisticalatlas.com/place /Texas/Houston/Race-and-Ethnicity.

Texas Associated Press Managing Editors Awards. n.d. http://www.txapme.com/awards.

Villafañe, Veronica. 2016. "Chronicle Lays Off 4 in *La Voz de Houston* Downsizing." *Media Moves*, April 15. https://www.mediamoves.com/2016/04/chronicle-lays-off-4-in-la -voz-de-houston-downsizing.html.

Larrazolo, Octaviano A.

(1859–1930)

Octaviano Larrazolo served as the second Hispanic governor of New Mexico from 1919 to 1921 and as the first Mexican American to serve in the U.S. Senate, sitting for New Mexico from 1928 to 1929. As governor, Larrazolo successfully championed the women's suffrage movement in New Mexico. Known as the "Silver Tongued

Octaviano Larrazolo was a Republican politician who served as the fourth governor of New Mexico in 1918. He later became the first Mexican American U.S. senator (1928–1929). (Library of Congress)

Orator," Larrazolo also worked to secure civil rights for Hispanics at the New Mexico Constitution Convention of 1910. In addition, Larrazolo was a successful entrepreneur (he started several Spanish-language newspapers) in Las Vegas, New Mexico.

Octaviano Larrazolo was born on December 7, 1859, in Allende in the state of Chihuahua, Mexico. In 1870 his parents sent the young Larrazolo to Tucson, Arizona, to study under Bishop Salpointe, in hopes that he would join the priesthood. In 1875, Salpointe and Larrazolo moved to Santa Fe, New Mexico, where Larrazolo enrolled at St. Michael's College. After completing his education, Larrazolo became a teacher in Tucson, Arizona. In 1878, Larrazolo moved to El Paso County, Texas, where he served as an elementary school principal until 1884.

In 1885 Larrazolo was appointed chief deputy of the district and county clerk of El Paso County. Simultaneously, he was also a clerk of the U.S. District and Circuit Courts in El Paso. In 1888 he was admitted into the Texas bar; two years later Larrazolo was elected district attorney for the 34th Judicial District in El Paso.

In 1895, Larrazolo moved to Las Vegas, New Mexico, where he opened a law firm. Between 1900 and 1908, Larrazolo ran three times as the Democratic Party candidate for territorial delegate to the U.S. House of Representatives, but each time he was defeated in the heavily Republican Party state. At the 1911 state Democratic Party Convention, Larrazolo requested that half of the statewide nominees be Hispanic to reflect their statewide census majority. The Anglo-majority delegates from the Democratic Party Convention denied Larrazolo's plea. Larrazolo resigned from the Democratic Party immediately.

Larrazolo was embraced by the predominately Hispanic majority in the Republican Party. As a Republican advisor, he played a critical role in the 1910 state constitution convention. Arguably one of his greatest political accomplishments, Larrazolo crafted language in the Education and Elective Franchise Articles guaranteeing Hispanics civil rights protections.

In 1918, Larrazolo was elected governor of New Mexico. During Larrazolo's first legislative term, he successfully passed a law restricting child labor and a compulsory education bill that included bilingual education. At the Western States governors' conference in 1919, Larrazolo was nominated president. Under his leadership, Larrazolo and the other participating governors developed the League of Public Lands, which ceded all surveyed public lands without minerals to the states.

With the support of Nina Otero Warren, during his final year as governor, Larrazolo led the successful final push for women's suffrage. Under his governorship, Otero Warren was appointed to the state health board. Larrazolo also mentored other female Hispanic politicians, such as Soledad Chacon, who became the first Hispanic woman to win a statewide election when she was elected as New Mexico's secretary of state in 1922. Larrazolo then went on to serve in the New Mexico House of Representatives from 1927 to 1928. At the 1928 Republican Party Convention, Larrazolo was nominated to fill the vacant U.S. Senate seat after the death of Senator A. A. Jones. In 1929, Larrazolo, who had fallen ill, served during the U.S. Senate session. One year later, on April 7, 1930, he passed away at his home in Albuquerque, New Mexico.

Steve Martinez

See also: Richardson, William "Bill" (1947–)

Further Reading

Chavez, John. 1984. *The Lost Land: The Chicano Image of the Southwest.* Albuquerque: University of New Mexico Press.
Gonzales, Phillip B. 2001. *Forced Sacrifice as Ethnic Protest: The Hispano Cause in New Mexico & the Racial Attitude Confrontation of 1933.* New York: Peter Lang Press.

Latin Builders Association (LBA)

Founded in 1971 and based in Miami, Florida, the Latin Builders Association (LBA) is the largest Hispanic construction association in the United States. It is a nonprofit association that represents the interests of builders, developers, contractors, architects, engineers, lawyers, electricians, real estate agents, tradesmen, and others in construction and development industries. The LBA has over 650 member companies representing south Florida's construction industry and most of the area's related business concerns. During the 1980s through the early 2000s, the LBA, a largely Cuban American organization, became one of the most politically influential business groups in Miami.

As Cuban exiles and Cuban Americans gained economic momentum in the Miami-Dade area, they established businesses and civic organizations to build political influence. The LBA was one of these organizations, and by 1990, it was a major player in south Florida business and politics. For example, the association was able to get the Dade County Commission to extend urban boundaries into previously reserved areas in the county—despite significant opposition by environmentalists. The LBA worked with city and county mayors in the region on development projects such as airport improvements, downtown redevelopment, and transportation. LBA board members and leaders have historically had close ties with south Florida's Republican Party that has elected officials such as Marco Rubio, the Diaz-Balart brothers, and Ileana Ros-Lehtinen.

In October 2016, LBA endorsed Hillary Clinton. This is the first time the conservative-leaning, largely Cuban American organization backed a Democrat for president. LBA president Alex Lastra said, "Throughout its 40-year history, the LBA has consistently endorsed candidates who have conservative principles, a pro-business mindset, believe in limited government regulation, and possess strong business ethics and family values that have closely aligned with ours. . . . In the past, these candidates have tended to be from the Republican Party."

Failing to win the LBA's endorsement represented a double political rejection for Donald Trump—a rejection from conservatives and from builders. The rejection also signaled a trend of less solid support for Republican candidates by Cuban American voters. The LBA's stance was also seen as a nod to Jeb Bush and Marco Rubio, who were Trump rivals—especially Rubio, a former LBA director. This also occurred in the context of the LBA breaking ties with Trump's business established just a year earlier. In 2015, the LBA left Trump's National Doral golf resort as the venue for its biennial gala, citing Trump's "recent pattern of bigoted, sexist and ignorant verbal assaults on immigrants, women and veterans."

Jessica L. Lavariega Monforti

See also: Díaz-Balart, Lincoln (1954–); Diaz-Balart, Mario (1961–); Ros-Lehtinen, Ileana (1952–); Rubio, Marco (1971–); Trump, Donald J. (1946–) and Latinos

Further Reading
Grenier, Guillermo J., & Max J. Castro. 1999. "Triadic Politics: Ethnicity, Race, and Politics in Miami, 1959–1998." *Pacific Historical Review* 68, no. 2: 273–92.

Lavariega Monforti, Jessica, Juan Carlos Flores, & Dario Moreno. 2013. "Manny Diaz and the Rise and Fall of the Miami Renaissance." In Sharon A. Navarro and Rodolfo Rosales, eds. *The Roots of Latino Urban Agency.* Denton: University of North Texas Press, pp. 81–96.

Portes, Alejandro. 1987. "The Social Origins of the Cuban Enclave Economy of Miami." *Sociological Perspectives* 30, no. 4: 340–72.

Latina Political Leadership in the South

In the United States, Hispanics, at 54 million, comprise the nation's largest ethnic minority. In 2015, Latinas were one in five women in our country and by 2060 will encompass almost one-third of the United States' female population. Between the 2000 and 2012 U.S. presidential elections, Latina voters increased from 5.5 percent to 8.3 percent. However, nearly 6 million eligible Latinas did not cast a ballot in the election. Although the Latino vote in 2016 was between 13 and 14 million, as a political force, Latinas have not realized their full political participation potential. However, the number of Latina elected officials increased by 47 percent between 2004 and 2014. Increased Latina representation in voting and in holding elected office could help support more Latina-friendly government policies (Gándara, 2015).

THE LATINA PIPELINE

According to the government study, "Fulfilling America's Future: Latinas in the U.S. 2015," women encompass one-third of all lawyers in the United States. However, Latinas are critically underrepresented at 6.7 percent of female lawyers. Between 2004 and 2014, Hispanic women increased their participation by about only one-third. This is a serious problem considering that the law is a venue into politics. Increasing the number of Latinas graduating from law schools and teaching at the higher education level could raise the number of Latinas in politics and serving at every level of government. In 2015, the National Hispanic Caucus of State Legislators launched the Latinas Lead Initiative to help accomplish this goal (Pérez-Litwin, 2012).

At the present time, Latinas are making progress, and this essay will highlight only a few of the growing number of successful and rising Latina leaders in the South. A sampling of Latina participation at the state, local, and federal level will be addressed, as well as community activity.

SOUTHERN LATINA ELECTIVE REPRESENTATION

The best place to start is at the state elective office level with Georgia state representative Brenda López Romero. Representative López Romero (D-99th) is a new and dynamic young female leader from the Atlanta metropolitan area. She has lived in Norcross in Gwinnett County, Georgia, for over 10 years and is principal attorney at the López Firm, LLC, that handles removal and family-based immigration cases. As a Georgia representative, she serves on the following committees: Education, Retirement, and State Planning and Community Affairs. She has served as vice-chair of the Latino Caucus for the Democratic Party of Georgia and was legal advisor to the Southwest Voter Registration Education Project for Cobb/Fulton Steering Committee. In 2014–2015, López Romero was treasurer of the Latino Caucus of the Democratic Party of Georgia. In the 2016 Democratic primary election, she beat a long-time party activist who was well supported. She saw her victory as a natural progression of her advocacy work. Her election signals the growing political strength of Georgia's booming minority population.

LATINA APPOINTIVE POSITION

The next display of outstanding Latina leadership is Rocio Del Milagro Woody, who was appointed to the Commission for the Board of Correction by Georgia governor Nathan Deal in 2013. Woody also serves on the executive board of the Georgia Association of Latino Elected Officials and on the board of the directors of the International Family Center. In 2012, she was appointed to the Georgia Supreme Court Unlicensed Practice of Law Standing Committee. She is founder and president of the Peruvian American Business Chamber and past president of the League of Women Voters of DeKalb County, Georgia. Woody was granted the 2015 National Association of Social Workers Distinguished Practice Award and the 2014 Georgia Latina of Excellence Award. She is the founder and president of The Road to

Recovery, Inc., based in Atlanta. To date, The Road to Recovery, Inc., is the only private Latina-owned clinical practice recipient of local, state, and federal contracts to provide behavioral health programs in Georgia. She feels like her most important contribution to the Latino community is serving as a female role model. For her, it is important to give back to the community in the form of advocacy to aid the immigrant's struggle. As the first Latina appointed to the Georgia Board of Corrections, she believes the selection represents a better understanding and approval of Latino immigrants, of women, and of their contributions.

U.S. EXECUTIVE BRANCH REPRESENTATION

Latina Miryam Gerdine, a native of Lancaster, Pennsylvania, recently celebrated 20 years working for the U.S. Department of Health and Human Services and was elected as the first president of the Health Resources and Services Administration's (HRSA) Hispanic Employee Resource Group. She volunteered for 12 year for the Proyecto Salud, an innovative public/private partnership seeking to improve the health status of the language-minority community in Montgomery County, Maryland. In 1996, Gerdine was the Congressional Hispanic Caucus Institute (CHCI) Edward Roybal Public Health Fellow, which opened the doors to her career in public service at the U.S. Department of Health and Human Services. Her first project was working on the Healthy People 2000 Progress review on Hispanic Americans. She was a legislative analyst in the HRSA, Office of Legislation, working on the health workforce portfolio. Gerdine has been enthusiastically engaged in the HRSA Mentoring Now program since its inception in 2012. In 2014, the Bethesda chapter of the Association for Women in Science awarded her with the Excellence in Mentoring Award. Miryam Gerdine is an example of Latina leadership within the executive branch of government and in her community at large.

NOT-FOR-PROFIT HEALTH SECTOR

Cheryl Aguilar is a licensed clinical social worker who has worked with the immigrant and Latino community in the District of Columbia metro area since 2006. In February 2017, Aguilar launched The Hope Center for Wellness, a behavioral health private practice, and serves as director and lead therapist. At La Clinica del Pueblo, she was the organization's first tele-mental health therapist to expand mental health access to Latinos through video. She has designed and implemented several culturally sensitive groups to work with the immigrant population and is a sought-after national speaker and trainer on culturally competent work with Latinos and immigrants. Before embarking in the social work profession, she worked in journalism and public relations for over a decade. From 2011 to 2014, Aguilar led communications efforts for national and local nonprofits, businesses, and individuals through her consultancy firm, Aguilar Communications. In her communications career, she was one of the leading media communicators engaging ethnic media nationwide on immigration, women empowerment, youth, and issues affecting low-income people.

HUMAN AND CIVIL RIGHTS SECTOR

Adelina Nicholls is the executive director of the Georgia Latino Alliance for Human Rights and a leader in grassroots organizing in the state. Since 2001, Nicholls has played a key role in organizing protests, workshops, and campaigns to support immigration reform and to end discriminatory practices and profiling for our community. She received the MALDEF Award for Community Service (2001), the ACLU Georgia Civil and Human Rights Award (2008), and *Mundo Hispánico*'s Best Organization of the Year 2013.

LAW AND JUSTICE SECTOR

Ana Maria Martinez is a staff attorney for Judge Dax Lopez and is the founder and director of the Georgia Latino Law Foundation. This is a nonprofit dedicated to increasing diversity in the legal profession by supporting the Latino legal community pipeline. Martinez identifies and matches students with mentors and provides educational and leadership programs for upcoming community leaders. In 2012, she received the Award of Achievement for Outstanding Service to the Public from the Young Lawyers Division of the State Bar of Georgia. She serves on the Atlanta Regional Commission's Millennial Advisory Committee and is a Lead Atlanta graduate.

Helen Hamilton Rivas, a Latina by heart, soul, and marriage, is the director of the Alabama Coalition for Immigrant Justice United. Rivas has dedicated her life to working to improve the lives of Alabama's immigrant community. She says that she grew up learning to prize fairness and justice and this inspired her participation in civic and political advocacy. For decades, Rivas has fought for social justice and equal treatment for all, but admits that Alabama has been less than welcoming to undocumented immigrants. She crosses social, ethnic, and faith lines as a founding member of Latinos Unidos de Alabama and is an at-large board member of the Birmingham Metro Diversity Coalition. However, most of her time is spent working as a member of the steering committee of the Alabama Coalition for Immigrant Justice, ensuring that immigrants and their families find the help they need.

Linda K. Mancillas

See also: Latinas in U.S. Politics

Further Reading

Bejarano, Christina E. 2013. *The Latina Advantage: Gender, Race, and Political Success.* Austin: University of Texas Press.

Gándara, Patricia. 2015. "Preface: Alejandra Ceja Executive Director White House Initiative on Educational Excellence for Hispanics." *Fulfilling American's Future: Latinas in the U.S.* https://sites.ed.gov/hispanic-initiative/files/2015/09/iFulfilling-Americas-Future-Latinas-in-the-U.S.-2015-Final-Report.pdf.

García, Sonia R., Valerie Martinez-Ebers, Irasema Coronado, Sharon A. Navarro, & Patricia A. Jaramillo. 2008. *Políticas: Latina Public Officials in Texas.* Austin: University of Texas Press.

Odem, Mary E., & Elaine Lacy, eds. 2009. *Latino Immigrants and the Transformation of the U.S. South.* Athens: University of Georgia Press.

Pedraza, Gilda (Gigi). 2017. "Women's History Month: Latinas in Georgia." *Latino Connection Georgia*, March. https://latinoconnectionga.com/2017/03/02/womens -history-month-latinas-in-georgia/amp.

Pérez-Litwin, Angélica. 2012. "The Need for an Innovative Approach to Latina Leadership Training." *Huffington Post*, September 29. http://www.huffingtonpost.com /angelica-perezlitwin-phd/the-need-for-an-innovativ_b_1715215.html.

Rivas, Helen. 2012. "Fighting the Anti-Immigrant Backlash in Alabama." *Americas Quarterly* (Spring). http://www.americasquarterly.org/helen-rivas. Personal email exchange. January 24, 2017.

Latina/o Gender Gap

The term "gender gap" refers to gendered patterns in political behavior or, more specifically, to how women's and men's behavior has or might differ. Although it is used most frequently in reference to partisan voting, "gender gaps" also emerge in voting turnout and in public opinion. Gender gaps related to women's higher level of turnout combined with a slight proclivity toward supporting Democratic candidates have garnered much attention for their potential impact on elections. As Latinos have increased their share of the voting-eligible population, so, too, has attention to the potential "racial gaps" in their political behavior increased. Although voter turnout among the Latino community remains much lower than for white and African American voters, the partisan gap is much more substantial than the gender gap. Earlier research consistently found the racial and ethnic political gaps were more distinct than the gender gap. Increased attention has been given to racial patterns of political behavior, but less is given to how gender and race intersect. Paying attention to the gender gap in the context of the U.S. Latino population allows us to examine the ways that gender and race (along with other relevant dimensions of identity and experience) intersect. This gives us a more complete account of Latino voting behavior and the significance for U.S. politics. It also provides important insights into the oversimplified account of the "gender gap."

Since 1980, women have consistently had higher voter turnout rates than their male counterparts. This contemporary gender gap in voter turnout has grown. Table 1 shows the U.S. Census data for the 2012 and 2016 elections. In both elections, women participated at a 4 percent higher rate than men. The racial gap in voting has generally shown white voters participating at significantly higher rates than any other group. The one exception to this was in the 2012 election, when 66.2 percent of black voters turned out compared to 64.1 percent of white voters. Latinos, as well as Asian American voters, have participated at much lower and less consistent rates than white and black voters. In both elections, only about 48 percent of Latinos voted. The gender gap in voter turnout is consistent across racial-ethnic groups, with the exception of Asian Americans in 2016 (which was close enough to be within the margin of error). The gap between Latino voters in 2012 was 3.8, and in 2016 it increased to 5. This was higher than the turnout gender gap between white and Asian voters but lower than that among black voters.

Getting more attention than voter turnout is the contemporary or "modern gender gap" in partisan voting. Whereas in the past women as a whole tended to vote

Table 1 Voter Turnout Rates, 2012 and 2016

	2012			2016		
	All	**Men**	**Women**	**All**	**Men**	**Women**
All	61.8	59.7	63.7	61.4	59.3	63.3
White	64.1	62.6	65.6	65.3	63.7	66.8
Black	66.2	61.4	70.1	59.4	54.2	63.7
Latino	48.0	46.0	49.8	47.6	45.0	50.0
Asian	47.3	46.0	48.5	49.0	49.7	48.4

Source: U.S. Census Bureau, https://www.census.gov/topics/public-sector/voting/data/tables.2012.html.

more conservatively, in the last several decades, U.S. women tend to favor Democratic Party candidates at rates slightly higher than men. These "gender gaps" vary from election to election, and the size or potential size of the partisan gender gap receives much attention and speculation. In 2012, 55 percent of women voted for Democratic nominee Barack Obama, as compared to 45 percent of men. In 2016, the gap increased from 10 to 13 percentage points in favor of Democratic nominee Hillary Clinton. In regard to racial trends in partisan voting, the gap has tended to be much more substantial than the gender gap. The largest and most publicized racial partisan voting gap is between white voters, who tend to vote more strongly in favor of Republican candidates, and black voters, who vote almost predominantly for Democratic candidates. Latino voters (as well as Asian American voters), however, have also shown a strong preference in favor of Democratic candidates. Although the gap is not as large as between white and black voters, it is still substantial. Table 2 shows the CNN exit polls for 2012 and 2016. In 2012, 39 percent of white voters voted for Obama, as compared to 93 percent of black voters and 71 percent of Latino voters.

When gender and race are looked at simultaneously, the stories of both the "gender gap" and the "racial gap" are altered. Although the gender gap in partisan voting holds across all three racial/ethnic groups, white women are more likely to support the Republican candidate. Although this received much attention in the 2016 election, it is a pattern that holds up for several decades with few exceptions. The size of the gender gap in partisan voting does, however, vary between the racial-ethnic groups. In 2012, Latino voters had the highest gender gap in partisan voting, at 11 percentage points, followed by black voters with a 9-point gap, and white voters with a 7-point gap. In 2016, black and white voters had the highest gender gaps, both with a 12-percentage point gap, whereas Latino voters had a 6-point gap. It is important, however, to note that there has been much debate about the quality of these exit polls, particularly in regard to their capture of Latino voting patterns. The exit polls run by Latino Decisions, which report a significantly higher sample size and more sophisticated sampling techniques to capture the complicated "Latino vote," reported that 79 percent of Latino voters voted for Democratic candidate Hillary Clinton. According to these polls, 86 percent of Latinas voted for Clinton as

Table 2 Support for Democratic Candidates, 2012 and 2016

	2012			2016		
	All	**Men**	**Women**	**All**	**Men**	**Women**
All	51	45	55	48.5	41	54
White	39	35	42	37	31	43
Black	93	87	96	89	82	94
Latino	71	65	76	66	63	69

Source: CNN Exit Polls, http://www.cnn.com/election.

opposed to 71 percent of Latino males, for a 15-point gap, higher than what CNN reports for any group.

Latinos are a diverse population, and therefore the gender gap also varies across a variety of factors, including national origin and generational status. Studies have shown that as Latinas acculturate, they are more likely than their male counterparts to develop strong partisan identities (Bejarano, 2014). Paired with their higher levels of political participation, it is increasingly important for political parties and party candidates to pay attention to Latinas as a part of their electoral strategy. This was something acknowledged and incorporated by Democratic presidential candidate Hillary Clinton in 2016.

Gender gaps in public opinion are also a contemporary phenomenon in U.S. politics. Since the 1980s, women have tended to hold more liberal policy positions than men on a variety of issues. This has included attitudes on public goods (i.e., education, social welfare spending, etc.) that might be attributed to traditional "feminine" roles within the family as well as "feminist" attitudes on gender equality. Studies on racial identity and public opinion often focus on the issues that different groups prioritize as well as their respective opinions.

Latinos have consistently listed several key issues as the most important facing their community: immigration, employment, education, and the economy (not necessarily in that order). Latinos generally support more liberal policy views, with Latinas generally more liberal than Latino men. The gender gap is evident across a variety of policy areas, including gender-related issues, reach of government policies (such as government income support), health care policies (such as retaining the Affordable Care Act), and immigration-related policies (such as disapproval of workplace raids). As a result of Latinas' increased support of more liberal public policies, they may also be more likely than Latino males to support the Democratic Party and their candidates.

Overall, Latinas exhibit significant gender differences in their political attitudes and behaviors, attracting more authority and voting power to influence American politics. Latinas also demonstrate distinctive political attitudes compared to their male counterparts, which has helped them become the central agents of Latino political participation. It is expected that this political gender gap among Latinos will only widen in future elections, which will bring Latinas increased political attention and power.

Christina E. Bejarano and Celeste Montoya

See also: Election of 2016 and Latinos; Latina Political Leadership in the South; *Essays:* Latino Mobilization and Voter Turnout: An Overview of Experimental Studies

Further Reading

Bejarano, Christina. 2014. *The Latino Gender Gap in U.S. Politics.* New York: Routledge Press.

Bejarano, Christina, Sylvia Manzano, & Celeste Montoya. 2011. "Tracking the Latino Gender Gap: Gender Attitudes across Sex, Borders, and Generations." *Politics & Gender* 7, no. 4: 521–49.

García Bedolla, Lisa, Jessica Lavariega Monforti, & Adrian D. Pantoja. 2007. "A Second Look: Is There a Latina/o Gender Gap?" *Journal of Women, Politics & Policy* 28, nos. 3–4: 147–71.

Montoya, Lisa J. 1996. "Latino Gender Differences in Public Opinion: Results from the Latino National Political Survey." *Hispanic Journal of Behavioral Sciences* 18, no. 2: 255–76.

Montoya, Lisa J., Carol Hardy-Fanta, & Sonia Garcia. 2000. "Latina Politics: Gender, Participation, and Leadership." *PS: Political Science & Politics* 33, no. 3: 555–62.

Navarro, Sharon A., Samantha L. Hernandez, & Leslie A. Navarro, eds. 2016. *Latinas in American Politics: Changing and Embracing Political Tradition*. Lanham, MD: Rowman and Littlefield.

Latina/o Identity Politics

At first glance, Latina/o identity seems like a straightforward and easily identifiable concept; on closer analysis, however, the very idea is a complex and contested one. A term whose meaning and content are perceptible yet always subject to debate, Latina/o identity can never be reduced to a single definition or strict set of attributes. Instead, it is characterized by diversity and multiplicity. Politically, this means Latina/o identity is ideologically ambiguous. One can claim a strong Latina/o identity while also being a far-right conservative or a militant leftist. In this way, Latina/o political identity can be understood as having multifarious political possibilities, capable of being invoked either to consolidate forms of corporate power or to support progressive movements for social justice.

Identities are based on the presumption that members of particular groups share a specific affinity based on similar experiences, social location, language, and/or shared ways of living. For Latina/os, then, we might understand identity to presume that the various Latin American national-origin groups share a sense of collective identity and cultural consciousness. We might assume that to identify as Latina/o implies being part of a political community with shared interests and a common policy agenda.

These assumptions, however, become complicated by the fact that *Latina/o* is an umbrella term used to refer to the diverse group of individuals living in the United States who trace their ancestry to the Spanish-speaking regions of Latin America and the Caribbean. Latina/os hail from Colombia, Mexico, Paraguay, Puerto Rico, and beyond—more than 20 countries in all. In other words, rather than distinguishing between members of specific and distinct ethnic subgroups (Mexicans, Cubans, Puerto Ricans, Dominicans, etc.), journalists, politicians, advertising executives, academics, and other influential elites generally prefer the descriptor *Latino*. At times, *Hispanic* is used interchangeably with *Latina/o*, and many, including U.S. government agencies, define Hispanic broadly to include people of Spanish or Portuguese heritage as well as those of Latin American descent. In recent years, the term *Latinx* has also gained popularity, since it avoids the problem of choosing a feminine or masculine gender (such as Latina/o) and is a more gender-inclusive term. However, because it remains the most common term used to designate these populations, this essay will use *Latina/o* when talking about Latina/o identity.

The term Latina/o has entered the United States' mainstream terminology and is routinely used to refer to a demographic group, a voting bloc, a market, a language, a cultural group, and a community. From Spanish-language television, to presidential speeches, to references in the mass media, *Latina/o* has become the term most commonly used to denote the United States' largest minority group.

In point of fact, however, many of the individuals grouped under the rubric may not even accept the idea that they have a common "Latina/o" identity with those who share this designation. This is partly due to demographic factors: while Latina/o communities are growing in size across the United States, there continues to be a great deal of regional concentration among the four largest national-origin groups, with Mexicans concentrated in the West and Southwest, Cubans in Florida, and Puerto Ricans and Dominicans in the Midwest and Northeast. Many Latinas/os in the United States have minimal contact with other national-origin populations; they know little, if anything, about the histories and cultural practices of the different subgroups. For these reasons, Latina/o identity is both indeterminate and variable, involving issues of colonialism, conquest, migration practices, region, race, color, gender, sexuality, class, and language.

As scholars have noted, the all-encompassing nature of the pan-ethnic designation means that the term *Latina/o* suffers from a serious lack of specificity. Saying someone is Latina/o tells us nothing about country of origin, gender, citizenship status, ideological orientation, economic class, or length of residence in the United States. An undocumented immigrant from El Salvador is Latino; so is a third-generation Mexican American lawyer. Moreover, the category is racially indeterminate: Latinas/os can be white, black, indigenous, Asian, and every combination thereof. When referring to "Latina/os in the United States," it's unclear whether the subjects under discussion are farmworkers living below the poverty line or middle-class homeowners, urban hipsters, or rural evangelicals, white or black, queer or straight, young or old, conservative or radical, religious or atheist, college educated or high school dropouts, undocumented Spanish monolinguals or fourth-generation English-only speakers. Because such broad inclusivity can erase cultural specificities, it's no wonder that scholars who study Latinas/os and the various subgroups that make up the pan-ethnic population often critique the concept's tendency to "erase our cultural specificities" to "homogenize and lump us all together as one undifferentiated mass" (Aparicio, 2011: 40–43).

While invocations of Latina/o identity are clearly capable of obscuring the differences between individuals and communities, the impulse to group Latinas/os into a singular identity category is neither accidental nor incomprehensible. That's because the process of identifying as Latina/o is simultaneously emotive, historical, experiential, *and* strategic. For example, Latina/o identity is sometimes constituted through the homogenizing effects of racism whereby the regional and cultural histories of people hailing from Latin America are erased. As with African Americans and Asian Americans, a racialized "otherness" has been applied to the diverse communities of Latinas/os living in the United States. As scholar Suzanne Oboler notes, despite internal and racial group differences, "people of Latin American descent in the United States have long been perceived homogeneously as 'foreign' to the image of 'being American' . . . regardless of the time and mode of their incorporation into the United States or their subsequent status as citizens of this nation" (Oboler, 1995: 17–18). Given this type of broad-based discrimination, it is unsurprising that identifying as Latina/o emerged in response to prejudice and racial stereotyping. In recent years, the rise in anti-immigrant rhetoric and violent border control policies has had a powerful impact on Latina/o identity and how Latinas/os understand themselves politically. More specifically, while increasing hostility toward immigrants (particularly the undocumented) has led some native-born Latinas/os to distance themselves from immigrants, it has also produced new forms of identification and solidarity among large numbers of Latinas/os who (regardless of their citizenship status) feel collectively offended and threatened by an increasingly xenophobic political climate. Indeed, the ongoing assault on immigrants has not only led to the rise of a large and powerful immigrant rights movement—the increased political salience of immigration is shaping the political content of Latina/o identity. In this way, Latina/o identity is capable of providing people with a shared history of racial struggle—a powerful sense of linked fate that sometimes serves as the basis for a collective politics.

Along with the homogenizing effects of racism, there is a long history of various Spanish-origin subgroups laying claim to a pan-ethnic Latina/o identity. This has been particularly true in Chicago and New York, cities where a diversity of Latino subgroups have lived and worked in close proximity to one another. For example, when revolutionary poet and Cuban activist José Martí founded the Partido Revolucionario Cubano (the Cuban Revolutionary Party) in New York in 1892, the Partido also organized a *Sección de Puerto Rico*, uniting "the two Caribbean nationalities in a joint struggle against Spanish colonialism" (Flores, 2000: 148). By the turn of the 20th century, a number of Puerto Ricans residing in New York were already identifying themselves as Latina/o or Hispanic. Beyond explicitly political forms of identification, Latinas/os were creating pan-ethnic cultural practices based on food, films, print culture, and music. Prior to World War II, Latinas/os in New York "read Spanish-language newspapers, saw Mexican and Argentine films, listened to Spanish-language radio stations, formed associations that promoted language, culture, and civic concerns, and danced and listened to Latino music" (Sánchez Korrol, 1988: 151–52). That such expressions of coalitional support, cultural crossover, and group affiliation have been present among some portion of the U.S. Latina/o population for over a century is a valuable reminder that "Latina/o identity" is both historically present and socially constructed. Rather than something natural or preexistent, Latina/o identity is the result of intentional collective practices capable of occurring in local, national, and hemispheric contexts.

Strategically, depictions of Latina/o identity often reflect the diverse political impulses of numerous communities and interest groups. Starting in the 1970s, for example, Latina/o identity became institutionalized through the combined effort of the U.S. government and Latina/o civic and business elites. In 1970, at the behest of the Nixon White House, the long-form U.S. Census questionnaire added the Hispanic-origin question; six years later, Congress passed the Roybal Act, requiring the Census Bureau and other federal statistical agencies to produce separate counts of persons of Hispanic origin. The production of a Latina/o identity was further reinforced in 1980, when a Hispanic-origin question was added to the short Census form, the one mailed to every American household. Such bureaucratic shifts reflect the strategic efforts of Latina/o civic elites who have found it beneficial to portray Latinas/os as a large population with a collective identity. For these advocates, locating subjects under the "pan-ethnic" umbrella expanded the population and geographical base for Latinas/os, depicting them as akin to African Americans and projecting them into the national political arena. When confronting an interest-group paradigm that rewards national over regional interests and sees strength in numbers, Latina/o elites found it strategically useful to create a new Hispanic Census category that sorted persons of Latin American descent into their own pan-ethnic classification. By emphasizing the idea of a shared identity, ethnic advocates and entrepreneurs were able to enhance Latinas'/os' visibility at the national level while acquiring data on these communities and securing federal resources for a variety of Latina/o populations.

In sum, Latina/o identity is best understood as historically constructed, strategically produced, and emotionally experienced. Like every other identity, it's a sense of self that is created, sustained, and transformed through contact and engagement with others. In other words, rather than an identity simply there to be discovered (something one *has*), Latina/o identity is a dynamic practice (something one *does*). Forever evolving, Latina/o identity is an assertion whose content is continually coming into being.

Cristina Beltrán

See also: Latino Political Power

Further Reading

Alcoff, Linda Martín. 2006. *Visible Identities: Race, Gender, and the Self.* New York: Oxford University Press.

Aparicio, Frances R. 2011. "(Re)constructing Latinidad: The Challenge of Latina/o Studies." In Juan Flores and Renato Rosaldo, eds. *A Companion to Latina/o Studies.* Hoboken, NJ: Wiley-Blackwell, pp. 39–48.

Barvosa, Edwina. 2008. *Wealth of Selves: Multiple Identities, Mestiza Consciousness, and the Subject of Politics.* College Station: Texas A&M University Press.

Beltrán, Cristina. 2010. *The Trouble with Unity: Latino Politics and the Creation of Identity.* New York: Oxford University Press.

Chavez, Leo. 2008. *The Latino Threat: Constructing Immigrants, Citizens, and the Nation.* Palo Alto, CA: Stanford University Press.

García Bedolla, Lisa. 2005. *Fluid Borders: Latino Power, Identity, and Politics in Los Angeles.* Berkeley: University of California Press.

Dávila, Arlene. 2001. *Latinos, Inc.: The Making and Marketing of a People.* Berkeley: University of California Press.

Dávila, Arlene. 2008. *Latino Spin: Public Image and the Whitewashing of Race.* New York: New York University Press.

Flores, Juan. 2000. *From Bomba to Hip-Hop: Puerto Rican Culture and Latino Identity.* New York: Columbia University Press.

Lavariega Monforti, Jessica L. 2014. "Identity Revisited: Latinos(as) and Panethnicity." In Tony Affigne, Evelyn Hu-DeHart, and Marion Orr, eds. *Latino Politics an Ciencia Política: The Search for Latino Identity and Racial Consciousness.* New York: New York University Press.

Migration Policy Institute. 2017. "Central American Immigrants in the United States." http://www.migrationpolicy.org/article/central-american-immigrants-united-states.

Mora, Cristina. 2014. *Making Hispanics: How Activists, Bureaucrats, and Media Constructed a New American.* Chicago: University of Chicago Press.

Nazario, Sonia. 2007. *Enrique's Journey.* New York: Random House.

Oboler, Suzanne. 1995. *Ethnic Labels, Latino Lives: Identity and the Politics of (Re)Presentation in the United States.* Minneapolis: University of Minnesota Press.

Rodríguez, Juana María. 2003. *Queer Latinidad: Identity Practices, Discursive Spaces.* New York: New York University Press.

Sánchez Korrol, Virginia. 1988. "Latinismo among Early Puerto Rican Migrants in New York City: A Sociohistoric Interpretation." In Edna Acosta-Belén and Barbara R. Sjostrom, eds. *The Hispanic Experience in the United States: Contemporary Issues and Perspectives.* New York: Praeger.

Sandoval-García, Carlos. 2017. *Exclusion and Forced Migration in Central America: No More Walls.* Geneva, Switzerland: Springer.

Latinas in U.S. Politics

Ethnicity and gender are both factors widely considered to affect a candidate's electoral chances. Latinas have and continue to change the political landscape as candidates in U.S. politics. According to the 2014 National Appointed and Latino Elected Directory, there are 6,100 Latinos, men and women, serving in elected office nationwide (NALEO, 2014). This is up from 4,853 Latina/o elected officials who held office in 2004, an increase of 25 percent over 10 years. NALEO also found 2,099 Latinas serving in elected office, comprising nearly 35 percent of the total number of Latino elected officials nationwide. This number marks a 47 percent increase from 2004, when only 1,427 Latinas were serving in an elected official capacity. Four states with the largest number of Latino elected officials are Texas, California, New Mexico, and Arizona. In these four states, Latina women made up an even smaller portion of elected or appointed officials.

At the federal level (see Table 1), there are 10 Latinas (nine U.S. representatives and one U.S. senator) serving in the 104th Congress (2017) with one serving on the U.S. Supreme Court.

At the state level, the number of Latina/os in state legislatures reached a new record. As of January 2015, there are 302 Latinas/os serving in the state

Table 1   Latinas Serving at the Federal Level

U.S. Representative	Michelle Lujan Grisham (D-NM)
U.S. Representative	Nannette Barajan (D-CA)
U.S. Representative	Jaime Herrera Beutler (R-WA)
U.S. Representative	Grace Napolitano (D-CA)
U.S. Representative	Ileana Ros-Lehtinen (R-FL)
U.S. Representative	Lucille Roybal-Allard (D-CA)
U.S. Representative	Linda Sánchez (D-CA)
U.S. Representative	Norma Torres (D-CA)
U.S. Representative	Nydia Velazquez (D-NY)
U.S. Senator	Catherine Cortez Masto (D-NV)
U.S. Supreme Court	Sonia Sotomayor

Source: CAWP 2017.

legislatures of 38 states, with 73 serving in state Senates and 229 serving in lower houses. Latinas/os serving in state Senates include 65 Democrats and 8 Republicans. Shifts in geographical representation as a result of election 2014 included Latino gains in Arizona, Colorado, Hawaii, and Kentucky, with losses in California and Missouri. This resulted in one Latino being elected in Kentucky and two Latina women winning seats to the Nevada and Alaska state legislature.

As of January 2015, there are 175 Latina/o Democrats and 54 Republicans serving in state lower houses. Immediately after the election of 2016, the Latina/o gains at the state lower houses were due to the success of Latina/o Republican candidates, with Latina/o Democrats losing 3 seats and Latina/o Republicans gaining 11 seats. Notable changes or contests at the state lower houses include the following: Attorney Liz Vazquez (R), Alaska's first Latina state legislator to serve from 2015 to 2017, and Victoria de la Guerra Seaman (R), elected to the Nevada Assembly (Larraz, 2016).

There are 74 women serving in statewide elective executive offices. Four of them are Latina. Nellie M. Gorbea (D-RI) is the first Latina elected to statewide office in New England ("Rhode Island's Secretary of State," n.d.). Susana Martinez (R-NM) is the only Latina to serve as governor in the United States and was elected in 2010 ("Welcome to the Office of Governor Susana Martinez," n.d.). In 2016, Susana A. Mendoza (D-IL) is the first Latina to ever run for and win a statewide office, comptroller. That same year, Evelyn Sanguinetti (D) was elected to serve as the lieutenant governor of Illinois. She is the first Latina to serve in this position in the United States.

THE THEORY OF LATINAS IN U.S. POLITICS

Most of the research on gender and politics does not take into account the experiences of women of color, especially Latinas. Once the field began studying race, it followed the larger U.S. political tradition of seeing race in terms of "black" and "white"; gender was either studied separately or seen as another "minority" (Hull, Schott, and Smith, 1982). Subsequent scholarship drew attention to the politics of "women of color," obscuring the difference there might be between women of different races/ethnicities.

Scholars then developed a more holistic way of thinking about ethnic, racial, and gender identities called intersectionality, where scholars examined individuals and groups at the intersection of demographics groups such as black women and Latinas. Some intersectionality scholars (Zinn and Dill, 1994; Crenshaw, Gotanda, Peller, and Thomas, 1995; Hancock, 2004; Hill Collins, 1990) argued that "the distinguishing categories within a society, such as race/ethnicity, gender, religion, sexual orientation, class, and other markers of identity and difference, do not function independently but, rather, act in tandem as interlocking or intersectional phenomena" (Manuel, 2006). This theoretical paradigm calls attention to the "triple oppression" faced by this group. This type of oppression includes racial, sexual, and cultural traditions that encourage or perpetuate passivity, submissiveness, and strict gender roles (Davidson, 1991). Others see also see a "Latina advantage" (Bejarano, 2013), or what Fraga, Martinez-Ebers, Lopez, and Ramirez (2005: 1) called strategic intersectionality. Fraga et al. suggest that "as ethnic women, their multiple identities better position [Latinas] to build cross-group coalitions that are more likely to attain threshold levels of legislative support" and hypothesize that "the intersection of gender and ethnicity might position Latina legislators to have a richer set of strategic options, relative to Latino male legislators." Hawkesworth's (2003) research reminds us that barriers for Latina women continue after they are elected and are institutionalized. Hawkesworth offers a framework that disentangles race and gender dynamics within institutions that in turn call attention to practices that maintain and reproduce marginalization.

RESEARCH ON LATINAS IN U.S. POLITICS

Currently, there are few works on Latinas in U.S. politics. In the 1990s, Carol Hardy-Fanta (1993) published one of the first books on Latina politics. Hardy-Fanta challenged two core assumptions about Latinas/os in mainstream political science research: Latinas were invisible and insignificant political actors, and Latino culture inhibits their political participation in the United States. In 2008, Garcia, Martinez-Ebers, Coronado, Navarro, and Jaramillo explored the obstacles faced by Latinas in politics. That same year Navarro (2008) focused on the lack of female minority representatives in Texas politics and the importance of race in the development of (Latina) female leadership ability. She also focuses on the barriers a Latina must overcome to be elected such as appointments to committees and serving as committee chairs, to name a few. A few years later, Christina E. Bejarano (2013a) proposed that the intersectional identities of Latinas could allow them to gather electoral resources that come from Latino communities and women groups. Bejarano's (2013b) second book, published in that same year, unpacks more aspects of the gender category for Latinos, including analyzing the gender differences in Latino political behavior across national origin, foreign-born status, and generational status. Hardy-Fanta et al. (2016) conduct an empirical analysis to determine if there were differences among minority groups elected to Congress. The authors examined differences in ambition, political ascension, and how they govern. Navarro, Hernandez, and Navarro (2016) examine Latinas as candidates, their campaign strategies, use of social media, and the role of stereotypes. These works have just opened the door for further research on Latinas in U.S. politics. There is so much we have yet to learn.

Sharon A. Navarro

See also: Latina/o Gender Gap

Further Reading

Bejarano, Christina E. 2013a. *The Latina Advantage: Gender, Race, and Political Success.* Austin: University of Texas Press.

Bejarano, Christina E. 2013b. *The Latino Gender Gap in U.S. Politics.* New York: Routledge.

Crenshaw, Kimberle, Neil Gotanda, Gary Peller, & Kendal Thomas. 1995. *Critical Race Theory: The Key Writings that Formed the Movement.* New York: The New Press

Davidson, Bruce. 1991. "Poor Treatment May Force Krier Out of Senate." *San Antonio Express-News*, May.

Fraga, Luis Ricardo, Valerie Martinez-Ebers, Linda Lopez, & Ricardo Ramirez. 2005. "Strategic Intersectionality: Gender, Ethnicity." Paper presented at the annual meeting of the American Political Science Association, Washington, D.C., August 31–September 4.

Garcia, Sonia R., Valerie Martinez-Ebers, Irasema Coronado, Sharon A. Navarro, & Patricia A. Jaramillo, eds. 2008. *Politicas: Latina Public Officials in Texas.* Austin: University of Texas Press.

Hancock, Ange-Marie. 2004. *The Politics of Disgust: The Public Identity of the Welfare Queen.* New York: New York University Press.

Hardy-Fanta, Carol. 1993. *Latina Politics, Latino Politics, Gender, Culture, and Political Participation in Boston.* Philadelphia: Temple University Press.

Hardy-Fanta, Carol, Pei-te Lien, Dianne Pinderhughes, & Christine Marie Sierra. 2016. *Contested Transformation: Race, Gender, and Political Leadership in the 21st Century America.* New York: Cambridge University Press.

Hawkesworth, Mary. 2003. "Congressional Enactments of Race-Gender: Toward a Theory of Race-Gendered Institutions." *American Political Science Review* 97, no. 4: 529–50.

Hill Collins, Patricia. 1990. *Black Feminist Thought: Knowledge, Consciousness, and the Politics of Empowerment.* Boston: Unwin Hyman.

Huetteman, Emmarie. 2017. "New Faces in Congress: Catherine Cortez Masto, First Latina Senator." *New York Times,* January 24. https://www.nytimes.com/2017/01/23/us/politics/catherine-cortez-masto.html.

Hull, Gloria T., Patricia Bell Schott, & Barbara Smith, eds. 1982. *All the Women Are White, All the Blacks Are Men, But Some of Us Are Brave.* New York: Feminist Press.

Larraz, Roland. 2016. "Unstable Victoria Seaman Running for Senate." *Las Vegas Tribune,* April 21.

Navarro, Sharon A. 2008. *Latina Legislator: Leticia Van de Putte and the Road to Leadership.* College Station: Texas A&M Press University.

Navarro, Sharon A., Samantha L. Hernandez, & Leslie A. Navarro. 2016. *Latinas in American Politics: Changing and Embracing Political Tradition.* New York: Lexington Press.

"Rhode Island's Secretary of State." n.d. http://sos.ri.gov/about-us.

2014 National Directory of Latino Elected Officials. http://www.naleo.org/at_a_glance.

"Welcome to the Office of Governor Susana Martinez." n.d. http://www.governor.state.nm
    .us/Meet_Governor_Martinez.aspx.

"Women of Color in Elective Office 2017." *Center for American Women and Politics.* http://
    www.cawp.rutgers.edu/women-color-elective-office-2017.

Zinn, Maxine Baca, & Bonnie Thorton Dill, eds. 1994. *Women of Color in U.S. Society.*
    Philadelphia: Temple University Press.

LatinoJustice PRLDEF

Formerly known as The Puerto Rican Legal Defense and Education Fund (PRLDEF), LatinoJustice PRLDEF is a national Latinx civil rights litigation and advocacy organization based in Manhattan, New York, with a southeast regional office in Orlando, Florida. It was founded in 1972 by three Puerto Rican attorneys from New York—Jorge Batista, Victor Marrero, and Cesar A. Perales—who aimed to end the discrimination they observed and experienced in their communities through advocacy and litigation. They were inspired by the NAACP Legal Defense Fund to create an analogous organization that would ensure that Puerto Ricans' civil rights would be protected. With funding from the Ford Foundation, they embarked upon class-action litigation so that the remedies obtained would benefit larger groups than in individual litigation.

In May 2017, it opened a satellite office at the Touro College Jacob D. Fuchsberg Law Center/Randolph Hearst Public Advocacy Center in Central Islip, Long Island, New York. Its current projects include Latinas at Work (LAW), designed to combat abuses against immigrant women workers in the metropolitan New York area, and the Rights Restoration Project, which seeks to end the systematic felony disenfranchisement of Latinos and other communities of color in Florida. Its current litigation concentrates on constitutional rights; immigrants' rights; voting rights; and discrimination in housing, education, and employment. The treatment of day laborers, freedom of movement, and all forms of bias that affect Latinx living in the United States are also areas of focus for LatinoJustice PRLDEF.

In its earliest case (1974), PRLDEF sued the New York City Board of Education on behalf of the Puerto Rican educational improvement organization. Once the city signed off on the August 1974 ASPIRA consent decree, the lawsuit established the right of public school students with limited English proficiency to be educated in a bilingual manner while they became fluent in English.

Another early case, *López v. Dinkins* (1973), secured parents of schoolchildren the ability to bilingual ballots and interpreters in Spanish, Chinese, and English for school board elections. Victories in employment discrimination and other landmark litigation soon followed, yet the founders realized the need for more advocates so the organization started a Legal Education Division. This division, which continues its activity to this day, partners with the Law School Admission Council for activities such as Law School Admission Test ("LSAT") preparation, Law Day, and LAWbound, a project whose aim is to increase the number of Latinx who successfully stay on the path to law school. LatinoJustice has also partnered with Pfizer,

Inc., to sponsor the Cesar A. Perales Leadership Institute, an effort to provide Latinx students with the tools to assist their communities and be the trailblazers of the future. For Latinx young professionals, the organization has created its LatinoJustice PRLDEF Lideres Board to assist in networking, leadership, and mentoring opportunities.

As the organization celebrates its 55 years, its litigation agenda continues unabated. One of the most recent important cases that it has been involved in include filing an amicus (friend of the court) brief in *U.S. v. Texas* (2016), urging the Supreme Court to lift the injunction that blocked the executive actions on immigration that President Obama announced in November 2014.

María M. Pabón

See also: Cartagena, Juan (1956–)

Further Reading

Berg, Bruce F. 2007. *New York City Politics: Governing Gotham.* Rutgers, NJ: Rutgers University Press.

Giovanni, Ziedah Ferguson. 2003. "Real and Imagined Threats to Our Voting Rights." *New York Amsterdam News* 94, no. 27 (July 3): 13.

LatinoJustice PRLDEF. n.d. "Four Decades of Protecting Latino Civil Rights." http://latinojustice.org/about/history.

Villarreal, Elpidio. 2006. "Keeping True to Our Fundamental Values." In *Vital Speeches, of the Day* 26: 784.

Latino Political Power

The foundational components of politics include power, community, struggle/change, and empowerment. There are demographics, conditions, and values that bring people together to express and promote policies and actions by governmental institutions (i.e. abortion, environmental protection, immigration reform, affirmative action, etc.) in United States (Garcia, 2017). The intersection of demographics and values can be seen within Latino communities. Communities seek remedies, protection, and favorable governmental policies so the exercise of power, influence, and representation serve as key elements that will increase their chances to be successful. As a result, political power (i.e., the capacity or ability to direct or influence the behavior of others and institutions) is an ongoing process for Latino communities (Garcia Bedolla and Michelson, 2014). This process includes struggles, challenges, obstacles, and strategies to both enact targeted social change and energize Latinos to become and remain politically engaged. Now the discussion of the key elements of power, community, struggles/strategies, and empowerment will follow.

EXAMINING LATINO POLITICAL POWER AND COMMUNITY

When discussing Latino political power, having a vibrant community is central. Community refers to a body of persons with a common history and common social, economic, cultural, and political interests. For Latinos, this involves their lives in the United States and their experiences in American society. This commonality lies within their own community and as part of the larger U.S. society. For Latinos such experiences can include negative treatment, attitudes, and injustices directed toward them. So if Latinos have affinity and identification with other community members, then such negative treatment can serve to seek change and redress. This type of connection reinforces group "membership" and a sense of a stake in the status and well-being of other Latinos. While an individual can be very connected with other Latinos in their social life and familial ties, our discussion of Latino political power involves the willingness to participate in collective actions in the public sphere. As a result, we can see how Latino collective action affects institutions', especially economic and political, response to Latino interests, issues, and needs. The role of racial/ethnic social identity and linked fate served as essential ingredients for attachment and motivation to act collectively. The very existence of Latino communities serves as a basis for continual actions on behalf of Latinos.

LATINO POWER: RESOURCES, LEADERSHIP, AND ISSUES

The use and success of exercising political power requires resources, leadership, identifiable issues, policy preferences, and targeted institutions. In developing these dimensions of political power, individuals should undergo an empowerment process in which they exhibit personal and political ability to act. In addition, Latinos generate political awareness, knowledge, and skills to engage in group settings and prioritized policy areas to direct their energies and policy preferences. Together, Latinos work through organizations (i.e., ad hoc and more structured organizations) to generate the necessary economic and human resources to advance strategies to pursue their interests. The recruitment and maintenance of a cadre of persons who serve in leadership roles is the link between the larger Latino community and the forerunners of carrying out the group's goals. As much of the political dynamics of the U.S. political system operates in this manner, Latinos are in competition with other communities of interest.

This discussion of Latino political power places great weight on the roles of organizations and active leadership. The combination of both provides greater clarity and articulation of Latino interests, as well as directing this community toward strategic actions and "appropriate" political targets. Linking Latino organizations with the Latino population base opens the way to activate a significant base of supporters, utilize their human resources, and recruit a pool of leaders and activists. We are talking about collective actions and accumulating political resources. Prioritizing a Latino issue agenda, determining effective strategies and arenas for actions can open access to powerholders. This "starts" the political effort to influence decision makers and remains a long-standing challenge for Latino communities. Because politics occurs at many levels of society, a diversity of Latino-based organizations built on national-origin appeals, as well as by neighborhoods, cultural practices, religious affiliation, gender, and familial ties are ways to get more Latinos involved.

This discussion of empowering Latinos centers on the clustering of Latinos as a larger "pan-ethnic" community drawing on a mixture of leaders from many national origins. In doing so Latinos can advance a variety of strategies to enhance their political power. Thus, growth of Latino political power would mean that persons of Latino origin over time come to accept the Latino label as meaningful. A large community can become a powerful voting bloc and an effective policy advocacy "bloc" so politicians must pay attention. Attention and successes provide greater motivation for Latinos to work together to fight for common causes.

NUMBERS: POLITICAL CONVERSION OF POPULATION GROWTH

A most visible aspect of the Latino political power base has been their significant population growth, especially since the 1970s. The combination of a young population, higher birth rates, and significant influx of international migrants has fueled Latino growth. A popular notion about the Latino community is seeing Latinos as predominantly an immigrant community, but that fails to capture Latinos as multi-generational residents and that a greater portion of Latinos' growth comes from U.S. births. In fact, over two-thirds of the nation's growth has come from the Latino community, which now numbers over 56.5 million (17.6% of the total population). While their population growth has leveled off, Latinos still contributed 50 percent of the U.S. growth in 2017. A more complete characterization of Latinos (i.e., national origin, nativity, language use, age structure, etc.) can accent the resource base of this community, as well as some challenges they face. The political and power potential of Latinos has been a long-standing theme in their political development. While a sizeable population base is a critical resource for empowerment and acquiring power, some other additional key "ingredients" are necessary.

ATTEMPT TO DEFINE A LATINO AGENDA

The connections of common group bonds and interests represent the bases for advancing an agenda and targeted actions for Latino interests and needs. One of the top issues has been education in which such issues as inadequate funding for public education, need for bilingual-bicultural education, access to higher education, reducing dropout rates, lowering suspensions, and improving the overall quality of education experiences represent long-standing priorities (Zambrana and Hurtado, 2015). Polls from the Pew Research Center have reinforced the importance of this policy area, as well as improving the economy, improving access to health care and affordability, civil and voting rights, climate change, environmental justice, and the criminal justice system and law enforcement. This list of policy areas, on the face of it, does not appear to be very different from other communities, yet Latinos' perspectives and preferences are distinctive.

For example, prevailing immigration policies have placed greater emphasis on border security, militarization of the border, criminalization of "illegal entrants," formal deportations, and placing Latino communities under heightened police scrutiny and "profiling." From Latinos' perspectives, immigration policies would include greater legal rights and protections for immigrants, stabilizing the undocumented community's status, providing a pathway for citizenship, providing legal protections and actions to "normalize" mixed-status households (both youths brought to the United States and undocumented parents of native-born children), and comprehensive legal immigration reform. The current national Republican agenda for the economy would mean revitalizing the coal industry, reducing governmental regulations for corporations, and tax cuts, whereas Latinos would prioritize workers' rights and protections, advocating for union activities, minimum wage increases, and improving access to affordable housing. The distinctiveness of Latinos' policy agenda comes in direct conflict with the current administration and the Republican Party that controls both chambers of Congress. Understanding the priorities of Latinos' interests and needs will provide the necessary directions of Latinos' efforts to exercise their power and challenge other groups/interests in the political arena.

CULTIVATING CIVIC ENGAGEMENT AMONG LATINOS

For broader Latino civic engagement to occur, there is a need for Latinos to gain greater political familiarity of the political processes and issue debates. By heightening knowledge and motivation to become more politically engaged, strategies and Latinos' energies can be directed into effective political actions. There is clear evidence of these dynamics working, particularly in the policy domains of immigration, voting rights, and health care. At the same time, sustained efforts are required at both the national and local levels. For Latino political influence to be effective in a competitive political context, Latino political power has assets that include a dramatically rise in their percentage of the electorate, a youthful population in which almost 1 million annually turn 18, and expanding activism. Data show that Latino participation rates are increasing and disproportionately more Latinos are aligned with the Democratic Party. In the case of the latter, the receptiveness and responsiveness of Democratic Party leadership to the Latino agenda may allow more opportunities to form coalitions with other groups holding similar policy preferences (i.e., other minority groups, labor unions, environmental advocates, etc.) and increase mobilization efforts.

Several foundational components have been discussed to illustrate how the coming together of the Latino community, based on common interests, can develop political resources. There is an emphasis on a persistent struggle, with uncertainty as what the future holds. At the same time, political involvement is a learning process, and these experiences carry over across encounters and across generations. This discussion of Latino political power includes both a looking backward and projecting forward from the perspective of improving and empowering Latinos and the communities they come from with greater opportunities, socioeconomic mobility, and the use of resources to affect their daily lives. This latter point is at the heart of political power. The ability to act and determine your own future and achieve your aspirations is fundamental to the development of power and its use. Since the latter part of the past millennium, Latino political power has been slowly expanding, with much of the responsibility falling on this community's efforts to promote its interests and needs with effectiveness and forcefulness. Understanding the dynamics of power and the impact of this community is the fuel to advance collective interests and actions. Better and more successful strategies are built upon Latinos' past and current efforts. The contemporary climate finds Latinos facing pushback and backlash because of their origins, culture, language, and negative stereotypes. While discrimination and racism have been a long-standing reality for Latinos trying to achieve and maintain power, Latinos confront the intersecting factors of immigration, xenophobia, and public attitudes that characterize Latinos as not really belonging to American society. Working within this negative climate involves devising strategies that factor in these elements and become more proactive. Latinos have used their resources to hold back "backlash" policies, but promoting policy alternatives is also part of their political agenda. There is a high level of polarization and hostilities that have put Latinos more on the defensive, and trying to hold fast for the gains they have made is a necessary part of the struggle. Continued advancement may become slower or even some retrenchment so that Latino power progress will require daily struggles, however small or large, as perseverance is necessary.

John A. Garcia

See also: Education and Latinos; Immigration as a Policy Issue

Further Reading

Barreto, Matt A., Loren Collingwood, & Sylvia Manzano. 2010. "A New Measure of Group Influence in Presidential Elections: Assessing Latino Influence in 2008." *Political Research Quarterly* 63, no. 4: 908–21.

García Bedolla, Lisa 2014. *Latino Politics.* 2nd ed. Cambridge: Polity.

Garcia Bedolla, Lisa, & Melissa R. Michelson. 2012. *Mobilizing Inclusion: Transforming the Electorate through Get Out the Vote Campaigns.* New Haven, CT: Yale University Press.

Garcia, John A. 2016. *Latinos Politics in America: Community of Interests and Culture.* 3rd ed. Lanham, MD: Rowman and Littlefield.

Garcia, John. 2017. "Navigating through Turbulence and Troublesome Times: Latinos, Election 2016, Partisan Politics and Salient Public Policies." In William J. Crotty, ed. *Winning the Presidency 2016.* New York: Routledge, pp. 170–93.

Le Espiritu, Yen. 1993. *Asian American Panethnicity: Bridging Institutions and Identities.* Vol. 171. Philadelphia: Temple University Press.

Sanchez, Gabriel, Amy Goodin, Amerilic Rouse, & Richard Santos. 2014. "Importance of Ethnicity on Attributes toward Health Care Reform." *Social Science Journal* 47: 326–43.

Sanchez, Gabriel R, Vickie Ybarra, & Lisa Sanchez. 2016. "Racialized Nativism in State Policy: The Great Recession and Punitive Immigration Policy in the American States, 2005–2010." *State Politics and Policy Quarterly* 16, no. 3: 313–39.

Vargas, Edward D., Gabriel Sanchez, & Melina Juarez. 2017. "The Impact of Punitive Immigrant Laws on the Health of Latinos." *Politics and Policy* 45, no. 3: 312–37.

Zambrana, Ruth Enid, & Sylvia Hurtado, eds. 2015. *The Magic Key: The Educational Journey of Mexican Americans from K-12 to College and Beyond.* Austin: University of Texas Press.

Zepeda-Millan, Chris. 2017. *Latino Mass Mobilization: Immigration, Racialization and Activism.* New York: Cambridge University Press.

Latinx Entrepreneurship

Entrepreneurship is a mechanism that can help to facilitate the social and economic integration of immigrants. It also serves to infuse ethnic communities with financial and social resources. Latinxs were once the ethnoracial group least likely to own a business, but their rates of business ownership are growing faster than any other ethnoracial group. This essay examines rates of Latinx entrepreneurship, why Latinxs might enter into entrepreneurship, and the challenges to mobility that Latinx entrepreneurs experience in a society that is stratified by race, class, and gender.

Research on Latinx entrepreneurs is limited compared to the large body of literature focusing on Asian immigrant entrepreneurs. Historically, scholars generally argued that business ownership was a traditional mobility ladder for Asian immigrants and their descendants but *not* for Latinxs (with the exception of Cuban exiles). Just a few decades ago, Latinxs trailed behind every other immigrant group in terms of business ownership. Indeed, most studies of Latinx entrepreneurs concentrated on low-wage, gendered entrepreneurial niches, such as domestic workers, gardeners, or street vendors in the informal or underground economy. These studies generally maintained that low levels of education and personal wealth and a lack of coethnic social capital (the information and resources found within

Jordi Muñoz wrote the code to create the first autopiloted drone. He built the drone, tested it, and posted footage online. Chris Anderson, former editor-in-chief of *Wired*, saw the footage and was so impressed by Muñoz that he cofounded 3D Robotics with him. The successful company works primarily with government agencies. (David Maung/Bloomberg via Getty Images)

networks that facilitates individual or collection action) impeded the entrepreneurial success of Latinx immigrants.

Though many scholars have historically expressed pessimism about Latinx business ownership, especially compared to other immigrant-origin groups, Latinx business ownership is growing at unprecedented rates. According to the U.S. Census Bureau's Survey of Business Owners (SBO), conducted every five years, Latinxs owned just over 1 million businesses in 1997. By 2007, the number of Latinx businesses more than doubled, with Latinxs owning 2.3 million enterprises. Between 2007 and 2012, Latinx-owned businesses grew by 46.3 percent. By 2012, there were 3.3 million Latinx-owned businesses in the United States, and these firms make up 12 percent of all U.S. businesses and generate almost $500 billion in economic activity annually. Latinxs now own more firms than any other ethnic minority group.

According to a recent survey conducted by the Stanford Latino Entrepreneurship Initiative (see https://www.gsb.stanford.edu/sites/gsb/files/publication-pdf/report-slei-state-latino-entrepreneurship-2016.pdf), immigrants own 29 percent of Latinx firms, with 40 to 50 percent being businesses with more than $1 million in revenue and more than 50 employees. Fifty percent of Latinxs at both startup and growth stages solely utilize internal funding sources, regardless of their size. Of the firms that received external funding, one-third use bank and business loans at the early stage, while two-thirds use bank and business loans at the growth stage.

According to the U.S. Census Bureau's Survey of Business Owners, people who identify racially/ethnically as Mexican American, Mexican, or Chicano headed nearly half of all Latinx-owned enterprises in 2012. The fastest-growing Latinx racial/ethnic group in business is Puerto Ricans. The number of Puerto Rican–owned firms grew 65 percent between 2007 and 2012 compared to 56 percent for Mexican American–owned firms and 12.4 percent for Cuban-owned firms. Three states have the largest number of Latinx-owned firms: California (815,304), Texas (687,570), and Florida (604,128). In 2012, Los Angeles County had the largest number of Latinx-owned firms compared to all other U.S. counties (332,967), followed by Miami-Dade County, Florida (319,653). Latinas have been strong contributors to the growing, and high, rates of entrepreneurship among Hispanics. Latinas are starting businesses at six times the national average, and they are the fastest-growing segment of women-owned businesses (Survey of Business Owners, 2012).

Why might Latinx entrepreneurship be increasing? There are several factors that might push and pull Latinx entrepreneurs into the world of business ownership. For low-skilled immigrants, limited English skills and blocked mobility in the mainstream labor market are push factors that can thrust Latinx immigrants into self-employment. Some low-income and undocumented Latinx entrepreneurs may enter into entrepreneurship in the underground economy as a form of economic survival because their legal status prevents them from obtaining stable jobs or to increase their earnings. Latinx immigrants might also view entrepreneurship as the essence of the American dream and as a pathway to independence and self-sufficiency in a society that values individualism and meritocratic ideals. Whether one views entrepreneurship as epitomizing the American dream or as a route to independence can depend on social class status (whether one is low income, middle class, or upper class). For example, one study finds that low-income Salvadoran immigrants were more likely than their higher-class Peruvian counterparts to relay that they started businesses because it was a "dream," in line with the American dream rationale. In contrast, higher-class Peruvian immigrants emphasized that entrepreneurship provides independence and autonomy (Verdaguer, 2009). Another study of Latinx restaurant owners finds that the desire to attain economic mobility and independence was also the driving factor behind business ownership, regardless of national origin, class, or gender (Valdez, 2010). Research on native-born Latinx entrepreneurs is lacking, but recent studies also find that native-born Latinxs who experience barriers to obtaining a college degree might enter into entrepreneurship because they believe the economic returns will be greater than those earned from low-wage jobs (Agius Vallejo, 2012).

A growing body of scholarship demonstrates Latinxs are increasingly entering the middle class via entrepreneurship in traditional immigrant gateway cities like Los Angeles and Chicago and also in regions and states where the Latinx population is increasing most rapidly, like the South and Midwest. One study conducted in Richmond, Virginia, demonstrates that many new Latinx arrivals to the city are middle-class professionals and entrepreneurs who create community-based organizations centered on business success (Schleef and Calvacanti, 2010). Other researchers employ an intersectional approach, concentrating on how gender and class intersect to affect the entrepreneurial experiences and business patterns of the middle class, especially as it relates to perceptions of opportunity and discrimination. One study finds that middle-class Latina entrepreneurs rarely perceived discrimination from society, but they felt disadvantaged because of their gender (Verdaguer, 2009). In a similar pattern, another study shows that low-class Latina restaurant owners dismiss gender inequality, whereas middle-class women, who have stronger connections to the male-dominated restaurant industry, feel that their gender hinders their mobility more than their race (Valdez, 2011). Scholars also demonstrate that experiences with gender and racial discrimination push middle-class Latinxs out of corporate America, while the growing Latinx population can be a concurrent pull factor that gives middle-class Latinxs the confidence to pursue professional businesses that aim to serve other Latinxs (Agius Vallejo and Canizales, 2016). Research also finds that middle- and upper-class Latinx entrepreneurs also retain an ethos of giving back to coethnics and communities and that they attempt to infuse Latinx communities with social and financial capital aimed at Latinx social and economic integration (Agius Vallejo, 2015).

Research has also examined the barriers that Latinx entrepreneurs face in accessing financial capital to start and expand businesses. This obstacle is related to an individual's race and class position and their access to personal wealth and other resources, including financial institutions, family, and coethnics that can be utilized for capital. Wealth (total assets, like home equity, savings, retirement funds, and investments, minus all debts) is especially critical, as it can be invested directly into the business or used as collateral to obtain loans, which can help businesses expand. Reflecting their lower levels of wealth and restricted access to banks, in part due to a historical legacy of discrimination in the financial sector, Latinxs are less likely than other groups to obtain business loans and instead use savings, credit cards, or home equity lines of credit to fund their businesses (Agius Vallejo and Canizales, 2016; Valdez, 2011). When Latinx business owners do obtain loans, they pay higher interest rates and are more often denied loans than white business owners, even after controlling for creditworthiness (Cavalluzzo and Wolken, 2005).

Jody Agius Vallejo

See also: Immigration as a Policy Issue

Further Reading

Agius Vallejo, Jody. 2012. *Barrios to Burbs: The Making of the Mexican American Middle Class*. Palo Alto, CA: Stanford University Press.

Agius Vallejo, Jody. 2015. "Levelling the Playing Field: Patterns of Ethnic Philanthropy among Los Angeles' Middle and Upper-Class Latino Entrepreneurs." *Ethnic and Racial Studies* 38: 125–40.

Agius Vallejo, Jody, & Stephanie Canizales. 2016. "Latino/a Professionals as Entrepreneurs: How Race, Class, and Gender Shape Entrepreneurial Incorporation." *Ethnic and Racial Studies* 39, no. 9: 1637–56.

Cavalluzzo, Ken, & John Wolken. 2005. "Small Business Loan Turndowns, Personal Wealth, and Discrimination." *The Journal of Business* 78, no. 6: 2153–78.

Estrada, Emir, & Pierrette Hondagneu-Sotelo. 2011. "Intersectional Dignities: Latino Immigrant Street Vendor Youth in Los Angeles." *Journal of Contemporary Ethnography* 40, no. 1: 102–31.

Farlie, Robert, & Alicia Robb. 2008. *Race and Entrepreneurial Success*. Cambridge, MA: MIT Press.

Farlie, Robert, & Christopher Woodruff. 2010. "Mexican-American Entrepreneurship." *The B. E. Journal of Economic Analysis and Policy* 10, no. 1: 1–42.

Gold, Steven J., & Ivan Light. 2000. "Ethnic Economies and Social Policy." *Research in Social Movements, Conflicts, and Change* 22: 165–91.

Ramirez, Hernan, & Pierrette Hondagneu-Sotelo. 2009. "Mexican Immigrant Gardeners: Entrepreneurs or Exploited Workers?" *Social Problems* 56, no. 1: 70–88.

Schleef, Debra J., & Hilquias B. Cavalcanti. 2010. *Latinos in Dixie: Class and Assimilation in Richmond, Virginia*. New York: State University of New York Press.

U.S. Bureau of the Census. 2007. "Survey of Business Owners." Washington, D.C.: Author.

U.S. Bureau of the Census. 2012. "Survey of Business Owners." Washington, D.C.: Author.

Valdez, Zulema. 2011. *The New Entrepreneurs: How Race, Class, and Gender Shape American Enterprise*. Redwood City, CA: Stanford University Press.

Verdaguer, María Eugenia. 2009. *Class, Ethnicity, Gender and Latino Entrepreneurship*. New York: Routledge.

Lau v. Nichols

(1974)

Lau v. Nichols is a U.S. Supreme Court case involving bilingual education. The case was a class-action suit brought on behalf of non–English-speaking Chinese students in the San Francisco Unified School District. The case bears the name of Kinney Kinmon Lau, one of many named petitioners. The suit claimed that, due to language deficiency, non–English-speaking students were being denied an equal education. Although stopping short of claiming that education is a constitutional right, the Court did find that a lack of language assistance was a violation of the Civil Rights Act of 1964.

In 1971, a federal decree required the integration of the San Francisco school system. At the time, according to court documents, 2,856 Chinese students in San Francisco schools could not speak English. The California Education Code stated that bilingual education was only permitted if it did not interfere with normal instruction. The Court estimated about 1,800 of the non–English-speaking Chinese students were not receiving any assistance in language comprehension, assistance understood as English-language instruction or other instructional procedures such as providing translators or teaching certain classes in Chinese. The suit argued that non–English-speaking students received an unequal education because they could not understand what they were being taught. This, in turn, violated the Equal Protection Clause of the Fourteenth Amendment. The Equal Protection Clause provides that laws and policies must protect and affect citizens in a nondiscriminatory manner. What is regarded as equal protection is often debated, with the disparate impact of a policy potentially deemed unintentional and, therefore, not discriminatory. If the Fourteenth Amendment had been applied to this case, the Court would have needed to determine whether the school policy of not providing language assistance resulted in an unconstitutional lack of equal protection or if, instead, any difference in levels of education was merely an unintentional impact of the policy.

This determination was not necessary, as the Supreme Court did not agree with counsel that the Fourteenth Amendment applied in this case. The justices did, however, find the situation to be a violation of the Civil Rights Act of 1964, which bans discrimination, based on, among other things, national origin. In this way, the Court linked language with ancestry and, in so doing, extended the protections against discrimination based on national origin to language rights. In the majority opinion, Justice Douglas argued that a policy that does not assist students in gaining the basic language skills necessary to understand instruction undermined any sort of meaningful education. The Court did not specify how to resolve the situation, leaving remedial actions up to the school system. In addition, Justice Blackmun purposely limited the reach of this decision in his concurring opinion. He wrote that the large number of non–English-speaking students influenced the case, noting that if fewer students had been affected by the lack of language assistance, the Court would have decided differently.

While this case involved non–English-speaking Chinese students, it has clear implications for the larger debate regarding bilingual education for other non–English-speaking children, including Latinx students. However, the *Lau* decision was not broad enough to protect language rights in other areas and, in fact, did not continue to protect bilingual education. For example, in response to the *Lau* decision, the Department of Health, Education and Welfare established guidelines for accommodating non–English-speaking students only to have the guidelines discontinued by the Reagan administration. However, this decision set the precedent that providing language assistance to non–English-speaking students might be necessary to maintaining an equal educational environment, leaving the door open for many more debates regarding bilingual education.

Mary McThomas

See also: Bilingual Education; *Plyler v. Doe* (1982)

Further Reading

Brown, Donathan, & Amardo Rodriguez. 2014. *When Race and Policy Collide: Contemporary Immigration Debates.* Santa Barbara, CA: Praeger.

Lau v. Nichols, 414 U.S. 563 (1974).

Moran, Rachel F. 2005. "Undone by Law: The Uncertain Legacy of *Lau v. Nichols.*" *Berkeley La Raza Law Journal* 16, no. 1: 1.

Sugarman, Stephen D., & Ellen G. Widess. 1974. "Equal Protection for Non-English Speaking School Children: *Lau v. Nichols.*" *California Law Review* 62, no. 1: 157–82.

League of United Latin American Citizens (LULAC)

The League of United Latin American Citizens (LULAC) is a civil rights organization established in Corpus Christi, Texas, in 1929. Leading up to its founding the Southwest had seen an increase in the Mexican population due to the Mexican Revolution of 1910 and the need for labor in the growing cities and agricultural regions of the Southwest. With this came an increase in anti-immigrant and anti-Mexican sentiment. In an effort to improve conditions, on February 17, 1929, Order Sons of America, the Latin American League, the Sons of America, and the Order Knights of America met in Corpus Christi, Texas, and decided to merge into LULAC.

Within LULAC there was an ideology to identify as "emerging Americans." They were a highly patriotic group that felt that Mexicans Americans deserve the right to integrate into U.S. society without barriers based on race or ancestry. They sought social, educational, and economic assimilation of the Mexican American people through reformist policies, voter registration and educational efforts. In their activist endeavors, they focused primarily on racial discrimination as the root cause of the lack of or low upward mobility of the Mexican American people.

They sought an integrationist perspective whereby they felt it necessary to prepare the community to integrate into Anglo society. They encouraged parents to speak to their children in English to conform to cultural and social expectations. The ultimate demonstration of their accommodationist agenda was their stance that, in fact, Mexicans should be considered white, not just legally but socially as well. They fought against being designated as "colored" in various poll tax policies and in the 1936 census. By asserting that they could not be categorized as black, this fed into a black/white notion of race in America, attempting to place themselves firmly in the category of white.

Women do not often feature prominently in the official documentation of the early days of LULAC, as it was not until 1933 that women were allowed to become members. In the early days of the organization, the women of LULAC primarily served through auxiliary organizations. Later, women organized official "Ladies LULAC" chapters, often focusing on social gatherings. An early member of LULAC, Adela Sloss-Vento, described herself as a collaborator of the cause and sought to elevate public knowledge of LULAC by writing the biography of LULAC leaders and lawyers J. T. Canales and J. Luz Saenz. LULAC went on to have three female presidents: Belen Robles (1994), Rosa Rosales (2006), and Margaret Moran (2010).

LULAC saw a resurgence after World War II as veterans were ready to engage with the inequalities that they thought would dissipate after they served their country. A significant population of second-generation Americans, they had little to no ties to Mexico and were committed to changing the structures that inhibited their upward mobility. They would be at the forefront of major civil rights battles regarding segregation and education, both locally and in the courts nationally, laying the foundation for future civil rights battles for the community.

In 1948, LULAC filed a desegregation lawsuit, *Minerva Delgado v. Bastrop Independent School District,* charging the district with continuing the practice of segregation of Mexican American children in the school system. Though they lost that battle, between 1950 and 1957 LULAC filed 15 separate suits or complaints against school districts. In 1954 LULAC, led by San Antonio lawyer Gus Garcia and Houston attorney John J. Herrera, successfully took a case to the U.S. Supreme Court challenging a ban on Mexican Americans serving on juries in some parts of Texas.

Outside the court battles, LULAC continued to advocate for the educational advancement of the community. In 1956, under the leadership of Felix Tijerina, The Little School of the 400 was created, ultimately a precursor to the federal Head Start program, offering free early childhood education. They devised a curriculum that would teach Mexican and Mexican American children 400 critical words in English that would help them when they started first grade.

LULAC was very active in encouraging individuals to vote and participate in politics. For example, LULAC was highly involved with the GI Forum in organizing the "Viva Kennedy" campaign. In November 1963, the LULAC chapter in Houston convinced President Kennedy and the First Lady Jacqueline Kennedy to stop by and speak to the members, he in English and she in Spanish. It is believed that on that day, November 22, that President Kennedy was the first sitting president to acknowledge a Latino voting bloc. The significance of this was overshadowed, as this would be President Kennedy's last public appearance before his assassination on November 23, 1963.

This era of heightened activity would slow down tremendously in the mid-1960s. LULAC's assimilationist agenda would begin to be criticized. With the rise of the Chicano Movement in the 1960s led by more radical organizations such as La Raza Unida and the Brown Berets, and the national interest in the Farm Workers movement, LULAC's relevance was questioned. They were often characterized as an elitist organization, primarily interested in the upward mobility of the middle class and therefore out of step with the needs of the broader poor and working-class Mexican and Mexican American community. Tactics differed as well; LULAC preferred dialogue and appeals to Anglo accommodation and did not question various institutional structures.

While LULAC was not in step with this new era in the civil right movement, it nonetheless survived and continues to remain active. As a moderate organization in the eyes of the federal government and corporate sponsors, they were able to secure grants to continue their social services programs such as early childhood education and housing projects. Today, LULAC has a robust array of direct service programs and advocacy efforts in the areas of education, civic engagement, health, and programs to empower local communities in regard to financial literacy. LULAC has evolved and currently takes an active role in advocating for the rights of farmworkers and immigrant rights, along with all the agenda items that have defined this organization for over 80 years.

Cynthia Duarte

See also: Brown Berets; Brown Power Movement/Chicano Civil Rights Movement; *Delgado v. Bastrop I.S.D., et al.* (1948); La Raza Unida Party (LRU); Mexican Repatriation; Rosales, Rosa (1944–); United Farm Workers (UFW); Viva Kennedy! Clubs

Further Reading

Contreras, Russell. 2012. "JFK's Last Night Recalled as Key Event for Latinos." *Associated Press*, November 26. http://www.startribune.com/jfk-s-last-night-recalled-as-key-event-for-latinos/180747041/.

Marquez, Benjamin. 1993. *LULAC: The Evolution of a Mexican American Political Organization.* Austin: University of Texas Press.

Marquez, Benjamin. 2011. "Choosing Issues, Choosing Sides: Constructing Identities in Mexican American Social Movement Organizations." *Ethnic and Racial Studies* 24, no. 2 (March): 218–35.

Orozco, Cynthia E. 2012. *No Mexicans, Women, or Dogs Allowed: The Rise of the Mexican American Civil Rights Movement.* Austin: University of Texas Press.

Lesbian Identity. See Politics of a Latinx Lesbian, Gay, Bisexual, and Transgender Identity

LIBRE Initiative

A 501(c)(4) nonprofit organization established in 2011 by its president, Daniel Garza, the LIBRE Initiative is widely known and acknowledged to receive much of its funding from Charles and David Koch. The Koch family is heavily involved in politics and raised hundreds of millions of dollars through an often mysterious network of nonprofit groups, such as Americans for Prosperity (AFP)—a massive political action group that promotes conservative policies and elected officials—and are credited for helping to transform the Tea Party movement from a group centered around the health care debate in 2009 into a wave of elected officials in the 2010 midterm elections.

According to Daniel Garza's biography, he was born in the Central Valley of California and traveled with his parents as seasonal agricultural workers, citing this experience as the foundation for his understanding of the "plight of the immigrant community."

The LIBRE Initiative gained practical relevance after multiple failures by the Republican Party to attract more Latino voters after decades of promoting anti-immigrant policies, such as Proposition 187 in California and SB 1070 in Arizona. LIBRE's stated mission is "informing the U.S. Hispanic community about the benefits of a constitutionally limited government, property rights, rule of law, sound money supply and free enterprise through a variety of community events, research and policy initiatives that protect our economic freedom."

The "freedom through economic empowerment" message is rooted in Libertarian ideology and promotes a message of self-reliance, free enterprise, and limited government. However, many argue that LIBRE is not promoting Latino empowerment, but policies that hinder progress within the Latino community. For instance, LIBRE is opposed to increases in the minimum wage, they are opposed to organized labor, they oppose universal health care, and they are supportive of voter ID laws that are widely seen to have a disproportionate impact on minority voters.

LIBRE is also criticized for promoting voucher programs and charter programs for education, a popular policy among conservatives that grew in response to school integration following the Civil Rights Movement. LIBRE recently announced their support of an education initiative in support of vouchers in Arizona to counter initiatives pushing for greater funding for public education. This program, however, is directed through a different LIBRE organization, The LIBRE Institute, which was formed under a different tax status, 501(c)(3). The different tax status situates the organization as a nonprofit with limited political activities, and is focused on issue-oriented programs, such as vouchers. The LIBRE Institute says that "The LIBRE Institute engages and informs the U.S. Hispanic community on the benefits of economic freedom because *Freedom Drives Progress.* Through Our Four Pillars: *Economic Prosperity, Education, Faith,* and *Family,* The LIBRE Institute is empowering Latinos to achieve the American Dream."

As a nonprofit organization, similar to a church or school, The LIBRE Institute holds education forums designed to promote the acculturation of Latinos into American society. These forums include classes in the English language, civics, and history. LIBRE offices are often located in Latino neighborhoods near schools, such as their office in Mesa, Arizona.

Their offices are furnished with computers, study rooms, conference rooms, and game rooms, providing resources for young Latinos to use after school. This outreach into Latino schools gives LIBRE organizers an opportunity to promote free-market ideals without the stigma of being associated with conservatives or the Republican Party.

Stephen A. Nuño

See also: Education and Latinos; Minimum Wage; Proposition 187 (1994); SB 1070 (2010); Voter ID Laws, Impact of

Further Reading

Abrajano, Marisa, & Simran Singh. 2009. "Examining the Link between Issue Attitudes and News Source: The Case of Latinos and Immigration Reform." *Political Behavior* 31, no. 1: 1–30.

Bautista-Chavez, Angie, & Sarah Meyer. 2015. "The Libre Initiative—An Innovative Conservative Effort to Recruit Latino Support." Cambridge, MA: Scholars Strategy Network.

Santillan, Richard, & Federico A. Subervi-Velez. 1991. "Latino Participation in Republican Party Politics in California." *Racial and Ethnic Politics in California:* 285–319.

Segura, Gary M. 2012. "Latino Public Opinion & Realigning the American Electorate." *Daedalus* 141, no. 4: 98–113.

Skocpol, Theda, & Alexander Hertel-Fernandez. 2016. "The Koch Network and Republican Party Extremism." *Perspectives on Politics* 14, no. 3: 681–99.

Longoria, Eva

(1975–)

Born to Mexican American parents in Corpus Christi, Texas, Eva Longoria is known for her work as an actor, philanthropist, producer, and businesswoman. Upon graduating with a bachelor's of science degree in kinesiology from Texas A&M University and being Miss Corpus Christi USA 1998, Longoria entered the television and movie industry. Since then she has been nominated for and won numerous awards, including a nomination for a Golden Globe in her most noteworthy role as Gabrielle Solis in the hit television show *Desperate Housewives*. Longoria is also the spokesperson for Padres Contra El Cancer (Parents against Cancer), where she has helped raise over $4 million for the organization through the annual fundraising gala "El Sueño de Esperanza," (The Dream of Hope) and other fundraising campaigns. She has contracts with companies such as L'Oréal and Hanes, owns her own clothing line, and is also a restaurant owner in Hollywood. All the while, Longoria has continued to use her platform to support various charitable organizations and provide a positive impact and voice to the Latino community.

Actor Eva Longoria in Los Angeles, 2018. In May 2014, she initiated the Latino Victory Project to raise funds for candidates and efforts to get out the vote. (Starstock/Dreamstime.com)

In 2013, Longoria graduated from California State University, Northridge with a master's degree in Chicano studies. Her thesis was titled, "Success STEMS from Diversity: The Value of Latinas in STEM Careers." Longoria took this initiative in order to gain a genuine understanding of her community and so she could create more effective changes.

The Eva Longoria Foundation, cofounded by Howard Buffett, is Longoria's most well-known organization. The organization addresses the disparity in education and poverty among Latinos. Additionally, it provides business programs and entrepreneurial guidance to help Latinas with career training and mentorship. Other organizations founded by Longoria include Eva's Heroes, started in 2006, which aims to aid developmentally disabled children with extracurricular activities and provide counseling to parents and family members. Furthermore, Longoria contributed as an executive producer on the documentary *The Harvest*. The movie brought to light issues surrounding migrant child workers all across the United States working up to 12 hours a day, seven days a week, in hazardous conditions without being protected under child labor laws. Longoria accepted the award in 2011 when *The Harvest* won an ALMA for Special Achievement.

Longoria has openly expressed herself and concerns on topics relating to politics and especially immigration. Longoria expressed her disapproval of Arizona's anti-immigrant law and openly supported the DREAM Act, a legislative act that would allow alien minors to eventually gain permanent residency over time.

Longoria was also an advisor to President Obama, advocating for the rights of Hispanic immigrant families and children. She has been an active spokesperson for immigration reform and representation. In the film *Food Chains,* Longoria, along with Eric Schlosser, follows a hunger strike led by the Immokolee farm workers. The strike followed the plight of farm workers fighting for their representation rights, wages, and safety in the farm fields from pesticides. The film helped bring much needed attention to the rights of farm laborers and the hardships they face and pressured companies and business to act with fairness.

As one of the founders of the Latino Victory Project, Longoria has also pushed the Latino population to exercise their right to vote and engage in politics, policy and civic development. The aim of the Latino Victory Project is also to develop future Latino leaders to engage as citizens and be representatives for the Latino community.

Longoria's efforts have led to her winning numerous awards and recognition worldwide. Notably, Longoria was named Philanthropist of the Year in 2009 by *The Hollywood Reporter* and was listed 42nd on a list of 200 in *Richtopia*'s Most Influential Philanthropists and Social Entrepreneurs Worldwide.

Zujaja Tehreem

See also: Immigration as a Policy Issue; Obama, Barack (1961–) and Latinos

Further Reading

"Eva Longoria: Charity Work & Causes." https://www.looktothestars.org/celebrity/eva -longoria.

"Mission & Vision." http://latinovictory.us/MISSION_VISION.

Los Angeles School Walkouts

(1968, 2006)

The Los Angeles School Walkouts of 1968 were organized by Chicano students to protest against the quality of education they received in high schools. These actions are considered the first massive demonstration of Latinx youth in Southern California; their importance has inspired other public tactics and demonstrations, like the Walkouts of 2006 (several days of public demonstrations against harsh restrictions on undocumented migrants proposed in the H.R. 4437 Act of 2005).

By the end of the 1960s, the Chicano Movement (also known as the Brown Power Movement) questioned the circumstances that students of Mexican descent experienced in high schools: a 40 to 50 percent chance of not graduating high school and an elevated chance to be among the lowest in the nation in terms of reading ability. Both the Spanish language and history of Latinx communities were not part of academic curricula, and students' skills and abilities were not noticed or developed. Additionally, teachers and counselors encouraged them to learn a trade and join the workforce without pursuing any further education. The average high school professor was Anglo-American, and some constantly harassed Chicano students with racial slurs.

In 1967, Sal Castro, a teacher at Lincoln High School, had the idea of organizing a series of walkouts in what would eventually be known as the East Los Angeles Walkouts or the Chicano Blowouts. Numerous schools in the area participated, gathering between 2,000 and 5,000 protestors who effectively shut down all East Los Angeles high schools for almost an entire week. Among the organizers was Moctesuma Esparza, who had previously been a key part of Chicano activist groups such as the Brown Berets and the UMAS (United Mexican American students), and both participated in the walkouts. After these demonstrations, students met with the board of education and presented a list of over 30 demands drafted by the central committee. The demands focused on academic, administrative, and infrastructure concerns, such as bilingual and bicultural curricula and textbooks, hiring more personnel of Mexican American heritage, the removal of teachers or administrators who showed any kind of racial prejudice against Chicano students, and building better premises and new schools. Unfortunately, even when the board of education agreed with almost all of these points, they did not comply with the demands, citing lack of funding. Several of the Blowouts organizers were arrested for disturbing the peace even when the protests had a nonviolent nature. Although these demonstrations were not immediately successful, they are still considered the largest mobilization of Chicano youth leaders in Los Angeles, and one of the pivotal moments in Chicano history. Its symbolic strength has been a point of reference for other movements, among them the 2006 Los Angeles Unified School District Walkouts.

In December 2005, the U.S. Congress passed the Border Protection, Antiterrorism, and Illegal Immigration Control Act (H.R. 4437), which contained provisions that would toughen requirements to attain residency status and would criminalize not only immigrants but also landlords, employers, and organizations that provide services, jobs, or help to undocumented immigrants. In March 2006, over 40,000 students, immigrants, and supporters commenced a series of walkouts that lasted several days and involved many high schools, showing the organizational power of a large Latinx community and the convening power of Latinx students, leaders, and Spanish-speaking mass media networks. The Act did not pass the Senate, although it paved the way for similar proposals and laws at local levels.

Pamela Fuentes Peralta

See also: Brown Berets; Brown Power Movement/Chicano Civil Rights Movement; Mega Marchas of 2006

Further Reading

Chávez, Ernesto. 2002. *"¡Mi Raza Primero!" (My People First): Nationalism, Identity, and Insurgency in the Chicano Movement in Los Angeles, 1966–1978.* Berkeley and Los Angeles: University of California Press.

García, Mario T. 2011. *Blowout! Sal Castro and the Chicano Struggle for Educational Justice.* Chapel Hill: The University of North Carolina Press.

Ludlow Massacre

(1914)

The Ludlow Massacre was an attack against 1,200 striking coal miners and their families by the Colorado National Guard and the Colorado Fuel & Iron Company. On April 20, 1914, troops opened fire with machine guns on the armed miners and set fire to the provisional settlement where the workers and their families were camping out in Ludlow, Colorado. The massacre is considered the culmination of the Colorado Coal Strike that started in September 1913. With a death toll of over a dozen, including 2 women and 11 children, the Ludlow Massacre has been often described as one of the most lethal strike repressions in U.S. history, and one of the most violent struggles between laborers and corporate power in the country's past. Most recently, it has been studied as a significant episode in the history of organized immigrant labor.

Coal production in Colorado reached a peak in 1910, dominated by a handful of businessmen. Among the most influential was the Rockefeller family, who owned

The Ludlow Massacre was a watershed moment in U.S. labor relations. Seen here is the funeral procession of the Ludlow victims leaving a Catholic church. (National Archives and Records Administration)

the Colorado Fuel & Iron Company, one of the most powerful companies in the country. Since the turn of the century the mining industry had tried to quash union efforts and strike attempts. One of the corporate strategies was to recruit immigrants, hoping that ethnic and racial differences within the workforce would make it impossible for laborers to unite. The largest groups of immigrant miners in Colorado were Italian, Mexican, Austrian, and Greek. It is worth noting that numerous workers labeled as Mexicans were actually U.S. citizens from Colorado and New Mexico. In spite of employers' increasing efforts, miners organized themselves in order to improve their harsh working conditions. By 1913 11,000 coal miners employed by John D. Rockefeller, Jr., were trying to form the United Mine Workers union and presented a list of demands that included recognition of their association, an eight-hour work day; the right to elect their own check-weight men, in order to ensure an honest measure of the coal they actually mined (as they were paid by results); the right to trade in any store; and the right to choose their own doctors. The major coal companies rejected the petitions, and the workers voted to strike. On September 23, 1913, the miners and their families were evicted from their coal camps, so they set up temporary tent colonies near their workplaces. The biggest one was the Ludlow camp, which housed more than 1,000 people.

The Colorado Fuel & Iron Company responded by harassing their workers and by bringing in strikebreaking professionals, as well as workers that would replace the strikers. On April 20, 1914, National Guardsmen engaged in a daylong gunfight with the workers. That afternoon, the members of the Guard set fire to the Ludlow colony. Thirteen residents who tried to flee were shot and killed and many more burned to death. The colony ended in ruins. Among the victims were Charles Costa, union organizer at Aguilar; his wife and two children, 4 and 6 years old; and Mrs. Chavez, a Mexican woman, and her three young children and nephew. Even though the workers were replaced by nonunion employees and failed to obtain their demands, in the long term the legacy of the strike and the massacre had an impact on labor relations and mining conditions, paving the way for discussions about health, working conditions, and other workers' rights.

Pamela Fuentes Peralta

See also: Gonzales, Rodolfo "Corky" (1928–2005)

Further Reading

Mauk, Ben. 2014. "The Ludlow Massacre Still Matters." *The New Yorker,* April 18. https://www.newyorker.com/business/currency/the-ludlow-massacre-still-matters.

Montoya, Fawn-Amber, ed. 2014. *Making an American Workforce: The Rockefellers and the Legacy of Ludlow.* Boulder: University Press of Colorado.

Scott, Martelle. 2008. *Blood and Passion: The Ludlow Massacre and Class War in the American West.* New Brunswick, NJ: Rutgers University Press.

Luján, Ben Ray

(1972–)

Democrat Ben Ray Luján has represented New Mexico's 3rd congressional district since his initial election to the seat in 2008. He is the eighth Mexican American elected to the U.S. House of Representatives from New Mexico since statehood (U.S. House of Representatives, 2013). Luján hails from a family of public servants; his father, Ben Luján, Sr., served in the New Mexico House of Representatives, and his cousins are former U.S. representative Manuel Luján (D-NM) and current U.S. representative Michelle Luján Grisham (D-NM). Prior to his election to the open 3rd congressional district seat vacated by Democrat Tom Udall, Luján was an elected member of the New Mexico Public Regulation Commission and gained public service experience as deputy New Mexico state treasurer and as an administrator for the New Mexico Department of Cultural Affairs (U.S. House of Representatives, 2013). Luján's political career reflects a commitment to representing the issues important to a diverse and often underrepresented constituency at the national level.

New Mexico's 3rd congressional district is rich in Hispanic/Latino and American Indian history. The district included New Mexico's capital city of Santa Fe, one of the United States' oldest Spanish Mexican settlements, and is home to 15 Pueblo tribes, the Jicarilla Apache Nation, and the Navajo Nation. The district spans a large, sparsely populated geographic area, but is socioeconomically and culturally diverse. Hispanics make up 41 percent of the district's population, and American Indians are 18 percent (U.S. Census, 2015), which reflects New Mexico's rich cultural diversity. Though not a majority-Latino district, New Mexico's 3rd congressional district is an important example of a majority-minority district, which helps explain Luján's decisive election and reelection victories (Bowler and Segura, 2012). Having been born and raised in northern New Mexico, where Hispanic and American Indian communities have lived in harmony for much of New Mexico's history, the native influences on his upbringing have made Luján a proud and effective advocate of American Indian issues at the national level.

Luján's advocacy for Hispanics and American Indians, as well as the energy and technology sectors, are features of his "home style" of representation, through which he has identified and cultivated his core constituencies in the early "expansionist stage" (Fenno, 2002) of his congressional career. Through his sponsorship of 100 and co-sponsorship of over 1,000 pieces of legislation, and over 200 declarations recorded into the U.S. Congressional Record during his tenure (Library of Congress, 2017), Luján has advocated for a wide range of issues important to Latino and American Indian communities in New Mexico and nationwide. In 2010, Luján co-sponsored HR 3553, the Indian Veterans Housing Opportunity Act (Public Law No. 111–269), which eliminated some restrictions on income for eligibility of housing assistance, making housing support more accessible. In 2014 he co-sponsored HR 2431, the National Integrated Drought Information System Reauthorization Act (Public Law No. 113–86), which helps small ranchers and farmers by improving drought warning systems. His leadership on issues as diverse as opioid abuse prevention, immigrant protections, community college energy training, water rights, and environmental protection has earned him endorsements and favorable ratings that reflect the congressman's acute attention to his "geographic and reelection constituencies" (Fenno, 2002).

Luján's identity, lived professional experiences, and service to his constituents have also led to his assignments to key House committees and to positions of leadership within the Democratic Party. He has been a House Democratic chief deputy whip and chair of the Democratic Congressional Campaign Committee. His experience as a state utilities regulator and his representation of the geographic area where the Los Alamos National Laboratory is located inform his substantive work as a member of the Energy and Commerce Committee, Communications and Technology Subcommittee, and the Health Committee. Luján also voices his advocacy of Latino and American Indian communities though his service on the Congressional Hispanic Caucus and the Native American Caucus.

Xavier Medina Vidal

See also: Lujan Grisham, Michelle (1959–); *Essays:* Hispanic Office Holders at the State and Local Levels; Latino Elected Officials on the Federal Level

Further Reading

Bowler, Shaun, & Gary Segura. 2012. *The Future Is Ours: Minority Politics, Political Behavior, and the Multiracial Era of American Politics.* Washington, D.C.: CQ Press.

Fenno, Richard F., Jr. 2002 [1978]. *Home Style: House Members in Their Districts.* Longman Classics Edition. New York: Pearson.

Library of Congress. 2017. "Legislation Sponsored or Cosponsored by Ben Ray Luján." https://www.congress.gov/member/ben-lujan/L000570.

Luján, Ben R. 2017. https://lujan.house.gov/.

U.S. Census. 2015. "My Congressional District." *American Community Survey.* https://www.census.gov/mycd.

U.S. House of Representatives. 2013. *Hispanic Americans in Congress: 1822–2012.* Washington, D.C.: U.S. Government Printing Office.

Lujan Grisham, Michelle

(1959–)

Michelle Lujan Grisham is a politician and lawyer who has represented New Mexico's first congressional district since 2013. A member of the Democratic Party, Lujan Grisham is a member of the House Agriculture Committee, the House Budget Committee, and the House Oversight and Government Reform Committee. Lujan Grisham advocates for public health programs, women's rights, veterans' services, environmental protections, and policies to protect seniors such as Social Security and Medicare. Prior to serving in Congress, Lujan Grisham held prominent positions in state government. She served as the director of New Mexico's State Agency on Aging under both Republican and Democratic governors. In 2004, Governor Bill Richardson appointed Lujan Grisham secretary of health, where she served until 2007 when she left to pursue elected politics. In 2016, Lujan Grisham was elected chair of the Congressional Hispanic Caucus for the 115th Congress and announced her intention to run for governor of New Mexico in 2018.

Born in Los Alamos, New Mexico, Michelle Lujan Grisham was educated at St. Michael's High School in Santa Fe before she attended the University of New Mexico, where she obtained a bachelor's degree and later returned for law school, receiving her JD in 1987. Lujan Grisham claims her motivation to pursue a career in public service came from watching her parents struggle to afford medical care for her sister who was diagnosed with a brain tumor at 2 years old and passed away at age 21 (Kim, 2013). Luján Grisham comes from a political family. Her uncle, Manuel Lujan, Jr., represented New Mexico in Congress before he joined President George H. W. Bush's administration as secretary of the interior, her grandfather was the first Hispanic chief justice of the New Mexico Supreme Court, and her cousin, Ben Lujan, was elected to Congress in 2008 to represent New Mexico's third congressional district.

In 2008, Lujan Grisham mounted an unsuccessful bid to win the Democratic primary for New Mexico's first congressional district, losing to Martin Heinrich, who went on to win the general election. Two years later, she was elected to office as Bernalillo County commissioner where she worked to bring accountability, transparency, and ethics reform to the county government (Committee to Elect Michelle Lujan Grisham, 2012). In 2012, Heinrich vacated his seat to run for the U.S. Senate, providing Lujan Grisham with a strategic opportunity; Lujan Grisham went on to win both the Democratic primary and the general election, joining the 113th Congress as the representative from New Mexico's first congressional district. Once in Congress, Lujan Grisham joined a number of policy caucuses and became an active member of the Congressional Hispanic Caucus. Reelected in 2014 and 2016 with large margins, Lujan Grisham became chair of the Congressional Hispanic Caucus in 2017, where she advocates for immigration reform and policies to reduce minority health disparities and improve economic opportunities for Latinos and other minority groups.

In Congress, Lujan Grisham has introduced legislation to improve access to food and nutrition assistance, expand access to health insurance programs such as Medicaid, and assist families when they face home foreclosure. She has also developed and introduced the National Care Corps Act, modeled after the Peace Corps, which would create new programs to provide high-quality care for aging and disabled Americans. In 2016, Lujan Grisham announced plans to run for governor of New Mexico in 2018.

Angelina L. Gonzalez-Aller

See also: Congressional Hispanic Caucus Institute (CHCI); Luján, Ben Ray (1972–)

Further Reading

Committee to Elect Michelle Lujan Grisham. 2012. "Michelle Lujan Grisham Accomplishments." http://www.michellelujangrisham.com/files/Michelle-Lujan-Grisham-Accom plishments.pdf.

Gustavus, Sarah 2012. "Grisham Has Already Defied Expectations." *NMpolitics.net*, May 24. http://nmpolitics.net/index/2012/05/grisham-has-already-defied-expectations/.

Hellwege, J., & C. Sierra. 2016. "Advantages and Disadvantage for Latina Officeholders." In S. Navarro, S. Hernandez, and L. Navarro, eds. *Latinas in American Politics: Changing and Embracing Political Tradition*. New York: Lexington Books, pp. 113–34.

Kim, S. M. 2013. "Sister's Death Drives Lujan Grisham." *Politico*, January 17. http://www .politico.com/story/2013/01/michelle-lujan-grisham-profile-086137.

Lujan Grisham, M. 2016. "Biography." https://lujangrisham.house.gov/about/biography.

"Meet Michelle." *Michelle Lujan Grisham: Democrat for Congress*. http://www .michellelujangrisham.com/meet-michelle/.

Lynching in the U.S. Southwest

Lynching refers to an extralegal murder of an individual at the hands of a mob for an alleged offense that has not been verified in a court of law. Lynchings often had a racial undertone, as both African Americans and Mexican Americans, among other groups, were often targeted for this violent act by white mobs for various reasons having to do with maintaining white supremacy (the belief that white people are superior to those of all other races and should dominate). Mexican Americans were frequent targets of lynching in the U.S. Southwest, which consisted of the following states: Arizona, California, New Mexico, and most violently, in Texas. The history of lynching in the Southwest had largely been ignored, but historians now believe the Mexican American population in the Southwest had been lynched at a rate similar to that of African Americans, though more African Americans were lynched overall. This equivalence in terms of comparable rates is due to the much smaller size of the Mexican American population in the Southwest between the years 1848 and 1928 (Carrigan and Webb, 2003). Delgado (2009: 303–4) notes that local Mexican American communities in the Southwest recorded a local history of lynchings through *corridos* (Spanish-language ballads composed to celebrate an event or hero) and *cantares* (Spanish-language poetry).

Historians have been able to comb through historical documents to verify 547 cases of lynching, although they admit this was a conservative estimate and that the real number could lie in the thousands (Carrigan and Webb, 2015). The U.S. Southwest was once part of Mexico, but was ceded to the United States following the Mexican-American War (1846–1848). A small population of about 100,000 Mexican Americans remained in the newly acquired U.S. territory and would be complemented by a small stream of Mexican migration. The Mexican Americans represented a challenge to the economic and social dominance of white Americans, and lynchings were a tool by which white mobs could render Mexican Americans politically powerless and economically subjugated. For example, white Americans turned to lynchings to eliminate economic competition from Mexican Americans, such as during the California Gold Rush when an estimated 163 Mexican Americans were killed due to the early success of that group in the gold mines (Carrigan and Webb, 2003: 422).

One distinct feature of the lynchings of Mexican Americans is the fact that law enforcement often colluded with the lynch mobs. The criminal justice system often did not investigate lynchings of Mexican Americans, and even when it did, they never prosecuted anyone. The Texas Rangers were a law enforcement agency with statewide jurisdiction that was the most infamous in their participation in lynch mobs. While they had been terrorizing the Mexican American population practically since their inception, their most brutal acts were carried out in periods of heightened tensions between Mexico and the United States, such as when the Texas Rangers and a local mob of white vigilantes killed 15 Mexican American men in the Porvenir Massacre in 1918, erroneously believing the men had been colluding with Mexican raiders (Carrigan and Webb, 2015).

The Southwest was also a region known as the borderlands (a region where two nations or societies shared an often-contested boundary) where Mexican, U.S.

American, and indigenous societies often came into contact and conflict. The most lynchings occurred in the decades that featured the greatest tension between the governments of the United States and Mexico. In the 1910s, U.S. white American fears about the Mexican Revolution and its potential supporters among the Mexican American population following the discovery of *Plan de San Diego* (a revolutionary document that called for Mexican Americans and other minorities to overthrow U.S. white American rule) led to one of the bloodiest periods in Texas history. The lynching of Mexican Americans in the Southwest would decline dramatically in the 1920s as the Mexican Revolution ended and the hysteria over *Plan de San Diego* dissipated. Diplomatic pressure from Mexico also forced the U.S. federal government to intervene in investigations of lynchings of Mexican nationals in the Southwest (Carrigan and Webb, 2003: 429).

Matthew S. Mendez

See also: National Security State and Latinos; Treaty of Guadalupe Hidalgo (1848)

Further Reading

Carrigan, William D., & Clive Webb. 2003. "The Lynching of Persons of Mexican Origin or Descent in the United States, 1848–1928." *Journal of Social History* 37, no. 2: 411–38.

Carrigan, William D., & Clive Webb. 2015. "When Americans Lynched Mexicans." *New York Times,* February 20. https://www.nytimes.com/2015/02/20/opinion/when-americans-lynched-mexicans.html?_r=0.

Delgado, Richard. 2009. "The Law of the Noose: A History of Latino Lynching." *Harvard Civil Rights-Civil Liberties Law Review* 44, no. 2: 297–312.

Mallea, Jose

(1977–)

Jose Mallea served as the national senior Hispanic outreach advisor for former Florida governor Jeb Bush's unsuccessful 2016 presidential campaign. Hired to Bush's political action committee, Right to Rise, Mallea advised the campaign on Latino outreach and engagement and worked to bring more Latinos to the GOP by focusing on issues like immigration reform and jobs. He is the owner and president of JM Global Consulting and co-owner of the Biscayne Bay Brewing Company in Doral, Florida, and Local Craft Food & Drink in Coral Gables, Florida (Minsky, 2017). A long-time Republican political leader, Mallea is a candidate for the Florida State legislature to replace Representative José Felix Diaz (House District 116). Representative Diaz, who will be termed out in 2018, announced his candidacy for the Florida Senate in May 2017.

Prior to his candidacy, Mallea held several political, government, and civic positions. In 2012, he served as the Florida State director for former Speaker of the House Newt Gingrich's unsuccessful bid for the presidency (Caputo, 2011). From 2011 to 2015, Mallea served as national strategic director for the LIBRE Initiative (Caputo, 2015). The nonprofit grassroots Latino political outreach organization is tied to influential philanthropists Charles G. and David H. Koch, who have made significant financial contributions to libertarian and conservative groups and campaigns since 2009.

In 2010, he served as campaign manager to Senator Marco Rubio, who successfully won a three-way race against Representative Kendrick Meek (D) and former Florida governor Charlie Crist, who left the GOP and ran as an independent, to represent the state in the U.S. Senate. Mallea is credited with engineering Rubio's victory, relying on his strong ties with Republican elites and the Latino community in Miami-Dade. Prior to this position, Mallea also served as chief of staff to Manny Diaz, the mayor of Miami from 2005 to 2007.

Mallea worked several years in Washington, D.C., serving in the Department of State as associate director in the Office of White House Liaison (2004–2005) and as a senior advisor in the Office of Commercial and Business Affairs (2003–2004). From 2001 to 2003, Mallea worked in President George W. Bush's administration in various appointed posts, including special assistant to the Administrator of the U.S. Small Business Administration Hector V. Barreto and personal aide to the White House Chief of Staff Andrew Card (Leadership Institute, 2017). In late 1990s, Mallea worked on gubernatorial and presidential campaigns, respectively, serving as regional field director for Jeb Bush's 2000 campaign in Florida, and as youth coordinator for Bob Dole's 1996 campaign where he worked to increase youth voter turnout in Miami-Dade County.

Mallea, who is of Cuban Ecuadorian descent, graduated from Hialeah-Miami Lakes Senior High School and Florida International University in Miami, Florida.

Atiya Kai Stokes-Brown

See also: Rubio, Marco (1971–)

Further Reading

Burton, Michael J., & Daniel M. Shea. 2010. *Campaign Craft: The Strategies, Tactics, and Art of Political Campaign Management.* Santa Barbara, CA: Praeger.

Caputo, Marc. 2011. "Gingrich Hires Former Rubio Campaign Chief José Mallea." December 12. http://www.kansas.com/news/nation-world/national/article1082243.html.

Caputo, Marc. 2015. "Bush PAC to Hire Longtime Rubio Friend and Aid for Hispanic Outreach." http://www.politico.com/story/2015/05/jeb-bush-pac-to-hire-longtime-marco -rubio-friend-and-aide-for-hispanic-outreach-117544.

Dulio, David A. 2004. *For Better or Worse: How Political Consultants Are Changing Elections in the United States.* Albany: State University of New York Press.

Johnson, Dennis W. 2007. *No Place for Amateurs: How Political Consultants Are Reshaping American Democracy.* 2nd ed. New York: Routledge.

Leadership Institute. 2017. "Jose Mallea—Former Guest Speaker at the Leadership Institute." https://leadershipinstitute.org/training/contact.cfm?FacultyID=1234671.

Minsky, David. 2017. "Biscayne Bay Brewing's José Mallea Announces Candidacy for Florida Legislature." *Miami New Times*, March 27. http://www.miaminewtimes .com/content/printView/9233035.

Thurber, James A., & Candice J. Nelson. 2013. *Campaigns and Elections American Style: Transforming American Politics.* 4th ed. Boulder, CO: Westview Press.

Trent, Judith S., Robert V. Friedenberg, & Robert R. Denton. 2015. *Political Campaign Communication: Principles and Practices.* 8th ed. New York: Rowman & Littlefield Publishers.

Marín, Rosario

(1958–)

Rosario Marín served as the 41st treasurer of the United States under Republican president George W. Bush from 2001 to 2003. She is the only U.S. treasurer to have been born outside U.S. borders, the first Mexican-born citizen to become treasurer, and was the highest-ranked Latina woman in the Bush administration. As treasurer, she encouraged financial literacy for Latinos and had a significant role in President George W. Bush's Partnership for Prosperity with Mexico. She was the first Latina to run for Senate in California in 2003, but her campaign was not successful; she ran as a Republican. Throughout her career, she has been an advocate for people with disabilities.

Marín was born Rosario Spindola in Mexico City, and when she was 14, she and her family moved to California on visas provided by her father's employer. Because she did not speak English, Marín failed her high school's standardized tests and was labeled mentally disabled by the school. This inspired her to work harder to learn English, and she graduated from high school with honors in 1976. While working full time at City National Bank, she attended East Los Angeles College and then California State University of Los Angeles (CSULA). She graduated from CSULA in 1983 with a bachelor's degree in business administration and marketing. By the time she graduated college, she had been promoted from a receptionist at City National Bank to almost being promoted to vice-president of the company. Before she was promoted, she and her husband Alex had their first son Eric in 1985. After they learned he had Down's syndrome, she stopped working in order to care for him and his younger siblings, Carmen and Alex, after they were born.

Her son, Eric, inspired her to become a champion of the rights of people with disabilities. She founded her own nonprofit, Fuerza, Inc. (Force, Inc.), as the first ever support group for Hispanic families of children with Down's syndrome who were Spanish-speaking, and it is still in operation today. In 1992, she became the chief of legislative affairs for the Department of Developmental Services and was later promoted to the assistant deputy director of the California State Department of Social Services.

In 1994, Marín was elected to the city council of Huntington Park, California, and the council elected her as mayor. She served two terms as mayor even though most of the population consisted of Democratic Hispanics, and she had been a proud Republican since becoming a U.S. citizen in 1984. While working as mayor and councilwoman, she served as deputy director of Governor Wilson's Community Relations Department in 1997 and later as the public relations manager for AT&T's Hispanic Market in the Southern California Region.

In 2004, she resigned from her job as U.S. treasurer to launch her campaign for the U.S. Senate, thus becoming the first Latina in California to run for Senate. However, she was not selected as the Republican candidate for the election. Between 2005 and 2006, she served as the chairwoman of the California Integrated Waste Management Board. From 2006 to March 2009, she was the secretary of the State and Consumer Services Agency under Governor Arnold Schwarzenegger. While there, she oversaw 17 state departments. In 2007, she published an autobiography entitled *Leading between Two Worlds: Lessons from the First Mexican-Born Treasurer of the United States*. From 2009 to 2010, she served as the vice-president of business relations for the Old Republic National Title Insurance Co. in Orange County, California.

Throughout her career, Marín has been awarded numerous honors because of her activism and work in the public sector. In 1995, she received the Rose Fitzgerald Kennedy Award by the Joseph P. Kennedy, Jr., Foundation in appreciation of her work for people with disabilities. In 1996, she was named to the Special Olympics board of directors. She was awarded the Lifetime Achievement Award at the League for California Cities Annual Conference in 2006. She has been awarded four honorary doctorate degrees from California State University, Los Angeles; Whittier College; St. Francis University; and Woodbury University.

Carolyn Phillips

See also: Acosta Bañuelos, Romana (1925–2018)

Further Reading

"Biography of Rosario Marin." 2003. *Rosario Marin '04*. http://digital.library.ucla.edu /websites /2004_999_042/en/about/.

Oliver-Mendez, Ken. 2002. "U.S. Treasurer Rosario Marin: The New Face of the American Dream." *Caribbean Business*, October 3. http://ehis.ebscohost.com/eds/pdfviewer /pdfviewer?sid=5136068c-8381-4271-974f-fae0d3b2df24@sessionmgr4007&vid =0&hid=4108.

Radelat, Ana. 2002. "Rosario Marin: A Latina Who's Right on the Money." *Hispanic* (June): 26. http://ehis.ebscohost.com/eds/pdfviewer/pdfviewer?sid=b1817e13-84b0-4d72 -9883-a47a372eb40e%40sessionmgr4009&vid=1&hid=4113.

"Rosario Marin: Former Treasurer of the United States." 2016. *American Program Bureau*, September 14. http://www.apbspeakers.com/speaker/rosario-marin.

"Rosario Marin: U.S. Treasurer—From Illiterate Immigrant to Honor Student." *Brief Biographies*. http://biography.jrank.org/pages/3399/Marin-Rosario-19-U-S-Treasurer -From-Illiterate-Immigrant-Honor-Student.html.

"Rosario Marin Receives Lifetime Achievement Award at League of California Cities Annual Conference." 2006. *Internet Wire*, September 7. http://rlib.pace.edu/login ?url=http:// go.galegroup.com/ps/i.do?p=ITOF&sw=w&u=nysl_me_pace&v=2 .1&id=GALE|A151063566&it=r&asid=963952d655be8aa2a66156fd0a1e2909.

Mark-Viverito, Melissa

(1969–)

Melissa Mark-Viverito is a politician and member of the Democratic Party from New York City. She is the current Speaker of the New York City council and New York City council member for the 8th district, which includes Harlem and the Bronx. She is the first Hispanic and Latina to hold that position.

Mark-Viverito was born and raised in Puerto Rico; she moved to New York for college. She attended Columbia University, where she received a bachelor of arts degree in 1991 and later Baruch College of the City University of New York, where she received a master's of public administration. Her involvement in politics predates her time as a New York City councilor, when Mark-Viverito was involved with local progressive activists such as those who hoped to end U.S. Naval training exercises on the Puerto Rican island of Vieques. She later helped found Mujeres del Barrio, an organization focused on helping women become involved in politics, worked as an organizer for Service Employees International Union (SEIU) Local 1099, and served as a member of Manhattan Community Board 11.

She first ran for New York City council in 2003, but lost to the incumbent Phil Reed, who had held the position since 1995. Two years later in 2005 when Reed was no longer able to run for office due to term limits, Mark-Viverito ran again and narrowly defeated Felipe Luciano in the Democratic primary. She won the general election later that year and became the council representative for New York City's 8th district. Mark-Viverito was reelected twice: in 2009 and 2013. Although New York City council members are currently limited to two consecutive four-year terms, Mark-Viverito was able to serve three terms due to a change in term limits laws in 2008 even though those changes were rolled back two years later. During her third and final term, in January 2014, she was unanimously elected Speaker of the New York City council. Mark-Viverito's third and final term expired on December 31, 2017. There is some speculation that she will run for New York City mayor. In the meantime, she has been critical of the lack of women elected to the city council and helped to found an organization to recruit and raise funds for women who hope to run for office.

Mark-Viverito was elected as a progressive and has supported many progressive policies while in office. She co-chaired the city council's progressive caucus. She supports raising the minimum wage, offering free birth control to all women in New York City, transgender people's rights, and the legalization of marijuana. She supports a proposal to close the Rikers Island Correctional Center. She has remained an active participant in political activism in New York City. She was arrested during the Occupy Wall Street protests in 2011.

New York councilwoman Melissa Mark-Viverito, who served as the speaker of the New York City Council from 2014 to 2017 as well as councilmember for the 8th district from 2006 to 2017, speaks at the unveiling of the PETA Icon postage sheet in New York City, 2013. (Taylor Hill/FilmMagic/Getty Images)

Mark-Viverito faced some criticism from other progressive Democrats. Although she initially supported the Right to Know Act, which would have required police officers to explain why they are searching someone, she did not call for a vote on the measure despite support from the majority of the city council. Others criticized her during her 2013 campaign after she accepted free consulting services from a lobbying organization for which she was fined.

She has been critical of President Donald Trump. During his campaign she supported Hillary Clinton and criticized Trump's campaign speeches through Twitter. In April 2017, she spoke with other leaders of cities who refuse to cooperate with federal immigration officials. During the discussion with other leaders, she said that she hoped they would be the Trump administration's "worst nightmare" (Durkin, 2017). She helped organize activists and leaders from other cities across the country to help strategize against the Trump administration's immigration policies.

Nathan Angelo

See also: Espaillat, Adriano (1954–); Farina, Carmen (1943–); Ferreras-Copeland, Julissa (1976–)

Further Reading

Barkan, Ross. 2014. "The Unlikely Rise of City Council Speaker Melissa Mark-Viverito." *New York Observer,* June 17. http://observer.com/2014/06/no-2-and-trying-harder.

Durkin, Erin. 2017. "Council Speaker Mark-Viverito Urges Sanctuary Cities Like NYC to Be Trump's 'Worst Nightmare'" *New York Daily News,* March 27. http://www.nydailynews.com/news/politics/nyc-pol-urges-sanctuary-cities-trump-worst-nightmare-article-1.3010841.

Goodman, J. David. 2016a. "New York Council Won't Vote on Police Reform Bills, But Agency Agrees to Changes." *The New York Times,* July 12. https://www.nytimes.com/2016/07/13/nyregion/new-york-city-council-will-not-vote-on-police-reform-measures.html.

Goodman, J. David. 2016b. "Mark-Viverito, New York Council Speaker, Pays Fine to End Conflict Case." *The New York Times,* January 6. http://www.nytimes.com/2016/01/07/nyregion/mark-viverito-new-york-council-speaker-pays-fine-to-end-conflict-case.html.

Grynbaum, Michael M., & Kate Taylor. 2014. "Mayoral Ally Elected Speaker, Furthering City's Liberal Shift." *The New York Times,* January 8. https://www.nytimes.com/2014/01/09/nyregion/mark-viverito-is-elected-city-council-speaker.html.

McGeehan, Patrick. 2014. "Higher Minimum Wage Gains Support." *The New York Times,* June 4. http://www.nytimes.com/2014/06/05/nyregion/higher-minimum-wage-gains-support.html.

Martinez, Susana

(1959–)

The first Latina to be elected governor in the United States, Susana Martinez was elected governor of New Mexico in 2010. Martinez, a Republican, was rumored to be in the running to join Mitt Romney's 2012 presidential ticket as a vice-president, but was not selected.

Susana Martinez, a Mexican American, was born on July 14, 1959, in El Paso, Texas. She is the daughter of Jacob Martinez, a former deputy sheriff and Marine. Martinez's mother, Paula Aguirre, worked in multiple offices while raising Martinez and her two siblings. She is the legal custodian of her older sister Lettie, who is developmentally disabled and has cerebral palsy.

Susana attended Riverside High School in El Paso. She served as student body president and graduated in 1977. Martinez chose to attend the University of Texas-El Paso and graduated with a bachelor's degree in criminal justice in 1981. After completing her bachelor's degree, Martinez moved to Oklahoma and pursued a law degree.

After completing her law degree, Martinez moved to Las Cruces, New Mexico, where she took a job as an assistant district attorney for the 3rd judicial district. As an assistant district attorney, Martinez focused on cases dealing with sexually abused children. She attended seminars related to sexual offenses against women and children. In addition, Martinez developed a team that specialized in these areas, including members dedicated to helping victims. The district attorney, Doug Diggers, promoted her to deputy district attorney. Upon the election of Gregory Valdez as the district attorney, Martinez was fired. She filed a wrongful termination lawsuit and received an out-of-court settlement. Martinez later ran against and defeated Valdez for the district attorney position.

In 2010, incumbent governor Bill Richardson termed out and was not able to run for reelection. Martinez ran in the Republican primary and beat five opponents to face Lieutenant Governor Diane Denish. Martinez defeated Denish 53 percent to 46 percent in what was the fourth time two women ran against each other in a gubernatorial race.

As governor, Martinez's first action was introducing a state budget. She also put in place a moratorium on vehicle purchases by state departments and barred state agencies from hiring former lobbyists. In addition, Martinez signed bills expanding a law that requires DNA samples from suspects booked on felony charges. This was an extension of Katie's Law, which focused on suspects booked for crimes of murder, kidnapping, and robbery. Martinez has also fought

Governor Susana Martinez, first female governor of New Mexico and the first Latina governor in the United States, speaks during the 2016 annual New York State Republican Gala in New York City. (Eduardo Munoz Alvarez/Getty Images)

for education reform and has proven to be a more moderate Republican. While Martinez has served as governor, there has been an increase of enrollment in pre-kindergarten. She has also championed for reading intervention programs and wants to increase the number of pre-K classes in New Mexico. Martinez has also pushed for higher education reform, as well as a bridge plan that allows high school students to earn a high school and associate's degree simultaneously. Martinez faced scandal when questions of her great-grandparents' documents arose. Martinez, like many multigenerational Mexican Americans, have one or more family members who came across the border and are not documented. Martinez's office maintained that neither she nor her father spoke to her great-grandfather and she could not be sure of their documentation.

Martinez has been married twice. She met her current husband, Chuck Franco, in Las Crusas. She has one stepson. Martinez was originally a Democrat; however, in 1995 she switched parties. As Martinez tells the story, she went to lunch with her husband and a few friends who intended to persuade Martinez to become a Republican. Martinez went to the lunch with the thought that she would listen to be polite. Upon leaving the lunch, she turned to her husband and said, "I'll be damned, we're Republicans."

Samantha Hernandez

See also: Richardson, William "Bill" (1947–); *Primary Documents:* New Mexico Governor Susana Martinez's First State of the State Address (2011)

Further Reading

Garcia, Lizeth, & Tony Affigne. 2016. "A Force to Be Reckoned With: Rethinking Latina Leadership and Power." In *Latinas in American Politics: Changing and Embracing American Tradition.* Lanham, MD: Lexington, pp. 181–92.

"Governor Susana Martinez." 2011. http://www.governor.state.nm.us.

Hellwege, Julia, & Christine M. Sierra. 2016. "Advantages and Disadvantages of Latina Officeholders in New Mexico." In *Latinas in American Politics: Changing and Embracing American Tradition.* Lanham, MD: Lexington, pp. 113–34.

Mega Marchas of 2006

Also known as the 2006 U.S. immigration protest marches, the Mega Marchas of 2006 were a series of demonstrations that began in Chicago and continued throughout major cities nationwide for a period of eight weeks. The spring of 2006 marked a significant historical moment for both Latinx political activism and the immigrants' rights movement in the United States. Latinx and immigrants' rights demonstrators staged massive protests throughout the nation between March and May 2006. Staged in major metropolises and small-to-medium cities alike, these demonstrations contained a dual purpose: to protest punitive legislation targeting undocumented immigrants, while also advocating for comprehensive immigration reform that would allow undocumented migrants to adjust their immigration status to permanent residency (legalization, also known as "green card" status). A major demonstration in Chicago on March 10, 2006, estimated at 100,000 people was the initial impetus for protests throughout the country. The largest single demonstration occurred in Los Angeles on March 25, 2006, with a march of more than 500,000 people through downtown. The largest nationwide day of protest occurred on April 10, 2006, in 102 cities across the country, with 350,000 to 500,000 in Dallas.

By the mid-2000s, the estimated number of undocumented immigrants living in the United States reached 12 million, causing controversy and resulting in local communities, states, and congressional lawmakers to sponsor or implement various legislative proposals aimed to crack down on the undocumented population. In April 2005, a grassroots citizen activist group known as the Minuteman Project began conducting armed patrols of the U.S.–Mexico border in Arizona and California to assist the Border Patrol in surveillance and apprehension of migrants attempting to enter the United States illegally. However, the main catalyst that triggered the 2006 immigration protests was H.R. 4437, a controversial bill approved by the Republican-controlled U.S. House of Representatives in December 2005. Also known as the "Sensenbrenner Bill" after its chief sponsor, Republican Congressman James Sensenbrenner of Wisconsin, the officially titled "Border

Protection, Anti-Terrorism, and Illegal Immigration Control Act" authorized the construction of 700 miles of fencing along the nation's southern border and contained provisions that would have increased undocumented presence in the United States from a mere *civil infraction* (a noncriminal, nonprosecutable offense) to a *felony* (the most serious category of criminal offenses).

H.R. 4437 sought to establish criminal penalties for any person who knowingly assisted an undocumented immigrant to remain in the United States or who provided shelter or other forms of assistance to undocumented migrants. While proponents of the Sensenbrenner Bill claimed that this provision was intended to crack down on immigrant smugglers, critics pointed out that the vague wording of H.R. 4437's text could be legally interpreted to criminalize churches, charities, homeless shelters, centers for abused women, and other humanitarian organizations that do not exclude undocumented immigrants from their services. Critics also noted that, as written, H.R. 4437 could be interpreted as legally encouraging or requiring U.S. citizens to report undocumented parents or relatives to authorities.

On March 10, 2006, approximately 10,000 immigrants' rights protestors staged a rally against H.R. 4437 and for humane treatment of the undocumented in Chicago. The popularity of this protest quickly spread nationwide as a result of discussions on Spanish-language media and social media use by high school students, with rallies soon taking place in New York, Los Angeles, Philadelphia, Washington, D.C., Atlanta, Dallas, Phoenix, and other cities.

During the first few weeks of demonstrations, the protestors sparked controversy and a backlash from right-wing, conservative pundits and media outlets for waving flags of Mexico and other Latin American nations while chanting in Spanish and displaying Spanish-language placards—tactics that immigration restrictionists claimed reflected the largely Latinx protestors' alleged refusal to assimilate and pledge their loyalties to the United States. Protestors soon shifted tactics by carrying mostly American flags and dressing primarily in plain white shirts, symbolizing peace, in subsequent rallies. Chants of *"Sí, se puede!"* ("Yes, We Can!") and signs reading "Today We March, Tomorrow We Vote!" became common sights during the weekly marches. The Mega Marches culminated with the "Day without Immigrants" boycott on May 1, 2006, in which undocumented workers were encouraged to take the day off from work and avoid purchasing products in order to demonstrate their importance to the U.S. economy.

The legacy of the 2006 Mega Marches is mixed. On one hand, H.R. 4437 failed to become federal law, as the bill did not gain approval in the U.S. Senate. The rallies also signified a growing political conscience and activism among a younger generation of Latinx voters. However, the intense activism of demonstrations did not lead to the passage of comprehensive immigration reform, as such legislation containing provisions for earned legalization status failed to clear Congress in 2006 and 2007, despite the support of President George W. Bush. More than a decade after the marches, the United States has yet to pass comprehensive immigration reform.

Justin D. García

See also: Immigration as a Policy Issue; National Security State and Latinos

Further Reading

Archibald, Randal C. 2006. "Immigrants Take to U.S. Streets in Show of Strength." *New York Times*, May 2. http://www.nytimes.com/2006/05/02/us/02immig.html.

Barreto, Matt A., Sylvia Manzano, Ricardo Ramirez, & Kathy Rim. 2009. "Mobilization, Participation, and Solidaridad Latino Participation in the 2006 Immigration Protest Rallies." *Urban Affairs Review* 44, no. 5: 736–64.

Chavez, Leo R. 2008. *The Latino Threat: Constructing Immigrants, Citizens, and the Nation.* Stanford, CA: Stanford University Press.

"500,000 March in L.A. against Immigration Bill." 2006. *Washington Post*, March 26. http://www.washingtonpost.com/wp-dyn/content/article/2006/03/25/AR200603 2501352.html.

Gonzales, Alfonso. 2009. "The 2006 Mega Marchas in Greater Los Angeles: Counter-Hegemonic Moment and the Future of El Migrante Struggle." *Latino Studies* 7, no. 1: 30–59.

Lavariega Monforti, Jessica, & Adam J. McGlynn. 2015. "The Awakening of the Sleeping Giant? An Examination of the Role of Ethnicity in the 2006 Immigrant Rights Protests." *The Social Science Journal* 52, no. 4: 550–60.

Mohamed, Heather Silber. 2017. *The New Americans? Immigration, Protest, and the Politics of Latino Identity.* Lawrence: University Press of Kansas.

Pallares, Amalia, & Nilda Flores-González. 2010. *¡Marcha!: Latino Chicago and the Immigrant Rights Movement.* Vol. 25. Urbana: University of Illinois Press.

Voss, Kim, & Irene Bloemraad. 2011. *Rallying for Immigrant Rights: The Fight for Inclusion in 21st Century America.* Berkeley: University of California Press.

Melon (Casita) Strike

(1966)

In 1966, farm workers struck against La Casita Farms and other large melon growers in Rio Grande City and other towns in Starr County, Texas. Starr County is one of the four counties that comprise the Rio Grande Valley (RGV) located in Deep South Texas. It was largely rural and economically underdeveloped. Agribusiness predominated the region, especially large growers such as La Casita Farms, which depended on manual labor to harvest crops. Melons were the largest crop harvested in Starr County and one of the most lucrative for growers such as La Casita Farms, producing an excess of $1,000,000 in profits per year.

In the 1960s, rampant discrimination and racism plagued the social, economic, and political life of Mexican Americans in South Texas. Segregation in schools, housing, and public services was commonplace, and poverty was a reality for 70 percent of Mexican American families in Starr County who had an annual income below the poverty line of $3,000; in some cases, families earned less than $1,000 per year. With an average annual income of approximately $534, Starr County was one of poorest counties in the nation, and most residents had low levels of education and very few employment options. The lack of industrial development and availability of higher-wage industrial jobs compelled many Valley residents to work in agricultural fields as farm workers earning anywhere from $0.40 to $0.85 per hour. These workers not only harvested melons and other produce in Rio Grande City for La Casita Farms, they migrated to other states such as

Arizona, California, Oregon, and Colorado to harvest other crops to make ends meet. The lack of unions and ability to negotiate with employers exacerbated the plight of farm workers because they did not have collective bargaining rights under the National Labor Relations Act (NLRA). Since Texas is a right-to-work state, had no minimum wage laws, and stringent labor laws that prohibited picketing, it was even more difficult for farm workers to organize and challenge grower abuses.

In 1962, César Chávez and Dolores Huerta formed the Farm Workers Association (FWA) to organize Mexican and Mexican American farm workers in Delano, California. By 1966, the Civil Rights Movement and Johnson's War on Poverty were in full swing and the FWA became the National Farm Workers Association (NFWA). The name change gave migrant workers from the RGV hope that they could become members of the same labor organization in Texas. In spring 1966, Chávez sent Eugene Nelson, one of his organizing picket captains, to Rio Grande City to help organize farm workers and negotiate a union contract. Nelson began speaking to groups of workers about the benefits of organizing and creating a union in the RGV. Hundreds of workers supported creating a union and agreed to join their independent Workers Association with the National Farm Workers Association led by César Chávez and have the UFW represent them in negotiating a union contract at $1.25/hour, the right to bargain collectively, and recognition of their union. Over 400 workers voted to go on strike against the melon growers of Starr County on June 1, 1966, forcing many packing sheds to shut down. Growers retaliated by hiring strikebreakers from Mexico to thwart unionizing efforts. Growers also resorted to threats and violence sanctioned by county officials and law enforcement such as the Texas Rangers to break the strike and force workers back into the fields.

Like the grape strikers in Delano, California, striking melon workers, their supporters, and community members planned and carried out a pilgrimage march (*La Marcha*) from Rio Grande City to the state capital in Austin to meet with Governor John Connally about conditions and wages in agribusiness. Marchers traveled 490 miles from Rio Grande City to reach Austin. Strikers and farmworkers were supported by members of other unions in Texas, religious leaders from all major faiths, UFW leaders César Chávez and Dolores Huerta, and thousands of sympathizers. *La Marcha* ended on Labor Day 1966 at the state capital where over 10,000 people joined them as they waited to speak to Governor Connally to no avail.

Strikers and workers maintained the strike through 1967 with the support of community members, the Texas AFL-CIO, and other organizations who helped by setting up a grocery store, a strike kitchen and strike store, and donating food, clothing, and other necessities to sustain workers during the strike. To stop strikebreakers from crossing into the United States from Mexico, strikers and supporters, including many women, established a picket line at the international bridge at Roma. One activist, Daria Vera de la Cruz, lay across the bridge to prevent workers from crossing. Key leaders included UFW leaders such as Eugene Nelson, Bill Chandler, Tony Orendain, and Gilbert Padilla as well as local leaders such as Rebecca Flores, Alejandro Moreno, Daria Vera de la Cruz, Lolita Serna, Natividad Bazan, Librado de la Cruz, Mike Díaz, Herminia Rodríguez, and Baldemar Díaz, to name a few.

Although the strike did not result in union contracts or an immediate increase in wages for striking melon workers, the event signified a watershed for civil rights and labor activism among Mexican Americans in South Texas, especially among women. Labor leader Rebecca Flores and other community leaders credit the strike with sparking the Chicano Movement and increasing political awareness among Mexican Americans and motivated many to participate in a movement to challenge the unjust social, political, and economic institutions that relegated them to second-class status. Two years later, Mexican American students from Edcouch-Elsa High School organized a massive walkout to protest discrimination, poor treatment, and unequal education. Like the grape strike of San Joaquin Valley in California, the Melon Strike of Rio Grande City played a key role in highlighting the plight of Mexican American farmworkers nationwide.

Maritza De La Trinidad

See also: Chávez, César (1927–1993); Delano Grape Strike (1965–1970); Huerta, Dolores (1930–); United Farm Workers (UFW)

Further Reading

"A Long Struggle with La Casita." 1966. *The Texas Observer: A Journal of Free Voices* 58, no. 11 (June): 1–5.

Bailey, Richard R. 1979. "The Starr County Strike." *Red River Valley Historical Review* 4 (Winter, 1976), 42–61.

Fishlow, David M., ed. *Sons of Zapata: A Brief Photographic History of the Farm Workers Strike in Texas.* https://libraries.ucsd.edu/farmworkermovement/ufwarchives /elmalcriado/Frankel/Strike.pdf.

Jepson, Wendy. 2005. "Spaces of Labor Activism, Mexican-American Women, and the Farm Worker Movement in South Texas Since 1966." *Antipode* 37, no. 4 (September): 679–702.

Kostyu, Frank A. 1970. *Shadows in the Valley: The Story of One Man's Struggle for Justice.* Garden City, NY: Doubleday.

Procter, Ben H. 1969. "The Modern Texas Ranger: A Law-Enforcement Dilemma in the Rio Grande Valley." In John A. Carroll, ed. *Reflections of Western Historians.* Tucson: University of Arizona Press.

Samora, Julian, Joe Bernal, & Albert Peña. 1979. *Gunpowder Justice: A Reassessment of the Texas Rangers.* Notre Dame, IN: University of Notre Dame Press.

"United Farmworkers, Texas." https://farmworkers2016.wordpress.com/2016/05/13/monitor -remembering-the-1966-rio-grande-city-melon-strike.

Méndez, Sylvia

(1936–)

Sylvia Méndez is best known for bringing national attention to one of the first cases that challenged the segregation of Mexican American children in the public schools in California. *Mendez, et al. v. Westminster School District of Orange County, et al.*, 64 F.Supp. 544 (S.D. Cal. 1946) was a federal district court case that confronted the existence of Mexican remedial schools in Orange County, California. The U.S. Court of Appeals for the Ninth Circuit, aff'd, 161 F.2d 774 (9th Cir. 1947) held that the forced segregation of Mexican American students into separate "Mexican schools" was unconstitutional and unlawful. U.S. District Court judge Paul J. McCormick ruled,

> The equal protection of the laws pertaining to the public school system in California is not provided by furnishing in separate schools the same technical facilities, textbooks and courses of instruction to children of Mexican ancestry that are available to the other public school children regardless of their ancestry. A paramount requisite in the American system of public education is social equality. It must be open to all children by unified school association regardless of lineage.

Attorneys for the plaintiffs argued that Mexicans were "white" and therefore should not attend segregated schools.

Sylvia Méndez was born in Santa Ana, California, to Gonzálo, an immigrant from Mexico, a farmer, and a successful agricultural businessperson, and Felicitas, a native of Puerto Rico. The family had moved to Westminster from Santa Ana to work a vegetable farm that her father had leased from the Munemitsus family, a Japanese American family who had been interned in Arizona as a result of an executive order by President Franklin Roosevelt on February 19, 1942, authorizing the incarceration of Japanese Americans to internment camps following the attack on Pearl Harbor.

Méndez was only eight years old when her parents brought a class-action suit representing five families against four Orange County school districts challenging the segregation policies in the public schools. The case gained national attention when Méndez began telling the story through public speeches of her parents' story. Méndez and her siblings were sent to the neighborhood school in the community of Westminster, only to be told that they had to go to the "Mexican school" across town. Although there were no existing laws that prohibited Méndez and her siblings from attending the school, practices were in place that gave education officials authority to treat students from Mexican ancestry differently.

The case was filed in the U.S. District Court, and the attorney representing the plaintiffs, David Marcus, a Los Angeles civil rights lawyer, argued that segregating children of Mexican ancestry was in violation of the

Civil rights activist Sylvia Méndez, of Mexican and Puerto Rican heritage, is presented with the 2010 Medal of Freedom by U.S. president Barack Obama. At age eight, she played an instrumental role in the *Mendez v. Westminster* case, the landmark desegregation case of 1947. (Alex Wong/Getty Images)

Equal Protection Clause of the Fourteenth Amendment of the U.S. Constitution and the California Constitution. On March 14, 1946, Judge Paul McCormick of the Southern District of California, Central Division struck down the segregation practices, and the Ninth Circuit Court of Appeals in San Francisco affirmed the decision on April 14, 1947. Not too long after the ruling, California governor Earl Warren at the time, who later became chief justice on the U.S. Supreme Court, successfully passed legislation repealing laws and practices that segregated Mexicans, Asians and Native American children in the state's public schools. The case is also significant since it was decided eight years before the U.S. Supreme Court struck down segregation in public schools in the 1954 landmark case, *Brown v. Board of Education*, which ruled that "separate but equal" is "inherently unequal." Thurgood Marshall, who was an attorney for the NAACP at the time of the *Méndez* case, wrote a "friend of the court" brief, and later used the decision as precedent when he argued the *Brown* case before the Court. The *Méndez* case successfully ended *de jure* segregation in California and paved the way to end legal segregation in all public schools in the nation.

Ultimately, Méndez was able to attend Westminster Main Elementary School, becoming one of the first Latinos to attend an all-white school in California. It should also be noted that because the Méndez family leased the land from the Munemitsus family, they did not lose their land, like so many other Japanese American families at the time. In 1998, the school district of Santa Ana paid tribute to the Méndez family by naming a new school after the parents. Commemorating the 60th anniversary of the *Méndez* case, the U.S. Postal Service issued a special stamp in 2007. President Barack Obama in 2011 awarded the Presidential Medal of Freedom, the highest civilian honor, to Méndez. Since her retirement as a nurse and assistant nursing director of the Pediatric Pavilion at the Los Angeles University of Southern California Medical Center, she continues to educate students about the *Méndez* case across the country and advocates for educational equity. Méndez continues to be a fierce advocate of her parents' legacy.

Sonia R. García

See also: Del Rio Independent School District v. Salvatierra (1930); *Delgado v. Bastrop I.S.D., et al.* (1948)*; Hernández v. Texas* (1954)*; Lau v. Nichols* (1974)*; Plyler v. Doe* (1982)

Further Reading

Arriola, C. 1995. "Knocking on the Schoolhouse Door: *Mendez v. Westminster*, Equal Protection, Public Education, and Mexican Americans in the 1940s." *Berkeley La Raza Law Journal* 8, no. 2: 166–207.

Robbie, Sandra. 2002. "*Mendez v. Westminister: For All the Children/Para Todos Los Ninos.*" (Emmy Award–winning Documentary). KOCE-TV.

Strum, Philippa. 2010. *Mendez v. Westminster: School Desegregation and Mexican-American Rights*. Lawrence: University of Kansas Press.

Valencia, Reynaldo, Sonia R. García, Henry Flores, & José R. Juárez. 2004. *Mexican Americans and the Law: ¡El Pueblo Unido Jamás Será Vencido!*. Tucson: University of Arizona Press.

Mendez v. Westminster (1947). See Méndez, Sylvia

Menendez, Robert "Bob"

(1954–)

Democrat Robert Menendez is the first Latino to be elected to the U.S. House and U.S. Senate from New Jersey. Menendez has been a staunch advocate for comprehensive immigration reform and has supported affirmative action. He was also a supporter of the Development, Relief and Education for Alien Minors (DREAM) Act, which did not pass, but eventually led to the Deferred Action for Childhood Arrivals (DACA) Act passed by President Barack Obama in 2012. Menendez is also known for being part of the "Gang of Eight" due to his support of a pathway to citizenship for undocumented persons.

The son of Cuban refugees, Menendez was born in New York City months after his parents had arrived from the island. Menendez's political career began when he became involved with the Board of Education in Union City, New Jersey, becoming the youngest school board member from 1974 to 1978. In 1976, Menendez graduated from Saint Peter's College, and soon after, attended law school at Rutgers University in Newark, New Jersey, where he received his juris doctorate in 1979. From 1986 to 1992, Menendez became mayor of Union City, New Jersey, a community largely described as the "Havana on the Hudson" due to its large Cuban population, second only to Miami, Florida. While in his role as mayor of Union City, Menendez became a state legislator for the New Jersey State General Assembly until 1991. In 1991, Menendez became a member of the New Jersey State Senate's 33rd district during a special election to fill the vacancy of Christopher Jackman. Upon completing his time as state senator, Menendez went on to represent New Jersey's 13th congressional district for two consecutive six-year terms. In 2002, he was elected as chairman of the House of the Democratic Caucus, which is considered to be one of the most powerful positions in the House of Representatives. Upon completing his role in the state Senate, in 2006, Menendez was elected to take Jon Corzine's vacated seat in the U.S. Senate. Menendez was later re-elected to the Senate in 2012. In his position as senator, Menendez has served as chairman of the Senate Foreign Relations Committee for the 113th Congress. In 2013, he was the first Latino to chair this committee. In the 115th Congress, Menendez was ranking member of the Subcommittee on the Western Hemisphere, Transnational Crime, Civilian Security, Democracy, Human Rights, and Global Women's Issues. Menendez has served on the Committee on Banking, Housing, and Urban Affairs, as well as the Committee on Finance and Committee on Foreign Relations.

On April 1, 2015, Menendez was indicted over corruption charges that he had used his position of power in the Senate to trade political favors with Salomon Melgen, an eye surgeon from Florida. The trial began on September 6, 2017. The jury was unable to reach a unanimous verdict, and the judge declared a mistrial on November 16, 2017. On January 31, 2018, the Justice Department dropped all charges against Menendez.

Melanie Z. Plasencia

See also: La Opinión; La Voz de Houston

Further Reading

Library of Congress: Hispanic Americans in Congress 1822–1995. 2010. "Robert Menendez." https://www.loc.gov/rr/hispanic/congress/menendez.html.

"Menendez, Bipartisan Gang of 8 Introduce Common Sense Immigration Reform." 2013. *Bob Menendez for New Jersey.* https://www.menendez.senate.gov/news-and-events /press/menendez-bipartisan-gang-of-8-introduce-common-sense-immigration -reform/.

Menendez, Robert. 2010. *Growing American Roots: Why Our Nation Will Thrive as Our Largest Minority Flourishes.* New York: Celebra.

Observer. 2015. "The 51 Most Influential Latinos in NJ Politics Elected and Nonelected." http://observer.com/2015/09/the-51-most-influential-latinos-in-n-j-politics-elected -and-nonelected.

Salant, Jonathan D. 2016. "See Which N.J. Lawmaker Is the Go-To Source for Washington's Spanish-Language Media." *NJ.com,* March 28. http://www.nj.com/politics /index.ssf/2016/03/in_dc_menendez_is_news_source_for_spanish-language .html.

Mexican American Legal Defense and Educational Fund (MALDEF)

The Mexican American Legal Defense and Educational Fund (MALDEF) is a civil rights organization founded by attorney Pete Tejerina and former state director of LULAC, Mario Obledo, on May 1, 1968, in San Antonio, Texas. The goal of MALDEF is to incorporate Latinos into U.S. political and socioeconomic life. Tijerina and Obledo, with the assistance of the Legal Defense and Educational Fund of the NAACP, obtained a $2,250,000, five-year grant from the Ford Foundation to implement "litigation and generation education activities." Today, it offers information about immigrants' and voters' rights through legal aid and advocacy, as well as educational opportunities such as scholarships and leadership programs. With headquarters in Los Angeles and satellite offices in San Antonio, Chicago, and Washington, D.C., MALDEF's governmental structure includes a president, general counsel, and a 30-member board of directors.

MALDEF was established at a time when Mexican Americans called for political advocacy after decades of discrimination and an upsurge of militant activism by Chicanos and other Mexican American activists rallying for voting, due process, educational, and farmworker rights. Even though there were other Latino organizations such as the League of United Latin American Citizens (LULAC) or the American GI Forum, MALDEF had a distinct vision that sought to fight against discrimination, mainly through the judiciary.

Successful due to the critical mass of lawyers and primary funding from the Ford Foundation, and modeled after the National Association for the Advancement of Colored People (NAACP) Legal Defense Fund, MALDEF began with the plan to inform the Southwestern Mexican American community about their civil rights and provide jobs to recent law school graduates.

The organization was headed by Pete Tijerina as the executive director, Mario Obledo as general counsel, three staff attorneys, and 14 board directors. In 1971, it moved its headquarters to San Francisco, where the first two female Mexican American attorneys, Graciela Olivarez and Vilma Martinez Singer, were appointed to the board of directors. From 1973 to 1982, Martinez became the first female president of MALDEF. She maintained that MALDEF needed to ensure that winning cases would also translate into the institutionalization of civil rights.

MALDEF first started off by participating in school funding cases. The 1973 case of *Demetrio Rodriguez et al. v. San Antonio Independent School District* was a loss, in which the Court ruled against the equal financing of education. However, in the same year, MALDEF achieved its first successful litigation before the Supreme Court in the case of *White, et al. v. Regester, et al.*, which resulted in the implementation of single-member districts for Texas county, city council, and school board districts, allowing for more minority voting power. This litigation helped eventually bring Texas into compliance with the 1965 Voting Rights Act, which required federal approval of state electoral practices. In 1989, MALDEF won another historic victory in *Edgewood ISD v. State of Texas,* in which the Texas Supreme Court unanimously ruled that the state's system of public finance for education to be unconstitutional.

In 1982, MALDEF achieved national legal victory with the Supreme Court case *Plyler v. Doe*, in which the Court struck down a Texas law that denied undocumented children enrollment in public schools. As a result, new lines were drawn for the 23rd congressional district, allowing the Latino community to be able to elect a congressional candidate of its choice. In addition to addressing school segregation, MALDEF has addressed police brutality, labor discrimination, anti-immigrant action, and denial of due process to members of the Chicano Movement. In *Morales v. Barnett*, MALDEF represented a Mexican American family of U.S. citizens attacked by a border vigilante in Arizona, where the court ruled in favor of the Morales family; in *Gonzalez v. State of Arizona*, MALDEF filed a suit against a provision of Arizona Proposition 200 that required new voters to show proof of citizenship. In 2012, the U.S. Court of Appeals for the Ninth Circuit struck it down. In 2015, MALDEF sued JP Morgan Chase & Co. for discrimination against an HIV-positive employee and also represented airplane cleaners facing harassment for speaking Spanish in the workplace. In 2016, MALDEF sued the University of Georgia for denying Deferred Action for Childhood Arrivals in-state tuition. The same year, it also filed a lawsuit against the exclusion of Mexican Americans from the "Whites Only" cemetery. In 2017, MALDEF released a number of statements on President Trump's "cruel and senseless immigration demands," such as ending the Deferred Action for Childhood Arrivals program as well as Temporary Protected Status for Haitian and Salvadoran Immigrants.

In addition to its strong emphasis on educational issues and leadership development, MALDEF devoted its resources to women's equity and voting rights. In 1974, it institutionalized the Chicana Rights Project (CRP) which helped Mexican American women fight sex discrimination against them. CRP's national office was located in San Antonio, and the project also had a regional branch in San Francisco. In the early 1980s, MALDEF discontinued the CRP when it lost its foundation support. In the 1970s, MALDEF partnered with the Southwest Voter Registration Education Project to fight voting inequities. This project filed 88 lawsuits between 1974 and 1984 and thereby successfully increased voter registration among Mexican Americans. MALDEF also lobbied to ensure that the 1975 extension of the Voting Rights Act of 1965 included citizens with Spanish surnames in the Southwest.

In 2008, MALDEF made the transition to the use of "Latino" in their description from Mexican American, signaling a move to encompass the growing and broader Latino community from other nationalities, leading the organization to be often called the "law firm of the Latino community." MALDEF holds gala dinners, often inviting famous Latino figures for performances or presentations.

Kimberly Cárdenas

See also: American GI Forum; League of United Latin American Citizens (LULAC); *Plyler v. Doe* (1982); *San Antonio Independent School District v. Rodriguez* (1973); Southwest Voter Registration Education Project (SVREP)

Further Reading

Ortega, Joe. 1972. "The Privately Funded Legal Aid Office: The MALDEF Experience." *Chicano Law Review* 1: 80.

Rios, Rolando, James Harrington, & Hector Gutierrez. 2016. "Political Power of Latinos in the Years to Come." *Texas Hispanic Journal of Law and Policy* 22: 57.

Rivas-Rodriguez, Maggie. 2015. *Texas Mexican Americans and Postwar Civil Rights*. Austin: University of Texas Press.

Vigil, Maurilio. 1990. "The Ethnic Organization as an Instrument of Political and Social Change: MALDEF, a Case Study." *The Journal of Ethnic Studies* 18, no. 1: 15.

Mexican American Political Association (MAPA)

A civic rights organization formed in Fresno, California, in 1960, the Mexican American Political Association (MAPA) was the first Mexican American group in U.S. history to openly declare itself to be political. Its origins are tied to a gathering of the California Democratic Council in 1959 where an auxiliary meeting of Mexicano delegates was called by Edward Roybal to discuss a growing dissatisfaction with the party's lack of support for Mexicano candidates across the state. The aims of MAPA were the following: to support the social, economic, cultural and civic betterment of Mexican Americans through political action; to elect and appoint Mexican Americans to public office; to take stands on political issues; to launch voter registration drives; to carry on political education; and to encourage increased activity in both major political parties.

Disaffected and frustrated by a series of electoral defeats in California involving Mexicano candidates for lieutenant governor, secretary of state, and other state assembly posts, MAPA sought to create an organization that would put the community's needs over and above the electoral needs of the Democratic Party (cited in Navarro, 2005: 273). For many years it was felt that Mexican Americans had been very loyal to the Democratic Party and that they had not received a commensurate return of the spoils for their efforts (Vigil, 1978). When Mexicanos ran for statewide offices in California, the Democratic Party wavered in their support and tacitly believed that Mexican American candidates could not carry majorities within

Mexican American Political Association (MAPA) protesters march in Dinuba, California, for equal representation on the school board, ca. 1992. (David McNew/ Getty Images)

the state (Navarro, 2005). These outcomes led to a feeling in the Mexican community that they were being taken for granted and simply used to further the purposes of the party establishment. These sentiments were aggravated when the Democratic Party sponsored a redistricting program that diminished the power of Mexicano voting blocs throughout the state (Gómez-Quiñones, 1990) and it prompted the need for a more independent and focused form of political action. Thus, MAPA initiated strong community campaigns that reached working-class populations in the barrio, and many of these locales became the pillars of their network (Ibid.). At its height, MAPA had 3,700 members in 36 chapters throughout the state of California (cited in Navarro, 2015: 275).

In addition to its hardened stance with the parties, MAPA distinguished itself from past accommodationist organizations by openly stressing ethnic identity, direct electoral politics, and electoral independence (Gómez-Quiñones, 1990). For example, in order to support a greater level of self-determination, MAPA strongly supported the incorporation of East Los Angeles so that Mexicanos would have a greater say in community deliberations, decisions, and outcomes (Gómez-Quiñones, 1990; Guzman, 1976; Vigil, 1978). "When the incorporation effort failed, MAPA turned its attention to individual campaigns elsewhere in the state" (Guzman, 1976: 145). Mexican American candidates were fielded and supported for all branches of government even though this explicit ethnic agenda would open them up to criticism of ethnic bias and cause partisan funding to wither. Despite these challenges, MAPA achieved a quantum victory in the election of Edward Roybal as the first Mexicano congressman from California in the U.S. House of Representatives (Servin, 1970; Vigil, 1978).

MAPA's trailblazing did not end there. Their ethnic brand of politics eventually would lead to confrontations around the cross-cutting and conflicting interests of Mexican Americans, immigrants, and government policy. While initially, MAPA generally supported immigration containment initiatives to protect citizen and worker rights in the United States, invariably, policy proposals in these areas were often used as a facile way to discriminate against Latino citizens and residents (Gutierrez, 1995). To shed light on these issues, MAPA opposed the Arnett Bill, an initiative that promulgated employer sanctions, on the grounds that it would cause employers to steer away from hiring qualified Latinos living in the United States. It was unprecedented that U.S. Latino politics was indirectly incorporating the concerns of immigrant populations coming from Latin America. Additionally, MAPA was one of the early groups to form a women's caucus (Vargas, 2011). The totality of these actions would prove to have profound consequences on the agendas of future Latino political organizations by precipitating the great diversity and multifront advocacy that one sees in Latino organizations today.

Over time, a series of pressing challenges and obstacles limited MAPA's effectiveness and influence in the wider political milieu. Because of the organization's political goals and their venture into more ethnocentric postures, they did not qualify for external funding and relied heavily on community and membership donations, which greatly diminished their capacity to grow and expand. Additionally, because they so powerfully used the Mexican American label, they were inhibited from expanding into other states like New Mexico and Texas, where identity labels took the form of Hispanos and Latins, respectively (Servin, 1970). Other constraining factors were the gap between its white-collar, professional-class leadership and its barrio, blue-collar rank-and-file membership, which caused classic divides in language, priorities, and agendas. Sometimes the powerful concerns of the grassroots constituency could not easily be filtered and integrated into the divergent goals of the organizational and political elite (Gómez-Quiñones, 1990; Guzman, 1976; Navarro, 2005; Tirado, 1970).

MAPA continued on as an advocacy and endorsement group for several decades, eventually morphing into a more bipartisan version stemming from changes in leadership; however, several factors contributed to its decline. Factionalism often divided the group to the point where important political posts were not successfully backfilled by Mexicano candidates. Additionally, because MAPA's mission was primarily electoral, they would often experience surges of activity during election season and membership exodus in the off season, thus impairing their ability to attain political constancy (Navarro, 2005). While MAPA's electoral mission could have had more widespread appeal and implications, the urban, ethnocentric emphasis it acquired was not easily transferable to more rural, conservative regions of other Southwestern states. MAPA's most enduring legacy might lie in its departure from the accommodationist postures of previous Mexicano groups who often unwittingly served as extensions of the established major parties. Their furtherance of ethnic identity as a form of political consciousness very likely influenced the nationalistic objectives of Chicano groups and organizations that were already tracking toward their formative stages.

Daniel Gutierrez

See also: Roybal, Edward R. (1916–2005); *Primary Documents:* Excerpt of an Oral History Interview of Congressman Edward Roybal (1975)

Further Reading

Gómez-Quiñones, Juan. 1990. *Chicano Politics: Reality and Promise 1940–1990.* Albuquerque: University of New Mexico Press.

Gutierrez, David G. 1995. *Walls and Mirrors: Mexican Americans, Mexican Immigrants and the Politics of Ethnicity.* Berkeley: University of California Press.

Guzman, Ralph C. 1976. *The Political Socialization of the Mexican-American People.* New York: Arno Press.

Navarro, Armando. 2005. *Mexicano Political Experience in Occupied Aztlan: Struggles and Change.* Walnut Creek, CA: AltaMira Press.

Online Archive of California (OAC). 2009. "MAPA's Program," http://www.oac.cdlib.org.

Servin, Manuel P. 1970. *The Mexican-Americans: An Awakening Minority.* Beverly Hills, CA: Glencoe Press.

Tirado, Miguel David. 1970. "Mexican-American Community Political Organizations: The Key to Chicano Political Power." *Aztlan* I (Spring): 53–78.

Vargas, Zaragosa. 2011. *Crucible of Struggle: A History of Mexican Americans from Colonial Times to the Present Era.* New York: Oxford University Press.

Vigil, Maurilio. 1978. *Chicano Politics.* Washington, D.C.: University Press of America.

Mexican American Youth Organization (MAYO)

The Mexican American Youth Organization (MAYO) was a civil rights organization formed in March 1967 in San Antonio, Texas, by five graduate and undergraduate students at San Antonio's Saint Mary's University. The five young Chicanos, known as Los Cincos, José Ángel Gutiérrez, Mario Compean, Willie C. Velásquez, Ignacio Pérez, and Juan Patlán, organized MAYO to address a variety of social justice issues facing Chicanos/as in Texas, including the impoverished conditions of the barrio. MAYO was a leading civil rights organization in the late 1960s and early 1970s, particularly for Mexican American youth in Texas and led to the formation of La Raza Unida Party (LRU) in 1970.

In building MAYO, Los Cincos aimed to create an "organization of organizers" interested in pragmatic, political action. MAYO broke from other established Latino organizations in Texas, such as League of United Latin American Citizens and American GI Forum, with its focus on developing the talent and energy of young activists. The young leaders familiarized themselves with more confrontational, political tactics by studying Saul Alinsky; African American civil rights and Black Power organizations; and fellow Chicano Movement activists, such as Reies López Tijerina's New Mexico movement, the Alianza Federal de Pueblos Libres. Although MAYO lacked a set ideology, the organization largely adhered to a Chicano nationalism and idea of "la raza unida," and its leaders were critical of what they deemed to be racist, gringo institutions and individuals. MAYO's preamble to its constitution details the organization's purpose: "The purpose of the Mexican American Youth Organization is to establish a coordinated effort in the organization of groups interested in solving problems of the Chicano community and to develop leaders from within the communities."

MAYO's pragmatism and cultural pride developed into a direct action approach to politics with unconventional, and sometimes eclectic, protest methods. In MAYO's first demonstration, Gutiérrez, Compean, and Pérez picketed an Independence Day celebration at the Alamo in San Antonio, declaring Chicano independence. MAYO sought to organize people for social justice through mass confrontations and demonstrations. The organizers initially focused on reform of the Texas educational system, a top priority given its widespread support among the Chicano community. Between 1968 and 1970, MAYO organized nearly 40 student boycotts or walkouts at schools with successes in a number of cities, including San Antonio and Crystal City. MAYO did not shy from confrontation or ridicule in its activism. For instance, in a Del Rio march in March 1969, MAYO protested the firing of some Chicano VISTA (Volunteers in Service to America) workers with a funeral for a dead rabbit named "Justice" and continued the protest tactic by throwing dead rabbits at the Texas governor's feet during his speeches in the following weeks. MAYO's unorthodox, militant image and vehement rhetoric aimed to energize action among the Chicano youth, but also attracted criticism from both the Anglo and Mexican American community, particularly from Texas Congressman Henry B. Gonzalez, a mainstream Mexican American politician, which also threatened their organization's funding sources.

By 1970, MAYO shifted priorities, with a larger focus on political empowerment and the creation of a third political party, La Raza Unida Party (LRU). LRU successfully fielded school board and city council candidates in the early 1970s in rural South Texas and increased Latino/a voter registration and turnout. LRU's first statewide, gubernatorial candidate earned 6 percent of the state total vote, but following elections failed to achieve similar levels of success. By the late 1970s, MAYO and RUP lost momentum, exhausted by divisions over gender, class, and place, and the organizations disbanded, with activists turning to other political organizations and efforts.

Emily M. Farris

See also: Brown Power Movement/Chicano Civil Rights Movement; González, Henry B. (1916–2000); Gutiérrez, José Ángel (1944–); La Raza Unida Party (LRU); League of United Latin American Citizens (LULAC)

Further Reading

Gutiérrez, José Ángel. 1998. *The Making of a Chicano Militant*. Madison: University of Wisconsin Press.

Montejano, David. 2010. *Quixote's Soldiers: A Local History of the Chicano Movement, 1966–1981*. Austin: University of Texas Press.

Navarro, Armando. 2014. *Mexican American Youth Organization: Avant-Garde of the Chicano Movement in Texas*. Austin: University of Texas Press.

Mexican Repatriation

Repatriation describes the return of migrants to their countries of origin, in this case Mexicans to Mexico from the United States. Although voluntary in definition, repatriation is euphemistically used to describe deportations, often in mass numbers. Repatriation is an ongoing reality for Mexicans since the establishment of the current U.S.–Mexico border; it has increased in times of economic decline and reversed during economic growth. Historically, the United States has repatriated more Mexicans than any other nationality. Repatriation also refers to the return to Mexico of deceased individuals. Posthumous repatriations have averaged around 10,000 annually in recent years.

Repatriation of Mexicans in the United States has its origins in the Mexican-American War. The Treaty of Guadalupe Hidalgo in 1848 ceded Arizona, California, Colorado, Nevada, New Mexico, Texas, Utah, and Wyoming to the United States. In the years following, the Mexican government encouraged its citizens to return home. Another surge of repatriation occurred after the Great War and the subsequent economic slowdown, which left Mexicans jobless and targets of discrimination.

The term repatriation, however, is most often used to describe the great exodus of Mexicans from the United States during the Great Depression. The prolonged economic slowdown of the Great Depression and discrimination toward Mexicans fueled the exodus. Repatriation efforts targeted all Mexicans in the United States but most left from California, Texas, the Great Lakes regions, and the Southwest where large Mexican populations resided and where emigration campaigns were prominent. Official entries into Mexico totaled over 458,000 from 1929 to 1937 according to official Mexican statistics. During the peak of repatriation, in 1931, over 138,000 individuals officially entered through Mexican checkpoints. Numbers might be much higher to account for unofficial departures.

Contributors to the great repatriation included federal agencies and officials—including Presidents Herbert Hoover and Franklin D. Roosevelt—as well as local and state politicians and organizations. The Mexican government played a dual role during the Depression. To help their citizens, Mexico ordered its consuls to protect Mexicans by providing advice and help to those targeted. On the other hand, the Mexican government also encouraged its citizens to return home by providing incentives. Mexico's desire to regain its citizens was largely a result of Mexican revolutionary nationalism, which intensified after the 1920s at the conclusions of the Revolution and the end of the Cristero Wars.

Growth during the Second World War once again encouraged Mexicans to travel north only to face threats of deportation following the war. Postwar anti-immigrant sentiment sought once more to exclude Mexicans from American society. The onset of the Cold War and the increased preoccupation with national security resulted in official deportation campaigns of which millions of Mexicans were the primary target.

In many surges of repatriation—particularly Depression-era repatriation—the Mexican government actively called its citizens back. Pull factors, like the promise of jobs, land, transportation, and education, added to the push factors of discrimination, racism, and marginalization of Mexicans in the United States.

More recently, the administration of President Donald J. Trump has vowed to be more active in increasing the power to repatriate Mexicans. Immigration and Customs Enforcement (ICE) has hired more officials to oversee deportations and has reinstated the 287(g) program, which allows the sheriff's office and local law enforcement to support deportations. Since January 25, 2017, arrests have totaled 41,000 individuals suspected of residing in the United States without documents—an increase of 37 percent over the same period in 2016.

Juve J. Cortes

See also: Depression-Era Repatriation of Mexicans; Immigration and Customs Enforcement (ICE), Expanded Powers of (2000s); Operation Gatekeeper (1994); Operation Hold the Line/Blockade (1993); Treaty of Guadalupe Hidalgo (1848)

Further Reading

Balderrama, Francisco E., & Raymond Rodríguez. 2006. *Decade of Betrayal: Mexican Repatriation in the 1930s*. Albuquerque: University of New Mexico Press.

Garcia, Juan Ramon. 1980. *Operation Wetback: The Mass Deportation of Mexican Undocumented Workers in 1954*. Westport, CT: Greenwood.

Nevins, Joseph. 2002. *Operation Gatekeeper: The Rise of the "Illegal Alien" and the Making of the U.S.-Mexico*. New York: Routledge.

Ngai, Mae M. 2004. *Impossible Subjects: Illegal Aliens and the Making of Modern America*. Princeton, NJ: Princeton University Press.

Mi Familia Vota

Mi Familia Vota is a 501(c)(4) nonprofit civic engagement organization founded in 2000 as part of a campaign by the Organization of Los Angeles Workers that focused on national social and economic issues affecting Latino communities. Originally called Mi Familia Vota 100%, the group focused on voter registration and increasing voter turnout among the Latino population of Los Angeles, California. Its main strategy was to promote voting as a social act to support the entire Latino community, rather than an individual and isolated task. After experiencing success in its community organizing efforts, new offices were opened in the greater Los Angeles area regions of Pico-Union and San Fernando in 2001. However, these new offices were closed just a year later in 2002. In July 2004, the group left California for Phoenix, Arizona, which has since been the location of its headquarters. Mi Familia Vota is known most prominently for its efforts in voter mobilization and voter registration, but also focuses on a number of key issue areas, including immigration reform, the expansion of affordable health care programs, environmental conservation, improvement of public education, promotion of workers' rights, and voter rights.

After two years without large-scale operation expansions, 2006 became a year of growth for Mi Familia Vota. Out of a desire to provide services to the historically large Texas Latino community, Mi Familia Vota opened offices in Houston, Dallas, and San Antonio in 2006. The group also extended its reach to Colorado during that same year and opened offices in Denver, Aurora, and Pueblo. In April 2006, Mi Familia Vota participated alongside the National Association of Latino Elected & Appointed Officials, Univision, Entravision, the National Council of La Raza (now called US Unidos), and Impremedia in the *Ya es hora ¡Ciudadanía!* ("Now is the time, citizenship!") campaign. This campaign came in the wake of national immigration reform protest marches in 2006, in which protesters in over 140 cities in 39 states demonstrated their opposition to House Resolution 4437, also known as the Sensenbrenner Bill. This bill included controversial provisions such as classifying as a crime the act of providing food, housing, and medical aid to undocumented individuals. In response to this legislative action, the *Ya es hora* campaign aimed to motivate 1 million legal permanent U.S. residents to apply for citizenship. In September 2006, the campaign superseded its goal with a total of 1.4 million legal residents applying for citizenship.

Ben Monterroso became the first full-time executive director of Mi Familia Vota in October 2006. Prior to his position as executive director of the organization, Monterroso maintained a high level of involvement in immigrants' rights campaigns and Latino community organizing. Monterroso decided to focus Mi Familia Vota on the goals of increasing both the number of registered Latino voters and Latino voter turnout in political elections. This led to the organization's key role in the mobilization of Latino voters for the 2012 presidential election. Similar to the *Ya es hora ¡Ciudadanía!* campaign of 2006, the *Ya es hora ¡VE Y VOTA!* ("Now is the time, go and vote!") campaign utilized Spanish media and grassroots groups to encourage Latino voters to turn up at the polls. The Mi Familia Vota Education Fund voter registration drives, voter education initiatives, and voter mobilization efforts across Arizona, California, Colorado, Florida, Nevada, and Texas contributed to the registration of over 83,000 Latino voters in 2012.

In February 2013, the organization was awarded the NASS Medallion by the National Association of Secretaries of State for its role in increasing civic engagement within the Latino community across the United States. In March 2014, Mi Familia Vota was awarded the Civic Engagement Advocate of the Year Award by the Nevada Hispanic Legislative Caucus. In April 2014, U.S. senator Harry Reid of Nevada awarded Mi Familia Vota with a Certificate of Commendation.

Raquel A. Centeno

See also: Immigration as a Policy Issue; National Association of Latino Elected and Appointed Officials (NALEO) Educational Fund; UnidosUS

Further Reading

Araújo, José Rúas. 2012. "La creciente importancia del voto latino en las elecciones presidenciales de los Estados Unidos de America." *Anàlisi: quaderns de comunicació i cultura* 45: 55–73.

Garcia-Rios, Sergio I., & Matt A. Barreto. 2016. "Politicized Immigrant Identity, Spanish-Language Media, and Political Mobilization in 2012." *RSF: The Russell Sage Foundation Journal of the Social Sciences* 2, no. 3: 78–96. doi:10.7758/rsf.2016.2.3.05.

Mi Familia Vota. 2017a. "Ben Monterroso." http://www.mifamiliavota.org/people/ben -monterroso.

Mi Familia Vota. 2017b. "History." http://www.mifamiliavota.org/about/history.

Ramirez, Ricardo, & Olga Medina. 2010. "Catalysts and Barriers to Attaining Citizenship: An Analysis of ya es hora¡ CIUDADANIA!." Washington, D.C.: National Council of La Raza.

Military Participation and Latinos

Latinos have played a significant role in the U.S. Armed Forces going back to the 19th century. Hispanic soldiers fought for both the Union and Confederate armies with the U.S. armed forces, highlighting the role of Hispanics fighting for the Union

Mexican American U.S. Army soldiers receive commands in both English and Spanish, Fort Benning, Georgia, 1943. (Bettmann/Getty Images)

Army in protecting the Southwestern United States from Confederate advancement there (U.S. Army, 2017). The Civil War also saw the first 3 Latinos earn the Congressional Medal of Honor, with 46 Latinos having been honored to date. The role of Latino soldiers increased in both World War I and World War II. The granting of citizenship to Puerto Ricans in 1917 with the passage of the Jones Act made over 200,000 Puerto Rican men eligible for conscription. Latinos already living in the United States went on to serve during World War I, with light-skinned Latinos incorporated into white units and dark-skinned Latinos segregated into units with African Americans, including the Harlem Hell Fighters (Oropeza, 2012). Many Puerto Ricans went on to serve during World War I although most were relegated to roles in service occupations such as cooks, although one group of soldiers took on the vital task of protecting the Panama Canal Zone (Oropeza, 2012).

Between 400,000 and 500,000 Hispanics served in the U.S. armed forces during World War II with more taking on combat roles than in the First World War. Despite their service, Latinos still faced discrimination at home at the conclusion of the war. A prime example of this was the denial of funeral services for Private Felix Longoria in Three Rivers, Texas, because of his Mexican heritage. The mistreatment of Hispanic soldiers by the military and Veterans Affairs led to the creation of the American GI Forum, which, led by Dr. Hector Garcia, helped obtain a full military funeral for Private Longoria at Arlington National Cemetery. The

American GI Forum would go on to play a prominent role in the burgeoning Chicano Movement.

The service and treatment of Latino soldiers continued to be a significant issue during the Vietnam War in Latino communities. Many Hispanics unable to attend college were not eligible for educational deferments, which allowed middle- and upper-income Caucasians to avoid the draft and Latinos of less economic means to be drafted at higher rates. For instance, in the state of New Mexico, Latinos accounted for 27 percent of the state's population but comprised 69 percent of the people who were drafted during the war (Tracy, 2006). This in turn led to high casualty rates for Latinos, as not only were they disproportionately drafted in some states, but they were also highly likely to serve in combat units (Tracy, 2006). This was one of the primary motivations for the Chicano Moratorium as social activism had been shown to influence the casualty rates for African Americans earlier in the Vietnam War (Talbot, 2003). However, the Chicano Moratorium, despite culminating with a protest of 30,000 Mexican Americans in East Los Angeles on August 29, 1970, never received the recognition of the antiwar protests of other groups either at the time or historically (Munoz, 2010).

The higher casualty rates faced by Hispanics persisted after the Vietnam War, as data published by the Department of Defense (2005) to compare African American and Caucasian casualty rates stated that Hispanics accounted for 9 percent of the military personnel fighting in Operation Desert Storm but were overrepresented by accounting for 11 percent of the casualties. More recently, the active duty military has shrunk in size by over 100,000 soldiers from 2010 to 2015; however, the percentage of active duty Hispanics has continued to grow (U.S. Department of Defense, 2015). As of fiscal year 2015, 12.3 percent of the U.S. military was Hispanic. In looking just at the U.S. Army, the percentage that is Latino more than quadrupled, going from 3 percent in 1985 to 14 percent in 2016 (U.S. Army, 2017; U.S. Department of Defense, 2015). Despite this growth, representation of Hispanics in the officer ranks remains something of an enigma. The reports cited do not present officer data by ethnicity, only by race. As of 2015, less than about a quarter of officers were nonwhite compared to nonwhite personnel compromising approximately one-third of the total active duty military. However, historical data show that Hispanics were also underrepresented when it comes to the officer ranks. Fiscal year 2001 data showed that at the time Hispanics were 9.49 percent of the active duty military but only 3.84 percent of the officer corps (Pew, 2003). The need for greater mentorship of Latino soldiers has been cited as a reason for fewer Latino officers in the military, and alternative mentoring strategies such as the use of the Internet have been proposed as a way to address this problem (Knouse, 2007). At the same time, Latino advancement in the military is hampered by the lower percentages of Latinos with college degrees, a requirement to serve as an officer, compared to other racial and ethnic groups. The educational attainment of Latinos presents a challenge for advancement in the military but also serves as a reason for some to enlist in the first place.

The increasing numbers of Latinos in the military has led to a greater discussion of the reasons for Latino military service. While an increasing Latino population is definitely one of the reasons, recent research (Lutz, 2008) finds that individuals from low-income backgrounds are more likely to enter into military service compared to those who are more affluent, Latinos included. As Latinos find themselves with lower incomes and levels of educational attainment compared to Caucasians, this has led some to theorize on the existence of a poverty draft, where the U.S. military targets low-income Latinos for recruitment given their increasing population and economic station. One example cited to support this theory is that recruiters have modified their recruitment strategy to appeal to Latinos including conducting in-home visits (which is not a common practice for other ethnicities) and launching a Spanish-language recruitment advertising campaign (Sanchez, 2013). Further, Latino soldiers are attractive to the U.S. military for their value system. Dr. Joseph Westphal, former undersecretary of the U.S. Army discussed in 2009 that Latinos hold the same values as the U.S. armed forces, "family, love of country, commitment to community, commitment to the nation, service to the nation and selfless sacrifices" (Henry, 2009). Further evidence exists for the poverty draft concept via the military's presence in U.S. high schools. First, Junior Reserve Officer Training Corps (JROTC) programs are disproportionately found in high schools in low-income communities. Finally, with the passage of the No Child Left Behind Act in 2001, schools were required to give military recruiters the same access to public schools as they would colleges and universities. In a joint letter at the time of the law's passage from Defense Secretary Donald Rumsfeld and Secretary of Education Rod Paige (U.S. Department of Education, 2002), it was stated in regard to military service that "[f]or some of our students, this may be the best opportunity they have to get a college education," reinforcing the idea that the U.S. military realizes that low-income students, including Latinos, will be sold on the idea of military service as beneficial given an absence of other opportunities available to them on their own.

Closely tied to the military's ability to recruit Latinos is the oft-proposed DREAM Act, which would create an opportunity to achieve citizenship by serving in the military, thus possibly creating a pipeline of recruits. As the proposal of the DREAM Act created a connection between military service and gaining citizenship, historically, military service has been viewed as a way for Latinos to demonstrate their patriotism to the United States even for those Latinos who are naturalized or native-born citizens. Perez (2010: 170) explains, "Given that the citizen-soldier is located at the pinnacle of citizenship hierarchy, one way marginalized communities of color have laid claim to full citizenship rights is precisely through military service and the performance or patriotism and loyalty. . . . Not surprisingly, many young Latinas/os have regarded their participating in the military as a [sic] one pathway to first-class citizenship." A debate exists over whether undocumented immigrants may be motivated to join the military specifically in an effort to gain citizenship. However, honorably discharged soldiers who fought in Iraq and Afghanistan have been deported, and in recent years the peak number of noncitizen service members granted citizenship was in 2010 when only 10,000 undocumented residents were granted citizenship (Lawrence, 2016). Lastly, survey research of Latino soldiers finds that gaining citizenship is not commonly cited when identifying their reasons for service (Dempsey and Shapiro, 2009).

While there is a debate regarding how the military recruits Latinos, why they choose to serve, and their advancement opportunities while serving, there is also research that identifies the benefits of military service for Latinos. Leal (1999: 153) found "that Latino veterans, and particularly draftees, exhibited higher levels of voting and low-intensity nonelectoral political activities," a finding that was not as significant for Anglo veterans. Whether this translates to Latino veterans running for office is uncertain, but overall, veteran representation in public office and especially Congress has been on the decline since the 1970s. In other work, Leal (2007) finds that ROTC programs, especially at the college level, are beneficial for Latino students to be able to pay for postsecondary education. Additionally, Leal, Nichols, and Teigen (2011) found that Latino veterans were likely to have higher incomes than Latinos who did not serve in the military, and in regard to patriotism and acculturation; Leal (2003) found that serving in the military led to greater knowledge of culture and history for Latinos and Anglos. Finally, Shapiro (2009) in a study of the attitudes of active duty members of the Army and cadets at the U.S. Military Academy found that overall Latinos were satisfied with their service and optimistic regarding their future opportunities.

In closing, the experience of Latinos in the U.S. military has been mixed, in that it has provided benefits to many in the form of the opportunity to attend college and improve their socioeconomic status, but there are problems of discrimination in recruitment and service that continue to exist today. Moving forward the study of Latino military service will to continue to examine how Latinos come to serve in the U.S. military and if their experience when enlisted and as veterans improves over time.

Adam McGlynn

See also: American GI Forum; Brown Power Movement/Chicano Civil Rights Movement; Chicano Moratorium (1970); DREAM Act; DREAM Act at the State Level; Education and Latinos; Jones Act (1917); Pérez García, Héctor (1914–1996)

Further Reading

Dempsey, Jason K., & Robert Y. Shapiro. 2009. "The Army's Hispanic Future." *Armed Forces & Society* 35, no. 3: 526–61.

Henry, Ashley. 2009. "Undersecretary Says Hispanic Community Shares Army Values." *U.S. Army.* https://www.army.mil/article/28898/Under_secretary_says_Hispanic _community_shares_Army_values.

Knouse, Stephen. 2007. "El Mentor: Mentoring for Hispanics in the Military." Paper Presented at the 2007 6th Biennial Defense Equal Opportunity Management Institute Research Symposium.

Lawrence, Quil. 2016. "Service Members, Not Citizens: Meet the Veterans Who Have Been Deported." https://www.npr.org/2016/01/13/462372040/service-members-not -citizens-meet-the-veterans-who-have-been-deported.

Leal, David L. 1999. "It's Not Just a Job: Military Service and Latino Political Participation." *Political Behavior* 21, no. 2: 153–74.

Leal, David L. 2003. "The Multicultural Military: Military Service and the Acculturation of Latinos and Anglos." *Armed Forces & Society* 29, no. 2: 183–226.

Leal, David L. 2007. "Students in Uniform: ROTC, the Citizen-Soldier, and the Civil-Military Gap." *PS: Political Science and Politics* 40, no. 3: 479–83.

Leal, David L., Curt Nichols, & Jeremy Teigen. 2011. "Latino Veterans and Income: Are There Gains from Military Service?" In David L. Leal and Stephen J. Trejo, eds. *Latinos and the Economy.* New York: Springer, pp. 193–209.

Lutz, Amy. 2008. "Who Joins the Military? A Look at Race, Class, and Immigration Status." https://surface.syr.edu/cgi/viewcontent.cgi?referer=https://scholar.google.com/&httpsredir=1&article=1002&context=soc.

Muñoz, Rosalio. 2010. "Why Commemorate the February 28, 1970 Chicano Moratorium." *LatinoLA*, February 24.

Oropeza, Lorena. 2012. "Fighting on Two Fronts: Latinos in the Military." https://www.nps.gov/heritageinitiatives/latino/latinothemestudy/military.htm.

Perez, Gina. 2010. "Hispanic Values, Military Values: Gender, Culture, and the Militarization of Latina/o Youth." In *Beyond El Barrio: Everyday Life in Latina/o America*. New York: NYU Press, pp. 168–86.

Pew. 2003. http://www.pewhispanic.org/2003/03/27/hispanics-in-the-military/.

Sanchez, Erika L. 2013. "U.S. Military, a Growing Latino Army." January 1. http://nbclatino.com/2013/01/01/u-s-military-a-growing-latino-army.

Shapiro, Robert. 2009. "Citizenship and Service Political and Social Attitudes of Active-Duty Army and Cadets at the U.S. Military Academy, West Point." *Institute for Social and Economic Research and Policy. Columbia University.* http://iserp.columbia.edu/content/citizenship-and-service-political-and-social-attitudes-active-duty-army-and-cadets-us-milita.

Talbot, Richard P. 2003. "White, Black and Hispanic Casualty Rates During the Vietnam Conflict: Any Differences?" Paper Presented at the 2003 Meeting of the American Sociological Association.

Tracy, James. 2006. *The Military Draft Handbook*. San Francisco: Manic D Press.

U.S. Army. 2017. https://www.army.mil/hispanics/history.html.

U.S. Department of Defense. 2005. "Who Is Volunteering for Today's Military? Myths versus Facts." http://www.defense.gov/news/Dec2005/d20051213mythfact.pdf.

U.S. Department of Education. 2002. https://www2.ed.gov/policy/gen/guid/fpco/hottopics/ht10-09-02c.html.

Minimum Wage

Minimum wage in the United States is a combination of federal, state, and local laws; this is a key civil rights issue for Latinos, given the high rates of poverty in Latino communities. While Latinos represent only 15 percent of the workforce, they comprise 25 percent of those who would benefit from a high minimum wage. As of July 2016, the federal government mandated a nationwide minimum wage of $7.25 per hour, and as of October 2016, 29 states have a higher wage minimum than the federal wage requirement. Aside from local districts, Washington, D.C., has the highest minimum wage in the United States at $11.50; this is a significant population center for Central Americans. This followed by Massachusetts, with large Puerto Rican and Dominican populations, and Washington with $11.00 each. Arizona, New York, Rhode Island, Colorado, New Jersey, Illinois, Florida, and New Mexico all pay more than the federal wage laws require and have significant Latino populations. Many cities have enacted even higher local minimums. They include San Francisco and Seattle, which will both see their minimum wage levels grow to $15 by 2018 and 2021, respectively.

In March 2017, 66 percent of Hispanics reported participating in the labor force along with a 5.2 percent Latino unemployment rate. According to Belman, Wolfson, and Nawakitphaitoon (2015), Latinos are on average more likely to be employed at minimum wage jobs relative to other demographic groups. One in five Latinos earns minimum wage, according to the Bureau of Labor Statistics. According to a 2015 Pew Research Center Report, Hispanics support raising the federal minimum wage at a higher rate than the U.S. population generally.

The highest increase of real median household income for Hispanics, relative to non-Hispanic white and black households was 6.1 percent from 2014 to 2015; additionally, the poverty rate decreased for Hispanics from 23.6 percent to 21.4 percent. These statistics suggest Hispanic post-recession recovery has been relatively larger than other demographic groups (U.S. Census Bureau, 2016).

A study on the Living Wage Ordinance passed in 1997 in Los Angeles suggested Latinos are among the groups who benefit through labor substitution from an increased minimum wage, especially if they possess skills relevant to the industry (Fairris and Bujanda, 2008). This suggests businesses are more likely to employ Latinos over others when an increase in minimum wage is enacted. Other studies suggest higher minimum wages do not affect Hispanic teen employment but it does have a negative effect on the amount of hours worked and no significant effect on earnings (Allegretto, Dube, and Reich, 2009). In other words, Hispanic teens would work less when higher minimum wages are enacted, making total income unaffected by the higher minimum wage.

There have been calls from groups like UnidosUS to increase the minimum wage in cities, states, and at the federal level. Countering calls from leading Latino organizations to raise state and federal minimum wages, the LIBRE Institute, a free-market Latino advocacy group, has published a study that finds minimum wage hikes would adversely affect Latino workers. Specifically, they say that employment opportunities for Latino workers are significantly diminished following minimum wage hikes.

Carlos Navarro Perez and Zujaja Tehreem

See also: Latinx Entrepreneurship; LIBRE Initiative; UnidosUS

Further Reading

Allegretto, Sylvia A., Arindrajit Dube, & Michael Reich. 2009. "Spatial Heterogeneity and Minimum Wages: Employment Estimates for Teens Using Cross-State Commuting Zones." Working Paper Series. Berkeley, CA: Institute for Research on Labor and Employment, UC Berkeley. http://irle.berkeley.edu/files/2009/Spatial-Heterogeneity-and-Minimum-Wages.pdf.

Belman, Dale, Paul Wolfson, & Kritkorn Nawakitphaitoon. 2015. "Who Is Affected by the Minimum Wage?" *Industrial Relations* 54, no. 4: 582–621.

Fairris, David, & Leon Fernandez Bujanda. 2008. "The Dissipation of Minimum Wage Gains for Workers through Labor-Labor Substitution: Evidence from the Los Angeles Living Wage Ordinance." *Southern Economic Journal* 75, no. 2: 473–96.

U.S. Census Bureau. 2016. "Income and Poverty in the United States: 2015." https://www.census.gov/content/dam/Census/library/publications/2016/demo/p60-256.pdf.

U.S. Department of Labor, Bureau of Labor Statistics. n.d. *Table A-3. Employment Status of the Hispanic or Latino Population by Sex and Age.* https://www.bls.gov/news.release/empsit.t03.htm.

U.S. Department of Labor, Bureau of Labor Statistics. 2017. *Characteristics of Minimum Wage Workers, 2016.* Report 1067. https://www.bls.gov/opub/reports/minimum-wage/2016/home.htm.

Minors, Unaccompanied and Undocumented

(2010s)

In the 2010s, the United States started to see an influx in the number of unaccompanied, undocumented minors crossing the border into the United States in hopes of seeking refugee status. In 2011, the number of unaccompanied, undocumented minors was around 16,000, but by 2014 the number of children making the journey across the border alone increased to about 68,540 (BBC News, 2014). The majority of these children were between the ages of 15 and 17. They came to the United States to escape gang violence in Central America and hoped to seek refugee status. Many turned themselves in to Border Patrol or were picked up by immigration officers and placed into detention camps where they awaited trial to see if they would face deportation. The number of unaccompanied minors increased so dramatically that in 2014 the Obama administration declared a humanitarian crisis.

While the majority of unaccompanied minors in the past had come from Mexico, this wave of children was predominately Central American. Many were from El Salvador, where the homicide rate has been steadily increasing due to the breakdown of a truce between MS-13 and the 18th Street gang. However, a number of minors were also coming from Guatemala, Honduras, and Nicaragua, countries that all have a great deal of cartel violence and high murder rates. The children who fled feared being forced to serve as mules for the gangs, being raped, and the possibility of death for not complying with the wishes of the gangs and cartels in their home countries. In many instances the families of these children pay thousands of dollars to have a guide known as a "coyote" cross these children over to escape the violence in their home countries. In some instances they make their way up North America by sitting on top of freight cars and then swimming across the Rio Grande. The majority of these minors end up entering the United States in the Rio Grande Valley in Texas. Local organizations like Catholic Charities of the Rio Grande Valley, led by Sr. Norma Pimentel, have stepped in to provide food and clothing, and even lodging to these minors.

Unlike immigrants from Canada and Mexico, who are quickly processed and deported back to their home countries, Central Americans detained by border officials are given a trial before a ruling is made. Because there is a waiting period between first being detained by Border Patrol and facing a judge, children are held in temporary holding facilities. While in temporary holding, family sponsors living in the United States are tracked down so that the child may be released to their family until their court date. When no such sponsor can be found, children must remain in these temporary holding facilities. Precedent for holding refugees or releasing them to their families can be traced back to George W. Bush, who signed the anti–human trafficking legislation, and international refugee treaties.

Despite the fact that these children have made the very long journey to the United States and are fleeing violence, the majority of the children are deported back to their home countries, with only 7 percent of the cases in immigration court resulting in the individual being allowed to stay in the country. This is due, in part, to the fact that few have legal counsel.

President Obama responded to the massive wave of unaccompanied minors by calling the National Guard to the southern border to help the children and relieve the Border Patrol. In addition he asked Congress for $3.7 million in additional funds to pay for extra immigration judges, medical services, transportation costs, and other services related to maintaining the children apprehended at the border. This humanitarian crisis was blamed on President Obama and the Democratic Party for being too soft on illegal immigration, with many Republicans pushing for more stringent border security despite the president's efforts to seek resources to process and deport those who do not meet the qualifications to stay in the United States. Many people erroneously believe that because children are released to their family to await a court hearing, they will not actually face deportation, when in actuality most of the children will be returned to the countries and the violence they sought to escape.

Angela E. Gutierrez

See also: Central American Migration; Immigration as a Policy Issue; Obama, Barack (1961–) and Latinos; Pimentel, Norma (1953–); *Primary Documents:* Full Congressional Testimony of Dulce Medina, Mayeli Hernández, and Saúl Martínez (Three Central American Youths Who Entered the United States as Unaccompanied Minors) (2014)

Further Reading

BBC News. 2014. "Why Are So Many Children Trying to Cross the US Border?" *BBC News*, September 30. http://www.bbc.com/news/world-us-canada-28203923.

Krogstad, Jens Manuel. 2016. "U.S. Border Apprehensions of Families and Unaccompanied Children Jump Dramatically." *Pew Research Center*, May 4. http://www.pewresearch.org/fact-tank/2016/05/04/u-s-border-apprehensions-of-families-and-unaccompanied-children-jump-dramatically/.

Markon, Jerry, & Joshua Partlow. 2015. "Unaccompanied Children Crossing Southern Border in Greater Numbers Again, Raising Fears of New Migrant Crisis." *Washington Post*, December 16. https://www.washingtonpost.com/news/federal-eye/wp/2015/12/16/unaccompanied-children-crossing-southern-border-in-greater-numbers-again-raising-fears-of-new-migrant-crisis/?utm_term=.99550855e984.

Meko, Tim. 2016. "What Happens When an Unaccompanied Minor Is Caught at the U.S.-Mexico Border." *The Washington Post*, January 16. https://www.washingtonpost.com/apps/g/page/national/what-happens-when-an-unaccompanied-minor-is-caught-at-the-us-mexico-border/1944/.

Park, Haeyoun. 2014. "Children at the Border." *The New York Times*, October 21. https://www.nytimes.com/interactive/2014/07/15/us/questions-about-the-border-kids.html.

Partlow, Joshua. 2015. "El Salvador Is on Pace to Become the Hemisphere's Most Deadly Nation." *The Washington Post*, May 17. https://www.washingtonpost.com/world/the_americas/el-salvador-is-on-pace-to-become-the-hemispheres-most-deadly-nation/2015/05/17/fc52e4b6-f74b-11e4-a47c-e56f4db884ed_story.html?utm_term=.7649dfcf8bf7.

"Rising Child Migration to the United States." 2017. *Migrationpolicy.org*, January 28. https://www.migrationpolicy.org/programs/us-immigration-policy-program/rising-child-migration-united-states.

"Southwest Border Unaccompanied Alien Children FY 2014." 2015. *U.S. Customs and Border Protection*, November 24. https://www.cbp.gov/newsroom/stats/southwest-border-unaccompanied-children/fy-2014.

Tobia, P. J. 2014. "No Country for Lost Kids." *PBS*, June 20. https://www.pbs.org/newshour/nation/country-lost-kids.

Miranda v. Arizona

(1966)

Miranda v. Arizona is a landmark Supreme Court case that extended and clarified protections of those accused of a crime. The decision clarified that police officers must inform a suspect of their right to counsel as guaranteed by the Sixth Amendment of the U.S. Constitution and the protection against self-incrimination as provided in the Fifth Amendment. Prior to this case, someone unaware of these constitutional protections could be interrogated by police without a lawyer present. After the decision, police are required to read suspects the appropriately named Miranda warning, informing them of their right to remain silent and their right to an attorney.

The case was a combination of four similar cases the Supreme Court agreed to hear involving police conduct during custodial interviews. The case bears the name of Ernesto Miranda, an Arizona resident of Mexican heritage. Arizona police officers arrested Miranda on suspicion of kidnapping and rape. After taking him into custody, he was placed in an interrogation room where he was questioned for approximately two hours. Miranda initially claimed his innocence but eventually signed a written confession. Miranda was 23 years old, poor, and only had an eighth grade education. The officers acknowledged that they had not informed Miranda of his right to legal counsel, believing they were not required to do so. At trial, Miranda's attorney attempted to keep the confession from being admitted into evidence but was unsuccessful. The jury found Miranda guilty on both counts.

The case was appealed to the Arizona Supreme Court. However, the justices found no constitutional violation of Miranda's rights since he did not request a lawyer, regardless of his lack of knowledge that he could do so. The U.S. Supreme Court agreed to hear the case. Contrary to Arizona's court, the justices found that Miranda's Fifth and Sixth Amendment rights had not been sufficiently protected, as he had not been informed of his right to have an attorney present during the interrogation and was similarly uninformed about his right to remain silent and not incriminate himself. They did not believe it was reasonable to assume that every suspect was aware of these rights, especially someone with limited education. The Court determined that Miranda's confession should not have been used as evidence against him, meaning the jury should not have heard it. As a result, the Court vacated his sentence, which, in essence, makes it as if the trial never happened. Miranda was retried. The confession was not admitted as evidence in the second trial. However, Miranda was still found guilty and convicted of kidnapping and rape.

While the decision may not have changed Miranda's fate, it forever altered the landscape of the rights of the accused. Because of *Miranda v. Arizona*, police officers are required to inform suspects of their Miranda rights, rights now so well known, called Miranda rights, that most people can recite them by heart merely from watching television police procedurals. Suspects are informed of their right to remain silent, thus protecting their Fifth Amendment right to not be compelled to be witnesses against themselves. They are also informed of their right to have the assistance of counsel as provided by the Sixth Amendment. Future cases would further delineate the rules regarding exceptions to Miranda requirements, for example, determining when a police interview is just a conversation or a custodial interrogation within the understanding of *Miranda*. In addition, the Supreme Court in *Berghuis v. Thompkins* (2010) and *Salinas v. Texas* (2013) held that a suspect must expressly and unambiguously invoke Miranda rights in order to be protected by them. That being said, this case provided the initial protections granted to the accused.

Mary McThomas

See also: Brown Power Movement/Chicano Civil Rights Movement

Further Reading

Kinports, Kit. 2011. "The Supreme Court's Love-Hate Relationship with Miranda." *The Journal of Criminal Law and Criminology* 101, no. 2: 375–440.

Miranda v. Arizona, 384 U.S. 436 (1966).

Scherr, Kyle C., & Stephanie Madon. 2012. "You Have the Right to Understand: The Deleterious Effect of Stress on Suspects' Ability to Comprehend 'Miranda.'" *Law and Human Behavior* 36, no. 4: 275–82.

Stuart, Gary L. 2004. *Miranda: The Story of America's Right to Remain Silent.* Tucson: University of Arizona Press.

Thomas, George C., III, & Richard A. Leo. 2002. "The Effects of Miranda v. Arizona: 'Embedded' in Our National Culture?" *Crime and Justice* 29: 203–71.

Moreno, Luisa

(1907–1992)

Labor organizer Blanca Rosa Rodriguez, later known as Luisa Moreno, was born August 30, 1907, to an affluent coffee-growing family in Guatemala. Renouncing her privilege and wealth in her home country, she would eventually become one of the most successful labor organizers of destitute laborers in the United States. It all started with her following her love for poetry by moving to Mexico City in the mid-1920s. There, she published her first book of poetry and married. Eventually, she and her husband moved to New York's Spanish Harlem, and in 1928, Rodriguez gave birth to her daughter, Mytyl. As leading labor historian Vicki Ruiz notes, Rodriguez became politicized by the conditions of poverty in New York, leading her to organize La Liga de Costureras, a union for neighborhood garment workers (Ruiz, 2007: 32). This early attempt at bettering the lives of the women she lived and worked alongside proved a harbinger of her life to come.

Though her interests in poetry had taken her to New York, it was her newfound love for labor organizing that led her to take a job in Florida in 1935 with the American Federation of Labor, the most prominent labor union in the United States. It was then that she decided to take on the alias "Luisa Moreno." Unlike "Blanca Rosa," which literally means white rose, and symbolized white femininity, Rodriguez chose "Moreno," because it means dark in Spanish—a creative way of distancing herself from her roots of privilege. "Luisa," a reference to Luisa Capetillo, a famed Caribbean labor organizer in Florida's cigar industry, invoked the region's women's labor history (Ruiz, 2007: 32). The poetic construction of "Luisa Moreno" ultimately helped Rodriguez accomplish her organizing goals with racialized and immigrant laborers throughout her career.

In a 1940 poetically tinged speech given in Los Angeles titled "Caravans of Sorrow," Moreno argued that immigrant workers were "not aliens" but were vital to the economies of the Southwest (Ruiz, 2007: 37). In fact, from the mid-1930s up until the 1950s, Moreno organized black, Caribbean, and Latino immigrants across the U.S. sunbelt to make sure that these workers were treated with the respect they deserved. For example, with the American Federation of Labor in the 1930s, Moreno successfully organized racialized women cigar workers in Florida's Tampa region. As a representative of the union she helped found, United Cannery, Agriculture, Packing, and Allied Workers of American (UCAPAWA), she organized Texas Mexican pecan shellers in San Antonio and migrant farmworker families in the Rio Grande Valley. Moreno is most known, however, for her organizing of fruit and vegetable cannery workers in Los Angeles's California Sanitary Canning Company (Cal San) in 1941. Appealing to the strong leadership of Mexican women workers across various Cal San plants, Moreno was able to negotiate for higher pay, hospital benefits, and free legal advice for workers (Ruiz, 2007: 38). Following intense surveillance and intimidation by the FBI for her labor organizing of the Southwest's most vulnerable laborers, Moreno was forced to "self-deport" in the 1950s on accusations of being a communist. Moreno argued that even though she was to be deported, her efforts to affect the lives of countless Latina/o immigrant workers would never be forgotten as long as her labor lived on in the Latina/o communities she worked alongside (Ruiz, 2007: 40).

Moreno was also involved in the legal arena. She was the co-chair of the Sleepy Lagoon Defense Committee (SLDC), where she advocated for the release of 12 Chicanos convicted in an unfair trial by an all-white jury of murdering a Mexican farm worker in 1942. As noted by Gaye Johnson, the Los Angeles police used the trial to demonize Chicano youth, already under surveillance for their dressing in Zoot suits—a style of dress that was deemed "a threat to public order" (Johnson, 2013: 28–29). Ultimately, Moreno, too, would fall under intense surveillance from the FBI as part of "Operation Wetback," a campaign to deport Mexican and Mexican Americans, for her labor organizing and legal mobilizations of the Southwest's most vulnerable communities.

Salvador Zárate

See also: Fierro de Bright, Josefina (1914–1998); Operation Wetback (1954); Sleepy Lagoon (1942); Zoot Suit Riots (1943)

Further Reading

García, Mario T. 1994. *Memories of Chicano History: The Life and Narrative of Bert Corona.* Berkeley: University of California Press.

Griswold del Castillo, Richard, & Carlos M. Larralde. 1997. "Luisa Moreno and the Beginnings of the Mexican American Civil Rights Movement in San Diego." *Journal of San Diego History* 43, no. 3: 284–311.

Johnson, Gaye T. 2013. *Spaces of Conflict, Sounds of Solidarity: Music, Race, and Spatial Entitlement in Los Angeles.* Berkeley: University of California Press.

Ruiz, Vicki L. 1987. *Cannery Women, Cannery Lives: Mexican Women, Unionization, and the California Food Processing Industry, 1930–1950.* Albuquerque: University of New Mexico.

Ruiz, Vicki L. 2004. "Una Mujer Sin Fronteras." *Pacific Historical Review* 73, no. 1: 1–20.

Ruiz, Vicki L. 2007. "Of Poetics & Politics: The Border Journeys of Luisa Moreno." In Sharon Harley, ed. *Women's Labor in the Global Economy*. Rutgers, NJ: Rutgers University Press, pp. 28–45.

Schmidt Camacho, Alicia. 2008. *Migrant Imaginaries: Latino Cultural Politics in the U.S.– Mexico Borderlands*. New York: New York University Press.

Movimiento Estudiantil Chicanx de Aztlan (M.E.Ch.A.)

The Movimiento Estudiantil Chicanx de Aztlan (M.E.Ch.A.) is a student-led organization established in 1969 as part of the larger U.S. Civil Rights Movement. The English-language translation of the name of the organization is Chicanx Student Movement of Aztlán, and members are known as Mechistas. The organization was founded as part of the Plan de Santa Barbara in 1969, a document that outlines proposals for a curriculum in Chicano studies, the role of community control in Chicano education, and the necessity of Chicano political independence, and was primarily aimed to empower Chicanx youth who at the time struggled with a public education system that negated their ethnic and cultural identities, among other issues. A current of the Chicanx Movement worked to push for the creation of Chicanx studies programs and departments in U.S. universities. The Plan worked toward this goal by calling for an organization of students at the university level that addressed the concerns of Chicanx students and acted as the student arm of Chicanx studies. Today, there are M.E.Ch.A. chapters around the United States; most are organized in colleges and universities, but there is also a strong presence among high school students.

As part of establishing Chicanx studies, El Plan called for existing organizations like MAYO (Mexican American Youth Organization) and UMAS (United Mexican American Students) and others to fall under the M.E.Ch.A. name, in part, to move away from the use of the term "Mexican American" and replace it with the politicized "Chicano." M.E.Ch.A. members, or Mechistas, placed a strong focus on political education. *Las Hijas de Cuauhtemoc*, for example, was an effort led by Mechista women to increase political consciousness among new recruits and to contribute to the vision of Chicanx liberation. This space within M.E.Ch.A. would also become a vehicle for Mechista women to discuss and organize against misogynistic tendencies within the organization and to challenge the oppressed role of women in society more broadly.

Although the Chicanx youth movement that preceded M.E.Ch.A. was known for its militancy and radical actions such as walkouts, sit-ins, and even street fighting, Mechistas also engaged in organizing cultural and social events. Organizing these types of events allowed M.E.Ch.A. to reach out to a greater community and campus-based audience. However, M.E.Ch.A. to this day is still a site for ideological debates as various Marxist and political currents continue to actively engage Chicanx youth and Chicanx liberation.

M.E.Ch.A. has evolved over the decades, incorporating and organizing for the rights of other oppressed minorities such as the lesbian, gay, bisexual, and transgender (LGBT) community. Chapters around the nation are currently guided by 14 main objectives, including eradicating sexism and homophobia from the organization and Chicanx communities, continuing the fight for educational rights, and building M.E.Ch.A. as a democratic organization.

The structure of M.E.Ch.A. allows for national-level coordination while still leaving space for a strong focus on local-level issues. M.E.Ch.A. consists of campus-based chapters, regions (geographic or state), state, and national levels. The main gatherings take place at the state and national levels and are led by an elected national board. Today, M.E.Ch.A. continues to organize for the creation and defense of Chicanx and ethnic studies programs in coalition with other student and community groups. For example, Mechistas were involved in reversing the mass under-funding of the College of Ethnic Studies (COES) at San Francisco State University. Mechistas were also instrumental in the founding of the Chicano/a Studies Department at the University of New Mexico in the spring of 2015.

Melina Juárez and Moises Santos

See also: Brown Power Movement/Chicano Civil Rights Movement; Gonzales, Rodolfo "Corky" (1928–2005); Mexican American Youth Organization (MAYO)

Further Reading

Blackwell, Maylei. 2003. "Contested Histories: *Las Hijas de Cuauhtemoc*." In Gabriela F. Arredondo, Aida Hurtado, Normal Klahn, Olga Najera-Ramirez, and Patricia Zavella, eds. *Chicana Feminisms: A Critical Reader*. Durham, NC: Duke University Press, pp. 53–59.

Gómez-Quiñones, Juan, & Irene Vásquez. 2014. *Making Aztlán: Ideology and Culture of the Chicana and Chicano Movement, 1966–1977*. Albuquerque: University of New Mexico Press.

Munoz, Carlos. 2007. *Youth, Identity, Power: The Chicano Movement*. London: Verso.

Rosales, F. Arturo, & Francisco A. Rosales. 1997. *Chicano! The History of the Mexican American Civil Rights Movement*. Houston: Arte Publico Publisher.

Murguía, Janet

(1960–)

A political activist and prominent national civil rights leader for Latino communities, Janet Murguía is the president and chief executive officer (CEO) of UnidosUS, formerly known as the National Council of La Raza (NCLR), the largest Latino advocacy and civil rights organization in the United States.

Murguía was born on September 6, 1960, in Kansas City, Kansas. She grew up in a small house with seven brothers and sisters in the Argentine section of Kansas City. Murguía's father worked as a laborer for a steel company, while her mother stayed at home to watch over her, her siblings, and other children from the neighborhood. Murguía's parents both migrated from Mexico to the United States in the late 1940s.

Murguía attended the University of Kansas where in 1982 she earned a bachelor of arts in Spanish language and literature and a bachelor of science in journalism. She continued her studies at the University of Kansas in law and obtained a JD in 1985.

She began her career in Washington, D.C., as counsel for former Congressman Jim Slattery (D-KS). She served as counsel for Congressman Slattery for seven years before she took a position at the White House. At the White House, Murguía worked as deputy assistant to President Clinton from 1994 to 2000. As deputy assistant, she provided strategic and legal advice on key issues. She also served as a deputy director of legislative affairs where she managed legislative staff and was a senior liaison between Congress and the White House.

Before joining the University of Kansas in 2001, Murguía worked as deputy campaign manager and director of constituency outreach for Al Gore's presidential campaign. Murguía oversaw the outreach efforts of the campaign toward national constituency groups. She was also a spokesperson for the campaign. Murguía joined the University of Kansas

Janet Murguía, civil rights activist, is president and CEO of UnidosUS, formerly National Council of La Raza, a Latino advocacy organization. (Starstock /Dreamstime.com)

as executive vice-chancellor for university relations. As vice-chancellor, she was in charge of managing internal and external public relations as well as governmental relations. Murguía also led coordinated efforts that pertained to the strategic planning of the university at its four campuses and the Alumni Association, the Athletics Corporation, and the Endowment Association.

In 2005, Janet Murguía became the president and CEO of the National Council of la Raza (NCLR), the nation's largest Latino civil rights advocacy organization in the United States, now known as UnidosUS. In her role as president and CEO, Murguía has testified before Congress on issues that affect the Latino community, such as education, immigration, health care, civil rights, and the economy. Murguía is a prominent leader in the Latino community who regularly appears in media outlets and speaks out on behalf of the Latino community. Since joining UnidosUS, Murguía has sought to strengthen and broaden the impact of the organization across the country.

Janet Murguía currently serves on the board of the Independent Sector, the Hispanic Association on Corporate Responsibility, and the National Hispanic Leadership Agenda (NHLA). Murguía is a member of the Merrill Lynch Diversity and Inclusion Council and is an executive committee member of the Leadership Conference on Civil Rights. Additionally, she serves on the Advisory Board of the National Hispanic University.

Murguía has received multiple accolades for her admirable trajectory as an activist and leader. She has been named as one of *Latino Leaders Magazine*'s "101 Top

Leaders of the Hispanic Community," *The Non-Profit Times*' "Power and Influence Top 50," *People En Español*'s "100 Most Influential Hispanics," *Washington Magazine*'s "100 Most Powerful Women in Washington," and *Hispanic Magazine*'s "100 Top Latinas" and "100 Most Influential Hispanics."

Angela X. Ocampo

See also: UnidosUS

Further Reading

Bordas, Juana. 2013. *The Power of Latino Leadership: Culture, Inclusion, and Contribution.* Oakland, CA: Berrett-Koehler Publishers.

Hispanic Scholarship Fund. 2017. "#HSFstories Janet Murguía." http://ee.hsf.net/en/media/hsf-stories/janet-murgia.

Huffington Post. 2017. "Janet Murguía." http://www.huffingtonpost.com/author/janet-murguia.

Rothschild, Scott. 2001. "KUED Janet Murguía." *Lawrence Journal-World.* http://www2.ljworld.com/news/2001/aug/11/kued_janet_murguia.

Torres, Lourdes. 2014. "Dismantling the Deportation Nation." *Latino Studies* 12, no. 2: 169–71.